HOME ORCHID GROWING

THIRD EDITION

Rebecca Tyson Northen

PRENTICE HALL PRESS
New York London Toronto Sydney Tokyo

Copyright © 1970, 1962, 1950 by Prentice Hall Press
A Division of Simon & Schuster, Inc.
All rights reserved, including the right of reproduction
in whole or in part in any form.

Published in 1986 by Prentice Hall Press
A Division of Simon & Schuster, Inc.
Gulf + Western Building
One Gulf + Western Plaza
New York, NY 10023

Originally published by Van Nostrand Reinhold Company Inc.

PRENTICE HALL PRESS is a trademark of Simon & Schuster, Inc.

Library of Congress Catalog Card Number: 74-90339

ISBN 0-671-60891-6

Manufactured in the United States of America

10 9 8 7 6 5

THIS BOOK IS FONDLY DEDICATED TO
HANK, BETTY, PHIL, AND TOM

PREFACE

Orchids, the most fascinating of flowers, can now be grown by anyone—in a greenhouse, a sunny window, or a basement with artificial light. This book will bring them to you, with cultural methods that will enable you to grow some of the 25,000 species no matter where you live. Since the second edition appeared in 1960, growers have increased by the thousands; many who started with a few plants a decade ago now have large collections. Busy people from all walks of life and in all occupations are finding not only relaxation and joy in orchids, but a keen and never ending interest.

The variety among orchids is one of their chief charms. They range from white through soft, delicate colors to the boldly gaudy and spectacular; from sweetly simple shapes to the sometimes incredibly fanciful and bizarre; from large plants with tremendous flowers to kinds with showers of small, gay blooms, and on down to miniatures that require a hand lens for viewing. The blooms of most are long lasting, some remaining fresh for months. All are delightful. To know a few is to want to know others.

They are not difficult to grow, but success depends on learning their basic needs and on adjusting the growing conditions you have to offer to suit their requirements. Because orchids come from many different environments, and because people live in such different climates, this book gives you those basic needs and suggests ways to handle the plants under various circumstances. Ingenious equipment is now available to make it easier for the small grower, even those who have to be away from home a good deal.

This book will take you through many adventures in orchid growing. It not only sees the beginner through the first steps, but advances him, and those who are already growing orchids, through all phases of orchid culture including breeding and experimentation. It enables the hobbyist to develop his interests in many directions, to try new things, to specialize in whatever field he finds most appealing. It is written in conversational style, minus technical language, to make it easy reading for all.

It takes up raising plants from seedlings to maturity, their potting, dividing, watering, and general care; pollination and seed germination; the control of flowering time in *Cattleya;* the breeding of hybrids, with basic genetics as a guide; polyploidy; meristem culture; diseases, pests, problems, and their control; construction and management of greenhouses and equipment for them; indoor artificial-light growing, as well as orchids in the garden; and the care and use of cut flowers. It also introduces the collecting and importing of wild orchids and the need for their conservation in their natural habitats.

The orchids are presented in related groups, or tribes, the most familiar along with their less well known and sometimes even more intriguing relatives. Thus those who begin with corsage types or kinds widely grown will learn of many others to add variety to their collections, in some of which they may eventually find a special interest.

This third edition has been carefully revised throughout to include changes and new developments even up to the time of printing. It is far more profusely illustrated than the second edition, and describes many more kinds of orchids. Of the 368 black and white photographs, over 160 are new in this edition; 233 picture species and hybrids, and 135 illustrate how-to-do-it methods, equipment, diseases and problems, collecting orchids, and so forth. There are also 28 helpful line drawings. In addition, over 90 color photographs illustrate new hybrids and delightful species.

Over 500 species of orchids from all over the world are described in the text, 275 more than in the second edition. Among them are the familiar ones that all orchid lovers should know, as well as kinds that are unusual or rare, some newly discovered, and some whose weird form or astonishing behavior gives them special appeal.

My grateful appreciation goes to all of those whose work has contributed to orchid knowledge in general, to those who have furnished information through visits, correspondence, and writings, and to those who have so kindly loaned me pictures for publication. The book could not have been written without their help.

Laramie, Wyoming   R. T. N.
1970

CONTENTS

COLOR ILLUSTRATIONS

1

ORCHIDS AS A HOBBY

Orchids are the most fascinatingly varied and beautiful of all flowers. There are close to 25,000 species, and new ones are being discovered every year. So different are they one from another that at first glance it is hard to believe they are related. Some are large and showy, others are almost microscopic; some have delicate coloring, others such bold colors and markings that one automatically compares them to tropical birds and animals; some are serenely simple in form, others are incredibly modified and complicated. It is as if nature, having invented the basic orchid theme, has, like a musician, played every conceivable variation on that theme. In fact, nature's imagination has gone far beyond the capabilities of human imagination.

Once you have grown a plant or two, you will find yourself under their spell. Call it magic, or just plain curiosity, it is legendary among orchid growers that one cannot stop with but a few. They are deeply satisfying plants. Even though the eventual reward is their flowers, there is joy in watching the new growths and roots, in seeing a plant that produced only one growth last year give rise to two this year with the promise of double the number of flowers. With the exception of a few whose flowers wink open, then close in a day or two, most of them give flowers that last for weeks or months. The familiar corsage orchid, the *Cattleya,* stays fresh and perfect for two to six weeks, and *Phalaenopsis* can last from two to five months.

Growers who embark on the orchid adventure today are fortunate. They will not experience the trials and tribulations with which orchid growing was fraught in its early years, or even the problems that faced those of us who began fifteen to twenty years ago. Plants are readily available and relatively inexpensive, growing methods are better understood, and materials and equipment are scaled to the needs of the small grower. There are still problems, as there are with all kinds of plants, but anyone who has grown flowers for a hobby will understand that plants are not machines, and that successful growing requires care in learning their needs, judgment in handling them, and a good deal of common sense. You may have read that orchids are as easy to grow as African violets. Well, they are, but you do not grow them like African violets. Nor do you grow an African violet like a cactus. Orchids come somewhere in between.

To understand the fortunate situation in which you will find yourself, you must know a little about the phenomenal history of orchids and orchid growing. In the late 1700's and early 1800's, many expeditions were sent to explore Central and South America. The myriad of plants intrigued the horticulturalists of Europe, and botanical collectors eagerly searched out new forms and kinds. Among these were a wealth of orchids. The Europeans knew their native orchids, but were overwhelmed by the tremendous quantity and variety of those being sent from the tropics. A kind of horticultural and scientific madness ensued, as more and more kinds were discovered. Much money went into the expeditions, and collectors suffered physical hardship, even risk to life, in order to gain the prized

Fig. 1-1 *Cattleya gigas,* the largest and most showy of the *Cattleya* species, typical of the large ruffled corsage orchid.

plants. Competition was keen as the searchers scoured the lowlands, the river canyons, the jungles, and the high mountain areas. The collectors were quite jealous of their finds, and often kept locations secret, even falsifying their reports to throw other collectors off the track. Thus it was that sometimes the habitat of a certain kind of orchid was lost for years until later collectors rediscovered it.

The botanists whose job it was to study and classify the orchids had a monumental task, for orchids from the western hemisphere did not fit into the known genera. Orchids are peculiar in that kinds that look very different may actually belong to the same genus, and kinds that look alike are not always closely related. Botanists today are still trying to straighten out the relationships. And the problems increased as orchids were found in the Pacific Islands, Asia, Africa, and Australia.

The people who first tried to grow these plants were faced with many difficulties. They found that they could not just put these strange plants in pots in ordinary soil. Nor could they grow them from seed in the usual manner. Their problems were multiplied by the fact that orchids came from widely different climates and temperature conditions. Some were found by waterfalls and streams, constantly bathed in spray and mists while some came from places boldly exposed to the drying sun. Some lived at low elevations where the temperatures were hot, others near the tops of mountains where the temperatures were cool day and night. Some perched on tree branches, and some grew on the ground in meadows and glades. Considering what we now know about the plants, it is a wonder any of them survived these early attempts to cultivate them. However, those growers who were successful fell into the same error as the early

collectors, and jealously guarded their secrets. The wealthy people who could afford the traditional conservatory greenhouse did not do their own growing but hired trained growers to care for their orchids. The cloak of secrecy was kept drawn about orchid growing long into the twentieth century, except that the barrier was broken now and then by an occasional amateur willing to learn by trial and error. It was so generally believed that only the initiated could grow orchids that most novices gave up after a failure or two and others were afraid to try when there seemed so little chance that they would succeed.

Commercial orchid growing expanded tremendously between 1900 and 1920, and by this time the number of patient amateurs was also increasing. The demand put a great pressure on the supplies of wild plants. Unless one could obtain divisions of plants already in cultivation, the usual way to obtain more was by importation. The reason behind this was that it was so difficult to grow orchids from seed. Although a seed pod contains close to a million seed, and although growers had learned to make hybrid crosses, attempts to germinate the seed often resulted in complete failure or in the production of but a handful of seedlings. Ruthless stripping of the native plants, especially of cattleyas, threatened their extinction in certain areas, and brought about eventual embargoes on their exportation.

A revolution in orchid growing was brought about by a discovery made by Professor Lewis Knudson of Cornell University in 1922. He was experimenting with the germination of various kinds of seed, including that of orchids. He found that orchid seed germinated readily in a glass flask containing an agar jelly to which chemi-

Fig. 1-2 *Cattleya* Bow Bells 'Serene', a fine modern white hybrid.

Home Orchid Growing

cal nutrients and sugar had been added. This medium is much like that on which bacterial cultures are grown. Orchid seed is tiny, as fine as dust, and contains little or no food for the developing embryo. The availability of the nutrients and sugar enabled the embryo to develop and grow. Dr. Knudson's discovery meant that instead of fifteen or twenty seedlings, thousands could be grown from one pod. It opened up a whole new world of possibilities to orchid lovers. Not only were they freed from the costly and wasteful importation of wild plants, but they could explore the promising field of hybridization. Orchid collecting still goes on, but for the purpose of obtaining the odd and unusual kinds, the "collector's items" as we call them, and of finding new species. Amateurs often go orchid hunting on vacation trips, for the pleasure of seeing orchids in the wild and of bringing home the plants they have found themselves. Whether you can go collecting or not, you should give yourself the pleasure of growing some of the species brought in fresh from the jungle.

As do all revolutions, the one in orchid seed germination brought about an explosive period, which led to some mistakes as well as some wonderful results. One of the mistakes, which we can view with humor in the light of history, was an abortive attempt by some commercial growers to keep this discovery a secret too, so that they alone could capitalize on the seedling business. The results of such scientific discoveries are, however, free to all; and it wasn't long before growers everywhere, both amateur and commercial, were trying their hand with Dr. Knudson's new method. As soon as the amateur entered the picture, particularly the special breed of American amateur who will try anything and persist until he finds a way to success, there could no longer be any secrecy.

Out of pure exuberance, growers excitedly crossed any orchid with any other orchid, to see what beautiful or bizarre results might be obtained. Growers sold millions of seedlings on the naive assumption that any cross would embody the best qualities of its parents. Then the truth began to emerge—that not all crosses were good, that often all of the seedlings, or a large proportion of them, were actually inferior. Occasionally good things would emerge from some crosses, and many of these older hybrids proved invaluable as the basis for further hybridization. Although much time and effort was spent in raising plants that eventually

had to be discarded, both by the growers and by the amateurs who bought them, much was learned.

Thoughtful growers began to slow down and study the problems more cautiously. They learned, for instance, that one fine flower when crossed with another equally fine might give good offspring, but that when crossed with a different flower might not. Some flowers seemed to have the ability to transmit their best qualities, while others did not. Perhaps most valuable of the information gained during the explosive years was that not only could related species be crossed quite freely, but even related genera. Hybridizers are still exploring the thrilling possibilities thus offered. We can't say that orchid breeding is fully worked out even now, but the chance of obtaining good plants from seedlings is far better now than it used to be. Now, in exploring the possibilities of new hybrids, growers make the untried crosses in full knowledge that they must wait for the results before judging their worth. And buyers who purchase them as seedlings also know that they must wait to see what comes.

As the amateur growers increased in number, the demand for small prefabricated, inexpensive greenhouses was met by the greenhouse manufacturers, so that greenhouses of all shapes and sizes can be had at reasonable prices. Many amatuers who are handy with tools have built their own. Dealers now have an array of equipment for the small grower, as well as pre-mixed fertilizers and insecticides, and special types of potting materials.

And what are these orchids that have provoked such love and excitement for generations? They are the most highly specialized plants in their line of evolution, topping the lilies and irises. They grow wild all over the world, except in regions of perpetual snow and in parched deserts. You probably know *Calypso* and the moccasin flowers, most showy of our native North American orchids. However, the tropics offer the greatest profusion, and it is the tropical orchids that are sought for greenhouse collections and which are the progenitors of our present hybrids.

Among the kinds you most frequently see, and which are widely grown for corsages, are *Cattleya,* whose showy flowers with their spectacular lips come in white and shades of lavender, pink, rose, yellow, bronze, and green; *Cymbidium,* of more modest style, but with a wide range of colors; *Phalaenopsis,* whose round white or pink flowers are serenely beautiful, and which now come in shades of yellow and green as well, often barred

Fig. 1-3 These are all orchids.. CENTER, *Phalaenopsis* Grace Palm. Clockwise from the LEFT side, *Pholidota imbricata, Oncidium ampliatum, Cycnoches aureum* (male flower), *Lycaste aromatica,* and *Oncidium papillio.*

and speckled; and *Paphiopedilum,* the waxy Asian ladyslipper, which can be delicately beautiful or boldly reptilian. Others, to mention but a few that are also the delight of growers, are *Dendrobium, Epidendrum, Oncidium, Odontoglossum,* and *Vanda,* all of which give sprays of charming, brightly colored flowers in varied designs and sizes.

Most orchids live in the tropics, and of these the greatest numbers inhabit the cloud forests at elevations between 3,000 and 9,000 feet. Orchids are found above and below this belt, but they become fewer in number and variety as the mountain tops or sea level is approached. In these jungles vegetation is dense and competition for light is almost vicious. Plants grow so thickly that the jungles are really forests upon forests. Giant ferns and other vegetation completely cover the ground. Plants that need more light than they can get on the ground contrive in some manner to reach up above the undergrowth. Vines grow up the tree trunks and form a tangled network among the branches. Some trees whose seedlings would die on the ground send their seed to germinate on branches of other trees, and when a seedling is developed it sends roots down into the ground and eventually smothers the tree that gave it support. Light- and air-loving orchids would have been pushed out of existence long ago if they had not evolved some way to live above the stifling mass of undergrowth.

The whole top of a forest is an aerial garden. Orchids and some other kinds of plants have learned to cling to the trees. Sometimes the burden of plants grows so heavy that a thick branch may break under its weight. Plants that live on other plants are called "epiphytes," "epi" meaning above or on, and "phyte" meaning plant. The epiphytes obtain no nourishment from the plants on which they grow—they are not parasites. They merely grow where they can find a foothold and a collection of humus material consisting of dead leaves and bugs. Outside of the forests epiphytic orchids may be found growing on thatched roofs (often placed there by the natives), stone walls fallen logs, or rocky cliffs.

The epiphytes have cleverly adapted their structure to their needs as air dwellers. Since they are cut off from a continuous supply of water, they must depend on catching rain and dew, and for this purpose their roots have a spongy coating that soaks up water. To withstand the period between rains their stems and leaves are thickened, like the stem of a cactus, for the storage of water. When such a plant is grown in a flower pot, the potting medium must be extremely porous to allow the roots plenty of air.

Many kinds of orchids may live on the same tree. Those that can resist drying most efficiently and which also require a lot of light live in the tops of the trees and on exposed branches. Those that cannot resist drying quite so well, or which do better when shaded somewhat more, may live lower down on the tree, and some miniature orchids often find protection among the roots and stems of a larger plant.

In addition to orchids which are epiphytic, there are other kinds that live on the ground and are not equipped to resist drying. They are found in more open forests, in meadows, or along the banks of streams where the break in vegetation allows light to reach them. These are called terrestrials. The ground in which they grow is always fluffy with humus such as rotting wood or thick layers of dead leaves, so that even these, when grown in pots, must have an open, well-drained compost.

Most amateurs start a collection with a few cattleya plants, and add other kinds as they go along. Each kind has its own blooming season, so that even with a small collection it is possible to have a spread of flowers throughout the year. We always suggest beginning with mature plants, either species or hybrids. In the first place it is hard to wait years for flowers, so we think it is fun to get something that will bloom soon. Also the mature plants are better able to withstand changed conditions and are more likely to survive what mistakes you may make in learning to care for them. In growing a mature plant, you learn to know the habits of the kind, how it makes its growths and roots, how the flowers develop, etc. After you have served an apprenticeship in this way, you are ready to try some seedlings, perhaps a few very young ones, just out of the flask, or some two- or three-year-olds.

Tiny seedlings just out of the flask are delicate, and even though they are about a year old, they are so small that they are put twenty-five to thirty in a community pot or small flat. Their growth for the next year is slow, still somewhat of a formative stage, and some do not survive. They need to be shaded carefully and kept quite damp. During their third and fourth years they are moved from small single pots to increasingly larger ones, and become robust and more demanding of light.

Fig. 1-4 In the damp tropical forests epiphytes cover the trees. UPPER, a tree growing alongside a river in Peru is heavy with orchids, bromeliads, aroids, and gesneriads. An agile Indian boy climbs where the author fears to go. LOWER, the tip of the smallest twig is an aerial garden.

Fig. 1-5 The variety to be found among orchids is half of their charm. Gathered together here from this varied collection are *Cattleya, Odontoglossum, Vanda,* and *Miltonia.* (*Courtesy Lord and Burnham*)

Fig. 1-6 Lovely cluster-type "cocktail" hybrids are being made with many small waxy flowers to the stem. LEFT, *Cattleya* Beverly Boswell (Celia X December Snow).

RIGHT, *Cattleya* Claesiana (*loddigesii* 'Stanley' X *intermedia* var. *alba*).

Seedlings are priced according to their age—a flask containing a hundred plants sells for from fifteen to twenty-five dollars, just a few cents a plant. Community pot size are from seventy-five cents to a dollar and a half; and larger seedlings from two dollars on up. Seedlings about ready to bloom are often just as expensive as mature plants, and because their quality cannot be known until they bloom, we would rather buy several younger ones for the same money. Not every plant in a cross will be of equal quality, and we feel we increase our chances of obtaining some good ones by buying several of a cross.

The suspense of waiting for a new hybrid to bloom, or any plant new to your collection, is beyond description. Day by day you watch the buds grow larger, until one day you see that the tip of the bud is opening. Within a few hours the sepals and petals swing out and the lip starts to unfurl. You can almost see the flower parts move. It takes about twenty-four hours for the flower to open, but it is somewhat limp during this stage, and the colors are pale. As another twenty-four to forty-eight hours pass, the color intensifies, the flower becomes firm, its parts stretch open to their fullest, and finally its peak of perfection is reached. Here is one of nature's most artful creations, and it is yours to enjoy for days or weeks, and will repeat itself for years to come.

2

BASIC HABITS AND STRUCTURE

The charming array of shapes, sizes, and habits made by just a few different kinds of orchid plants adds to the fun of orchid growing, and keeps an amateur constantly adding new kinds to his collection. Also, it makes an orchid grower something of a marvel in the eyes of his friends.

GROWTH HABITS

In general, there are two basic growth habits, or patterns of growth, among orchids. Essentially, one type makes a new growth (or lead) each year from the base of the preceding growth, and this new growth produces flowers, makes its own set of roots, and in turn gives rise to another new growth the following season. Such a plant consists of several stems arising from a creeping ground stem, or "rhizome." In the other type of growth pattern there is but one main upright stem that grows taller each year, adding new leaves to the top but not making any new growth from its base. It has no rhizome and forms no pseudobulb. Flowering stems and aerial roots come from between the leaves, following each other in succession up the stem year after year. While the plant does not form new vegetative growth from its base, it may branch from buds in the axils of the leaves.

The names for these two growth habits are rather descriptive. The kind that makes new seasonal growths from a rhizome is called "sympodial"

which freely translated means "feet together." The type that has but one main stem is called "monopodial," or "one-footed." There are far more sympodial than monopodial kinds, but each type contains some of our best loved orchids, so you will undoubtedly have both types in your collection.

When you first glance at a cattleya plant, you will be struck by how stiff and strong it is. The heavy, thickened stems and the thick, hard leaves may remind you of a cactus plant. Actually, there are some similarities, because both are built to withstand periods of dryness. The cactus has been reduced to a water-storing stem (its spines are its "leaves"), because it must subsist through long periods of drought. In the cattleya and other orchids like it, the enlarged stem and thickened leaves are reservoirs for water and food. In addition, a heavy coating of wax protects the leaves. While in nature a cattleya actually has to withstand only short periods of drying between rains or baths of fog or dew, some other kinds live where there are definite seasons of dry weather. These orchids, including the cattleya, have the capacity to go for weeks without water.

The thickened stems of sympodial orchids are called "pseudobulbs." Actually, the stem of the cattleya is not as bulbous as is the stem of many other kinds in which it is truly spherical or pear shaped. The term pseudobulb is used to distinguish these fat stems from true bulbs because their structure is quite different. A true bulb, a lily for instance, is made up of scale-like leaves. An orchid pseudobulb is purely a stem, actually a jointed stem.

In the cattleya the new growth, or "lead" as it is called, comes from a bud at the base of the growth made the preceding year. The bud swells, breaks through the dry covering scales, and elongates. It grows horizontally for an inch or so and then curves upward. The horizontal part becomes an extension of the rhizome or ground stem, and the upward growing part produces the new pseudobulb, leaves, and eventually the flowers. The new growth is covered with tight sheathing leaves that give it a criss-cross or braided look. When it is about three or four inches long, the true leaf emerges from the tip of the growth. Some cattleya species have a single leaf; others have two or three. As the growth continues the leaf expands, and within it you can see the "sheath," a thin green envelope that grows from the top of the pseudobulb and encloses the flower buds during the early part of their formation. It takes five or six months for the new growth to reach its full size, during which time it is soft and succulent. At the end of the growth period the pseudobulb becomes plump and the leaf also becomes thick and hard, a process called maturation or "hardening." Soon afterward the thin sheathing leaves dry to white tissue. Good light and proper care contribute to a good, hard plant and to flowers of good substance.

Flower buds in cattleyas are "initiated," that is, the flower parts are formed microscopically, at the tip of the pseudobulb; in some while the growth is developing, in others as the growth matures. But you may not be able to see the buds for some time. Some cattleyas flower as soon as the growth is formed, in which case the bud expansion follows right along as the growth approaches or reaches its full size. Others wait for several months before the flower buds start to grow. At any rate, when the buds begin development, they appear as little dark shadows at the bottom of the sheath, enlarging slowly at first, and then growing more rapidly until they push out through the tip of the sheath. The growth from base to tip of the sheath takes about six weeks, and another three weeks or so are required before the buds reach full size and are ready to open. The species normally flower once a year, each in its own season, but many hybrids make new growths and flower two or three times a year.

After flowering, the cycle starts over again when this growth gives rise to a set of roots and a new shoot. Thus one growth follows another. A pseudobulb does not flower again (there are exceptions

among some other kinds of orchids). The pseudobulbs and leaves remain green for a number of years, sometimes as long as six to eight years. On a plant that makes but one growth a year, you can tell the age of the oldest pseudobulb by counting back from the youngest growth. Eventually the older leaves die and fall off, and finally the old pseudobulbs shrivel and die.

Each pseudobulb, with the portion of rhizome at its base, is essentially a plant in itself. Pseudobulbs divided singly from each other will give rise to new plants. But a plant started from a single pseudobulb is quite weak; its new growth is small, and it takes several years' growth to attain flowering size again. Therefore, divisions are usually made of clumps of pseudobulbs, at least three, preferably four. There is a bud at each joint of the rhizome, but not all of the buds become active and develop into new growths. This is one of nature's safety factors. When a plant is divided, the removal of the growing end stimulates the development of one or more dormant buds on the older part, so that division results in two active halves.

Sometimes two buds will develop simultaneously from the base of a single lead, giving rise to two

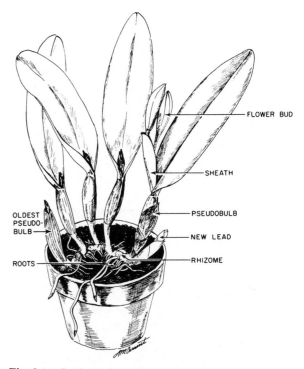

Fig. 2-1 Cattleya plant. Sympodial type of growth, with many stems arising from a creeping ground stem or rhizome. The new growth of the season, the "lead," comes from the base of the growth of the previous season.

Fig. 2-2 Vanda plant. Monopodial type of growth. A single upright stem grows taller year after year, adding new leaves at its tip. Aerial roots come from the stem between the leaves, as do the flower stems.

new pseudobulbs from one. Each of these in turn will produce a new growth, so that the plant becomes forked into two growing parts. Sometimes a bud farther back on an older pseudobulb will also start development, establishing still another line of growth. A plant with many leads is most desirable; it gives a greater number of flowers and yields many separate plants when divided. The habit of breaking extra leads is inherent in some plants, but is encouraged by good culture.

The roots of cattleyas and of all epiphytic orchids are covered, except for the green tip, with a white, spongy coating called "velamen," which probably has several functions—to soak up water, to protect the inner root tissues, and to cling to surfaces to give the plant support. As the roots

start to grow from the rhizome the green tip appears; then as the root elongates the velamen develops behind the green tip. The roots grow along in an exploratory manner, some penetrating the growing medium, others gliding across it to go down over the side of the pot. They cling tightly to any surface they meet, and those that do not meet with anything solid simply hang out in the air. This is their habit in nature, where they cling to the tree bark or hang down from the branch. The roots usually remain unbranched the first year, but if the growing tip is injured after the root has reached a fair length, branch roots will develop behind the tip. Older roots send out new branches each year.

Sympodial orchids that you will come to know,

in addition to cattleyas, are: epidendrums, whose plant forms run from those with fat round pseudobulbs to some with three-foot reed-like stems; oncidiums and odontoglossums, some of whose pseudobulbs are compressed laterally almost to a knife edge; dendrobiums, many of which have rather tall stems; and paphiopedilums which do not form pseudobulbs at all. These last are terrestrial plants and do not withstand drying well.

The stately vanda is a monopodial plant. It has a single main stem and grows quite tall, adding several new leaves to its tip every year. The leaves grow close together, alternating on the right and left sides to give a beautifully symmetrical plant. The flower stems also alternate sides, coming from the axils of the leaves on the upper part of the plant. The huge aerial roots make their appearance farther down, splitting the base of the leaves as they force their way out from the stem. Each new root comes somewhat above the one made previously. The vanda seems always to be making new leaves, but the roots occasionally undergo a period of dormancy. The tips cease growth and velamen covers the end. Then sometime later, the roots resume growth from the same tip. At the same time, branch roots grow along the length of the root.

The vanda shown in the accompanying illustration is of the strap-leaf type, with rather broad, flat leaves. There are also kinds whose leaves are cylindrical, pencil shaped.

You will come to know several other lovely monopodials. *Phalaenopsis,* which grows slowly, adds but one or two broad, flat leaves a year. Its flower stems develop near the base of the plant, giving a graceful, arching spray. *Aerides* grows quite like a vanda and gives drooping sprays of the most delightful little flowers.

The monopodials listed above are all epiphytic, and can withstand some drying. Their leaves are thick, sometimes tough and leathery, and store some water. Perhaps also the main stem and the large roots are reservoirs.

FLOWER STRUCTURE AND POLLINATION

The orchid flower is built on a very simple pattern of three outer and three inner flower parts, albeit the often fanciful shapes these parts take make some flowers look quite complex. The outermost flower parts are the three sepals, which can be identified as they enclose the rest of the

flower in the bud. Within these are three petals, one of which has been so modified that its appearance is entirely different from the other two and is therefore called by its own name, the "lip" or "labellum." The lip is not only shaped differently from the other petals, but it is embellished with its own markings of color and is often fantastically decorated with crests, horns, tails, or other protuberances. The lip is usually the most striking part of the flower, but there are some kinds in which the sepals or the petals are more elaborate. You may come across the term "tepals" in your reading, a word coined to refer to sepals and petals together.

The least conspicuous part of the flower is most diagnostic of an orchid, its hallmark. This is the column, a fleshy structure that sits in the center and consists of the fused reproductive parts. It adds charm to the flower, however, and if you take time to look at it you may decide that it is the most delightful part of all. Surely it is the most cleverly designed, both outwardly and from the point of view of function. It may be quite simply shaped, a white or pink or green cylinder, or it may look like a little figure, a doll, a bird, an insect, a face wearing goggles, or the neck of a swan. Often the column is decorated with wings, or a cap, or a fringed bonnet. At the tip of the column is the

Fig. 2-3 Parts of the orchid flower, illustrated by a cattleya.

Home Orchid Growing

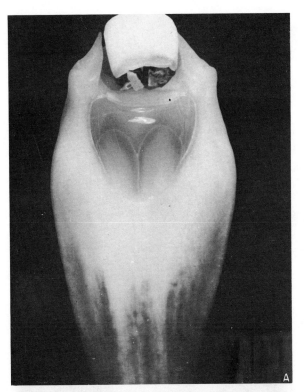

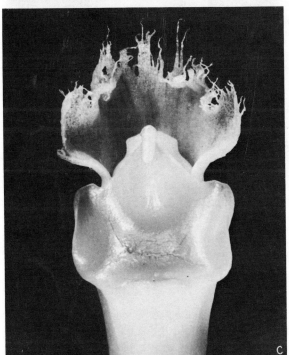

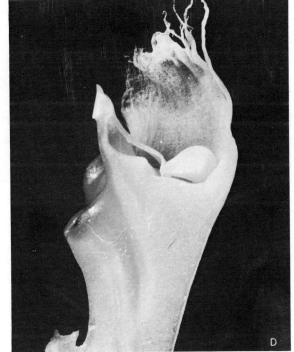

Fig. 2-4 A. A cattleya column. At the very top is the anther cap, tipped up to show the fuzzy tails of the pollinia within. Below the anther, separated from it by the rostellum, is the stigma.

B. A bee which has visited a cattleya flower and bears on its back the four pollinia that became fastened to it as it crawled out from under the column.

C. The column of *Trichopilia suavis,* decorated with a fringed bonnet. The "beak" of the column is the viscid disc.

D. The column with the anther cap removed and the side sliced away to show the pollinia lying in the anther chamber. The pollinia are attached by a tail-like band (caudicle, or stipe) to the viscid disc. The viscid disc will adhere to an insect touching it, and as the insect leaves it will bear the pollinia on its back.

Basic Habits and Structure   **13**

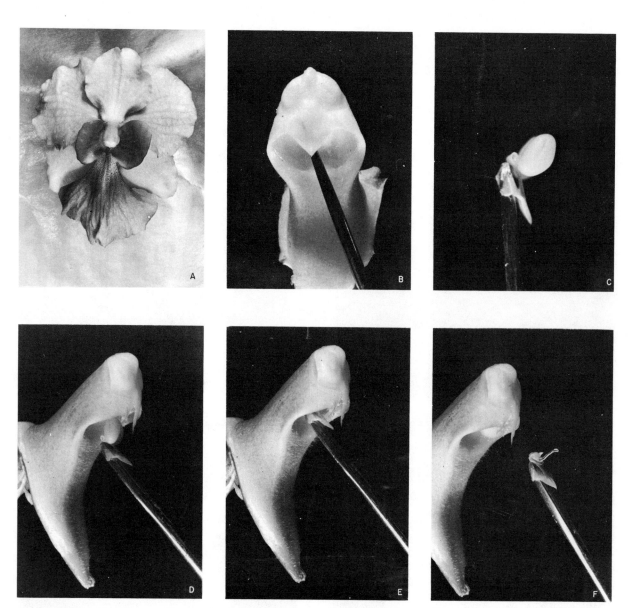

Fig. 2-5 Steps in pollination, as it would be performed by an insect.

A. A Vanda flower.
B. The column with flower parts removed. The swellings of the anther cap show the location of the pollinia within. Touch the underside of the "beak" and the viscid disc will stick to the needle.
C. The pollinarium attached to the needle.
D. Put the needle bearing the pollinarium into the stigmatic cavity.
E. Touch the pollinia to the sticky fluid of the stigma.
F. Pull out the needle. The pollinia will be left on the stigma, held so strongly by the sticky fluid that they are torn off the caudicle.

anther which bears the pollen, but instead of being dusty, the pollen grains are molded by wax into hard pellets. The pellets, called "pollinia," lie in a cavity covered by a hinged cap, where they look like a pair of eyes. Just below the anther, separated from it by a partition, is the female receptive organ, the "stigma," a shiny depression filled with extremely sticky fluid. The column may be stubby and upright or may arch out over the base of the lip.

By offering nectar to a visiting insect, the lip lures it into an ambush, for the column poised over the lip is equipped with a tricky device to fasten its pollen to the insect. The pollen-fastening mechanism is so designed that it applies the pollen to the insect as it *leaves* the flower, causing it to carry the pollen off and deposit it on the next flower it visits, ensuring cross-pollination. Some kinds of orchids are pollinated by only a single kind of insect. It is fun to discover this mechanism in the column

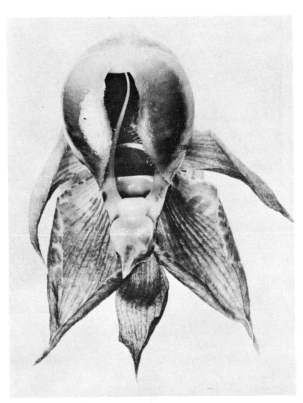

Fig. 2-6 *Catasetum macrocarpum.* When a visiting insect touches the whip-shaped trigger within the hoodlike lip, the pollinia fly up and become attached to it by means of the viscid disc.

able to fly, and spend their time helplessly crawling around over the plant. Others make attempts at wobbly flight. One may become well enough adjusted to visit another flower, whereupon, as it forces its way into the throat, the pollinia are caught in the viscid fluid of the stigma and are torn off the caudicles. The bee emerges from the second flower with the stubs of one set of caudicles, bearing on top of them the new set of pollinia it has just acquired.

Some kinds of orchids have even more ingenious methods. Instead of having a gland on the rostellum, the pollinia are themselves attached by a little strap to a disc that is viscid on its under surface and hangs down like a beak from the end of the column. Pollinia, strap, and viscid disc are together called the "pollinarium." As an insect enters the flower it does not touch the sticky side of the disc. But as it backs out, or flies up from the lip, it hits the viscid surface, which instantly becomes stuck to

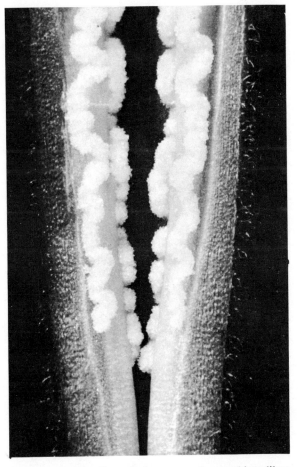

Fig. 2-7 Section through the ovary of a paphiopedilum flower, showing the rows of ovules. When fertilized, each ovule becomes a seed.

of any orchid you may have. In the cattleya, the partition (rostellum) that separates the anther from the stigma bears a gland that secretes sticky fluid. The pollinia within the easily tipped-up anther cap have fuzzy tails (caudicles) that lie just under its edge. In search of nectar an insect, usually a bee, has to crawl underneath the column, between it and the lip. As it backs out, it presses against the gland on the rostellum, ruptures it, and becomes smeared with "glue." At the same time, its movement tips up the anther cap and the fuzzy tails of the pollinia are caught in the glue. It flies away with one or two, sometimes all four, of the pollinia attached to its back.

I am sure that the South American bees that are accustomed to orchids think nothing of this, but the bees in this country are puzzled by the sudden burden they have acquired. Although we do not like to have bees in the greenhouse (because a pollinated flower quickly wilts and is therefore ruined), we have had a lot of fun watching an occasional bee that has happened to enter. The pollinia on its back are just like a load of suitcases, and they throw the bee off balance. Some are unthe insect. So, as it flies off, it pulls the attached pollinia out of the anther and bears them off on its back to another flower. Try this yourself, with a needle or the tip of a pencil. Touch the under side of the beak and you can pull out the attached pair of pollinia, golden globules as shiny and beautifully shaped as jewels.

The pollinia are usually in an upright position when they are withdrawn from a flower, but in many kinds the stalk goes through motions afterward to bring the pollinia into a better position for contacting the stigma of the next flower visited. In some kinds the stalk bends forward to point the pollinia straight ahead. In *Vanda* Miss Joaquim, illustrated herewith, the stalk does a triple turn— it bends forward, then backward, then forward again in an S curve, which results in shortening the stalk and at the same time presenting the pollinia in a higher position so that they will touch the arching stigma. In some other kinds the stalk bends forward and then the pollinia rise up at its tip.

Fig. 2-8 A female *Aëdes* mosquito leaving a flower of *Habenaria obtusata* with a pollinarium attached to its right eye. (*Courtesy Warren P. Stoutamire*)

Much fun can be had in learning just what the pollinarium does in various species.

Among orchids, some are pollinated by bees, flies, moths, butterflies, beetles, ants, spiders, or even birds. Many are quite selective and rely on just certain species, or only one species, to do the job. These are adapted in peculiar ways to their pollinators. Some imitate the female of the species of insect so that the male is lured into attempting to mate with the flowers, performing pollination in the process. Such are the two species of *Trichoceros* shown later on. Some have devious ways of forcing their servants to perform pollination. The catasetum has a sensitive trigger, which, when touched, causes the pollinarium to shoot out and stick to the bee with a fast-setting cement. If you imitate a bee by touching the trigger with a pencil, you can actually feel the recoil of the flower when this happens, and you will have difficulty removing the pollinarium from the pencil, so tightly does it adhere.

Many species place the pollinia on a certain part of the anatomy of an insect, in a position where they are sure to be brought into contact with the stigma of the next flower visited. Some of our native orchids are pollinated by mosquitoes. Drs. Warren Stoutamire and Leonard Thien have confirmed the observations of others and are independently conducting detailed studies. A fascinating example they describe is the pollination of *Habenaria obtusata*, which they have observed in the field and in the laboratory with mosquitoes caged with the flowers. Oddly, it seems that only female mosquitoes are attracted to the flowers. The flower has a divided anther, each half with its own viscid disc standing on either side of the stigma. The lip bears a projection extending backward over the entrance to the nectary, so that the mosquito is forced to probe into the flower on one side or the other. As it retreats from the flower, its head comes in contact with a viscid disc, and it leaves with a pollinarium stuck to its eye—the right eye if it probed into the right side of the nectary, the left if it probed on the left side!

There are two orchids whose entire life cycle is a mystery since they live underground. Of all the strange habits of orchids, it would seem that this was a most inefficient way to survive. Yet they manage to make use of their environment to do so. One is *Rhizanthella gardneri*, which never sees the light of day. It has been found only accidentally, never by deliberate search. Probably it is often ploughed up and goes unnoticed. It produces a

16

Fig. 2-9 The underground orchid *Rhizanthella gardneri.* The head of small flowers is produced and seed is formed entirely underground. (*Courtesy Alex S. George*)

head of small flowers, perfect in every way, which open and form seed without ever appearing above the surface. We can wonder about them: Are they pollinated by small soil dwellers who crawl in and out of the flowers, or are they self-pollinating? Do ants, perhaps, distribute the seed? But we cannot know the answers. The other is *Cryptanthemis slateri,* which also lives, blooms, and produces seed underground. This one, however, is thought to push the flower head to the surface for seed dispersal. Both of these strange orchids are natives of Australia.

TEMPERATURE GROUPS

When the many and varied climates to which orchids are native are put together and analyzed, it turns out that there are three basic temperature ranges into which most of the kinds can be fitted. Winter temperatures are kept somewhat cooler than summer temperatures, partly because we can control the winter temperatures whereas we have less control over the summer's, and partly because when artificial heat is used moderate temperatures give healthier plants and better flowers. The night temperature is critical; in fact, some kinds of orchids will not flower if the night temperature runs above a certain limit and others do poorly if it goes below a definite point. The three temperature

groups that have been established are therefore based on *winter night* temperatures. Winter day temperatures are kept about ten degrees higher than those of the nights. Summer temperatures, particularly where the days become very hot, offer special problems that will be dealt with later on.

The three temperature groups are: "cool," with nights held between 50° and 55°; "intermediate," with nights of 55° to 60°; and "warm," with nights of 60° to 65°. A different group of plants is grown in each temperature range, except that if the temperature runs a little warmer or a little cooler in some spots in a greenhouse it may be possible to add plants from another temperature range. In choosing orchids to grow it is of utmost importance to learn first their temperature requirements and be sure that you can give each the range it needs. It is of no avail to put a "warm" orchid in a "cool" greenhouse, or vice versa.

The cool greenhouse (50° to 55°) is used widely throughout this country for many kinds of plants; in fact it is used for many of the florists' cut flower crops such as carnations, stock, snapdragons, and camellias. If you already grow some of these flowers, you can slip in a few cool orchids such as cymbidiums, some paphiopedilums, and others that come from cool climates or high elevations. It is the most economical of the three ranges, since heating costs are lower. However, many orchids that demand cool conditions in the winter also prefer cool summers, so that in general the cool types are better grown in the cooler part of the United States. With special coolers and attention to keep environmental factors in balance, they may sometimes be grown in warmer climates.

The "intermediate" greenhouse (55° to 60°) accommodates by far the greatest number of kinds. It is often referred to as the "cattleya house" because it is the range in which cattleyas are usually grown. Along with the cattleyas you can grow epidendrums, laelias, oncidiums, dendrobiums, vandas, some kinds of miltonias, paphiopedilums, odontoglossums, and a tremendous array of odd and unusual kinds called "botanical" orchids.

The "warm" greenhouse (60° to 65°) is used for kinds that do not do well with nights under 60°. These include phalaenopsis, some paphiopedilums, and others, in general kinds that come from lower, warmer climates.

You may ask why, since the upper range of the intermediate and the lower range of the warm greenhouse meet at 60°, should there be a distinction between the two; why not grow everything at

60°? In running a greenhouse, it is almost impossible to keep the temperature at an exact point. There is always a fluctuation of a few degrees as the heat goes on or off. By keeping the air circulating we narrow the margin of fluctuation, but about five degrees of difference inevitably occurs. These five degrees can be critical for many kinds. If you run the temperature repeatedly below 60°, Phalaenopsis and some others will do nothing. If you run it repeatedly above 60°, you automatically eliminate many kinds that you otherwise could grow. While some people grow cattleyas at 60° to 65°, problems often arise that are eliminated in the 55° to 60° range. In the intermediate range we feel that cattleyas are stockier, flowering is more regular, and the flowers are of better substance and last longer. Since cattleyas do so well at 55° to 60°, and since using this night temperature range allows you to grow so many other kinds, there is a real reason for adhering to it, and for separating it from the warmer 60° to 65° range.

3

THE CARE OF ADULT CATTLEYAS

Since cattleyas are the most widely grown of all orchids and since most growers start with them, the conditions that suit cattleyas and their method of culture have become a sort of base, or point of departure. For orchids that are to be treated exactly like cattleyas (as to light and water in addition to temperature), it is customary to say "handle like cattleyas," or "likes cattleya conditions." Then, for those that vary a bit one way or another from the needs of cattleya we say "cattleya conditions except a bit more shade, or more frequent watering, etc." We shall therefore spend the longest time and give most space to cattleya culture, and in this section you will find the basic rules for all orchid culture. When we take up other kinds, we will give their specific needs and tell you how to vary the basic rules for them.

Adult cattleyas include plants just matured from the seedling stage and propagations made from older plants. The matured seedlings show a succession of leaf sizes from the small leaves up to the larger flowering lead. A propagation is a division of a plant. It may be made from the lead end of a plant—the youngest growth plus the two or three pseudobulbs just behind it, in which case it should flower on its next new growth—or it may consist of the older half of the plant. If these older pseudobulbs (or backbulbs as they are sometimes called) are plump and still have their leaves, the first new growth they make may flower.

But if the pseudobulbs are shriveled and have lost their leaves, the first new growth may be quite small, and it may require another two years before a flowering size growth is produced. It is therefore preferable, in buying mature plants, to get those in flowering condition, unless you know that the backbulbs are from very good plants and that it would be worth waiting the several years for them to flower again. The plant should be vigorous and healthy. If it is a propagation it should show evidence, by cut flower stems on each pseudobulb, of having flowered regularly.

You can buy species or hybrids. There are two groups of species. One, the "labiata" group, has the wide frilled petals and lip with which most people are familiar, and its pseudobulbs bear a single leaf. The other, the "bifoliate" group, has smaller, more waxy flowers, some with a spade-shaped or fiddle-shaped lip and a remarkable array of colors and markings. The species are usually quite inexpensive and dependable, and some offer exceptional interest to any collection. The hybrids are priced according to their quality. Those that come in the six-to-ten-dollar class (the price of most of the species) will be about average in quality. For your first plants it would be wise to buy in this price range. Later on, when you are sure of your growing ability, you will want to have some of superior quality, which you may buy as higher priced mature plants, or raise from seedlings that cost less. If you live near a professional orchid grower, you will benefit from picking out your plants in flower so that you know exactly what you are getting. However, this is possible for relatively few of us. Otherwise, send for catalogues of reputable dealers, and buy but a few plants at a time until you know with whom you like best to deal, and which growers furnish the best plants.

Cattleya flowers come in many sizes and a great range of colors. Orchid hybridizers for years were so intrigued by their ability to produce ever larger flowers that giant flowers became the vogue, and small ones, unless they had exceptional coloring or some other unusual quality, were rather looked down upon. Truly, some of the nine- and ten-inch cattleyas are spectacular, and if their color and shape are good, they are very handsome. But many people had the feeling that grace and daintiness were lost in the giant size, and that the smaller flowers should be loved for their special appeal. Now the small flower has come into its own. More frequent crosses are being made using the delightful smaller species, which offer their waxy substance and unusual coloring along with more flowers to the stem. Their three-to four-inch flowers are often called "cocktail" orchids and are, along with the standard five- and six-inch flowers, most popular for corsages.

In judging the quality of cattleya flowers, regardless of the size, there are certain characteristics to look for. A strict point system is used in judging flowers for awards. The color must be pure and fresh. It may be dark or light, but never dull or muddy, and the color in the lip should be in harmony with, or make a pleasing contrast to, the rest of the flower. The flower should have an aristocratic, graceful bearing. Its parts should be generous according to its kind (in some of the species the parts are normally slender). In the large-flowered hybrids, we especially look for broad, straight sepals and broad, flat or gently curving petals that do not fold back on themselves, as well as a nicely ruffled lip that opens fully to show the markings in the throat. Good substance is important. The more turgid, waxy flowers are better looking, do not become floppy, and last longer. Fragrance is an added attraction. Most cattleyas have a delightful, delicate perfume, and in some the fragrance is so aromatic that it fills the house.

The plants may be shipped to you out of their pots. Many growers like to save shipping weight and packing difficulties by removing the plant from the pot and substituting a polyethlyene bag. You should have some pots of various sizes on hand in which to put these when they arrive. Plants are also shipped "bare root." Since most of the potting material has been shaken off these, you will have to furnish them with fresh potting material. If you prefer to receive them in their pots, inform the dealer. Perhaps your first plants should arrive this way, to give you a chance to get used to them before you tackle a repotting job.

Up until a few years ago, practically all orchids in this country were grown in osmunda fiber, the roots of the osmunda fern. Its fibers are tough and springy so that they give the roots plenty of air, yet in the process of decay it furnishes all the nutrients the plants really need. It is somewhat difficult to learn to use it properly, and potting with it is a slow process requiring a strong arm. Also, it has become scarce and rather expensive with increased demand. A number of other potting materials have been tried, and it has been proved that orchids will accept a variety of materials if they have the basic qualities of giving the plants a firm foothold, of not breaking down rapidly, and of furnishing good drainage and aeration. Out of the experiments to find new materials came the discovery that the chopped bark of various trees, principally fir and Douglas fir, worked beautifully. Chopped bark has the advantage of being easier to use and less expensive than osmunda fiber. Growers in Hawaii introduced "hapuu," tree fern which is similar to, but tougher than, osmunda fiber, and this is now quite widely used. Slabs of tree fern are useful for growing some of the "botanical" orchids. Various prepared mixes are on the market, some especially useful for certain kinds of plants or certain climates. In the section on potting, Chapter 5, we will tell you how to handle the various materials and how to transfer plants from one to another.

TEMPERATURE, HUMIDITY, AND LIGHT

Plants do not keep accounts, of course, but if balance sheets were published for them, they would be quite similar to those you receive from the bank each month. If you spend more than you earn, you end up in debt. If you earn more than you spend, you have money left over for savings, and philosophically savings mean better living. The earning of plants is the food they make, and their spending is the food they use for energy. Their savings go into growth and flower production, with a reserve kept over toward launching the next season's growth.

During the day a plant carries on three activities: the making of food (sugar) for which light is necessary, the use of food (respiration, similar to our own use of food for energy), and growth. At night no food is made, but respiration and growth continue, drawing on the food made during the day.

Temperature regulates the rate of the plant's activities. Low temperature slows down the processes; rising temperature speeds them up, although not all at the same rate and not indefinitely. The reason behind what we call an optimal temperature range is that within this range the plant can carry on all of its life processes in a normal way, with no activity out of balance with the rest.

The ideal night temperature chosen for a particular kind of orchid is the temperature at which growth and respiration are in good balance so that the plant makes good growth without using too much of its food reserve. For cattleyas this is between 55° and 60°. At lower temperatures growth is slowed down; at higher temperatures there is a tendency for respiration to exceed growth and for the plants to become depleted.

With abundant light, food making increases as the temperature rises up to about 85°. The day temperature should ideally be about ten degrees higher than it is at night. In the winter and in cool weather, this is easy to maintain. Problems come with hot weather. The plant's activities remain in pretty good balance up to about 85°, but over this the equilibrium is upset. With higher temperatures there comes the danger of burning and finally death. Plants can tolerate 95° for a few hours, and 100° for shorter intervals, but when the temperature rises above this the situation rapidly becomes critical, for the lethal point is not far off.

There are ways to modify the greenhouse conditions with shading, ventilation, humidity, and air circulation, so that we can pretty well control the environment. We don't wait for extremes to arrive, we anticipate them, and we use the various means in coordination with each other throughout the year so as to give the plants a good balance of the various factors; a balance between day and night temperatures, between the amount of light and the day temperature, and between humidity and all the other factors.

Temperature. Winter for most of us means cold weather, but for some it is merely a cool season.

In some regions winter brings dull skies, long periods when the sun shines but rarely; in others, winter is a season of bright sun. For these reasons no one set of rules can be made as to just what to do in what month. The basis must therefore be the needs of the plants themselves, and each grower must adjust his own conditions accordingly.

In the winter we can maintain what we consider the ideal temperature conditions for cattleyas, 55° to 60° at night, and days of 65° to 72° degrees. On a dark day, or during a spell of dull weather, it is good to let the days hover between 65° and 68°. With the lessened amount of light the plants cannot make as much food as they can when the sun is shining, and a higher day temperature would cause them to use the food as fast as it is made. On a sunny day, however, let the temperature run up to 70° or 72°. We welcome the sun. In itself it helps to warm the greenhouse with a heat more natural than that produced artificially, and the good light allows the plants to make a generous amount of food. On these nice bright days, open the ventilators a crack to give the plants fresh air. We try always to maintain a buoyant atmosphere for orchids. The winter greenhouse tends to become a bit dank, and airing it out whenever you can gives the plants a lift and helps prevent disease. Always open the ventilators away from the direction of the wind.

Day and night, winter and summer, the air within the greenhouse should be kept in circulation. Circulation of the air keeps the temperature more uniform, preventing layering of hot and cold air or pockets of dead air. The air should be moved from one end to the other under the benches and returned up and over the plants. In a small greenhouse a single fan may do the job, blowing the under-bench air against the opposite end of the greenhouse, where it rises against the wall and naturally flows back toward the end where the fan is located. In a larger greenhouse it may help to have a second fan placed at the opposite end, pointing vertically to keep the air in circular motion. Nearly all makes of natural gas heaters come equipped with a fan. Often the wiring directions that come with the heater cause the fan to run only when the heat is on. The wiring should be changed to make the fan run constantly. If you have no fan in connection with the heating system, which would be the case with hot water heat, one can be installed separately. Not only is moving air a means of keeping a uniform temperature, but it is an important aid in disease prevention. Moving air does not hurt the plants as long as it is of the proper temperature and moisture content. Hot dry air blowing on them is harmful, as is a current of cold air.

More on heating systems will be given in Chapter 24, but we should say here that *artificial gas should never be used within a greenhouse, nor should gas that has any amount of artificial gas mixed with it, for it is fatal to orchids.* Natural gas is safe to use, but even with this the heaters should be vented to carry out all fumes of combustion. These fumes contain constituents that are harmful to cattleyas, causing what is known as "sepal wilt," and injuring other kinds as well. (See Chapter 23) Buds just ready to open are aged prematurely so that the buds may be blasted before opening or, if they open, the sepals are thin and tissue-like and the flower is ruined. Strong fumes can even injure the plants, aging them prematurely, so that they lose their older leaves before they normally should.

During an unusual cold spell it may not be possible to keep the greenhouse temperature quite up to normal. We experience this in Wyoming if the wind is blowing on a night when the outdoor temperature goes to minus 20°. A few nights of 50° or 45° will not harm cattleyas, although it may retard their flowering somewhat. Some kinds that grow with cattleyas may possibly drop their buds. Plants should be kept from contact with the cold glass, else they may have some leaves frozen. In England during World War II, fuel rationing forced growers to run their greenhouses at low temperatures, and although growth and flowering were poor, they were nevertheless able to keep their valuable plants. Heat may be conserved by tacking up sheets of polyethylene film on the inside of the greenhouse. Growers have reported that this works very well.

Problems with the heating system, power failure, etc. can bring on emergency conditions. We have no data on the length of time cattleyas can stand freezing or near-freezing temperatures. We have had a number of near fatal experiences ourselves, and have learned of others which have been worse. It is not as bad for the temperature to dip to freezing for half an hour and then rise again as it is for the temperature to stay at freezing for a longer period. During a short interval perhaps only some leaf tips and flowers may be frozen, but during a longer interval freezing may progress to the whole plant. We will give the treatment and handling of frozen plants in the section on ailments. Two aids against such emergencies are the installation of a temperature alarm, which rings a bell in the house to warn you of a dangerous drop (or rise) in temperature, and having on hand some form of auxiliary heat.

Spring brings such changeable weather that you have to watch the greenhouse rather carefully. The sun is traveling more nearly overhead, and the days are becoming warmer. On a bright, warm day the greenhouse can heat up in a short time. For a comparable example, consider how hot a closed car becomes when it is parked in the sun. Shading is an important means of controlling day temperature. We shall go further into shading under "light," but the relation between light and temperature and humidity and temperature makes it difficult to separate these three factors. As the days brighten, you can control midday heat for a while by opening the ventilators. The afternoon temperature drops quickly so be sure to close them by mid-afternoon. Automatic ventilator controls can be bought and might be necessary for those who have to be gone from home all day. Soon, however, you must apply a thin coat of shading to the glass to prevent the burning of the plants. This must be done by February in some areas. As spring advances a heavier coat will be needed. The aim is to keep the day temperatures between 70° and 80°, yet allow the plants enough light to get their season's growth off to a good start.

Summer brings the real problems in temperature control. We do not worry about summer nights. They will usually run somewhat higher than the winter nights, in fact, we simply have to accept what the outdoor night temperature brings. Cattleyas probably prefer a summer night temperature not exceeding 65°, but nights may go to 70° sometimes. There is always a contrast between day and night temperatures in the summer. The cooler night air brings the plants relief from the hot days. During hot weather we like to keep the ventilators open both day and night. It takes some time for the greenhouse to cool off—everything is warm, the pots, the benches, etc. Open ventilators during the night bring about cooling earlier than would be the case if the greenhouse were closed up, and keep it cool during the early morning.

When you can keep the summer day temperatures under 85° you are doing the plants a favor. As the leaves absorb light they become warmer than the surrounding air. If the greenhouse air goes to 100°, the leaves are even hotter and a further rise in air temperature will take them dangerously close to the burning point. Thick-leaved cattleyas and other kinds are more susceptible to burning than are some of the thinner-leaved kinds. Keep the fans running to circulate the cooler ground air, and step up the humidity to keep a current of moist air moving through and over the plants. Additional shading will be necessary, but try not to cut the light below the needs of the plants, about which more in a moment. Keep the ventilators open a few inches to let the heated air move out.

Evaporation of water into the air cools the air and the surfaces from which it is being evaporated. Air blown through a mist of water or a wet pad becomes cooled in the process. An evaporative system of one sort or another is a great help in cooling a greenhouse as well as in supplying humidity. A unit cooler such as those built for home use is satisfactory for a small greenhouse. Pads are incorporated in the walls of the unit and are kept wet by means of a circulating pump. Air is drawn through the wet pads by a blower which blows the damp cool air into the greenhouse. For most efficient cooling, the unit should be placed so that it draws air from outdoors. Another cooling arrangement is a "pad and fan," which can be operated in two ways. The pad, with a circulating water system (see Chapter 22 for details), is set in the wall of the greenhouse at one end, and a fan is installed to draw air through it. The fan may be an exhaust fan placed in the wall at the opposite end of the greenhouse, which pulls air through the pad and through the greenhouse and exhausts it at the other end. Or the fan may be placed directly in front of the pad so that it pulls air through the pad and pushes it through the greenhouse. A ventilator must be open at the opposite end to allow air to move out. Such evaporative cooling systems are capable of lowering greenhouse temperatures by as much as fifteen degrees.

Humidity. The older growers used to say that they could gauge humidity with "their noses." We like to be more specific, but you can sense when the atmosphere is right, or nearly so. When you walk into a greenhouse and it smells dry to you, when you can "smell the heat" as it were, chances are that the walks and ground are dry, and that the dry air will soon dessicate the plants if they are not quickly given some moisture. Or, if the air is stagnant and dense with moisture, oppressive to the point where you feel as if you must open the door for some relief, trouble of another kind is in store. But if, when you enter a greenhouse, you feel that you have opened the door on a spring morning, if the air is light and invigorating, moving as if in a gentle breeze, and you smell the gentle, damp, earthy fragrance of the plants, then you know that the atmosphere is right for orchids.

Warm air can hold much more water vapor than cool air, and relative humidity, expressed as a percentage, indicates the amount of water actually held by the air compared to the amount it could hold at a given temperature. For instance, at noon of a day when the temperature is 80°, the air may actually be holding only 35 percent of the water it could hold, so the relative humidity is expressed as 35 percent. But in the cooler evening, if the temperature drops to 50°, without any change in the actual amount of water, the air is now saturated, and the relative humidity becomes 100 percent. It is the temperature that determines whether the air can hold more or less water. Warm air therefore tends to attract water, to draw it from surfaces and from plants. You have seen garden plants wilt on a hot day when the warm air is drawing water from them faster than they can replace it by root action. And you have seen these same plants become turgid again in the evening when the cooler air allows them to replace the lost water.

Plants lose water through pores, or stomata, and it is through the stomata, also, that they take in carbon dioxide with which to make sugar. They

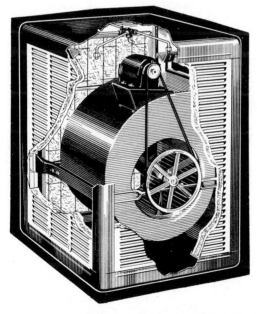

Fig. 3-1 An evaporative cooling unit. Pads built into three sides are kept wet by means of a circulating pump and distributing tubes. A blower draws outside air in through the wet pads and forces it into the greenhouse. (*Courtesy International Metal Products Div., McGraw-Edison Co.*)

lose water to the air faster when the relative humidity is low than when it is high. The thick-leaved cattleyas do not wilt; but if the air is too dry for them over a period of time, they cannot replace it fast enough through the roots, and the plants become emaciated, the leaves become thinner, and the pseudobulbs shrivel. Flower stems may be weak, unable to hold the flowers up properly, and the flowers themselves may be of poor substance.

In the winter, with moderate greenhouse temperatures, a relative humidity of 40 to 60 percent creates a good moisture balance for the plants. It is helpful to have a humidity gauge in the greenhouse so that you can actually know what the relative humidity is at all times. If your climate is mild and naturally humid and artificial heat is needed only occasionally at night, you may not have to add much moisture to the greenhouse air. But in a dry climate or one where artificial heat is needed throughout the winter, the greenhouse air becomes very dry, and humidity must be added.

You can add moisture to the air by "damping down," wetting the walks and under-bench areas with the hose. With a fan in operation the air picks up and circulates the moisture. Damping down is the old, standard method; but it requires that someone be home to do it. Those who are gone

from home all day or who object to getting their shoes wet may prefer to add a humidfier of some sort. Various types with various capacities are manufactured. These may be controlled by an electric humidistat, which turns the humidifier on or off according to the setting. A simple system, which we use, is a mist sprayer installed in front of the heater, so that the air blown by the fan picks up the moisture. We also damp down the floor on bright days when the sprayer does not furnish quite enough moisture. The number of mist sprayers could be increased, so that there are several at intervals under the benches. There is now an overhead mister that gives a very fine fog. It can be mounted high in the greenhouse and controlled by a timer, with the intervals adjusted to avoid excessive moisture. Overhead mist sprayers that put out a lot of water are dangerous to use because they keep the plants too wet.

Although the natural state of affairs is for the relative humidity to rise at night as the temperature drops, in the winter the air may become quite dry when the heat is running. A factor that contributes to this is condensation (or freezing) of moisture on the cold glass, taking it out of the air. When we were new at running a greenhouse, we did not realize that this was happening, and only learned

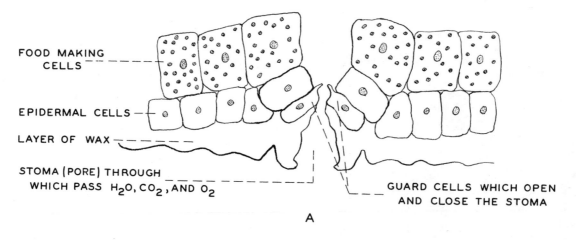

FOOD MAKING CELLS

EPIDERMAL CELLS

LAYER OF WAX

STOMA (PORE) THROUGH WHICH PASS H_2O, CO_2, AND O_2

GUARD CELLS WHICH OPEN AND CLOSE THE STOMA

A

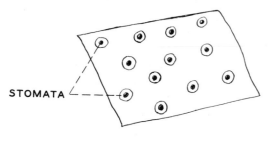

STOMATA

B

Fig. 3-2 A. A section of a cattleya leaf, showing the structure of a single stoma and the cells surrounding it. Note particularly the guard cells that regulate the opening and closing of the stoma, and the heavy layer of wax. B, a microscopic view of the undersurface of a leaf showing how the stomata appear externally. In such a view what are actually seen are the pits in the waxy covering of the leaf.

Home Orchid Growing

Fourteen Genera of Orchids: Gold Medal Exhibit (*Courtesy Lager and Hurrell*)

Cattleya Henrietta Japhet 'Colossal'

Cattleya intermedia var. *aquinii*

Blc. Mem. Helen Brown 'Sweet Afton' HCC/AOS

Lc. Mem. Albert Heinecke

it when plants began to show some dehydration. We then made it a practice to damp down the floor in the evening, and now let the sprayer in front of the heater run during the night as well as in the daytime. One exception to this is that after we have watered the plants, and the ground and benches are thoroughly wetted, we turn off the sprayer until the next day, or until needed again.

Hosing the plants with a sprayer, often called "syringing," is a practice that was once used rather freely, but is now used with caution, especially in the winter. The need for it has been reduced by the more general use of humidifiers. When a current of sufficiently moist air is kept moving through the greenhouse, it is ordinarily not necessary to mist the plants directly. There are circumstances when it is helpful, such as when it is necessary to protect plants from drying, and in warm seasons to help cool them when the sun is hot. The plants can absorb some water through their leaves, and water on the foliage also creates a saturated atmosphere for the plant, preventing excessive evaporation from the plant tissues. Syringing is therefore advised for newly potted plants until their root systems are again functioning, for hanging plants that dry out faster than benched ones, for seedlings, and for kinds that are more moisture demanding than cattleyas. In the winter, on a bright day, if the air is dry, a light syringing can be given to all the plants, cattleyas included, but this should never be done on a dull day, or when it is chilly in the greenhouse, or when the humidity is already high enough. Syringing should always be an extremely fine mist, applied with just a quick swish of the sprayer over the plants. (See Figure 4-1) Heavy syringing tends to wet the potting medium and may actually serve to keep it too wet.

Any syringing, or watering, should be done early enough in the day to allow the plants to dry off before night. This does not mean that the air or the potting medium should become dry, but simply that no water should be left standing on the plant parts. Fungal and bacterial spores can germinate only on wet surfaces. Water standing on the plants gives the spores a chance to germinate and infect the plants. Dry foliage and rhizomes discourage infection. Often a spreading infection in a greenhouse has been traceable to too frequent syringing. Crowding plants too close together on the bench also contributes to over-damp conditions. The air does not move as freely between the pots or through the plants as it does when they are well spaced.

This is particularly important to watch in damp climates and where the winters are dull.

Signs of too much humidity or of stagnant, over-damp conditions are the appearance of brown watery spots on the leaves, little brown or pinkish spots on the flowers, and blackened sheaths. A local spot of infection can be quickly treated, but if spotting becomes general throughout the greenhouse, the first thing to do is lower the humidity, dry off the plants, and increase the circulation of air. Sometimes water that has condensed on the glass drips onto the plants below, keeping the foliage or the potting medium too wet. If you can't cure the drip, move the plants. Diseases and their treatment will be taken up in a later chapter. We mentioned earlier that a relative humidity of 40 to 60 percent is good in the winter. We rather like a fluctuating humidity; 60 percent at night and for most of the day, but dropping to 40 percent sometime during the day. We feel that a brief period of lowered humidity—a short "drying off" time each day—contributes to the general health of the plants.

In spring and summer as the temperatures rise, it is necessary to open the ventilators more often to allow the heated air to move out. This, of course, lets some of the moisture escape. We have found that wide open ventilators do not reduce the temperature appreciably more than having them open only a few inches, and that the saving in humidity is worth the difference. If you have had the ventilators open all night, you will not have to worry about opening them early in the morning; but if they have been closed, be sure to get out to open them before the greenhouse heats up.

Although it is a challenge to do so, the humidity should be stepped up in hot weather, so that it reaches 70 percent some of the time if possible. With rising and falling temperatures and the need to have the ventilators open the humidity will fluctuate, but this is a healthy condition provided that the plants do not lose too much water during the heat of the day. Be sure that the current of air moving over the plants is moist enough to help them conserve water. Dry air in motion will only serve to hasten water loss. A vertical fan, in addition to the one running horizontally, is helpful in keeping the damp air moving upward. If your humidifier or evaporative cooler plus damping down does not supply enough moisture, a light, quick syringing by hand with a mist spray will help. This can be done several times a day in hot weather, provided you have the foliage dry by nightfall. In order to determine when the plants need misting, feel the leaves with your cheek. Your hands are usually cooler than your cheek, so the leaves may feel warm to your hand but cool to your cheek. When they feel hot, it is time to syringe them.

Light. Good light is important at all times of the year. Gone are the days when cattleyas were grown with heavy shade. When it was discovered that cattleyas made more flowers with bright light, the pendulum swung all the way in the other direction to where "all the light short of burning" became the slogan. This is a little too close for comfort and most of us prefer not to keep our plants under the constant threat of burning. Burned areas on the leaves and leaves in which chlorophyll has been destroyed cut down the efficiency of the plant. We strive to give them as much light as they need, anticipating from season to season what changes to make in the amount of shading, and keeping the light balanced with temperature and humidity.

The plants themselves show whether they are receiving the right amount of light. In good light the pseudobulbs are plump and hard, the leaves thick and firm, and the color is a medium to light green. Plants that give colored flowers may show red or purple pigment in the newly developing leads and often in the sheaths, and some leaves will retain a tinge of purple on their undersides. Plants that give pure white flowers do not show any of the purple pigment. Flowering is the final clue to light conditions; plants that flower well, giving flowers with strong stems and good substance, show that they have had enough light during the important period of growth and maturation, as well as during the time of flower bud development and the opening of the flowers.

Insufficient light leads to spindly growth that tends to be soft and succulent. The pseudobulbs do not round out well; the leaves may bend over at their juncture with the pseudobulb; and the plant may fail to flower. Growths that produce no sheaths, or sheaths and no buds, are called "blind" growths. (Don't write off such growths entirely, though. Sometimes flower buds come without a sheath, and a blind growth occasionally flowers later on.)

Too much light causes the loss of chlorophyll, the leaves becoming yellow or bronze and dry looking. Extremely strong light can burn the foliage. A burn first appears as a scorched area that later becomes dry and brown. It can be distinguished from a diseased spot by the fact that the latter remains soft and spreads if not arrested by treatment. Burning is actually a heat effect, produced when strong light raises the leaf temperature to the killing point.

These various signals are used to determine how much light to allow the plants at each season. It is not possible to bring all of the plants to the same shade of green, or to have them all make pseudobulbs of the same dimensions. Under the same light conditions, among plants standing side by side on the bench, one may have bulldog proportions and another be slim and dainty, one a light shade of green and another somewhat darker, depending on inherited differences, yet all may be doing well and all may flower eagerly. Watch their flowering and their new growths. When you have made all the adjustments that seem necessary for the plants in general, let well enough alone. If any one plant fails to flower, or if its new growths are smaller than the previous ones, you can suspect that this one needs more light. (We shall see later that watering and potting are other things to check.) Some individual plants may be more light-demanding than their neighbors. Some of the hybrids between *Cattleya* and *Laelia* (*Laeliocattleya*) are

Fig. 3-3   Burned spot caused by too intense light.

Home Orchid Growing

in this category. Find a brighter spot for them, stand them on an inverted pot or hang them above bench level where they will not be shaded by other plants.

It is helpful to have some measure of the amount of light to give cattleyas. It has been found that they need, and can take, between 2,000 and 4,000 foot-candles, or about 20 to 30 percent of full sun. The lower levels may have to be used in the summer when the heat of the sun, added to the warmer air temperatures, would make the greenhouse too hot. The level may even have to be reduced a bit more in some areas, but try not to go below 1,800 foot-candles. The higher level is possible in the winter when the sun is not as strong and the air is cooler. It is also possible to give more light in the summer when the air can be cooled by means of an evaporative cooler. Foot-candles can be measured by some photographic light meters, those which have an attachment with which foot-candles can be read directly, or a conversion table that translates the reading into foot-candles. If yours cannot be used, perhaps you can borrow one. The reading should be taken during the brightest part of the day, with the meter pointed directly toward the sun through the glass, making sure that you do not get any shadows from the framework of the greenhouse.

The usual method of shading a greenhouse is to apply a white shading compound to the glass itself. Such compounds can be obtained from a greenhouse supply company. Mixed according to directions, it is sprayed or painted on the glass to the desired thickness. There are also types of fixed shading, such as louvered-aluminum or wooden-slat shading, that can be fastened by sections to the outside of the greenhouse. And there are roller blinds that can be raised and lowered according to the weather, and various types of plastic netting. These are described more fully in Chapter 24.

In many regions in the winter, in order to give the plants enough light, the glass must be clear (unshaded), but in parts of the West it is necessary to keep a thin skim of shading through the winter. The bright fall sun can necessitate keeping some shade on the glass, but this is gradually thinned out by the weather. As winter approaches, watch the plants carefully. Don't let them burn by allowing the shading to become too thin during October and November. If it is necessary to do so, give the glass a thin coat of shading, perhaps only touching up the spots that have worn clear, or tack up cheese-cloth where additional shading is needed. By the end of November or early December, judge whether to let the rest of the shading wash off. Perhaps you will have to scrub off the stubborn remnants. Only you can tell, by watching the signals from your plants, whether to let the glass become clear or to keep some shading on all winter.

Toward the end of winter, as the days lengthen and the sun becomes stronger, keep an eye on the plants for the time when shading must be applied again. During the first warm days you can regulate the temperature by ventilation and a mist spray at noon, thus giving them the advantage of increasing light to make up for the short, often dull days of winter. When you see leaves becoming yellow, it is time to put on some shading; since spring often bursts upon us without much warning, do it before the plants become burned.

Cattleyas do better if light is not increased too suddenly. Plants that have been grown "hard" (with good light) can take sudden changes better than soft plants, however. A few days or a week of dull weather will not soften plants enough to keep them from taking the usual clear weather that follows, unless the rain or snow has washed off needed shading. (*Watch this carefully.*) But six weeks to two months of continuous dark weather can make them susceptible to burning when the sun comes out, hence the warning to beware of the onset of bright spring weather following a dull winter.

At one time growers hoped to develop a system whereby the greenhouse could be kept closed and unshaded, using brisk movement of nearly saturated air to cool the plants, with the intention of giving them full sun. There are very few places where this can be practiced fully. It is true that more light can be allowed with judicious use of moving air and humidity, but most growers have to use ventilation and shading as well. Fiberglass, a substitute for glass (see Chapter 24), has been experimented with for some years. It transmits 85 percent (a new type has been developed that transmits 95 percent) of outdoor light in a diffused manner, and with this it was again hoped that plants could be grown without any additional shading with the aid of an exhaust fan and humidity control. Some growers are apparently able to do so in areas of mild summers. However, it has been the experience of many that the approximately 7,500 foot-candles transmitted by fiberglass is too much, and that shading must be used during much of the year. Incidentally, plants that have been grown in the usual 2,000 to 4,000 range must have the light increased gradually if you wish to experiment with higher light intensities. Terrific burning will occur if you move them directly into the 7,500 foot-candle range which fiberglass gives in most areas or even into a much lesser increase of intensity. Cattleyas in nature do not have full sun. They are shaded by the moving foliage of the trees in which they grow, so that in our temperate zone, a zone of extremes, it seems logical to aim at some wise modification of outdoor light.

4

MORE ON THE CARE OF ADULT CATTLEYAS

WATERING

Although in nature cattleyas receive almost a daily rain or a drenching fog, in cultivation they rarely need a daily watering. On their native branches their roots grow in a shallow substratum of mosses and lichens, perhaps an inch thick, or hang free in the air. Some cling to almost bare bark. Hence they are freely aerated at all times, and are subjected to alternate wet and dry periods. In pots they have most of their roots confined to the potting medium, which dries out relatively slowly since it is enclosed. The difference is comparable to that between the drying rate of a shirt hung on the line and one left crumpled in the laundry basket. The former dries in a few hours, the latter may stay damp for days. The roots in the pot receive a good wetting when the plant is watered, and then for some days can absorb all the water they need from contact with the damp potting medium.

The various media used for potting have been chosen purposely for their porous nature and water-holding capacity. They allow free drainage, excellent aeration, and at the same time hold water while allowing the interstices to be filled with air. With these media it is a temptation to water more frequently than necessary; it is difficult to realize that it is actually possible to overwater them. The secret is to be very observant, to check the medium

from day to day, and *not to water until you are sure it is needed.* Beginners are usually cautioned to "err on the dry side," because it is much easier to step up the frequency of watering if you haven't been watering quite enough than it is to recondition a plant whose roots have become rotten from too much water.

Osmunda fiber and mixes with a high fibrous content, such as those made with bark, redwood fiber, peat moss, and perlite, hold water well from the start. If properly watered, they have a clean feel and remain firm up to two years or longer. Each watering should be thorough. Run the hose over the surface of the pot until the water runs copiously out of the bottom. It is not good just to give the pot a dribble, for this does not soak it uniformly or wet it through. After a thorough watering, the medium should be allowed to become *almost* dry before watering again. Feel the medium, press it with your fingers, or force your fingers between it and the pot. If it is at all springy and if your fingers feel cool from it, it still has enough water for the plant. If it is crisp and nonresilient, it is bone dry. Try to judge a point when it is *approaching dryness,* just before it reaches the crisp state, to water again. If you let it become bone dry it is difficult to get it thoroughly wet again, and this means that you will have to water it two or three times over at intervals of a few minutes, or else soak the pot in a bucket of water. When it is slightly damp it will readily take up more water.

Usually you can tell when it is ready for water by the weight of the pot; when nearly dry, it is light; when damp, it is heavier.

The barks, being in chunks, allow the water to run through very quickly, so you must be careful, again, to let the hose run in the pot long enough to insure getting the bark wet clear through. Bark of small size pieces, used for seedlings and plants with fine roots, and even the larger chunks of bark before they are well held by roots, are easy to wash out of the pot with a strong stream of water. Use a water breaker on the hose such as a "rose" or a Dramm "400," which breaks the water into gentle streams. After a thorough watering, watch the bark from day to day, and *do not water again as long as it is damp.* The surface bark may dry out before the rest, so you will have to dig down a bit to see what is going on within the pot. New bark does not hold water well at first. It takes a while for bacterial action to get going and for the process of breakdown to set in. Fresh bark therefore is not very absorbent and it may be necessary to water it every day or two for several months. After this period you will notice quite a difference in it; it stays damp much longer, and becomes a shade darker in color. When this stage is reached, it will not be necessary to water so often. Douglas fir bark takes longer to reach this point than white fir, as it is much harder in texture and sheds water more readily. Straight tree fern falls somewhere between bark and the fibrous mixes as to water-holding capacity. Some tree fern is softer and holds water well, other types are more wiry and dry more quickly.

Frequency of watering depends on many things; so it is not possible to give an absolute watering schedule. Small pots dry out faster than large ones; drying is more rapid in warm weather than in cool; and of course dry air causes more rapid drying than damp air. Plastic pots hold water longer than clay ones. The condition and size of the plant in the pot also has much to do with the drying rate. A plant with many growths and an extensive root system will use water more rapidly than one with just a few pseudobulbs. Therefore a plant that has been in the pot for two or three years and is just about ready for division will use more water than one just becoming established after division. A big old plant that has a heavy aggregation of pseudobulbs and which is becoming root-bound is harder to water. It is necessary to run the hose around the rim of the pot and through the pseudobulbs for quite a time to be sure that

enough soaks down in all parts to water it uniformly. To help in watering, it is a good idea to keep plants sorted as to size and condition. Plants in small pots that need frequent watering can be put together in one place, newly potted ones that need special care (see "potting") in another, and larger plants that should be watered less frequently in still another spot.

Seasonal differences in the frequency of watering are based on the actual use of water by the plant coupled with the effects of environmental conditions. Even though in nature cattleyas may not be subjected to appreciable changes in either moisture or temperature, they have periods when their outward activity pauses. In our greenhouses, they have periods of activity when new roots and new growths are developing or flowers are being produced, and periods when, so far as we can see, no activity is going on. A species or a hybrid that flowers as soon as its new growth is formed makes a set of roots and then shows no further activity for several months until eventually new growth starts again. Another will make and mature its new growth and then rest for several months before producing flowers. But the plants are not inactive during these periods of rest. Internal changes are going on which, when the time is ripe, will trigger the start of new vegetative growth or the production of flowers. During a period of rest the plant's processes may be slowed down, but it is still making and using food, and still needs water for the job. There are a few species, especially of laelias, which are crossed with cattleyas, that require less water than cattleyas when at rest. And these hybrids may need to become thoroughly dry between waterings in the winter. If cattleyas and cattleya hybrids are given water *according to how they use it,* they maintain their schedules regularly.

During the winter, because of cooler temperatures and shorter days, the plants do not use water as fast as in the summer. Also, the cooler temperatures retard the rate at which the potting medium dries. It may not be necessary to water large plants in a fibrous medium (pots of eight to ten inches or so) more often than once every two weeks, and those not quite so large (five- to seven-inch pots) once every week or ten days. The barks usually have to be watered somewhat more often, especially the coarse grades; eight- to ten-inch pots every week or ten days, and five- to seven-inch every four to seven days.

It is well to take the chill off the water in the winter, to have a means of mixing some hot water

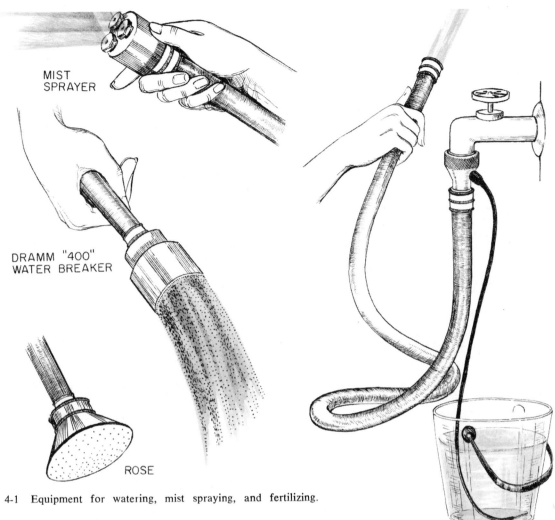

MIST
SPRAYER

DRAMM "400"
WATER BREAKER

ROSE

Fig. 4-1 Equipment for watering, mist spraying, and fertilizing.

with the cold to bring it to about fifty or fifty-five degrees.

In the summer you will have to water more frequently, perhaps twice as often as in winter, depending on conditions, especially humidity, in your area. When it is necessary to syringe the plants with a mist spray, as during hot weather, be sure you do not actually water them at the same time.

When over-watered, osmunda and the fibrous mixes gradually become soggy and have a sticky feel, and the air spaces become filled with water. Eventually they deteriorate into soft mush. Not only does the absence of air hinder the efficiency of the roots, but it allows the accumulation of toxic substances and promotes the growth of harmful bacteria and algae. This combination of conditions causes the roots to die. A potful of continually wet, soggy medium is usually full of rotten roots. The growth of algae over the surface and on the pots themselves is an indication of too much moisture.

Mosses often appear. While these are not harmful to the plants, they may conceal the condition of the fiber and form a hiding place for slugs and insects.

Many of the same problems are met when bark is over-watered, although the aeration is not so much interfered with until the bark begins to break down. It first becomes quite dark in color, almost black, and the pieces may have a slippery feel to them. A plant in over-watered bark does not do well; its roots may become stunted and its growths gradually lose their vigor. Badly decomposed bark becomes compacted into a hard mass in the bottom of the pot.

Since over-watering contributes to the death or lack of vigor of the root system, it naturally follows that the plant itself cannot grow well. Water-logged roots can absorb neither water nor minerals for the use of the plant. The leaves become yellow, especially the older ones, new growths fail to flower and are smaller than the previous ones. A plant that has been over-watered for a short time can be assisted toward recovery if the potting medium is allowed to become thoroughly dried out and to remain dry for several weeks. The plant must then be put on a schedule of less frequent watering. One that has been over-watered for a long time and which shows decayed roots had better be repotted and be watered infrequently until new roots form. This is the way all newly potted cattleyas are handled.

The emphasis on watering thoroughly rather than in dribbles has an additional reason. Salts can accumulate in the medium and on the inner surface of the pots, even plastic pots to a lesser extent, and there can also be a build-up of toxic substances. Both can damage the roots. You can see the results when a healthy root turns brown at the tip on coming in contact with the pot. Flushing out the medium at each watering helps prevent this. If fertilizer is given at each watering (of which more later), the pots should be flushed with plain water at regular intervals. Some water contains a good bit of dissolved minerals, so that even if you do not add fertilizer to it salts may accumulate. The addition of fertilizers, of course, adds that much more to the salt content so that flushing the pots between "feedings" is a good general practice.

QUALITY OF WATER

Most contemporary greenhouse growers, of orchids as well as other crops, are able to use their community water supply. Collecting rain water, which was once thought to be the best way to obtain water for orchids, is far too expensive and unreliable a method. Instances where the local water supply has not been suitable are few and far between, but they do exist. Visit other growers in your area. If the greenhousemen use the city water successfully, and if gardens and house plants do well with it, it will be all right for you to use it. *Do not use water that has been softened by the addition of sodium, used in most home water softeners.* The sodium replaces calcium and magnesium, two nutritional salts, and it in itself is toxic in the quantities that result. With too much sodium, plants start many growths that reach an inch or two in length and then cease to grow. Water softened by the ion-exchange method is safe, and a small portable unit is available for amateur growers.

Cattleyas like a slightly acid medium, one of about pH 6.2. This refers to the pH of the potting medium itself. Tap water is often less acid than this, usually somewhat alkaline. Osmunda, tree fern, and the fibrous mixes are able to maintain their normal pH even though the water used upon them is of a different pH, provided the difference is not extreme. Bark does this also, to some extent. We say they are "self-conditioning." (Bark is fairly acid at first but becomes less so after being put in use.)

The numbers in the pH scale make reference to the degree of acidity or alkalinity. The mid-point in the scale, pH 7, is neutral. Below pH 7 decreasing numbers refer to increasing acidity, and each number is ten times more acid than the preceding number. For example, pH 6 is moderately acid, pH 5 more acid, and pH 4 still more acid, and so on. Above pH 7, the numbers refer to increasing alkalinity; pH 8 is moderately alkaline, pH 9 more alkaline (very alkaline as far as plants are concerned), and so on. Cattleyas have been grown successfully with water up to pH 8. However, water that is above pH 8 should probably be treated to bring it closer to neutral, not necessarily below pH 7.5. The pH can be measured with hydrion paper, which reacts by turning different colors, or with other types of measuring devices. Many dealers have a variety to offer.

If your water is more alkaline than pH 8, you can rectify it rather easily by adding a little acid to it as you use it. We suggest doing it as you use it rather than attempting to keep a quantity acidified between waterings. Phosphoric acid is probably the best to use for this purpose, although acetic and hydrochloric acid are also good. It will not take much to do the job. You can use phosphoric acid full strength, but should obtain a one-tenth normal solution of hydrochloric or acetic rather than handle them full strength. First you must find out how much acid to add to your water. Measure a gallon of water in a clean container. Check its pH with hydrion paper. For measuring the acid, you should have a graduated cylinder marked in cubic centimeters (cc.). Let us say that you put 5 cc. of acid in the cylinder. Pour a very small amount into the gallon of water, stir thoroughly, and test with hydrion paper. If the acidity is not yet down to where you want it, add a little more, stir, and test again. Do this until the pH level you wish is reached. (It is not necessary to take it below pH 7.) Now write down the amount of acid it required to bring the one gallon of water to that level, and keep this information handy.

Perhaps the easiest method of acidification is to

Home Orchid Growing

add the acid to the water by means of a Hozon siphon or other proportioner usually used for adding fertilizer to the water. Hozon is a device that is screwed on between the faucet and the hose. It has a little side vent to which is attached a small tube that goes into a bucket of water. The force of water as it travels from the faucet through the hose draws the water out of the bucket and adds it to the main stream of water, at the rate of one part from the bucket to sixteen parts of hose water. The solution in the bucket is therefore used in a concentration sixteen times as strong as you wish the final product to be. To acidify the water, measure the amount the bucket holds, and add sixteen times the amount of acid it would take to bring this quantity to the proper acidity. For instance, if it takes one cc. of acid to acidify one gallon of water, add 16 cc. for each gallon in the bucket. Before watering the plants, check the *p*H of the water delivered by the hose. There is also a jar-siphon mixer, called Hydro-mix, which holds enough solution to treat 25 gallons of water. Therefore you add to the jar enough acid to adjust 25 gallons of water. Other proportioners are available, some more expensive than others, and some designed for large greenhouses. Always follow directions when using them.

Such proportioners require good water pressure to work accurately. If you have low water pressure, you might have to resort to a gravity tank or one with a pump. The former is a tank installed above bench level, with a hose through which the water will run by gravity. Determine the amount it holds, add the right amount of acid to bring it to the desired *p*H, stir thoroughly, and check the *p*H as the water comes through the hose. If you prefer a tank at floor level, a small pump can be used to deliver the water through the hose. Be sure to keep the tank clean, and if you do not mix the acid solution fresh each time, be sure to check the acidity frequently.

We should say here that if your water is far too acid, which is an almost unheard of situation, you can make it less acid by adding potassium hydroxide solution. The same method of measuring and testing with Hydrion paper is used, this time to bring the water up the *p*H scale from a lower level to something in the neighborhood of *p*H 6 or *p*H 6.2.

FERTILIZING

Osmunda fiber. Osmunda fiber gives the plants a balanced diet of minerals, and the plants will grow and flower without any added fertilizers. However, dilute applications of fertilizers will give them a boost and produce somewhat stockier growth and more and heavier flowers. You must be cautious about applying fertilizers to osmunda fiber, partly because only a slight supplement to the minerals already present is needed, and partly because overfeeding is a danger. Too much feeding leads to soft growths that do not harden up properly and also tends to discourage flowering. The fertilizer should be one in which nitrogen (N), phosphorus (P), and potassium (K) are in equal proportions, a so-called 10-10-10 or 20-20-20 formula. There are many brands put out especially for orchids. These are obtainable from orchid supply houses, but any of the complete fertilizers on the market will do, provided that these three minerals are in equal proportions. A concentration of one-half teaspoon per gallon of water is as strong as you should use, and many growers feel that one-quarter teaspoon per gallon is sufficient. Use every third or fourth watering.

In order to put the extra minerals to use, plants in osmunda must be in active growth and have enough light to make sufficient amounts of carbohydrates to balance the minerals. Most cattleyas make their new growth during the spring and summer, some starting as early as January, maturing the growths by July, and others starting later and maturing the growths in the fall. They should be fertilized only during this period of activity, and be given no fertilizer during the rest of the year. Some hybrids inherit the growth habit of one or another of their species ancestors, and should be fertilized accordingly. However, some hybrids are continually in a state of growth or flowering, often making two or more sets of growths a year, and starting new growths before the previous ones have matured. Such types can make use of some fertilizer through the winter, although because of the short days (fewer daylight hours) the concentration should be reduced to half, or the applications should be spaced farther apart.

Bark. By analysis, the various barks differ somewhat in the amount of available minerals, and all are lower in nitrogen than is osmunda fiber. Bacteria which feed on the bark and bring about its breakdown (a normal process that releases minerals for plant use) may use almost all of the available nitrogen, leaving little for the plant. Because of this, at least nitrogen should be added to the bark. There are those who prefer to add nitrogen alone, and those who like a complete fertilizer in which nitrogen is in greater amounts, such as a 30-10-10, or a 30-10-20 ratio. Staunch advocates of one or another are to be found wherever you go. There are also advocates of fish emulsion, an organic fertilizer, which is quite as acceptable as the inorganics. Many use it altogether, and some use it occasionally in place of one of the regular applications of inorganic fertilizer. Lack of absolute agreement on what is best is to be expected, because of differences in handling the plants, because of climatic differences in environment, and because of personal differences in what individuals look for in their plants. Orchids are slow to respond, and cattleyas are not "heavy feeders." It is difficult to diagnose why plants may produce fewer flowers one year than another, and equally difficult to know just what brings about more flowers. Bumper crops may be as much due to a happier combination of environmental factors, such as fewer cloudy days, a cooler summer, etc., as due to what fertilizer you used or whether you gave it at every watering or at every other watering. If all this seems to leave some questions as to where you should start, remember that, fortunately, in general orchids will grow and thrive with a variety of fertilizers.

An overabundance of nitrogen will usually encourage vegetative growth over flower production. In general, higher levels of fertilizers may be used when the plants are making vigorous growth and when light conditions are at their best, with the concentration reduced when the plants are less active and when the days are shorter or the weather cloudy. As a starting point, we suggest that you try the 30-10-10, or the 30-10-20 ratio, giving it in a concentration of one-half teaspoon to a gallon of water, at every other watering. This schedule may be kept up for plants in active growth during seasons of bright light. For plants that are resting, or during spells of dull weather, reduce the concentration to one-quarter teaspoon per gallon of water. If you happen to have on hand a quantity of 10-10-10 fertilizer but wish to increase the nitrogen value, you can do so by mixing equal parts of ammonium nitrate and 10-10-10, then measuring the amount to use per gallon as above. Some growers like to furnish a continuous supply of nitrogen by incorporating a slow-dissolving material such as uramite (just a light sprinkling) in the potting material, and then using a 10-10-10 fertilizer on it. This can also be accomplished by using dried powdered blood, one-fourth teaspoon sprinkled on the surface of a six-inch pot, or one teaspoon dissolved in a gallon of water and poured on at the rate of one cup per pot.

If you are of an experimental nature, you might try fertilizing half of your plants at every watering and the other half at every second watering, or set up some other trial program, and compare the results. If you fertilize at every watering, you must find some time to flush the pots with plain water. A possible method might be to give fertilizer as usual one week and the next time give plain water all around before applying the fertilizer.

Tree Fern. While it is necessary to learn by experience how often it must be watered, it is handled essentially the same as bark as to kind of fertilizer and frequency of application.

Fibrous Mixes. There are many mixes on the market, some under brand names and some put out by individual dealers. Most of them consist of various proportions of fir bark, redwood bark (either in chips or shredded), peat moss, and perlite or a similar substance. Some of them have added to them slow release fertilizers such as bone meal, hoof and horn, superphosphate, and urea-form nitrogen.

Those which do not have the added fertilizers may be treated like bark—being given a complete fertilizer, such as a 30-10-10 or 30-10-20 formula, one-half teaspoon per gallon at every other watering, with modifications in quantity according to the season or the activity of the plants.

Those which contain the fertilizers will not need as much fertilizer applied to them. If directions come with the product, follow them implicitly. If no directions are given, begin by trying a 30-10-10 formula at the rate of two teaspoons per five gallons of water, at every other watering.

Gravel and aggregates. The use of inert, decay-proof substances such as gravel and the light weight aggregates (Holite, Idealite, Solite etc.) was once looked to as a solution to orchid potting problems. Methods designed for experimental work in nutrition were adapted by growers. Most of those trying such methods eventually gave them up because of difficulties in furnishing the plants with a fully balanced diet of minerals. However, an occasional grower returns to gravel culture for special reasons, and is perhaps able to make improvements that work under his conditions. Details are given on pages 303-305.

Using aggregates (or volcanic tuff etc.) in pots is essentially gravel culture. In areas where plants remain out-of-doors much of the year where there are heavy rains, some growers find that the aggregates are useful because they do not break down. One must use a completely balanced fertilizer and watch carefully for symptoms of nutritional deficiency. (See Chapter 22.) Plants grown in organic media have the benefit of some nutrients always present, which is why organic media are really preferable. One must flush out the pots at intervals if the rains don't do it, to prevent accumulation of salt. If the medium is used over, it must be sterilized just as are old pots.

Application of fertilizer. Proportioners make fertilizing easy. These are described above in the section dealing with acidifying water. In using the Hozon, you make the concentration sixteen times as strong as you wish the solution for the plants to be. For a strength of one-half teaspoon per gallon, this would be sixteen one-half teaspoons, or eight teaspoons, for each gallon the bucket holds. In the Hydromix jar you would put twenty-five times the amount of fertilizer needed for one gallon, since it holds enough solution to treat twenty-five gallons of water. For other types follow directions. If the water pressure in your area is low, you might have to use a tank for fertilizing, also described above.

CARE OF FLOWERING PLANTS

Flowering cattleyas are all treated in the same way as those not in flower. They are watered on the same schedule and are allowed the good light that brings the flowers to their fullest color and firmest substance. Perhaps in hot weather they might be given a bit more shade after they are fully open to help them last. Once the flowers mature, that is, after they have been open three or four days, the plant can be brought in the house to be enjoyed, and can be placed on a table or the mantel or wherever it can be shown off, for the flowers do not need light in order to keep well. If you bring a plant into the house before the flowers are open, keep it in a bright (but not too hot) window until they are fully open.

We used to try to move flowering plants in the greenhouse to an area set aside for them so as to avoid getting water or insecticides on them. Moving plants, especially large ones, is a chore often

involving shifting several others to make room for one. Sometimes new growths are damaged, or buds broken off in the process. We have learned that water does not hurt the flowers provided they can dry off quickly. Some prepared fertilizers have a coloring material added (so that you can know whether the proportioner is working properly); as this dries it will leave a deposit on the flowers, as will insecticides. Try to avoid splashing the flowers during watering, and avoid spraying them. But if some do become wet with these materials, rinse them off with a fine spray of plain water before the materials have a chance to dry. Dust carried in by the wind may also be washed off.

It takes five to eight weeks for the buds to grow up to the tip of the sheath, depending on the individual plant. The length of time from the moment the buds break the tip of the sheath until they are open also varies. Some develop very quickly, requiring about a week, but most take two weeks or more. The flowers are not ready to cut until they have reached their fullest color and substance, at least two full days, sometimes four days, after the flowers open. Cattleya buds will not open in water, nor will flowers mature if they are cut too soon. The latter remain limp and green and soon wilt. After you have lived with your plants for a while, you come to know when the flowers have reached their prime, and how long it takes them. If you intend to use them for decoration or for corsages, or to sell them, it is important to avoid the disappointment of not having them last.

Cut flowers keep a long time in water, in a narrow necked vase so that the flower parts are not submerged. Their life can be lengthened by putting them in a cool place at night, or in a refrigerator at not lower than forty-five degrees. To keep a corsage, lay it on a little shredded wax paper in a polyethylene bag, close the bag tightly, and put it in the refrigerator. We learned some time ago that carnations can be kept for six to eight weeks after cutting when wrapped in polyethylene film and stored in a refrigerator or in a cool place, so we have tried this with orchids a few times. Usually some can be kept for longer than they would last on the plants, and can thus be saved for special occasions. Not all flowers will keep equally well. Those of heavy substance last better than thin ones, but the keeping qualities are sometimes a matter of individuality. They should be cut while in their prime, not necessarily during the first few days after opening, but not past the middle of their normal life. A fading flower or two can shorten the life of others stored with them. The flower stems are put in tubes, and they are then laid on shredded wax paper in a shallow box. The box is wrapped tightly in polyethylene film and stored at forty-five degrees. Among those we have tried, phalaenopsis kept particularly well; but some cattleyas kept for two weeks longer than they would have otherwise.

All cutting instruments must be sterilized between plants, when cutting flowers, potting, or trimming, to prevent spreading disease from plant to plant, particularly virus disease. Virus may be present even though no symptoms show, so it should never be assumed that a plant is free from it. Flaming is the best way to sterilize instruments, although boiling for ten minutes will also do it. An alcohol lamp is easy to use and to carry with you in the greenhouse. In a stationary potting area a Bunsen burner or a blow torch can be used. One system we suggest is to have a large supply of razor blades or "re-usable throw-away" knives sold by some dealers, sterilize them all and then as each is used drop it in a can to be re-sterilized later. When flaming, be sure to hold the blade in the flame long enough to heat thoroughly the entire surface. Also, wash your hands frequently and thoroughly. Don't go from plant to plant, as I have seen some do, pinching off an old flower here and an old stem there. Fingers and fingernails can carry virus just as well as a knife.

As plants come into bloom, watch to see that the buds are not cramped in the sheath or prevented from coming out through its top. Sometimes a sheath becomes dry before flowering time, or is too long in proportion to the length of the flower stems, or is too tough for the buds to force open. Except for those with a double sheath, you can see the buds by holding the plant against the light. If the stems become bent back on themselves, cut off the top of the sheath or open it with your fingers; otherwise the stems will become distorted and the flowers may not grow fully out of the sheath before they are ready to open. Watch to see that a sheath is not growing up under an adjacent leaf which would cause the buds to be injured or bent. You can slip one leaf behind another to allow room for the flowers, or tie back leaves that are in the way. If the group of flowers on a stem is too heavy for the stem, the stem may bend with their weight, in which case the stem should be staked so that the flowers will be held upright. Occasionally a flower has difficulty in opening; its parts may be very tightly clasped together. Let it alone for a couple of days to see whether it can open by itself, but if

it doesn't you can ease the petals apart or unfold the rim of the lip with your fingers, or perhaps accomplish this by blowing into the flower.

The keeping qualities of the flowers are partly due to a protective covering of wax, but this is also an individual characteristic. In general, those of heavy substance last the longest, but some not particularly heavy can last for weeks. Good culture, of course, contributes to this.

As the flowers fade they should be cut; when the last flower on a stem is removed, the stem and sheath should be cut off close to their base. Dying flowers in the greenhouse are something of a hazard. They give off ethylene gas, which can cause sepal wilt in flowers just ready to open. Two or three fading flowers will not produce enough to harm others, but a large number of them may do so. Also, old flowers are susceptible to spotting by the Botrytis fungus; and once this fungus is on the increase in the greenhouse, fresh flowers may become infected. Whenever such spots make an appearance, remove the flower at once. (See Chapter 23 for diseases that show up in flowers.)

Thrips, red spiders, and aphids are enemies. Thrips chew the surface tissues leaving little silvery or brown scars. Red spiders and aphids puncture the tissues, leaving small wounds surrounded by a transparent halo. Insects also spread disease. The control for these is given in the chapter on pests. "Honey" is secreted at the tips of the sepals and also at their juncture with the stem. This is a pleasant sweet-tasting substance. When the flowers are growing close together, sometimes a bit of this honey becomes smeared on an adjacent flower part and a transparent streak results. Wash it off with a touch of water and the streak will disappear.

Keep a record on the label of each plant as to the flowering time, the number and quality of the flowers, and how long they last. When your greenhouse becomes crowded, you will wish to dispose of some plants in favor of better ones, or ones which flower at a different time of the year. Don't discard a plant on the basis of its first flowering, unless the flowers are exceedingly poor on a well-grown plant. If they are nicely shaped, but small or poorly colored, see if better culture won't bring them along to be larger or brighter. A plant that consistently gives poor flowers is, of course, not worth keeping, nor is one that refuses to flower in spite of good culture. Sometimes a recalcitrant plant can be encouraged to flower by giving it better light, or a slightly warmer or cooler night temperature. It is worth a bit of experimenting to find out. However,

Home Orchid Growing

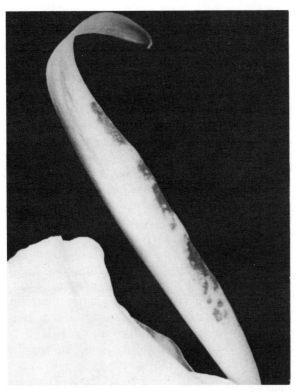

Fig. 4-2 LEFT, closeup of flower damaged by red spiders.   RIGHT, a flower ruined by slugs.

often we find ourselves giving our best locations and our most earnest care to a plant that performs poorly, when it would be better to discard it in favor of a more rewarding plant. The value of keeping records is proved when you have an opportunity to trade plants with a friend, or to sell some, or when you wish to make room for new plants by culling out poor ones.

GENERAL SUGGESTIONS

When an orchid plant is making new leads, help it to maintain a nice upright position by staking the leads as they develop. Some leads will assume a good position by themselves, but others may lean out too far. Newly developing growths are quite soft and easy to break, so be gentle. You can't do much until a lead is about half grown, and then you can begin to train it. Place a stake (steel) in the center of the pot or use a clip-on stake. Usually one stake is sufficient for a medium-sized plant. Using soft string, make a turn around the stake, then bring the string out and around the lead and back to the stake to be tied. You can

snug in a young lead by placing the string fairly close to its base, where it is strong, to bring the main curve closer to the plant. When this lead is more fully grown, replace the string with another placed at the juncture between the pseudobulb and leaf. Never constrict a stem by looping the string around it; always tie the leads with a "sling" of string. A plant with many leads becomes a challenge to keep staked. Don't try to pull all the leads in close to the stake; just give them a good position and leave room between them for flower buds to emerge without crowding.

Keep the pots free from weeds. Oxalis is a particular pest, because it shoots its seed as the pods become ripe, thus insuring a new crop as soon as you have pulled out one. It is best to get oxalis plants out while they are tiny. The barks are free from weed seeds, and osmunda can be treated before being put into use. Hand weeding is safe, of course. The only chemical weed killer recommended at all is Simazine 80-W, a Geigy Chemical Co. product. This is injurious to kinds without pseudobulbs, and has also caused injury to plants with pseudobulbs that are particularly sensitive or are not well established. Some growers have found it safe for cattleyas, both seedlings and mature plants, in a concentration of one tablespoon to one gallon of water, and even up to two tablespoons per gallon, sprayed lightly over the surface of the pot. A stronger solution of three tablespoons per gallon may be used for weeds under the benches. It would be well to be cautious, to use it only for a bad infestation of weeds, and then on a few plants first. Use the same caution before trying any other products.

As the sheathing leaves that surround the pseudobulbs become dry and start to fall away from the stem, they may be removed. They come off more completely when they are wet. Do not peel the still green ones from the young pseudobulbs. When you have finished weeding, cutting old flowers etc., gather up all trash and remove it from the greenhouse.

Consan-20 (20 percent Consan) is an aid in keeping a clean greenhouse. It's general use is as a disinfectant and algae control in swimming pools and evaporative coolers. In a greenhouse it may be used to wash the benches, glass, and walks to free them from the unsightly algae that grow wherever it is constantly damp, and which cut down the light through the glass. One ounce per eight gallons of water, or one teaspoon to one gallon, is sufficient for the job. This is quite an alkaline substance. Insufficient information is available as to its safety for plants, and it is possible that it may be injurious to some kinds. Caution is therefore advised in allowing it to come in contact with them.

Whenever you are in the greenhouse, working or just looking, you may discover something that needs attention—crowded flower buds, a new lead that needs tying, a few weeds to be removed, bugs on some flower buds, a light burn, or a disease spot. Don't forget to look over the plants in the back row; they sometimes become neglected. A regular program of spraying for insects should be established as a preventive measure to keep insect populations under control. Keep a little hand sprayer ready in between times, in case you find a few aphids, red spiders, or other pests on flower buds. And if you find a plant with a few suspicious spots, treat it with a little fungicide right away. See Chaper 23 for disease and pest control.

Two frequent pests are slugs and snails. The former are easier to control than the latter, but both are killed by preparations containing metaldehyde. Do not use an arsenic preparation on orchids. Chewed leaves and flowers, as well as root tips, are evidence of slugs, and you often see a slug lying along a stem or a newly developing lead. Regular treatment with a "slugicide" will keep them under control. More difficult to control are the snails, a very small, hard-shelled, flat-coiled kind, the largest of which reach about three-sixteenths of an inch in size. They remain in the potting medium for the most part, wreaking destruction on the new root tips; but occasionally they will be seen on the rhizome or the developing young growths. When you see new root tips badly chewed off, and do not find slugs, you can suspect that snails are present. It doesn't take many to keep the new root tips whittled off as fast as they form. The metaldehyde preparations should be used repeatedly. Metaldehyde has some residual action, but it does not necessarily get all the individuals or all the eggs. The treatment must therefore be repeated every few weeks, and then at intervals of three or four months. Where a bad infestation is found, we remove the plant from the pot, take off all the potting medium, pick off all the snails we can find, wash the bare roots with the hose, and dust the roots and the base of the plant thoroughly with metaldehyde powder before putting it in fresh medium. Other chemicals for snail control are given in Chapter 23.

Occasionally a plant is found whose roots just simply stop growing. Perhaps the plant was over-watered unwittingly at some time, possibly by drip from the roof, or salts may have been allowed to accumulate. Remove the plant from the pot to ascertain the cause. Perhaps the bark is moldy. Various kinds of mold can invade the medium, a slippery feeling slime mold, a granular, dry looking mold, and a cobwebby kind. The latter two can interfere with water-holding capacity of the medium. Not all harm the plants, but where you find mold and root injury or lack of growth together, it is best to put the plant in fresh medium. Many growers feel that the addition of one-third part redwood bark helps hold down the development of mold.

As you go along the bench watering the plants, glance back from plant to plant to see whether the water drains rapidly through the pot. Once in a while fine material becomes washed out of the bark into the bottom and clogs up the drainage hole. With your fingers or a screwdriver, push up the crock over the hole to let the water run out. Then flush out the pot thoroughly to remove the material that was clogging the drainage. If this doesn't remedy the situation, remove the plant from the pot to see what was causing the trouble.

Sometimes a grower is disappointed in the flowering of a plant which he bought while in bloom, and from which he expected a duplication of the flowers he saw. Changed conditions can alter the quality of flowers. A plant that gave brightly colored flowers under good light may give paler ones with less sun. An unusually hot summer, or a dull chilly fall can cause poorer blooming than usual. You will find this so from year to year with your own plants, so if it happens to one you have recently bought, see whether improved conditions won't remedy the situation.

5

POTTING MATURE CATTLEYAS

Most potting will be done in the spring, since this is the time when most plants start their growth. Those that make new roots as early as January and February can be potted then, and those that do not start new growth until May or June can be potted at that time. Plants make their best growth during spring and summer, and it is well to put them in fresh medium in time to take advantage of the good growing weather. Individual plants that start new growth at some other time of the year may have to be potted accordingly. We do not like to shift a plant that has finished its active growth phase and is going into a rest period. Disturbing it at such a time will force it to sit for months without an active root system.

MATERIALS

As described in the previous chapter, various media can be used for orchid growing. The oldest, osmunda fiber, has never been excelled but is in short supply, is expensive, and requires much time and effort. It is still preferred for certain things. Sometimes a plant that is "touchy" in bark will do well in osmunda. Also, it is useful for growing plants on driftwood, where a pad of osmunda can be wired on to form a base for establishing the plant, or in baskets. It is good to have some on hand.

The barks are satisfactory and are far easier to work with. They can be used straight, or incorporated in various mixes. Plain bark comes in various grades or sizes of pieces: 0 to $\frac{1}{4}$ inch, $\frac{1}{4}$ inch, $\frac{1}{4}$ to $\frac{1}{2}$ inch, $\frac{1}{2}$ to $\frac{3}{4}$ inch, and chunks up to $1\frac{1}{2}$ inch for special purposes. The smaller sizes are used for seedlings and small species, the larger for larger plants. The size you choose depends on your personal likes and on the conditions under which you grow your plants—the medium sizes for dry climates, for instance, and the larger for damp climates and for outdoor growing where there is high humidity and much rain.

There are several different kinds of bark. At present fir bark is most widely used. This is composed largely of white fir (*Abies concolor*) with some red fir (*Abies magnifica*) occasionally mixed with it. These come from California and are essentially alike as to characteristics. Douglas fir (*Pseudotsuga menziesii,* also known as *P. taxifolia*) comes from the Pacific Northwest. It is hard and very solid and at first more resistant to water, but eventually cannot be told from the others. Redwood bark, which is much softer and shreds easily, is often mixed with fir bark (one part redwood to three parts fir). Some growers feel that it lessens the growth of mold or fungus. It is seldom used alone.

Various mixes using bark as a base are on the market, or you can make your own. Descriptions of mixes preferred by one grower or another appear frequently in the orchid publications, and many commercial growers package their own for sale. When used for the kinds of plants specified and following directions they give good results.

In buying bark and bark mixes, be sure to get carefully prepared material. The barks used should have been screened, and heat treated to eliminate snails.

Tree fern, or hapuu as it is called in Hawaii, comes from many countries. It can be bought as slabs and logs on which plants can be grown directly, or made into "pots," figurines, and balls. It also comes shredded or chopped, to be used in pots just as bark is used, in grades determined by the length of the fibers. Tree fern from different areas varies sometimes in quality, some being quite hard and wiry, some softer and more pliable. The latter holds water better. The type you choose depends on personal preference, and it may take a bit of experimenting to find out which you like best. Tree fern can be mixed with bark.

The inert media, gravel, Holite, Solite, Idealite, etc., and types of volcanic tuff or scoria, are less widely used than the ones just described and require much more careful treatment as to fertilizers. Growers who keep their plants out of doors in areas of heavy rain often try them because they do not break down, and rapid breakdown of organic media is often a problem. Sometimes the added problems found with the inert media are not offset by this one quality.

Plastic pots have come into quite general use. Because orchids require free aeration of the roots, they were looked upon with suspicion at first. But with the more open media such as bark and tree fern it has been found that they are quite satisfactory. Since the pots come with only small drainage holes, it is recommended that plenty of drainage material be provided in the bottom. This can be gravel or one of the aggregates. When clay pots are used, the drainage material usually consists of broken pieces of pot. Naturally this is not available when only plastic pots are at hand.

The advantages of plastic pots are that they are less expensive, that they can be shipped without the drastic breakage that occurs with clay pots and for less transportation cost, and that they do not allow the accumulation of salts to as extensive a degree as clay pots. For dry climates they offer the added advantage of not drying out as fast. One disadvantage is their light weight, noticed especially when a tall heavy plant such as *Cycnoches* is more susceptible to being tipped over.

Hanging baskets of wire or redwood strips offer variety in any greenhouse and are necessary for kinds with pendulous flower sprays. Osmunda is the usual medium used for them. They must be watered more often than pots.

NEED FOR REPOTTING

A plant needs to be repotted (1) when it has outgrown its pot and (2) when the potting material is no longer in good condition. The first is easier to judge, but the second is more important from the point of view of the immediate health of the plant.

Outgrown pot. As a plant adds successive leads these come closer to the edge of the pot. Soon the leads will grow out over the edge, and the new roots will travel down the outside to wind around the pot or go along the bench. It does no harm for one lead to extend beyond the edge, provided it maintains a nice upright position, or can be tied up straight. In fact, if the potting material is in good condition, it does no actual harm to the plant if two successive leads grow out of the pot. Roots hanging in mid-air seem to remain healthy, but they are subject to injury when the plant is moved, and if they cling to the bench they will, of course, have to be broken off eventually. A plant should not be allowed to grow for too long a period in this manner, for subsequent leads will grow downward, flower stems will stick out horizontally, and the shape of the flowers may be impaired. It must be confessed that almost all growers have a few plants that do not get repotted when they should be. Especially is this true with plants in osmunda, with which potting is a time-consuming job. Once the plants are in bark, moving them on is easier, although even so, when one has many plants and little time, or when family emergencies prevent attending to the plants at the right time, some are inevitably skipped. As long as the medium is good, and care is given to watering and fertilizing, the plants will survive in good condition.

Condition of the medium. Potting media will remain in good condition for varying lengths of time, depending on how the plants are watered and on the relative humidity of the environment. They break down more rapidly when they are watered to excess or kept in a very humid atmosphere. Two years may be as long as most will be good under

Home Orchid Growing

these conditions. When moderately watered, or in a dry climate, or in a greenhouse where the relative humidity is kept only moderately high, they may last for three years. Thus plants can be left longer in the same medium under the latter conditions, provided they are doing well and still fit their pots.

How can you tell when the medium is not in good condition? Osmunda fiber becomes soft and spongy to the touch, and if you take a plant out of the pot you will find that the fibers have disintegrated into a soft mush. In such a pot you often find good roots only in the upper half or third of the pot where they are able to get more air and remain somewhat more dry than in the wet mush toward the bottom. Or you may find no good roots at all. Somewhat the same situation exists when other media have broken down. The lower half will have disintegrated more thoroughly than the upper half, and the broken down material will have compacted into a solid mass. Here again, you may find good roots only in the upper part. In order to find out how the potting medium holds up for you, check a plant or two after a year and a half. If the medium is deteriorating, you will know that you have been keeping it too wet and should therefore cut down on the frequency of watering. Possibly, also, you have been keeping the relative humidity too high.

TIME TO REPOT

Best time. The best time, in fact, the ideal time, to repot a plant is just before it starts the new roots of the season, or just as these roots begin to show. The new roots come from the base of the recently matured lead. Their first sign is little swellings underneath the curved basal section (rhizome) of the lead. The bright green root tips then push out through the brown covering of the rhizome. The root tips are very tender and are easily broken. By the time they have reached a length of half an inch it is difficult to repot a plant without injuring them. When a root tip is broken, the root ceases to grow from that point. Older roots will form branch roots behind the tip if the tip is broken, but the very new ones may simply stop growing for the season. At the time the new roots make their appearance, the older roots undergo a wave of activity that causes them to branch, and you can then see new root tips all through the medium. There is a real advantage in potting a plant just when this activity starts so as to let the new roots and branch roots grow into fresh medium.

Next best time to repot. If the new roots develop before you can take care of a plant, wait

Fig. 5-1 LEFT, new roots too long to be handled without damage. Better to pot just as roots are starting or else wait until they are five or six inches long and capable of branching.

RIGHT, plant that was potted just as new roots were starting, allowing them to grow immediately into fresh medium.

until they have grown to a length of five or six inches rather than to risk breaking them. They are then old enough to form branch roots themselves. The older roots are still actively branching and if any of them are injured in the potting process they will form additional branches. Potting a plant at this time interrupts its growth for a few weeks, necessitating a period of recovery, and is therefore not as ideal a time as that given above. But it does offer a second chance to take care of plants you miss when the roots are first starting. Some species and hybrids habitually form new roots just when the flower buds are developing in the sheath. To prevent any setback to the flowers, such plants can be handled at this "next best" time.

A hybrid that flowers two or more times a year will probably start growth cycles at various times of the year. Some may start a new set of growths before the last have flowered. Try to repot such plants during the spring or summer, catching them when they are forming a new set of roots.

Problem plants. An occasional plant may show signs of deterioration while its neighbors are in perfectly good health. If there is not a disease involved (See Chapter 23), the cause is almost certain to be root loss, for which two possible reasons are over-watering and snail damage. More and more we have found the latter to be the cause of what seemed a mysterious cessation of root activity, with the roots still alive but blunted and crooked. The snails may have done their work and moved on to another plant, so that none, or perhaps only one or two, can be found. Since the roots are already inactive, whether from over-watering or damage by snails, and since you have the plant out of the pot, you might as well put it in fresh medium. This is particularly easy when the plant is in bark or a mix. Often a plant will make a remarkable recovery. Sections of roots that are still alive sometimes respond quite quickly with branch roots. An interesting phenomenon takes place when a plant with absolutely no roots starts a new lead. Ordinarily roots are formed only by a mature lead, but when no roots are present to support the young developing lead, it will often start its own set when it is still very small, barely an inch or two in length. The first new growths from plants that have been badly set back because of root loss may not be large enough to flower. But at least you will have rescued them from a bad situation and put them on the road to recovery.

TOOLS AND POTTING AREA

A sharp, long-bladed knife, scissors, pruning shears, and a metal potting stick are about the only tools needed. *All of these should be sterilized by flaming between plants. Metal stakes that are re-used must also be sterilized.* We suggest an alcohol lamp for the purpose. Some growers use a small blow torch. A Bunsen burner would be fine if you have an outlet for gas.

Used pots should be washed and soaked in 10 percent Clorox (one part Clorox to nine of water) for at least ten minutes, and then be rinsed in several changes of water until no odor of chlorine remains. Clay pots will hold chlorine longer than plastic ones and should therefore be rinsed more times, and be left to air out for several days. Rinse them again just before use. This also goes for broken crock that is to be re-used for drainage, and for gravel and any of the aggregates to be re-used.

A plant to be potted must not come in contact with debris from other plants. A good method is to cover the potting area with paper and when you finish with a plant gather up all the debris in the paper and put it in a trash can, spreading fresh paper for the next one. Newspaper will work, but freezer and butcher's paper are better as they keep the potting area dry.

HOW AND WHEN TO DIVIDE PLANTS

Each pseudobulb with its individual basal part, that is, its section of rhizome, is potentially an individual plant. It makes its own set of roots, and gives rise to new leads from buds at the joints of the rhizome. If a plant is cut up into individual pseudobulbs, however, the new growths from them will be very small, almost like those of young seedlings. It will take several years for a one-bulb division to become a flowering plant. A new growth, if it is to be of flowering size, requires the support of several pseudobulbs behind it. For this reason, divisions are made of groups of connected pseudobulbs, three or four in a clump if possible.

Not all of the buds along the joints of the rhizome will develop into leads. Many remain dormant throughout the life of the plant, a sort of safety factor. The buds most likely to grow into new leads are the two located, one on each side, at the juncture of the pseudobulb with the rhizome. Sometimes a plant activates only one bud at a

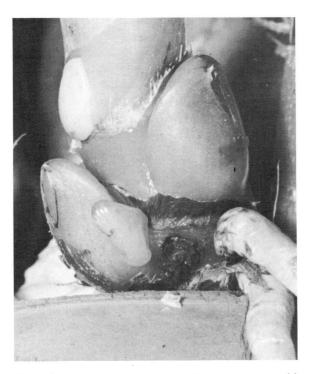

Fig. 5-2 Nature's safety factor. Base of a lead with covering tissues removed to show the buds, one at each joint. Usually one or two buds become activated and will develop into leads. Here two have enlarged and are growing. The small buds remain dormant, possibly to develop later or when the plant is divided. If the leads should suffer a catastrophe, one or the other of the dormant buds will become active. Note, also, roots growing from the base of the lead.

time from the base of each recently matured lead. This we call a one-lead plant. It grows along in a straight line, its pseudobulbs marching across the surface of the potting medium in single file. Sometimes, a plant will break two buds, causing a fork in its growth line, each of which then continues to give a new lead each year—a two-lead plant. If one of the forks breaks two buds concurrently, the plant will then have three growing ends. Some individuals grow so lustily that they break two buds from almost every pseudobulb, and quickly develop into plants with six, eight, ten, or more leads.

The decision of whether to divide a plant depends partly on its habit, and partly on its size. A plant that consistently gives but one lead a year should definitely be divided when it has made enough pseudobulbs to give two strong divisions. This would be when seven or eight pseudobulbs had been formed, allowing for a lead division of four pseudobulbs and a backbulb division of three or four. Removing the growing end will stimulate one of the dormant buds on the back part to

develop, so that you will have two plants. The lead division should flower on its next growth; the backbulb division, being not quite so vigorous, may take two years to flower.

Some growers like to anticipate the division of a one-lead plant by encouraging a bud on the back part to break and develop into a good growth ahead of time. This can be done by notching the rhizome (cutting it halfway through) between about the third and fourth pseudobulb. Do this some time before new growth starts at the front end, so that hopefully the two will begin at the same time. Thus both will be in the same stage for repotting.

Interestingly enough, an occasional plant keeps the habit of giving but one lead a year from the time it is a seedling until it is divided. The stimulus of division may cause two or three buds to break simultaneously on one or the other half, so that from that time onward that division becomes a plant with several leads.

A plant with two or more leads may not require a pot any larger than a one-lead plant, and for the same amount of space will give you double or treble the number of flowers. So if you have a plant with several leads, that is compact and growing in an orderly fashion, it would probably pay not to divide it. Such a plant can be moved along into a larger pot, perhaps removing only the back-bulbs, and may become a very fine specimen. It is more thrilling to have a huge plant covered with flowers than to have several small ones with a few flowers each. Eventually, a plant becomes too large to handle conveniently, and then will have to be divided. You will have the choice of breaking it up into a number of smaller plants and waiting

Fig. 5-3 Two leads developing from buds situated as in Fig. 5-2.

Fig. 5-4 A. A plant that is growing in two distinct lines. Each half has two or more leads. This plant should be divided in the center, and probably each half kept intact. B. A plant with several leads on the front half. Divisions should consist of the front half, to be carried on intact, and a back half, which will probably give several new growths.
C. A compact plant with five leads in a seven-inch pot. Such plants give many flowers in little space.

while some of these regain specimen size, or of making two or three large divisions.

The accompanying diagrams, Figure 5-5, give some types and suggestions. A shows a one-lead plant that should be divided. B shows a plant with two leads that also should be divided. The plant

is growing in two definite lines, but each line has produced only one lead since the original break that caused it to fork. Dividing it may stimulate it to make more leads at a time. Each growth line can be separated at the point where it forked from the original part of the plant. The group of back-bulbs can be potted if they are still plump and have some leaves, or be discarded if they are no longer vigorous. You will probably want to keep them if the plant is valuable, and in time they will make a third flowering plant.

C shows a two-lead plant that is not ready for division, but from which the backbulbs can be removed. Make the cut just behind the pseudobulb that gave rise to the two leads, so that they remain connected. The backbulbs are probably more vigorous in this plant than they are in A and B because they are younger. D shows a three-lead plant that should be divided in the same manner as the two-lead plant just described, keeping the three leads together and removing the backbulbs.

E shows a plant that has branched and re-branched, offering an opportunity either to keep it as a unit, removing just the backbulbs, or of making two or three divisions. The dotted lines show where it might be cut to make three plants, the solid line where it should be cut to make two divisions. F shows a similar plant that has made even

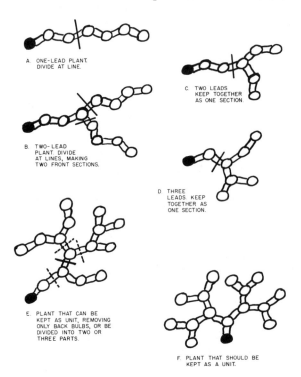

Fig. 5-5 Diagrams showing how to divide plants. In each one the oldest pseudobulb is shown as solid black.

Home Orchid Growing

more leads, each growing end making two leads a year. This plant surely should be kept as a unit as long as possible, for it is a beautifully symmetrical specimen.

Diagrams cannot possibly include all of the shapes your plants can take. Some will make all of their growth forward, producing a plant heavy with leads on one side of the pot and practically nothing on the other side. Then there are those whose many leads cross over each other, or force each other up in the air, offering a real challenge when it comes to dividing them. Each plant has to be dealt with according to its own needs. You can make a neater plant in some cases by removing one or two crowded leads with their connected pseudobulbs, leaving the rest of the plant intact. Also, a plant may send one lead over the edge, keeping the others neatly within the pot. The overhanging section can be clipped off and potted separately, leaving the rest of the plant undisturbed for another year or so. Its removal will stimulate into growth a bud behind the cut, so that a new lead will develop at that point on the old plant.

POTTING IN BARK AND MIXES

Choose a pot that will accommodate about two years' growth. For a plant that makes one lead a year, or one set of leads, judge the size needed by the distance between the pseudobulbs, estimating how much larger the plant will be with two years' growth added. For a plant that makes two or more sets of growths a year, the pot will have to be relatively larger. Ordinarily, a plant of four pseudobulbs that makes one growth a year will require a six-inch pot. A two- or three-lead plant that makes two or three growths a year should go into a seven- or eight-inch pot. If you are familiar with the discussions that have gone on during the period of trial and error in the use of bark, you will have heard that, "You may over-pot in bark," and "You must use larger pots with bark." This has caused some confusion and should perhaps be explained. Many growers got so much better growth in bark that they found their plants were outgrowing their pots sooner in bark than they did in osmunda. Especially was this true where there had been a tendency to overwater in osmunda, a tendency that was almost automatically relieved when the plants were put in the more open, more rapidly drying bark. When using osmunda, growers are cautioned

not to put a small plant in a large pot because the osmunda stays wet longer in the center where the roots of the small plant are concentrated. Bark and bark mixes are not as dangerous in this respect. However, putting a plant in a larger pot than it needs is purely a waste of material and space, and a plant will do no better in an oversize pot than in one more fitted to its size. You must therefore judge the size of the pots according to your own observations of how the plants do for you. If they outgrow their pots before the two years are up, next time use a larger size.

We like to dampen the medium before using it. It seems to make it easier to settle in the pot and around the roots. Some growers use bark dry, just as it comes from the bag, so you may take your choice.

To remove a plant for repotting, first soak it in a bucket of water or water it thoroughly to loosen the roots that cling to the pot. It can then usually be knocked out of the pot quite easily. With your fingers work loose the roots clinging to the outside, then turn the pot upside down and, holding the plant with one hand, tap the rim on the bench. The plant should drop down into your hand. If it does not come out this way, run a knife around inside the pot to separate the roots that cling stubbornly to it. You may also have to do this with the roots on the outside.

Much of the old medium will fall away as you shake the plant a bit and gently move the roots apart. Run the hose through the roots to remove as much of the remaining material as will come free, but do not try to pull away those pieces that cling tenaciously to the roots. Look for evidence of slug and snail injury. Decayed roots should be cut back to healthy tissue, or removed entirely if completely rotted. The healthy roots need not be cut back if their shape and length will allow them to be put into the new pot without being broken. Roots that have grown on the surface can be left on the surface. Any that have grown outside of the pot, and which would be broken in repotting, should be trimmed back to a stub of three or four inches in length. Cut off any shrivelled pseudobulbs (backbulbs) by severing the rhizome.

Pull off the old tissue-like scale leaves that cover the pseudobulbs. Do not remove the coverings from the rhizome unless they are particularly dry and loose, lest you injure dormant buds. Leave the covering on the young pseudobulbs. As you clean off the old tissue, look for scale insects which have a habit of hiding under it. The young scale in-

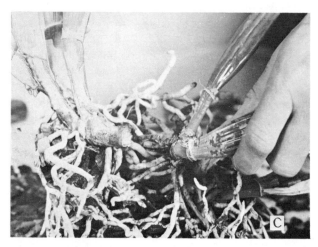

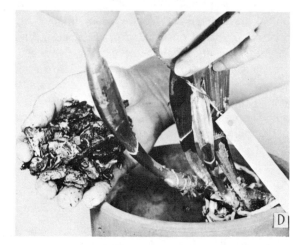

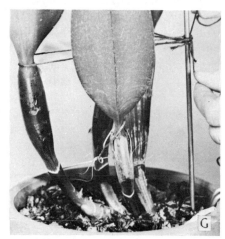

Fig. 5-6 Potting in bark.

A. A one-lead plant that will be divided. Growth has reached edge of pot. New roots are just starting at base of lead.

B. Remove plant from pot. Cut through rhizome to make a "lead" division of four pseudobulbs.

C. The plant divided. Ease the sections apart. Trim back any roots broken in the process and cut off any dead roots. Shake off most of old bark.

D. Pot has been prepared with several pieces of crock in bottom and enough bark to hold plant at right level.

Place plant in pot with older end against one side. Scoop bark into pot, thumping it at intervals to settle it.

E. Fill pot, thump again, and press bark down around edges with thumbs for extra firming. Note that rhizome is in a trench on surface, with bark lying against sides and top part exposed. Level of bark is one-half inch below rim.

F. Attach stake to rim to give plant rigid support. (There are several types made to use with bark.)

G. Tie each pseudobulb to stake. Use a "sling" of string, making tie at stake.

48   Home Orchid Growing

sect is free-moving, and crawls around until it finds a sheltered spot, where it then settles down, sticks its proboscis into the plant tissues, covers itself with a dome of hard material, and remains permanently. Eggs are laid under the shell, and as the young hatch, they move out and find a new location. Clusters of scales with whitish or brownish shells may be found in protected places, along the grooves and joints of the pseudobulbs and at the juncture of leaf and pseudobulb. We do not see as much scale as we used to. In fact, it rarely occurs in greenhouses that are regularly sprayed with Malathion. But it can occur, especially on old plants that you may have acquired from neglected collections. If you find scale, scrub it off with a soft toothbrush dipped in an insecticide, and then dip the whole plant in the same solution. If you do not find scale, it is not necessary to scrub or dip the plant.

Decide whether to divide the plant, and how best to do it, and cut through the rhizome. Put a label on each division. If snail and slug damage is present, dust the roots with metaldehyde powder or dip them in a metaldehyde solution. You are now ready to pot.

Choose a pot of appropriate size. There is a three-quarter height that is excellent in the larger diameters.

Put a generous layer of drainage material in the bottom, and over this a handful or two of potting medium. With one hand hold the plant in the pot so that the rhizome comes about half an inch below the rim and the back end touches one side, giving room at the other end for new growths. With the other hand pour handfuls of the medium in around the roots, filling it among them with your fingers. When the pot is about two-thirds full, thump the pot on the bench to settle the medium, still holding the plant in position with one hand. Then add more medium up to the rim, thump the pot again to settle it, and then with your fingers or the blunt end of a potting stick press it down firmly around the inside edge of the pot. The rhizome should lie in a trench on the surface, with the medium lapping up against its sides and the upper surface exposed.

If the plant does not have many roots to hold it a piece of stiff wire cut a little longer than the inside diameter of the pot can be placed across the rhizome and its ends wedged against the sides of the pot. Clip a stake to the side of the pot and tie the pseudobulbs to it.

MOVING PLANTS FROM OSMUNDA FIBER

For moving plants from osmunda fiber to other media there are two methods in use. Some growers like to leave a chunk of fiber under the front end of the plant, their reasons being, first, to give something to help anchor the plant, and second, to leave the roots of the younger part somewhat undisturbed. Other growers, including myself, prefer to remove practically all of the osmunda fiber. It does not hurt to leave a few shreds clinging to roots here and there, if by so doing you can prevent breaking the roots, but a large chunk of fiber holds water longer than the surrounding medium and creates a "wet spot" in the pot. If the plants are repotted when new roots are just forming, or when the roots are actively branching, as we described on page 43, the plants will become reestablished rapidly. To give the plants an anchor, stakes are made which clip to the pot and furnish a rigid support, eliminating the need for a chunk of fiber for this purpose.

POTTING IN OSMUNDA FIBER

One must remove the plant from the pot as described above and follow the steps in Figure 5-7. Remove the fiber from the core and from the back part. Study the plant to see whether to divide it, and where to make the cuts. Now ease apart the sections of the plant. Try to leave a firm chunk of fiber under each growing end, with as many roots intact as possible. Remove the rest of the old fiber from each part. Cut off any decayed roots, and cut back any healthy ones (except those in the solid ball) to a four-inch stub. Remove the old tissue from the pseudobulbs, and treat for scale or slug and snail injury if these are found.

Prepare the fresh osmunda fiber by soaking it in water, wringing it out thoroughly and letting it drain until it is just damp, no longer dripping. With a hatchet, chop the pieces into chunks about three inches wide. Fill a clay pot to about one quarter its depth with crock, and lay a piece of fiber over the crock.

Now take the plant in your hand and place chunks of fiber under the rhizome and between the root stubs to re-form a good ball. Set the plant with its ball of fiber in the pot, pressing the back end of the plant tightly against the back of the pot. With one hand squeezing the ball of fiber against the pot, push in additional chunks at the

  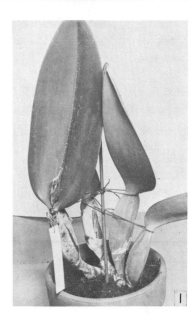

Fig. 5-7 Potting in Osmunda Fiber.

A. A two-lead plant to be divided.

B. After removing oldest few backbulbs, plant is divided where it forked into two leads.

C. The front divisions. Each must be trimmed up.

D. Prepare osmunda by chopping into chunks.

E. A division ready for potting. Roots have been trimmed back so that stubs remain in a solid ball of fiber.

F. Pot has been prepared by filling it one-fourth full of crock, and adding enough fiber to hold plant at desired level. Set division in place, with older end at side of pot. Place a large notched chunk of fiber under the lead.

G. Press fiber back with your hands and insert additional pieces, vertically, until no more can be put in by hand.

H. Work in more fiber with a potting stick. Place a chunk on edge of pot, catch it in middle with stick, and force stick down and toward center of pot. Continue until fiber is uniformly hard.

I. Stake and tie the plant.

Home Orchid Growing

front end and at the sides, between the fiber that is already in place and the side of the pot. The chunks should be inserted vertically. Do not build up layers of fiber on top of each other, but instead add them as you would add books at the end of an already crowded bookshelf. Osmunda fiber requires pressure from the sides to hold it in place. When you have put as much fiber in the pot as you can with your hands, lay a chunk on its side on the rim of the pot and force it in with a potting stick, pushing one edge down into the pot to bring it vertically alongside the rest, and always maneuvering the potting stick down and toward the center of the pot. Do not let the rhizome of the plant hump up. If it does this, pull out one or two pieces of fiber, settle it down, and start again. The rhizome should lie in a groove on the surface of the fiber, with its lower surface in the fiber and its upper surface exposed. Mature plants should be potted "hard," that is, the fiber should have about the consistency of sod. If you can easily push your fingers between the pot and the fiber, it is not hard enough. Add more chunks of fiber to tighten it up. Drive a steel stake into the center of the pot, and tie the plant to it.

CARE AFTER POTTING

All roots that are either bruised or broken in the potting process, and even those not visibly damaged, are subject to rotting if they are kept wet. They heal nicely if they are allowed to dry out and remain dry for several weeks. For this reason we let the potting medium go without water until we see the new roots developing. The barks dry more quickly than osmunda fiber, but the latter, even though it is damp when used, will dry in a few days. During the period of root recovery it is necessary to protect the plants from water loss through the leaves and pseudobulbs. We give them a little extra shade and a light mist spray twice a day on bright days. Just swish the sprayer over the plants, to dampen the pseudobulbs and leaves. A bit of the spray will also dampen the rhizome and the merest surface of the potting medium. This will encourage new roots to form. As the root tips become visible throughout the medium, give light waterings for a while, not enough to soak clear through, and then as the roots develop further increase the depth of the watering. When the roots are growing vigorously, remove the extra shade and put the plants on a regular watering and fertilizing schedule.

SPECIAL NOTES

Sometimes shortly after it has first been wetted, osmunda fiber develops a little fuzzy white mold. This is not dangerous to the plants. It disappears as the fiber dries out and does not come back. We do not know what it is—nor does it always appear. Just ignore it.

A few growers have advocated soaking the bark in a fertilizer solution several hours before using it. Either ammonium nitrate or a complete fertilizer may be used. Since the roots are inactive for a while and since the bark is kept dry, this will not immediately benefit the plants. However, when you do begin to water, the developing roots can then absorb the nutrients. A system that is perhaps more beneficial to newly potted plants is foliar feeding— adding a fertilizer (one-half teaspoon per gallon) to the water with which you mist the foliage. This, also, can be either ammonium nitrate or a complete fertilizer. The leaves will take up only a small amount of the chemicals but the plants will thus receive a little boost until their roots are again active.

Backbulbs can be encouraged to start new growth by being enclosed in a polyethylene bag. Put some damp medium in the bag, set the backbulbs in it, and close the bag tightly with a rubber band. In time a bud may start growth. When this new lead has roots starting, remove from the bag and pot as you would any division.

6

THE CATTLEYA SPECIES

Many wonderful things have been discovered by accident, and it was an accident that introduced the first cattleya plants to European botanists. The story goes that in 1818 a Mr. Swainson was collecting mosses and lichens in Brazil, and gathered some heavy, thick-leaved plants to tie around some of his collections for shipment to England. When this material arrived, William Cattley, an eminent horticulturalist, realized that the odd plants were something unusual and rescued them from oblivion. The first of these plants bloomed in 1824, and was studied by Dr. Lindley, a renowned botanist, who found it to be of a genus entirely new to science. Lindley described the plant and gave the new genus the name *Cattleya,* after its happy possessor. The founding specimen he named *Cattleya labiata autumnalis,* because of its beautiful lip and its habit of flowering in the autumn.

For many years these were the only *Cattleya labiata* in Europe, for no one could rediscover its native habitat. It seems odd that this was so, for many other cattleyas were discovered in the following decades, *Cattleya mossiae* in 1838, *Cattleya gigas* in 1848 or '49, *Cattleya trianaei* in 1856, and so on. No great numbers were imported and many plants did not survive the long voyage. The cattleyas were highly prized by horticulturalists and brought high prices from wealthy collectors, but their future in the commercial market was not realized until 1891. In that year tremendous numbers of *Cattleya labiata* were found, and their purchase by two different companies, one English

and one Belgian, caused quite a stir in orchid circles. There ensued a heated argument as to whether these were indeed the true *Cattleya labiata autumnalis,* each company hoping that it alone held the prize. Finally it was established that all of them were the real *labiata.* Possession of so many of the same species caused the price to drop from about $20 to about $1 per plant.

That was the beginning of the great demand for cattleyas for the commercial market. Improved steamship travel sent a stream of collectors to South America who sent back hundreds of thousands of cattleya plants to importers in their various countries. These were sold at auction to commercial growers, horticulturalists, and amateur growers.

As the kinds of cattleya were discovered one after another, in great profusion, and were classified by the botanists of the time, many were found to be so similar to *C. labiata* as to be considered varieties of that species rather than as separate species. These varieties of *C. labiata* are the ones with which the public early became entranced because of their large, showy flowers, and they have occupied the center of attention ever since. For convenience and brevity, it has become customary to treat them as separate species, but *C. mossiae* was named *C. labiata,* variety *mossiae, C. trianaei* was named *C. labiata,* variety *trianaei,* and so on for the rest of this group, *dowiana, eldorado, gaskelliana, lawrenceana, lueddemanniana, mendelii, percivaliana, rex, schroederae, warneri, warscewiczii* (called *gigas* more commonly). These and two other species, *luteola* and *maxima,* which are similar, are together

Fig. 6-1 *Cattleya labiata,* the species upon which the genus was founded, has played many important roles in orchid culture.

referred to as the "labiata" group. They all bear a single leaf to the pseudobulb, and for this reason are sometimes also called the "unifoliate" group.

The other group of cattleyas is called the "bifoliate" group because its stems bear two, sometimes three, leaves. They are distinctive and delightful, quite different from the labiata type, and are rapidly coming into their own both from the point of view of popularity and for use in hybridization. Their flowers are usually smaller, with more slender parts, but many are very waxy and some produce their flowers in clusters of from five to twenty to a stem. The lip is small, often pointed, and may be kidney shaped or fiddle-shaped, having a break between the side and mid-lobes referred to as a "spade" lip. They exhibit a fantastic array of colors and markings—yellow, green, yellow-green, brownish green, brown, orange, red-orange, white, bluish white, and tones of pink and pink-magenta that are often very brilliant. Many are spotted with brown or purple. The lip is often in complete contrast to the rest of the flower; for instance, *C. bicolor* is brownish green with a bright pink lip. With the interest now tending toward smaller flowers, these little species offer their individual charms both to the collector and to the hybridist. In crossing them

with the larger labiata types, growers combine the characteristics of many smaller flowers to the stem, distinctive coloring, unusual shapes, and heavy substance with the fuller, rounder form of the labiata type.

Except for a few which retain their popularity, the species of the labiata group are found less often now in amateur collections than in former years, when they once formed the bulk of cattleyas available both to amateur and commercial growers. The more luxurious hybrids, with their wider range of colors, have almost entirely supplanted them. However, good specimens of species have a real value, the very best of them being almost unobtainable because they are retained by the hybridists and by collectors who prize them, and who often return to them in breeding programs. The value of the species to the amateur lies in their dependability for flowering times, and in the interest they have as the types that have gone into the making of the hybrids. Even though one may love his hybrids, he will know them better if he is familiar with some of their progenitors. If you have a good plant of any of the species, keep it.

The species of the bifoliate group, on the other hand, are becoming rapidly better known, and amateurs are eagerly adding them to their collections. This is a reflection of the widespread interest in the odd and unusual kinds of orchids. It also shows that the present-day amateur has come of age—he does not feel that he must have just the huge and the showy, although they have great attraction, but that he places value on the particular qualities each kind, large or small, has to offer. As a matter of fact, a single plant with many bright little flowers creates just as much of a show as one that gives larger flowers, and a tiny, dwarf plant holds it own by sheer contrast.

I should like to translate for you a bit from an old book, *Les Cattleya* by Léon Duval, a French orchid grower, 1907. "It is no more just to establish comparisons or classes of beauty among certain cattleya than it would be to compare certain works of art; let us leave to beautiful plants their own special qualities, which command our admiration for these same qualities, and not establish a royalty among the cattleya. . . ."

Cattleyas have many relatives that are delightful and charming in themselves, and with which they have been crossed to make an array of inter-generic hybrids. Among them are *Epidendrum, Laelia, Sophronitis,* and *Broughtonia.* In the general plan of this book related genera are grouped together as

Home Orchid Growing

tribes. An exception is made here since this first part of the book is based on cattleyas and their culture. The species of cattleya will be described apart from the rest of their tribe, and the other members will be given in a later chapter.

THE SPECIES

The cattleyas are all epiphytic, that is, growing naturally on trees and rocks. Their stems vary in height from two inches to three feet; in some they are club-shaped and in others cane-like. They have from one to three thick, hard leaves, borne at the top of the stem, and the stem is clothed with thin sheathing leaves that dry after the first season. The flower parts are free and spreading, the sepals similar, the petals broader than the sepals. The lip usually has three parts—two side lobes that fold up around the column and a middle lobe that is spreading. In some the side lobes are quite distinct from the middle lobe, and are often more fleshy, especially among members of the bifoliate group. In others the side lobes are continuous with the middle lobe, as in the labiata group. The column is plain, not decorated with wings, and bears four pollinia, two in each of the two sacs in the anther. Most of the species are delightfully fragrant.

The Labiata Group

Cattleya dowiana. This variety of *labiata* is a beautiful nankeen yellow with a large purple lip lined with gold. It has contributed its yellow color to many hybrids. The flowers are between six and seven inches across; from two to six occur on a stem. It was discovered in Costa Rica in 1848 by a Polish gardener, Joseph Warscewicz. However, the specimens that he sent to Europe arrived in poor condition, and it was not until 1864 that good specimens were obtained by Mr. Arce and purchased by Messrs. Veitch and Sons, English horticulturalists, who flowered it for the first time. The species was named for Captain Dow, whose ship carried many an orchid hunter and many a cargo of orchid plants. It is the most celebrated of Costa Rican orchids, but is quite rare now, having been nearly cleared out by collectors.

C. dowiana variety *aurea.* This species occurs in Colombia, entirely separated from the *C. dowiana* of Costa Rica. The flowers are a deeper yellow and the lip is more copiously marked with gold. It is a large plant, similar in every way to *dowiana.* Its period of vegetative growth is from May to September, and flowering follows immediately in September and October. It rests during the winter. The species is used a great deal in hybridization.

C. eldorado. Pale rosy-lilac with slender petals. The lip of this flower is the same color but marked with a central orange blotch surrounded by white and purple. It is a variety of *labiata,* but not well known, which was discovered in Brazil in 1866. It flowers in late summer and fall.

C. gaskelliana. These large, fragrant, handsome flowers are six to seven inches across. The sepals and petals are usually purple-violet, suffused with white, occasionally marked with a median band of white. The lip is generous in proportions, and the tube is the same color as the petals. The front lobe of the lip is deep violet with a pale border, the throat streaked with yellow and marked on each side by a spot of yellowish white. French growers used to call this species *"Cattleya chou"* (Cattleya cabbage) because it is so easy to grow. It is a variety of *labiata* and is still quite popularly grown by amateurs. Vegetative growth starts in about April and flowering follows immediately, from July to September, after which it rests during the winter. The species occurs in Venezuela and Brazil, where it grows on rocks at elevations from five hundred to three thousand feet. It was introduced into England from Venezuela in 1884 or '85 and was named for a Mr. Gaskell of Woolton. There is a white variety, *alba,* and one that has white petals and sepals with the front lobe of the lip crimson.

C. gigas. This species should be correctly called *warscewiczii,* but the name *gigas* is commonly used and will be found in lists and catalogues. It was discovered in 1848 or '49 in Colombia by the same man who found *dowiana.* This is the largest flowered of all the cattleyas, the blooms being seven to nine inches in diameter and most showy. The petals and sepals are rosy-lilac, and the huge, rich red-violet lip is marked with two brilliant yellow eyes. The edge of the lip is ruffled and has a pale border. *C. gigas* is demanding in its cultural needs. New growth starts in January or February, occasionally a bit later. Flower buds push up before the growth is mature, to open in June, July, or early August. New roots form right after flowering, and this is the time to repot. These roots have to carry the plant on through fall and winter and the next spring's flowering. A curious habit is to make a second growth in the summer which does not flower. Some growers try to prevent this by withholding

Fig. 6-2 A wedding bouquet made with flowers of *Cattleya gigas* 'Firmin Lambeau', a rare white variety of this species. (*Courtesy B. O. Bracey and Co.*)

Blc. Natoma

Lc. Pink Fairy

(*Courtesy Rod McLellan Co.*)

Lc. Golden Girl

Cattleya Bow Bells (*Courtesy Clint McDade and Sons*)

water after flowering, but are not always successful and may put the plant off cycle. In my opinion, it is a mistake to refuse water during the period of root growth, food making and storing, and maturation. If a second growth starts, better let it mature because the next flowering growth must come from it. Then give a decided rest, watering only sparsely from October until new growth starts. The swelling of the eyes will be the plant's own signal of renewed activity and the need for regular watering. It likes a bright airy place, except that when the flowers are open a bit of shade helps keep them fresh longer. The white variety, 'Firmin Lambeau,' is very valuable.

C. labiata. These beautifully proportioned flowers, of wonderful texture, are a rich, vibrant rose, almost luminous in quality. The dainty lip is modest in size, with the throat more open than tube-like. The front lobe of the lip is ruffled, deep red-violet with darker lines which run through two orange spots into the yellow throat. The flowers keep a long time. The flowering time of *labiata* and its hybrids can be controlled by manipulation of daylength and temperature. *C. labiata* starts its growth in March or April, and flowers without pause in the fall, from October through November. The flower buds are produced in a double sheath, one sheath within the other. The period of rest is from the end of flowering to the start of new growth in late winter. Among the many color variations are a white form, var. *alba,* and one which has white petals and sepals with a crimson lip, var. *cooksoniae.* This native of Brazil was discovered in 1818.

C. lawrenceana. A small flowered species, not well known, has reddish-brown pseudobulbs. The flowers are four to five inches across with five to eight in a cluster. The petals are rather slender, and the lip small and tube-like. The color varies from pale rosy-purple to white, and the front lobe of the lip is purple with a maroon blotch. The species occurs in British Guiana, where it was discovered about 1882. It grows actively during the summer and remains through the winter with the sheaths formed, to flower in the spring.

C. lueddemanniana, also called *speciosissima.* This species closely resembles *labiata.* The flowers are rose-purple, suffused with white, the front lobe of the lip is amethyst-purple, and lines of this color extend into the throat between two yellow blotches. It is one of the few whose handling is rather tricky. The clue to its behavior is probably that it grows natively under such a variety of conditions that the plants show more individual differences than are found in most species. It grows actively from spring to fall, and can flower anytime from April to September. Its period of lessened activity is November to February. The species occurs in Venezuela, where it was discovered in 1850. It was named by Professor Reichenbach for Mr. Lueddeman, for many years his chief gardener and a well-known horticulturist. There is a white form, var. *alba.*

C. luteola. These charming little yellow flowers are only two inches across with petals about the same width as the sepals, and a small tubular lip that is yellow or whitish, often streaked with purple. The pseudobulbs are two to three inches tall and leaves three to four inches long. The species occurs in Brazil, where it was discovered in 1853. It flowers in early winter.

C. maxima. The flowers, though large and nicely colored, have slender parts and lack compactness. Sepals and petals are lilac or pale rose, the front lobe of the lip is ruffled, pale rose or a deeper shade, with a central stripe of yellow from which radiate darker lines, and a pale border. The plant is not grown much now, though it was once very popular. It occurs in Ecuador, Peru and Colombia and flowers in the fall.

C. mendelii. One of the most distinct of the labiata group, this species has large delicately colored flowers, seven to eight inches across. The sepals and petals are whitish or pale rose, and the lip is generous in size with the outer lobe very much ruffled and marked with a clean-cut patch of purple. The throat is yellow, more or less streaked with crimson. It is easy to grow, and much loved by amateurs. Its native habitat is Colombia, where it was discovered in 1870, and named for Samuel Mendel, an English orchid lover. In habit it is similar to *mossiae* (below). The species grows from June through September, and waits through the winter after the sheaths are formed to bloom in April and May.

Cattleya mossiae. Once called the Easter orchid, this beautiful species rivals *gigas* in richness of coloring. Its spring flowering season gave it great value for Easter and Mother's Day. It is rosy-lilac in color, with wide, beautifully ruffled petals. The lip is as wide as or wider than the petals, the broad front lobe frilled, mottled with violet-purple, with a pale border. The throat is yellow, striped with purple. It was discovered in 1836 in Venezuela, where it grows in large quantities, and flowered for the first time in the collection of a Mr. Moss, after

Fig. 6-3 *Cattleya mossiae.*

whose wife it was named. It was collected so ruthlessly that it was threatened with extinction, and the Venezuelan government had to place a temporary embargo on its export to give it a chance to reproduce. There is wide variation in this species including some that are thin and poorly shaped, but a good specimen is very pretty. There are many magnificent named varieties, of which the best known are var. *wageneri,* white with a yellow spot on the lip, and var. *reineckiana,* white with purple lip. The species grows during the summer and early fall, and waits through the winter with its sheaths formed to flower in April and May. Some individuals flower as late as August.

C. percivaliana. This is one of the smaller flowered of the labiata group, but a lovely orchid. The richly colored flowers are four to five inches across, varying from light to deep rose, and are nicely proportioned. The dainty, rather short lip has a pale, exquisitely frilled border surrounding a deep maroon center. The throat is orange, variegated with deep violet. It flowers at Christmas time. The species, which occurs in Venezuela was introduced in 1882 to England by Sander. It is named after Mr. R. Percival, an English orchid grower. There is great variation in the species from good to poor quality. Growth may start in January, without any rest after flowering, or it may wait to begin new growth in April or May. Sheaths are formed by the end of the summer, but the flower buds wait until October to begin development, and mature in December.

C. rex. These large cream white to pale yellow flowers are attractive but seldom grown. The lip is of good size, the throat yellow, veined with purple, the front lobe crimson, lightly veined, with a white, ruffled border. The species occurs in the Peruvian Andes. Growth starts in April, and the plants flower in the summer, after which they rest during the winter.

C. schroederae (also spelled *schröderae*). Lovely fragrant flowers are entirely pale rose faintly suffused with white, except that the lip has yellow or deep rose in the throat. It was orginally designated a variety of *trianaei,* and therefore belongs in the labiata group. However, it is much more ruffled than *trianaei* and has a later blooming season, rivaling *mossiae.* It is another of the handsome Colombian orchids, discovered in 1885 or '86, and named for Baroness Schroeder, wife of a famous orchid grower. The plant grows from May through September, and then, like *mossiae,* waits through the winter with the sheaths formed. The flower buds start to develop about the first of January, and open from March to May. The flowers mature more slowly than those of some other species, and should not be cut until they have been open four or five days. There are many named varieties, a white form and several near-white ones.

C. trianaei. The flowers of this species are a little more plain, the petals and lip a little less ruffled than others of the labiata group, but they are still lovely, and a handsome specimen ranks with the best of the cattleyas. The sepals and petals are pale pinkish-lavender. The lip is a little narrower than the petals, but sometimes equals their width. The front lobe is usually purple, but is often a brilliant crimson hardly rivaled among the cattleyas. The pale border of the lip varies in width, being fairly wide in some and hardly discernible in others. The throat is yellow, faintly streaked with deeper yellow. The average size of the flower is about six to seven inches. It is a species in which there is a great variation in coloring. *C. trianaei* is a native of Colombia, where it was discovered in 1856 by the celebrated traveler, J. Linden. The species was named for José Triana, a well-known botanist of Bogotá, who died in Paris. The blooming season extends from late December through March, with the largest number flowering in January. New growth starts a short time after flowering, in about March or April, and continues until August, at which time the sheaths are completely formed. The flower buds wait until October to begin developing. Among the varieties is a white form.

C. warneri. A lovely member of the labiata group, this species is similar to *labiata,* but with larger flowers. The sepals and petals are rose-lilac, the front lobe of the lip is heavily ruffled and

Home Orchid Growing

Fig. 6-4 *Cattleya trianaei.*

bright purple. The throat is yellow-orange, streaked with white or pale violet. Growth starts in February and the flowers develop as soon as the sheaths are formed, opening during May and June. Its period of lessened activity is during the winter. The species occurs in South Brazil where it was discovered in 1859. There is a lovely white form, var. *alba,* that has a yellow throat.

The Bifoliate Group

Cattleya aclandiae. Greenish-yellow flowers are barred and spotted with chocolate brown, with a bright rose-purple lip. The short fleshy side lobes curve up beside the column, and the spreading middle lobe is fleshy in the center and kidney-shaped. The extremely broad rosy column is a decorative attribute of the flower. The plants are dwarf, the little two-inch stems spaced rather widely on the creeping rhizome. Each stem bears a pair of small rounded leaves. The four-inch flower is startlingly large for the size of the plant. The species,

which was discovered in Brazil in 1839, blooms variably almost any time of the year.

C. amethystoglossa. Daintily colored, attractive flowers, three and one-half to five inches across, grow five to eight in a cluster. Sepals and petals are white suffused with rose-purple, and spotted with amethyst. The lip has small, white erect side lobes, and a broad, rounded middle lobe that is violet-purple marked with radiating ridges of papillae. The plants are very tall, with pseudobulbs reaching three feet, and bearing two leaves six to twelve inches long. The plant, discovered in Brazil in 1862, flowers in mid-summer.

C. aurantiaca. A small, dainty plant with rather drooping racemes of little red-orange flowers, about an inch and a half in diameter. The flowers hold themselves partially closed and have the peculiar habit of being self-pollinating. Popular in itself for its brilliant color, it is proving useful in making red hybrids, crossed with *Sophrolaeliocattleya* and *Laeliocattleya.* It is native to Guatemala and surrounding countries, and blooms in late winter and early spring.

C. bicolor. This remarkable flower is olive-green tinged with copperish brown, with a bright crimson tongue-like lip that has no side lobes and leaves the column completely exposed. The pseudobulbs are tall and jointed, one to three feet high, bearing two leaves four to six inches long. This species has been used in hybridization with members of the labiata group. It was discovered in Brazil in 1837. It usually blooms in the fall, sometimes in the spring as well, giving four to six very waxy flowers to a stem.

C. bowringiana. A strong growing plant that sometimes produces as many as twenty flowers on a stem and is often used in hybridization with members of the labiata group. The cane-like stem has a fat, bulbous swelling at its base. The flowers are small, less than three inches across, the sepals and petals rose-purple. The lip is similar to that of the labiata type, deep purple with white in the throat. It grows on rocks and rubble near streams in British Honduras, and needs a little more water than most cattleyas. The species grows during the spring and summer, flowers in October and November, and has a short mid-winter rest. It was discovered in 1884.

C. citrina (also considered a member of the Encyclia division of *Epidendrum*). This attractive

Fig. 6-5 The delightful fragrance of *Cattleya citrina* attracts a young orchid admirer. (*Photo by Ted Dully, courtesy H. Phillips Jesup*)

plant is a conversation piece in or out of bloom. It grows in a pendant manner, and should be put in a hanging basket or on a piece of driftwood. The egg-shaped pseudobulbs bear two or three silvery green leaves that have a "bloom" upon them. The flower buds appear from the growing lead and expand before the growth is mature. The lovely lemon yellow flowers have a border of white around the frilled lip and are very waxy and spicily fragrant. In order to appreciate the beauty of the upside down flowers, you must look up at them. Discovered in Mexico in the 17th century by the Jesuit, Hernandez, it was not until 1859 that any large numbers reached Europe. It flowers in late spring and early summer, and prefers a cool spot, which possibly can be furnished in an intermediate house.

C. deckeri. Similar to *skinneri* and *bowringiana,* this species was once thought to be a variety of the former. The three-inch flowers are rose-purple and the lip is without the white patch in the throat. It occurs in Mexico, Guatemala, Costa Rica, and Panama and flowers in the fall.

C. dolosa. This charming dwarf plant resembles *walkeriana,* of which it was once thought to be a variety. It is probably a natural hybrid between that species and *loddigesii.* The four-inch flowers are waxy, rose-magenta, with the front lobe of the lip amethyst-purple marked with yellow. The little side lobes of the lip are erect. The flowers are produced from the top of the pseudobulb. It is rather rare.

C. elongata. A large, tough species that grows in Bahia, Brazil, on sparsely vegetated volcanic rock, where it endures almost desert conditions and full sun. Its roots grow into rock crevices where they find moisture and protection. Its canes are sturdy, one foot tall, and it bears a cluster of three-and a half-inch flowers at the top of a two foot stem. The flowers are waxy, fragrant, and of a rich red color with a lighter purple lip. Sepals and petals are narrow, the latter charmingly waved. The lip has long side lobes that enfold the purple column and a generously spreading mid-lobe decorated with a triangle of yellow.

C. forbesii. These pale yellow-green or tan-green flowers are three to four inches across, several to a stem. The somewhat tubular lip is colored most subtly; its side lobes are pale pink on the outside, striped with red on the inside, and the ruffled mid-lobe is bordered with white and has a deep yellow throat marked with wavy red lines on either side of a central yellow crest. The plant is dainty, with stems about the thickness of a pencil and eight to

Home Orchid Growing

Fig. 6-6 *Cattleya forbesii.*

ten inches tall. It was discovered in South Brazil in 1823. It flowers in mid-summer and rests during the winter.

C. granulosa. This species is well worth growing because of its striking flowers which are olive-green, sometimes yellowish brown, spotted with crimson-purple or red, occurring five to nine in a cluster. The white side lobes of the lip form a tube that is yellow or rose inside, while the long spear-shaped middle lobe is marked with crimson papil-

lae. The flowers are very waxy, the lip so stiff as to appear to be carved out of wood. The flowers, which appear in the summer, last a long time. The plant is now being used in hybridization. The species occurs in Guatemala and Brazil; it was discovered in the latter country in 1840.

C. guttata. These beautiful yellow-green flowers are spotted with deep purple. The lip has long pink or white side lobes that enfold and almost completely conceal the column and a short, spreading middle lobe that is amethyst-purple marked with papillae. The pseudobulbs reach thirty inches in height, and bear two leaves five to nine inches long. The flowers are three to four inches across, five to ten in a cluster. Discovered in South Brazil in 1827, its flowering season is from November to January. The plant is frequently used in hybridization.

C. intermedia. Charming, delicately colored flowers make this a most desirable species. The four- to five-inch flowers vary from pale rose to milky white and are sometimes dotted with amethyst. The lip has smooth side lobes that enfold the column in a long tube, while the spreading middle lobe is ruffled and of a rich amethyst color. The slender pseudobulbs are about eighteen inches tall, and bear two or three leaves. The flowers

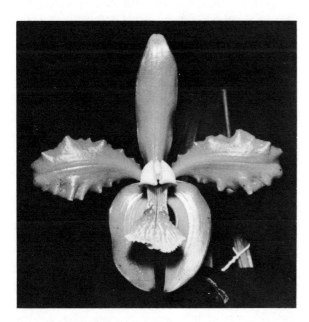

Fig. 6-7 *Cattleya granulosa. (Courtesy Jones and Scully, Inc.)*

Fig. 6-8 *Cattleya intermedia. (Courtesy Jones and Scully, Inc.)*

occur in a cluster of four to five. This is another of the species now being used in hybridization. It occurs in South Brazil where it was discovered in 1824. The flowers appear through the summer. There is a white form.

C. intermedia variety *aquinii*. This very rare form perhaps merits species standing as *C. aquinii*. The petals are broad, somewhat ruffled, and carry the coloring of the lip, having the tips deeply marked with rich amethyst. This characteristic is contributed to some of the hybrids made with *C. intermedia* var. *aquinii* as one parent, called "splash petal," hybrids.

C. leopoldii. A Brazilian species much like *guttata,* and possibly only a variety of it, differing in the shorter, more squared side lobes of the lip which expose the end of the column, and in its flowering season which is summer. The variety with pure white lip and green sepals and petals, long known as *guttata* 'alba', should be called *leopoldii* 'alba'.

C. loddigesii. This is a lovely species which grows in a variety of locations in Brazil. There is another very much like it, heretofore considered a separate species as *harrisoniana,* now felt to be

a variety of *loddigesii,* and so recognized in current literature. It is difficult to tell them apart. *C. loddigesii* has light rose-lilac flowers, and a lip with more or less erect side lobes and a central lobe with a smooth disc. There is a pure white form 'Stanley' that has been much used in hybridization. The variety *harrisoniana* has possibly somewhat darker flowers, whose lip has longer side lobes that enfold the column and a crest marked with papillae or little raised protuberances. In both, the color of the lip shades into yellow in the throat. Both flower in late summer and early fall.

C. nobilior. This species produces its flowering growth from the base of the pseudobulb, as does *walkeriana* which it resembles, and of which it is probably a variety. The purple-lilac flowers are very fragrant, three to four and one-half inches across, but only one or two grow on a stem. The lip is fleshy, the side lobes entirely enfolding the column; the middle lobe is broad and yellow. It occurs in Brazil.

C. pachecoi. Rather recently discovered, this species resembles *aurantiaca,* with flowers two and one-half to three inches across, six to ten on a stem, lemon-yellow with a buff to light yellow lip. The lip does not have distinct side lobes, but is rather tubular with the outer portion slightly expanded, and a disk with three slightly raised central veins. The plant occurs in Guatemala.

C. schilleriana. These rather large, striking flowers are four to five inches across, olive-green tinted with brown and spotted with black-purple. The side lobes of the lip are white externally, marked with purple inside, while the middle lobe is kidney-shaped, crimson, with a white margin and streaks of white. It was discovered in Brazil in 1857, and flowers from June to September. A small plant, it somewhat resembles *aclandiae,* and is suspected of being a natural hybrid between that and *guttata*. It is rather rare.

C. skinneri. Called the "Flower of San Sebastian" in Costa Rica where it is the national flower, this plant is used by the natives to decorate their altars and the roofs of their houses. The flowers are three and one-half inches across, entirely rose-purple except for white in the throat. Five to ten grow on a stem. They have a sparkling, almost crystalline texture which gives them a radiant quality. They are not of heavy substance, but keep a long time. The lip is similar in character to the labiata type, but somewhat more tubular. This is a popular species and widely grown. It occurs

Fig. 6-9 *Cattleya loddigesii* var. *harrisoniana,* typical of the bifoliate group with its slender stems bearing two or three leaves. (*Courtesy Rod McLellan Co.*)

Home Orchid Growing

from Mexico to Guatemala, where it was discovered in 1836. The flowers appear in late winter or spring. There is a pure white form.

C. velutina. The tawny-yellow flowers, spotted with maroon-purple, make this a striking species. The small side lobes of the lip are white, streaked with purple inside, while the middle lobe is white marked with a yellow spot and radiating purple lines at its base. It blooms in late summer and is fragrant. The plant is native to Brazil.

C. violacea. These very lovely fragrant, bright rose-purple flowers of heavy substance are four to five inches across. The lip is fleshy, deep purple-violet, with triangular side lobes that enclose the column, and a rounded, ruffled front lobe marked with a patch of yellow streaked with purple. The plant occurs at rather low altitudes in the northern part of South America, where the temperature is quite hot. It can be adapted to the usual cattleya temperatures but needs a warm place in the greenhouse and rather more water. The flowers appear through the summer. It was once known as *C. superba.*

C. walkeriana. A dwarf species whose stocky little pseudobulbs bear single leaves but whose flower characteristics put it in the bifoliate group. The flowers are among the most beautiful of all, with their perky shape, velvety texture, and sweet fragrance. They are three to five inches in diameter, rich rose-lilac, and hold themselves very flat. The side lobes of the lip flare open to form a collar for the enormous rose-colored column. The mid-lobe of the lip is triangular and spreads flat. The flowers may be produced from either the top or the base of the pseudobulb, most often in the latter manner. When the flowering stem comes from the base, it looks at first like a vegetative growth, but it remains slender and gives rise to a stem bearing flowers. From its base comes the next vegetative growth. The old flowering growths remain, looking like little aborted and leafless pseudobulbs, alternating along the rhizome with the regular pseudobulbs. This habit does not seem to carry over into its hybrids. It is a native of western Brazil, where there are definite wet and dry seasons. Discovered in 1839, it was brought to Europe for the first time in 1848. Its flowering season is irregular, extending from fall to spring, and its flowers last for six weeks. It requires much less water during its period of rest.

NATURAL HYBRIDS

The apparent ease with which the species within a genus will cross with each other, and even with the species of related genera, is one of the remarkable features of the orchids. Because this is true it is to be expected that natural hybrids would occur in areas where related, kinds grow together. That they do occur has led to some confusion in identification. Kinds which were at first thought to be species have later been found to be hybrids, and occasionally one that was thought to be a hybrid has been given the status of a species. Some of the natural crosses have been repeated in cultivation, thus proving their origin.

C. hardyana. Found in Colombia, this is a hybrid between *dowiana* var. *aurea* and *gigas.* The flowers are large, bright rose-purple. The richly colored lip resembles the lip of *dowiana* var. *aurea* but has the two yellow eyes of *gigas.* This natural hybrid has been repeated in cultivation. The man-made hybrid *C.* Hardyana is one of the best known of the older hybrids and has been used as a parent in a long line of subsequent hybrids.

C. guatemalensis. This hybrid between *skinneri* and *aurantiaca,* has pale rose-purple flowers. The lip has side lobes that are pale orange on the outside, and a middle lobe of purple with a red-spotted orange-yellow disk. Some plants give flowers that resemble the *skinneri* parent and others have flowers that are more like the *aurantiaca* parent. There is sometimes an orange tone to the flowers when they first open. It blooms in late spring and summer and is found in Guatemala.

C. victoria-reginae. This plant grows with *labiata* and *leopoldii,* and is probably a hybrid between the two. Its pseudobulbs are tall like those of the latter and bear one or two leaves. The flowers are attractive, intermediate between the two species in size, and have the three-lobed lip of the *leopoldii* parent, although the middle lobe is broadened by the influence of the *labiata* parent. The sepals are purple tinged with yellow, the petals purple; both are veined with red. This Brazilian plant, which was discovered in Pernambuco in 1891, is quite rare.

A few other natural hybrids have been found, and are sometimes described as species. They are rarely seen at present, and some may not be known in collections.

7

CONTROL OF FLOWERING IN CATTLEYAS

The *Cattleya* species come from areas where the length of the days reaches neither of the extremes of short or long days that exist in our latitudes, and where the temperature changes from season to season are small. Yet the small changes in daylength and temperature are apparently critical for their flowering in their native habitats. These species exhibit their sensitivity to daylength and temperature in various ways when grown in our country. Our greater seasonal differences in daylength are imposed upon their inherent flowering habits, and the temperatures we maintain in our greenhouses may influence their response to the length of days.

Important to the understanding of their flowering habits is a knowledge of when and under what conditions flower buds are "initiated," and what conditions bring about the subsequent growth of the flower buds. Initiation of flower buds means the laying down of the flower parts in microscopic size by the meristematic tissue at the tip of the pseudobulb. The buds are not visible in the sheath at this time, in fact, in some species several months elapse between the initiation of the buds and the time they can be seen growing in the sheath. Since our daylength is constantly changing from shorter to longer, or longer to shorter, each species has to find a specific daylength compatible with its inherent habit and the stage of development of its pseudobulbs for the initiation of flower buds. The

daylength that prevails during the period which follows initiation, and the temperatures of the season or in the greenhouse, may or may not be conducive to their further development. Thus after initiating their buds, some species can develop them immediately, while others must wait for several months after initiation for the proper set of conditions to occur that will cause these buds to resume growth. *With cattleyas (and other orchids as well) we must deal with two sets of conditions, one that causes initiation of buds and another that brings them into active growth.* Once the buds have been put into active growth so that they are elongating rapidly, they will continue to grow regardless of the length of the days.

The sensitivity to daylength of many garden and house plants, and control of their flowering by manipulation of daylength, has been known for many years. Plants, such as chrysanthemum and aster, initiate flower buds and develop them immediately following initiation. The conditions that bring about initiation also bring about flowering. Thus when we speak of daylength in connection with their flowering, we mean the daylength necessary for the whole process from bud formation to the opening of flowers. Among the plants of house and garden are "short-day" plants, which initiate buds and produce flowers when the days are less than 13 hours long (some require days less than 12 hours, and a few respond on a 14-hour day); "long-day" plants, which initiate flower buds and produce flowers when the days are longer than 13 or 14 hours, and "day neutral" plants which flower regardless of the daylength. Chrysanthemums and asters are typical short-day plants. They can be brought into flower at any time of the year by controlling the length of day—by giving them long days by means of electric lights until it is desired to have them start the flowering process, and then short days to bring about bud formation and blooming. Calceolaria and scabiosa are examples of long-day plants. Their flowering can be brought about in mid-winter by giving them artificially lengthened days. Night temperature can alter the flowering of many kinds. For instance, foxglove does not flower when grown continually with night temperatures of 55° to 60°; it will flower only after a period of nights of 40° to 50°. Stocks flower during the winter at a night temperature of 50° but not at 60°. Temperature can even change the response of a plant to daylength. Poinsettia will flower with short days when grown at night temperatures of 63° to 64°, but becomes a long-day plant with nights of 55°.

Comparison of a few *Cattleya* species on which work has been done will illustrate the role of both daylength and temperature on their bud initiation and flowering. The following table gives the normal dates of flower bud initiation at Ithaca, New York, as discovered by Gavino Rotor from microscopic studies of the tips of pseudobulbs. The plants were growing in normal seasonal daylengths and temperatures. These species and some other kinds of orchids were then grown experimentally under continuously short and continuously long days, at continuous night temperatures of 55° and 65°, and compared to groups grown normally. The short days were held at 9 hours in length by covering the plants with black cloth when the normal daylength exceeded this, and long days were kept at 16 hours by using artificial lighting.

Normal dates of bud initiation under greenhouse conditions in Ithaca, New York*

	1949	1950
Cattleya gaskelliana		March 1
C. labiata	June 25	June 25
C. percivaliana	September 3	September 1
C. trianaei	September 3	September 15
C. mossiae	November 15	November 1

* Bulletin #885, Cornell University Agricultural Experiment Station, "Daylength and Temperature in Relation to Growth and Flowering of Orchids" by Gavino B. Rotor, Jr.

When *C. gigas* (similar to *C. gaskelliana* in above table) is grown with a night temperature of 55° and normal daylength, it initiates its buds during the short days of late February and early March. The daylength of the following weeks is conducive to the further development of the buds, and they grow rapidly and come into flower before the pseudobulb is fully mature. The buds are thus initiated and begin development during the short days of spring. If instead of 55° nights, *C. gigas* is grown continuously with nights of 65°, it will not flower. If the plants are grown with continuous 16-hour days and either 55° or 65° nights, they generally fail to flower. From the point of view of both flower bud initiation and triggering the buds into growth, *C. gigas* is a short-day plant. Even though it completes its flowering during the long days of June and July, the significant daylength is that which causes the buds to begin growing up in the sheath. Once the buds have started this growth they will continue regardless of the daylength.

C. trianaei normally initiates its flower buds in mid-September when the days are short, and waits until the even shorter days of November to start the buds growing up in the sheath. Temperature is not critical in its case, for it will initiate and develop its flowers with either 55° or 65° nights. The daylength is critical, however, for flowering is entirely prevented by continuous days of 16 hours at either night temperature. *C. trianaei* is, therefore, another short-day plant.

C. mossiae initiates its buds during the short days about November 1, at a night temperature of 55°, and waits through December and part of January to start the buds growing up in the sheath. Continuous long days entirely prevent flowering. In work done on *C. mossiae,* it appeared that this species would initiate some buds with 65° nights and short days, but the flowering was delayed and spread erratically over a number of months. Experience in growing *C. mossiae* has shown that its best and most reliable flowering comes when it has at least two months of short days with nights of 55° to initiate the buds and start them growing in the sheath. Here, therefore, is another short-day species.

C. labiata, under normal seasonal conditions, initiates flower buds during the longest days of the year, close to June 21. The long days and warm nights that usually prevail through the summer prevent these buds from going ahead and developing, and this species waits until the shorter days and cooler nights of fall to resume growth of the buds and bring them into bloom. Experiments with *C. labiata* turned up some remarkable interrelationships between temperature and daylength. When it was grown with continuous long days and nights of 65°, it was entirely prevented from blooming (although we would expect from the above information that flower buds had been initiated). Grown with continuous long days but with nights of 55°, some plants flowered, though not all. A night temperature of 55° is apparently capable of somewhat offsetting the influence of long days. Grown with continuous short days and 65° nights, about half the plants flowered; and better flowering was had with short days and 55° nights. As a matter of interest, when we sort out this data we find the following to be true: (1) as far as flower bud initiation is concerned, *C. labiata* is day neutral, for it initiates buds with either long or short days, regardless of night temperature: (2) at a 55° night temperature it is day neutral for it can both initiate and develop flower buds at this temperature with either daylength; (3) with 65° nights it is a short-day plant as far as growth of the buds and blooming is concerned; (4) the only combination that entirely prevents the growth of the buds and therefore prevents flowering is long days plus 65° nights; (5) growth of the flower buds resulting in flowering requires either 55° nights, or short days, or both.

Not enough work has been done on other species of *Cattleya*. We can only speculate about the habits of those not actually studied. But if we were to speculate on the basis of what we know of those that have been described here and from the flowering times of others, we might guess that the kinds that flower in winter, spring, and early summer are all short-day plants. Where fall flowering is concerned, we would not know whether the plants follow the habits of *C. labiata*, or whether they have a pattern of their own. There are many *Cattleya* species, some quite unfamiliar and little grown. We do not know what any of these would show themselves capable of under experimental conditions. So far, the only patterns discovered are "short day" and "day neutral."

Hybrids inherit their growth and flowering patterns from their ancestors. Some members of a cross may inherit the pattern of one of the species in their makeup, others that of a different species. There are hybrids, however, that make several growths a year, and flower whenever a growth matures. We have a cross in which a number of flowering patterns appear. There are individual plants that always flower in the spring, others always in the fall, and still others always in the winter. There are some that flower regularly twice a year, both in the spring and in the fall. All of these we would call short-day plants. In this same cross there are some individuals that flower three or four times a year, and which, through a period of several years, have hit nearly every month in the year. We have not studied their actual bud initiation, but we feel it would be safe to say that these individuals are day neutral.

Control of flowering has been worked out very exactly for *C. labiata* and its hybrids. *C. labiata* contributes its habits of bud initiation and flower development to its progeny. The more labiata there is in a hybrid, or the more recently it has been introduced into the strain, the more exactly can its flowering be controlled. The flowering of these hybrids can be timed for any date one wishes. Flowering has been prevented experimentally for as long as two years, and the plants then brought into flower. Hybridists have created crosses especially for the control of flowering, and greater success will be had in using them. This does not mean that you should not try control on any labiata hybrids you may have.

Essentially, the method of control is to give the plants long days and a night temperature of 65° to withhold flowering until it is desired to have the buds start to grow up in the sheath, and then to give them the short days that will bring about blooming. It has been found that complete control is had by starting the long-day, 65° night treatment in June. You might wonder why it must be begun so early, since these plants normally do not flower until fall. As a group, the labiata hybrids flower from September through November. Without studying each plant individually, there is no way of knowing exactly when the flower buds start to grow up in the sheath. If exact control is desired, it is best to keep the night temperature at 65° by means of thermostatically controlled heating, otherwise a cool spell of weather might trigger some plants into starting the flower buds up in the sheath, thus bringing them into bloom ahead of the date you wish. Also, since the days begin to shorten after June 21 and we do not know just what the critical daylength is for the start of flower bud growth, the days are held to 16 hours by means of electric lights from this date. It takes about two months, more or less (you would have to time this for your own plants), for the flower buds to grow up in the sheath and be ready to open, so the long days and

65° nights are continued until about two months before the crop of flowers is desired. Day temperature during the long-day treatment is run ten degrees higher, around 75°. Suppose you wish to have the flowers for the Christmas holidays. The long-day treatment is continued until the middle of October, at which time the plants are allowed to have the normally short days of the season. The night temperature can now be dropped to the usual 55° to 60° range, although the buds will come along a little faster if 65° nights are continued. If you wish to have the flowers for Easter, you continue the long-day treatment until approximately two months before Easter, and then give short days. However, if you wish the flowers for June, the time for starting short days is April 1. Because the days are becoming longer at this time, you will have to shorten the daylight hours by covering the plants with black cloth from five o'clock in the evening to eight o'clock in the morning. The accompanying drawings show both lighting and darkening techniques.

For merely prolonging the daylight hours, the light intensity does not have to be high. The lights should be of the incandescent or Mazda type. Forty- to sixty-watt bulbs, placed in reflectors two to three feet above the plants and at intervals of about eight feet, will be sufficient to withhold flowering. They are turned on at sundown and kept on long enough to give a total of 16 hours of light. In a greenhouse where other plants are grown, you must be careful to enclose the group of plants being lighted so as not to affect the flowering of other things. During the period of high night temperatures and long days, the plants should be given regular applications of fertilizer, and they must have as good sunlight during the day as possible, short of burning. Watering should be watched carefully to conform to what the plants actually need, so that they become neither dehydrated nor too soft. For shortening the days artificially, it is necessary to build a framework over which black cloth can be drawn every night, and the cloth must be light proof.

From the time the buds show in the sheath, the length of time to bloom can be somewhat regulated by temperature. If the night temperature is 50° or 55°, the flowers will take about two weeks

Fig. 7-1 Arrangement of lights for long-day treatment.

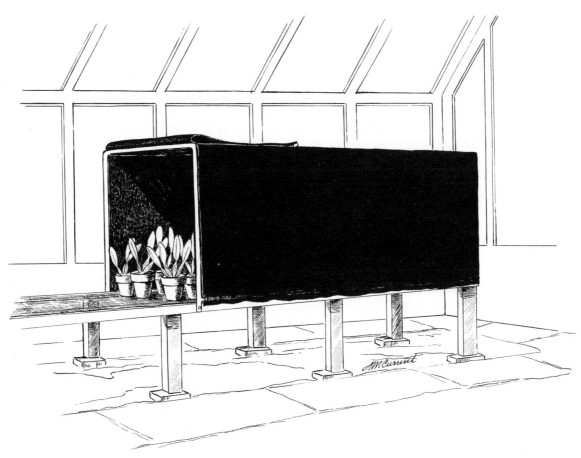

Fig. 7-2 Black cloth for short-day treatment. The cloth is arranged on a framework, so that it can be pulled over the plants to cut out the light, or drawn back to allow light.

longer to develop than when it is held to 65°. If the night temperature is pushed to 70°, development time can be reduced further. This can be useful if for some reason you find that you are going to miss the date for which you have planned. If the buds are farther along than they should be at a certain time, you can hold them back a week or two by dropping the night temperature. We do not advocate a 70° night temperature for anything but an emergency, but if it is a matter of meeting a certain date or losing the income from a crop of flowers, it would be worth raising the nights to 70° for the short time necessary to gain flowers a week or two earlier.

A number of growers are producing two sets of flowers a year from the labiata hybrids. They have found that by using higher light intensities to prolong the days they can stimulate plant growth so much that the year's cycle can be telescoped into six months. They use bulbs of 100-150 watts, spaced about six feet apart and two to three feet

above the plants. They maintain nights of 65° and days of 80° to 85°. Extremely good air circulation is necessary because of the heat from the lights. Careful attention must also be given to the humidity, watering, and fertilizing. The long-day treatment is given from June to the middle of October, and the naturally short days from then on will bring on the flowers for the Christmas holidays. As soon as the flowers are cut, or by the first of January, the plants are put under long days again. The long days and 65° nights speed up the growth that normally starts at this time of the year. About the first of April, the plants are given short days, and the flowers are ready to cut by June. As soon as this crop is cut, the long-day treatment is started again, the plants now start another new growth, and the flowers can again be timed for Christmas.

It is a problem for an amateur with one greenhouse and a mixed collection of orchids to do much with control of flowering. Keeping a high night temperature for much of the fall and winter to control *C. labiata* hybrids, prevents many other kinds from flowering. Many amateurs have experienced difficulty in preventing light leaks when giving the long-day treatment, and if enough light reaches other plants it may prevent the flowering of some of them. To attempt the control of more than one kind of cattleya presents additional problems. If you are giving labiata hybrids long days and 65° nights, and then must give mossiae hybrids short days and 55° nights, you can see how the troubles would multiply. About the only way an amateur can do much with controlling flowering is to have two greenhouses, one maintained at fifty-five degrees and the other at sixty-five degrees at night. In each greenhouse there can be lights installed and a framework for cloth. Groups of plants would then be moved from one situation to another as their schedule demanded. In the 55° house you could grow a few of the intermediate kinds of orchids, and in the 65° house perhaps a few of the warm kinds, so as to have more variety than just two or three types of cattleya hybrids.

We cannot give you much in the way of schedules for types other than the labiata hybrids. Most commercial growers have found it easier to handle just these, since they comprise a wonderful array of richly colored flowers and can be managed so exactly. But if you have a large number of plants that flower regularly in the winter or spring, you might use what has been given earlier in this section as a basis for some experiments. It seems to be difficult to do much about controlling the kinds which, like *C. gigas*, start their growth in the winter and bloom on this young growth in early summer. At best they can be speeded a bit into flowering by extending the normal daylength in gradual stages, starting after the buds are well up in the sheath. Mid-winter blooming kinds can (if they are amen-able to the treatment) be brought into bloom early, say for Christmas, by giving them short days starting in September. Timing of these must include a period for bud initiation which means a few weeks longer than the usual two-month period. These mid-winter blooming kinds are usually prevented from flowering by long days, so to delay their flowering until spring necessitates giving them long days until about three months before you wish to have them in bloom. Kinds that make up their growth in the fall and do not flower until spring, do not offer much chance of control. The short days of November and December do not normally trigger the flower buds into growth at that time, yet many of them require this period of short days and 55° nights in order to bloom at all. Their flowering can be brought about a little earlier than usual, say for Easter rather than in June, by giving the plants long days and 65° nights *after* the buds are well up in the sheath.

Remember that kinds other than labiata hybrids have not been much worked with. We do not know just what influence the various species have on their hybrids. Hybrids of complicated ancestry may have six or a dozen species in their makeup, often more. The fact that a certain hybrid has *C. mossiae* in it does not mean that it will behave like *C. mossiae*. As a matter of fact, it may behave more like some other ancestor whose habits have not been studied. We do know that most of the *Cattleya* species and hybrids grow well and flower faithfully with the normal daylengths of the seasons and with a night temperature range of 55° to 60°. An amateur who has a mixed collection of cattleyas and other kinds can have something in bloom most of the time by choosing plants for their natural flowering period.

8

GENETICS AND THE BREEDING OF HYBRIDS

In 1852 orchids were still new to Europeans. People were busy just learning to know and grow them. The possibilities of hybridization were apparently unthought of until a surgeon saw how it could be done and suggested it to an orchid grower. The surgeon was a Dr. Harris of Exeter, and the grower, Mr. J. Dominy, foreman of the firm of Veitch and Sons. In 1852 with Dr. Harris' help, Mr. Dominy performed the first hand pollination, and in 1856 the first hybrid orchid flowered, *Calanthe* Dominyi (*Calanthe masuca* × *Calanthe furcata*). Mr. Dominy worked for twenty years, and produced about twenty-five hybrids, among them, in 1863, the first bigeneric hybrid, *Laeliocattleya* Exoniensis (*Cattleya mossiae* × *Laelia crispa*).

The exciting note injected into orchid growing by Dr. Harris had a powerful reaction. The best of the newly produced hybrids created a sensation at exhibitions. Old orchid books are full of glowing accounts of the new marvels, and predict wonderful things to come. Mr. Dominy worked alone in the field for most of the twenty years, for it was not until 1871 that a hybrid was produced by someone else. No one at that time could have foreseen the future extent of hybridization during the next seventy-five years. In 1890 there were 200 crosses registered. Now there are thousands upon thousands, and the number grows each year.

A large proportion of the best hybrids have been made by experienced growers, but amateurs have had a hand in hybridization, too. Success on both sides was largely a matter of chance, and indeed still is. Curiosity plus the desire to create something unusual prompted nearly everyone to cross whatever orchids he had at hand, in the hope that he would achieve some striking result. Many of the crosses made between hybrids of doubtful quality have not been wise, and have only cluttered the lists. Crosses between species have always been valuable for the tremendous amount of knowledge they have given us, and crosses between genera have contributed even more. All such crosses are the result of the burning curiosity possessed by human beings—the desire to see "what would happen if—." The early growers tried all sorts of things. During the first fifty years of hybridization, from 1856 to 1906, crosses were made in many genera, including *Cattleya, Calanthe, Dendrobium, Aerides, Paphiopedilum, Cymbidium, Lycaste, Zygopetalum, Miltonia, Odontoglossum, Stanhopea, Vanda, Epidendrum, Laelia, Phaius,* and many others. At least fourteen bi-and tri-generic hybrids were created, including combinations between genera of the Cattleya tribe, as well as such things as *Odontioda* and *Odontonia.* Considering the difficulties with germinating seed, this is a phenomenal record, for the crosses numbered over 1,500. Of these some

750 were in *Paphiopedilum* alone, the most difficult of all genera.

The nature of orchids themselves, being slow to mature and flower, necessitated accurate records, lest the parentage of seedlings be forgotten. The great interest in hybrids led to the registration of crosses, not only to insure credit to the first person to think of a cross, but to save others from repeating what had already been tried. The fortunate result of these factors has been the development of an orchid genealogy as accurate and complete as any family history in existence.

It early became the custom to give a hybrid a name of its own. At first this was done to honor the creator of a hybrid or someone who had achieved fame in the orchid world. The system gives us a handy way to identify the complicated hybrids that exist today. It would be impossible to call an orchid by the names of a dozen or more ancestors. It is even awkward to give the immediate parentage of a plant every time we want to speak of it. For instance, how much more simple it is to say *Cattleya* Hardyana, than to say *Cattleya dowiana, aurea* by *Cattleya gigas.* Nowadays growers are pressed to find names that have not already been used. Hybrids are named after the gods of ancient mythology, the letters of the Greek alphabet, presidents, generals, opera stars, the grower's own relatives and friends, or names fanciful or descriptive. In writing out the parentage, it is customary to give the pod or female parent first.

Once a name has been given to a cross, it stands for any repetition of that cross. For instance, *Cattleya* Fabia is *Cattleya dowiana* × *Cattleya labiata,* and every time those two species are mated the offspring must be called *Cattleya* Fabia. *Cattleya* Fabia × *Cattleya* Hardyana produced *Cattleya* Princess Royal, while the mating of the white forms produced *Cattleya* Princess Royal, alba. Knowing the name of any hybrid enables you to trace its ancestry back to the species involved in all the branches of its "family tree."

Sander's *Complete List of Orchid Hybrids* covers crosses up to 1946, and three addenda, each covering a three year period, brought the listings up through 1954. These lists are straightforward and simple. They include the name of the hybrid, the names of its parents, the date of registration and the name of the person who registered the cross. Each volume consists of two tables. Table I enables you to look up a hybrid by its name and gives you its parentage. Table II lists under each species and hybrid the species and hybrids with which it has been crossed and the resulting hybrid names. These volumes are a monument to Mr. Fred K. Sander, of Sanders (St. Albans) Ltd., England, who devoted over fifty years of loving work to their compilation, all done without remuneration except for the gratitude of orchid growers all over the world.

David F. Sander continued the work up to 1960 and produced the ingenious one-table form, beginning with a set of two volumes containing hybrids from 1946 to 1960. Registration of hybrids and the issuing of further volumes are now conducted by the Royal Horticultural Society. Additional volumes are published at intervals. All are obtainable through the American Orchid Society, Inc., as are forms for registering hybrids. If you wish, you may write directly to the Registrar of Orchid Hybrids, The Royal Horticultural Society, Vincent Square, London, S. W. 1. Registration fee is $3.00.

Primary crosses, crosses between two species, are likely to yield plants that are intermediate between the parents, and more or less uniform. But crosses between two hybrids are more complicated and show great variety among the offspring. A hybrid is made up of factors inherited from each of its parents and, when two hybrids are mated, these factors recombine in many ways. The offspring will show various combinations of the characteristics of the parent plants, as well as combinations reminiscent of many of the types found in their ancestry. For an interesting series showing this see page 195. The same thing happens when a hybrid is self-pollinated, for its inherited characteristics also recombine to give a number of different kinds of offspring.

During the earlier years of hybridization it seemed sufficient to know the names of the two species or hybrids crossed to make a certain hybrid. Through the years it has become obvious that certain individual plants have been better parents than others, and that some have been more consistent in transmitting their characteristics to their offspring. Often it is not a question of superiority but rather of distinctive characteristics obtained from certain individuals. It has become important to know exactly what individual plants have been used as parents. To mark an outstanding plant it is given a varietal name, a name added to the hybrid name and set in single quotes, for example *Cattleya* Bow Bells 'Serene.' Thus this plant is set apart from other members of the cross, and the varietal name is carried with it and all of its divisions, which together form a "clone."

We have seen that once a name has been given

to a cross, that name stands for any repetition of the cross. Here we must explain lest some difficulties in understanding lead to confusion. Let's say that a certain cross proves to be so successful that there is more demand for seedlings than there are seedlings available. The originator of the cross may *remake* the cross, using the *identical parents* again. Another grower, who has *divisions of these same parents,* may also *remake* the cross. However, a grower who has other plants from the same hybrid groups, different individuals from those used in the original cross, will not get the same results by crossing them. It is true that the resulting seedlings will have the same hybrid name, and if his plants are superior his cross may be better, but the offspring will exhibit quite a different array of characteristics. Let's say that there is a hybrid named *Cattleya* Alpha which has progeny ranging in color from pink to green, and one named *Cattleya* Beta that ranges from pale lavender to dark purple. A cross between a green Alpha and a pale Beta will be quite different from a cross between a pink Alpha and a dark purple Beta. Or let's say that in a cross which we shall call *Cattleya* Delta one individual occurs that is tetraploid, having double the normal number of chromosomes. Crosses in which this tetraploid Delta is used as a parent will be different from crosses in which other Deltas, diploid plants, function as parents. One can readily see the need for distinguishing individual plants used in hybridization.

It was at one time hoped that new hybrid lists might include the clonal name of parent plants. Although the American Orchid Society tried to work out some method, it has not proven feasible. There are often dozens of outstanding clones in a single cross, and registration of each hybrid made with each clone would, the authorities felt, cause awkward duplication and unnecessarily long lists. Technically, the cross would be the same no matter

Fig. 8-1 Modification of characteristics of two species parents in their primary hybrid. UPPER, *Cattleya bicolor,* a bifoliate species which has slender sepals and petals and a lip without side lobes.

CENTER, *Cattleya dowiana,* a member of the labiata group, with broad petals and a broad lip with the sides rolled over the column.

LOWER, *Cattleya* Iris, *Cattleya bicolor* × *Cattleya Dowiana.* The lip, though wider and more ruffled than in *C. bicolor,* is still not as wide as in *C. dowiana,* and is still somewhat tongue-shaped as in *C. bicolor.* The side lobes of the lip have been reduced to the merest trace at the very base of the lip. (*Cattleya dowiana,* courtesy *H. A. Dunn and H. Griffin*) which clones were used; the hybrid name would of course be the same. It was felt that the registration lists were not the place for this information; rather, the hybridizer should be responsible for keeping the records, and that those who wished to buy offspring from certain clones should be able to obtain the information from him. Additional information regarding a clone should also be kept in its record, such as its chromosome number, its color, and the characteristics of its offspring.

The results of a cross cannot be known until a fair percentage of the seedlings flower. The fact that the parent plants are handsome does not necessarily mean that their offspring will be equally good. If the seedlings are good, however, the grower will be encouraged to use their parents again in other combinations. Proving the merit of parent plants is a long job, for they must be tried in a number of crosses, not just one. Failure in one cross may not mean that the same plants will fail when combined with other individuals. Again, the need for records and for identification of plants used as parents can be clearly seen. How disappointing it would be for a cross to turn out exceptionally well and then not to know which plants produced this cross! Equally sad is a situation, which has often occurred, in which divisions of valuable plants have been lost

because of the lack of proper labeling. In the field of hybridization it is not enough to guess or think that a certain plant is a division of a particularly famous one. If a grower is going to represent his seedlings as offspring of certain famous parents, he must know beyond all doubt that this is so. If a buyer is desirous of obtaining a division of a certain plant, he must be given the assurance that the plant he receives is in fact that plant.

How do such differences among individuals occur? How are characteristics carried from parent to offspring? How is it that a characteristic that occurs in one generation may not show up in the next, but may instead be exhibited in a later generation? It is the purpose of this chapter to show, by highly simplified examples, the basic workings of inheritance. These basic principles will not cover all of the complications that arise in the passing on of traits from one generation to another, but will give a glimpse into the general methods by which this takes place. When you have read through the "A B Cs" of inheritance in this chapter, you will be better able to understand things that you can see in your own plants, and you will appreciate the work of the cytogeneticists who are now studying inheritance in orchids. Compared to what is known of genetics of the fruit fly, we know as yet

Fig. 8-2 Two plants from the same seed pod, showing possible variation from good to poor in the same cross. Both have the same lip pattern, but one has inherited large size and fairly good shape, while the other has inherited small size and less good shape.

Home Orchid Growing

very little about the genetics of orchids. The problem is complicated by the thousands of kinds of orchids, by the fact that transmission of characters in different genera may be accomplished by different gene groups, and by the length of time from seed to flower.

The discussion of genetics in this chapter will be based on *Cattleya* and some of its intergeneric crosses with *Laelia, Sophronitis,* and *Brassavola.* Descriptions of the latter genera will be found in the chapter on the Cattleya tribe, along with such related genera as *Epidendrum, Diacrium,* etc.

GENETICS

The foundation of the individual in all species of living things, both plant and animal, lies in its genetic makeup. Every cell in a plant, whether of roots, leaves, or flowers, contains in its nucleus a set of microscopic structures called chromosomes. On each chromosome there are still smaller structures called genes, so tiny that they cannot be seen with the ordinary microscope. The genes (derived from genetics, which in turn comes from genesis, the beginning) control every single characteristic of the individual. Try to list all the observable traits of an orchid plant, from the most obvious to the most minute, including such things as: pseudobulbs, tall or short, thick or thin; leaves, long or short, wide or narrow; sheath, single or double; lip, bordered or plain, "eyes" present or absent, throat, open or tubular; texture of flower; substance, whether waxy or thin, and so on. You would soon have quite a list. The internal structure of the plant, if you could discern it, should be added to your list, as should its growth and flowering habits and the keeping quality of the flowers. Every one of these items is controlled by genes, and it probably takes several thousand, working together in a most complicated way, to produce the plant under scrutiny.

Environment cannot be overlooked in the making of a plant. Without the necessary growing conditions, a plant cannot develop properly. But proper growing conditions only give the genes a chance to express themselves. A plant that gives poor flowers under the best of care will never give good ones. It does not have the genetic makeup for good flowers. Such characteristics as petals that fold back too far, or misshapen flower parts, are genetic faults. (However, if a plant that has consistently produced good flowers suddenly gives

Fig. 8-3   A cell with two pair of chromosomes.

defective ones, you might look for insect injury, disease, or some environmental cause. Freak flowers appear occasionally but seldom repeat themselves.)

Every species has its own standard number of chromosomes. In man there are forty-six. In the fruit fly there are eight. The garden pea, used by Mendel in the experiments which gave the world the fundamentals of genetics, has fourteen.

Chromosomes exist in pairs, but the members of each pair actually stand side by side only during reduction division (see below). The two members of each pair of chromosomes are identical in shape and size, but not necessarily in gene content. Genes also occur in pairs, one member of a pair on each of the matched chromosomes. Each pair of chromosomes is different from every other pair in the cell. Fig. 8-3 shows a cell that has two pairs of chromosomes, which have been made black and white to distinguish the individual members of each pair. The shape and size of the chromosomes, as well as the total number, are standard for the species. Of the forty chromosomes in *C. trianaei,* there are twenty distinct kinds, two of each, and every cell in the plant, except the reproductive cells, contains the full complement.

Certain tissues of a flower are set aside for the formation of reproductive cells. In these tissues the cells divide in a special way, called reduction division. The chromosomes come together in pairs. Then the members of each pair of chromosomes separate, and travel to opposite ends of the cell, which then divides in half to form two new cells. Fig. 8-4 shows this process. Each of the new cells now contains one member of each pair of chromosomes, or half of the original number. This is called the "haploid" number. The haploid cells later develop into sperm and egg cells, which in genetic terminology are called gametes. When fertilization takes place, see Fig. 8-5, and a sperm and egg come together, the full number of chromosomes, the

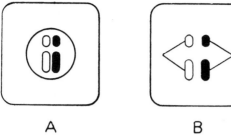 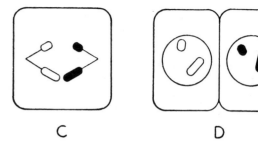

| A | B | C | D |

Fig. 8-4 Reduction division, A, the chromosome pair. B and C, they separate. D, new cells are formed with half the original number.

"diploid" number, is again present. The new individual that develops from the fertilized egg thus receives half of its chromosomes from one parent, half from the other. The chromosomes never fuse, but remain separate and distinct from each other. Each chromosome carries with it its own gene content, and when it goes into the making of a new individual it takes its genes along with it to that new individual.

The haploid number is referred to as "n" for brevity and convenience. The diploid number then becomes "2n." We shall later talk about triploids, "3n," and tetraploids, "4n," plants that have three and four times the haploid number of chromosomes, and even pentaploids, "5n." Plants with more than the 2n number of chromosomes are called "polyploids."

During the development of reproductive cells, it is pure chance which member of a pair of chromosomes will go into a resulting sperm or egg cell. We can think of the chromosomes as pairing with one to the right of the other, but just as often, the position is reversed. If the members of each pair are identical in gene content, it does not matter how they separate, for the resulting reproductive cells will be identical. But where the members of

a pair differ from each other, if by only one gene, it makes a great deal of difference. Fig. 8-6 shows the possible combinations of genes in the reproductive cells arising from one that has two pair of unlike chromosomes. Where only one pair of unlike chromosomes is involved, there are two types of reproductive cells, or 2 to the first power, 2^1. Where two pair are concerned, there are four types, or 2^2, and where there are three pair of unlike chromosomes, there will be eight different types of reproductive cells, or 2^3. The figures become almost astronomical for cells that contain a large number of chromosomes. For instance, where there are 20 pair, if each member of every pair is unlike the other, the possible types of reproductive cells is 2^{20}, or 1,048,576 different kinds.

Such a figure gives some idea of the problems confronting geneticists who try to make a complete analysis of a plant or an animal. The genetic makeup of an individual cannot be known from its appearance. The only way to find out what genes it contains is to breed it and see what comes out in the offspring. This reveals why geneticists usually choose subjects that have a short life cycle. In contrast to orchids, the fruit fly produces a new generation every few days, and wheat and corn in a matter of months. A planned study of orchid genetics started now would take several lifetimes to complete. We do have quite a body of facts, how-

Fig. 8-5 Fertilization brings together a set of chromosomes from each parent.

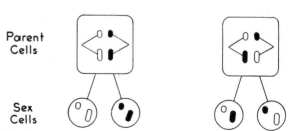

Parent Cells

Sex Cells

Fig. 8-6. Four types of sex cells arise from a cell having two pair of unlike chromosomes.

76

Home Orchid Growing

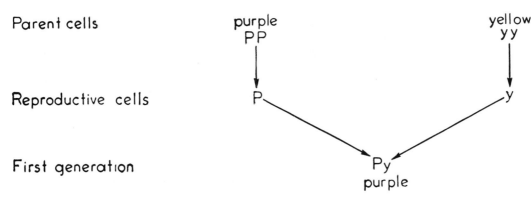

Parent cells   purple   yellow
                         PP   yy

Reproductive cells   P   y

First generation   Py
                              purple

Fig. 8-7 A hypothetical cross between *C. gigas,* in which purple is dominant, and *C. dowiana,* in which yellow is recessive, produces all purple flowers in the offspring.

ever, collected by careful observers, that show how certain factors in orchids behave, and their pattern follows the same general behavior seen in plants that have been studied in more detail.

Genes are of two general types, "dominant" and "recessive." Dominant genes have the power to induce the appearance of the characteristic they govern whenever they are present. Recessive genes can manifest themselves only in the absence of the dominant. For instance, in cattleyas purple is dominant over yellow. A cross between *Cattleya gigas* (purple) and *Cattleya dowiana* (yellow) gives all purple offspring. In Fig. 8-7, the dominant gene for purple is indicated by P, and the recessive gene for yellow by y.* *Cattleya gigas,* the parent plant, has the pair of genes PP, and gives one to each reproductive cell. *Cattleya dowiana,* similarly, has the pair yy, so that each reproductive cell contains one y. Each individual among the offspring inherits a gene for purple, P, and a gene for yellow,

y; and, since purple is dominant over yellow, the offspring have purple flowers. On the other hand, the yellow of *Laelia* is dominant over the purple of *Cattleya,*† so that a mating between *Laelia flava* and *Cattleya gigas* would give all yellow flowers. This is shown in Fig. 8-8 where Y now stands for dominant yellow and p for recessive purple.

There are cases where the dominant gene can manifest itself fully only when present in a double dose, that is, when two dominants are present for the same characteristic, instead of one dominant and one recessive. This seems to be true of flower size; see Fig. 8-9, where L stands for large size and s for small size. If a large cattleya, LL, is crossed with a small one, ss, each of the offspring will inherit one gene for large size and one for small, Ls. The size of the resulting flowers will be intermediate between the two parents. The gene for large size, when present in a single dose, is dominant to the extent that it can make the flowers of the

* The system of symbols used here has been devised for the sake of simplicity. It may well be that our single symbols may represent groups of genes.

† Species of Laelia that have been used to produce hybrids of various shades of yellow, orange, red-orange, and bronze, are *cinnabarina, flava, harpophylla, tenebrosa,* and *xanthina.*

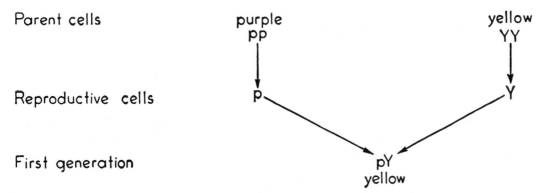

Parent cells   purple   yellow
                         pp   YY

Reproductive cells   p   Y

First generation   pY
                              yellow

Fig. 8-8 A cross in which the purple of *C. gigas* is recessive to the yellow of *Laelia flava* will produce all yellow flowers in the offspring.

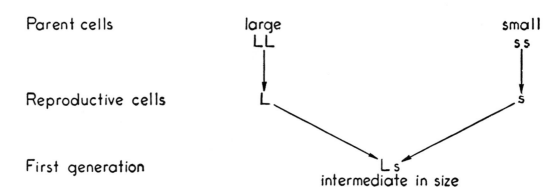

Parent cells	large LL		small s s

Reproductive cells   L   s

First generation   L s
                    intermediate in size

Fig. 8-9 Incomplete dominance. The incompletely dominant gene, L, for large size, when coupled with the recessive gene, s, for small size, gives offspring intermediate in size.

new generation larger than the smaller parent, but it is not able to bring them up to the size of the larger parent. This is called "incomplete dominance."

When species of extremely different size are crossed, for example a large cattleya and a small epidendrum, the resulting flowers do not come all the way up to the mid-point, or average, between the two. For instance, a 2-inch crossed with an 8-inch flower gives offspring of 4 inches rather than the 5-inch size one might expect. And a 1-inch by a 9-inch gives a 3-inch flower instead of a 4.5 inch one. Some years ago we reported an observation made on the number of flowers per spike in Cymbidium primary hybrids, (see page 182) which showed that the number corresponds with the geometrical mean rather than the arithmetical mean or average. Dodson and Gillespie in their book *The Biology of the Orchids* state that the geometrical mean also operates in flower size. The geometrical mean is found by multiplying the two sizes and taking the square root of the result, whereas the arithmetical mean is found by adding them and dividing by two. For the examples above, $2 \times 8 = 16$, and square root of $16 = 4$; $1 \times 9 = 9$, and square root of $9 = 3$. When the size of the parents are closer to each other, e.g. 6 and 8 inches, the size of the offspring comes closer to the arithmetical average, because this is also closer to the geometrical mean—geometrical mean, $6 \times 8 = 48$, square root of $48 =$ approximately 6.9; arithmetical mean, $6 + 8 = 14$, $\frac{14}{2} = 7$. Thus one need be concerned only when the parents are of quite widely separated size. It does point out, however, some of the difficulties faced by a hybridizer who wishes to combine the characteristics of a large flower with those of a small one, as in creating a large

red cattleya type by breeding with a small laelia or sophronitis.

Plants that have identical genes for any one character are said to be homozygous (pure) for that character. For instance, a plant that contains two genes for large size, LL, will give every one of its sperm and egg cells one of those genes, and when used as a parent, will transmit this gene to every individual among the offspring. The same is true of a plant that has identical recessive genes, such as one with two genes for small size, ss, which is said to be homozygous for this character.

A plant that contains unlike genes for any character is called heterozygous (impure, or mixed). If it is heterozygous for size, it means that it contains one dominant gene for large, and one recessive gene for small, Ls. The offspring of the two yellow-purple crosses described above are heterozygous for color, those of the cattleya cross being Py, and those of the laelia × cattleya, pY. When used as parents, heterozygous plants give half of their offspring the dominant gene and half the recessive.

The species tend to be homozygous. However, there are various types within a species, and these types pass their characteristics on to their progeny. There are, for example, good *Cattleya trianaei,* and poor ones. If the types are well separated geographically, the chances are that the good and the poor are respectively homozygous. But if there has been interbreeding among them, they may be heterozygous. The only way to tell whether a flower is homozygous is to pollinate it with its own pollen (self-pollinate it). If all the offspring are identical to the parent, you may know that the parent is homozygous. But if the progeny differ markedly from each other in any way, you will know that the parent is a mixture. A plant that is homozygous for all of its good qualities can be used

Home Orchid Growing

as a "stud" plant. One that proves to be heterozygous is not a "stud" plant. Self pollination is not only valuable in "proving" an individual, but is a means of obtaining pure strains, strains that are homozygous and which will all breed "true."

There are many dominant characters among *Cattleya* and its relatives which can be detected in their hybrids. The bifoliate type of growth, with its slender, jointed stems and two or three leaves is dominant over the thick pseudobulbs and single leaf of the labiata group. So, also, is the spade lip dominant over the labiate lip, and although through successive generations it may be broadened, it can often be identified by the notches that separate the middle lobe from the side lobes. The heavy substance of bifoliate flowers is transmitted to their hybrids. The characteristic veins in the lip of *C. dowiana* and the mottling in the lip of *C. mossiae* both persist in their hybrids. *C. labiata* contributes its day-length sensitivity to its hybrids. The reed-stem epidendrums are dominant both for their growth habit and the character of their flowers. Of course, segregation of these dominant characters through successive generations will cause them eventually to appear only in a percentage of the hybrids.

Whether you intend to enter into a serious breeding program or just cross two orchids for the fun of it, it makes the work more interesting and insures a greater measure of success if you follow some plan based on genetic principles. If what you want is merely a large number of good flowers, perhaps to make your hobby profitable, you will be saved from making crosses that would produce a large number of poor flowers. Or if you want to obtain a unique combination of characteristics from two individuals, you will be spared much pain in know-

ing ahead of time that the type you want may be only one out of a wide assortment of types in the offspring.

It is interesting to go a little further into the inheritance of yellow in cattleyas. The purple *Cattleya gigas* crossed with the yellow *Cattleya dowiana, aurea* gives a first generation (F_1 to geneticists) that is all purple, *Cattleya* Hardyana. Suppose *Cattleya* Hardyana is self-pollinated, and a second generation (F_2) of seedlings is raised. A person who did not know the inheritance of *Cattleya* Hardyana would be astonished to get some yellow flowers in this second generation. But those who knew its genetic makeup would have expected just that. Fig. 8-10 shows how this happens. *Cattleya* Hardyana is heterozygous. Its color genes are Py. In the formation of reproductive cells these genes segregate so that half of them contain P and half of them y. The second generation will recombine these genes in three ways, PP, Py, and yy. One-fourth of the plants will be homozygous purple, one-half of them will be heterozygous purple, and the remaining one-fourth will be homozygous yellow.

Again, someone who did not know genetics might think he could increase the "potency" of that homozygous yellow by crossing it back to the yellow *Cattleya dowiana, aurea*. It is true that he would get all yellow flowers, but the yellow always remains a recessive gene. If he is looking for a plant to use for breeding yellows when crossed with purple, he will not get it this way. Fig. 8-11 shows why. The only way to get a yellow that will always be dominant over purple is to use a yellow laelia as a parent, as described below under Laeliocattleyas.

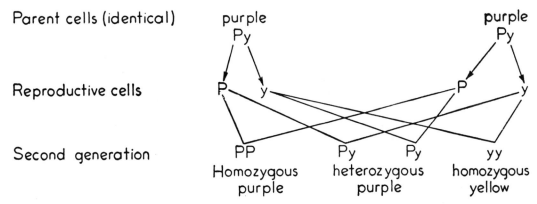

Fig. 8-10 The F_2 generation obtained by crossing members of the F_1 will be three-fourths purple and one-fourth

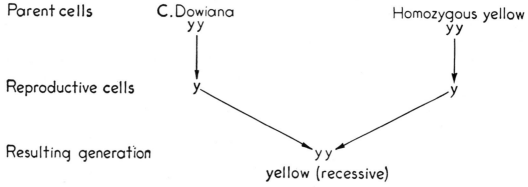

Parent cells   C.Dowiana   Homozygous yellow
                     y y   y y

Reproductive cells   y   y

Resulting generation   y y
                       yellow (recessive)

Fig. 8-11 The back cross of the homozygous yellow F₂ hybrid to *C. dowiana* simply produces another homozygous recessive yellow.

Laeliocattleyas

Laelia is used in crosses with *Cattleya* to lend bright coloring to the hybrids. *L. harpophylla,* a bright red-orange, can produce hybrids of the same color. *Laelia tenebrosa,* which is reddish brown with coppery suffusion and a darker lip, when crossed with *Cattleya* produces bronze flowers with deep purple lip, in which the bronze ranges from yellow-bronze to purple-bronze. *L. purpurata* has perhaps been used more than any other in hybrids with *Cattleya,* partly because of the deep velvety purple of its lip, and partly because it is itself a large flower and the resulting hybrids are of good size from the beginning. Hybrids that have a small laelia parent have to be crossed again with a large cattleya to bring the size up to the desired dimensions.

In the discussion of yellow-purple crosses above you will remember that the yellow of *Laelia* is dominant over the purple of *Cattleya.* The great value of this type of cross is that it is possible to breed a stud plant that is homozygous for yellow (that carries the double dose) and in which the

yellow is dominant. Such a stud plant should also be a yellow laeliocattleya that has the desirable cattleya shape. Two steps are necessary to achieve this.

Suppose we choose the all-yellow *Laelia flava* and cross it with any purple cattleya. Here we will be dealing with two characters, size and color. Fig. 8-12 shows the primary cross between these two, giving the first (F₁) generation. The cattleya is LLpp, where L represents the gene for large size, and p the gene for purple, which in this cross is recessive. *Laelia flava* is ssYY, where s stands for the gene for small size, and Y for yellow, which is dominant. The reproductive cells from the cattleya are all the same, Lp, and from *Laelia flava* similarly are sY. The offspring combining these genes are therefore identical, LsYp. They are of a size somewhere between the two parents, and all yellow, though the yellow is not quite as clear and pure as where the double dose of Y is present.

The plant we want to make in the next step is one that will be homozygous for both large size and yellow color, LLYY. Off hand, you might think that the way to get it would be to cross a member

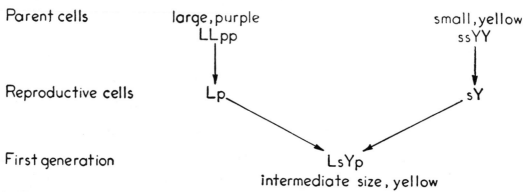

Parent cells   large,purple   small,yellow
                     LLpp   ssYY

Reproductive cells   Lp   sY

First generation   LsYp
                     intermediate size, yellow

Fig. 8-12 The F₁ generation obtained by crossing a purple cattleya with yellow *L. flava* gives all yellow flowers, which are heterozygous for both size and color.

of the F_1 generation back to the laelia parent. The laelia parent gives only one type of reproductive cell, sY. The plant from the F_1 generation gives four types, LY, Lp, sY, and sp. Combine sY with each of these and you get LsYY, LsYp, ssYY, and ss Yp. These come out in equal proportions as to the numbers of plants of each type. There are two types that are homozygous for yellow, LsYY and ssYY, but of these one is intermediate in size and the other is small. Nowhere can you find the plant you want, the LLYY type. The back cross to the cattleya would not give it either, for here you would get Lp combined with the four types of germ cells from the F_1, and the results would be LLYp, LLpp, LsYp, and Lspp. Two would be homozygous for large size, but none for yellow. So we have

to go at it another way, by mating members of the F_1 generation to get the F_2 generation in which the genes will be sorted out into the various possible combinations, and in which homozygous plants will occur. Incidentally, this is the real value of using the F_2 generation in any breeding program.

Look at the four types of reproductive cells that arise from a member of the F_1 generation, LY, Lp, sY, and sp. The homozygous large yellow plant we want would have to come from the fertilization of an LY egg cell by an LY sperm cell, and we can get this by self-pollinating a member of the F_1, or by mating one F_1 plant with another. Fig. 8-13 shows all of the possible combinations, in checkerboard style. The four types of reproductive cells are written horizontally and vertically, and each line

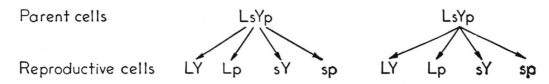

checkerboard to show all possible combinations in F_2

	LY	Lp	sY	sp
LY	LLYY homozygous large yellow	LLYp	LsYY	LsYp
Lp	LLYp	LLpp	LsYp	Lspp
sY	LsYY	LsYp	ssYY	ssYp
sp	LsYp	Lspp	ssYp	sspp

Fig. 8-13   Inheritance in the F_2 generation when members of the F_1 generation from Fig. 8–12 are crossed.

contains the combination of the genes at the left with each group on the top. The proportions of types in the second generation, F_2, are given in sixteenths. In the checkerboard the type LLYY occurs only once, so that this type will be one-sixteenth of the total number of offspring. (The large yellow plants in the offspring would have to be self-pollinated in order to discover which ones are the LLYY type.) Perhaps you will think it is hardly worth the trouble of making the cross to get only one out of sixteen. A plant breeder would consider it very worthwhile, for this LLYY plant when self-pollinated will give a whole generation of large yellow flowers, and when bred to any large cattleya will carry its dominant yellow to every member of the offspring. Among the other types on the checkerboard, some will give good flowers of large and intermediate size, both yellow and purple, plants that will be an addition to your collection, though not useful in breeding.

Brassocattleyas

The naming of species has been a long and complicated business. Often, a modern taxonomist does not agree with the name used by a predecessor and finds some botanical difference which causes him to feel that a certain species belongs more appropriately with a different group. Sometimes a new genus is set up for plants that do not quite fit the one in which they have been carried. Clearly, the names should be straightened out, for the record and for future generations of orchid lovers. But difficulties arise when the names of species used frequently in hybridization are changed, and when the hybrids have appeared in many lists.

"Brassocattleya" and "Brassolaeliocattleya" are terms long familiar. They represent a very particular concept of hybrids made with *Brassavola digbyana,* the species with the large fringed lip and lemony fragrance. Some years ago it was felt that this species and *B. glauca* fitted better with *Laelia* and they were moved to that genus. We all tried to get used to calling them *Laelia digbyana* and *L. glauca,* and their hybrids, *Laeliocattleyas.* In 1918 Rudolf Schlechter created the genus *Rhyncholaelia* for these species because of botanical differences he found to be significant, among them the beak-shaped seed pod. That was many years ago, of course, but the authorities of today have decided that that is where *digbyana* and *glauca* belong botanically. However, to avoid further confusion at

this time, we are going to follow the advice of a leading taxonomist and keep the old name *Brassavola,* provided that everyone is well warned and will remember that it is synonymous with *Rhyncholaelia,* and may some day be changed to that.

Brassavola digbyana has long attracted hybridists, not only because the lip is fringed but because it is so huge and actually rolls around the column. In a primary cross with a member of the labiata group of *Cattleya* the sepals and petals are reduced toward the size of those of *digbyana,* but the lip is broadened and shaped more like that of *digbyana,* with the fringe present though not as long. (See Fig. 8-14 for a picture illustrating this.) When *digbyana* is crossed with *Cattleya dowiana* the colors are diluted with green, which makes them very delicate and beautiful. Subtle coloring is also obtained when *digbyana* is crossed with a lavender cattleya, lovely tones of pink suffused with green for example. The colors become stronger when first generation hybrids are crossed with species or hybrids of darker tones, and some of the brilliant hybrids with large, full lip are among the handsomest of orchids. In a secondary cross, segregation of the genes causes both lip types to show up, so that there are some with the cattleya lip as well as some with the *digbyana* lip, some with fringe and some without it, or with the barest denticulation of the edge of the lip. The fragrance of the *digbyana* hybrids, reminiscent of citrus fruits, is another

Fig. 8-14. *Brassocattleya* Mrs. J. Leemann, which shows the huge rolled lip and fringe of *Brassavola digbyana.*

Home Orchid Growing

characteristic that frequently follows through a line of breeding.

It is interesting to note that a successful method for breeding yellows has been achieved through the use of *Lc.* Luminosa, *L. tenebrosa* × *C. dowiana,* a hybrid made in 1901, crossed with various hybrids containing yellow *Laelia* species and with some containing *digbyana,* such as *Bc.* Mrs. J. Leeman.

Red Hybrids

Sophronitis grandiflora, a gem of a flower in itself, has been made to contribute its redness to *Cattleya* and *Laeliocattleya* hybrids. The primary cross of *Sophronitis grandiflora* with a cattleya necessarily gives quite small flowers, and even smaller and less well shaped with a laelia. But when either of these is recombined with a cattleya or laeliocattleya, larger flowers of various deep rosy or red-violet tones appear. It has been hoped that the clear red tones would, through self-pollination or further breeding, be combined with the desirable size, but this happens rather infrequently. It may be that the chromosomes from *Sophronitis* are so unlike those of *Cattleya* and *Laelia* that they fail to pair at reduction division and that many reproductive cells are therefore non-functional. This may account for the fact that the types of desired color and size are frequently lost from seedling progeny.

Potinara is the name given to the quadrigeneric cross, *Brassosophrolaeliocattleya.* It can easily be imagined that a combination of all the desirable qualities of the four genera would be an outstandingly handsome thing. However, plants in which all the desired qualities show up occur in only a small proportion of the offspring, and the percentage of plants homozygous for all qualities even less often. A rather extensive breeding program would be necessary to achieve the ideal results. Many lovely combinations do occur in *Potinara* crosses, although relatively few have been made.

The search for a way to breed large red hybrids has been given a new boost with the discovery of *Laelia milleri.* It is hoped that this species will not offer the genetic difficulties that have plagued hybridists using *Sophronitis.* Some encouraging results have already been achieved.

Blue Hybrids

Blue is the most illusive color in cattleya hybrids, and hybridizers will not be content until they achieve it. Thus far only a few hybrids classed

as blue have a clear blue color, being mostly a lavender-blue or having off-white sepals and petals with lavender-blue in the lip. Genetic study is under way and it is felt that progress is being made toward understanding how blue is inherited.

White Cattleyas

Breeding white orchids has its own special problems genetically, as well as its own special appeal esthetically. The genetic problem has been pretty well worked out for cattleyas, so that you will not have the troubles experienced by some of the early growers. You will not have the sorrow of crossing two pure white flowers only to raise from them a batch of all purple offspring.

Before we discuss their genetics, we must first define what is a pure white orchid, odd though it may seem to have to define "white." From the point of view of its appearance, a pure white orchid is one in which there is not the slightest trace of purple pigment, either in the plant or in the flower. Plants that give purple flowers show purple pigmentation in the plant, in the new growths, sheaths, or leaves, even though their flowers may be extremely pale. Plants that give pure white flowers are all pure, bright green. Nor is there any trace of purple in the flowers. Green and yellow plastids are present, and the white flower may have yellow markings in the throat, but the rest of the flower must be a chaste paper-white, not tinged with color in any way.

The necessity for this definition arises from the carelessness of people who call any very pale flower white, even one that has the veins or the tips of the petals and sepals obviously tinged with color. These tinged whites are nothing but dilute color forms. It is not so significant when the tinged whites are sold by the florist for pure white, because the recipient of the corsage probably does not mind the slight tinting, may even prefer it that way. But a tinged white cannot be crossed with a pure white without giving colored offspring, at best a mixture of colored and white. Pure whites must be used if you want all pure white progeny. Or, if you are buying seedlings with the intention of having all pure white flowers, be sure that the parents are pure, and not "almost white" or "nearly white."

As if purposely to confuse the matter and make the breeding of whites more difficult than colored orchids, white cattleyas (and other genera, too) divide themselves into two groups genetically. It is simple when understood, but it puzzled early growers to find that combinations of the albino forms of some species gave all purple flowers, while different combinations of the same parents would give all white.

The mystery was solved by Charles C. Hurst, an English geneticist, who published his interpretation in *Experiments in Genetics* in 1925. He figured out the probable genetic makeup of white orchids from the way they behave in breeding. His deduction is briefly this. Manifestation of color in orchids depends on at least two types of genes working together. In order that a specific color may appear, there must be a gene, which Hurst calls R, to govern what color it is to be. And in order for that color to manifest itself, there must be another gene that allows color as such to be formed, which he calls C. In a colored orchid these two types are both present in their dominant form. However, if only the recessive form of the first type is present, no color may be made in the flower, even though the gene for color as such, C, is present. Or, if the situation is reversed and the plant contains only the recessive form of the second type, c, no color will show, even though the gene for specific color, R, is present. The two types of albinos are therefore, according to Hurst, ccRR and CCrr.

Any pure white when self-pollinated will give all white offspring, and any two of the same type when crossed will produce all white. You can see at a glance, however, that if ccRR and CCrr are crossed, the offspring will inherit c and R from its ccRR parent, and C and r from the CCrr parent, so that both types of genes will be present in the dominant form. The offspring will have the genetic makeup CcRr, and the resulting flowers will all be colored.

Hurst figured out to which of the groups, ccRR or CCrr, the various albino forms of the species belonged, according to the way they behaved when intercrossed. The *Cattleya* species from his list are given below, with the addition of other species that have shown their makeup by their behavior.

Any of the members of Group I when intercrossed will give all white offspring, and any of their hybrids may be crossed to produce all white. Similarly, any members of Group II and the hybrids derived from them will give all white offspring. But a member of Group I crossed with one from Group II will give colored offspring, as will a hybrid from Group I mated with one from Group II. An interesting example of crossing members from the

Group I, ccRR Whites

C. gaskelliana var. *alba* (H)
C. intermedia 'Alba' (H)
C. labiata 'Alba' (H)
C. labiata 'Harefield Hall' (M)
C. loddigesii 'Alba' (C and D)
C. loddigesii 'Stanley' (M)
C. lueddemanniana 'Alba' (C and D)
C. mossiae var. *wageneri* (H)
C. Obrieniana 'Alba' (M) (Nat. hybrid, *dolosa* X *loddigesii*)
C. skinneri 'Alba' (H)
C. speciosissima 'Alba'
C. trianaei 'Alba'* (C and D)
C. trianaei 'Broomhills' (M)
C. trianaei 'Verdonck' (M)
C. warneri 'Alba' (C and D)

Group II, CCrr Whites

C. eldorado 'Alba' (H)
C. harrisoniana var. *alba* (H)
C. mendelii 'Alba' (H)
C. percivaliana 'Alba' (H)
C. schroederae 'Alba'
C. trianaei 'Alba'* (C and D)
C. warneri 'Alba' (H)
C. warscewiczii (*gigas*) 'Firmin Lambeau'** (C and D)

* *C. trianaei* 'Alba' seems to include both genetic types. Only breeding with other whites can prove to which group a particular plant belongs.
** Pure white *C. warscewiczii* are very rare. The 'Firmin Lambeau' by its behavior seems to fit in this group, but there is no data on other whites of this species.
(H) Hurst's original list.
(M) Added by Melquist.
(C and D) Added by Curtis and Duncan.

The above expanded list from "Hybridization and Inheritance in Orchids," Lenz and Wimber, in *The Orchids*, edited by Withner.

two groups took place when the purple *C.* Enid resulted from *C. mossiae* var. *wageneri* X *C. gigas* 'Firmin Lambeau.'

Semi-Alba

Cattleyas and their hybrids which have pure white sepals and petals and a purple lip are called semi-albas or are designated W-L-C, white-colored-lip. We prefer the term semi-alba. Here we must emphasize that by pure white we mean the absolute absence of any color in the sepals and petals. Flowers that have a tinge of color in the sepals and petals, no matter how slight, would not come in the category of semi-alba, but instead would be considered colored flowers. There was for a while a tendency to call white with purple lip "alba," which was very confusing. Since the term alba means white, it should be used only for flowers that are all white. Semi-alba indicates half white, in other words, white sepals and petals and a colored lip.

The fact that a flower with pure white sepals and petals could have purple pigment in the lip indicated long ago that inheritance of lip color was separate from inheritance of color in the rest of the flower, and was therefore governed by an independent set of genes. We saw, above, that a flower will be white if it has a double recessive in either the C or R category, that is, if its makeup is ccRR or CCrr no color at all will be formed. It would follow that for color to appear in the lip, there must be at least one dominant C and one dominant R present. How, then, would another set of genes operate to prevent this color from showing in the sepals and petals, but allow it to be expressed in the lip? G. A. L. Mehlquist proposed a solution, upheld by W. B. Storey and H. Kamemoto, based on studies of various crosses.

They postulate (and this is a clever piece of deduction and seems very logical) that a pair of genes, **PP**, or **Pp**, or **pp**,* are present in all flowers, which control the distribution of coloring, whether the sepals and petals and lip shall all be colored, or only the lip. (These genes have nothing to do with the yellow coloring in the lip of a flower.) When the genes C and R are both present in a flower, the gene **P** (whether present along with **p** or as **PP**) causes the color to appear in both sepals and petals and in the lip; but where the genes for color distribution are recessive, **pp**, color shows up only in the lip. White flowers, in which no color at all can be manufactured, due to the genetic constitution cc or rr, are obviously not influenced by the color distribution genes. White flowers can have **PP**, **Pp**, or **pp**.

Great confusion as to how to breed semi-albas has arisen from the fact that sometimes a cross between two semi-albas gives all semi-alba, sometimes both semi-alba and white, in the offspring. In crosses between two colored flowers, semi-alba and white sometimes occur among the colored flowers in the offspring. Two white flowers can give all colored progeny or a mixture of white and semi-alba, or even all semi-alba. The great difficulty in predicting what a cross will yield stems from the fact that you cannot know the exact genetic makeup of a flower by looking at it. Re-

* By coincidence these workers chose the symbols **P** and **p** to represent color distribution, while I have used them to represent simply purple in the flower. In order to distinguish the two different sets they are given here in boldface type.

cessive genes are hidden when the plant is heterozygous, that is, when dominant genes are present to counteract their influence. Fortunately, hybridizers have been using for breeding only whites that have been proven to give all white progeny, and their descendants when crossed in the proper cc or rr group will give only whites. The danger of getting mixed progeny in a white cross would come from using whites of unknown heredity, such as whites that crop up in crosses between semi-albas or from colored parents. Let's look at the possible theoretical makeup of white, colored and semi-alba flowers, and then see how these could react with each other.

White flowers can have the following genetic makeup: ccRR**PP**, ccRR**Pp**, ccRR**pp**, CCrr**PP**, CCrr**Pp**, CCrr**pp**, and to these we would have to add Ccrr and ccrR, each combined with **PP**, **Pp**, and **pp**. In other words, white flowers are always homozygous for either the cc or rr genes, and may have any combination of the color-distribution genes.

Possible colored types are CCRR**PP**, CCRR**Pp**, CcRr**PP**, CcRr**Pp**, CCRr**PP**, CCRr**Pp**, CcRR**PP**, and CcRR**Pp**. They must have at least one C, one R, and one **P**, but the other member of each pair may be dominant or recessive.

Possible semi-alba types are: CCRR**pp**, CcRr**pp**, CCRr**pp**, and CcRR**pp**. They must have at least one C and one R, and are always homozygous for the **pp** genes.

As you glance through the lineup of types, you can see that whenever you mate two flowers that could bring together a combination of C, R, and **P** in the offspring, you will get some colored flowers. Whenever you mate flowers that offer the possible combination of C, R, and **pp**, you will get some semi-albas. And when two flowers offer the combinations of cc or rr, regardless of the **P** or **p** genes, you will get some white.

Let's work out a few semi-alba crosses. These must be considered hypothetical crosses, because not all of them have actually been performed, or if performed have not been studied. First we will self-pollinate a homozygous semi-alba, or cross it with another homozygous semi-alba. This would have the genetic makeup CCRR**pp**. Only one type of sex cell could be produced, CR**p**, and the recombination of these would re-create the CCRR**pp** makeup. In other words, a homozygous semi-alba crossed with a homozygous semi-alba always gives semi-alba. Incidentally, if you wish to find out what a semi-alba contains in the way of genes, the best thing to do is self-pollinate it.

Next let's take a heterozygous semi-alba, CcRr-**pp,** and self-pollinate it or cross it with one exactly like it. This is more complicated because four types of sex cells are produced. **CRp, Crp, cRp,** and **crp.** The following checkerboard shows this cross and the resulting types of offspring.

	CRp	Crp	cRp	crp
CRp	CCRRpp semi-alba	CCRrpp semi-alba	CcRRpp semi-alba	CcRrpp semi-alba
Crp	CCRrpp semi-alba	CCrrpp white	CcRrpp semi-alba	Ccrrpp white
cRp	CcRRpp semi-alba	CcRrpp semi-alba	ccRRpp white	ccRrpp white
crp	CcRrpp semi-alba	Ccrrpp white	ccRrpp white	ccrrpp white

Self-pollination of a semi-alba having genetic make-up CcRrpp. Ratio of offspring = 9 semi-alba to 7 white.

A third possible cross would be between the **CCRRpp** and the **CcRrpp** semi-albas. Here the single type of sex cell from the first plant, **CRp** would combine with the four types from the second, **CRp, Crp, cRp** and **crp,** to give offspring **CC-RRpp, CCRrpp, CcRRpp,** and **CcRrpp,** all semi-albas.

The possible combinations among white types are almost too numerous to give, but let's try a few. As we said before, crosses between any of the ccRR types will give all white, regardless of the **P** or **p** content, as will crosses between any of the CCrr ones. But when we mate plants from opposite sides of the table (see page 84) many combinations might result. The color distribution genes now become significant because we are crossing plants that contain the dominant C with those that contain the dominant R. A ccRR**pp** white crossed with a CCrr**pp** white gives sex cells cR**p** from the first and Cr**p** from the second, which combine to give CcRr**pp** offspring, all semi-albas. A ccRR**PP** white mated to a CCrr**PP** white would give sex cells cR**P** from one and Cr**P** from the other, which would combine to form CcRr**PP** all colored flowers in the offspring. A third cross might be between a ccRR**Pp** white and a CCrr**Pp** white, both heterozygous for **Pp.** The first would give sex cells cR**P** and cR**p,** and the second, sex cells Cr**P** and Cr**p.** Combined in the offspring these would give CcRr-

PP, CcRrPp, CcRrPp, and **CcRrpp,** a ratio of three colored flowers to one semi-alba.

It is not to easy for plant breeders to attain the desired results as for us to set up crosses on paper. They must come at it the other way, by making the crosses, raising large numbers of progeny and then, by studying the types and the ratios among them, figure out what the various contributions of the parent plants may have been. Geneticists who study these problems are often foiled by not having access to large enough populations of the progeny from certain crosses, or by not having complete records of crosses to study. They can be greatly assisted by growers, and will therefore be of greatest help to them in return, (1) if growers would call them in when a large population of seedlings from one cross is in flower; (2) if growers would note the characteristics of the offspring as to size, color, whether the color is dilute or strong, pattern of color, blooming period, and other characteristics of each plant, and the numbers of plants among the various types; and (3) if growers would be willing to make certain critical crosses that would give the geneticists needed information. The ratio of one type to another in a generation of seedlings gives the geneticist a great deal of information, because it shows what the parents contain in the way of dominant and recessive genes.

POLYPLOIDS

A polyploid is a type of plant that has one or more extra sets of chromosomes. In a normal cattleya, the basic number of chromosomes is forty, and the reproductive cells (gametes) contain the haploid number, or twenty. We refer to this haploid number as "n," and to a plant that has two sets as a 2n, or diploid plant. Each haploid set represents the set of chromosomes inherited from one parent. A plant with three sets of chromosomes is a 3n, or triploid plant. One with four sets is a 4n, or tetraploid. Five sets makes a 5n, or pentaploid, and six sets a 6n, or hexaploid.

Polyploids occur occasionally in nature, usually arising from an abnormal genetic event. The first polyploids among orchids occurred in some such way, either in their native habitats or in the greenhouses of orchid growers. Only when the science of cyto-genetics was developed, however, did growers know about polyploids as such.

If the chromosomes of a plant give it a happy

combination of good qualities, the plant may be superior to other members of its group. If a plant has an extra set of the chromosomes that bear genes for the good qualities, it is likely to be quite superior. This is the case with the polyploids. Tetraploids, with four sets of chromosomes, are likely to be very large, heavy plants, with large flowers of heavy substance, broad parts, and wonderful keeping qualities. Triploids are also large and heavy, somewhat faster growing than tetraploids, and they often give more flowers. We must not give the impression that all polyploids are superior to all diploids. A diploid with all dominant genes for its good qualities may compare very favorably with the polyploids. The triploids have the disadvantage of being partially or completely sterile. This means that they may fail to make functional reproductive cells, or they may make but few, and are seldom successful as parents. If the triploid is exceptionally fine, or embodies qualities that are most unusual, the grower may be happy to have the few offspring he can obtain from it. Whereas diploids may produce eighty to ninety per cent viable seed, triploids may give as little as five per cent, and sometimes five-tenths per cent viable seed. Pentaploids have been rare, and have not always been of as good quality as triploids and tetraploids, although some are very fine. With the help of the geneticists we are learning much more about them and they may soon be more abundant.

Through the years, growers have selected the best individuals for hybridization, and the best often included some that were polyploid. Thus polyploids began to play their role in hybridization without anyone's having knowledge of their genetic makeup. Some of them became famous as extraordinary parents, such as the tetraploid *Cymbidium* Alexanderi 'Westonbirt' and *Cymbidium* Pauwelsii 'Compte d'Hemptinne,' the triploid *Paphiopedilum insigne* 'Harefield Hall,' and the hexaploid (6n) *Phalaenopsis amabilis* 'Elizabethae.' It is almost impossible to tell just when, and through what plants, polyploidy entered many of the lines of cattleya hybrids. Chromosome counts made upon named varieties of a number of species have turned up the fact that some are polyploid, for example a tetraploid *Cattleya labiata* 'alba,' the tetraploid *Cattleya trianaei* 'Llewellyn,' and the triploid *Cattleya mossiae* 'Mrs. Butterworth.' Undoubtedly other polyploid cattleyas have existed and been used as parents, both species and hybrids, but in the ensuing years their identity has been lost and they are not now available for study. Even now,

crosses are being shown to be largely polyploid which had not been created with that intent, and often it is not known through what ancestors the polyploidy entered the line.

What brought about the occasional polyploid in nature and the first ones to occur in cultivation? The spontaneous appearance of triploids and tetraploids in an otherwise diploid population is felt to be caused largely by nonreduction in a few reproductive cells. It occasionally happens that in the formation of reproductive cells, one or more may fail to go through reduction division, and these thus become functional gametes with the full or 2n complement of chromosomes. Fertilization of a 2n gamete by one that has the normal haploid number creates a 3n individual, a triploid plant. Fertilization of a 2n gamete by another 2n gamete creates a tetraploid or 4n individual. There are other possible ways in which polyploidy can be caused. One is the chance fertilization of one egg by two sperms. Another is that in the interval between pollination and the arrival of the pollen tubes in the ovary, a few egg cells may undergo division of the nuclear material without dividing into two separate cells, thus doubling their number of chromosomes. As soon as man got hold of polyploids he, of course, began creating more and more of them by breeding them.

It should be emphasized that only an actual count of the chromosomes, in material especially prepared for microscopic study, can show the chromosome number of a plant. The large size of a plant or its flowers cannot be taken as an indication of its ploidy. Although a cross can be almost entirely polyploid, the discovery of a number of polyploids in a certain cross does not mean that all of the other members of the cross are also polyploids. In fact, it is often the case that 2n, 3n, 4n, and even occasionally 5n plants occur among the plants from the same seed pod. Individuals whose chromosome number is ascertained should have this information recorded both in the grower's file and on the label that stays with the plant. If the plant turns out to be diploid when it was hoped that it might be a polyploid, the information is no less valuable, for fine diploids are very important in hybridization. Counting chromosomes is a time-consuming process, and can be done only by people who either are trained or who have the background to train themselves to do it. Therefore it is not practical for a grower to have chromosome counts made on any and all plants. Plants which have proved valuable in breeding, or which have qualities that lead the grower to think they should be useful as parents, or plants which win awards or are interesting for some particular characteristic or behavior pattern, are worth having counts made upon. Geneticists make numerous counts in species and in hybrid progeny in order to obtain information on how polyploidy occurs and is transmitted.

Much breeding at present is aimed toward the production of triploids, which, because they flower so profusely are often preferred by amateurs and by the commercial cut-flower grower. Triploids are made by crossing a diploid by a tetraploid. Both diploids and tetraploids, having even sets of chromosomes, form abundant numbers of reproductive cells, and the combination of the haploid gametes from the diploid and the 2n gametes from the tetraploid give the 3n number that creates the triploids. Given an abundance of tetraploids, tremendous numbers of triploids of a wide variety of colors and types can be bred.

While the tetraploids themselves are very handsome plants, their value lies especially in the field of hybridization, for, at least up to now, they have not been available in large numbers. A rare tetraploid can show up in a 2n × 2n cross, but they occur more often in crosses involving one or more polyploid parent, in 3n × 2n or 3n × 4n crosses. A cross between two tetraploids regularly produces a tetraploid progeny, so that, now that growers have increasing numbers of tetraploids to work with, they can create more by mating them with each other. The chief lack of tetraploids is in certain color ranges, or in certain lines. Cymbidium growers, for example, are hopefully waiting for tetraploid greens to show up. Since tetraploids have a double dose of genetic material, their influence is quite strong in crosses where they are mated with diploids. Hence, once a tetraploid of a certain type or color occurs it can be used in crosses with diploids to produce triploids that come close to having the desired characteristics.

The more equally balanced in number and character are the chromosomes in a plant, the more regular is the formation of reproductive cells. Each chromosome must have a like chromosome to pair with at reduction division in order for the process to proceed in a regular fashion. The members of each pair are called homologous chromosomes, and are inherited, as you will remember, one from the male and one from the female parent. Pairing is less efficient when chromosomes are unlike, as is often the case when they are derived from species that are quite widely separated, and when odd numbers are present. Lack of pairing of the chromosomes gives rise to reproductive cells with odd numbers, and these cause the formation of aneuploid plants.

The term "aneuploid" is used to describe the condition of having a chromosome number over or under an exact multiple of the basic haploid or "n" number for the species. It is derived from the term "euploid" which means "true ploid." Euploid forms have exactly twice, or three times, or four or five times the n number. If *Cattleya* is used as an example, the euploid forms have exactly 40, 60, 80, or 100 chromosomes. Aneuploid means "not true ploid," and refers to plants that have something over or under 40, 60, 80, or 100 chromosomes. In plants that have two sets of unlike chromosomes, inherited from widely separated parent species, these chromosomes may not be able to pair at reduction division. Instead, they become assorted in odd ways, and, if functional sex cells are formed at all, they will probably contain odd numbers of chromosomes, such as 17 and 23, or 15 and 25, instead of the even 20 chromosomes each. Such sex cells will, when fertilized, give rise to aneuploid individuals, plants with chromosome numbers such as 37, 43, etc. The many failures to form functional sex cells accounts for the relative sterility of hybrids from quite unlike parents, as for example, *Cattleya* with *Schomburgkia*. (See Hybridization in *Vanda,* Chapter 12, for other examples.)

Aneuploids can also result from polyploid crosses. For example, in a triploid plant, which has three sets of chromosomes (60 in *Cattleya*) you might think that 30 of these would pair with the other 30. This is not what happens. A chromosome can pair only with its homologue. In a triploid there are three of each homologous type, instead of the usual two. Some chromosomes may form pairs, leaving the third homologue standing alone. Sometimes three will come together. As reduction division takes place, some of the pairs will separate normally. The unpaired chromosomes may drift to one pole or the other, but some may get stranded and, not arriving at either pole, fail to be included in the newly forming nuclei. The chromosomes that have come together by threes may separate so that two of them go to one pole and one to the other, or they may travel together so that one newly forming nucleus will receive all three while the other is left entirely without the genetic material they took with them. Some cells may be formed

Home Orchid Growing

with only a few pairs and a few stragglers and thus have a very incomplete gene content. Most of such erratically formed cells cannot develop into functional sex cells, which accounts for the high degree of sterility in triploids. The same thing takes place in pentaploids.

A higher percentage of aneuploids occurs in some crosses than in others, showing that some plants are less regular in the formation of reproductive cells than others. Studies upon aneuploids show that those that have just one or two more or less than the euploid number can be quite normal. But plants whose chromosome numbers range far to one side or the other of a euploid number may suffer lack of vigor or be quite abnormal in some way. For instance, aneuploids with chromosome numbers of 58, 59, 61, 62, or 78, 79, 81, 82, etc. may be normal plants, while those with something like 50 or 70 may be abnormal.

We mentioned earlier that occasionally gametes are formed without having their chromosome number reduced. The cells which are destined to form the sex cells go through the process retaining their full complement of chromosomes. It appears that some of the functional sex cells of triploids are of this nature. Crosses between triploids and diploids, and triploids and tetraploids seem to be more fruitful if the triploid is used as the female, or pod, parent. Diploids and tetraploids, having even sets of chromosomes, produce large numbers of functional reproductive cells, and when these types are used as the male, or pollen, parent, there is greater likelihood of obtaining some viable seed than if the triploid were used as the male parent. Although the fertility of triploids is notoriously low, *Cattleya* Bow Bells seems to be an exception. A number of triploid Bow Bells have been the parents of a long line of successful hybrids. We do not have all the data we could wish on these crosses, but it appears that successful matings have been made between triploid Bow Bells and diploid plants, as well as with triploid Bow Bells and tetraploids. Both tetraploids and pentaploids are among the progeny. The unusual fertility of these Bow Bells individuals seems to indicate that they are better able to form non-reduced gametes than many other triploids, and form them more freely. Since these Bow Bells crosses have appeared, some other crosses between triploids and tetraploids have been unexpectedly successful. It may well be that success depends on finding the more fertile of the triploids in any one group and then finding plants that will be compatible with them.

Pentaploids have been far fewer in number than tetraploids and triploids. Individual pentaploid plants have sprung from various polyploid crosses. In some cases these have not been as handsome or as vigorous as triploids and tetraploids, but this is not continuing to be true. Pentaploids can be formed by $3n \times 4n$ matings, where the 3n parent contributes a non-reduced gamete and the 4n contributes a 2n gamete. A fairly high percentage of pentaploids occurs in crosses where *Cattleya* Bow Bells has been mated with a tetraploid.

Attempts to create pentaploids and to use them as parents have been frustrating. However, work that is being done now may point the way. Theodore Zuck reports that efforts to cross the pentaploid *Lc.* Rosa Kirsch with 2n and 3n plants failed, but that a fairly good number of seedlings was obtained when it was crossed with a tetraploid *C.* Titrianae. From among the seedlings ten plants, counted at random, were all pentaploid. This would seem to have been brought about by fusion of 3n gametes from *Lc.* Rosa Kirsch with 2n gametes from *C.* Titrianae. Whether the 5n *Lc.* Rosa Kirsch also produce 2n gametes is not known, but if such were produced and functioned, it would be expected that this cross would also produce tetraploids. It is possible that no 2n gametes were functional. Another case of the successful use of a pentaploid as a parent is reported by D. H. Niimoto and L. F. Randolph, who are doing other valuable work in orchid genetics. This case involves the mating of a pentaploid with a diploid, a type of cross that has failed heretofore. The pentaploid parent is *C.* North Star 'Niimoto,' one of several pentaploids from a cross between a 3n *C.* Bow Bells and a 4n *C.* Helen P. Dane. Large numbers of vigorous seedlings are now being raised, but their ploidy has not yet been reported. Much information should result from their study. It should be added that the pentaploids *Lc.* Rosa Kirsch and *C.* North Star are very lovely, vigorous plants, which gives hope that a new horizon in *Cattleya* breeding is in view.

COLCHICINE

The chemical compound colchicine has been used by horticulturalists for a good many years to create giant sized plants and flowers (tetraploids) and to make otherwise sterile hybrids capable of producing seed. Both results come from the same function of the chemical, which is to double the number of chromosomes. We often see tetraploids advertised in garden catalogues, for instance tetraploid snapdragons. The progenitors of most of these have been man-made tetraploids, formed by the use of colchicine.

In orchid genera where there is a lack of tetraploids in certain colors, for instance green in *Cymbidium,* it would be a great boon if desirable diploids could have their chromosomes doubled so that the resulting tetraploids could be used in breeding. Where hybrids are sterile, because of being triploids, or because they contain chromosomes from unlike parents, for example in *Schombocattleya,* semi-terete *Vanda* hybrids, etc., or because of aneuploidy, they would become fertile if their chromosomes could be doubled. A number of workers have pioneered with colchicine, among them R. A. McLeod, Gavino Rotor, and H. Y. Nakasone and H. Kamemoto. However, progress has been uncertain until just recently, when Emma Menninger achieved a breakthrough with one method, and Donald Wimber and Ann Van Cott with another.

Colchicine upsets the normal process of cell division. Vegetative cells divide by a process different from that of reduction division. The process through which vegetative cells divide (as in the growing parts of plants) is called mitosis. In this process each chromosome duplicates itself so that each resulting cell receives the full complement of chromosomes. As a cell with forty chromosomes divides, each newly forming cell receives a complete set of forty chromosomes.

The steps in mitosis are diagrammed briefly in Figure 8-15, using a cell with 4 chromosomes for the sake of simplicity. In this diagram, A shows a resting cell. In B, the chromosomes are shown after each one has duplicated itself. In C, the chromosomes are lined up in the center of the cell, with a protoplasmic strand attached to each. This arrangement of protoplasmic strands or fibers is called the "spindle." In D, the strands appear to pull the attached chromosomes to the poles of the cell, half of them to one pole, the other half to the other pole. In E, the chromosomes are reconstituted into two nuclei, and a cell wall grows between them, forming two separate cells.

The cell with 4 chromosomes has, for a brief interval, 8 chromosomes. In a cell with 40 chromosomes, at the time when these have duplicated themselves the cell would momentarily contain 80. The peculiar action of colchicine is to interfere with the division process just at the point when the chromosomes have become duplicated. The cell is made to cease its activities and return to a resting condition, carrying the double number of chromosomes. When the effects of colchicine wear off, the cell begins the division process all over again. This time, the 80 chromosomes duplicate themselves so that there are 160. Half of these are drawn to each pole, so that the two new cells each receive 80 instead of the original 40. Thus the cells become tetraploid. Typical action of colchicine is shown in Figure 8-16.

The action of colchicine is not always perfectly regular. Sometimes an odd number of chromosomes is produced. Occasionally the doubling action is repeated, giving rise to cells that have four or eight times the normal chromosome number. Often not all cells are affected, so that the resulting plant may have some tetraploid parts mixed with normal parts. The ultimate aim is to produce plants that have tetraploid flowers, which will give reproductive cells bearing double the number of chromosomes.

Colchicine is poisonous to plants and to human beings. It must be used on plants in very

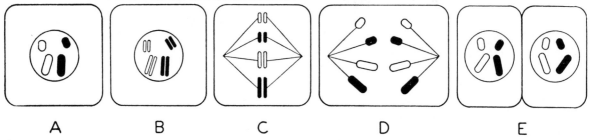

A B C D E

Fig. 8-15 Mitosis, the division of vegetative cells.
A. The resting cell.
B. Each chromosome duplicates itself.
C. The chromosomes gather in a plane through the center of the cell.

D. Opposite duplicates of each chromosome are drawn to opposite poles.
E. The new cell wall comes between the newly separated sets of chromosomes, and two cells, each with a full complement of chromosomes, are formed.

Home Orchid Growing

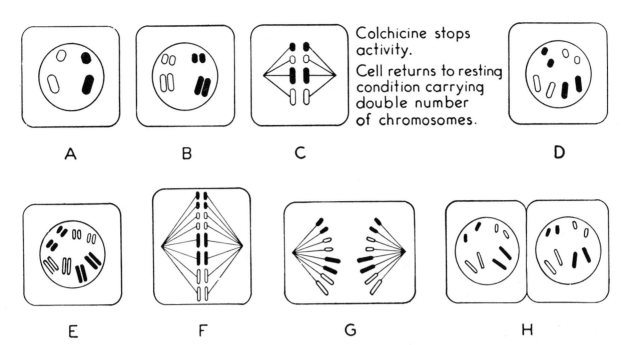

Colchicine stops activity.

Cell returns to resting condition carrying double number of chromosomes.

A B C D

E F G H

Fig. 8-16 Action of colchicine. Mitosis proceeds normally, A, B, and C, until colchicine is applied. Colchicine prevents the migration of the chromosomes to the poles, C, and returns the cell to resting condition, D. D. When mitosis resumes, after the influence of colchicine has worn off, the chromosomes duplicate themselves again, E. The process goes to completion, F, G, and H, producing new cells with double the original number of chromosomes.

weak dilutions, measured very carefully. Too strong a concentration may kill the plants, yet the dose, to be effective, must be very near the lethal strength. Workers are cautioned not to let colchicine remain in contact with the skin, and particularly not to get it in the eyes. It should be kept out of the reach of children.

Mrs. Menninger reported her work in the *American Orchid Society Bulletin,* November, 1963. She treated a dormant backbulb of *Cym.* Coningsbyanum 'Brockhurst,' first cleaning it and exposing the eyes. She pierced each eye several times with a very fine needle in order to allow the colchicine solution to reach the growing point within the sheathing leaves. She then soaked the base of the bulb including the eyes in a 0.3 percent solution for 1 hour and 14 minutes. Ten days later, fearing that the solution might not have been strong enough she re-treated it with a 1 percent solution for about the same length of time. Two years later root tip counts were made from the one growth that developed, and were found to contain 80 chromosomes, the 4n number. This growth eventually gave rise to a large plant, which was divided, and finally one of the divisions flowered. The flowers were found to be significantly larger than those of the original diploid plant, and root tip counts

showed that the plant had continued to maintain an 80 chromosome count.

The work of Donald Wimber and Ann Van Cott is reported in the *Proceedings of the Fifth World Orchid Conference,* 1966, and further results by Wimber and Doris R. Wimber in the *American Orchid Society Bulletin,* July, 1968. Seeds from diploid *Cymbidium* hybrids and a meristem culture from another diploid *Cymbidium* hybrid were treated. The seeds were first germinated in a liquid nutrient medium on a shaker until protocorms were developed (four to six weeks). The meristem tissue was cultured in liquid medium on a shaker, then was cut up and put in fresh medium and returned to the shaker for two weeks. At this point sufficient 2.5 percent aqueous colchicine solution was injected into the flasks of both to make a concentration in the flasks of 0.05 percent, and the flasks were kept on the shaker for from ten days to three weeks. The protocorms of both were then transferred to flasks of solid agar-nutrient medium. Five to six months later the plants were transferred to flats and from then on were grown under ordinary greenhouse conditions.

Approximately 40 percent of the treated seedlings and about 43 percent of the meristem plantlets proved to have become tetraploid. The rest

Genetics and the Breeding of Hybrids   91

had remained diploid except for a few chimaeras (plants in which there was some diploid, some tetraploid tissue). Ploidy determination was made by chromosome counts on root tip cells in some cases, and by measuring the stomata in others. (Wimber has done statistical studies on stomatal size in diploids and tetraploids and believes that they can be distinguished with fair certainty in this way.)

The later report (1968) on the flowering of the seedlings of one cross showed that in the tetraploids the flower parts were both broader and thicker, giving the flowers a more full shape and heavier substance.

Wimber's and Van Cott's treatment of protocorms was more fruitful than attempts of others to treat older seedlings, and had several advantages. For one thing, there was not the problem of trying to avoid injury to roots, which is a factor with older seedlings since colchicine can cause root damage, and for another, with such small masses of cells not covered by layers of protective tissue full penetration of colchicine was more likely.

In treating an eye on a cymbidium backbulb, Mrs. Menninger had the problem of providing for penetration of the outer layers of tissue, which she solved by pricking the eye. The eye at the base of a leafless and rootless cymbidium backbulb is positioned for easy submersion in a solution.

Treating a developing eye on an active plant with roots, such as a cattleya or dendrobium, is another matter. Perhaps it could be accomplished by inverting a vial containing an agar gel with colchicine over the elongating eye, having first pricked it to allow penetration.

A different problem is met in working with monopodials such as vandas and phalaenopsis. Here one would have to treat the stem tip of the main plant or of a side bud beginning to develop into a "keiki." If one could catch such a side branch in *Vanda* as it was just starting (or induce one by air layering), or treat plantlets forming on stem cuttings of *Phalaenopsis,* one could use the method of inverting a vial over them. After leaves have started to form, perhaps packing the tip with cotton wetted with solution would work.

Several attempts have been made to treat early stages of inflorescences, with the object of doubling the chromosome number of the flowers. Rotor did obtain viable seed from a plant of the sterile triploid *Cattleya* Mary Schroeder by first treating some developing flower buds and then using their pollen on other flowers of the same plant. Produc-

tion of viable seed where none had been possible before indicated that very probably the chromosome number of the flowers had been doubled (making them hexaploid since the plant was triploid). The disadvantage of this method is that only the flowers of the particular inflorescence treated would have the ploidy changed; that of the plant would remain unaffected. It would be more desirable, of course, to change the ploidy of a developing growth, which would lead to a plant with double the original number of chromosomes.

If you wish to try colchicine, it would be wise to use several different concentrations on several different plants (or groups of plants). One might also use each concentration for two or three different lengths of time. From such an experiment one might find what combination of concentration and length of treatment would be most successful, and this then could be used to treat other plants. Choice of concentrations might be made according to the type of material to be treated. There is a wide difference between that used by Mrs. Menninger on the cymbidium eye (0.4 percent and 1.0 percent) and that used by Wimber and Van Cott (0.05 percent). It might seem logical to use a stronger solution on the developing eye of a mature plant than on tender protocorms. However, the weak solution was in contact with the protocorms for ten days to three weeks, while the stronger ones were applied to the cymbidium eye for only a little over an hour each. We do not know whether the strong concentration would injure protocorms if they were exposed for only a short time, or whether the weak solution would be effective on a cymbidium eye over a longer period of contact.

Therefore, there is still much experimental work to be done. The success of these two pieces of work portends success with colchicine in the future, and anything that is accomplished will add greatly to this field.

DNA AND RNA

The scientific inspiration of Drs. Watson and Crick in 1953 revealed the structure of DNA, Deoxyribonucleic acid, the giant molecule that holds the coded information within each gene. This huge molecule, made up of thousands of chemical units, is in the form of a spiral ladder, which if magnified to a size we could climb would rival that in Jacob's dream and come close to reaching heaven. Its discoverers call it a double helix. The units can be described, purely schematically, as being "T" shaped, with the bar formed of a sugar (Deoxyribose) linked to a Phosphate, and the leg formed by one of four kinds of nitrogen bases, Adenine, Thymine, Guanine, and Cytosine. The units are called nucleotides, and the four kinds can be represented thus, using the initials D for Deoxyribose, P for Phosphate, A for Adenine, T for Thymine, G for Guanine, and C for Cytosine:

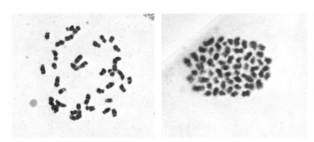

The nucleotides are manufactured by the nucleoplasm, within the nucleus of the cell.

The D-P sections line up to make the sides of the ladder, while the A, T, G, C sections link across to make its rungs, A always joining with T, and G with C. A portion of the ladder would look something like this, flattened out from its spiral formation:

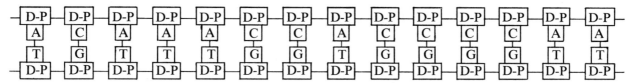

When cells divide and the chromosomes duplicate themselves, each DNA molecule also duplicates itself. It zips open up the center of the "ladder." Each A, T, G, C base attracts to itself its customary partner to form the other half of the DNA molecule, and thus two are formed identical to the original one. These are distributed equally to the new cells during mitosis.

And what does the DNA molecule do? It dictates the manufacture of a messenger to carry its information into the cytoplasm. The messenger is an RNA molecule, Ribonucleic acid, a single strand

molecule slightly different chemically in having Ribose sugar instead of Deoxyribose, and Uracil in place of Thymine. RNA moves out of the nucleus into the cytoplasm, and there "tells" the cell to make a certain enzyme for a certain activity. Each DNA molecule (gene) therefore brings about the manufacture of its own RNA counterpart, which controls a certain function of the cell.

Considering that there are thousands of genes, each composed of a huge DNA molecule containing a thousand or more nucleotide units in a definite order, one must marvel at the exquisite precision with which cell division takes place. A "mistake" or a change in the succession of nucleotides would result in a new message being carried to the cell. Such a change in message would bring about an altered activity, and therefore a change in the individual, or in other words, a mutation. Many of the "mistakes" never come to light because they result in failure or death of the organism. Many others, not lethal, have resulted in new forms; in orchids perhaps joined sepals, or longer stems, or a different lip pattern. Long accumulation of such changes has brought about new species. The myriad forms of life on earth today are the result of changes in the codes within the genes.

Many mysteries still remain to be understood. We do not know, for instance, from where the impulse comes to initiate cell division, to cause the unzipping of the DNA molecules and their reconstitution. Thus while the discovery of DNA and RNA and the elucidation of their structure and function were great milestones in scientific understanding, we remain in awe of, and with gratitude for, the orderly mechanisms of nature.

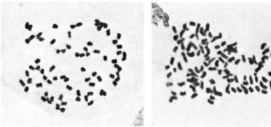

Fig. 8-17. Chromosomes in root tip cells of *Vanda*. From LEFT to RIGHT: a diploid, with 38 chromosomes; a triploid, with 57 chromosomes; a tetraploid, with 76 chromosomes; a pentaploid, with 95 chromosomes. (*Courtesy H. Kamemoto*)

9

GROWING AND SOWING YOUR OWN SEED

One of the main cares of nature, after assuring the nourishment and growth of a plant, is to insure its reproduction and the continuation of the species. Various ways have been devised for scattering the seed, for moving it away from the parent plant to more open ground.

The diversity of such mechanisms is a fascinating study in itself. There are plants that have ways of forcibly ejecting the seed from the pod or capsule, such as the Siberian pea and oxalis. Others offer fruits tender and tasty, brightly colored, which attract birds and animals that carry away their seed. The cockleburs make a nuisance of themselves by their method of forcing their seed upon whatever agent happens their way. The exquisite forms of wind-borne seed are well known for their delicate umbrellas and parachutes.

But not every seed that is produced finds conditions suited to its germination. Only those fortunate enough to land in just the right spot can grow to maturity. Hence plants in even the best of circumstances must produce more seed than will ever grow.

Epiphytic orchids face a special problem in seed dispersal. The chances are slim that a seed will find some obscure crevice in the bark of a tree where it can germinate, or that it will have there the necessary conditions of air and light, moisture, and mineral nutrients. If only one seed from each capsule should germinate and survive to maturity the continuation of the species would be well assured. In order to guarantee this against such odds, each plant produces hundreds of thousands of seeds every year. A scientific count of the seed in a capsule of *Cycnoches chlorochilon* revealed that it contained 3,770,000.

The formation of so many seeds by rather small plants means that the seeds must be very tiny, which is true of all epiphytic orchid seeds. The seed of cattleyas is as fine as powder, and close to a million are formed in one capsule. Its small size allows it to be carried by the gentle air currents in the jungle which are not strong enough to lift heavy particles to great heights. As the seed capsule ripens and splits open, the drift of pale yellow powder is picked up by the moving air and dusted from branch to branch. Some of the seed is blown away by stronger winds that meet the upward air currents above the jungle. Much of the seed, of course, drifts down to the ground where it has no chance to grow.

Because of its small size, the seed contains little, if any, food to nourish the embryo during germination. It must find a ready supply where it falls. In a pocket of decaying vegetable matter, there will be available minerals and sugars released by the decomposing action of fungi and bacteria. And as will be seen in a moment, the presence of sugars is all-important to bring about the germination of the seed.

Even after successful germination, the seedling

still faces hazards of destruction, over-growth of fungi, burning by the sun if it has not enough shade, or even desiccation if it does not receive frequent enough rain.

The first growers who tried to germinate orchid seed ran into problems that plagued them and their followers for three-quarters of a century. Various methods were tried to induce germination. The seed was sown on leaf mold, decaying bark, sphagnum moss, etc. More often than not, if the recalcitrant seed did germinate, much of it was killed by invading bacteria and fungi. When these attempts failed, growers set to work on the theory that germination might be induced by contact of the seed with some fungus found in association with parent orchid plants. The experiments that followed were intricate, and consisted of infecting the seed with isolated strains of fungi, called the symbiotic method. Enough success came from this work to carry the fungus method on for many years. But it was a technique that could be used only by experts, and even in their hands there followed frequent destruction of the seed by the fungi.

It remained for Dr. Lewis Knudson of Cornell University, in 1922, to find a completely controlled, standardized, simple method for germinating orchid seed. He had done previous work which showed that sugars had a favorable influence on plant growth, which suggested to him that orchid seed might require the presence of sugar in order to germinate. He interpreted the success with fungi, not to its effect on the seed itself, but to digestion by the fungi of some of the carbohydrates and nitrogenous substances present in the growing medium. Sugars would be among the materials released in this process.

This proved to be true. Dr. Knudson found that the seed germinated readily without the presence of fungi when sown on an agar jelly to which had been added the necessary mineral nutrients plus sugar. Patiently he worked to find out what was the best sugar to use, and in what concentration. He also had to adjust the proportions of the mineral nutrients. The flasks containing the agar-nutrient mixture were sterilized, and the seed was disinfected to kill foreign organisms that might enter the flasks with it. The flasks were stoppered after being sown, and left untouched until the seedlings were well developed, some eight months to a year later. The flasks were perfect little glass houses, protecting the tiny plants from insects and contamination, and providing them with a constantly moist atmosphere until they were well developed. This is called the asymbiotic method.

Dr. Knudson's method revolutionized orchid growing. He removed the guesswork, the confusion and the hazards, and gave growers a technique that was easy to use and certain of success. It is simple enough to measure out the ingredients for making the agar-nutrient jelly, and now it is even possible to buy the mixture all prepared except for the addition of water.

In the jungle, only an occasional seed of the tremendous numbers produced has a chance to germinate. Now, in the hands of man, nearly every seed may become a plant. Growers who once zealously guarded every hybrid seedling, now hardly know what to do with the countless thousands they produce. One grower estimates that he has 80,000 seedlings in flasks at present. This has put orchids on a par with other greenhouse crops, and made orchid plants available to all who would buy.

Needless to say, Dr. Knudson's flask method has given a tremendous impetus to orchid growing, not only by increasing the numbers of plants grown commercially, but by making it possible for amateurs to grow their own.

POLLINATION

A simple maneuver with the forceps starts a seed pod on its way in your greenhouse. The human hand can perform in an instant the function of pollination, which in nature requires the most elaborate preparation and clever groundwork. Few orchids are capable of self-pollination. In fact, most orchids are constructed so that self-pollination in nature is impossible. It almost looks as if, in the long struggle for survival, those orchids which were perpetuated by cross-fertilization were the more vigorous, and lived to maintain their kind.

The relationship between orchids and their pollinators is one of the marvels of nature. They are equipped with fascinatingly ingenious mechanisms by means of which insects are practically forced to carry the pollen from one flower to another. Each mechanism is so well designed as to be almost foolproof, but an individual orchid lives under a perpetual handicap. Its mechanism will work only if an insect of just the right size and shape enters the portals so attractively spread for its reception. A tiny orchid, just one-quarter inch in diameter, requires a very small insect, while another, whose nectar tube is in the form of a spur ten-inches long, needs the services of a species of moth with a ten-inch proboscis. A flower may be visited by scores of insects, yet may wither and die before the kind comes along that can serve as bearer of its pollen. However, when the right one does visit the flower, the insect is not allowed to leave without carrying with it a parcel of pollen glued to its anatomy.

The pollen grains are fastened together in rather large waxy masses called pollinia, each of which contains enough pollen to fertilize another flower satisfactorily. Cleverly enough, in order to insure cross-pollination, orchids fasten the pollen masses to the insect as it leaves the flower.

Fig. 9-1 A and B show in detail the reproductive parts of the cattleya. The column is shown from its under side in A, and cut in half lengthwise in B. The anther (*a*), the cap that covers the pollinia, is fastened by a tiny hinge (*h*) to the end of the column. Protruding slightly from under the anther are the tips of the four caudicles (*c*) attached to the pollinia (*p*). The rostellum (*r*), the partition between the anther chambers and the stigma, has on its under side a gland that secretes a sticky fluid. The stigma, which is really two stigmas grown together through the processes of evolution, is indicated by (*s*). The lip (*l*) presses up close under the column, forming a narrow passageway down which an insect must travel to reach the nectary (*n*) at its base. Fig. 9-1C shows the pollinia as they are situated in the anther chambers, after the anther has been raised, and Fig. 9-1D shows a single pollinium with attached caudicle.

The flower is pollinated by any rather large bee. When the bee lights on the lip its weight depresses the lip somewhat, and it then passes down the tube to get nectar. As it backs out of the tube, it pushes against the rostellum (*r*), ruptures the gland and becomes smeared with its sticky secretion. The force of the bee against the rostellum tips up the anther cap, touching off the spring. The anther flies back, rotating the pollinia so that the caudicles are exposed. As the bee backs further out, the caudicles are caught in the sticky fluid on its back, and the pollinia are pulled out.

When the bee visits the next cattleya, the pollinia on its back are forced into the stigmatic cavity. The stigmatic fluid is so sticky that it grips the pollen masses and tears them from the caudicles. After its feast of nectar, the bee leaves the flower with only the stumps of the caudicles attached, but in the process it will take with it the pollinia from this flower (if they have not already been removed) and bestow them on the next one it visits. You can imitate this by using a cotton swab for a bee. Push it down between the column and the lip, and as you pull it out watch the pollinia come with it. Then push it back into the flower and watch the pollinia stick to the stigma.

The simple sleight of hand that human beings can substitute for the natural process is to remove the pollinia from one orchid and place them directly on the stigma of another. But there is a difference between your responsibility and that of the flower where pollination is concerned. The flower makes elaborate preparations to insure pollination and the production of a huge number of seeds, from which possibly only one or two seedlings will grow. Your preparation consists of giving great care to the choice of parent plants so that the innumerable seeds you germinate will be worth your energy to raise.

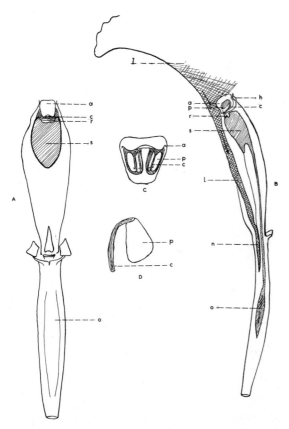

Fig. 9-1 Reproductive parts of a cattleya: A, the column from its under side, with the flower parts removed; B, a view of the column cut in half wherein it is seen that what appears to be the stem of the flower is actually the ovary: (a) anther, (h) hinge that holds the anther in place, (p) pollinium, (r) rostellum, (s) stigma, (l) lip, (n) nectary, (o) ovary; C, a view of the anther from its underside, showing the pollinia; D, a single pollinium with its caudicle.

If the flowers you wish to cross are of about the same size, and the plants are equally strong, it does not matter which one bears the pod. However, if one flower is much smaller than the other, it is better to put the pollen from the larger one on the stigma of the smaller. The reason is of a purely mechanical nature. The pollen from the small flower may give rise to pollen tubes too short to reach into the ovary of the larger flower, or at best they may reach only as far as the apex of the ovary.

The cross might then produce little or no viable seed (seed containing an embryo).

A seedling blooming for the first time, or a propagation having only two or three bulbs, should not be allowed to bear a seed pod. The production of seed would take more food than it can afford and still be able to make good growth. Such a plant should donate the pollen and the larger, stronger plant should grow the seed. A very large, heavy plant may carry two or three pods at the same time

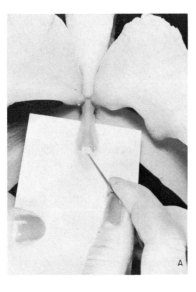
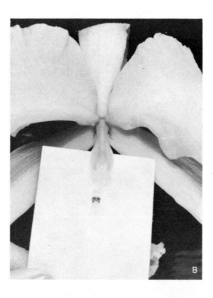
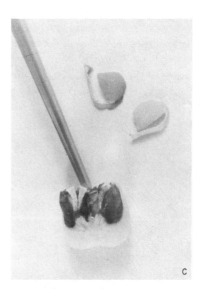
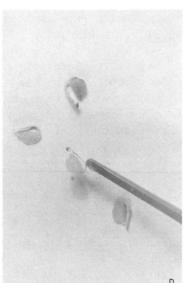

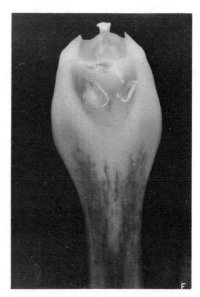

Fig. 9-2 Steps in pollination:
A. Remove the anther from the flower selected as the parent. Hold a clean piece of paper under the column and tip off the anther onto it.
B. The anther is separated from the column.
C. Nudge the pollinia out of the anther.

D. In order to pick up a pollinium, use a clean toothpick. Touch its tip to the sticky fluid of the stigma and then touch the caudicle of a pollinium. The pollinium will adhere to the drop of fluid.
E. Place the pollinium on the stigma.
F. Pollination is completed, with two pollinia on the stigma.

Home Orchid Growing

or may bear pods in successive years. If you wish to cross the same plant with two or three different others, use a separate flower for each kind of pollen. Never put two kinds of pollen on one flower.

A flower must be allowed to reach its prime before it is pollinated, that is, it must have been open for several days. Remove its own pollinia before placing on its stigma the pollen with which you desire to cross it. If you have a particularly handsome flower with nothing else at the moment to match it in quality, it is possible to keep its pollen for use in the future (see below under storing seed and pollen).

It is not necessary to use all four pollinia in the pollination of one flower. Actually, nature has provided enough pollen in one pollen mass to produce a pod full of seed. The other three might be called a safety factor. However, it is customary to use two pollinia, one on the left lobe and one on the right lobe of the stigma.

To obtain the pollinia, hold a clean piece of paper under the tip of the column and gently tip up the anther cap with a clean toothpick or other pointed instrument. The anther chambers (actually the whole tip of the column) will come loose and fall onto the paper. Push the pollinia out of their chambers with the same instrument, being careful not to touch them with your fingers. An easy way to transfer a pollinium to the other flower is to touch the stigma with your instrument and then touch the pollen mass. The pollinium will stick to the viscid drop on the instrument. Pollination is performed simply by pressing the pollinia well into the stigmatic fluid, one on each side. Once covered by the sticky substance, they will not fall off.

The first reaction of the flower after pollination is to wilt, sometimes within a few hours, certainly after two days. After the flower parts have wilted they should be cut off at their base to prevent decay and possible infection of the column. The column is, of course, left intact during formation of the seed pod.

DEVELOPMENT OF THE SEED POD

Within a week after pollination, the tip of the column becomes swollen and the pollinia seem to have been drawn deeply into the cavity. At about the same time, the ovary begins to enlarge. These reactions are merely the first responses to the presence of the pollen in the stigma. They are not a sign that fertilization of the eggs has taken place.

Each pollen grain, stimulated by the action of the stigmatic fluid, sends out a long slender tube. The pollen tubes grow down through the channel of the column, along the walls of the ovary, and eventually each tube penetrates an ovule. Fig. 9-3A shows this process, and Fig. 9-3B pictures sprouted pollen grains. During the growth of the pollen tube, two sperm cells are formed within it, one of which unites with the egg nucleus in the ovule. (The other sperm cell unites with other nuclei in the ovule to form the endosperm, tissue used as food by the developing embryo.) It takes sixty to ninety days for the pollen tubes to complete their growth and penetrate the ovules.

Every viable seed formed is the result of the penetration of an ovule by a pollen tube. Production of 500,000 seeds means that 500,000 pollen tubes were able to find their mark. How the 500,000th tube manages to find a still unfertilized

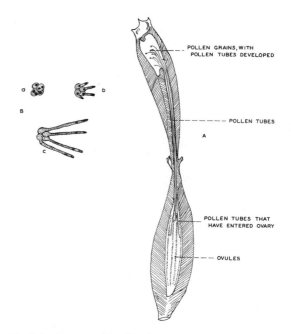

Fig. 9-3 Process of fertilization:
A. The column and ovary sixty days after pollination. The pollen tubes have grown from the pollen grains in the stigma down into the ovary, which by this time is definitely enlarged. During this sixty days the ovules have been maturing so that they are now ready to receive the sperm cells brought to them by the pollen tubes.
B. Pollen grains at various stages: a, as they originate, usually in groups of four; b, with tubes just starting; c, tubes elongating, and the nuclei carried along near their tips.

ovule is something to puzzle over, let alone the millionth or three millionth. That many pollen tubes are not successful is attested by the fact that often the greatest concentration of viable seed is found near the top of the ovary.

Incompatibility between the pollen and the flower on which it is placed often occurs. Sometimes it shows up within a few days by the shriveling of the column. The same pollen used on another flower might, however, have effected a successful mating. Sometimes a seed pod that seems to be progressing will turn yellow and drop off after two or three months. The ovules are immature at the time of pollination. Their maturation proceeds and the ovary enlarges while the pollen tubes are growing the necessary length. If for some reason the pollen tubes finally fail to effect fertilization, growth of the seed pod ceases.

If the cross is compatible, the ovary enlarges steadily. During its development it becomes marked with three deep flutings, corresponding to the three faint linear depressions visible on the ovary before pollination. The seed pod is completely hollow, containing three broad bands (placentae) to which the ovules are attached.

At six months the seed pod is about the size of a lemon and it does not enlarge much after this time. It ripens at about nine to ten months, occasionally later, and cracks open down the center of the flutings. The time to remove the pod is just when the cracks begin to show, before they have opened wide enough to allow the seed to spill out. To prevent losing any seed, it is a good idea to tie tissue paper over the seed pod a few weeks beforehand, and examine it from day to day. When the time comes for its removal, cut the stem that holds it to the pseudobulb, and place the pod in a clean glass jar to dry. Set the jar in a dry place, leaving it uncovered. Do not leave it in the greenhouse. If your climate is damp, the seed pod should be wrapped lightly in tissue paper and dried in a desiccator containing calcium chloride. When the pod is dried and split completely open, the seed can be shaken out into a clean container. It is ready to be sowed at this time, if you desire, but excess seed should be properly stored.

STORING SEED AND POLLEN

A desiccator is a glass container having two chambers, one holding calcium chloride which absorbs water vapor and the other containing the stored material. They can be purchased, but are rather expensive. A makeshift one will do as well. Use a wide-mouthed jar, and put two tablespoons of calcium chloride in the bottom. Make a shelf, out of hardware cloth or screen, that will rest in the center and divide the jar into two compartments, separating the calcium chloride from the upper part. A layer of paper over the screen will afford additional protection, yet still allow free circulation of air. Put the material to be stored in the top section, and screw on tightly a vacuum sealing lid. While drying the seed pod in the desiccator, let it remain at room temperature, as it will dry more rapidly this way than under refrigeration.

After the seed is removed from the pod, it should be kept under refrigeration. Cut pieces of writing paper (not wax paper) about four inches square, and in the center of each write the names of the parent plants so that the label will be visible after the seed is wrapped. Then put a small amount of seed in each paper, and fold carefully, fastening the ends with a paper clip. Place the packages in the desiccator, screw on the lid, and put in the refrigerator.

Seed retains its viability for a long time when stored in this manner, sometimes as long as six years. The percentage of germination decreases gradually, however, so that it may give only twenty to forty per cent after a long period.

Pollen does not remain viable for as long as seed, but may be kept for at least six months. Its viability is highest during the first few weeks. To store, place the pollinia in a glass tube, cork tightly, and dip the corked end in paraffin. Keep it in the refrigerator or at room temperature away from heat. Some advise the addition of a few granules of calcium chloride to the tube (in which case the pollinia must be wrapped in tissue paper to prevent contact with the calcium chloride), or the use of a small packet of silica gel. The pollinia may be dried in a desiccator for two days before placing in the glass tube.

CHECKING VIABILITY OF SEED AND POLLEN

Crosses between closely related species usually produce viable seed and pollen. Sterility is more likely to occur in complicated hybrids, particularly those derived from extremely dissimilar flowers.

Home Orchid Growing

Testing the viability of seed and pollen is a simple matter, though in nine cases out of ten it is not necessary for amateurs to bother with it. Commercial growers and those who are carrying on serious breeding programs find it a necessary procedure. Discovery ahead of time that a certain pollen is not viable enables the grower to choose some other pollen for use on a choice flower. Otherwise he may have to wait another year to mate that particular plant. The benefit of checking the viability of the seed before sowing a hundred or more flasks is obvious.

To test the pollen, place a little of it on a flower that you do not wish to save, a "cull." Pollen tubes commence to grow within forty-eight hours and can be seen under a microscope. Remove some of the stigmatic fluid on a pin point, mix it with a drop of water on a microscope slide, and cover with a cover glass. The sprouted pollen can be seen unstained, but if you wish to stain them add a drop of crystal violet solution to the water. Fig. 9-3B mentioned above, shows the pollen grains with tubes in various stages of growth. If you do not have a spare flower for this process, the pollen may be tested in a 0.2-molar sucrose solution (about one teaspoon of sugar in thirteen teaspoons of water) with agar added, kept at seventy-two degrees.

In any batch of seed there are some that do not contain embryos. Fig. 9-6 A and B shows a sample of cattleya seed, with and without embryos, as seen under a microscope. To observe your own seed, mix a small amount with water and place on a slide under a cover glass. Count the seed with and without embryos and estimate the relative percentage of good seed; eighty to ninety per cent is good. If no seeds have embryos, the lot must be discarded. You will have to use your own judgment as to whether to use seed that shows only a low percentage with embryos. Perhaps it will pay to try it for the sake of obtaining a few seedlings from a most unusual cross, or from one that rarely gives seed.

A further check of seed viability, and the one of real significance, is to sow a flask or two and see how well it germinates. This necessitates waiting three or four weeks, or until the seed swells and turns green. It sometimes happens (though rarely) that seed that appears under the microscope to be good is actually not living. This check would be well worth your while for seed that has been stored an excessively long time or has not been kept under good conditions.

PREPARATION OF THE FLASKS

The agar-nutrient medium for growing flask seedlings can be bought ready-mixed, so that beginners need not be awed by the list of chemicals involved. It can be obtained either from the Difco Company, Julius Leuschner, or Daniel M. Hill. Daniel M. Hill has two preparations, Hill's Standard Orchid Culture Medium for the germination of seed and for embryo culture and meristem culture, and Hill's Replating Medium for re-flasking seedlings. Complete directions are given for all, requiring only the addition of distilled water and warming, and if followed carefully results should be perfect. The mixtures are adjusted to the correct pH, so that the beginner does not even have this to worry him.

If you wish to have the seed germinated for you, there are individuals who make a business of this. Also, some commercial growers offer the service. It is a fine arrangement for those who wish to raise only a few seedlings each from their own crosses, or who do not have the time or place to care for flasks.

Usually, 500 cc. Ehrlenmeyer flasks are used, but wide-mouthed clear glass bottles are frequently preferred. The latter may have bakelite screw caps or be fitted with rubber stoppers. They must be capable of sterilization, and be large enough to give several square inches of suface of agar. Large test tubes may also be used, although these will hold fewer seedlings. Everything should be washed thoroughly and be rinsed several times.

Rubber stoppers are much easier to handle than the conventional cotton plug. They should be boiled for fifteen minutes before being used. The stopper should have a hole in the center, through which is put a piece of glass tubing bent over at the top, for ventilation of the bottle or flask. The bent-down end of the glass tubing is closed with cotton. This arrangement helps prevent the latent contamination of the flask, which is a nuisance with the cotton stoppers. Also, it is easier to sterilize the rubber stopper and neck of the flask at the time of seed sowing or transplanting.

When the agar-nutrient mixture has been prepared, it is ready to be poured into the flasks or bottles. These may be slanted, if you wish, or kept in an upright position. If you prefer them slanted, build a rack beforehand to hold them in the desired position. Many prefer the "slants" as they afford a somewhat larger surface area, and their horizontal position helps to prevent the entrance of mold

Fig. 9-4 Preparing flasks and sowing seed.

UPPER LEFT, add measured amount of prepared agar-nutrient mixture to one liter of distilled water in double boiler. Heat until thoroughly dissolved.

LOWER LEFT, pour the melted agar-nutrient mixture into flasks, using a long-stemmed funnel. The flasks are then stoppered and sterilized in a pressure cooker.

UPPER RIGHT, disinfecting the seed. Calcium hypochlorite solution from the flask at the left is put in a small vial, to which is added a bit of seed on the tip of a knife. The dropper to be used in the sowing process is put to soak at the same time in a cup containing calcium hypochlorite solution. The vial of seed will be shaken for twenty minutes.

LOWER RIGHT, flasks are taken one at a time from the pressure cooker, in which they were sterilized and allowed to cool. Here we have used cotton stoppers, but it is recommended that rubber stoppers be used instead (screw caps for bottles). These last should be put in a dish of sterilizing solution while the seed is being sown. Place a few drops of the suspended seed in the flask and replace the stopper. Cover the stopper and neck of the flask with foil or film.

spores while opened for sowing. Use a long-stemmed funnel for pouring the agar, so that it will reach down into the flask and obviate splashing agar on the sides or, most important, on the neck. This is essential to prevent the sticking of the stopper and to avoid giving molds a place to grow. The agar should be about an inch and one-half deep.

The flasks or bottles should be stoppered before sterilization. Screw caps should be tightened firmly and then released one-quarter turn.

Laboratory workers will be able to sterilize the flasks in an autoclave, but home canning equipment does just as well, preferably a pressure cooker. You must be sure that no water enters the flasks. In a pressure cooker, twenty minutes at fifteen pounds pressure is sufficient. After sterilization, remove the flasks while still hot, pour out the water from the cooker, and quickly put the flasks back in and cover with a clean cloth. This will allow them to cool without becoming contaminated. If possible, keep them thus protected until you are ready to use them. They are ready as soon as they are cool and the agar is jelled.

SOWING THE SEED

This process is so simple that the doing of it takes no longer than the telling. In fact, none of the procedures is difficult, and if the detailed descriptions make any part of them seem so, you have only to try it all, step by step, to realize that each is essentially easy. The second time you go through the process, you will wonder that you could ever have thought it complicated.

Sowing the seed consists of two main steps: (1) disinfecting the seed by soaking it in an antiseptic solution, and (2) putting a little of the suspended seed in each flask. We shall give you several methods—take your choice. In each method cleanliness is an important factor. The air is filled with mold spores. You are going to have to open the sterile flasks briefly to insert the seed, and you must take every precaution against contamination of the flasks during this time. Wait until the day's activities are over in the kitchen and the air has had time to settle before you begin your work. I like to spread damp dish towels on the work surface as a protection against dust, and the effect is better if they are wrung out of a 10 percent Clorox solution (one part Clorox to nine of water). Ingenious "kitchen

sowers" often find ways to make a temporary protected area or "tent" of plastic film, such as that which comes on dry cleaning. With the towels wrung out of Clorox on the work surface, the tent can be erected and everything be put inside. The worker then slips his hands under the front flap of plastic and quickly performs the operations.

Method #1. Equipment you will need in addition to the prepared flasks includes a one-quarter-ounce vial with a cork, a new medicine dropper, a glass or china cup, a graduated cylinder that holds 100 cc., two empty bottles, filter paper, glass funnel, an open flame (gas burner or alcohol lamp), a small bowl and a paring knife.

The seed may harbor mold spores acquired during handling and must therefore be disinfected. A solution of calcium hypochlorite * is standard for this purpose. Buy a bottle of it at the drugstore and keep it tightly stoppered in the refrigerator. To make up the solution put ten grams of the solid calcium hypochlorite in one bottle and add 140 cc. of distilled water. Shake thoroughly, let stand for one hour, shaking it at intervals. Then filter off the clear solution into the other bottle. This must be used at once. (Any amount left over must be thrown away, and fresh solution made up each time you prepare to sow flasks.)

Fill the little vial two-thirds with the calcium hypochlorite solution, and add a tiny bit of seed. The amount you can pick up on the tip of a paring knife will sow ten or a dozen flasks. (The knife, incidentally, should be sterilized by flaming and completely cooled before touching the seed.) Cork the vial tightly. The seed must be thoroughly wetted with the calcium hypochlorite solution, which requires that it be shaken vigorously and continuously for at least twenty minutes to break up the minute air bubbles that surround each seed.

While you are shaking the seed, put some of the remaining calcium hypochlorite solution in the cup and place the dropper in it to soak, being sure to fill the bulb as well as the glass part. You might also check on the arrangement of your equipment. Everything should be close together, the flasks, still in their covered container, and the cup with the dropper. In the bowl put a solution of 10 percent Clorox, for disinfecting the stopper while it is removed during sowing.

* Note that calcium hypochlorite is an entirely different chemical from the calcium chloride used in the desiccator. Calcium hypochlorite may be purchased as chlorinated lime.

When the seed has been disinfected, you are ready to sow the flasks. With *Cattleya* and some other kinds, the good seed sinks to the bottom and the chaff floats on top. This top portion may be poured off. The work will move more smoothly if you can have a helper at your first session, either to attend to the flasks or to drop the seed into them, but you can manage alone if you must. The following operations must be performed quickly so that the flask will be open to the air for as short a time as possible.

Take one flask at a time from the covered container and remove the stopper or screw cap. Place this in the bowl of Clorox.

Seed that has sunk to the bottom of the vial, or which in some cases has stuck to the sides, must be stirred up. This can be done by inserting the dropper into the fluid and forcing a few drops of air out of it. The bubbles will swirl the seed, and you can then take up a few drops of seed and fluid together to be transferred to the flask. Hold the dropper in the neck of the flask so that the drops will not run down the sides. Four drops is a good amount to put in each one, and if you move the dropper slightly in a circle you can put each drop in a different place on the agar. As soon as the seed is dropped in, take the stopper from the bowl, drain off any excess Clorox so that none will enter the flask, and replace it on the flask.

When all of the flasks are sown, pick up each one and gently tilt it back and forth to spread the seed over the surface of the agar. The screw cap or stopper must be covered, preferably with foil fastened with tape. Be sure that all flasks are labeled and dated.

One or two of the flasks may have become contaminated at the time of sowing and they will show growth of molds on the agar within a few days. It is to be hoped that not all of them will be so affected. If you work very carefully you may be able to get rid of a spot of mold, provided you find it while it is still small. Swab the neck, rim and stopper with 10 percent Clorox. Sterilize a long-handled instrument. Working in an area prepared as for flask sowing, open the flask, reach in and cut out the spot with the surrounding agar, and gently lift it out. Be sure that you do not touch the sides of the flask in the operation, else the mold may thus be spread. Drop a few drops of Wilson's Anti-Damp or Natriphene, both in a 1:2000 solution, on the area and re-stopper the flask. The more quickly this procedure is done, the less chance for further contamination. As your speed and dexterity increase with experience you will be less likely to have contamination in the flasks.

Method #2. This method employs a hypodermic syringe to inject the seed into the flask. Instead of a bent glass tube in the rubber stopper, a short straight tube is used, with cotton placed in it as before. Put a few drops of 10 percent Clorox on the cotton. The seed in suspension is picked up with a sterile hypodermic (a large bore needle is necessary). The needle is then dipped in 10 percent Clorox, forced between the cotton and the glass of the tube, and the seed squirted into the flask. R. H. Higgins suggests that if the seed tends to stick to the needle, this can be alleviated by adding a bit of 10 percent warm agar solution to the vial containing the seed and disinfectant. The stopper should be covered with foil after the flasks are sowed.

Method #3. The McEwan Flask Method. This method is detailed further on, under transplanting flasks. It is an entirely new method, the equipment and procedure designed by William S. McEwan, and if you plan to sow many flasks over a period of time, it would be well worth your consideration.

Method #4. The actual process of sowing the flasks is the same as described in Method #1, but the danger of contamination is reduced by the use of a "sleeve box." This is a box constructed with a slanting hinged glass lid and holes in the front or ends through which you can put your hands. Some growers like to add sleeves made of cloth and fastened on the outside of the holes. These have elastic in the ends so that they fit well up over the forearm. Wipe or spray the inside surfaces of the box with 10 per cent Clorox before use.

Place everything you need in the box before inserting your hands: sterilized flasks, sterilized dropper in cup of calcium hypochlorite solution, vial of disinfected seed, saucer of 10 percent Clorox for holding stoppers or lids, and squares of foil or polyethylene film for covering the flasks. You may wish to wear rubber gloves while working. It is not recommended that these be fastened to the ends of the sleeves, as the struggle to put them on often causes air to be sucked into the case with some force. After you have everything in readiness, put on the gloves, wash them in Clorox solution, insert your hands through the sleeves, and then wipe off

A

C

Fig. 9-5 A bio-clean work area for aseptic procedures. A, a unit suitable for work on a small scale. B, sowing seed. C, transplanting flasks. (A, *Courtesy General Acoustics Corporation*. B and C, *Courtesy the John Walters family*)

CARE OF FLASKS

Cattleya seed germinates and grows best at temperatures between 70° and 75°. The temperature may rise a little in warm weather. Ideally the temperature should be 70° to 75° at night also, but if you cannot maintain this, let the night temperature drop to 65°. A fluctuation of more than 10 degrees either way is not good for the developing seedlings and will retard their growth. Flasks may be kept on a shaded shelf in the greenhouse, or in a glass case with added humidity in the house. The latter is necessary to keep the flasks from drying in the drier atmosphere of the house. They need only 200 foot-candles of light. Flasks do very well under Gro-Lux lights, placed 12 inches under two 40 watt tubes.

In extreme cases of drying, it is necessary to add a little sterile distilled water to the flask. This is a risky procedure, however, and unless done expertly may result in contamination. The screw cap or stopper and the rim and neck of the flask must be thoroughly swabbed with 10 percent Clorox before opening. Then lift the lid only high enough to admit the dropper (previously sterilized) and replace it quickly after the water is added. If you have used a stopper with a short straight tube, as in method #2, put a few drops of 10 percent Clorox

B

the gloves with a cloth wrung out of Clorox solution placed in the box for this purpose.

Ready-made flasking "areas" are available. A plastic dome-like case with holes for inserting the hands can be bought with or without racks for holding the flasks. Another and more expensive arrangement is a self-contained air-conditioned unit. The unit keeps sterile air moving through "absolute" filters, out through a shielded work space. In the air-conditioned area, where air is moving, dry seed cannot be exposed else it will be blown away.

on the cotton and inject the sterile distilled water by means of a hypodermic syringe, inserting the needle between the glass and the cotton. Cover the stopper with fresh foil afterward.

During the development of the seedlings, disturb the flasks as little as possible. Jostling the flasks sometimes allows mold spores that have settled on the neck or the stopper to drop into the agar and cause contamination.

DEVELOPMENT OF THE SEEDLINGS

About ten days or two weeks after the seed is sown it begins to swell. Within six weeks the seed turns green, showing the development of chlorophyll. Fig. 9-6 shows the stages of development of the seedling. The embryo continues to increase in size until it is a little green spherule, about $\frac{1}{16}$ inch in diameter, shaped like a top, with a depression in its upper surface. Absorbing hairs soon cover the surface. Between two and three months after the seed was sown, the first leaf point makes its appearance in the middle of the depression, and the spherule becomes larger and somewhat flattened.

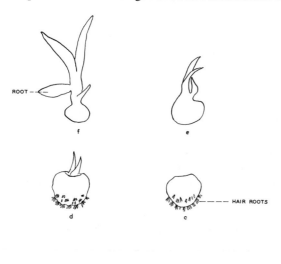

Fig. 9-6 Development of cattleya seedlings. A, a seed with an embryo. B, a seed without an embryo. C, protocorm developed; the embryo increases in size until it bursts the seed coat, and then enlarges. Absorbing roots (small hair roots) develop on its surface. D, protocorm, the first leaves developing (two to three months after sowing). E, elongation of the stem, with more leaves appearing. F, seedling at about four to six months, showing first root growing from the stem, below the second leaf.

This disc-like structure is called the protocorm. Soon a second and third leaf appear, the stem elongates, and the first root grows down. By the sixth month the seedling is well developed. During the following months the leaves grow larger, and additional roots may form. Nine to twelve months after sowing, the seedlings are ready to transplant to community pots.

When the flasks are first sown, it is not possible to control the number of seeds per flask. Some will be very crowded, others not so heavily populated. There is always some difference in the growth rate among individual seedlings; some take hold and grow rapidly while others develop more slowly. Some never go past the protocorm stage. The differences are more marked in crowded flasks where competition for the nutrients allows the faster growing ones to gain an advantage over the slower ones. After about six months, the growth rate in general slows down a little, due possibly to the accumulation of metabolic products in the agar as well as to depletion of the nutrients.

At the six-month stage, or even earlier, commercial growers and many ambitious amateurs like to transplant the seedlings to fresh flasks. The seedlings receive quite a boost by being put into fresh medium. The commercial grower has a dual purpose, first to produce flasks with a uniform number of plants so that one customer will not receive 500 plants and the next only 50, and also to have plants of transplantable size ready for the market in a shorter time. Amateurs are motivated by the desire to have their seedlings come along as fast as possible, and also to have them as large as possible when the time comes to put them into community pots. Transplanting flasks is, however, a ticklish business, and the average grower need not feel at all compelled to undertake it. The process is described later on in this chapter.

KNUDSON'S FORMULA "C"

After you have grown seedlings with the prepared products, you may want to mix your own medium. You should start with a standard formula, and later, if you want to join the ranks of experimenters, you may want to try the addition of vitamins or other growth promoting substances to the medium. It should be said here that, up to now, research has produced no better formulas than those of Dr. Knudson. Therefore, Knudson's "C," is given as the standard.

Home Orchid Growing

Chemical	Symbol	Amount
Calcium Nitrate	$Ca(NO_3)_2 \cdot 4H_2O$	1.00 gram
Monobasic Potassium Phosphate	KH_2PO_4	0.25 gram
Magnesium Sulfate	$MgSO_4 \cdot 7H_2O$	0.25 gram
Ammonium Sulfate	$(NH_4)_2SO_4$	0.50 gram
Sucrose	$C_{12}H_{22}O_{11}$	20.00 grams
Ferrous Sulfate	$FeSO_4 \cdot 7H_2O$	0.025 gram
Manganese Sulfate	$MnSO_4 \cdot 4H_2O$	0.0075 gram

These chemicals must be weighed with extreme care, using a fine balance. Any discrepancy in the proportions of the chemicals, even of the sugar, may be disastrous to the seedlings. If you do not have access to a fine balance, or are unaccustomed to its use, you had better ask your druggist to do the weighing for you. (Incidentally, he will also assist you with the name of a chemical supply house where you can buy the ingredients, or will sell them to you himself.)

Add the ingredients, one at a time, to one liter (1000 cc.) of distilled water, and dissolve completely. Then add fifteen grams of plain agar, and warm in a double boiler until all of the agar is dissolved.

After the medium is thus prepared, and before sterilization, it is necessary to check the *p*H (which means hydrogen ion concentration). The *p*H scale is based on units from zero to fourteen, which indicate the degree of acidity or alkalinity of a solution; seven is neutral. Below seven the solution is acid, and the lower the number the more acid it is. Above seven it is alkaline. Cattleya seed (and that of most orchids) grows best in a solution that has a *p*H of 5.0-5.2. This degree of acidity is necessary to make the minerals available for the use of the seedlings. Too great an acidity often kills the seed, and a too alkaline condition impoverishes the seedlings by preventing the plants from obtaining the necessary minerals. Equipment to test *p*H can be bought from most supply houses, and ranges from the expensive electrode type to the cheaper color indicator kind. Full directions come with the equipment.

Checking the *p*H consists of removing a small amount of the agar-nutrient medium as soon as it is prepared (before sterilization), and testing it with whatever type of equipment you have. If it is found to be too alkaline, add a drop or two of 0.1 normal hydrochloric acid to the whole amount of medium, mix thoroughly, and then remove a small quantity again for checking. Continue until the *p*H reads between 5.0 and 5.2. If the medium as first mixed turns out to be too acid, add 0.1 normal potassium hydroxide solution, and proceed in the same manner.

USE OF WIRE LOOP FOR SOWING SEED

Experts prefer a fine wire loop instead of a dropper for sowing seed. The loop is a bit difficult for beginners to use, so the dropper has been suggested to simplify things at first. The loop has the advantage of picking up the seed with very little of the sterilizing solution clinging to it, and in an expert hand the seed may be spread evenly on the agar. It is particularly useful in handling seed that sticks to the sides of the vial—cymbidium seed, for instance.

The end of a fine platinum wire is made into a loop about $\frac{3}{16}$ inch in diameter, and attached by the other end to a long slender handle. When the loop is dipped into a suspension of orchid seed, it comes out with a thin film of fluid spread within the loop, holding a good number of seeds. For seed that floats, the loop is dipped only into the upper surface. Where the seed sinks, the sterilizing solution can be poured off first, leaving the collection of seed in the bottom of the vial.

The loop is sterilized by flaming, and completely cooled before touching the seed. To be sure that it is cool, you might dip it into another vial of the disinfecting solution you are using. To sow the seed, the loop is drawn lightly across the agar, not really touching the agar but merely the moisture that has exuded on its surface.

OTHER METHODS FOR DISINFECTING SEED

Calcium hypochlorite solution has long been the standard means of disinfecting seed. It is gentle yet efficient, and it does not harm sensitive seed such as vanda, phalaenopsis and cymbidium. Cattleya seed can remain in it for several hours without harm, giving the beginner the advantage of extra time and allowing the seed to be kept over in case of an interruption during the seed sowing process. Some growers like a three percent hydrogen peroxide solution as a disinfecting agent, and some prefer a solution made by adding one Clorazene tablet to two ounces of distilled water. With these last two time is saved by not having to make up the calcium hypochlorite solution, but the seed should be sown within an hour or two.

It may be that some mold spores are not killed by disinfecting agents, resulting in flask contamination. Soaking the seed for 8 to 12 hours in a sugar or honey solution (2 teaspoons to 1 cup distilled water) will activate the spores so that they are more easily killed.

For seed that is not sensitive to a disinfecting agent, Clorox may be used, but always with extreme caution. The solution must be quite weak and the seed should not stand in it for very long. We recommend one part of Clorox to ninety-nine parts of water, although one of Clorox to fifty-four of water has been used. Shake the seed in the solution for exactly ten minutes, no longer, as after this length of time the percentage of germination may be reduced. As much as possible of the Clorox solution must then be removed and be replaced with sterile (boiled and cooled) distilled water. If the seed has sunk to the bottom of the vial, gently draw the Clorox solution off from above it with a sterilized dropper. If the seed is floating, insert the dropper below it and draw the solution into it. Replace with sterile distilled water and shake thoroughly. This may be enough rinsing for most seed, but the process can be repeated. Then sow the seed at once.

OTHER MEDIA FOR GERMINATING SEED

Research goes on to find new media for germination—media that will speed up the growth of seedlings and shorten the time they must be in flasks. So many things enter into such research that obtaining results that can be generally useful is a long, slow process. A substance that may stimulate the growth of one species may inhibit, or at least not benefit, the growth of another. A substance may be beneficial to some kinds in one concentration and to others in a different concentration. Thus it sometimes occurs that a report by one group of workers may seem to be in conflict with that of another, simply because seed from different

individuals was used, or because of other differences in the work. It would take a tremendous amount of space to summarize what work has been done on various modifications of formulas and on the additives and substitutes that have been tried, for instance, additions of substances from various plants, different sugars, numerous vitamins, growth promoting chemicals. Such work is discussed in a number of publications: Carl Withner in his chapter "Orchid Physiology" in *The Orchids,* edited by him, 1959; Kunio Kano, *Studies on the Media for Orchid Seed Germination,* 1965; and Joseph Arditti, "Factors Affecting the Germination of Orchid Seeds," Bot. Rev., Vol. 33, no. 1, 1967. The excellent bibliographies these include give references to other works.

However, from among the various plant substances tried in media, three have been found useful in germinating seed. These are coconut milk, tomato juice, and banana. Not all genera respond when tomato juice is used alone, but a mixture of coconut milk and tomato juice seems to be quite satisfactory for most genera. Coconut milk has been used in a great deal of work with seed germination. It and banana contain some substances that stimulate growth, but their exact nature has not yet been found.

Rev. Masao Yamada of Hawaii, who has in the past published formulas using coconut milk and tomato juice, has kindly given me by letter a revised formula. He emphasizes that best results are obtained with milk from green coconuts, in which the meat has just begun to harden. The milk at this stage is at its sweetest and is also in greatest quantity. Obviously, his formula will be most useful in areas where coconuts can be obtained at just the right stage of development.*

YAMADA'S FORMULA

For one liter of medium:
250 cc. of coconut milk
750 cc. distilled water
  5 teaspoons granulated table sugar
  1 teaspoon Peptone (powder, Difco Co.)
  ¼ teaspoon Gaviota Organic Orchid Fertilizer
  3 tablespoons canned unsalted tomato puree (any standard brand)
 15 to 20 grams of agar (Difco Co. plain agar)

A tomato juice formula as reported by J. Meyer is very simple and may be useful for some things,

* Other workers state that the ripeness of the coconut is not a factor in the effectiveness of the milk.

Home Orchid Growing

although not for cattleyas, according to some workers.

TOMATO JUICE FORMULA—J. Meyer
250 cc. fresh strained tomato juice
250 cc. distilled water
7.5 grams stick agar

Joseph Arditti outlines a method for using banana in the A. O. S. Bulletin, Feb., 1968, as follows:

1. Peel a sufficient number of greenish-yellow "Chiquita" brand bananas to obtain 150 grams (about 5 ounces) of fruit tissue.
2. Place tissues in a blender with one pint (distilled) water.
3. Homogenize for one minute.
4. Allow homogenate to stand in blender for 5 minutes.
5. Homogenize again for one minute.
6. Line a colander with a sheet of Whatman No. 1 filter paper, or a few pure white paper towels, or with 4 layers of cheesecloth, and filter the homogenate. Save the liquid, freeze until used.
7. Collect the portion which has accumulated in the colander and freeze until used.
8. Add one third of the liquid to 1 pint of culture medium and make up total volume to one quart plus 2 ounces. Adjust the pH to 5.0-5.2. Grow the seedlings on this for 90 days.
9. When seedlings are 90-95 days old add the insoluble portion (pulp kept frozen until now) to a pint of culture medium, homogenize to achieve maximum dispersal, and make up total volume to one quart plus two ounces. Transfer seedlings to this medium.

The culture medium may be Knudson's "C" or the Vacin and Went medium given below.

VACIN AND WENT CULTURE MEDIUM

Tricalcium phosphate	0.20 gm.
Potassium nitrate	0.525 gm.
Monopotassium acid phosphate	0.25 gm.
Magnesium sulfate	0.25 gm.
Ammonium sulfate	0.50 gm.
Ferric tartrate	0.028 gm.
Manganese sulfate	0.0075 gm.
Sucrose	20.0 gm.
Agar	16.00 gm.
Water	1,000 ml.

Adjust pH to 5-5.2.

To this may be added 25 percent by volume of coconut water, or if banana is used, follow Arditti's directions.

Note: Donald Nail finds that banana can foam badly, and suggests using three drops of Dow Corning DC200 or other dimethyl silicone to the medium before sterilizing.

If you wish to try a new medium, or to experiment on your own, it is advisable to have on hand a large quantity of seed from one seed pod. You can then germinate some on a standard medium such as Knudson's "C," or the Difco or Hill prepared media, for comparison, as well as for safety. Don't risk precious seed of which you have only a small amount on a medium with which you are not familiar.

GERMINATING GREEN SEED: EMBRYO CULTURE

Cattleya seed is easy to disinfect and germinates readily. Some kinds, however, are sensitive to disinfecting solutions and others are reluctant to germinate. Research has been carried on with a view to finding some stage in the development of the seed when it may be removed from an unripe pod and will germinate when thus planted green.

Experiments have shown that the immature seed can be germinated soon after fertilization has taken place, which varies in length of time from species to species, being, for instance, between 60 and 90 days for *Cattleya* and 70 and 130 days for *Epidendrum*. Since the exact time can be known only through study of each species or hybrid, it might be best to wait for several months after pollination, or until half the time usually required for the ripening of the pod is achieved.

Sowing seed from the green pod can be helpful in many ways. The seed within the unopened pod is absolutely clean and sterile, free from any contaminating organisms. If the pod is harvested before it begins to split and is thoroughly washed with a disinfecting agent, the seed can be removed under sterile conditions and be sown without having to be treated itself with a disinfectant. This eliminates the danger of harming sensitive seed, and also does away with one step in the usual procedure. Some kinds that are slow to germinate may do so more rapidly if sown before the seed coat is fully hardened. Although not all growers have difficulty with *Vanda, Phalaenopsis,* and *Cymbidium,* some definitely do, and these find that sowing the seed green gives them a better percentage of germination in these genera. *Paphiopedilum* is a problem unto itself. Poor germination is caused largely by the genetic makeup of the plants, but often apparently viable seed fails to germinate. It is thought that in *Paphiopedilum,* as in many other kinds of plants, the seed coat contains an agent that inhibits germination. Sowing the seed before the seed coat is fully developed has given better germination in some instances.

The flasks are prepared in the usual way and are kept covered until time to use them. In a pressure cooker or an autoclave sterilize the following equipment, wrapped in a towel: a small glass vial with a stopper for the seed, an eye dropper, a sharp stainless steel knife, and a shallow bowl. Also, sterilize at the same time a flask of distilled water. Prepare a sleeve box by spraying the inside with 10 percent Clorox solution and lay on its floor a towel wrung out of 10 percent Clorox. Place the prepared flasks in it, along with the sterilized package of equipment and the flask of sterile distilled water. Also place in the box a small towel wrung out of the Clorox solution, for wiping your hands.

Wash the seed pod thoroughly with 10 percent Clorox, scrubbing it gently all over including the seams with a soft brush, and then wrap it in a piece of toweling also wrung out of the Clorox. Some growers like to peel the outside layer off the pod at this point, and re-dip the peeled pod in Clorox. There is danger in doing this, for you may cut too deeply into the pod and expose the seed, so be careful. Exposure to the air will contaminate the seed, and contact with the Clorox will injure it. Place the wrapped pod in the sowing box.

If you have many flasks to sow, or if you are sensitive to Clorox, you should wear rubber gloves. Rinse the gloves in 10 percent Clorox after you have put them on, and then wipe them with the Clorox towel after inserting them through the sleeves. No Clorox may touch the seed. Open the sterile package. Pour some of the sterile distilled water into the bowl, and rinse your gloves in it to wash off the Clorox. Then pour a little distilled water from the flask into the seed vial. Now rinse the seed pod in the bowl, and cut it open with the sterile knife. Scoop out some of the seed with the knife and put it in the vial. Stopper the vial and shake it to suspend the seed. Sow the seed with the dropper, stoppering each flask as you do so. Some

workers prefer not to suspend the seed in water, but to drop it directly into the flask from the pod.

In this method, as soon as the protocorms have formed they are transplanted to new flasks and scattered evenly over the surface. It has been suggested that large test tubes be used for the germination stage to save culture medium, since the time in these would be short.

Placental culture, another form of embryo culture, is being carried on by Robert Scully, Jr. Instead of sowing the immature seed, the seed pod itself is cut in thin slices and the slices are laid on the agar medium with the cut surface in contact with the agar. When protocorms develop they are scraped off and put in fresh flasks. The advantages or disadvantages of this method are yet to be determined.

TRANSPLANTING FLASKS

Seedlings are given a great boost by being put in fresh medium during their development. The chief hazard in transplanting flasks is the danger of contamination. The flasks must be open for quite a while, and you must move an instrument in and out of them as you transfer groups of seedlings, thus multiplying the chances for mold spores to enter the flasks. The professional grower, whose first failures are but a dim memory, can turn out clean flasks day after day, but the amateur is lucky if he doesn't have some troubles. Amateurs, being what they are, however, usually persist until they are successful!

The stage at which seedlings are reflasked (replated is a term often used) is a matter of choice. They may be moved in late protocorm stage, when the first leaf point becomes visible and before roots have developed, or when the first root is still very short. It is easier to handle them then, and they may be simply scattered on the agar and will orient themselves as growth progresses. If one waits until the roots have grown long, the seedlings will be tangled together and separating them becomes a problem that involves time. The more quickly the operation can be done, the less likely the chances of contamination.

To prevent contamination at any stage, many growers remove the seedlings to a solution of Wilson's Anti-Damp or Natriphene, and from this to the new flasks. If you are transplanting older seedlings, this gives an opportunity to sort them

Home Orchid Growing

as to size, to put larger ones together in one flask and smaller ones in another.

Flasks for transplanting are prepared in the same way, and with the same medium, as the original ones, again 1½ inches deep. The work of transplanting must be done under cover, and the usual equipment is the sleeve box described above. The fresh flasks are placed in the prepared work space (sprayed with 10 percent Clorox, etc.). The flasks from which the seedlings are to be taken are thoroughly washed off on the outside with 10 percent Clorox, including caps or stoppers and the area between rim and stopper. The instrument for moving the seedlings may be a wire loop on the end of a handle, or a long-handled spoon with a small bowl. It should be sterilized with 10 percent Clorox after it is placed in the case and must then be rinsed in sterile distilled water just before use.

Open the flask from which seedlings are to be removed, and a flask into which they will go, placing the stopper of the latter in the dish of 10 percent Clorox. Gently dip out a group of seedlings, skimming them off the old agar, and place them in the new flask. Repeat until you have enough, perhaps about fifty, and then with the same instrument nudge them apart so as to space them more or less evenly. They will regain an upright position as their roots go into the new agar. Their growth can be accelerated by Gro-Lux lights, 16 hours a day.

An apparatus for transplanting seedlings was devised by William S. McEwan,* and is pictured herewith. The advantage of this device is that it has a small volume of air and, being glass, can be sterilized more efficiently than the sleeve box. It is a custom-made glass sphere to which have been fused two bell-shaped glass collars on the lower side and a single collar on the upper side. The sphere has a handle on top by which it is held in place by a clamp on a ring stand. The flasks to be sown, or the flasks to be transplanted, are held in the lower collars by rubber bands hooked over horns fused to the sides of the collars. You reach in through the upper opening with long-handled instruments to sow the seed or transplant the seedlings.

The general method for transplanting seedlings is as follows. The inside of the sphere and the collars are swabbed with 50 percent Clorox, and

* Wm. S. McEwan has made arrangements to have these flasks made for any who care to buy them. Interested persons may write to him at 513 A Lexington Ave., China Lake, Calif.

then with 10 percent Clorox by means of a piece of toweling wrapped around the end of a stick. The stopper and the neck of the fresh flask are thoroughly washed with 10 percent Clorox, and then, under cover of an inverted cereal bowl, the stopper is removed to a saucer of 10 percent Clorox where it remains until it is reinserted in the flask. Keeping the open flask in a horizontal position so as to prevent spores from entering, move it into one of the collars and hook it into position. The flask from which seedlings are to be taken is then washed off with 10 percent Clorox, opened and inserted into the other collar. The seedlings are moved from one flask to the other by means of a long-handled spatula, or handle with a wire loop, which has been sterilized before use. When the new flask is ready, the stopper is removed from the dish of Clorox, and the flask is edged out from under the collar just far enough to allow the stopper to be inserted while still under the protection of the collar.

Seed sowing is accomplished in much the same way. The sphere is swabbed with the Clorox solution, the flask is swabbed before opening and the stopper placed in a dish of Clorox. The flask is hooked into one of the collars. The sterilized seed is transferred from the vial to the flask either by means of a long pipette or, as McEwan prefers, by means of a little beaker holding 1 cc. and held by a ring on the end of a rod.

Dr. McEwan has developed a professional model for the use of those doing a great deal of flasking. This is illustrated in the *A. O. S. Bulletin,* October, 1966. It would be equally helpful for amateurs. By the addition of a pump that forces air through a filter and then through a solution of potassium permanganate a constant flow of sterilized air is kept moving through the flask. It resembles in principle the larger bioclean area described earlier. For the amateur with little available space, its size is a definite advantage. And it is not as complicated as it seems.

MERISTEM CULTURE

In the last few years a new method for propagation has made it possible to raise thousands of plants from a single individual, all identical to the parent plant, and to each other. Although different from raising plants from seed, it involves the same sterile techniques, much the same equipment, simi-

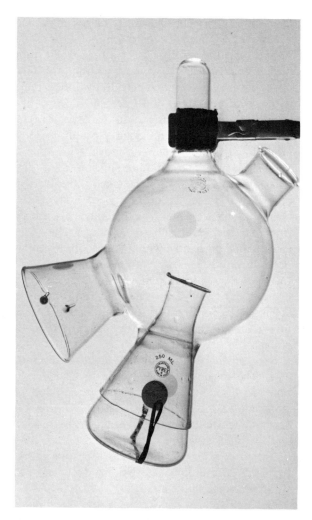

Fig. 9-7 The McEwan flask for sowing seed or transplanting flasks. LEFT, the McEwan flask, with two projecting bells into which the flasks are inserted for working, each attached by rubber bands to hooks on the sides of the bells. At the upper side is an open neck through which sowing or transplanting tools are inserted, and a handle by which the flask is held in a clamp. UPPER RIGHT, transplanting seedlings from one flask to another. LOWER RIGHT, stoppering the finished flask. (*Courtesy W. S. McEwan*)

lar nutrient formulas, and even the handling of protocorms, so it seems logical to place it in this chapter.

The method is called meristem culture, and the resulting plants are called mericlones. The work was pioneered by George Morel, and further developed by Donald Wimber, Michel Vacherot, Robert M. Scully, Jr., and others. The orchid nursery of Vacherot and Lecoufle was the first to carry it out on a commercial scale, contributing a great deal both to experimental work on various genera, and to the spread of knowledge and interest in meristem culture. Some amateurs are now doing their own meristeming, and for those who wish it, there are a number of laboratories that offer meristeming service.

Meristem culture was undertaken originally by Morel and Martin on dahlia and potato as a means of ridding individual clones of virus. Morel then turned his attention to *Cymbidium*. The theory was, and practice has shown, that the undifferentiated cells of the growing stem tip (the meristem) are often free from virus that infects the rest of the plant. This is only because these cells increase so rapidly that they stay a "step ahead" of the spreading virus. If this very small group of cells can be cut out without taking with it cells into which the virus has already penetrated, new plants free from virus can be raised from it. If infected cells are included in the culture, the resulting plants will still bear the virus. Of course, the production of virus-free plants does not mean that

Home Orchid Growing

they may not be subject to later infection in a new environment, just as any plants can become infected. But it does give a chance to have healthy plants from valuable individuals that may have become infected.

The technique is not limited to freeing plants from virus, however. It is a means of rapidly propagating an outstanding species or hybrid which could otherwise be increased only slowly by older means of division, and of obtaining large numbers of meristem divisions from plants that are beautiful but sterile. A number of genera have been successfully meristemed: *Cymbidium, Cattleya* and its intergeneric hybrids, *Dendrobium, Miltonia, Oncidium, Odontoglossum, Odontonia, Phaius, Calanthe, Zygopetalum,* and others.

An approximately $\frac{1}{16}$ inch cube of tissue is removed from the very tip of young vegetative shoots. Such shoots are those which are just starting into growth and have reached a length of an inch or an inch and a half. The tissue from the tip of the shoot is used, as is also that from the tips of buds in the leaf axils along the shoot. The cube of tissue is removed under sterile conditions with aid of a dissecting microscope. Each bit of tissue is placed in a vial or a small flask of liquid medium such as the Vacin and Went medium described on page 109, without the addition of agar. Scully added 25 percent by volume of coconut milk for *Cattleya.* The containers are then placed on a rotary shaker, which agitates them at a predetermined rate. The motion keeps the fluid constantly oxygenated, and bathes the pieces of tissue uniformly.

Within a few weeks each cube of tissue develops into a mass of protocorms, similar to those that develop from germinated seeds. The mass of protocorms can be removed from the flask and each protocorm be cut into several pieces. Pieces put into fresh liquid medium and returned to the shaker will develop into new masses of protocorms. Pieces put on solid medium, medium containing agar (and not kept on the shaker), go through the stages from protocorm to plant, producing leaves and roots in a matter of four to eight weeks. The cultures in liquid medium can be continued many times over—cutting up each mass of protocorms and returning the pieces to fresh medium on the shaker—until the desired number of potential plants has been obtained. Then the hundreds, or thousands, of pieces of tissue are grown on solid medium just as are flask seedlings. Thus from

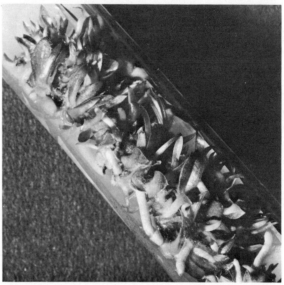

Fig. 9-8 TOP, A mass of protocorms developed from a single meristem of *Cattleya.* Each may be cut into several pieces if more plants are desired, or the protocorms may be separated and transferred intact to solid medium where each will form a plant. BOTTOM, Young plants four months after sectioning has stopped. (*Courtesy* The Cymbidium Society News *and George Morel*)

one original bit of meristem tissue, great numbers of new plants can be obtained.

The implications for the future of orchid growing are tremendous. Any awarded hybrid or otherwise desirable plant, including rare species, can theoretically be multiplied. Not all kinds may respond equally well, for cattleyas proved more difficult than cymbidiums. Growers who supply the cut flower market can now have the best forms and those which flower at desirable times in whatever quantity they desire. Amateurs may own examples of particularly appealing plants at a frac-

Fig. 9-9 Model G33 Rotary Action Bench-Top Shaker, manufactured by the New Brunswick Scientific Co., Inc.

tion of the cost of pseudobulb divisions. The fear that this would discourage further hybridization seems now unfounded, for orchid lovers will always want something new. And in a group of plants as varied as orchids, the chief appeal is the unusual.

Some method of reward to the hybridizer must be worked out, however, for unless he can make a living he will not be able to go on. It seems that patenting valuable plants is a possibility, with a royalty to the originator.

Techniques continue to be refined, and experimental work with kinds as yet untried must be done. Background and details of technique can be obtained from a number of articles in the *American Orchid Society Bulletin:* George Morel, July, 1960 and June, 1964; Donald E. Wimber, February, 1963; Yoneo Sagawa, T. Shoji and T. Shoji, February, 1966; Walter Bertch, January, 1967; and Robert M. Scully, Jr., February, 1967. Reprints of all but the 1967 articles are published in a pamphlet by the American Orchid Society, price $.25. A complete survey of literature dealing with meristem culture to date, giving details of methods and results, has been published by Margaret E. Marston and Pisit Voraurai of the University of Nottingham. This work, Miscellaneous Publication No. 17, "Multiplication of Orchid Clones by Shoot Meristem Culture. A Review of the Literature," is available from the Department of Horticulture, University of Nottingham School of Agriculture, Sutton Bonington, Loughborough, England.

10

SEEDLINGS FROM FLASK TO BLOOM

Even if you do not indulge in growing your own seed and sowing flasks, you will at some time or other want to obtain some flask seedlings, certainly some community pot seedlings. Flasks can be bought for between twenty-five and thirty dollars, and are usually transplanted flasks. That is, the seedlings have been moved from the flasks in which they were germinated into fresh flasks, and are of fairly uniform size and close to an estimated number. The price is low per plant, something like twenty-five cents each. The seedlings will be ready to go into communities as soon as you receive them.

Community pots may be bought, either freshly established from the flasks or with the seedlings ready to be moved on. Prices vary according to the number of plants per pot and their size. However, seedlings of community pot size are often sold individually, ranging from seventy-five cents to a dollar and one-half each. They are ready for individual pots. They are removed from the community pots or flats in which they are grown, and are shipped in little polyethylene bags. The grower with limited space or a desire for greater variety can thus obtain a few each of many different crosses.

Seedlings of larger sizes are also obtainable, on up to flowering age. We suggest that you buy them not larger than two-and-one-half-inch pot size, however, as their price is still very reasonable at

this age and you can have several for the price you would pay for one nearly mature plant.

When you buy seedlings, you make your choice from a list that gives the names of the parents, and usually a description of their size, coloring, and flowering season. The grower often adds helpful information as to what he expects from the cross, based on how the parents have behaved in previous crosses. Occasionally, crosses are offered that are repetitions of previous crosses, which have proved successful and for which there is still demand. If you know the history of the cross, and if the re-make is done with the original parents, it will undoubtedly be a good value. However, when re-makes are not done with the original parents, you have to be wary. Such a cross is bound to be different from the original—it may be better or it may be worse. If you know the hybridist, and his work, and if he has selected parents superior to the original ones for a definite purpose, you might like to try some of the seedlings on an experimental basis.

FLASK TO COMMUNITY POT

The flasks are packed carefully in boxes and sent by railway or air express. Sometimes they arrive in perfectly undisturbed condition, depending on the care with which they are handled and the distance they travel. Occasionally the soft jelly is jumbled and the little plants are clustered in tangled masses, which does not seem to harm them. If the flasks arrive in the latter condition, it is necessary to transplant them at once, but undisturbed flasks may be kept for a time.

If you have not seen flask seedlings before, nothing I can say will prepare you for their sheer beauty, the delicacy of their little shiny green leaves, and their tiny translucent roots. The plants are so small and fragile that you will handle them with tender awe, wondering that it has taken a year for them to grow to this size. In transplanted flasks the plants will be quite uniform. In non-transplanted flasks there will be a few larger seedlings, perhaps an inch and a quarter from tip to tip, with several leaves and three or four roots, some with leaves and roots a quarter of an inch long, and some with leaves and roots just starting to form. Also, in non-transplanted flasks, you will see some that are no farther than the protocorm stage (see Fig. 9-6), the little round green ball stage that precedes leaf formation.

These little seedlings, when removed from the flasks, will be put into "communities," either pots holding about fifty or flats holding around a hundred plants. The communities not only save space and facilitate handling a large number of seedlings, but they can be kept more uniformly moist, thus providing better growing conditions than small individual pots afford. They will remain in communities about a year.

Before removing the seedlings from the flask, prepare the pots or flats, whichever you decide to use. The former should be the shallow type called bulb pans, three inches or, preferably, five inches in diameter. Flats may be made at home using strips of wood two inches wide for the sides and hardware cloth for the bottom, making them about six by eight inches large.

Of course, osmunda may be used for communities, and it is good in many ways. As the roots grow into it there is little danger of washing the plants out of the pots, and they need not be watered very frequently. However, removing the seedlings from the fiber after their roots have become intermingled causes many roots to be broken. We are going to suggest that you use bark or a seedling mix or screened sphagnum moss.

For plants just out of the flasks the bark should be very fine and should contain some of the "screenings," the material screened out of the coarser grades. A seedling grade of bark is available in which the size is given as zero to one-quarter inch, undoubtedly containing much fine material. If you have a bag of any grade of bark, you may be able to obtain enough material for a

Fig. 10-1 A flask of seedlings ready for community pots.   (*Courtesy Rod McLellan Co.*)

Home Orchid Growing

few community pots by screening it through a one-quarter inch mesh screen. Although the coarser grades are pretty clean as they come from the producer, there is still some fine material in them.

Some growers like a mixture of three parts bark screenings, mixed with one part sand. Another mix is one part one-quarter inch bark, one part finely screened peat moss, and one part sand. Still another is eight parts screened peat moss, two parts sand, and one part granulated charcoal. Growers in areas where fresh sphagnum moss is obtainable, as in the Pacific Northwest, can use it to advantage in the seedling mix. A fine grade of chopped tree fern is good, either plain or mixed with seedling grade bark. Whatever the composition of the mixture, it should be fluffy or open, and should not pack hard in the pots. It should be easy to keep damp.

Flask seedlings are subject to "damp-off," an infection by a soil fungus that rots the stem at ground level and can destroy seedlings overnight. Although bark is less likely to carry infection than osmunda or soil, it is wise to sterilize it, or any of the mixtures, before putting seedlings in it. Put the potting material in a large pan, dampen it, and bake it for an hour at 250° in the oven. After it has cooled you may need to dampen it again before using it.

Pots should have one-third of their depth filled with drainage material; flats should have a layer of fine gravel laid over the screen. They are then filled with potting medium to within one-half inch of their rim.

Fig. 10-2 Transplanting flask seedlings into a flat. Make a little hole in the medium, set a seedling in place, and press the material around its roots.

Now remove the seedlings from the flask. Open the flask and pour into it one-half cup of water that is about room temperature. Swirl the flask, and pour out the water and the seedlings that have come loose from the agar into a shallow bowl. Repeat a time or two. If some of the seedlings are deeply embedded in the agar, reach into the flask with a dinner knife and cut out the section of agar containing them. Let them remain in the water until all of the agar is dissolved from their roots. You can tease away stubborn bits if necessary.

The seedlings are then put in a fungicide solution, such as Wilson's Anti-Damp, made up by adding two teaspoonfuls to a quart of water, or Natriphene made up according to the directions on the label. They will remain in this until you pot them. Set out three shallow bowls and put some of the fungicide solution into each. Then sort the seedlings as to size, putting the largest into one bowl, the average size into the next, and the smallest ones and those that have not gone beyond the protocorm stage in the last. Sorting them at this time will facilitate potting, because it is wise to put plants of about equal size together. Also, it saves the eye strain that results from looking through the whole batch each time for another seedling of the size you want at the moment.

I like to use small forceps to pick up the seedlings and put them in the pot. An old pair from someone's high school biology dissecting kit is good. Bend the tips a little so that they come together with just enough space between them to lift a seedling but not to pinch it. A pointed stick or a pencil will do for a tool to make the hole into which the seedling will go.

Beginning at one side of the pot or flat, make a little hole in the potting material, set a seedling in it, and gently push the material together around its roots. The seedlings should be set so that the level of the potting material comes just at the juncture of roots and stem. Some little plants will have nice straight short roots that are easily put in the hole. Others may have long curled roots that defy being set in place. Don't worry if the tips of the roots protrude above the surface. They will continue growth, and the plant will make new ones that will go into the medium. Just be sure that the plant itself is firmly in place. Place the seedlings about a half inch apart, allowing perhaps a little more space between very large ones. Fill a pot by putting the plants in concentric circles, and a flat by putting them in rows.

Prepare a dilute fertilizer solution, one-quarter

teaspoon of any complete orchid fertilizer to a gallon, and give each pot or flat a mist spray with this as soon as you finish potting it. Label each community with the name of the cross and the date.

After you have potted all of the large and average size seedlings, you are faced with the problem of what to do with the smallest ones and those that are still protocorms. If the flask yielded a generous number of seedlings, you may by now have all that you can take care of, and you may not wish to keep the less well developed ones. But if the flask was sparsely populated, or if the cross is a particularly valuable or intriguing one, you should save every plant. The left-overs may take longer to reach flowering size, but on the other hand, if their small size was the result of crowding in the flask, they will make a spurt of growth when they are transplanted. Early in my growing experience, after potting a tremendous number of seedlings, I ran out of pots, yet I didn't want to discard the least seedlings. So I put clean sand in a glass pie plate, wet it with nutrient solution comparable to "Ohio W.P." and set the little plants in it, even the protocorms. I covered it with a pane of glass and set it on the living room table. As the months went by I sprayed the plants with nutrient solution whenever the sand appeared to be drying. Each day I propped open the glass lid for a little while for ventilation. A large percentage of the seedlings grew very nicely. About half of the protocorms died, but to my surprise the rest developed good little leaves and roots. Although these were way behind their sisters out of the flask, they eventually matured into flowering plants.

A better method for handling these smallest seedlings is to put them in a community pot in bark screenings dampened with fertilizer solution, and then put the whole pot in a polyethylene bag and close the top with a rubber band. In place of the pot a glass jar can be used, filled two-thirds of its depth with bark screenings dampened with fertilizer solution, and then covered with polyethylene film fastened by a rubber band. Such pots or jars may be kept along with regular communities in a seedling box. Protocorms may be put in flasks if you can prepare them.

Community seedlings need a constantly damp environment, which is most easily furnished by a box or case such as shown in Fig. 10-3. One can be made from a fruit lug, or any wooden box about eight inches deep. The lid can be covered with polyethylene film or be made of glass, and should be hinged to the box. If you have a great many

Fig. 10-3 Community pots and flats need a damp atmosphere. A wooden box with a glass lid makes a good growing case for them.

community pots you can keep them on a bench with board sides and covered by a hinged sash.

A night temperature of 60° is necessary to keep the seedlings growing well, and they can be grown at this night temperature until maturity. They will grow a little faster if you can give them a night temperature of 65°. Perhaps a heating cable in an enclosure will do the job.

Community seedlings should be started with about the same amount of light they had in the flasks, about 200 foot-candles. Strong light will bleach the leaves and stunt their growth. Shade can be furnished by laying two thicknesses of cheesecloth over the lid of the box, or the boxes can be kept in an area curtained by cheesecloth. After about two months, gradually increase the light so that by the latter part of the year they are receiving 500 foot-candles. Growth can be accelerated by giving extra hours of light, up to a 16 hour day. See page 123.

It is important to keep the seedlings growing vigorously, and for this reason they should not be allowed to dry out. Spraying with a fine mist once a day may be all the watering necessary. The spray will wet the box and the pots, and so help maintain a humid atmosphere. But watch the potting material closely, checking down into the pots from time to time. It must be kept soft and moist, and water should be given in the pots when needed. Young seedlings require more water than mature plants, yet they must not be allowed to remain sopping wet. It doesn't take a very strong stream of water to wash the little plants out of the pots. For watering, either let the mist sprayer run long enough to wet the medium thoroughly, or use a

Home Orchid Growing

Fig. 10-4 Glass jars containing fir bark screenings (with sand added if desired) make good growing cases for seedlings just out of the flask. The jar at the right has newly transplanted seedlings, the one on the left older ones. This method is especially useful for the smallest, least well developed seedlings from a flask. (*Courtesy A. J. Pillichody*)

very gentle water breaker. Once a week add fertilizer to the water, one-quarter teaspoon to the gallon at first, and then increase the strength to one-half teaspoon per gallon.

Although the seedlings require a humid atmosphere, they will benefit from some ventilation. Moisture will condense in drops on the lid during the night. During the warm part of the day, prop the lid open a few inches to let this excess moisture dry off. Then close the lid. Ventilation will discourage the development of fungus infections. If the box stays too wet even with ventilation, drill a few holes in opposite sides to allow a little air movement, or leave the lid open for longer periods. Pots enclosed by film do not have to be opened in this way, for the film excludes fungus spores. However, spores that were present when the film cover was put on can germinate, so watch them carefully.

Damping-off can occur even though the potting medium and seedlings were disinfected originally. Use an occasional preventive spray of Wilson's Anti-Damp or Natriphene. If you notice any seedlings turning brown and watery, remove the whole container from the box and drench it thoroughly with the fungicide.

Slugs and snails are vicious enemies. One slug can mow down a pot full of seedlings in short order. Slugs are easier to control than snails, however, and they are easier to see. Poisons containing metaldehyde are used to control both, but you should not wait until you see them. Dust the communities with a powder form, or spray them with a liquid containing metaldehyde every month or six weeks.

Some seedlings may make exceptional growth during the first six months of their stay in communities. Even though you may be tempted to put them in individual pots at this time, it would be best to separate them and replant them in communities, with more space per plant, continuing their care as before.

INDIVIDUAL POTS

After spending a year in communities, most of the seedlings should be ready for individual pots. They will now be fat little plants, with thick waxy leaves. Some will have outstripped the rest, so that while the average plant may be an inch and one-half tall, with leaves one-half inch wide, others may be taller or broader. As always, a few will lag

Seedlings from Flask to Bloom   119

Fig. 10-5 A flat of husky seedlings ready to be moved into individual pots. (*Courtesy Rod McLellan Co.*)

behind the rest, and these slower ones can well go back into communities for another few months.

You may now switch to osmunda fiber if you prefer it for your plants in general. Little seedlings are not difficult to pot in osmunda, as are larger plants, and the fiber holds them firmly in the pot.

For osmunda we generally choose two sizes of pots, one-and-three-quarter-inch for the average plants, two-inch for the largest ones. For bark we put the average plants in two-inch pots and the largest ones in two and one-half inch ones. Bark may be a seedlings grade of perhaps one-eighth to one-quarter inch size, or you may continue with the 0-¼" grade. A mixture of bark and tree fern may also be used. Osmunda fiber should be the soft brown kind, sometimes called "golden." Pots should have two or three pieces of crock in the bottom. One ingenious grower uses styrofoam coffee cups as pots, with holes punched in their sides.

Chunks of osmunda fiber should be thoroughly wetted and allowed to drain, and then be cut into various size pieces. Take a seedling in your hand and lay a small chunk of fiber on each side of the roots, forming a cube-shaped sandwich. The circumference of the cube should be about twice that of the pot. Then, squeezing the sandwich together firmly, push it into the pot. If the amount of fiber was correctly estimated, it should completely fill the pot and be quite firm in consistency, not as hard as for adult plants, but not open or loose either. If you underestimated the amount of fiber to give the desired result, work in a little more, pressing it between the sides of the pot and the fiber already in place. The plant should be situated with the level of the fiber just above the root crown.

To prepare bark or any of the mixes dampen them first, then drain off the water. Hold a seedling in the pot so that its root crown comes just below the level of the pot rim, and pour the medium in around it, wiggling it in among the roots with your fingers. When the pot is full, thump the pot firmly on the bench a few times to settle the medium, and add more if needed. Then gently press it down all around the inside edges of the pot with your fingers. Do not force it in too roughly, else you may break the roots. A piece of stiff wire, cut just longer than the diameter of the pot, can be used to hold the plant in place. Press it across the rhizome, wedging it into the pot.

Put a label in each pot. This should be a routine part of the potting process, not only because it is more interesting to know what each plant is, but because a plant without a label is technically an "unknown" for the rest of its life. You may think you can remember that this group is cross such-and-such, and that that group is cross so-and-so. But pretty soon the plants will all look alike to you. Groups may be shoved together to make room for additional plants, and soon their identity is lost.

The newly potted seedlings should be shaded for the first few weeks to receive about 500 foot-candles of light. During this time, which is a recovery period, they should be syringed lightly several times a day in bright weather to reduce loss of water until their roots are again active. Night temperature can be 60°, but as with communities, they will grow a little faster with nights of 65°. They benefit from somewhat higher humidity than needed by adult plants, and although they should not be kept in as close an atmosphere as the communities, some means of giving them a humid atmosphere should be devised. A covered bench, suggested above for accommodating a large number of community pots, can be used for seedlings newly put in individual pots. The cover of the bench should be propped open for a fair part of each day. Another method is to fasten polyethylene film to a frame built around the seedlings. After the recovery period, the light should be gradually increased until they are receiving 1,000 foot-candles.

As with younger seedlings, plants of this age should not be allowed to become dry. Water them often enough to keep the medium damp. For bark, this will mean a daily watering until the bark begins to hold water efficiently, then perhaps they will need watering only every other day, or in cool weather every third day. Osmunda fiber will not need to be watered as frequently. Use a water breaker for either medium, as the full force of the hose can not only wash the plants out of the pots, but can tip over the pots themselves.

Plants in bark and mixes should be given fertilizer every other watering. One-half teaspoon of fertilizer to a gallon of water is a good concentration. Plants in osmunda fiber should not be fertilized until they are making active new roots, and then they may be fed every other week with the same strength used for plants in bark. For osmunda fiber use a 10-10-10 fertilizer, and for bark a 30-10-10.

TO THREE- AND FOUR-INCH POTS

After the first eight months in the individual pots, the plants will be sure to show quite a striking difference in size. They are then between two and a half and three years old. A few will be large enough to go into four-inch pots, while most will require only three-inch ones. Seedlings appreciate being shifted to fresh medium, so that even those that have not made much progress should be re-potted at this time.

It is a simple matter to remove a seedling from any of the mixes. Tap it out, give it a few gentle shakes and separate the roots a bit to loosen the bark and allow most of it to fall away. It is not necessary to remove bits that cling tightly to the roots. This is a good time to check for evidence of snails. If any are found, or if the roots look as if they have had bites taken out of them, dust the roots with a metaldehyde powder or dip them in a metaldehyde solution. Examine the roots and trim away any that are rotted. Roots that have grown over the side of the pot may be put inside of the new one if they will conform to the space. Otherwise trim them back to a two-inch stub. All of the roots, including the cut stubs, will send out branch roots in a short time.

Place the plant in its new pot, prepared with drainage material and fill in with fresh, dampened medium. This time bark may be a little coarser, perhaps the one-quarter to one-half-inch size. But in a dry climate it may be well to continue wtih the seedling grade for another year, or to use some tree fern mixed with the bark. To hold the rhizome down in the pot at the proper level, use a piece of wire described above.

If osmunda fiber is to be used, prepare the fiber and the pots as before. It is not necessary to remove the fiber from around the plant; many growers just transfer it intact. We like to loosen the ball a little by pulling away some sections of fiber that do not have roots in them. We then fit a few pieces around the old ball, set it in the new pot, and fill in with chunks of fiber that can be worked in with a potting

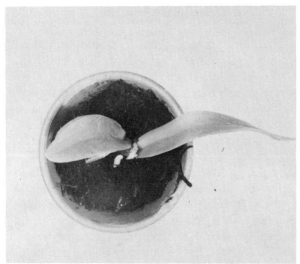

Fig. 10-6 Transplanting from community pot to individual pot in osmunda fiber. UPPER LEFT, a community pot of seedlings removed from the pot. UPPER RIGHT, seedlings separated from the fiber. Note difference in rate of development. LOWER LEFT, place a chunk of fiber on each side of the roots. Judge amount necessary to fill tightly the pot into which the seedling is going. LOWER RIGHT, the potted seedling. If fiber is not firm, press the ball toward the center and add a few more pieces of fiber.

stick. The fiber should be quite firm, but not hard.

Plants of this age should be staked as the next growth will double the present height of the plant. Stakes especially made for use with bark can be obtained from orchid supply companies, and these are a great help. They come in a number of designs, but all hold firmly to the rim of the pot, giving a rigid support for the plant. A straight steel stake can be used for osmunda, driven into the center of the pot beside the plant. Gently tie the tallest growth to the stake.

Seedlings in three- and four-inch pots can be placed on the open bench. Starting with 1,000 foot-candles of light, gradually increase the light so that by the end of the year they are receiving 2,000 foot-candles. Since they now occupy a larger area, it may be difficult to continue the 65° night temperature for them. They will do very nicely with the 55° to 60° nights usually maintained in the cattleya house. If you have a way of maintaining a 60° to 65° night temperature, they will grow a little faster, however. After this, their fourth year, the vigorous ones are going to be treated in the same way as adult plants, and should be gradually worked up to adult conditions. Keep them growing steadily. Do not let them dry out, and give them a mist spray on bright days. Continue the same vigil against slugs, snails and insects, and include the seedlings in the general treatment of the greenhouse for these pests. As before, give fertilizer to the plants in bark at every other watering, and to those in osmunda every other week.

FOUR- AND FIVE-INCH POTS

All the plants that have outgrown the three- and four-inch pots are shifted on to the next size, the threes into fours, and the fours into fives. Some will have developed two or three leads, an indication of vigor that is most welcome. Do not divide them. These are the specimen plants of the future. If they are large enough to justify it, move them into six-inch pots. If one of these plants with many leads turns out to be of fine quality, and if it carries on its eagerness to multiply its leads, some day you will have many wonderful plants from this one seedling.

Heretofore we have not had to consider any particular growth phase in repotting seedlings. But from now on it is best to pot them just as a new set of roots begins to form. Those in osmunda should be potted hard, as for adult plants. When they have resumed active growth, put them alongside the mature plants in your greenhouse and care for them in every way as you do the older plants.

FIRST FLOWERING

It would be quite difficult to choose any one stage in the life of a seedling as the most exciting. Their development in the flask is beautiful to watch. Their year in communities, which sees them transformed from fragile little things into husky youngsters, is a joy. Their further development in individual pots is most rewarding, for you can see that they are beginning to grow up. An array of healthy, perky, bright green seedlings is a sight almost as lovely as an array of flowers, and an achievement to be proud of. But it is really thrilling as they approach maturity and you know that flowering is not far off. A few may flower at the age of four years, many at the age of five years, while some will take longer. The average age of flowering used to be seven years, but better cultural methods have shortened the time and we do not have to wait so long nowadays for their first blooms.

There are always some laggards in any group of seedlings. Some may still be only large enough for three-inch pots when the rest have moved on to fours and fives. The rate of development is not necessarily related to the quality of the flowers they will eventually produce. Some of the slow ones may give just as good flowers as the faster growing ones, a few even better.

The most vigorous of the plants are usually the first to flower. Others may produce sheaths but no flowers, showing at least that they are nearly ready to bloom. The first flowers may or may not show what a plant is capable of doing. A big stocky plant should give good flowers its first time, with more than one to the stem. But many give only one flower, and often the first effort is smaller and not so well colored or of as heavy substance as subsequent flowers will be. The second flowering is a better test of the capabilities of a plant. Don't write off a plant that performs poorly the first time. We can't say that it will necessarily do better the next time, but at least give it a chance to do so. Sometimes the second flowering is an incredible improvement.

You can get some idea of the value of the cross from the flowering of the first group of seedlings. If it is uniformly good, it indicates that the rest will also be good. If only one or two of a fair number have good flowers, you may have a cross in which the percentage of good plants will be low, but perhaps the good ones will by themselves make up for the trouble of raising the cross.

ACCELERATING THE GROWTH OF SEEDLINGS

Most seedlings make their best growth during the long days and warmer nights of summer. Their growth is speeded up somewhat during the winter by giving them a night temperature of 65°, as suggested earlier in this chapter. Growth can be speeded up even more by giving them a 16-hour day by means of artificial lighting and for this Gro-Lux lights are sufficient, or a combination of Gro-Lux with cool white fluorescent, two tubes per 25 inch wide bench. It is not too difficult a matter to give additional light to a few community pots. The light is turned on at sundown and turned off when it has brought the total daylength to sixteen hours. Care must be taken not to let the light reach other plants in the greenhouse whose flowering schedule might be altered by it (See Chapter 7). Long days may be started while the seedlings are in the flask, and continued until the plants approach flowering size. Each phase of their growth should thus be shortened by a few months, bringing them into flower perhaps a year or a year and a half earlier than normal. Perhaps, however, you can manage lights only while the plants are in flasks and communities, finding it difficult to light the greater area they will occupy when they go into individual pots. Giving them long days for just their first year or two will give you an advantage in the ultimate time it takes them to reach flowering size.

Herbert Hager worked out a schedule which brings 10 percent of a batch of cattleya seedlings into flower in two and a half years from seed. About 80 percent of the batch will flower at three years, and the remaining few will flower a year or so later. His program involves stepping up the night temperature, increasing the daylight intensity by faster jumps and giving them a 16-hour day all year round. It is truly a forcing program, but its advantage is that you can very soon learn whether a cross is a valuable one or whether it should be culled. Mr. Hager warned that in order to make use of the higher night temperature along with the 16-hour days, the plants must have a great deal of natural sunshine, and that it is therefore wise to try his program only in areas where this is possible. At the time of his published report he was growing his plants for the most part in osmunda fiber. He did not specify the concentration of fertilizer to use, or the frequency of applying it, but indicated that the plants should be fertilized heavily. We would venture a guess that in a bark medium this would mean fertilizing at every watering, either with the one-half teaspoon per gallon concentration we have recommended elsewhere, or possibly even up to one teaspoon per gallon. In order to carry out Mr. Hager's program, an amateur should have a place where the high night temperatures will not affect other plants, where he can maintain a high humidity, and where the continuous long days will not affect the flowering of other things.

Here is his schedule. The night temperature maintained through all stages of growth is 68° to 70°. Daylength of 16 hours is produced in winter and summer by the use of 100-watt incandescent bulbs in reflectors placed two feet above the plants and five to six feet apart. The day temperature for plants in flasks should be between 80° and 85°, and the relative humidity should be between 50 and 70 percent. Natural light intensity is started at 200 foot-candles and is gradually increased to 400 foot-candles after germination. Plants are left in flasks from four to six months.

For plants in flats, the day temperature should be between 80° and 90° and the relative humidity is from 50 to 70 percent. The natural light intensity is started at 400 foot-candles and is increased to a maximum of 600 foot-candles. Plants are left in the flats for about six months.

The plants are then put in one- and one-half inch pots for a year. During this time the temperature and relative humidity are the same as they are for the flats, but the light intensity is increased up to 1,500 foot-candles. The seedlings are then moved into three-inch pots. The day temperature is kept between 80° and 90°, and the relative humidity usually between 50 and 70 percent although it may sometimes reach 80 percent. The intensity of natural light is gradually increased from 1,500 to 4,000 foot-candles. The first 10 percent will flower at two and one-half years; about 80 percent will flower when they are three years old.

OTHER KINDS OF ORCHIDS

All of the techniques described in this chapter may be used for any kind of orchid. In some kinds the seed pod takes a longer or shorter time to mature than in *Cattleya,* and the length of time for the various stages—flask, community pot, etc.— may be different. Some kinds reach flowering size earlier. But essentially the same methods are used for handling the seed, sowing the flasks, transplanting to community pots, and carrying the plants on to flowering size.

11

THE ORCHID TRIBES

When Nature drew the designs for the orchid family, she combined and recombined the basic flower pattern in every conceivable way and decorated her handiwork with all of the colors at her command. She created forms of beauty so serene, so pure, as to be almost sublime. She created other forms rich and showy, almost sensual. And then she turned or twisted, reduced or enlarged, shortened or lengthened each floral part to make thousands of new forms, lurid or beautiful, giant or pigmy, satanic or humorous. If a mathematician or a statistician were to try to compete with her, he would find that he could put together no new combinations that did not already have a counterpart in her work.

Man has been at work for more than a hundred years, naming and classifying the myriad orchids that have so far been discovered. Yet many are still hidden in jungle wilds or remote places, and each passing year brings to light some form new to his knowledge. It is characteristic of human beings that they must put a name to everything. And it is characteristic of scientists that the name must be so definite, so specific, that there can be no possible confusion of one object with another.

When a new orchid is found, even after it has bloomed and its major characteristics have been observed, it takes patient hours of dissection and study to determine with what group of orchids it belongs. Perhaps it does not fit with any established genus or tribe, and a new category must be made for it. Often the experts do not agree. One may feel that some slight difference is significant enough to warrant the creation of a new genus. Others

may insist that it is only a variation of a kind already classified. When you look up almost any orchid in Bailey's *Standard Cyclopedia of Horticulture,* or any comparable work, you see evidence of past confusion in the chronology of names that have been given to a single species.

The major sorting process, which gives a starting point in the classification of the 25,000 species, is the division into tribes. Each tribe of orchids might be compared to a deck of cards, which you sort into a pack because of the distinctive design on the back of each one. As the deck is divided into suits, each with its outstanding mark, so the tribe is divided into genera, (sing., genus) each with its own characteristic features. Every card in a suit differs from every other by the picture on it, or the number. Which brings us to the final division of the genus, the species (sing., also species). The species belonging to any one genus bear the hallmark of the genus, but each is different from the rest by some individual feature.

When you see the six of hearts, you have no doubt in what suit it belongs, or which card in the suit it is. But you cannot say just "six" or just "hearts." Similarly you cannot specify what member of the genus you mean by saying just *"Cattleya,"* for there are many members of the genus *Cattleya.* Nor can you say just "labiata," for that name may refer to a member of another genus. As soon as you say *"Cattleya labiata"* you erase all confusion, for there is no other kind of orchid that goes by those two names together. For clarity and convenience, it is an established rule to give the name of the genus first, as *Cattleya,* and then the specific name, as *labiata.*

Through the years past it has been more or less customary to capitalize those species names which have been created from proper nouns and to use lower case for all other species names. It is now becoming a general practice to use lower case uniformly for all species names, whether purely descriptive or made from proper nouns. Therefore, in this book (and in most current literature) you will find that species names are not capitalized. *Cattleya Mossiae* becomes *Cattleya mossiae; Cattleya Trianaei, Cattleya trianaei,* and so on. When writing scientifically about the species the name of the person who described each particular one is given immediately after the species name, *as Cattleya labiata* Ldl. (the abbreviation for Lindley). This not only gives credit to the botanist who established it, but points out exactly which designation you mean when there are possible synonyms.

Hybrid names are capitalized and are not italicized, but the generic name is retained in italics. A hybrid name is now written, for instance, *Cattleya* Bow Bells. We are not using in this book the system of putting an x in front of the hybrid name, as *Cattleya* x Bow Bells.

Not quite so easy to follow is another ruling, recently adopted in practice, that generic names are italicized only when the fact of their being genera is emphasized. We might, for instance, write, "He has many kinds of orchids—cattleyas, oncidiums, cymbidiums." But if we were to write specifically of the genus, we might put it this way "In *Cattleya* there are four pollinia."

A species often has a number of botanical variations distinct enough to merit an additional descriptive or varietal name. For instance, *Cattleya dowiana* has a yellow form designated *Cattleya dowiana,* variety *aurea, Dendrobium fimbriatum* has a form with a spot of deep purple on the lip called *Dendrobium fimbriatum,* variety *oculatum.* These botanical varieties (which might also be considered subspecies) occur in nature, usually in some numbers and often in a separate geographical location. The word variety may be abbreviated var., or v.

A grower who owns a particularly fine individual plant, whether species or hybrid, may designate it by a varietal name of its own. This name is added to the full name of the plant and is set off in single quotes. A famous example is *Cymbidium* Alexanderi 'Westonbirt,' which has become the ancestor of many of the fine modern hybrids. Suppose you own a particularly beautiful *Cattleya trianaei,* of richer color or heavier substance than other members of the species, and you wish to mark this plant to separate it from the others. You could call it *Cattleya trianaei* 'Supreme' or *Cattleya trianaei* 'Aristocrat,' or 'Jones,' or anything else you wished. When you divide this plant you would put this name on each division, and when you again divide the divisions the name would still follow, so that you would keep track of each and every division made from the original plant. The original plant and all of its divisions are called a "clone." The importance of identifying with certainty the divisions of a valuable plant is obvious. The members of a clone have an additional value in experimental work, because results are more decisive when the plants used are identical in every way. An individual plant designated by its own varietal name is considered a horticultural variety, as opposed to a botanical variety.

Most orchid tribes are so prolific that it would take a lifetime to collect a single specimen of all of the species included in just one tribe, to say nothing of the varieties of each species. Should you start on such a project, you might run into difficulties. Some tribes spread over a geographical area that includes all sorts of climatic conditions, so that its members may not be suited to the conditions of a single greenhouse. In any tribe, of course, there are some members more desirable for cultivation than others. Unless you have the urge to own every species in a tribe, you will select from many tribes those that have a special appeal for you. You may choose a plant for its graceful habit, its showy flowers, its intriguing shape, unusual coloring, delightful fragrance, or even for its size, for instance, a dwarf plant whose minuteness is a charm in itself.

Botanists are interested in all kinds of plants, however insignificant they may seem to most people. Because of this, orchids that are of no value as cut flowers, or that are not widely known, are often called "botanicals." Many of the botanicals are every bit as lovely as those with which we have better acquaintance, and these are now finding a place alongside their more popular relatives. Many amateurs find their chief interest in orchids not usually seen in the florist shop or in general collections.

Genera are known which have as many as 2,000 species. For others only two or three species are known, and the rest run somewhere between these

Home Orchid Growing

extremes. Obviously nothing less than an encyclopedia could describe all of the species.

Certain genera have been acclaimed by the public as the most beautiful and the most useful. Others, not as valuable commercially, are loved by collectors. Instead of presenting them to you as disconnected genera, each will be introduced along with the other members of its tribe. Many lovely orchids exist in the less well-known genera. To learn to know them in their relation to the more famous ones is to acquire a better understanding of them.

The presentation of the orchids in this book follows the system given in Bailey's *Standard Cyclopedia of Horticulture*. Another system of classification, held in high esteem by botanists, is that of Rudolph Schlechter, a very comprehensive work organized somewhat differently from Bailey's. Schlechter divides the orchids into four large tribes, and groups the closely related genera within these tribes into sub-tribes. Bailey carries his division directly to the groups of related genera, which he calls tribes, and does not employ sub-tribes. Bailey's tribes include essentially the genera grouped by Schlechter into sub-tribes. Bailey's key carries the classification to genera and is therefore especially useful to amateurs, particularly beginners. Bailey's *Standard Cyclopedia of Horticulture* is available at most libraries, another point in its favor. By using Bailey's key, a person wishing to find out "what kind of orchid this is" can usually track it to its genus. Many kinds can then be identified as to species by the descriptions in Bailey's text. The text does not contain every species of every genus, nor does any other work. We have added some not included in Bailey. There are 1,000 species of Dendrobiums alone, perhaps that many Oncidiums and Epidendrums, and hundreds in many others of the over 600 genera. Bailey gives many of those with which we are likely to come in contact, and books devoted to the orchids of specific regions are a great help.

The key to the tribes is given in Appendix A and contains more kinds than can be included in this book, for example the terrestrial ones native to the temperate zones. The tribes we shall discuss are those that contain the kinds most popular with and interesting to amateurs, and their less well known relatives, some of which are becoming better known every day.

The genera included in any one tribe are closely related. Certain basic structural similarities bind them together in spite of such apparent gross differences as size of plants and flower parts. Also, they are closely related genetically, for most of the genera within a tribe will interbreed. Inter-generic crosses are more fruitful with some genera than others, however, and, of course, some are more desirable aesthetically.

Hybrid names are made in two ways. Where only two species are involved the name is usually a convenient combination of them, for example *Epicattleya* (*Epidendrum* × *Cattleya*). Where more than two are involved the combinations can become quite awkward, although many are used, as in *Brassolaeliocattleya* (*Brassavola* × *Laelia* × *Cattleya*). Such tri- and quadri-generic hybrids are otherwise given the name of a person, usually someone outstanding in the orchid field, for example *Kirchara* (*Epidendrum* × *Sophronitis* × *Laelia* × *Cattleya*). The names are too numerous to list in this book, although some are given with each of the more important tribes. New combinations of genera are being made from year to year, with consequent new hybrid generic names. Occasionally the same name has been used in the past for completely different hybrid genera. Old spellings have been improved upon for greater clarity. Taxonomic changes have been made with consequent confusion as to which names, the old or the new, to continue in registration of hybrids. Sometimes little confusion would ensue and the new name is adopted by the registration committee. Sometimes utter confusion would result and it is decided to keep the old name for purely horticultural purposes, emphasizing meanwhile that the correct botanical name should be used scientifically.

Two works will greatly aid the orchid grower in keeping hybrid names straight and in identifying the parentage of labeled plants. One is "Natural and Artificial Hybrid Generic Names of Orchids" by Leslie A. Garay and Herman R. Sweet. The other is "Handbook of Orchid Nomenclature and Registration," published by The International Orchid Commission on Classification, Nomenclature, and Registration. It is available through the American Orchid Society, Inc.

12

THE AERIDES TRIBE

The genera belonging to this tribe number about eighteen, and include some of the loveliest orchids known—*Phalaenopsis* and *Vanda,* whose sprays of subtly tinted, sweetly rounded flowers are sublime among flowers; *Angraecum,* one species of which was made famous by Darwin's speculation about its long spur; and *Aerides,* which has dense clusters of fragrant little flowers of crystalline or waxy texture. Many of the other genera are equally attractive.

The growth habit of the Aerides tribe is monopodial, illustrated by the drawing on page 11. They do not have a rhizome, but instead have a single upright stem and grow by adding new leaves to the top and new roots from between the leaves along the stem. Flower stems come from the axils of the leaves. They are epiphytic, but do not withstand drying as well as kinds equipped with pseudobulbs. Their fleshy leaves, heavy stems, and large roots do store some water, however.

The genera range natively from the Philippine Islands through the Asiatic tropics and into Australia and Africa, although each genus inhabits its own particular area in this vast range. For the most part, they live in climates that are warm and humid, some being subjected to heavy rains the year round, others to more moderate amounts of precipitation. They are found growing mostly on trees, occasionally on rocks.

PHALAENOPSIS

The "moth orchid" (Greek, *phaluna* meaning moth, *-opsis* meaning resembling) receives its name from its similarity to some tropical moths. There are about fifty species, not all of which are well known in cultivation. Some which are quite rare are now proving their worth in hybridization. The beautiful flowers would be worth growing even if they lasted only a few days, but the fact that many last for from two to five months and that bloom succession keeps them in flower for much longer makes them all the more desirable. They are not light-demanding, a fact which, together with their preference for 65° nights, makes them easy to grow in the house. (See chapter 24.)

The foliage is attractive. The long, broad curving leaves may be shiny or leathery, plain green or mottled with grayish green, often purple underneath. They are from four to fifteen inches long, so that a mature plant can cover a fairly broad area. The plants increase in height only slowly, and add but one or two new leaves a year. Mature plants retain an average of five or six leaves, although a few individuals may retain more. The robust, often flattened roots appear from the stem between mature leaves and grow down into the pot or outside of it to wander to some lengths. The flower spikes come from the axils of the lowermost leaves, often from the region where leaves have fallen, and therefore from the older portion of the plant.

The flowers divide themselves structurally into two groups. The first group, called Euphalaenopsis, is characterized by appendages on the lip and by petals much broader than the sepals. The second group, Stauroglottis, has petals similar to the sepals, and a lip without appendages. In both groups

Fig. 12-1 A house of Phalaenopsis, where breath-taking beauty abounds for months on end. (*Courtesy Jones and Scully, Inc*)

the variously shaped lip is united with an extension of the basal part of the column, called the column "foot."

In general, the growing season, the period during which new leaves and roots are produced, is from spring through fall, with the flower spikes appearing from late summer into winter. Some individuals are quite orderly in this matter, but a large percentage vary, particularly among the hybrids, so that flower spikes may be started at almost any time of the year without regard to the state of growth of the plant.

The flower spike is tall and arching in most species, usually unbranched in the white species, branched in some others. Some plants develop all of the buds on a spike at about the same time so that the whole spray is open at once. Others open the basal flowers first, while the tip of the spike continues to form more buds. Plants with the latter habit can remain in flower for the better part of a year, since individual flowers keep for several months and new ones open to replace those that fade. Do not cut off a spike until you are sure it has ceased to form new buds. There is sometimes an interval between fading of the first flowers and development of succeeding ones. In many of the species and hybrids, if the flower stem is cut just below the node that produced the first flower, a branch stem may come from one of the lower nodes, giving a second spray of flowers. Such branch stems may not bear as many flowers as the original spike and sometimes the flowers are smaller. But this is not always true, for we have had excellent secondary spikes of twenty flowers.

When a plant is grown under less than ideal conditions it may not form new flower spikes when an old one is making a branch, so the grower must decide from experience whether to remove a spike entirely or leave it to form a secondary one.

Culture

Potting. Phalaenopsis require rather small containers in proportion to their size and in general need be repotted infrequently. A plant should never be allowed to become run-down, however. With these plants perhaps more than with any other kind you have to find just the right medium for your conditions and your individual type of culture. Some growers simply cannot manage them in bark, for instance, while others like it, and other growers may have difficulty with some other medium. Osmunda fiber is still regarded by many experts as the best medium. A preferred mix among many Florida growers is one-third each of shredded redwood chips, tree fern, and fir bark. Various other media used successfully are: osmunda mixed with tree fern; plain tree fern; plain bark; chunks of coconut fiber; chunks of charcoal; and some of the proprietary mixes.

A plant should be repotted when the medium is no longer good, or when the plant has lost a good many lower leaves and roots, leaving the active part of the plant standing above the medium on a naked stem. Repotting should be done when new roots are developing, preferably when flowering is finished.

To repot, remove the plant and clean off the old medium. With your fingers break off the old inactive stub of the stem below the ring of living roots. Cut back the lower roots to a length that will fit in the new pot. These stubs will branch, giving new roots that will go directly into the medium, providing a firm foothold for the plant. Allow the upper roots to maintain their natural position, whether in or out of the pot. Osmunda fiber need not be packed as hard as for cattleyas, but it should be firm. Bark, or chunks of charcoal, should be of very coarse grade (large size pieces), and potting is done as directed for cattleyas. The plant should be centered in the pot, and in any medium the basal part should be placed an inch or so down into the potting material.

Many growers place the plants on racks so that they are tilted to prevent collection of water in

Home Orchid Growing

the leaf crown, but they may also be grown upright on benches. Delightful hanging containers and mounts made of tree fern are used in areas where the humidity can be maintained sufficiently high. On the latter the plant is fastened with string or wire until the roots take hold, and these are particularly attractive for kinds that make young plantlets from flowering stems, which can then be trained to root at intervals around the mount, covering it eventually with a solid mass of plants.

After potting, water sparingly until new roots are well formed. Keep the atmosphere humid (60 to 70 percent relative humidity) and spray the plants with a fine mist once or twice a day. Since Phalaenopsis is not grown in strong light, additional shade after potting is not always necessary, but if the leaves become limp in spite of mistings the light should be reduced to about 500 foot-candles till the plants recover.

Temperature.   These plants from the hot, humid tropics of Asia must be kept gently warm. The night temperature should not go below 60°, as temperatures below this cause growth to be poor and flower buds to drop. Actually, the plants do better with temperatures somewhat above 60° at night, preferably closer to 65°. Day temperature should be ten degrees higher in the winter, but can go higher in the summer with the usual precautions about excessive heat.

Water.   The plants should be watered frequently enough to prevent the medium from ever becoming bone dry, but they do not like to be kept sopping wet. Watering needs to be more frequent in dry climates than in damp ones, and of course, more frequent when plants are in bark than in osmunda fiber. The atmosphere should be kept humid, by damping down and spraying the benches between the plants if humidity is not a great problem in your area, or by means of humidifying equipment in dry climates. The plants welcome light mist sprays on bright days, but they must dry off by night. The growth tends to be succulent and is particularly liable to damage if kept wet. During the winter, watch for drip from the roof and move any plants that might catch the water.

Feeding.   Phalaenopsis benefits from applications of fertilizers. In osmunda a 10-10-10 formula given every two or three weeks at a concentration of one-half teaspoonful to a gallon of water is about

right. A 10-10-10 formula may also be used for charcoal and coconut fiber, at every other watering. With bark a 30-10-10 formula should be used, unless some other means is devised for giving the higher nitrogen needed. Watch the plants carefully and adjust the frequency and concentration to their needs.

Light.   Strong light makes small hard plants that do not do well. Phalaenopsis does best in less than half the light intensity allowed cattleyas. During the summer they should be given between 500 and 1,000 foot-candles. Toward fall increase the light gradually to encourage flowering and toughen the plants somewhat, and by winter let them have about 1,500 to 2,000 foot-candles.

Ventilation and air movement.   In a greenhouse, air movement is absolutely necessary for Phalaenopsis. The moving air should be damp, and this means that unless the climate provides a high humidity some means of adding water to the moving air should be provided. Whenever possible open the ventilators, at least a crack, but do not let cold air blow on the plants. Ventilation and air movement help keep the plants healthy at all times but are particularly important to prevent spotting of flowers by the Botrytis fungus.

Phalaenopsis mite.   The most vicious enemies of Phalaenopsis, and of many other genera, are the false spider mites. The species *Tenuipalpus pacificus* is called the Phalaenopsis mite because of its affinity for this genus but it also attacks other orchids. There are also very similar species of the genus *Brevipalpus* that resemble it in appearance and activity and which also attack *Phalaenopsis* and other genera. The false spider mites wreak devastating damage to the leaves, causing first irregularly shaped yellow flecks or spots that become pitted or sunken then necrotic, remaining white or gray or turning brown, and causing early death of the leaves. The damage looks much like some fungus or virus diseases. The mites themselves are invisible to the naked eye, one thing that makes them such cunning enemies, and can just barely be seen with a ten power lens. They are best seen with a low power binocular microscope. Figure 23-15 in section on pests shows a greatly enlarged photograph of *Tenuipalpus pacificus*. Once you have seen this mite and its relatives, or their empty skins, you will not mistake them for the common two-

Fig 12-2a   Phalaenopsis leaf injured by Phalaenopsis mite, *Tenuipalpus pacificus,* one of the false spider mites. Note grayish or whitish scars.

Fig. 12-2b   Closeup of same leaf to show sunken and pitted areas. (*Photos by Tom Northen*)

spotted mite or "red spider." Often each little injured spot on a leaf is occupied by one or more mites, and others may be found hiding along the leaf veins and in the leaf axils. They can usually be found on either leaf surface, and the damage they do involves both surfaces. They spin no webs. The mites are orange or reddish, and their oval eggs are of the same color, laid either free on the leaf or under a deposit of scabby looking material. Not all miticides will kill false spider mites—a few will get both them and the two-spotted mites. Among those effective for both kinds are Dimite, Kelthane, and Chlorobenzilate. Dimite is said to have a particularly long residual action. Two sprayings should be given seven days apart, and then repeated in two weeks. An occasional preventive spray should then be included as part of the regular spray program. The best defense is to examine leaves with any suspicious yellow, brown or gray pits or spots, and take action if false spider mites are found.

Propagation.   Phalaenopsis do not lend themselves as well to vegetative propagation as some other kinds. When side shoots develop on the plants, they can be removed after they have started their own roots. Sometimes young plantlets form from nodes on the flower spike. If a plant that you are repotting is fairly tall and has a good array of roots, you can divide it to leave a basal stump with a few living roots. Often a young plant will develop at the top of the old part. When growing rapidly it can be removed. Any young plantlets such as those described should be potted in sphagnum moss or soft osmunda fiber, and then pot and all should be enclosed in a polyethylene bag to give a damp atmosphere. When such plants are growing vigorously, they can be cared for like seedlings of a comparable size. Very rarely a plantlet is developed on a root.

A method to encourage the formation of plantlets from buds on the basal part of flowering stems has been achieved by Robert M. Scully, Jr. The stem is cut in sections bearing one bud to each, and these are then grown in a seed germinating medium with banana or coconut milk added.

A clean, healthy stem is selected, cleaned thoroughly with 10 percent Clorox or 100 percent ethyl alcohol. The bracts covering the buds are then removed, scraping off the basal part where the bract is attached with care not to injure the bud. Sections are then cut leaving one-half inch above and one and one-fourth inch below the bud. The cuttings are then soaked in 10 percent Clorox for 15-20

Home Orchid Growing

minutes, swirling them at intervals to make the soaking more thorough. Test tubes or vials with screw caps with an inch or so of medium are used, one for each cutting. These must be prepared in advance, and the transfer of the cuttings to them is done under sterile conditions as for seed sowing. The cuttings are removed from the Clorox solution and drained on a sterile surface. A slice from the bottom of each stem (the long end) is taken off to give a fresh surface, and the stem is inserted into the medium in the test tube. The mouth of the tube or vial is flamed, and quickly stoppered. The cuttings are, of course, placed so that the bud points upward. The cultures are grown with 150 foot-candles of light, sixteen hours a day, or can be grown with constant light. The buds start to grow quite rapidly, making little plants ready for potting in four to five months, sometimes longer. Some cuttings may fail along the way, but a fair percentage survive. If contamination occurs, the cutting may be removed, re-sterilized, and put in fresh medium. Sometimes a dark pigment diffuses out of the stem into the medium, and this seems not to be harmful. The young plantlets are grown in the same manner as seedlings.

Growing Phalaenopsis from seed. Pollination is carried out by hand as for other genera. The seed pods mature quickly, about five to six months after pollination. When the pod matures it dries and splits open quite suddenly, so that it should be covered in advance to prevent loss of seed. The seed loses its viability rather soon after it ripens, and while it may be stored in a refrigerator for a while, it should be used before very long. Also, it is more sensitive to disinfecting agents than other kinds. Calcium hypochlorite is the safest to use, and the seed should be sown rapidly so that it does not remain in the solution any longer than absolutely necessary. If you are very speedy, you can use a solution made by dissolving one clorazene tablet in two ounces of water.

The best method is to sow the seed from the green pod. Remove the pod at least a month before it would normally ripen; four to four-and-a-half months from pollination is generally accepted as the best time. Proceed according to the directions given in Chapter 9.

The seedlings grow rapidly and are ready to move out of the flask in six months or so. They may be transferred to flats or to five-inch community pots. They should be kept covered with glass to give them a warm, close atmosphere. When they are ready for individual pots, use the three-inch size. They reach flowering size in about three years, sometimes even less.

The Species: Group I, Euphalaenopsis

The lip in this group bears a pair of appendages, either antenna-like cirri, or slender horns. The petals are broader than the sepals and are contracted at their base into a slender "claw."

Phal. amabilis. This is one of the most popular of the genus, and, with its several varieties, is the basis for most of the modern white hybrids. The leaves are plain green, six to twelve inches long. The tall arching flower stems carry many flowers, each three to five inches in diameter. The pure white sepals and petals are set off by a lip which is tinted with yellow and spotted and streaked with red, and which bears two wavy cirri that fold back from the outer end. Secondary sprays will develop if the stem is cut just below the node that produced the first flower. The plant—which occurs in Java, Borneo, Amboina, New Guinea and Queensland— flowers in the fall and early winter. A form with large well shaped flowers is var. *rimestadiana,* and one that is pink or deep rose is var. *sanderiana.* Two famous plants which formed the background for the breeding line that led to our present day hybrids were the polyploid (6n) *P. amabilis* 'Elizabethae' (*amabilis* × *amabilis* var. *rimestadiana*) and *P. Gilles Gratiot* (*amabilis* var. *rimestadiana* × *aphrodite*). From this line came *P.* Doris, Chieftain, and Winged Victory. With the advent of the tetraploid Doris new possibilities arose as this hybrid proved to have far better keeping quality than others. *Phal.* Doris has contributed this quality to subsequent hybrids such as Grace Palm, Juanita, Dos Pueblos, Vallemar, etc. Recrossing of selected individuals of these, plus back-crossing to plants used previously has led to a group of hybrids that are very much alike genetically and which exhibit near uniformity of perfection.

P. aphrodite (now considered a variety of *amabilis*). White flowers, sometimes flushed with pink, similar to *amabilis* but smaller, and borne in a drooping raceme. The lip is tinted pink and yellow and has two fine, twisted cirri. The leaves are brownish green, ribbed down the center, and about a foot long. Occurs in Java and the Philippines. Flowers in the spring and summer.

P. schilleriana. Marvelous drooping flower

sprays, branched and carrying as many as a hundred flowers in tones of rosy-lilac, make this a favorite species. The plants have long leaves, mottled with grayish white, and purple underneath. The roots are flat and rough. The flowers are about three inches across. The rosy tone of the petals and sepals pales toward the edges. The lip is of the same color, dotted with red. Instead of cirri, it has a pair of divergent horns at its tip. It occurs in the Philippines and flowers in the spring. This species is much used in hybridization, for the purpose of combining its branched, heavily flowered inflorescence with the heavier substance and larger size of the white hybrids.

P. stuartiana. This charming species has small, oddly colored flowers. The leaves are mottled when young, grayish-green with purple undersides when mature. The sepals are white, the lateral ones pale yellow on the inner half and speckled with red at the base. The petals are white, lightly dotted with purple at the base. The golden-yellow lip is margined with white, spotted with purple, and has a pair of horns at its tip. The flowers have especially good keeping qualities and are borne on generously branching sprays. This species occurs in the Philippines and flowers in the winter. It is also used in hybridization.

P. intermedia. A natural hybrid between *aphrodite* and *equestris* (*rosea*), which has been repeated in cultivation. The leaves are generally green above, purple underneath. The flower stem is sometimes branched and bears flowers two inches in diameter. The sepals and petals are white, the petals speckled with rose at the base. The lip has violet side lobes dotted with crimson, and a deep crimson middle lobe bearing a pair of short horns at its apex. It occurs in the Philippines and flowers from March to October.

The Species: Group II, Stauroglottis

The lip of this group is without appendages, and the petals are more nearly the size of the sepals. The plants are in general smaller than those in Group I, and the flowers, though also smaller, are usually brightly colored, often strikingly barred or spotted. The species in this group have been less widely grown than those in Group I, but now that the ultimate in white hybrids has been reached, hybridists have turned to this group, and to the pink species in Group I, for the variety they offer in the creation of new things.

P. amboinensis. From the island of Ambon, west of New Guinea. It is pale yellow with concentric cross bars of cinnamon brown. The sepals are broad, the petals somewhat less so, and the lip is a broad diamond shape. The two- to three-inch flowers are borne on a sometimes branched stem six to nine inches in length. The markings do not show up, or come through only slightly, in hybrids made with white or pink species. Very interesting color and marking combinations are present in hybrids made with species of similar characteristics.

P. cochlearis. A newly discovered species, it is yellow-green with two faint brown bars at the tip of the sepals and petals, and has a pretty lip, decorated with crimson on the white side lobes, with the deeper yellow mid-lobe having radiating lines of red-brown. The flowering stem reaches over a foot in length. It is native to Borneo.

P. cornu-cervi. Yellow-green flowers barred with brown and having a white lip are produced freely on a stem whose shape resembles that of a stag horn. The species is deciduous natively, but apparently requires no rest period in a greenhouse. It occurs in Burma and Java and flowers throughout the year.

P. decumbens. See *Kingiella decumbens.*

P. equestris. This is the correct name for the species so familiarly known as *P. rosea.* The plant has small leaves, plain green with a pronounced notch at the tip. It produces several flower spikes a year and the flowers open over a period of months, keeping the plant in flower nearly all year long. The one inch flowers have rosy purple sepals and petals bordered with white. The side lobes of the lip are pink, while the mid-lobe is brown at

Fig. 12-3 *Phalaenopsis cornu-cervi.* (*Courtesy J. A. Fowlie*)

Home Orchid Growing

the base and bright rose-purple at the end, sometimes striped. The crest can be yellow or white. It occurs in the Philippines and is now being used in hybridization. Its offspring have good substance and shape, and often appear with candy stripes or pink lips.

P. fimbriata. This is another new introduction, and promises green coloring among its hybrids. The flowers are about one to one and a half inches in diameter, with sepals and petals of light lime to apple-green, with a few amethyst spots near the tips of the lateral sepals. The lip is medium to dark amethyst, fringed in white and with a "tooth brush" of hairs on the upper side of the mid-lobe. It is a native of Java.

P. gigantea. This species is so named for its huge plant size, rather than flower size. In nature the leaves reach several feet in length, but in cultivation do not seem to grow so large. The flower spike can be from six to fifteen inches in length and is closely packed with fleshy, two-inch flowers. The very round flowers have a white ground and are spotted with brown or purple-brown. The lip is red-purple. The plants are rare in nature, but have been raised from seed. Mature plants require a coolish spot, with considerable shade. They cannot be kept too wet but like a very humid atmosphere. They are best mounted in a hanging position, and should be misted early in the day in bright weather. The species is native to a narrow region on the island of Borneo.

P. lindenii. The pretty one-and-a-half-inch flowers of this species are pink with an overlay of fine dotted lines of pale purple. The three-lobed lip is unusually large, and the oval mid-lobe is striped with purple. Its hybrid offspring often inherit its lip characteristics and have striped sepals and petals. The generously long flower spike produces many flowers over a long period. It is native to the Philippines, and flowers from March to August.

P. lowii. The plants of this species are not so vigorous as some, and the flowers are small, one and a half to two inches in diameter. They make up for their size by their lovely coloring. The sepals and petals are white, flushed with amethyst toward the base. The middle lobe of the lip is deep violet-purple. The sprays may carry as many as twenty flowers. The species is deciduous in its native environment, Borneo and Burma. It flowers in the summer and requires a drier atmosphere than some.

P. lueddemanniana. This remarkable species has over thirty color forms. A number are rosy-purple of glistening waxy texture, some almost solid color, others striped sparsely or profusely with white. There are also many forms which run from cream to yellow, some with pronounced mottling or bars of brown, one of which bears the most descriptive varietal name *hieroglyphica* and another the name *ochracea*. From these have come a wide variety of hybrids, and the yellow forms are proving valuable in producing yellow offspring. The plants are small and give but few flowers at a time, which are long lasting. The sepals are broader than the petals, and the lip is narrow with a sharp, raised crest down the center bearing a few bristly hairs. It occurs in the Philippines and flowers throughout the year. Plantlets form frequently on old flower stems. An odd characteristic is that after pollination the flowers turn green and remain fleshy while the seed pod ripens.

P. maculata. This species is interesting because of its bright red lip. The flowers are less than three-fourths inch in diameter, creamy white with red-brown markings. It is native to Sarawak, Borneo.

P. mannii. This species gave the first break in the creation of yellow hybrids, and recently a number of succeeding yellows have been made. It is a small flower with slender sepals and petals, yellow, heavily overlaid with brown markings, and an anchor-shaped lip, white with some purple markings at its base. With most of the species in this group their potentialities as parents were not known until they were bred, often giving surprising results. This was true of *P. mannii* with which Lewis Vaughn did pioneering work in breeding yellows. The species is native to Assam, India. It has leaves six to twelve inches long, green, spotted with purple, and a flower spike that is branched and bears ten to fifteen flowers, fragrant and long lasting.

P. mariae. Resembling *lueddemanniana,* this species has yellow flowers that are marked with four transverse bars. The flowers are one and one-half inches across, and the lip is rose-purple with white margins, without bristles. It occurs in the Philippines.

P. micholitzii. Another species that resembles *lueddemanniana.* This one has white or yellow flowers that are not barred. It occurs in the Philippines.

P. sumatrana. A medium sized plant with two-inch flowers that are quite heavy in substance. They are cream-white, barred with red-brown, about two inches in diameter. The lip has erect side lobes with orange spots on the inside, and a long mid-lobe

Fig. 12-4 *Phalaenopsis micholitzii.* (*Courtesy J. A. Fowlie*)

that is white with purple lines on each side of the dense tuft of hairs down the center. It is native to Sumatra, Borneo, and the Malay Peninsula, and flowers in the spring.

P. violacea. This lovely species has two quite definite forms. One from Borneo is pale green or greenish white with a purple lip and a purple suffusion at the base of the dorsal sepal and petals, over the back of the column, and on the inside basal half of the lateral sepals. The lateral sepals converge toward the lip. The form from Malaya is more or less uniformly rosy-purple, with the lateral sepals wide spreading. There are forms of the Malayan type that are paler, as well as an albino variety. Plants of the Malayan type are somewhat smaller than those of the Borneo type, having leaves from six to nine inches in length and flowers of two inches, while those from Borneo run to twelve inches in leaf length and three inches in flower size. Also, the Borneo form is a reluctant breeder, while many hybrids result from the Malayan one.

PARAPHALAENOPSIS

The genus *Paraphalaenopsis* was created for three species which may or may not be justifiably separated from *Phalaenopsis.* They have terete leaves and are all native to western Borneo. To date they have not been bred successfully with *Phalaenopsis.*

Paraphal. denevei. This species has leaves to about two and a half feet long which may be upright or pendulous, usually the latter. Several flowers of two-inch diameter are produced on an erect stem from spring to summer. They are very attractive and long lasting. The petals and sepals are flat with wavy edges, light greenish-yellow to dark yellow-brown. The lip is three lobed with a narrow, blunt, tongue-shaped mid-lobe, and the tips of all lobes are red or red-violet. The crest of the mid-lobe is striped with transverse red lines.

P. laycockii. Much like the former, but with larger flowers that are white suffused with pinkish lavender. The three-lobed lip has erect, twisted side lobes spotted with brown on the inside, and a mid-lobe that is lavender at the tip shading to brown, striped at the base. It is summer flowering.

P. serpentilingua. The name is descriptive of the mid-lobe of the lip, which is long and narrow and forked at the tip. The flowers have quite wavy, moderately broad petals and sepals, which are white with a faint tint of pink. The lip is yellow with stripes of red transversing the mid-lobe, brown tips to the tall, upward-spreading side lobes, and spots on the tall, fleshy, double-pointed crest.

DORITIS

The single species of this genus was originally named *Doritis pulcherrima,* but was later placed in the genus *Phalaenopsis* as both *P. pulcherrima* and *P. esmeralda.* Although it breeds freely with *Phalaenopsis,* certain differences cause it now to be accepted by its original name.

Doritis pulcherrima. The plant grows tall, with many pairs of close-ranked, tough, stiff, six-inch long leaves, and produces young vegetative growths from its base. The three-foot flower stem is branched and gives rise to twenty or so flowers on each branch, opening in succession over a long period. The delightful little flowers are one inch in diameter and of a pale rose-purple varying to darker shades. The side lobes of the lip range from purple to orange to brownish red, while the mid-lobe is purple and pointed in shape. Two cirri are situated behind a crest at the base of the mid-lobe. It spreads natively over an area of Southeast Asia and the Malay Peninsula, and flowers in fall and winter. The variety *buyssoniana* has larger, more richly colored flowers, with more flatly spreading parts.

KINGIELLA

A genus of several species, only one of which is well known, and this has recently been removed from *Phalaenopsis* where it has been called *P. decumbens* and *P. amethystina*.

Kingiella decumbens. Rather a small plant, with narrow, five-inch leaves that are quite thin in substance. The eight-inch flower stem holds many little flowers barely more than half an inch in diameter. The sepals and petals are white, the former purple spotted toward the base; the lip is purple. It flowers more than once a year. It spreads natively through Southeast Asia into Malaysia and the Philippines.

VANDA

This genus of sun-loving, robust plants has won the hearts of orchid growers everywhere. Their flowers are beautifully shaped and exhibit a wondrous blending of colors. They are of excellent substance, keep well, and are adaptable to many uses. According to the habit of the species, from three to eighty blooms may occur on one stem. Their name is the Sanskrit word, Vanda, which was applied in ancient India to the Vanda of Bengal and related orchids.

The fifty or more species range natively through a variety of climates in tropical Asia. If the native habitat of each kind had to be reproduced in cultivation, it would make their culture quite difficult. Fortunately, vandas are most adaptable. They can be grown in either an intermediate or a warm greenhouse, with the possible exception of *Vanda coerulea* which prefers cooler nights. Even this species can be grown in a cool spot in a cattleya house.

The majority of the species have strap-shaped leaves, a few have cylindrical leaves, called the "terete" species, and a few come in between and are called "semi-terete." Each group breeds freely within itself. However, hybrids between leaf types can usually be carried no farther than the primary cross, for they are almost entirely sterile. The low degree of fertility in the inter-type groups and the few exceptions to this are discussed later.

Large, fleshy roots are produced from the stem between the leaves, which may grow into the pots, but which are likely to grow straight out into the air or into the pots of neighboring plants. The flower sprays arise from the axils of the leaves on the newly matured part of the plant. (See illustration, page 11.) The flower stems alternate from

Fig. 12-5 *Vandanthe* Waipuna 'Hodama', A.M./A.O.S., A.M./H.O.S. (*Vandanthe* Ellen Noa × *Vandanthe* Rothschildiana). (*Courtesy Wm. Kirch*)

side to side of the plants, each one being produced from the axil of the next higher leaf. One, two, or sometimes three sprays appear at once, or they may come in succession through the year.

The sepals and petals are usually similar in size, though in some the lateral sepals are larger. They are narrowed toward the base, rounded toward the apex, and usually flat and spreading. The lip is attached to the short foot of the column and is spurred at its base, with the side lobes fleshy and erect, the middle lobe spreading. Colors include white, yellow, rose, purple, blue, and brown, often fantastically combined or fused in single flowers.

CULTURE

Potting. Vandas require a large amount of growing medium and much nourishment. Osmunda fiber and tree fern have long been used, but bark is quite satisfactory for them. In fact, since bark allows the grower to keep up with the rapid growth of young plants, and since all ages do well in it, it is rapidly becoming the preferred medium in this country. The pots should have good drainage. Potting young seedlings simply requires that they be moved on into larger pots as they outgrow the smaller ones. After a plant has matured and flowered, it need be repotted only when the medium breaks down or the pot is no longer adequate. One could never use pots large enough to contain all the roots, so the aim is to furnish a size in proportion to the plant and its need for water and fertilizer.

Vandas increase rapidly in height. Some will grow to six or seven feet. This is not always an advantage. A large, heavy plant will produce more flowers for a while, but when it begins to lose the basal leaves and becomes straggly, flowering is sometimes reduced and the plant is no longer neat and handsome. Rather than allow them to become so tall, it is better to cut off the top half and pot it in fresh material. New hybrids tend to be more compact and height is less of a problem with them.

To divide a plant, make a cut through the stem so as to leave a goodly number of roots on both halves, and a number of leaves on the older part. Choose a time when new roots are growing and old roots are branching. Wet the roots thoroughly to make them more flexible; it may then be possible to wind them around in the new pot without injury. If they break, cut them off at the break and put the stubs in the medium. Roots that grow too high upon the stem to go into the pot are left as they are. Center the plant so that the base of the stem is two inches or so in the medium. Fill in with bark (or osmunda or tree fern). Stake the plant so that it will not wobble. Repot the good section of the old part. Given a damp atmosphere, new growth may break from a dormant bud along the stem. If the roots of the old part remain good, the new growth can be allowed to continue to grow upon it. However, most growers prefer to remove the new plantlet when it has made roots of its own. It will take such a plantlet several years to reach flowering size. Incidentally, any plantlets that develop along the stem of a plant may be removed in like manner.

Air layering may encourage a new root to start if none is present where you wish to divide the plant. Cut a notch in the stem just under a leaf, place a ball of damp sphagnum moss around the cut and the stem and wrap this in polyethylene film tied securely. When a new root has formed, the upper section bearing it can be removed and potted.

Water. Vandas require abundant water during their growing season, with somewhat less during the winter, though not to the point of dryness. They can withstand drying far better than phalaenopsis, however. After potting, water sparingly until the roots take hold again. Roots that have been dis-turbed by potting will rot if they are kept wet, whereas they will start branch roots if they are kept on the dry side. Although vandas can take a drier atmosphere than phalaenopsis, they appreciate a humidity of 40 to 50 percent. In a very damp atmosphere, the plants will be larger and less tough than in a drier environment, although they will grow and flower well with a lower daytime humidity. A mist spray on bright days is beneficial, both to aid in furnishing humidity and in giving water to the aerial roots. Where an evaporative cooler or a humidifier is used, misting is not necessary.

Temperature. Vandas will do well with a night temperature of from 55° to 65°. This means they can be grown well either with cattleyas or with warmer growing kinds. They can very well withstand an accidental cold spell, such as that produced when trouble arises with the heating system, although they should, of course, not be allowed freezing temperatures. While they are not as susceptible to burning as some, they should be protected from excessive daytime heat.

Light. The terete-leaved species require stronger light than the strap-leaved ones, and in warm areas are grown out-of-doors in full sun. The strap-leaved kinds and hybrids between these and the terete will adapt themselves to about the same amount of light as cattleyas. Not all of them do well where winters are dull, however, but selected kinds, chosen for their adaptability, may. If you live where the sun shines all year round, you can grow almost any kind of vanda. If you have long spells of dull weather, buy vandas from growers who have chosen kinds for that type of climate. Give them the brightest spot in either the cattleya house or the warm greenhouse.

Ventilation and air movement. Just as moving air and ventilation help to keep other orchids healthy, so do they benefit vandas.

Feeding. Vandas are heavy feeders. In osmunda fiber and tree fern they may be given a complete fertilizer every two weeks. In bark they should be fed at every watering, with a fertilizer of high nitrogen content.

Training roots. If you have but few plants, you can control their habit of sending their heavy roots in all directions. Roots that have extended to some distance from the plant can be brought back toward the pot and finally trained to go into the medium. Newly growing roots can also be trained into the pot. Wet the root thoroughly to make it flexible, and then tie a sling of string around the root and the plant stem. Pull it in the direction you wish it to go until it resists the pull. Let it alone for a few days, and then every now and then, tighten the string. Finally, it will be in a position for you to maneuver the tip into the potting medium. Growers with many plants will probably not have time to do this; so when they water or use fertilizer solution, they should wet the aerial roots as well.

Vanda from seed.   Vandas may be readily grown from seed, using the methods recommended for *Phalaenopsis.* The wide variety represented in the genus gives an opportunity for a wealth of hybrids. Inter-generic crosses with other members of this tribe add to the possibilities. Growers in Hawaii and in the Orient have led the way with tremendous numbers of hybrids, fascinating in their combination of colors and shapes. The interest is spreading to other parts of the world.

The Species

Of the large number of species, fewer than half are well known. Some that are rather rare are now being used in hybridization. The outstanding species are popular with amateurs, as are the many hybrids.

Vanda amesiana. This is a smaller plant than some, with semi-terete leaves. It bears sprays of fragrant flowers which range from white to rose-purple on foot-long stems. It occurs in Burma and Thailand at elevations of 5,000 feet and flowers in mid-winter.

V. coerulea. This is the famous blue vanda, much loved for its own sake as well as for its contributions to hybrids. It varies from clear cobalt to both paler and deeper shades of blue. Its dense sprays carry ten to twenty flowers which are each three to four inches across. The sepals and petals are nearly equal and overlap each other, giving the effect of a round, flat, compact flower. The little lip is three-lobed, the front lobe a rich blue. The flowers last about a month when kept cool. This strap-leaf species occurs under sunny, cool conditions at high elevations in northern India and Burma. It flowers anytime from fall through winter and spring and it can be grown either in a cool spot in a cattleya house where it can have plenty of light or with cool orchids. *V. coerulea* crossed with *Euanthe sanderiana* produced one of the best known of all hybrids, the large, flat, blue *Vandanthe* Rothschildiana.

V. concolor. Rather rare in collections, this strap-leaf species is a tetraploid which has been used somewhat in hybridization. Its yellow-brown flowers are borne about seven to ten to a stem. The plant occurs in China and flowers in the summer.

V. cristata. Smaller than many, it has six-inch, leathery leaves, and an erect, short flower stem with half a dozen two-inch blooms. The flowers are delightfully fragrant, very waxy, and long lasting. They range in color from cream-yellow to yellow-green with blunt, oval, incurving sepals, and rather downward-bent petals. The lip is green underneath, tawny above with dark red stripes and spots. It flowers from spring to summer, and occurs at high elevations in Nepal, Bhutan, and Sikkim.

V. dearei. The fragrant, long-lasting flowers are creamy white with a yellow lip, qualities that endear them to growers although the species is not as striking as some. The cross *Vanda dearei × Euanthe sanderiana* produced *Vandanthe* Ellen Noa, one of the outstanding strap-leaf hybrids. *V. dearei,* a strap-leaf species, occurs in the Sunda Islands, Borneo, and Java and flowers in the summer.

V. hookeriana. A tall, terete-leaf species, its cylindrical leaves are channeled on the upper surface and pointed. Each stem bears five or six flowers which are about two and one-half inches across. The sepals are white flushed with purple, the petals, which are larger and wavy, are white flushed and spotted with purple. The side lobes of the lip are amethyst with pale lines, the middle lobe, which is broad and spreading, is white stained with deep purple. This species is very common in Malaya and also occurs in Borneo and Sumatra. It should best be grown out-of-doors in bright sun. The flowers appear in the fall. The plant has contributed its huge lip to the hybrid *Vanda* Miss Joaquim, which is grown in fields in Hawaii and imported into this country in large quantities.

V. kimballiana. A semi-terete species requiring cool conditions. The plants are slender, and rarely grow taller than fifteen inches. The lovely flowers are pure white except for the lip, the middle lobe of which is deep rose, marked with deeper veins; the side lobes are yellow. The base of the lip forms a spur about an inch long. The plant grows on the faces of cliffs, exposed to the sun, in the high altitudes of Burma and flowers in late summer or early fall.

V. lamellata. A dwarf strap-leaf species with slender recurved leaves. It bears many-flowered stems of light yellow blooms that are stained with brown and measure about two inches across. There is a more brightly colored variety, var. *boxallii* that is more commonly grown and is used in hybridization. It occurs in the Philippines and flowers in the winter.

V. luzonica. This striking species has two-inch flowers borne in generous numbers on sprays up to fifteen inches long. They are white with crimson markings and a bright red lip. The plant is rather short, growing about two feet high, with strap-shaped leaves which are fifteen inches long. It occurs in the Philippines and flowers in the spring. This species has been used a great deal in hybridization and contributes its coloring to its progeny.

V. merrillii. Although it was discovered only fairly recently, this species is already becoming popular. Its small creamy flowers are stained with red to red-brown and have a shiny waxy texture. The lip has side lobes of white with purple dots, and a fiddle-shaped mid-lobe streaked and stained with red. It is a strap-leaf species which occurs in the Philippines and flowers spring and summer.

V. sanderiana. The name of this famous species has been changed to *Euanthe sanderiana.* See below.

V. spathulata. A tetraploid with tall spikes of golden yellow flowers, this tall plant has strap-shaped leaves that are only three inches long. Both leaves and flower stems are spotted with red. The flowers are small, only an inch or so across, and have a lip of darker yellow marked with red-brown. It is a native of India and Ceylon that is being used in hybridization.

V. sumatrana. Although not commonly grown, this species is being used in hybridization. It is similar to *dearei* in general aspect, with shiny greenish-brown flowers. The plant occurs in Sumatra and flowers in the winter.

V. teres. This very lovely species has played a great role in introducing vandas to this country. Its flowers are large, with broad wavy parts. The petals and sepals are similar in size; the sepals are white tinged with rose and the petals are a rich deep rose. The lip has large, yellow side lobes that fold over the column, and a triangular outer lobe that is rose, veined and spotted with yellow, spread-

Fig. 12-6 *Vanda teres,* a terete leaved species. (*Courtesy H. A. Dunn*)

ing at its outer end and split in the center. The plant occurs in Burma and flowers from May to September. The hybrid *Vanda* Miss Joaquim, *hookeriana × teres,* was the first hybrid to be widely distributed. *V. teres* is a terete-leaved species, which is very popularly grown, although it may be too light-demanding for parts of this country.

V. tessellata. This is the correct name for the species better known as *roxburghii.* It is the one upon which the genus was founded in 1820 by Dr. Brown, who adopted the name given it in Bengal, "Vanda," as the name of the genus. It is a medium sized plant with strap-shaped leaves and a spike of six to eight greenish-yellow flowers. The wavy sepals and petals are white on the back, reticulated with olive-brown on the front. The long middle lobe of the lip is violet. This native of Bengal flowers from May to August. It has been used in hybridization. Varietal forms range in color from pink through yellow.

V. tricolor. A well-known species which has thick, waxy or leathery flowers, heavily spotted with bright red-brown on a yellow ground. The flowers are white to cream colored on the back. The middle lobe of the lip is lyre-shaped, rich purple, and decorated with elevated lines. The flowers are fragrant and long lasting. The variety *suavis,* some-

Home Orchid Growing

times treated as a distinct species, has sepals and petals of white, spotted and barred with reddish purple. The front lobe of the lip is pale rosy purple, the side lobes deep purple. Both are tall, strong plants with strap-shaped leaves. They are native to Java and flower variably.

HYBRIDIZATION IN VANDA

Hybridization in Vanda is beset by special problems that arise from mixed hybrids made between species of different leaf types. Hybrids within each leaf type group are, with rare exceptions, entirely fertile, except that any triploids produced are by their nature quite sterile. Inter-group hybrids can be made by crossing a terete species with a strap-leaf species, or by crossing a terete hybrid with a strap-leaf hybrid, but most of the resulting hybrids are almost entirely sterile.

The basic haploid chromosome number in Vanda is 19 and (except for the tetraploid species) the species all have a diploid number of 38. In the inter-group hybrids, the 19 chromosomes from the terete species will not pair at reduction division with the 19 chromosomes from the strap-leaf species, and hence, because the distribution of chromosomes is very erratic, sterility results. Production of any viable seed by such hybrids is usually the result of non-reduced gametes. The situation is most unfortunate because the semi-terete hybrids are very lovely, and one can imagine the wondrous hybrids that would result if they could be used freely as parents. When two striking exceptions to the sterility of the semi-terete hybrids occurred in Hawaii, W. B. Storey and H. Kamemoto, by dint of a great deal of work with the microscope, worked out a fascinating genetic detective story.

Vandanthe Mevr. L. Velthuis (*V. Miss Joaquim × Euanthe sanderiana*) is a semi-terete diploid hybrid and would be expected to be quite sterile. One individual plant of *Vandanthe* Mevr. L. Velthuis crossed with *V. coerulea* gave a small hybrid progeny, *Vandanthe* Nora Potter. Nora Potter immediately became famous, in the first place because they are very handsome; in the second place, because it was most unusual for a hybrid such as Mevr. L. Velthuis to be a successful parent; and in the third place because the Nora Potters were discovered to be pentaploid. The question of how two diploid parents could give rise to a pentaploid progeny was worked out by W. B. Storey from a study of the formation of sex cells in Mevr. L. Velthuis. He discovered that it produced giant 4n

Fig. 12-7 *Vandanthe* Mevr. L. Velthuis, a diploid semi-terete hybrid, whose genetics is described in these pages. (*Courtesy Jones and Scully, Inc.*)

gametes, sex cells that contained 76 chromosomes. These, united with the 19 chromosomes from *V. coerulea,* gave the 95 chromosomes of the pentaploid Nora Potter.

V. Emma van Deventer is a semi-terete hybrid between *V. teres* and *V. tricolor.* Since the parents were diploid, it was assumed that the offspring *V.* Emma van Deventer were also diploid. Several plants of Emma van Deventer, owned by different people, were crossed with plants of *E. sanderiana.* At best a few seedlings might have been expected, but in each case seed formation was abundant and thousands of vigorous seedlings were raised. The unusual fertility was astonishing. The cross, *Vandanthe* Nellie Morley, proved to be triploid in each of the progeny, and all were quite uniform. It was thought that the triploidy had resulted from non-reduced 2n gametes from Emma van Deventer. Another cross between Emma van Deventer and *sanderiana* produced a pentaploid progeny, and this inspired H. Kamemoto to investigate the parents of both types of offspring. He found that the pentaploid progeny was produced in the same manner as the pentaploid progeny from Mevr. L. Velthuis; in this case a diploid Emma van Deventer had given rise to giant 4n gametes. Chromosome counts on the Emma van Deventers that had given the triploid offspring proved them to be, not diploid as had been thought, but tetraploids. The discovery of their tetraploid nature explained their unusual fertility, for tetraploids form reproductive cells with ease. The 2n gametes that had given rise to their triploid offspring were then known to be normally

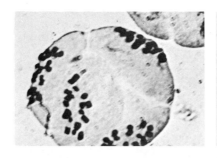 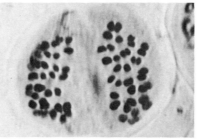 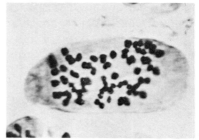

Fig. 12-8 Variation in the formation of reproductive cells in *Vanda,* which leads to differences in ploidy. LEFT, a quartet of normally reduced haploid cells, containing 19 chromosomes.

CENTER, a pair of nonreduced diploid cells, containing 38 chromosomes.
RIGHT, a giant tetraploid cell with 76 chromosomes, formed by doubling of the diploid number. (*Courtesy H. Kamemoto*)

reduced (from the 4n cells of the parents) rather than to have been non-reduced gametes of a 2n parent.

Tetraploids of the type of Emma van Deventer are called "amphi-diploids," for they contain the full diploid number of chromosomes from two unlike parents. The significance of this is that whereas the plant would be sterile, or nearly sterile, with 19 chromosomes from the terete parent and 19 from the strap-leaf parent, it has been made fertile by the doubling of these chromosomes. Each set of 19 terete chromosomes now has another set to pair with, and the 19 chromosomes from the strap-leaf parent also have a set to pair with. It is not known how this amphi-diploidy, usually a rare event, occurred in several plants from the same seed pod.

The ability of some additional semi-terete hybrids to give progeny in the two ways just described is testified by the recent findings of both triploid and pentaploid progenies. Thus the sterility barrier is being broken by the ability of individual plants to produce non-reduced gametes and occasionally to double their own chromosome number. Hybrids which give but very few viable seed may still be most useful if their polyploid offspring can in turn be used as parents. There are still large numbers of semi-terete hybrids that appear to be completely sterile. If they could be made to double their chromosomes, they, too, would become fertile. Here is a way in which colchicine might be useful (see Chapter 8), if a proper technique could be worked out.

We should not leave the subject of hybridization without mentioning the delightful small-flowered crosses being made. They combine *Vanda* and *Aerides* with *Rhynchostylis, Saccolabium, Ascocentrum,* and others to give plants of smaller dimensions that have clusters of flowers the size of a dime or a quarter, in a range of rainbow colors. Much

more suitable to small greenhouses, these are jewels in themselves and sparkle alongside their larger and more stately relatives.

EUANTHE

The single species in this genus has so long been known as *Vanda sanderiana* that it is going to be difficult to become accustomed to changing its name, and the names of the many hybrids that have come from it.

Euanthe sanderiana. This is one of the most beautiful orchids known. Because of its beauty, size, and shape it has been used most frequently in hybridization. It is a magnificent broad, flat flower, with rounded parts. The lateral sepals are especially large and are the most striking feature of the flower. The coloring is a fusion of hues. The dorsal sepals and the petals shade from white to rose. The lateral sepals are yellow-green suffused with reddish brown and marked with a network of brown. The little lip is dull crimson, with a squarish middle lobe and side lobes that form a little cup under the tip of the column. The color variations in this species are quite remarkable, some tending to purple, others to red. It is a strap-leaf species which occurs in the Philippines and flowers in the fall. *E. sanderiana* contributes its broad, flat, rounded shape to its hybrids, one reason why it is so frequently used. Its hybrids are likely to have the reticulation (network) of deeper color which is one of its charms. In *Vandanthe* Rothschildiana this reticulation is of a deep blue. The influence of its shape is clearly seen in two of its hybrids— *Vandanthe* Nellie Morley and *Vandanthe* Ellen Noa.

AERIDES

Aerides, the type genus of the tribe, is very much like *Vanda* in plant characters and cultural require-

Home Orchid Growing

Fig. 12-9 *Aerides fieldingii.*

ments. It offers drooping sprays of delicately beautiful flowers.

Aerides fieldingii. The nickname of this species is "fox brush" orchid, and although the flower spray is a fat cylinder about the size of a fox tail, the name in no way does justice to the flowers. About a hundred (or more) dainty, one-inch flowers are borne on the stem, each a bit of perfection that has to be looked at closely. They are saucer shaped with an open pointed lip, solid pink in color, or with a bit of white at the edges. They have a sparkling crystalline texture, and a dainty perfume. The plant occurs in Sikkim and Assam, and flowers in the spring and summer.

A. lawrenceae. These tall Philippine plants produce sprays of fifteen to twenty flowers, each about one and one-half inches across. The waxy flowers are greenish white, tipped with amethyst. The

lip is closed at the tip like the tip of a Persian slipper, and the basal section together with the erect side lobes forms a pouch. The lip has a central strap that curves backward completely covering the column. The flowers, which are sweetly fragrant, appear during the late summer and early fall.

A. odoratum. This species is similar to *lawrenceae,* but it has a stronger fragrance and some differences in flower shape. The "horn" of the lip is more sharply curved, and the pouched portion is not as wide. The plant occurs in the Philippines, and flowers in late summer and early fall.

A. quinquevulnerum. Most common of the Philippine species, found growing on trees within twenty miles of the city of Manila. The flowers are white, each petal and sepal tipped with reddish purple, the "five wounds" from which it derives its name. There is a form common in the Islands of Mindoro which is burgundy colored, var. *purpuratum.* The flower spikes are quite long, many flowered, and a plant may produce several at a time. Flowers during late summer.

Fig. 12-10 *Aerides quinquevulnerum.*

ANGRAECUM

Native to tropical Africa, Madagascar and the Seychelle Islands. There are numerous species, but only a few are really known in cultivation in this country. The plants are similar to *Vanda,* and they may be grown with cattleyas. However, the night temperature should not go below 55°. The lip typically produces a long spur at its base.

Angraecum dasycarpum. An enchanting miniature, whose little white flowers are star-shaped with a rather long, tongue-like lip, apparently without a spur. The short plant stems bear alternate very fleshy, broadly oval leaves.

A. eburneum. A scoop shaped, shiny white lip and slender green sepals and petals, make this species from the Comoro and Seychelle Islands most attractive. The spur is but three inches long. The large, heavy plants branch freely and the young plantlets can be removed. Flowering stems come several at a time and hold fifteen or more blooms, delightfully fragrant.

A. eichlerianum. A tall, climbing plant that reaches five feet in height. It has leaves four to five inches long, and produces usually one flower opposite each leaf base. The flowers are fragrant and long lasting, three inches in diameter, with pointed oval sepals and petals and a lip which Bailey says is "extinguisher" shaped. Webster

Fig. 12-11 *Angraecum eburneum,* one of the most widely grown of the genus. (*Courtesy Jones and Scully, Inc.*)

comes to the aid here defining an extinguisher as a candle snuffer! There is a short spur which is curved in the middle. The sepals and petals are green to yellow-green, the lip white with an emerald green patch in the throat. Flowering time is summer and it is native to West Africa.

A. giryamae. This is the largest of the genus, and is so like *A. eburneum* that it may be but a variety of that species.

A. infundibulare. A rather dainty climbing plant, with oval leaves and thin roots at each node. It is similar to *A. eichlerianum* but produces larger flowers. The sepals and petals are brownish green, quite slender, while the lip is rounded trowel-shaped, white shaded to yellow-green and then to deep green in the throat. The tapering yellowish spur is five inches long. It flowers from fall to winter, and is native to West Africa.

A. scottianum. This species has terete leaves, deeply grooved on the upper surface, three to four inches long. The plant grows to between one and two feet in height. The flowers are held upside down, one to three to an inflorescence, and are very fragrant and waxy, about two inches in diameter. The parts are slender and whitish yellow, and the broad concave lip is white with a reddish-brown four-inch spur. Native to the Comoro Islands, it flowers in the fall.

A. sesquipedale. Waxy white, five-inch star-shaped flowers with spurs ten inches long are produced on generous sprays and create a handsome species. The long spur and the close association of orchids with specific insects, caused Darwin to

predict that there must be a moth with a proboscis long enough to obtain the nectar from the base of the spur and so perform the act of pollinating this species. Later, the Sphinx moth of Madagascar, home of *sesquipedale,* was thought to be the elusive species in question, but according to Dodson its role has not been verified. A Christmas flowering season has given *sesquipedale* its nickname of "Star of Bethlehem."

A. superbum. Another species from Madagascar, this is similar to *eburneum* and may be a variety of it. It has a spur even longer than that of *sesquipedale.* The flowers are three inches across, and are very fragrant.

MYSTACIDIUM

This is a genus of several species, two of which are well known to most lovers of botanicals. Perhaps others will become more familiar as time goes on.

Mystacidium capense. A dainty plant, almost a miniature, with but a few narrow leaves that are two to three inches long. The inflorescence emerges laterally and holds a generous number of delightfully fragrant white blooms of waxy texture a little over an inch in diameter. The sepals and petals are pointed, as is the slightly broader lip, and the spur is about two inches long. It flowers in the spring, and is a native of southeast Africa.

M. distichum (preferably *Angraecum distichum*). A completely charming miniature, with little short curved leaves tightly clasping the sinuous stems to give a braided effect. Tiny white flowers appear at intervals along the stem. A plant with many growths is extremely decorative. The species flowers in the fall. It is native from West Africa to Uganda.

RENANTHERA

Renanthera is a genus similar to *Vanda,* grown for its brightly colored flowers, which, though small, are produced in great numbers and make a striking display. Subtle variations of yellow marked with red, and red with orange, are the general color schemes of the species. The purpose of crossing this genus with *Vanda* and other members of this group is to introduce its brilliant red and orange tones as well as its free flowering habit and perky forms. The resulting hybrids have a wide variety of fanciful shapes which gives them a fascination all their own. *Renanthera* has four pollinia (in contrast to the two in *Vanda, Phalaenopsis, Ae-*

Fig. 12-12 *Angraecum infundibulare.* (*Courtesy Benjamin C. Berliner*)

Fig. 12-13 *Angraecum sesquipedale,* the lovely "star of Bethlehem." (*Courtesy Jones and Scully, Inc.*)

Fig. 12-14 *Mystacidium (Angraecum) distichum.*

rides, and *Angraecum*), and the lip is movable. The plants are slender, with short fleshy leaves, and some reach such great height that they are almost too tall for the average greenhouse. They need exceptionally good light.

Renanthera coccinea. This species grows six to ten feet high. The branched flower stem comes from an upper leaf axil, and bears a hundred or more flowers that are two inches wide and four inches long. The very slender petals and dorsal sepal are bright red marked with yellow. The lateral sepals are longer and wider, and are clear red. The tiny yellow lip is tipped with red. A native of Cochin China, it flowers in the fall.

R. imshootiana. Similar to *coccinea,* but growing only about two feet tall, this species produces a wealth of flowers on a freely branching stem two feet long. The dorsal sepal and petals are short and slender, standing up above the broad lateral sepals and giving the flower the look of a butterfly. The dorsal sepal is dull yellow, the petals the same but dotted with red, and the lateral sepals are cinnabar red on the upper surface, dull yellow beneath. The species is a native of Assam.

R. lowii. Once called *Arachnanthe lowii,* this huge, spectacular plant grows very tall and produces flower stems six to ten feet long. Its heavy leaves are much longer than other members of the genus, being two to three feet in length. Of the forty to fifty flowers produced on the stem, the lower two are quite different from the rest. They are small and fleshy, tawny yellow with crimson spots, while the others are larger, less fleshy, with a pale yellow-green ground and irregular blotches of reddish brown, and a small yellow lip spotted with purple. The species comes from Borneo.

R. matutina. This smaller species from Java has flowers of bright yellow shaded with crimson.

R. monachica. The short leaves of this species are one-half inch thick and dark bluish green. The flower stem bears twenty-five or more flowers, one to one and one-half inches in diameter. They are bright orange with deep red spots. This native of the Philippines flowers in early spring.

R. storei. Called the "fire orchid" in the Philippines, this species is quite similar to *coccinea.* The dorsal sepal and petals are brick-red; the lower sepals are brilliant crimson marked with lighter tones. The lip is crimson with yellow bars and a white center. The flowers last for two months. This is perhaps the most widely used species in hybridization.

Other Members of the Aerides Tribe

Arachnis is a genus also used in hybridization with *Vanda.* Its name means "spider-like." The genus was at one time designated as *Arachnanthe,* and later was included in *Renanthera* by some authorities. The genus *Arachnis* is not given as such in Bailey. Some of the species are now retained in *Renanthera. Arachnis* is characterized by four pollinia and by having the lip hinged to the base of the column and readily movable. The genus likes light, as much as or more than *Vanda.*

Arachnis flos-aeris. Native to the Philippines, these plants grow eight to ten feet tall and produce short flower stems with about ten three- to four-inch flowers. They are yellow barred with purple-brown and have a musky scent. The flowers appear from July to March.

Fig. 12-15 *Opsisanthe* Juliet (*Euanthe sanderiana* × *Vandopsis gigantea*). (*Courtesy Wm. Kirch*)

A. moschifera. These striking cream or yellow-green flowers are spotted and barred with deep red or purple. They have the texture of enamel. The stems are slender and climbing. The flowering time is variable.

Vandopsis, a genus whose name means "like Vanda," resembles *Vanda* except that the lip has no spur. The plants are very robust and heavy. The members of the genus are frequently crossed with *Vanda.*

Vandopsis gigantea. Heavy pendulous plants produce flower stems ten to fifteen inches long with flowers three inches across. The flowers are golden yellow, blotched with cinnamon, and have a white lip. The species occurs in Burma.

V. lissochiloides. This is the most familiar of the species, and is sometimes mistakenly called *V. batemannii.* The flower stem bears a dozen or more three-inch flowers which are yellowish, spotted with purple on the upper surface and reddish-purple underneath. The flowers are somewhat coarse in texture and last a long time. It occurs in the Philippines and flowers from spring through summer.

Saccolabium is a genus of delightful dwarf plants which produce dense sprays of charming little flowers. The lip is sac-like, as the name implies. They can be grown with cattleyas, with plenty of water during the growing season, less during the winter. All of the species are brightly colored. *S. hendersonianum* has bright rose flowers, *S. cerinum* flowers that are red-orange, and *S. coeleste* flowers that are white tipped with blue.

Ascocentrum, once included in *Saccolabium,* has the delightful species, *curvifolium* which grows only six inches tall and which has half-inch flowers ranging from purple to red-orange, and *miniatum,* which is a foot tall and bears an upright stem of twenty to forty tiny bright orange flowers.

Cyrtorchis. A genus of about fifteen species as yet little known in this country, except for one species, *Cyrtorchis arcuata.* It has delightful fragrant, waxy, white flowers, about an inch and a half in diameter, which are perfect symmetrical stars because the lip is the same size and shape as the other floral parts. They have a three-inch, curved, green spur. The plants are stiff, with strap-shaped leaves, and the flower stem grows out horizontally, bearing a dozen or more blooms. Native to East, Central, and South Africa, it flowers in winter and spring.

Fig. 12-17 *Antheranthe Jack Warne (Euanthe sanderiana × Renanthera storei). (Courtesy Jones and Scully, Inc.)*

Neofinetia is a genus of but one species, a lovely miniature, *N. falcata.* It grows to about two and a half inches tall and branches freely. The little white flowers are very fragrant at night. They have slender sepals and petals, a triangular lip, and a long curved spur. They are borne three to seven on short inflorescences. It is native to Japan and Korea.

Aeranthes has spectacular, handsome, waxy green flowers that are boldly spider-like. The sepals and petals form a five-pointed star, with broad bases and slender, pointed tips. The rather square lip is large, with the side lobes molded into two portions and the mid-lobe fleshy and tongue-like. There is a short spur at the base of the column foot. The plants are similar to *Angraecum,* quite large and heavy, and the flowers are borne on long wiry stems, occasionally singly but more often two or more together or in succession. These natives to Madagascar may be grown in the same manner as *Angraecum,* and flower from summer into winter.

A. arachnites has three-inch flowers of lime green, whose white lip has a green mid-lobe. The flowers are borne on upright stems about as tall as the leaves.

A. ramosa has exceedingly dark green flowers, about three inches across. The petals curve upward, while the lateral sepals curve downward.

Fig. 12-16 *Cyrtorchis arcuata.*

Home Orchid Growing

Sarcochilus includes some of Australia's most charming and best loved natives. The genus also spreads from the Malay Peninsula through the Pacific islands. The four given here are all from New South Wales and Queensland. They have small round flowers, sepals and petals alike, and a fleshy little hinged, cup-shaped lip. *S. ceciliae,* called "fairy bells" is about five inches tall with coarse little slender tufted leaves. The round half-inch flowers are bell-shaped, bright pink, with a velvety lip. *S. falcatus,* nicknamed the "orange blossom orchid," is but a few inches tall with six-inch sickle-shaped leaves. It has flowers up to one and one-half inches across, pure white except for the pink, yellow, or orange lip. *S. fitzgeraldii* grows on damp, cool rock faces of ravines. It is a large, branching plant with one-inch flowers of white or pink. The sepals and petals have crimson stippling at their base, and the lip is orange or yellow. *S. hartmannii* is a sturdy plant with heavy channelled leaves. Its flowers are more full, with round parts of a clear crystalline white. It flowers most profusely of all, and is often covered with blooms.

Trichoglottis, best known for two exceptionally lovely members, has about thirty-five species ranging from the Philippines and other islands to the Malay Peninsula and the countries of Southeast Asia. The plants have rather heavy stems clothed with short, oval leaves, and some can reach five feet in height. The flowers are very long lasting.

Fig. 12-18 *Rhynchostylis densiflora* 'Ratana', C.B.M./A.O.S., an exceptionally fine example of the delight offered by many of the less well known members of the Aerides tribe. (*Courtesy Jones and Scully, Inc.*)

T. brachiata has round, dark wine-red, velvety flowers, two inches across, which come singly from the upper leaf axils. The broad, oval sepals and petals have a narrow border of yellow. The mid-lobe of the five-lobed fuzzy lip is in the form of a cross. The lip coloring, yellow and white with wine markings, accents the dark, rich flower. The species occurs in the Philippines in Mindanao, Luzon, and other islands, and its fragrant flowers are produced over several months.

T. philippinensis is similar to *T. brachiata;* in fact the latter is sometimes given as a variety of it. It is a taller plant with flowers a bit smaller, less rich, but nevertheless very attractive. They tend to greenish yellow with brown mottling. It covers the same geographical range as *brachiata.*

Other genera of the Aerides tribe, most of them well worth knowing, are *Acampe, Aerangis, Camarotis, Cleisostoma, Diaphananthe, Gastrochilus, Listrostachys, Luisia, Rhynchostylis, and Sarcanthus.*

Inter-generic Hybrids

Inter-generic hybrids in this tribe are numerous, and more will undoubtedly appear as time goes on. The combining names given to the bi-generic hybrids do not as readily show their origin as do those in the Cattleya tribe, although some ingenuity was used in creating them. Some of them are as follows: Aeridopsis = Aerides × Phalaenopsis; Aeridovanda = Aerides × Vanda; Arachnopsis = Arachnis × Phalaenopsis; Aranda = Arachnis × Vanda; Aranthera = Arachnis × Renanthera; Ascocenda = Ascocentrum × Vanda; Luisanda = Luisia × Vanda; Opsisanda = Vandopsis × Vanda; Renantanda = Renanthera × Vanda; Renanthopsis = Renanthera × Phalaenopsis; Renanopsis = Renanthera × Vandopsis; Sarcothera = Sarcochilus × Renanthera; Trichovanda = Trichoglottis × Vanda; Vandaenopsis = Phalaenopsis × Vanda; Vandanthe = Euanthe × Vanda.

For additional intergeneric hybrid names, including a multitude of tri- and quadri-generic hybrids, consult Garay and Sweet, *Natural and Artificial Hybrid Generic Names Of Orchids,* and the new *Handbook on Orchid Nomenclature and Registration,* 1969.

13

THE CATTLEYA TRIBE

The cattleyas, the most showy members of this tribe, have already been described. However, these handsome orchids should not be allowed to overshadow their lovely cousins.

EPIDENDRUM

Epidendrum is a wide-spread genus of one thousand species, loved by amateurs everywhere. They are easy to grow, and flower profusely, some producing their beautiful clusters of brightly colored flowers almost all year round. The flowers vary from one-fourth inch, each a dainty miniature, to six inches in diameter. Many are worth growing for their fragrance alone.

They grow wild in tropical and subtropical America, from Florida south to Brazil. They are so abundant in parts of Central America that they could almost be classed with weeds. Yet when they are transplanted to our greenhouses, they match their true quality with that of their more exalted relatives. Epidendrums were among the first epiphytes to be imported into Europe. In fact, the first epiphytic orchid to flower in England was *Epidendrum cochleatum,* in 1787.

There is some variation among the widely distributed species as to cultural needs, but in general they do well in a cattleya house, with night temperatures from 55° to 60°. Some may like a spot that runs a little cool and others one that runs a bit warm. Many do well in hanging positions, in baskets, or on slabs of tree fern, or fixed with a piece of osmunda fiber to a slab or log. They may be grown in osmunda fiber or bark, and the reed stem kinds may even be grown in a fluffy soil compost. These last are often grown in gardens in warm climates. They should all be watered like cattleyas.

Epidendrums can be divided into two general groups according to the characteristics of the plants. Although we shall not use the divisions here, it is well to be familiar with them. In the group called Encyclia, and for which *Encyclia* can be used as the generic name, are placed those with true pseudobulbs, such as *atropurpureum* and *prismatocarpum*. In the group called Euepidendrum (Eu- meaning true) can be placed the reed-stem types such as *ibaguense* and *evectum,* and for these the generic name *Epidendrum* is retained. There are too many species ever to be included in any one list, and only the experts can rule on the less well known ones or the borderline cases, hence we shall include them all as Epidendrums.

The Species

Out of such a large genus it is possible to give here only a handful of species, which have been selected for their variety, and popularity, or because of some unique characteristic that makes them particularly interesting and shows the wide scope of this genus.

Epidendrum alatum. Its fragrance is one of the charms of this species. The two-inch flowers are variable in color, being yellow-green with purple at the base of the petals and sepals, and raised purple lines in the central part of the three-lobed lip. The pseudobulbs are pear shaped, about five inches tall, and bear two leaves that are long and slender and contracted almost to a tube at their base. It likes intermediate to warm conditions, and flowers from spring to fall. It occurs from Mexico to Nicaragua.

E. anceps. One of Florida's native species, this is also found all the way to Peru. It is not showy, except that the rather tall, vigorous plants are handsome, for its little flowers are only a half-inch in diameter. They are greenish tan with a green column, but are very waxy and prettily shaped. They occur in tight clusters at the tip of the cane-like pseudobulb, and the same stem produces clusters in succession throughout the year, and year after year. It likes to be mounted on a driftwood log with osmunda fiber, but can also be grown in a pot.

E. aromaticum. Some may find the heavy fragrance of this species a bit overpowering. It has round two-inch tall pseudobulbs with one or two leathery, often purplish, leaves. The panicle of flowers may reach three feet in length, and holds many long-lasting one-and-a-half-inch flowers that are cream colored except for the three-lobed lip which is veined with red-brown and sets off a reddish column. It flowers from summer to fall, and occurs from Mexico to Guatemala.

E. atropurpureum. This is one of the loveliest of the genus. The mahogany and green sepals and petals spread wide, the tip of each curving forward gracefully. The spreading lip is white with crimson stripes. Six to ten of these attractive, long-

Fig. 13-2 *Epidendrum boothianum.*

lasting flowers are borne on a long spray rising from the top of the short, oval pseudobulb. It ranges from Mexico to Venezuela and flowers in late spring and early summer. A plant on a slab makes a magnificent display with its leads growing upward and a fan of flower spikes. The variety *randianum* (or *randii*) has the sepals and petals outlined in light green, and a white lip centered with a purple-rayed blotch. The variety *roseum* has a bright rose-colored lip that forms a pleasing contrast to the dark sepals and petals.

E. boothianum. A delightful, almost miniature species, whose little flat, round pseudobulbs have earned it the nickname "little dollar" orchid. One to three slender upright leaves are borne from the pseudobulb, and usually do not exceed three or four inches, although they can grow taller. The flower stem is erect, about twice the height of the leaves, and bears several bright, saucy, inch-wide flowers, yellow, spotted or barred with red. The strangely shaped little lip gives the impression of a pair of walrus tusks hanging under the column. It flowers in summer and fall, and occurs in south Florida, the Bahamas, Cuba, Mexico, and British Honduras.

E. boothii. It does not seem quite fair for two species to have names so much alike. This and *E. boothianum* could never be mistaken for each other, however. *E. boothii* has quite insignificant flowers, cream colored, with slender parts, two or three borne at a time on a short stem that barely appears above the tip of the slender pseudobulb. Total height of the plant is about six inches. It

Fig. 13-1 *Epidendrum atropurpureum,* one of the most striking of the genus. (*Courtesy H. A. Dunn and H. Griffin*)

Phalaenopsis Fiery

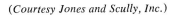

(Courtesy Jones and Scully, Inc.)

Phalaenopsis mannii

Phalaenopsis Golden
Sands 'Orchidglade'
SM/SFOS

Phalaenopsis violacea

Aeranthes ramosa

Phalaenopsis Clara
Knight

Vandanthe
Rothschildiana

Antheglottis Ulaula

Phalaenopsis Moonclurie
'Orchidglade' AM/AOS

Angraecum Veitchii

Aeranthes arachnites

Brassavola nodosa

Diacattleya Chastity

Cattleya Porcia 'Cannizaro' AM/AOS

Bc. Heaven's Sake

Schombocattleya Angel
Wings

Cattleya walkeriana var.
alba 'Orchidglade'
CBM/SFOS,
FCC/AOS

Cattleya Little Angel

Cattleya guttata

Slc. Falcon 'Alexanderi'
FCC/RHS, FCC/AOS

Cattleya guatemalensis

(Courtesy Jones and Scully, Inc.)

Cattleya aurantiaca

Cattleya dowiana var.
aurea

occurs in Costa Rica and Mexico, and from Cuba to Surinam.

E. brassvolae. Flowers in tones of brown and green, with slender, long-pointed parts make this a striking species. The lip consists of a long claw (stalk) by which it is attached and a pointed outer lobe. The plants are husky, with tall pseudobulbs. It flowers in late summer and fall, and occurs from Mexico south to Panama.

E. ceratistes. With this beautiful little species, of apple green flowers, begins a story of past confusion. When it first bloomed in our own collection of plants brought back from Costa Rica, it seemed to key out as *E. oncidioides,* but since it looked nothing like an oncidium to merit such a name, I sent it to Dr. Schweinfurth. He gave me its proper name, *ceratistes.* Another plant, also from Costa Rica, quite different in general appearance, also proceded to key out as *oncidioides.* Dr. Schweinfurth again helped out; this time, while giving me its correct name *E. mooreanum,* he explained that both of these had first been named separately and then had been reduced to varieties of *E. oncidioides,* and then had been returned to their original names. It comforted me that the confusion was not mine alone! It is revealing that in species that somehow look very different, so much so that the amateur would not think they could possibly be the same, their actual structure and relation of the parts can be close enough to warrant the same diagnostic specifications. At any rate, *E. ceratistes* is a delightful plant. Its slender sepals and petals are the same length, the latter a bit narrower at the base and slightly broader toward the tip. The side lobes of the lip are a darker green and lie along the column with their tips upturned. The lip is almost round, coming to a sharp point at its end with its lateral edges slightly turned down, and is white with raised lines of red. The flowers are held on an airy spray that can be simple or branched. The plant is small, with onion-shaped pseudobulbs that bear three or four leaves. It is apparently widespread natively, from Mexico to Venezuela and flowers in the summer.

E. ciliare. One of the best known, this species is loved for its easy-going habit. The plant looks like a cattleya and grows about a foot tall. The slender, graceful flowers are about five inches across and are borne in clusters of three to seven. The sepals and petals are yellow-green, set off by a dainty, three-lobed, white lip, with a needle-like mid-lobe and fringed side lobes. It grows abundantly in Mexico and flowers in the winter.

E. cochleatum. The shape of these attractive, upside-down flowers suggests an octopus. The slender, yellow-green sepals and petals stream down from the shell-like, green- and purple-striped lip which is almost black on the reverse side. The flower stem elongates through a period of five to seven months, producing a succession of flowers, with four or five open at a time. The slender, conical pseudobulbs are five to eight inches tall, bearing a pair of leaves. They may be found from Florida to Colombia. The variety *triandrum,* so called because it has three anthers, is native to Florida. The Costa Rican form is a much smaller plant and its flower stem is shorter with smaller flowers spaced evenly along its length and with more open at a time.

E. coriifolium. Of the sheerest pale green wax, the few flowers per stem are extremely beautiful. The stem that bears the flowers is zig-zag, and at each joint there is a huge bract that almost prevents the flower from opening. The lip is broad and spreading, very stiff. The sepals are narrow and the petals almost threadlike, so delicate that they often do not separate completely away from the sepals, and are often not noticed for that reason. The plant has flattened stems with a few spatula-shaped leaves on the upper section, quite rough and leathery. The species occurs from Mexico to Peru. There is also a dark form.

E. difforme (syn. *umbellatum*). A delightful small species, this one has slender stems and alternate pale green leaves. The waxy, fragrant, greenish-white one-and-a-half-inch flowers are borne directly at the top of the stem in clusters of three to five. The sepals and petals are slender, while the lip is spreading and wavy at the edge. The plants occur from Mexico south to Panama and flower in summer or early fall. There are slight variations in the flowers and the plant size from region to region.

E. endresii. This is a beautiful, dainty species, discovered long years ago and then "lost" until rediscovered recently by Clarence Horich in Costa Rica. The flowers are white, subtly touched with purple on the edges of the column and the center of the lip. They are about one inch in length, and are borne at the top of the delicate, reed-like stems, which are leafy from top to bottom. The plants are somewhat difficult to keep growing well, but are well worth the effort, as this little species will outshine many larger things around it. It is said to occur in Panama as well as Costa Rica, and blooms in the winter.

Fig. 13-3 TOP, *Epidendrum exasperatum:* A, the whole flower: B, detail of the column. CENTER, *Epidendrum laucheanum:* C, part of the chain of flowers; D, a single flower. BOTTOM, *Epidendrum cochleatum:* E, the column of the variety *triandrum,* which has three anthers; F, the type form of the flower.

E. exasperatum. The charming flowers have brown petals and sepals, in front of which the little white lip hangs straight down. With its divided front lobe and split side lobes, it looks exactly like a child in a white snowsuit, with even the zipper flap outlined in purple, and with the column forming the head and face. The plants may retain a modest size in a greenhouse, but in nature they can grow several feet tall. The branching stems are slender, with alternate leaves their whole length, and the flowers appear in short sprays from their tops. The species flowers in the winter. It occurs in Costa Rica and Panama.

E. fragrans. The flowers of this species are spicily scented and pretty, simliar in shape and size to *E. cochleatum* but creamy white with a red peppermint-striped lip. Pseudobulbs are from four to five inches tall, bearing a short single leaf. Since the flower stem is short, the cluster of blooms nestles close to the leaf. The plants occur from Guatemala through the West Indies to north Brazil and flower in late summer and early fall.

E. ghiesbreghtianum. Almost a miniature, rarely more than five inches tall, this species produces a flower huge for its size. The slender pseudobulbs hold a pair of narrow leaves that fold somewhat together. From within their bases comes a short flower stem that gives rise to one or two blooms. The sepals and petals are gold-green or yellow-green with dotted lines of brown, and are plain green on the back. The large squarish lip is white, with a few short purple veins at its base. The striking flower is about two and a-half inches long. It is a rare species in nature, coming from a restricted area in Mexico, but was raised from seed by the late John Lager who distributed it. L. O. Williams in *Orchidaceae of Mexico* states that it is closely related to *E. mariae.*

E. ibaguense. This is the preferred name for the species familiarly known as *E. radicans.* The plant is vinelike, having a tall, slender stem with rather widely spaced short leaves and long aerial roots. It should be trained to a support in the greenhouse. The tall and erect flower stem bears a dense cluster, actually a sphere-shaped head, of one-inch, brilliantly colored flowers, ranging from red to orange to yellow. Each flower is a little jewel, having waxy little sepals and petals and a fringed lip. *E. ibaguense* crossed with a number of other reed type species has given an array of "reed-stem" hybrids. Selection has produced plants that are more compact and shorter than their parents, making them more suitable for small greenhouses. The flowers run through all the tones on the yellow to red sec-

tion of the color circle, including peach, pink, red violet, brick red, etc. The best known of the reed-stem hybrids is *Epidendrum* O'brienianum, *E. ibaguense* × *E. evectum*, registered in 1888. The latter is a little known species which is nevertheless useful in hybridization. *E. ibaguense* occurs throughout Central and South America, growing in open weedy soil in dense masses and flowering throughout the year. The reed-stem species are very dominant for plant character and flower size and shape, which may be due to the fact that some are tetraploid.

E. ionophlebium. This species is rather like *E. fragrans* in general shape, but greenish rather than creamy white, and with a fuzzy, squarish callus on the lip. It occurs from Mexico to Panama, and flowers in the winter and spring.

E. latilobium. The flowers of this species are somewhat reminiscent of those of *coriifolium,* appearing to be made of transluscent green wax, but they are larger and are borne in a fascicle-like cluster. The plants are quite different, as well. The side lobes of the lip are extremely broad, shaped like butterfly wings, and have wavy edges. The small mid-lobe is divided into two divergent parts. The sepals are very narrow, and the petals even narrower. The plant can be from a few inches to a foot tall, and has rounded leaves clasping the stem in funnel-like manner. It occurs in Costa Rica and flowers any time from fall to spring.

E. laucheanum. Long chains of tiny flowers, extending from the tips of rather slender, few-leaved stems, make this species just as deserving of the nickname "necklace orchid" as *Dendrochilum* to which the nickname is usually applied. The chains can be anywhere from a few inches to almost two feet in length, and the latter bear over a hundred little yellowish, fleshy flowers, all open at once. They are delicately fragrant, an additional charm. The stems may lose their leaves seasonally. The plants produce many new growths at a time, which gives many chains of flowers simultaneously. The species occurs through most of Central America and in Colombia, and flowers in the winter.

E. lockhartoides. A delightful miniature resembling the genus *Lockhartia* in its braided appearance, this species is as decorative when not in flower as when blooming. Six to eight tiny green flowers are borne on a short stem, each barely exceeding its bract and folding back upon it. The plants occur in Costa Rica and Panama and flower in the fall. They like a bit more shade than others, and do well in an orchid case.

E. mariae. A very lovely species, it has two-inch

pseudobulbs and leaves only four inches long. The flower stem is about eight inches tall and bears one to three large flowers. The petals and sepals are small, greenish-yellow, while the huge lip is spreading, with a deeply indented outer portion, white with green veins in the throat. It occurs in Mexico, and likes a cool spot in an intermediate house.

E. (Nanodes) medusae. José Strobel, Ecuador's well-known and lamented collector, found this species after it had not been seen in the wilds for years. He described it as looking almost animal-like among other plants on the branches. Indeed, it does have an animal-like quality, perhaps of some marine creature with many swimmerettes. But it is a beautiful plant, one that does not need to bloom to draw attention in a greenhouse. The stems, which can be a foot long, hang downward, and are clothed with fleshy, three-inch, slender-oval, curving leaves that clasp the stem tightly with their bases. The three-inch flowers appear at the tip of the stem, barely extending beyond the last leaf. They are spectacular, with green petals and sepals stippled with red, and a huge, round heart-shaped ruby red lip that is fantastically fringed and lacerated on its edge. It takes the new growths two years to mature. In the meantime, many young growths are developing, crowded close together. The flowers appear in the spring, two or three at a time, but sometimes singly. It occurs only in Ecuador, and likes a cool spot in the greenhouse, fairly shaded in the summer but somewhat brighter in the winter. It is best mounted on a log or grown in a hanging container. Do not let it dry out.

E. mirabile. The lovely rosy-lilac flowers of this species are more like a small cattleya than an epidendrum in general appearance, but the plant gives no doubt as to its identity. The climbing, sprawling canes branch and re-branch every which way, but since they are not too large they can be accommodated easily on a piece of log padded with osmunda fiber. The flowers are produced at the tip of the cane in clusters of three or so. They are about three inches in diameter and last for two or more weeks. The name *mirabile* probably stems from their beauty, but also perhaps from the fact that such attractive flowers could be produced by such an unlikely plant. The species is confined to a few places in one range of mountains in Costa Rica. It flowers in the fall and prefers a cool spot in a cattleya house. It has a lemon fragrance.

E. mooreanum. Compare this species with *E. ceratistes* to see how much it resembles it, but at the same time how different it is in aspect. The petals

and sepals are more nearly the same in shape, and flare back from their bases. The side lobes of the lip are broader and are colored pink like the lip, rather than being a different color as in *ceratistes*. The mid-lobe of the lip is quite square, instead of being round, and has a notch where *ceratistes* has a point. The plant itself is larger and tougher, and the bloom spray is much longer, reaching four feet. It occurs in Costa Rica and Panama, and flowers in late summer.

E. nemorale. This is a very showy, fragrant species, with a wealth of two- to four-inch flowers, soft rose-red in color. The plant has large, fat pseudobulbs with foot-long slender leaves. The flowering stem can reach three feet in height, and produces many blooms that last a long time. It is native to Mexico where it grows at fairly high elevations, but it takes kindly to cattleya conditions, and it flowers in the summer.

E. nocturnum. Spidery, white flowers grace rather tall cane-like pseudobulbs. The flowers with their slender parts resemble those of several other species, among them *E. obesum* and *ciliare*. *E. nocturnum* is one of Florida's well-loved native species, and spreads from there through Mexico and Central America, into South America, and through the West Indies. It is adaptable either to intermediate or warm conditions. Its evening fragrance is one of its charms.

E. obesum. The name hints that this species is fat, but it is a misnomer. The stem is about one-fourth inch wide, and somewhat flattened, and the plant grows to 15-24 inches tall. What deceives the viewer is that the bases of the leaves encircle the stem in a rather open funnel-like manner, giving the impression of a thick stem. The leaves themselves are almost spatulate, about four to five inches long and two and a half inches wide in the middle. The flowers are of the spidery type, with very slender brown sepals and petals. The white lip is joined to the column, at the end of which its two side lobes flare out, and its needle-like mid-lobe hangs down. The species is native to Costa Rica and Panama.

E. oncidioides. The cause of much confusion, and with a long story behind it, this species is apparently rare even in its native Brazil. Robert Dressler had searched long among the various things called *E. oncidioides* without being convinced that any of them could be the plant originally described by Lindley in 1833. Finally he received some specimens from Brazil which gave masses of yellow flowers when they bloomed. Sweetly scented, they matched Lindley's description and also had the

A

B

C

D

E

F

Fig. 13-4 TOP, *Epidendrum sophronitis;* A, a single flower; B, a plant with several growths in bloom. CENTER, C, *Epidendrum prismatocarpum;* D, *Epidendrum mirabile.* BOTTOM, E, *Epidendrum endresii;* F, *Epidendrum latilobium.*

A

B

Fig. 13-5 *A, Epidendrum ceratistes; B. Epidendrum mooreanum.*

E. paniculatum. Luxuriant panicles of tiny green and white flowers with a touch of pink make this a charming harbinger of spring. The tall canes may not grow higher than two to three feet in a greenhouse, but are said to reach six feet in nature. They are clothed with rather thin, prominently veined leaves, making them quite attractive plants. Each slender flower is about an inch long. The fleshy sepals are green, quite rough on the back, slender and sharply pointed. The petals are much more slender, thread-like in fact, each with a little oar-like tip. The white lip is roundish and bulged on its top surface, with the mid-lobe split into two divergent horns. Delicate red lines decorate the convex lip crest, which is furrowed in parallel channels. The species is widespread from Mexico to Brazil and Argentina.

E. parkinsonianum (syn. *falcatum*). This peculiar and very beautiful species is widespread through Mexico and Central America. It grows in a pendant position, with the stout rhizome climbing upward and the long, flat, channeled leaves hanging down from short pseudobulbs. The two to three six-inch pure white flowers are held on short stems so that they are backed by the green of the foliage, giving the appearance of an arranged bouquet. The slender sepals and petals spread flat. The side lobes of the lip spread wide like a pair of wings; between them the needle point of the mid-lobe gives a sharp accent. The variety *falcatum* differs in having a less stout rhizome, pendant, thin pseudobulbs, and much more fleshy leaves. Also, the flowers are smaller and have more slender parts, and the petals and sepals are tinged with green and purple.

E. pfavii. A waist-high plant with each leafy cane topped by a cluster of eight or more large, bright rose-magenta flowers, it is a sight indeed. The flowers are bold, two inches or more long, with somewhat the shape of our native "shooting star," that is, with the sepals and petals bent backward along the ovary and the column and lip projected forward. They are fleshy and velvety. The lip is a lighter color with a white center, the side lobes bent down beside the mid-lobe, and the mid-lobe divided at its tip. It grows at the edge of cloud forests in Costa Rica and in cultivation it should not be allowed to dry out.

E. polybulbon. This is a charming miniature that spreads quickly into a mat of tiny pseudobulbs about an inch tall, each with a pair of perky, slightly longer leaves. A single flower per pseudobulb is borne on a short stem that arises from a tiny sheath.

long, slender pseudobulbs he described. Another diagnostic feature these plants had, mentioned by Lindley but not possessed by those confused with it, were petals much broader than the sepals. Dressler spoke amusingly of the woes of the amateurs who had been trying to identify various species which always keyed out to *E. oncidioides,* but which were not really that. Their experience completely matched mine with *E. ceratistes* and *E. mooreanum,* described above! Another that falls in this category is *E. gravidum,* or *E. oncidioides* var. *gravidum.*

The half-inch flowers are yellow, tinged with red, and have straight, spreading sepals and petals, with a broad, flaring white lip. The tip of the column is marked with bright purple. It flowers in winter and spring, and occurs natively from Mexico through Guatemala, Honduras, and Costa Rica, to Cuba and Jamaica.

E. porpax. The habit of this plant is somewhat similar to *schlechterianum,* but it is larger. The fleshy, waxy leaves are purplish green, and the incredibly waxy flowers are dark greenish brown, borne singly on short stems that project barely beyond the leaves. The flower has slender sepals and petals and a very round heart-shaped lip whose surface is convex. Three lighter colored ridges decorate the base of the lip. The column is heavily hooded. The branching stems form a mat as they extend out in all directions. It is native from Mexico to Panama and from Venezuela to Peru.

E. prismatocarpum. One of the most showy of the genus, this species has large, airy clusters of two-inch, boldly-marked flowers. They are waxy, pale yellow-green, spotted with purple-black. The sepals and petals are slender, and the spear-shaped lip is slender and pointed, pale purple with a yellow tip and a white border. It occurs in Central America and flowers in the summer. Some plants are quite tall, other specimens smaller, the conical pseudobulbs being from three to six inches in height and the leaves a foot long.

E. pseudepidendrum. This species is very similar to *E. pfavii* in general character and size, but is even more striking with its brilliant flowers, which have fluorescent green sepals and petals and a waxy bright orange lip. Its canes grow three or four feet high, and both old and new ones produce clusters of six to eight flowers each year. The flowers are almost three inches long, with their narrow petals and sepals bent backward. The broad, spreading, finely fringed orange lip is decorated with several yellow keels on the crest, and has no side lobes. The column is pink, adding another color note to the flower. The species is native to Costa Rica (and possibly Panama?), but was "lost" after its original discovery in 1871 until it was rediscovered by Costa Rica's well-known botanist Alexander Skutch in 1958. Now it is very popular and much sought after. It flowers in the fall, and must not be allowed to dry out.

E. pseudo-schumannianum. This species, newly named by J. A. Fowlie, is the Panamanian native previously mistaken for *E. schumannianum* (see below). Its flowers are blue-violet on the under-

surface. The sepals and petals are dusty yellow on the front, marked with brown spots. The longish lip is violet, shading to a paler tone at the tips of the lobes and is not spotted. The side lobes are narrower than those of *E. schumannianum* and do not spread as sharply sideways. The mid-lobe is deeply divided. The slender pseudobulbs reach a height of about four feet. It flowers in the spring, with blooms of one and one-half inches.

E. pseudo-wallisii. This dainty spring-flowering Costa Rican species is less rare than *E. wallisii* of Panama and Colombia. The reed-like stems have six to eight leaves on their upper part. The leaf bases are speckled with fine red warts. Usually two clusters of four or so two-inch flowers come from the top leaf axils. The waxy, yellow, pointed-oval sepals and petals are spotted with red. The large wavy lip is white with red spots, and has long down-pointing side lobes. The mid-lobe has a long central keel and two short side ones. The less divided lip of *E. wallisii* is decorated with purple lines. Both like intermediate conditions.

Fig. 13-6 *Epidendrum radiatum,* a waxy, creamy flower with candy-striped lip. (*Courtesy Rod McLellan Co.*)

E. radiatum. This species is similar to *E. cochleatum* and *E. fragrans* in plant character and flower shape. The flower is more round than *E. fragrans* and heavier in substance, with the lip less pointed and the striping of a deeper shade. It occurs from Mexico to Venezuela and flowers variably.

E. schlechterianum. This little creeping plant is so stiff that it is almost impossible to bend a stem or leaf. The whole plant is waxy with very short leaves that clasp the stem in close-ranked order, and with flowers which open against the end leaves and are colored so much like the plant that they could go unnoticed. There is some variation in color and size; for instance, one from Costa Rica has light green leaves, the younger ones tinged with pink, and flowers of a pinky tan, and one from Panama which is larger and heavier, is of an almost purple-green with flowers of green tinged with red. All are finely toothed on the edges of leaves and flower parts, and the latter are also papillose (covered wth fine little waxy bumps). The species spreads all through Mexico and Central America, Brazil and Peru, Trinidad and Surinam. It flowers in the spring, and also at other times.

E. schumannianum. Long confused with a better known plant from Panama, this species seems to be restricted to Costa Rica and to be the original one described by Schlechter. The flowers are of a bluish violet, their rounded sepals and petals spotted on the inner surface with red-violet. The lip has distinct, flat side lobes, widely separated from the mid-lobe which spreads from a narrow central portion. It is colored like the rest of the flower, but has fine dots down the center. The flowers are a bit over an inch in diameter, and occur on a tall stem from the slender pseudobulb.

E. sophronitis. Surely one of the most unusual of all orchids, the bluish green leaves have a bloom upon them, an overlay of silver. They are oval and short, attached by twos to tiny unseen pseudobulbs. A plant with many growths therefore looks like a whorl or rosette of leaves. From within the leaves and nestled close down into them come very strange flowers. The name *sophronitis* does not describe them at all; *stapelioides* would be better, or something reminiscent of star fish. The sharply pointed, fleshy petals and sepals spread out like the arms of a starfish and are brownish-green with dotted lines of red. The lip is broad at its base, purple and "juicy" looking, with a point that hangs down from its central edge. As the flowers age they become reddish, and if these are what Lindley saw as he described the species, he may be excused for the

name he chose. The column is a very decorative part of the flower, short and with broad wings that lie over the basal part of the lip. Each growth gives three or four flowers, open one or two at a time, through late winter and spring. The species is native to Peru and Ecuador and is cool growing.

E. stamfordianum. This is a popular species, though it is a little hard to get started when shipped in from the wild. It produces its flower stalk from the base of the tall pseudobulb, instead of from the apex. The flowers are produced in generous numbers, and are fragrant. The sepals and petals are narrow, yellow spotted with red. The lip, which resembles a bird with its wings spread, is white to yellow. The plants are found from Mexico to Colombia and Venezuela.

E. tampense. A native of Florida, this is an attractive, though not showy, orchid. The small greenish flowers are borne on a slender stem. The little lip is tinted with purple. This is the little orchid that for a while was rather widely sold by non-orchid dealers as the "butterfly orchid." It flowers any time of the year.

E. vespa. This distinctive species has chunky, waxy, boldly marked flowers that are held upside-

Fig. 13-7 *Epidendrum vitellinum* makes a bright spot of orange-red in the greenhouse. (*Courtesy Rod McLellan Co.*)

Fig. 13-8 *Epiphronitis* Veitchii, one of the earliest bigeneric crosses, made in 1890. It is *E. ibaguense* (*radicans*) × *Sophronitis grandiflora*. (*Courtesy Rod McLellan Co.*)

down on a stiff, erect spike. The plants can have rounded or elongated pseudobulbs, with conspicuous joints at the top where the second and third leaves are attached. The flower spike holds ten to twenty flowers, which are sweetly fragrant in spite of their somewhat reptilian coloring—greenish tan with red spots. The lip has no side lobes, and the mid-lobe is very short, with a fat several-lobed crest, and a flaring outer portion that looks like a mustache, vertically striped with red. The species is widespread through tropical America; one of its native haunts is Machu Picchu, Peru. It likes to be grown cool, and flowers in the spring. It is also commonly known as *E. crassilabium*.

E. vitellinum. The small plant, with pseudobulbs barely two inches tall, bears two slender leaves six to nine inches long. The flower stem is about eighteen inches tall and carries a dozen or more one-and-a-half-inch flowers that are entirely orangered. The variety *majus* is a heavier plant with larger, more brilliant flowers, and is the one usually imported. The species occurs in Mexico at high altitudes and likes a cool spot in the cattleya house. It flowers in early fall.

BARKERIA

This genus of several delightful species was for a while included in *Epidendrum* but has now been moved out again. The plants are slender, with no thickening of the stem and with but a few slender, pointed leaves at the top. The flower spikes are also slender, and are tall and erect, with many sometimes closely spaced, showy flowers. The leaves are deciduous and fall during the winter rest period, at which time the plants must be kept quite dry. The species like intermediate temperatures.

Barkeria elegans. The sepals and petals are dark rose while the rectangular lip is white or near-white with a large shield-shaped spot of crimson on the front half. The huge column is yellow spotted with purple. The flower is shaped much like that of *B. lindleyana.* It is native to Mexico and flowers in the fall.

B. lindleyana. This very lovely species has tall stems of two-inch flowers of a brilliant rose-lavender, almost cerise. The dorsal sepal bends forward, while the lateral ones flare back above the petals. The petals are turned over so that their dorsal surface is uppermost. They are oval-pointed, and the sepals are keeled. The lip is large, rectangular, a bit wavy on the edges, with a paler central area and two raised crests down the middle. The plants vary a bit in color in their range from Mexico to Costa Rica. They flower in the fall.

LAELIA

Laelia is the most nearly like *Cattleya* in appearance, differing from it in structure by having eight pollinia, while the latter has four. Their similarity has given rise to some disagreement among botanists as to whether certain of them should be classed with *Cattleya* or *Laelia*. The special contribution of *Laelia* to hybrids is the brilliant coloring of some species which includes yellow, coppery-bronze, scarlet, and red-orange, as well as deep tones of violet. Their flower parts are slender, and with a few exceptions, the flowers are small. The object in hybridization is to combine the *Laelia* coloring with the better *Cattleya* shape.

The genus consists of about thirty species occurring in Mexico, Central America, and South Brazil; none of the species is common to all these regions. They are found on rocks and trees, often at quite high altitudes. Their culture is the same as for cattleyas, with care to shift plants that do not thrive to warmer or cooler spots until the right conditions are found. Some may do well suspended from the roof of the greenhouse for maximum light. They need quite thorough drying between waterings, especially when not flowering or making active growth.

There is great variety among the species as to height of plants, shape of pseudobulbs, size, and other characteristics. They are often divided into different groups according to plant characters, and this was followed in previous editions of this book. However, we feel that there is little purpose in continuing the practice, so for greater convenience we have put them now in alphabetical order.

The Species

L. albida. These small, fragrant flowers are two inches in diameter, pure white except for a yellow streak down the lip and crimson dots at its base. The lip has small, erect side lobes and a rounded middle lobe. The species occurs in Mexico and flowers through the fall and winter. It is popular in collections.

L. anceps. One of several species with large, showy flowers, this is perhaps the one most widely grown. The pseudobulbs are long-oval, about four or five inches tall, and are slightly compressed on two sides to sharp ridges. They bear single leaves. The flower stems are tall and arching, occasionally reaching three feet in length, and each holds a group of three or so flowers. A plant with many leads or a group of plants makes a beautiful show when in bloom. The flowers are four inches across, with slender, pointed sepals, petals slightly darker and almost twice as wide, and a brilliant three-lobed lip. The side lobes fold over the column, and are purple on the outside, yellow with red stripes within. The front lobe curves downward, and is deep red-purple with a wide yellow ridge down the center that divides into three parts as it passes out onto the crest. It is said that a feature that helps distinguish this species from *L. autumnalis* is a green line on the back of sepals and petals, but this is not always clearly apparent. The flowers last a long time, two months or more on the plant, but do not keep well when cut. A native of Mexico, it flowers in mid-winter.

L. autumnalis. Similar to *L. anceps* in size and general shape, its pseudobulbs are somewhat conical, becoming furrowed with age, and bear two or three leaves. The sepals and petals are bright rose-purple. Side lobes of the lip are erect and partially enclose the column, and are white or light rose on the outside. The mid-lobe has three raised ridges down the middle, the outer two white with purple dots, the inner one yellow. A native of Mexico, this species flowers in the fall. A fine variety goes by the name of *L. gouldiana* and is winter-blooming.

L. cinnabarina. Its charming flowers are bright red-orange, verging on red in some individuals, with slender sepals and petals that are flat and open. The lip has short, pointed side lobes, and a larger, ruffled mid-lobe. The pseudobulbs taper from a swollen base and are five to twelve inches tall, topped by a single foot-long leaf. The inflorescence is from one to two feet tall, and may hold from five to fifteen flowers. This has become very important in hybridizing. It is one of the rock-dwelling species native to Brazil and blooms in the summer.

L. crispa. A popular, summer-flowering species, its blossoms are large, fragrant, and white, except for yellow and purple in the lip. The petals and lip are attractively ruffled. Five or six flowers are produced per stem. The plants are large and cattleya-like, with pseudobulbs to seven inches tall, and a single leaf up to a foot long. The species is native to Brazil. It was crossed with *C. mossiae* in 1863 to form the first bi-generic hybrid.

L. flava. Bright yellow two to two-and-a-half-inch flowers are borne in groups of four to eight on a stem a foot high. The lip has blunt side lobes and a ruffled midlobe with four elevated ridges down the center. The plant tends to be dainty, with slender pseudobulbs tapering from a swollen base to about eight inches in height, bearing single, stiff, often purplish leaves. A rock dwelling type, it occurs in Brazil and flowers in the fall. It plays a role in hybridization.

L. harpophylla. A delightful species which has five to ten brilliant scarlet-orange flowers on a short stem. It is quite similar to *L. cinnabarina.* The tubular lip has a ruffled edge. It is valuable in hybridization. It grows as an epiphyte although akin to the rock living species. A native of Brazil, it flowers in February and March.

L. jongheana. These small plants are quite rare. They have pseudobulbs of two inches and solitary leaves up to six inches, and produce large flowers. The sepals and petals are light rose, the sepals slender and the petals twice their width. The remarkably beautiful rose lip is ruffled, chrome-yellow inside, with seven keels that end in wavy ridges. It is native to damp mountainous areas of Brazil, but where the light is bright.

L. lundii. A true miniature, with slender, almost terete stems and leaves, this species has beautiful

Fig. 13-9   Two species of *Laelia*.
LEFT, *Laelia crispa,* which has plant characters very much
like *Cattleya.*

RIGHT, *Laelia flava,* a small plant with a tall flower stem.
(Courtesy Rod McLellan Co.)

Fig. 13-10   *Laelia lundii,* a miniature.

Fig. 13-11   *Laelia tenebrosa*

The Cattleya Tribe

little one-inch flowers. The petals and sepals are pale pink, while the much ruffled generous lip is marked with branched veins of cerise that converge into solid color in the center. The flowers come on the new growths soon after they make a start, and open before the leaves begin to emerge. After flowering, the growth procedes to form leaves and pseudobulbs. Flowering time is mid-winter. The species is native to Brazil.

L. milleri. This is a new species, named in 1960 by Almiro Blumenschein, and is causing great excitement for its brilliant red color and promising use in bringing red into crosses with *Cattleya.* It is one of the rock dwelling species of Brazil. The pseudobulbs are rounded at the base and tapered at the top, three to four inches tall, with the single, narrow-oval three- to four-inch leaf held at an angle. The flower spike is twelve to twenty inches high and bears four to ten star-shaped flowers, rather like those of *L. cinnabarina.* There seem to be two types of flowers, according to Carl Withner; one a larger flower with narrow sepals and petals and of red-orange color, and the other smaller, but with more rounded parts and blood-red in color. The latter is, of course, the more desirable.

L. perrinii. This is one of the species quite close to *Cattleya* in plant characters and size of flower, which reaches five and a half inches. The dorsal sepal is erect but the lateral sepals curve toward each other. The petals are slightly broader than the sepals and their edges are wavy. The labiata-type lip holds its outer lobe reflexed. The flower is pale rose-purple, the lip deeper purple and streaked inside with yellow. Flowering time is winter. It is native to Brazil.

L. pumila. This pretty dwarf species has a flower almost as broad as the plant is tall. The moderately broad sepals, petals, and the tube of the lip are rose colored, while the outer lobe of the lip is bright red-violet with a tiny patch of white at the tip. The plant has little oval pseudobulbs and stiff shiny, somewhat wrinkled leaves, and is about five inches tall. Flowering time is variable, mostly in the fall. It occurs in Brazil.

L. purpurata. The largest of the genus, it has flowers up to eight inches in diameter. The petals are white, suffused with light rose, and the handsome, bell-shaped lip is a rich velvety purple. The plant occurs in Brazil and flowers in the spring. It and its many varieties are used in hybridization more than any other *Laelia.*

L. rubescens. This is the "Flor de Jesús" of Guatemala, but it occurs all through Central America and Mexico, often dwelling on rocks. There are many color variations, from pink to dark lavender to white. A white form with a dark purple patch in the lip is somewhat reminiscent of a mariposa lily. The plant has round, flattened pseudobulbs that become quite wrinkled with age and a single narrow eight-inch leaf. The flowers are held on a tall stem, several in a cluster. They are two to three inches in diameter, with the petals broader than the sepals, and the lip three-lobed, the lateral lobes enfolding the column and the mid-lobe rounded.

L. sawyeri. See *Schomburgkia galeotiana.*

L. speciosa. Another almost dwarf plant with a large flower, it is one of Mexico's loveliest species. The plant has two-inch oval pseudobulbs, tightly covered with white papery sheathing leaves, and a single stiff five-inch leaf. The single flower is held on a short stem, and can reach six inches in diameter. It is of a pinkish lavender color, and has good shape, with broad petals and a wide open ruffled lip. The lip is white inside with a long raised yellow crest from which radiate a few purple lines, and has a broad lavender border. It blooms in the spring.

L. tenebrosa. Sometimes given as a variety of *L. grandis.* This species has flowers which are a little better shaped than many. They range from coppery-bronze to citron-yellow. The lip is trumpet-shaped, deep purple with a border of white, marked with darker veins. A very striking and unusual flower, it is the parent of many hybrids. The plant occurs in Brazil and flowers in the spring.

L. xanthina. These are yellow flowers, somewhat variable in intensity, ranging from buff to yellow to yellow-green, three to five to a stem. The front lobe of the lip is white streaked with crimson. The flowers have a somewhat leathery texture. This species occurs in Brazil and flowers in winter or spring.

RHYNCHOLAELIA

Two species formerly included in *Brassavola,* and for a while removed to *Laelia,* are now given the generic name *Rhyncholaelia.* Other species of *Brassavola* remain in that genus. The name *Brassavola* will continue in use horticulturally, however.

Rhyncholaelia digbyana. Slender pseudobulbs bear a single fleshy leaf. It is rather slow growing and not too floriferous. The greenish white flower, while waxy, has a remarkable satin sheen. The huge lip, often four inches across, is white or cream colored, its edges marvelously fringed. The lip remains wide where it folds up over the column, carrying the fringe around to meet at the top of the tube. The sepals and petals are slender and plain, pale green tinted with pinkish lavender. The flowers have a strong scent of citrus fruits. The species has eight pollinia, occurs in Honduras, and flowers in July and August.

R. glauca. Rather short, slender pseudobulbs, somewhat compressed, bear a single leaf. The usually single flowers are fragrant, yellowish-green with a large spreading lip that is streaked with red in the throat. The plant occurs in Mexico and Guatemala and has eight pollinia. This species is used in hybridization as well as *digbyana,* but with a view toward small, neat flowers.

BRASSAVOLA

Of the twenty or so species in this genus, some are little known; but many are grown widely for their individual charms and are crossed with other members of this tribe. The plants have terete leaves, or leaves that are slender and so thick as to be almost terete, topping slender stem-like pseudobulbs. The flowers are basically similar, having very slender sepals and petals and a lip whose outer lobe spreads open from a slender tube. It occurs in Central and South America.

Brassavola cordata (syn. *subulifolia*). This plant has pale green sepals and petals, with a pointed heart-shaped lip that is white. The flowers occur three to six on a stem shorter than the leaves.

B. fragrans. As many as twelve of these fragrant flowers can occur on the stem. The sepals are yellowish-white, faintly spotted with purple; the petals are yellowish-white, and the white lip has a green spot at the base.

B. nodosa. These flowers are delightfully fragrant from evening to the middle of the night, earning the nickname of "Lady of the Night." The sepals and petals are white or faintly greenish white. The front lobe of the lip is white, shaped like a long spade. Several flowers are borne on long graceful stems.

Fig. 13-12 *Brassavola nodosa* 'Orchidglade'. Nicknamed "the lady of the night." (*Courtesy of Jones and Scully, Inc.*)

SOPHRONITIS

This is a genus (of about six species) of which one, *Sophronitis grandiflora,* is frequently used in hybridization for the sake of its red color. All are dwarf plants, with brilliantly colored flowers that bear eight pollinia. Both like a coolish spot in the cattleya house.

Sophronitis cernua. These are very small plants. The flowers are colored like those of *S. grandiflora,* but are smaller and borne in clusters of four to eight. The species occurs near Rio de Janeiro and flowers in the winter.

S. grandiflora or *coccinea.* This is a beautiful little plant, compact, with short, egg-shaped pseudobulbs and oval leaves, of a total height of three to four inches. The single flowers are bright scarlet, sometimes red-orange, one and a half to two inches across, very plain and neat. The sepals are spatula-shaped, the petals very round, and the narrow, orange lip folds over the column. It occurs in the Organ Mountains of Brazil and flowers through the winter.

SOPHRONITELLA

A single species makes up this genus, one often included in *Sophronitis* as *S. violacea.*

Sophronitella violacea. It has pseudobulbs one inch long and leaves of two to three inches. The tiny flowers are only an inch across and are bright rose in color. The species occurs in the Organ Mountains of Brazil and flowers in the winter.

NEOCOGNIAUXIA

This genus has only two species, the better known of which was for many years called *Laelia monophylla,* but now bears the name *Neocogniauxia monophylla.* It is restricted to Jamaica, where it grows in the cool rainforests. It is a delicate plant with slender stems three and a half inches tall, covered with red-speckled sheaths. The single leaves are also slender. The one- to two-inch flowers are borne singly atop arching stems. They are brilliant orange-scarlet, with oval petals and sepals and a tiny yellow lip that enfolds the column, just allowing the purple anther cap to be seen. It flowers in the fall and should be grown cool.

SCHOMBURGKIA

Schomburgkia galeotiana. Native to Mexico, it has tall cylindric, fluted, pseudobulbs and bears a wealth of red-violet laelia-like flowers on long arching stems. Its hollow pseudobulbs are inhabited in nature by nests of biting ants. An especially handsome type was found by H. D. Sawyer in 1942 in the mountains of Acuitlapan and named *Laelia sawyeri* by L. O. Williams. Since then some uncertainty has arisen as to its justification as a separate species, and it is tentatively being referred to as *S. galeotiana.*

S. lyonsii. This native of Cuba and Jamaica has two-inch white flowers spotted with purple, their petals and sepals very much ruffled. They are borne in a cluster of ten to twenty at the end of a five-foot stem. The plant is smaller than *S.*

A

B

Fig. 13-13 *A. Sophronitis grandiflora* or *coccinea,* a delightful miniature. The plant is scarcely four inches tall, often only two inches. (*Courtesy Rod McLellan Co.*)
B. A fine form of this species.

tibicinis but quite similar. It flowers in late summer.

S. lueddemannii. The flowers of this species have long slender sepals and petals, very much twisted and ruffled. They are brown, against which the small purple lip, decorated with a yellow crest, forms a nice contrast. Many flowers are borne in a dense head atop a fairly tall stem. It occurs from Panama to northern South America, and flowers in the summer.

S. superbiens. Once included in *Laelia,* this is a large plant with pseudobulbs a foot high from which arise flower scapes five to six feet long. At the end of the scape is a huge cluster of ten to twenty six-inch flowers of a rich lilac-purple. The parts are slender, rounded at the tips, very much ruffled at the edges. The lip has yellow side lobes with purple stripes, and the mid-lobe is yellow with crimson margins and several toothed crests. It is native to Mexico, Guatemala, and Honduras, and has a variable blooming season.

S. thomsoniana. Much smaller than some, it has solid, fluted pseudobulbs six to eight inches tall. The flowers are borne on a three- to four-foot stem, and are a bit over two inches in size, creamy

Fig. 13-14 *Schomburgkia undulata,* the ultimate in ruffles. (*Courtesy H. A. Dunn and H. Griffin*)

white or light yellow, with a purple lip. The sepals and petals are undulate. It is native to Cuba, Haiti, and the Cayman Islands, and flowers in the spring.

S. tibicinis. Huge, hollow, ant-infested pseudobulbs reach two feet in height and are three inches in diameter. The flowering stem can reach as much as twelve to fifteen feet, and holds a dense panicle of two- to three-inch flowers. Their color varies from purple to brownish-orange, and they have slender, twisted, wavy sepals and petals. The lip has rounded side lobes that enfold the column, and a small mid-lobe. It occurs from Mexico to Costa Rica and Cuba and flowers in the summer.

S. undulata. Waxy flowers, purple or brown-purple, with very ruffled sepals and petals are held in a dense head of twenty or more. The small, three-lobed lip of dark lavender exposes the nearly white column. The ridged pseudobulb stands on a long slender stalk. The species is native to Colombia, Trinidad, Venezuela, and Panama, and flowers in early spring.

Other Members of the Cattleya Tribe

Broughtonia is a genus native to the West Indies, containing two or three species sometimes included with *Epidendrum.* Best known is *Broughtonia sanguinea,* a little plant with pseudobulbs two inches long and leaves two to four inches long. It gives a cluster of one-inch, crimson to blood-red flowers which have slender sepals and nearly round petals and lip. It likes somewhat warmer temperatures than cattleyas, and can be grown in the warm greenhouse, or possibly hanging in a warm spot in the cattelya house. Great interest is now being shown in this species for creating small and delightful hybrids with other members of the tribe.

Cattleyopsis is very similar to *Broughtonia* except that it has eight pollinia while *Broughtonia* has four, and the leaves are toothed on the edges. *Cattleyopsis ortgiesiana,* from Cuba, and *lindeni* from Cuba, the Bahamas, and Jamaica are both dwarf plants that have a real appeal.

Diacrium (now being changed to *Caularthron*) contains few species, one of which, *bicornutum,* is superbly beautiful, and is called the "Virgin Orchid" because of its purity of form and grace. The flowers are sparkling white; the oval, pointed sepals and petals are about the same size. The little bifurcated lip is faintly dotted with purple.

Fig. 13-15 *Diacrium bicornutum,* a beautiful species. (*Courtesy H. F. Loomis*)

The flowers are borne on an erect stem which produces up to twenty buds successively. The plant is rather tall, with horn-shaped pseudobulbs that are nine inches tall and have several leaves at their apex. The plant occurs in northern South America, Trinidad, and Tobago, and is often found on sea cliffs where it is bathed with salt spray. It flowers over a period of two months or more, usually during the summer. A very similar species is *bilamellatum.*

Laeliopsis is quite similar to *Cattleyopsis. Laeliopsis domingensis* has four pollinia, and was once included in *Cattleya.* It is grown like *Broughtonia* and occurs in Haiti and the Dominican Republic.

Leptotes. *Leptotes bicolor* is a dwarf plant, with short terete stems only an inch long and a little terete leaf about three inches long. The flower stem bears two to four two-inch flowers that are white with purple in the lip and which have six pollinia. Even smaller is the all-purple *L. unicolor.* They occur in Brazil and flower variably.

Inter-generic Crosses in the Cattleya Tribe

The bi- and tri-generic crosses between *Cattleya, Laelia, Brassavola, and Sophronitis* have already been described. In addition to these, many others have been made. *Diacattleya* and *Dialaelia* are crosses between *Diacrium* and *Cattleya* and *Laelia,* respectively. *Epicattleya, Epidiacrium, Epilaelia,* and *Epiphronitis* reveal their origin as crosses between *Epidendrum* and *Cattleya, Diacrium, Laelia,* and *Sophronitis. Leptolaelia* is the hybrid between *Leptotes* and *Laelia. Liaopsis* is the hybrid between *Laelia* and *Laeliopsis.* The ease with which the various genera may be crossed shows how closely related they are. An amateur might have a good bit of fun trying various combinations. The current interest in the smaller flowered but distinctive hybrids made from the bifoliate cattleyas has spiked a renewed interest in the possibilities offered by epidendrums as parents, particularly the larger flowered kinds such as *E. atropurpureum, E. mariae* etc.

For the names of the myriad other hybrid genera see the booklet on this subject by Garay and Sweet, 1966, and the *Handbook on Orchid Nomenclature and Registration,* 1969.

14

THE CYMBIDIUM TRIBE

The genus *Cymbidium* far surpasses the other genera in this tribe. The tribe grows natively from Japan to Australia, through China, India, Burma, Malaysia, and even the Philippines. Yet within this tremendous area the various species are restricted to rather segregated geographical regions. Some inhabit the cool higher elevations; others dwell where it is warmer. Many have been revered since ancient times; others have been discovered more recently.

CYMBIDIUM

Cymbidiums are among the loveliest of orchids and the most useful. The familiar kinds have tall, arching sprays of waxy, delicately colored flowers which make a wonderful display in shades of yellow, green, rose, and white—plain or subtly blended. The plants themselves are attractive for their grassy foliage. The keeping quality of Cymbidiums is unusual even among orchids, and the blooms last in perfection a minimum of six weeks and sometimes as long as three months.

The serene beauty of the flowers gives them a charm quite different from that of the showy, ruffled *Cattleya* or the curiously flagrant *Paphiopedilum*. Their oval, pointed sepals and petals are of nearly equal size and shape and are colored similarly. The dorsal sepal often bends slightly forward over the lip. The lip is fleshy, with side lobes that stand erect beside the column, and a front lobe that bends down in tongue-like fashion. It is from the somewhat boat-shaped lip

that the genus gets its name (*Cymbid,* Greek for boat). The lip is usually marked with a pattern of spots and lines, bears one or more ridges, and is sometimes downy. The column is nearly erect, often flushed with color, and frequently speckled or lined with the same shade that marks the lip. The species bear from one to thirty blooms on a spike.

Most of the cymbidiums grown today are hybrids, and until now these have been almost entirely the cool-growing types bred from the species with large showy flowers, which range natively through high elevations in the Khasia Hills and the Himalayas. These hybrids flower well only in areas where they can have cool summer nights, nights below 60° and preferably around 55°. With ingenious handling, and especially with the help of cooling systems, some growers have been able to flower them where the nights are warmer. It has been found that the delightful miniature cymbidiums from China and Japan along with a few small flowered "pendulous" species will do well in warmer areas. This along with the current interest in smaller flowers, has opened a new field in breeding. Not only is there opportunity for much variety and beauty in the creation of miniature hybrids, but there is a possibility, in crossing them with the large-flowered kinds, of broadening the temperature tolerance of the latter.

Cymbidiums are evergreen plants, with abundant fleshy roots. The pseudobulbs vary according to the species from robust spheres larger than your fist to a slender and barely apparent thickening of the stem, and are sheathed with the bases of the

Fig. 14-1 *Cymbidium* Peri 'Beefeater.' A very floriferous hybrid. (*Courtesy Armacost and Royston, Inc.*)

leaves. The leaves remain green for several years, and as they fall, their dried bases remain attached to the pseudobulb. The plants are compact and cover a circular area. The leaves are slender, of leathery texture, not particularly fleshy, and vary in length from about a foot in the smaller species to sometimes three feet in the larger ones. The species differ somewhat in the number of leaves per pseudobulb, from nine to fifteen being usual. New growths arise from the base of mature pseudobulbs.

The flower spikes appear from June through October, according to the habit of the plant. Spikes that appear early may flower in the fall, while those that appear later may flower through the winter and spring. However, the development of the spikes and the time of opening of the flowers is not always thus conveniently associated. In some plants spike development, enlargement of the buds, and opening of the flowers proceed in a swift, continuous sequence. In others, although the spikes appear at about the same time, the growth through fall and winter is slow, so that the buds are not ready to open until late spring.

The spike is at first similar in appearance to a vegetative growth, but by the time it is three or four inches long its character becomes apparent. The spikes are rounded and their tips are sharply pointed. The stems are clothed in sheathing leaves

that remain tightly clasped during their early development. As the spike lengthens, the tip which encloses the buds is fatter than the rest of the stem. When the spike has reached about half of its ultimate length, the buds emerge from the last sheathing leaf. The section bearing the buds elongates, giving space between the buds, and the buds enlarge until finally they are ready to open. Usually the buds at the base open first and the rest follow in succession. If a stem is cut after several flowers are open, and is kept in water in the house, the rest of the buds will open and attain really quite good color and substance, although the last few will probably not be up to the quality of the rest. *Cymbidium* is one of the few orchids that will do this. It is therefore unusually useful in cut flower arrangements. However, if you wish perfection in each flower, the spikes should be allowed to mature on the plant.

There are two types of growth and flowering habits. In one type flower spikes are produced from the immature pseudobulb. In the other the spikes come from the fully mature bulb. In the

Fig. 14-2 Vegetative growth and flower spike coming from pseudobulb at nearly the same time. Note how tightly pointed the flower spike is.

Home Orchid Growing

first type, new growth starts in late winter or early spring. This growth is not completely mature when, in late summer or early fall, it gives rise to flower spikes. It continues to grow and mature while the flower spikes are developing. In the second type, new growths are started during the summer, making their appearance shortly before flower spikes arise from the same pseudobulb. These are sometimes so close in development that one cannot tell which are the vegetative growths and which the spikes. However, the flower spikes soon outstrip the vegetative growths, which develop slowly through fall and winter. In the spring they take on a new spurt and grow rapidly so that by mid-summer they are fully mature and ready to start new vegetative growths. Soon thereafter, their flower spikes appear.

It is possible that some of the difficulties encountered in flowering cymbidiums with regularity are due to a mixing of these basic habits in the hybrids. Plants in both categories (those which flower on the immature bulb and those which flower on the mature bulb) must have reached just the right stage of development by late summer in order for flower spikes to be triggered into development. As the end of flowering approaches, push the plants into rapid vegetative growth; step up fertilizing and watering, give all the sun you can, and let the night temperature run about 55°.

Cymbidiums have become so important, for commercial growers and the cut flower market as well as for amateurs, that people all over the country are determined to grow them. There is great need for exact information as to what initiates cymbidium flowers. Research is being done, but is hampered by a number of things. Species cymbidiums are not too numerous in this country, and when available are not obtainable in large numbers. Information gained from the study of species is basic and helps us understand the hybrids. But one cannot assume that because certain species behave in certain ways that other species will behave in the same way, or that hybrids containing them will do so. When research is done on hybrids, it is desirable that the plants studied should be identical, which means that they should be members of the same clone (divisions of the same original plant), and the advent of meristem culture will help here. The accumulation of measured information is slow, and we still have to go pretty much by what has been learned by general experience. Added to these problems is the fact that certain plants just won't do what you expect of them. Certain of the

modern hybrids, which by the flowering of the first seedlings look wonderful, may show themselves to be quite tricky, flowering just often enough to keep you hoping, or flowering for some people and not for others. Reluctant flowering may be caused by chromosomal aberrations, or it may be that certain individuals simply need a different combination of environmental factors.

GREENHOUSE CULTURE

Temperature. In general, we know that cymbidiums flower with greater regularity in areas where the summer nights are cool, rarely up to or over 60°, close to 55° for most of the time, and where they get good bright sun. They tolerate the higher daytime temperatures that go with bright sun, and although temperatures above 85° are not advantageous, with plenty of water and circulation of moist air they will tolerate 95° to 100° if not of too long duration. Cymbidiums do not burn as easily as the thicker leaved kinds. It was at one time thought that perhaps what they needed was a wide difference between day and night temperatures rather than a specifically cool night temperature. This has not proven out, however, for regardless of the day temperature and the spread between day and night temperatures, they actually flower better when the summer nights are close to 55°. Also, vegetative growth is better with cooler nights, the plants being more vigorous and the leaves tougher and stronger.

Flower spikes start forming during the summer and may appear on into the fall. Those spikes that appear last of all may have actually initiated buds earlier but have been slower in growing and therefore tardy in making their appearance. At any rate, the initiation of flower buds and the appearance of spikes in general seem to be brought about by the combination of low night temperatures and long bright days. Plants that fail to make spikes during this period rarely start spikes later on (in winter), undoubtedly inhibited by the short days of winter even though by then the night temperature is favorable for their formation.

If, during the summer (the period of long days) the plants can be furnished the necessary cool nights, flowering should take place. We have found that on our occasional warm nights (in Wyoming) we can lower the temperature by several degrees if we run the evaporative cooler. If the natural humidity in your area is such that an evaporative cooler would not reduce night temperature, we suggest instead using a refrigerative unit. Compact units of modest size are available for use in homes, motel units, etc., and one of these should reduce the night temperature in a small greenhouse. They are more expensive than evaporative coolers, and perhaps would run into too much money for a large greenhouse.

In order to allow the bright light necessary, less shading should be applied than to a cattleya house. The greenhouse temperatures therefore tend to go very high. Although the plants can take short periods of high temperature, they will do better if the temperature can be kept under 85° for the most part. This is possible with extremely free ventilation, all the ventilators open, and someone on hand to damp down the walks and benches and mist the plants several times a day. Far more efficient and easier on both grower and plants is an evaporative or refrigerative cooler, or a pad and fan arrangement, or mist nozzles with fans to move the air upward.

Growers in moderately warm areas have had some success with cymbidiums by putting them outdoors during the summer. The nights may be a few degrees cooler outdoors than in a greenhouse, and the freer air movement is a help. The plants are set on cinder or gravel beds, or are placed on low stands, either in a lath house, or under a roof of lath or plastic shading, or under a tall tree that will give some protection at noon. Cymbidiums that are grown outdoors all year long can take full summer sun. Greenhouse plants that have had nearly full sun and which are put outdoors early enough to become hardened to it may also be able to take full summer sun. There is no advantage in letting them burn, however. Be sure they get plenty of water and spray them for red spiders. They must be brought indoors before frost.

A trick that has been tried, but without consistent success, is treating the plants with ice water during the latter part of the summer. The plants are watered in late afternoon or early evening with water that has been cooled with ice, and some growers even pour ice cubes or crushed ice into the pots. The jubilant success of one summer does not necessarily show up the next. The general plaint is "ice water worked last summer but it didn't work this summer." A possible reason for its not always working is that the roots may be cooled so much that they are not able to absorb nutrients fast enough to supply the needs of the plants. Reports of spikes' dropping their buds would indicate poor

nutrition. Chilling the roots while the air surrounding the leaves is still quite warm may upset the physiological balance of the plant.

During fall and winter temperature is less of a problem. The ideal night temperature is 50°, with a fluctuation to just one side or the other. Some growers confine the fluctuation between 50° and 55°, others prefer to keep it between 45° and 50°. Winter day temperatures are held close to 60° in dull weather, and allowed to rise to 65° on bright days. Too high temperature day or night can cause erratic opening of flowers or the dropping of buds. This brings up a problem dealing with early flowering. The aim of many growers is to beat the season, with flowers as early in the fall as possible. However, spikes that come very early and have the flower buds out of the last sheathing leaf by September, may drop their buds due to the high day temperatures still prevalent through that month. Such early flowering plants should be kept as cool as possible.

Light. During the summer cymbidiums can take, and should have, a great deal of light, a minimum of 4,000 foot candles, and up to 8,000 foot candles where the temperature can be kept from going to dangerous extremes. If this cannot be furnished them in a greenhouse, even with methods to keep down the heat, it is better to move them outdoors. If any burning shows up, move them to where they will receive partial shade during the middle of the day, or provide a lath or plastic screen roof that will admit 70 to 80 percent of full sun.

During the winter the plants must still have good light, clear glass except possibly in areas with extremely bright winter sun, in order to develop the flower buds. Those which have flowers in shades of pink and red will have richer coloring if they develop in bright light. Shade added after they are open helps them keep longer. However, those which have green or yellow flowers should be given shade from the time the buds emerge as these colors tend to fade in bright light. Remove the extra shade as soon as flowering is finished.

CO₂ enrichment of air. The addition of carbon dioxide to greenhouse air has been toyed with for many years, with a history that goes all the way from burning briquettes, using dry ice, and burning candles to dispensing the gas from pressurized cylinders. Few advocates have developed during this time. Recently, carnation producers in the West have had good results. As far as I know, there is as yet little or no data from scientifically controlled work with orchids, but several cymbidium growers on the West Coast are most enthusiastic about their results. It is being used largely for seedlings and meristem propagations, and is said to increase their growth rate and bring them to maturity in a shorter time. One grower also believes it enhances the growth of seedlings and young meristem plants of *cattleya* and other genera. Measured results on mature plants are lacking, but it is generally thought that it is of very little real benefit.

There are CO_2 generators on the market for large greenhouses: the Tecrol CO_2 Generator made by the Whirlpool Corporation, and the HY-LO CO_2 Producer distributed by Geo. J. Ball, Inc. A testing apparatus is available, called the Dioxor Test Kit, which consists of a glass tube filled with a chemical that changes color in proportion to the amount of CO_2 present and is matched to a color scale. No equipment for small greenhouses seems to be on the market at this time; but if the method should prove valuable for amateurs, and if there is a demand, it may be produced in the future. Use of a pressurized cylinder is probably the best means of adding CO_2 to the air of a small greenhouse, controlling it with a pressure gauge and using the testing kit to determine the proper flow.

According to one grower, a concentration of 1,000 parts per million parts of air gives good results. Another uses 1,200 ppm. Below these amounts, the increase in growth is not appreciable, and the benefit does not increase with higher concentrations. Extremely high concentrations may be injurious. It is reported that plants use more fertilizer with added CO_2 and can stand higher day temperatures.

The CO_2 is distributed through the greenhouse by means of perforated plastic tubing (see page 337). It is used only in the daytime. Circulating fans operating in a closed greenhouse keep it diffused throughout the air. Where the air is not circulated, as when only turbulator fans are used, it collects at and below bench level since it is heavier than air, and it remains undisturbed when ventilators are open if exhaust fans are not in use. However, when the air is moved out of the greenhouse, as is done by pad and fan cooling systems, the CO_2 would be removed with it. In the latter situation, CO_2 enrichment would be of benefit only during the months when cooling systems were not in operation.

Potting. Selection of a compost for cymbidiums is a matter of personal choice, the main requisite being that the compost hold water well and furnish free drainage. Types of compost used range from straight osmunda fiber (shredded), to straight bark, with various mixtures of materials in between. Composts consist of half osmunda and half fibrous loam; half osmunda and half dried oak leaves; one-third shredded osmunda, one-third loam, one-third sand; sandy loam mixed with shredded redwood fiber (Palco Pete) and dried oak leaves; bark mixed with sand, peat moss, and oak leaves. Some of the mixes turn out to be largely of fibrous content, others are more soil-like. Some growers package and sell their favorite cymbidium mix. To various mixes some like to add hoof and horn or bone meal for the slow release of phosphorus, and uramite for the release of nitrogen.

Cymbidiums do not like to be disturbed too often, preferably not more often than every two or three years. Mature plants should therefore be given a pot large enough to accommodate a good many new growths. Often from one bulb two growths will come, and from each of these two more the next year. The plants will do better and give more flowers if they are carried on into ten- or twelve-inch pots instead of being divided frequently. A plant needs repotting when its pseudobulbs become crowded against the edge of its container. This will usually happen before the medium has become unfit for growing. If a plant is not doing well, however, remove it from the pot and determine the cause, and then put it in fresh compost.

Plants should be repotted immediately after each one has finished flowering. This will mean that some will be ready in March or April (a few earlier) and some not until May or June. The former will not yet have started new roots, which is ideal, but the latter, even though root tips may be active, should be potted if they need it. Try to disturb the new roots as little as possible. Plants that did not flower should be included with the early group for repotting.

A plant that is not to be divided can be moved into a new pot with very little disturbance. Prepare the new pot with a fair amount of crock for drainage and add a layer of potting medium over the crock. Remove the plant from its pot, shake off the old compost (or if osmunda, dig out as much of the core fiber as you can without tearing the roots), and trim off any dead roots. We usually do no root trimming other than this, unless some roots are so long that they would be broken in the potting process. There are growers who prefer to trim the roots back to a four-inch stub.

Set the plant in the pot so that the level of the new compost will come about half an inch above the rounded base of the pseudobulbs and half an inch below the rim of the pot. Pour in enough of the potting material, previously dampened, to fill the pot to half its depth. Work it in among the roots with your fingers and thump the pot on the bench to settle it. Then proceed to add compost and thump it in place until the pot is full. With your thumbs or a tamper, firm the surface around the inside edges of the pot. If osmunda is used, dampen the chunks first and then tear them apart so that the fiber is softly shredded. Stuff some of it into the central part of the root ball and among the roots, then set the plant in the pot and work the fiber into the space between roots and pot, finishing it with a potting stick. It should be firm, but not as hard as for cattleyas.

In moving plants on into larger pots, it is well to remove any leafless backbulbs that are situated where they can be cut off without disturbing the green part of the plant. If the plant consists of a complete circle of green bulbs with a few backbulbs in the center, these had best be allowed to remain. When the plant has made its new growth toward one side, backbulbs can easily be removed from the other side. Sometimes when a large plant has had the backbulbs removed from one side it leaves a long narrow green section that is awkward to pot. This had best be divided to make two or more plants of better shape.

Dividing a cymbidium is more of a challenge than dividing a cattleya. The pseudobulbs grow so close together that often it is difficult to tell which one comes from which other one. The rhizome that connects them is rather short, and the bulbs must be pressed apart to reveal it. A one-lead division should consist of the lead bulb and at least the bulb behind it. However, since two leads so often come from each bulb, the smallest division it is wise to make often consists of two leads and the bulb from which they arose. From the point of view of flower production, it is better to keep together five or six bulbs. Smaller divisions often do not flower the first year.

After removing the plant from its pot, turn it around in your hands to study it. Press the bulbs apart a bit to see how the bulbs are connected, and gently wiggle or twist a group here and there to see which ones are held together. This will help you plan where to make the divisions. Some growers

feel that it is safer to break the bulbs apart so as to avoid the possible spread of infection from cutting tools. However, the rhizome is woody and hand-breaking sometimes tears good buds away from the base of the pseudobulbs. If you prefer to use a knife or pruning shears, *flame the tool* before going on to each new plant. Each break or cut should be treated to prevent the entrance of fungi or bacteria. Swab it with a strong solution of fungicide or a slurry of Tersan. Dividing a plant of necessity causes many roots to be broken. Trim broken roots back to four-inch stubs. Then pot the divisions as described above.

Two diseases of cymbidiums often are not revealed until potting time. Since leafless pseudobulbs are sheathed with leaf bases, and since these bulbs often remain on the plant for some time, it is often not suspected that they may be internally rotted. However, if pseudobulbs lose their leaves too soon, resulting in a plant that has leaves only on the youngest bulbs, or if the bulbs are soft, infection may be present. Cut through the rhizome between the backbulbs. Infection is shown by brown, dark purple, or black tissue. Discard any bulbs that are

Fig. 14-3 UPPER, when dividing a Cymbidium, press the pseudobulbs apart to determine the "lines" of growth. LOWER, strip the old leaf bases away from the backbulbs. Insert base of pseudobulb in a sand-peat moss mix (or other mix), or use polyethylene bags as described in text.

Home Orchid Growing

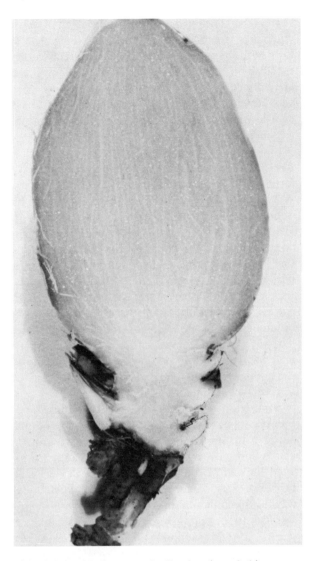
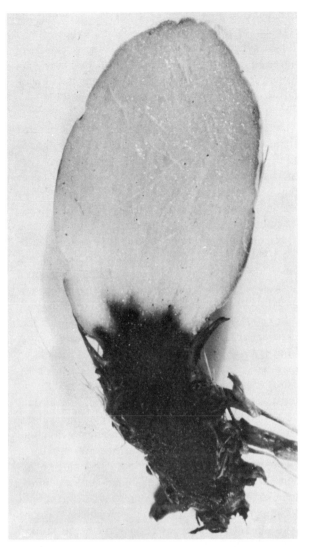

Fig. 14-4 A black or purple discoloration of rhizome or pseudobulb indicates a rot. LEFT, a healthy pseudobulb, RIGHT, a diseased one, cut in half to show internal tissues.

Note the healthy white buds at the base of the one at the left, and the blackened killed buds on that at the right.

infected. Continue to cut forward (flaming the knife between cuts) until clean white or cream-colored tissue is found. The infection spreads from bulb to bulb through the rhizome so that if it is found in the rhizome the chances are that it has already entered the next bulb. The bulbs become rotted inside, which kills the leaves. New growths from infected bulbs often show watery areas on the leaves, and, of course, the leaves soon die. A bacterial soft rot causes the brown to purple watery decay of the pseudobulb. A fungus, *Pythium ultimum,* produces the jet black color in the pseudobulb which soon shrivels and becomes "mummified." Plants from which infected areas have been removed should be soaked for twenty-four hours in Wilson's Anti-damp, Natriphene, or some other

fungicide, and then dried bare-root for ten days. If infection recurs after potting it is best to perform surgery again and re-treat, but if it persists the plant should be discarded.

Care of newly potted plants. Growers differ on this subject. Some put the newly potted plant directly on a regular watering schedule; others prefer to water only lightly until new root growth is evident and then start heavier watering, and this last seems to work best for me. Cut roots seem to heal better when kept on the dry side (the compost just damp), and the formation of branch roots is encouraged. A mist spray of the foliage on bright days helps to prevent water loss and makes up for lessened activity of the roots after potting. Whether the plants should be given extra shade during the recovery period depends on day temperatures. Those which are repotted early in the season may not need extra shade, while those repotted later may benefit from it for a few weeks. Do not start giving fertilizer until root action develops.

Starting backbulbs. Backbulbs may be started right away, or, as some prefer, they may be allowed to dry for ten days or so first. In the latter case, set the backbulbs from each plant in a separate paper bag with a label (a carboard box will also serve) leaving them open to the air and in a dry place. They can be started in polyethylene bags, in which a bit of damp potting medium has been placed. Set the bags on the bench between pots of plants, where they will be shaded by the foliage and kept in an upright position. If the bulbs fall over, the new growth will assume awkward angles. The bulbs may also be started in pots or flats, in a mixture of fine bark and peat moss, or either of these with sand. The new growths will start their own roots when they have reached a length of three inches or so. Those bulbs already in pots can be carried on in them, but those in polyethylene bags or flats should be potted as soon as roots reach a length of about an inch. New growths on backbulbs will come along faster if they are kept a little warmer for a while, with nights of about 58°. This can be accomplished by putting them in the cattleya house, for example. But if you do not have a warm spot for them, they will still make growth. A strong bulb should make a flowering growth the second or third year.

Watering. Except for the period right after potting, cymbidiums should not be allowed to dry out. Depending on the medium you use, water frequently enough to keep the medium quite moist. In bright hot weather, with the luxuriant foliage transpiring water rapidly, you may have to water every day. Large plants that fill the pot will use water more rapidly than newly potted ones. During the cool days of winter, watering will not need to be as frequent.

Humidity and ventilation. Cymbidiums need good ventilation and air movement. The relative humidity should be around 50 percent as an average. If you do not have humidifying equipment, help the plants through the heat of the day by giving them a mist spray over the foliage, and by damping down the ground. The relative humidity may be

kept higher during the growing season than when the plants are in flower. Flowers are susceptible to *Botrytis* spotting under too damp conditions, especially if there is not good air circulation. Fresh air brought into the greenhouse, either by open ventilators or by fans, greatly helps to keep plants and flowers clean and healthy. Ventilators may be left open all night in summer.

Fertilizing. There are almost as many systems of fertilizing cymbidiums as there are compost mixes. For plants growing in a mix containing a good bit of organic material, or in osmunda fiber, a 30-30-30 fertilizer used about every other watering is sufficient. However, for plants grown in bark or a mix that is largely bark, a high nitrogen fertilizer is necessary with every watering. When organic materials such as bone meal, leaf mold etc., have been added, the materials which these release need not be duplicated in a chemical fertilizer applied with the watering. For instance, if uramite has been added to bark before potting, it is not necessary to use a high nitrogen fertilizer; rather, a balanced fertilizer should then be used.

Some growers use the same fertilizer throughout the year, but most like a schedule of additional nitrogen in the spring to speed vegetative growth, and a low nitrogen-high phosphorus fertilizer toward the end of summer to encourage flower spike formation. This can be accomplished in different ways. Ammonium nitrate can be added to a soluble fertilizer in the spring, one part to two of the latter, or dry fertilizer applied as described below. In August, superphosphate can be sprinkled on the potting medium and among the pseudobulbs (this is slow dissolving and gradually releases extra phosphorus through a long period), or one can buy a fertilizer low in nitrogen.

A dry feeding program for plants grown in a soil mix is outlined as follows by Paul Gripp: May 15 and July 1, give blood meal. August 1 and September 15, give a mixture of four parts blood meal, four parts single superphosphate, and one part potassium sulphate. October 30, give a mixture of four parts blood meal, four parts single superphosphate, one part potassium sulphate, and one part dolomite lime. Apply a small handful over the surface of each 12-inch pot, proportioning accordingly for smaller pots. He cautions that this is applicable only for plants in a soil or soil-like mix. Plants in bark may be injured as the material would quickly filter down through it and burn the roots. On soil it remains on the surface where the minerals are slowly released and carried to the roots by water.

Garden Culture

In regions where the temperature does not fall below 26°, cymbidiums may be grown out-of-doors. Large trees will furnish noon shade with a little sunlight filtering through, or a lath house may be used in lieu of trees. The laths should run north and south so that the sun will cast moving shadows, and the space between laths adjusted according to the intensity of the sun in your area. Where day temperatures are moderate or where the sun is not too intense, the plants may be able to take full sun. When the thermometer shows signs of falling below 26°, the plants should be covered for frost protection.

The plants may be grown in beds, with soil prepared in a ditch one foot deep and one foot wide. In the ditch put a layer of leaf mold six inches deep, and then a layer of horticultural peat to an equal depth. This is tramped down, and a layer of sandy soil added on top. Then, the compost is thoroughly mixed by turning it over two or three times with a shovel. Moisten the compost and wait a day or two before planting.

Remove the plants from their containers, and carefully loosen up the ball of fiber or compost. If it is possible to do so without injuring the roots, spread them out about three inches below the surface, cover them with pure peat, and put some peat directly around the pseudobulbs. Then fill in with the compost. If the roots are too tightly tangled, set the loosened ball in the trench and fill the compost in around it. Water lightly until new growth starts, giving frequent syringings of the foliage. When the plants are established, they may be watered rather abundantly.

Cymbidiums are attractive grown among rocks along with other plants, where their location is carefully prepared with sufficient compost.

Seedlings

Cymbidium seed is obtained by hand pollination and sown in flasks after the method described for cattleyas. It sticks to the sides of the tube of disinfecting solution, but may be handled either by keeping it agitated when a dropper is used, or by picking it up with a platinum loop. The seed is somewhat slow to germinate, but the seedlings grow well.

When the seedlings are removed from the flasks, they may be put either into five-inch community pots, or, better, in flats. Pure osmunda fiber is satisfactory for their growth, as are the composts described earlier. The community pots should be kept in a covered box, or the flat covered with a pane of glass, to furnish them the close, damp atmosphere conducive to rapid growth. At this stage, they benefit from a night temperature of 58° to 60°. When the plants are three or four inches tall they may be moved from the community pot into three-inch pots. If those in flats still have room to grow, they may be left there for a while longer.

Seedlings may be shifted to larger pots as the need requires without disturbing the ball around the roots. They grow rapidly, and often flower at five years of age, though the naturally slower ones may take seven or eight years.

Cymbidium seedlings are reasonably priced and are a good buy for the amateur. Since it takes back-bulb propagations two or three years to reach flowering size, two- or three-year-old seedlings will actually flower about as soon. Unless you have a particular interest in obtaining propagations from certain plants, the young seedlings will give the greatest satisfaction.

Fig. 14-5 A seedling in a five-inch pot developing its first flower spike.

The Species

Of the sixty or more species of *Cymbidium,* only half have gained importance from a cultural point of view. Even these appear less and less in cultivation as their place is taken by the superior hybrids. In addition to the large flowered species there are a number with smaller flowers, some most generous in the numbers they produce, which may increase in importance and popularity because of their tolerance for warmer temperatures. Lastly, there are the charming miniature species, many of which may also be grown under warmer conditions.

The Species: Large Flowered, Mostly Cool Growing

C. eburneum. This species seems to be rather hard to grow, and is now rarely cultivated. But it has had a great influence on hybrids, in fact it was one of the parents (with *C. lowianum*) of the first *Cymbidium* hybrid, made in 1889, the famous *C.* Eburneolowianum. The broad flower parts of *C. eburneum,* its round shape, and delightful fragrance have come down through a long line of hybrids, largely through mating other species with the primary *C.* Eburneolowianum. Its flowers are rosy-white, or pure white, with a creamy lip, dotted with rose-purple and having a yellow ridge down the center. The flowers are three to four inches across, usually only one to a stem. The plant is rather weak growing, with slender pseudobulbs and leaves one to two feet long. It grows in the Khasia Hills at elevations of 5,000-6,000 feet and flowers in late winter and early spring.

C. erythrostylum. So called because of its red column, this species has flowers that are white with a few rose colored dots at the base of the petals and sepals. The creamy lip is heavily lined with red-violet. The petals are held forward, meeting at the top edges, and give the appearance of a hood over the lip. This hooded aspect is often inherited by hybrids that include this species. The early flowering habit of this species is one of the characteristics sought in its hybrids. The plant is small, with pseudobulbs one and a half to two inches tall, and leaves ten to fifteen inches long. The arching flower spike bears four to eight flowers. It occurs in Annam, and flowers in the fall and winter.

C. giganteum. In spite of its large, fragrant flowers and early flowering habit, this species is not used as much now as it was at one time. It does not have the good keeping qualities that we now expect, and its hybrids are often dull in color. It is found

in the ancestry of many hybrids, however, to some of which it has contributed its yellow-green color. It occurs in Nepal, and flowers in fall and winter.

C. grandiflorum (preferably called *hookerianum*). These handsome plants are distinguished by having the base of each leaf expanded into a ribbed sheath, striped yellow and green. Their growth is tufted, the pseudobulbs scarcely thickened. The fragrant flowers reach five inches in diameter, and occur five to fifteen on a curving spray that originates from the base of the newly formed pseudobulbs. The petals and sepals are clear green, and the large lip is pale yellow spotted with red-purple. In using this species in breeding, growers have had to eliminate its only poor feature, that of frequently dropping its flower buds before they open. Sometimes the buds sit on the stem for weeks apparently ready to open, only to turn pink and fall off. The hybrids we now have flower satisfactorily, and many of them trace their green color to *C. grandiflorum.* The species grows natively in Nepal, Sikkim, and Bhotan.

C. l'ansoni. This species was once thought to be a variety either of *lowianum* or *tracyanum,* but its distinct differences make it a valid species. Its striking flowers have yellow sepals and petals, heavily lined with purple-brown, and the large spotted lip is pale in contrast. Its most outstanding hybrid is *C.* Ceres (*l'ansoni* × *insigne*) which ranges from pink to red and which, in turn, has been a most successful parent. Although it occurs in upper Burma, only a few plants have ever been found.

C. insigne. One of the most valuable of the species, it is prized for its vigor, its compact growth, and its tall, upright spikes of twelve to twenty flowers. The spikes grow three to four feet tall. The flowers range in color from white (var. *album*) and near white, to rose-lilac, with rosy dots at the base of the sepals and petals. They are three to four inches in diameter. The lip is rounded, dotted with rose, and has a yellow keel. Both the white and colored forms have been used in making many fine hybrids, which have since been combined in various ways to give a wide variety. Two of the important hybrids are the tetraploids *C.* Alexanderi 'Westonbirt' (Eburneo-lowianum × *insigne*), and *C.* Pauwelsii 'Compte d'Hemptinne' (*lowianum* × *insigne*). *C. insigne* was discovered comparatively recently, in 1901. This species occurs in Annam and flowers in early spring.

C. lowianum. This is another handsome and much used species. The plants are large, with pseudobulbs up to nine inches tall and leaves two to three feet long. The flower spike arches gracefully, and bears fifteen to thirty-five large flowers. It has many varieties that are almost as desirable as its hybrids. The flowers keep for two months or more, and this desirable quality, along with its floriferousness, has been handed down to its progeny. The flowers are greenish-yellow with faint red or brownish veins. The rather pale yellow lip is downy and has a V-shaped red-brown blotch on the front lobe. One of its often-used varieties, var. *concolor,* has clear yellow-green petals and sepals, and its lip is marked with a light orange-buff patch. It occurs in Burma, and flowers from late winter to early summer.

C. parishii. This rather rare species resembles *eburneum,* except that the pseudobulbs and leaves are larger, and the spike bears three to six flowers instead of one or two. The fragrant, white flowers are four inches in diameter, with the lip decorated with large purple spots. The parent of the many hybrids made from this species was the variety 'Sanderae,' distinguished by much more color in the lip, and broader and more pointed petals and sepals. It has been combined with many of the other fine species. It grows natively in Annam, and it flowers in the summer.

C. schroederi. This species is found in the ancestry of many hybrids, but does not add much to them in quality. Therefore it has not continued in use. It has greenish yellow flowers and a lip marked with dull red blotches. It occurs in Annam.

C. tracyanum. This species has contributed its early flowering season to its descendants. The yellow-green flowers are fragrant and occur five to twenty-five on a spray. The plants are vigorous and are grown with ease. It is said that, while the species is often used out-of-doors, its flowers keep better in the damper conditions of a greenhouse. The flowers are yellow-green, marked with bright red, and have a yellow lip also marked with red. The plant occurs in Burma and Siam. Flowers are produced in the fall.

The Species: Small Flowered, Pendant Spikes, Warm Growing

The plants in this group are smaller in general than in the previous one, and the flower spikes, instead of arching upward from the pseudobulb, travel across the potting medium and down over the edge of the pot. With one exception, they like intermediate or warm temperatures, and may be grown in bark or a loose cymbidium mix. They like plenty of sun. They are not common in cultivation as yet, but will probably be more readily available as time goes on. Some of them may be grown out-of-doors in such places as Florida and Hawaii. In a greenhouse be careful not to over-water them, and to pot them high to give their spikes a chance to grow out over the surface of the medium.

C. aloifolium. These straw-colored or tawny flowers have a yellow lip with brown markings. They are borne on a pendant spike, and are about one and one-half to two inches across. The plant, which occurs in Burma, blooms in winter and spring.

C. atropurpureum. A dozen or more heavy little flowers are borne on a drooping spike about a foot long. The sepals and petals are maroon-purple with a velvety sheen, and the lip is white. The plant, which is epiphytic, occurs at elevations of 500 to 3,000 feet in mountainous areas of Malaya, and the Philippine Islands. It flowers in late spring and early summer.

C. devonianum. The flower spike of this odd plant will burrow down through the potting medium if not trained over the edge. It is said to have an unpleasant odor, which may not carry on to its hybrids. The dense flower spike carries over twenty olive to tawny flowers that have a rosy lip decorated with a dark purple spot on each side. A number of hybrids have been made with this species. The leaves are broad and fleshy and taper to a narrow base or petiole. It occurs in northern India, needs cool temperatures, and flowers in the spring.

C. finlaysonianum. These large plants give many two-inch flowers that are borne on a pendant spike that reaches two to four feet in length. It grows natively along with *C. atropurpureum,* and is also epiphytic. The flowers are dull yellow with a central stripe of reddish-brown, and are fragrant in the morning. It flowers in the spring and summer. The plant grows easily in warm areas.

C. pendulum. The plant has stiff, upright leaves and a short pendant flower spike. The pretty little flowers are light yellow trimmed with purple, and have a purple lip with yellow lines. This species is native to northern India. It flowers variably.

The Species: Miniatures

We are indebted to orchid lovers of Japan for making us aware of the charms of the miniatures native to Japan and China, which the Japanese cherish for their beautiful foliage as well as for their flowers. The species *pumilum, devonianum,* and *tigrinum* were the first to become known and used

 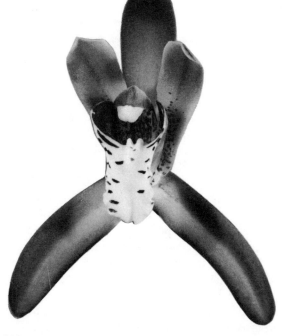

Fig. 14-6 LEFT, *Cymbidium devonianum.* RIGHT, *Cymbidium tigrinum.* (*Courtesy Fred A. Stewart, Inc.*)

in hybridization in England and subsequently in this country. Species from other countries are now making their way to our shores and offer a new array of possibilities in hybridization.

Fortunately for growers in this country, all of the miniature species and their hybrids (at least those made so far) can be grown along with cattleyas, although a few require a warm spot in a cattleya house. A few are epiphytic, identified by their velamen-covered roots. These do well in bark, while the others will do well either in bark or in a cymbidium mix. Japanese growers apparently keep their plants somewhat cool during the winter, with night temperatures between 40° and 50°, growing them warmer in the summer and with "half-sun." Whether they would do better in our greenhouses if kept this cool during the winter we do not know, because they seem to do very well with cattleya temperatures all year round.

C. canaliculatum. This is an epiphytic plant which gives dense spikes of attractive little flowers in a wide range of colors, including brown, green, yellow, magenta, and maroon. The variety "Sparkesii" is the favorite with its deep maroon petals and sepals and its pink lip with red dots. The species occurs in Australia. It has fleshy deeply channelled leaves from whence it gets its name. It flowers in the spring.

C. ensifolium. (Called *Kenran* in Japan, meaning "Sword Cymbidium.") The small flowers, many to the spike, are fragrant, yellow-green, and have a white lip blotched with dull red. The blossoms appear in the fall. It occurs in China and, rather rarely, in Japan.

C. faberi. The Japanese call this species *Ikkei-kyuka,* which means "many flowers on a scape." There are three color forms—reddish, greenish, and white. The plant needs plenty of water, especially during the growing season, and will do well with a bit less light than some other species. A native to China, it flowers in late spring and early summer.

C. forrestii. In Japan this species is known as *Shina-Shunran* or "Chinese spring orchid." The very fragrant flowers are green tinged with red and are borne singly on short stems. The plant occurs in China and flowers in the spring.

C. gyokuchin. The name is derived from *Gyo-chin,* meaning "young fish in the water." It was described in an ancient Chinese book on orchids and was imported into Japan over a century ago. The sepals and petals are pure yellow-green, and the lip is pure white. Less fine varieties have touches of red. Some have the foliage striped or mottled with white or yellow. It occurs in China and Formosa, and flowers in the fall.

C. kanran. ("Winter orchid.") The spikes of

Home Orchid Growing

this species carry many fragrant little flowers, which vary from green to red. The deep green foliage is glossy, and in some varieties the margins of the leaves are white. A native of Japan and Formosa, it flowers in late fall and winter and cannot take too strong light.

C. hoosai. This species has up to fifteen fragrant flowers to a spike. Two forms occur. Those from China are called *Shina-hoosai,* and are such a dark purplish red that they are often called the "black cymbidium." Those from Formosa are called *Taiwan-hoosai,* and are of a paler color. Both flower in the early spring.

C. madidum. Another of the delightful Australian species, this one is a fairly large plant but has miniature flowers, as many as forty or more, one inch in diameter, on a stem. They are very fragrant, chartreuse except for a dark spot in the lip, and have rounded parts. In spite of the fact that it is difficult to breed, Mary B. Ireland, who has created many miniature hybrids, has made many crosses between it and both diploid and polyploid standard types.

C. pumilum. This very floriferous little plant bears thirty flowers to a spike. The blossoms are purplish red with a white lip dotted with red. Many of the plants have variegated foliage. They like a cool spot in the cattleya house, although the hybrids can be grown somewhat warmer. The species is native to China and flowers in early summer. The famous *Cym.* Minuet is *pumilum × insigne.*

C. suave. This is the third one of the Australian species, and a newcomer to this country, introduced by Emma Menninger. Except that it has a foot-tall stem rather than a pseudobulb, and produces grassy foliage, it is quite similar to *C. madidum.* Fragrant in nature (not always in cultivation), it has one-inch apple green flowers with a brown spot on the lip. Its parts are rounded, the lip tongue-shaped. Emma Menninger, leader in miniature breeding, is the first to make any headway in hybridizing it, and progress is being made.

C. tigrinum. A truly dwarf species, the pseudobulbs are about an inch tall and leaves four inches long, although the flowers are rather large, sometimes reaching three inches in diameter. Two or three blooms occur to a stem. The sepals and petals are green tinged or spotted with brown, and the large lip is white or cream colored marked with red-purple. The plant, which occurs in Burma and Thailand and flowers in the fall, is frequently used in hybridization.

C. virescens (syn. *goeringii*). In its native Japan this species is called *Shunran,* "Spring Orchid."

The little plants have grass-like leaves about six inches long, often margined with yellow or white. The flowers are green with tinges of red, and are borne singly on short stems. They do not open fully. The species is spring flowering.

Cymbidium Hybrids

The destiny of the large-flowered cymbidium was determined by the discovery of *Cym.* Alexanderi 'Westonbirt' (*Cym.* Eburneolowianum × *Cym. insigne* 'Westonbirt') registered by H. G. Alexander in 1922. This lovely large white hybrid was so successful in transmitting its size, shape, and substance to its progeny that it became the most popular parent in cymbidium history, and its value in hybridization has become legendary. Many, many crosses have been made with Alexanderi 'Westonbirt' as a parent. The best of the progeny, selected for their size, shape, and substance have been in turn crossed with each other, and back again to Alexanderi 'Westonbirt.' Thus has developed a long line of Alexanderi 'Westonbirt' hybrids. It was not known until fairly recently that Alexanderi 'Westonbirt' was a tetraploid, having 80 chromosomes (four times the haploid number of 20, and thus designated as 4n). In addition, many of the selected individuals from among its progeny have also proven to be tetraploid. Where crosses are made with both parents tetraploid, progeny that are almost entirely tetraploid are possible.

The dominance exhibited by Alexander 'Westonbirt' includes a strong influence on the color of the progeny. This influence causes a paling of the expected color, regardless of how brilliant the other parent may be, so that the offspring are almost entirely white, cream, or pale pink. This does not detract from the beauty of the hybrids themselves, for they are wonderful large flowers. From this line of hybrids have come the best of the white cymbidiums, as well as many that are of delicately lovely coloring; but it has meant that other breeding lines have had to be developed in order to achieve more color. *Cym.* Pauwelsii 'Compte d'Hemptinne' (*insigne × lowianum*), a buff-pink tetraploid registered in 1911, is now being used with great success as a parent. It imparts good size and substance and, when used with brightly colored hybrids, does not dim the colors. Apparently, when used with Alexanderi 'Westonbirt' hybrids, its presence allows succeeding generations to be more brightly colored and to show a wide range of colors.

Numbers of tetraploid hybrids stemming from these two great progenitors are themselves proving to be excellent parents. Some may in time become as valuable as their older counterparts. The four which we shall name are all English crosses, proven by count to be tetraploids, and have shown their worth in recent crosses. (While these individuals are known to be tetraploids, this does not mean that all the other individuals in these crosses are tetraploids. A good many more have been found to be, and the chances are that some crosses may be entirely tetraploid, but only a count can prove it.*)

Balkis 'Silver Orb,' Balkis 'Luath,' and Balkis 'Perfection,' from the cross registered in 1934 by Lionel de Rothschild, Exbury: Alexanderi 'Westonbirt' × Rosanna 'Pinkie.' The colors are white and blush pink.

Babylon 'Castle Hill' and Babylon 'Carpentier' from the cross registered in 1952 by H. G. Alexander: Olympus 'Rex' × Pauwelsii 'Compte d'Hemptinne.' They are rich pink in coloring.

Rosanna 'Pinkie' and Rosanna 'Warringal,' from the cross registered in 1927 by H. G. Alexander: Alexanderi 'Westonbirt' × Kittiwake. These are blush pink.

Nam Khan, from the cross registered by Lionel de Rothschild in 1941: Pauwelsii 'Compte d'Hemptinne' × Rosanna 'Pinkie.' The colors range from pink to yellowish pink.

Growers who have obtained divisions of these plants, as well as other fine members of these crosses, are using them to great advantage. Some of their progeny may in the next decade equal or outshine them, if that is possible. Results of breeding the above plants have shown them capable of allowing other colors to come through.

The breeding of tetraploids should not overshadow the variety of diploid hybrids. Many of the diploids rival the tetraploids in quality, and many outshine tetraploids in brilliance and variety of colors, if not in size. In general, the diploids produce more flowers to the spike. The majority of good greens, yellows, and reds are diploids. Growers are constantly on the alert for the spontaneous appearance of tetraploid plants in these colors. These might arise from the accidental non-reduction of reproductive cells, allowing a 2n sperm cell to fertilize a 2n egg cell. If such plants should occur, and should be capable of transmitting their color to all of their progeny, they would be invaluable.

* D. E. Wimber, G. A. L. Mehlquist, and E. W. Wells have made over 300 chromosome counts in cymbidiums.

(See under Colchicine, Chapter 8, work on creating tetraploids from diploids.) Growers are crossing many of the diploid greens, yellows, and reds with Balkis, Babylon, Rosanna and Nam Khan (and their offspring) to produce triploids (3n). In the triploid progeny, a variety of colors come out, but a percentage have the desired color of the diploid combined with the better size of the tetraploid. Some of the diploid hybrids being used for this purpose are Apollo 'Exbury' (yellow); Saigon and Flare (red); and Blue Smoke and Vale of Kashmir (green). In purchasing seedlings from such crosses, one should know in advance that they will not be uniform in coloring—for instance, a cross with a green diploid will give only a percentage of greens out of a variety of colors. With the swing to wider variety in sizes, (as evidenced by hybridizing the smaller-flowered species) a diploid with brilliant color or a subtle combination of colors, which is also graced by nice form and heavy substance, should be admired for its own intrinsic qualities. With cymbidiums, as with cattleyas, we have passed the stage at which everything has to be big to be of value.

In conjunction with the polyploid breeding of cymbidiums, there occasionally occur pentaploids (5n) and plants with odd numbers of chromosomes, aneuploids. The pentaploids are said not to be superior to tetraploids and triploids in quality of flowers and plant characters. The aneuploids may be abnormal in some way, either in plant growth or in the flowers themselves. It is possible that reluctance to flower or failure to flower may be caused in some cases, but not all, by the presence of extra chromosomes which may upset the physiological balance of the plant. A certain amount of sterility is encountered among the aneuploids as well as among hybrids between unlike species, for example, crosses between miniature and large species.

An interesting observation has been made on the number of flowers produced to a spike in the primary hybrids of the Himalayan species. You might expect that if you crossed a species that usually produced one bloom with one that produced twenty-five, the resulting hybrid would give something close to the mean (average) between these two, or thirteen. But that is not the way it happens. Actually, a hybrid between a species that gives one and a species that gives twenty-five will itself produce about five or six flowers to a spike. Mathematically, five is the geometrical mean between one and twenty-five, arrived at by multiplying one by

Fig. 14-7 LEFT, *Cymbidium pumilum album*, a true miniature. (*Courtesy Yoshio Nagano*)
CENTER, *Cymbidium devonianum*, with pendulous flower spike. (*Courtesy Fred A. Stewart, Inc.*)

RIGHT, *Cymbidium* Flirtation 'Princess Royal', a hybrid between *Cym. pumilum* and *Cym.* Zebra. (*Courtesy Fred A. Stewart, Inc.*)

twenty-five and taking the square root of the product. Studies of various crosses have shown that cymbidiums follow this general rule, and the rule may be used to predict the number of flowers you will get in any primary hybrid. As inheritance becomes more complicated in advanced hybrids, it is not possible to trace this feature through the maze of habits represented in any one plant. This rule may not hold true in hybrids between the Himalayan species and the small-flowered ones. In *Cym.* Jean Brummit (*devonianum* × *eburneum*), the number of flowers per spike comes close to the number produced by *devonianum*.

Miniature hybrids have taken a great hold on the fancy, both of hybridizers who are excited by the challenge they present and growers who love them for their appealing qualities.

The first crosses were made in England in 1944; McBean's *C.* Pumander (Lois Sander × *pumilum*), and Brummitt's *C.* Jean Brummitt (*devonianum* × *eburneum*). The first American hybrid was Stewart's *C.* Flirtation (*pumilum* × Zebra) in 1955. These sparked a wave of hybridization in which Emma D. Menninger and Mary B. Ireland played large roles. Crosses were made almost entirely between the miniatures and diploid standard types, mostly with *pumilum* at first and then with *tigrinum, aloifolium, ensifolium,* and *madidum,* this last one of the most recently introduced species. This type of hybrid is called "miniature," although the size of the flowers is increased and the shape influenced by the larger parent. However, they are still delightfully small, and are more usable than the miniatures themselves.

Then followed crosses between miniatures and tetraploid standards, which are euphoniously called "polymins." Although the first was made by Bowers in 1955, Sweetheart (*pumilum* × Alexanderi 'Hamilton Smith'), it was a Menninger cross that started the wave of polymins. This was Fairy Wand (*pumilum* × Princesse Maria) in 1957.

These crosses proved discouragingly sterile as parents, except for one, Bowers' *C.* Sweetheart, which he found to be fertile and with which he made hybrids with such famous parents as Blue Smoke (*C.* Lynette), Alexanderi 'Westonbirt' (*C.* Showgirl), and Nila (*C.* King Arthur). The results have so far been splendid.

The future in miniature breeding is promising. Barely a start has been made. It is to be hoped that in carrying on further hybridization the real meaning of "miniature" will be remembered, and small size kept as one of the sought-for attributes.

Other Members of the Cymbidium Tribe

Cyperorchis is a genus closely related to Cymbidium, and native also to the Khasia Hills and the Himalayas. It has very few species. The flowers differ from *Cymbidium* in having narrower sepals and petals, which remain closed for nearly their entire length, spreading apart only at the tips. The flowers are small and are borne close together on the stem.

Grammangis differs from *Cymbidium* in that the leaves arise from the apex of the tall pseudobulb About four species are known, and these are nat⁻ to Madagascar and Java.

Grammatophyllum is a genus ranging from Southeast Asia through Borneo, New Guinea, and the Philippines. It became famous for the gaint species *G. speciosa,* which can reach ten to twenty-five feet in height and bear flower spikes ten feet long, each with up to a hundred flowers. Plants in New Guinea (called *G. papuanum* but possibly not differentiated from *speciosum*) have weighed over 2000 pounds. The flowers are six inches in diameter, clear yellow, spotted with purple. *G. fenzlianum* is not as large, but gives flower spikes of five feet with sixty flowers each, green or yellow-green, spotted with brown. *G. measuresianum* has pseudobulbs about one foot tall with very large leaves, two feet long and five inches wide.

Its flower sprays can also be five feet long, with thirty to fifty two-inch blooms, cream with dark brown markings. *G. scriptum* is similar in size to *G. measuresianum* and has very handsome four-inch flowers. The are greenish brown with elongated spots of red-brown. All prefer warm conditions but can be grown in an intermediate house. They require frequent watering and heavy fertilizing while growing, a bit less after growth is made up.

Cymbidiella is native to Madagascar, and requires warm, very humid conditions. *C. rhodochila* is quite like *Cymbidium* in plant characters and has four-inch flowers, many to a spike, which are light green marked with many purple spots.

Home Orchid Growing

Cattleya aclandiae

Cattleya Brabantiae: first hybrid to receive an award—1863, RHS

Cattleya leopoldii 'Alba'

Sophronitis coccinea

Cattleya walkeriana

Barkeria lindleyana

Epidendrum endresii

Laelia flava

Brassavola digbyana

(*Rebecca T. Northen*)

Laelia milleri

Broughtonia sanguinea

Epidendrum medusae

Cym. Stanley Fouraker 'White Magic'
    HCC/AOS

Cym. Balkis 'Silver Orb' AM/AOS

(Courtesy Fred A. Stewart, Inc.)

Cym. Earlyana 'Ivory Gem'

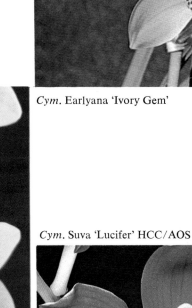

Cym. Suva 'Lucifer' HCC/AOS

Cym. San Francisco 'Meadow Mist' AM/AOS,
    AM/RHS

15

THE CYPRIPEDIUM TRIBE

The Cypripedium tribe consists of four terrestrial genera, one genus native to the north temperate zone, one to southern Asia, and two to South America. The first two genera are well known, and both have been called *Cypripedium* in common usage. However, the name *Cypripedium* accurately belongs only to the ladyslippers of the north temperate zone, found in the woods of North America, northern Asia, and Europe. The southern Asiatic genus is *Paphiopedilum*. The South American genera are *Phragmipedium* and *Selenipedium*.

Paphiopedilum is the genus usually cultivated by amateur and commercial growers, and once nicknamed the "Cyps." Included in this genus are some of the most striking of all orchids. In florist shops they compete for admiration with cattleyas and cymbidiums and are becoming increasingly popular. They have been favorites of English growers for generations. Their marvelous range of colors—from yellow, green, brown, red, and purple, to white—is often subtly combined in single flowers. *Phragmipedium* and *Selenipedium* are genera interesting to collectors, although not widely grown. Our native cypripediums are known by all who love and study wild flowers and may be grown with special care in gardens.

The flowers of the Cypripedium tribe are distinct, differing markedly from those of other tribes. The most appealing floral part is the lip, which is shaped like a pouch or slipper and which suggested their name (*Cyprus*, sacred to Venus, and *pes*, *pedis*, Latin for foot). Conspicuous, too, is the dorsal sepal standing guard above the lip, often broad and brilliantly marked. The petals extend laterally and are slender in proportion to the dorsal sepal. The other two sepals are fused together and lie behind the pouch. Usually they are hidden in a front view of the flower, but when they are enlarged, they add one more touch of beauty.

It would seem that these structures would be enough to distinguish the tribe. But botanically speaking, the number of fertile anthers is more important. All members of the Cypripedium tribe have two fertile anthers, whereas other tribes have only one. A third anther, which is sterile, is modified to form the conspicuous shield-like body called the staminode, which projects forward from the column and covers the reproductive parts.

The members of the Cypripedium tribe lack pseudobulbs and so are not equipped for storing water. There is a short stem from which grow the leaves. After the leaves have formed on a new growth, the flowering stem rises from the tip of the stem, between the leaves.

PAPHIOPEDILUM

This genus of handsome Asiatics has an almost lurid beauty. The flowers, of heavy substance and unexcelled keeping quality, may be enjoyed either on the plant or cut for a month or more. Some few remain fresh for as long as three months. The species vary in their flowering season so that blooms may be had at any time during the year. One of their chief attractions is their ease of culture. They are a good choice for amateurs who do not have a greenhouse, for a pot or two will grow beautifully on a window sill or in a Wardian case.

Fig. 15-1 Reproductive parts of *Paphiopedilum*. The petal has been removed and half of the lip cut away. The column has three parts. The structure at the top is the staminode, a shield that covers the other parts. The footlike structure that swings down into the lip is the stigma, the undersurface of which receives the pollen. There are two anthers, one on each side just above the stigma. The pollen grains are contained in a soft sticky wax, exposed on the lower surface of the anther.

The species, except the rare ones, are inexpensive, and a few dollars will buy many years of pleasure. The hybrids are more costly, particularly the more recent ones.

The fifty or so species are native to tropical Asia, Malaya, and the near-by islands. Some are found at relatively high altitudes in the mountain chains, where rainfall is abundant and temperatures are cool. Here they grow on accumulations of decaying vegetation, on ledges, or in crevices of limestone rocks, partially shaded by overhanging cliffs or trees. Other species occur at lower elevations where the temperatures are higher.

Temperature. Culturally, the cool- and warm-growing ones may be distinguished by their foliage. Those with plain green leaves require a night temperature of between 50° and 55°. Actually, the temperature need not be held as low as 50°, as long as it usually remains close to 55°. The day temperature should be kept between 65° and 72° in the winter, and it would be ideal if the summer day temperature could be kept not over 75°. However, the cool species, like most orchids, will accept and tolerate summer temperatures above this, but will do their best if they do not often exceed 85°. In order to protect the cool paphiopedilums where the heat of summer is prolonged, some growers put the plants out-of-doors in the shade of large trees. The pots may be set on cinder beds or on benches to assure drainage. They should be elevated to keep slugs and cutworms from reaching them.

The warm-growing species are those with mottled foliage, and hybrids between the plain and mottled foliage kinds come in this category. They prefer a night temperature that does not go below 60°, but which, on the other hand, may go above this in the summer. They may be grown comfortably with cattleyas, with day temperatures that suit cattleyas and companions.

Both the cool- and warm-growing kinds can be accommodated in a cattleya house, as a matter of fact, if the former can be given a spot that runs a bit on the cool side. Shade will have to be adjusted for them as described below.

The good keeping qualities of the paphiopedilums make it possible to have them for most holidays. Occasionally, however, it is desirable to slow down the opening of the blooms for a certain purpose. When the stem has reached its full length and the buds are almost fully developed, the temperature may be lowered a few degrees. Flowering is thereby slightly delayed. The temperature must not be lowered too soon or the stems will remain short and the plant will not be as handsome in bloom. Slightly lowered temperatures will allow the flowers to last longer, so that many growers, in order to keep a group of flowers as long as possible, keep the temperature a few degrees cooler after the plants have come into full bloom.

Potting. Paphiopedilums thrive when potted in soft, brown osmunda fiber. Some growers prefer a mixture of three parts osmunda to one of live sphagnum moss, but it is difficult to keep the sphagnum alive. Others are now successfully using bark, preferably a seedling grade, or one in which the largest size pieces are one-half inch. A mixture of 80 percent bark and 20 percent dried crushed oak leaves is also popular, as are bark mixed with tree fern, and plain tree fern. The choice of a compost is a personal thing. The chief essential in any compost is that it should have free drainage, because the roots, although never allowed to become dry, do not thrive in a sodden compost.

The plants are best repotted soon after flowering, at which time they may be divided into groups of not less than three growths. Remove all dead leaves and roots and all decayed compost. After adding crock for drainage, hold the plant at such a depth for potting that the base of the plant will be about one-half inch deep in the medium. If the plant

Fig. 15-2 LEFT, the new growth appears from within a leaf axil of the mature growth. RIGHT, the fuzzy root tips grow down among the pieces of crock in the bottom of the pot. These roots must not be allowed to become dry.

is set too high the new roots will not thrive, and if too deep, the base of the plant may rot. If osmunda is used, pot firmly but not as hard as for cattleyas. Mixed compost should be firmly tamped. After potting water only enough to keep the compost damp until new root growth begins. In the meantime, give the plants a light mist spray once a day—just enough to dampen the outer portions of leaves and not so heavily as to allow water to collect in the leaf axils. Water standing in the leaf axils encourages bacterial infection. The plants will become re-established in about three months.

Water. Since growth is continuous in this genus, and because the plants have no pseudobulbs, the potting medium should not be allowed to dry out. The frequency of watering depends so much on environmental conditions and on the type of medium used that it is difficult to give any set schedule. During bright weather two waterings a week may be sufficient, with longer intervals between waterings in dull weather. Misting the plants is usually not necessary except in very hot weather. Always

water thoroughly so that water runs out of the bottom to flush out excess salts, for accumulation of salts is injurious to the roots.

Light. Paphiopedilums do best in diminished light. During the winter, when days are short and the light slants from the south, they need between 1,000 and 1,500 foot candles. As the days lengthen into spring, shading should be applied to cut the amount of light gradually down to 800 or 900 foot candles. In areas where summer heat is great, this may even be reduced to 700 foot candles. However, let the plants themselves be the guide. The foliage of the plain leaved species should be a good green; yellow-green shows they have too much light. The mottled-leaved species can be an even richer green.

Humidity. These plants require the same humidity as do cattleyas. Good air circulation is a must. Excessive moisture on the leaves encourages disease.

Fig. 15-3 Water standing in the heart of the growths encourages a bacterial rot that can spread quickly through the plant. Note the blackened areas of the leaves in the center.

Fertilizers. Paphiopedilums are perhaps more resentful of over-feeding than any other kind of orchid. If the salt content of the growing medium is too high, root growth is reduced or, in extreme cases, eliminated. In osmunda fiber no extra nutrients are required. This is one thing that makes osmunda fiber such an excellent medium for this genus; all you have to do to get fine root and top growth is to water properly. In mixed composts an occasional feeding with a 10-10-10 fertilizer may be beneficial, perhaps no more than once a month, with the pots thoroughly watered with plain water in between times. In straight fir bark, a 30-10-10 fertilizer is essential, given every other watering. Again, flush the pots thoroughly in between times. If root growth is lessened in any case where fertilizer is given, try reducing the frequency, perhaps giving an additional application of plain water in between times.

Propagation. Paphiopedilums are easily propagated by division, with three growths to a division. However, while this increases the number of plants of a kind, it does not usually increase the number of flowers from a group of plants. Plants may be allowed to become large specimens with many leads, which are extremely handsome. They actually need division only when the growths have extended out so far from the center of the plant that the center is empty of leaves. In such cases, the growing sections of the plant often separate themselves naturally, falling away from the old dead portion of the rhizome. When dividing a plant it is best to break the rhizome with your fingers rather than cut it. Just give the rhizome a quick twist to break it.

Growing paphiopedilums from seed is not so easy as it is with other kinds. Part of the difficulty lies in a reluctance of the seed itself to germinate, and part in breeding the plants. Experts have used many and varied formulae for germination. The problems and methods are discussed later.

The Species

The genus is divided into three sections according to certain features of the flowers.

Section I has flowers nearly round, made so by the large, round petals. All have mottled leaves and require somewhat warmer temperatures than the plain-leaved species.

Section II has elongated, slender petals, and a plain pouch with the top not eared. All have plain green leaves and require cool treatment.

Section III has the pouch eared or notched on the posterior edges. Plants with both mottled and plain leaves are represented.

Section I

P. bellatulum. This species is attractive for its foliage as well as for it charming flowers. The leaves are up to ten inches long and are three and one-half inches wide. They are deep green, mottled with lighter green on the upper surface, purplish underneath. The flower is round, shaped like a deep saucer, with the almost egg-shaped lip backed by the broad petals. They are white to pale yellow marked with purple spots, which run nearly into lines on the dorsal sepal, and which are smaller on the lip. (See Fig. 15-9.) The species occurs in China and flowers in the summer.

P. concolor. The plants are about the same size as *P. godefroyae,* with leaves mottled green on their upper surface and spotted with deep crimson below. The flowers are yellow, spotted with purple. The dorsal sepal is concave and almost round, and the broad petals point downward. The paler lip is nearly cylindric and somewhat flattened on the

Home Orchid Growing

sides. The species grows in Moulmein. It blossoms in the fall.

P. delenatii. This beautiful little plant has oval leaves that are dark green mottled with light green above, light green mottled with red-violet underneath. The rounded flowers have an oval, pointed dorsal sepal that is velvety on the back and margins, white flushed with rose, and round white petals. The spherical lip is white and rose, lightly flushed with lavender. It occurs in Indo-China and flowers in late winter and early spring.

P. godefroyae. This small species has leaves six inches long by one and one-half inches wide. They are mottled green on the upper surface, and green spotted with brown-purple underneath. The short flower stem bears one or two white or pale yellow flowers that are lightly spotted with magenta. The petals are oval and point downward. The species occurs in Cochin-China and flowers in the summer.

P. niveum. The plants are about the same size as the two preceding species, with the foliage strikingly colored, green mottled with gray-green above and brilliant purple underneath. The flowers are white with a scattering of purple dots, and the dorsal sepal is red on the back. The edges of the flower are prettily waved. This species occurs

Fig. 15-4 *Paphiopedilum niveum. (Courtesy J. A. Fowlie)*

naturally in the Loncavi and Tambilan Islands. The flowers appear in the spring.

Section II

P. praestans. The striking flowers are large and brightly colored. The two-inch tall dorsal sepal is whitish, decorated with sharp lines of purple. The spirally twisted petals are yellowish, veined with brown, and are about five inches long. They have hairbearing warts on their margins. The lip is rather long, somewhat flattened on the sides, and is shiny yellow, suffused with red. A native of New Guinea, it flowers in August.

P. rothschildianum. A handsome species, the plants have two-foot long, green leaves, and a spike that may bear several flowers. The flowers are stunningly colored. The dorsal and lateral sepals are yellow striped with black-purple. The fused lateral sepals in this species are larger than in many others and give the effect of a mirror image of the dorsal. The long, slender petals extend five inches and are pale green, spotted with purple, distinctly lined or nerved with dark green. The long lip is purple, veined with a darker shade and yellow toward the top. It stands sharply forward. A native of Borneo and Sumatra, it flowers in the winter.

P. sanderianum. This is a remarkable species. The petals are one and one-half feet long, twisted, pale yellow, barred and spotted with purple. The dorsal sepal is narrow and pointed, yellow-green with brown stripes. The long, projecting lip is brown-purple and yellow. It occurs in the Malay Archipelago, and flowers in early spring.

P. stonei. Three to five stunning flowers are borne on a stem. The dorsal sepal is white, trimmed with two or three crimson streaks and the lateral sepals almost equal it in size. The twisted petals are five to six inches long, tawny, with crimson spots for two-thirds of the length, and solid crimson at the end. The lip is rose, reticulated with crimson; the upper sides fold in and are white. This species is from Borneo and flowers in the fall.

Section III

P. argus. This species has distinctive, medium-sized flowers. The dorsal sepal is oval and pointed, white striped with green, or sometimes with both green and purple. Occasionally it is spotted with blackish purple at its base. The wavy petals have a white ground with green veins for two-thirds of their length, and clear purple tips. Blackish warts decorate the inner surface of the petals. The lip is

Fig. 15-5 *Paphiopedilum argus.* (*Courtesy J. A. Fowlie*)

brownish purple, green underneath, and the narrow, infolded lobes are light purple spotted with a deeper shade. The foliage is mottled. Native to Luzon, it flowers in April.

P. barbatum. This is an attractive species whose deep purple tones often approach red. The nearly round dorsal sepal is folded at the mid-vein. It is white, green at the base, stained and striped with purple. The petals, which bear blackish warts on their upper edges, are brownish green at the base changing to purple at the tip. The lip is deep brownish purple. The foliage is mottled. It occurs in the Malay Peninsula and usually flowers in the summer.

P. callosum. This species contains beautiful, large flowers, noted for their huge dorsal sepal, which may be three inches across. It is folded at the mid-vein and somewhat wavy at the top, white, with alternately long and short veins changing from purple at the base to green above. The petals are pale green with purple tips and have a sprinkling of blackish warts on the upper margin. The brownish purple lip is green beneath. The foliage is mottled. A native of Siam, it flowers in the spring.

P. charlesworthii. This is a charming species with mottled foliage and medium-sized flowers. The large and spreading dorsal sepal is white, suffused and spotted with rose-purple. The petals are yellow-green, reticulated with brown, and the lip is rosy-

purple. It occurs in Bengal. The blossoms appear in the fall.

P. curtisii. Distinctive flowers are borne on rather tall stems that rise above the leaves which are mottled on their upper surface. The flowers have a very long brownish purple lip whose infolded lobes are decorated with darker warts. The petals are long and slender, downward hanging, pale purple tending to white along the mid-vein, and covered with lines of small purple spots or warts from which arise blackish hairs. The small dorsal sepal is green with a white margin, marked with alternately short and long green veins. Its upper edges fold together to form a pointed peak. It occurs in Sumatra and flowers in May and June.

P. dayanum. An attractive species with mottled foliage, it produces slender flowers on a long stem. The dorsal sepal is prettily shaped, with the lower sides folded back and the upper edges folded forward to form a point at the top. It is white with green veins. The long, slender petals are greenish brown changing to rose purple. The slender lip is somewhat pointed at the tip, brownish purple, veined with green. The plants are native to Borneo. Flowers appear in May and June.

P. exul. The lightly marbled foliage is bordered with white. The yellow-green dorsal sepal has a white margin and brown spots. The petals and lip are yellow with faint brown markings. This species occurs in Siam.

P. fairieanum. Small plants with light green leaves have attractive, medium-sized flowers. The

Fig. 15-6 *Paphiopedilum curtisii.* (*Courtesy J. A. Fowlie*)

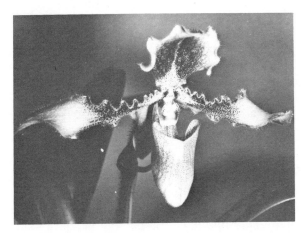

Fig. 15-7 *Paphiopedilum hirsutissimum.* (*Courtesy J. A. Fowlie*)

nearly round dorsal sepal is large in proportion to the size of the flower, with an undulating margin. It is greenish white, reticulated with violet. The upward-curving petals are yellow to white, streaked with purple, bearing tufts of hairs on their wavy margins. The smallish lip is green and white. It occurs in Assam and flowers in the fall.

P. hirsutissimum. Large, dark colored, hairy flowers make this a striking species. The roundish wavy dorsal sepal is heavily marked with black-purple and bordered with green. The petals are slender near their base, wider toward the end, and somewhat twisted. They are mottled with deep purple on a green ground near the base, becoming bright purple at the tip. The deep green lip is tinged with purple. The foliage is plain green. The plant is native to Assam. It flowers in the spring.

P. insigne. This is the easiest to grow and one of the most popular of the genus. It appears everywhere, in collections and in the florist's show window. Perhaps its most attractive feature is the shiny appearance of the flowers; they almost look as if they had been varnished. The broad, oval dorsal sepal has the top turned slightly forward. The central part is apple green, spotted with purple along the darker green veins, and the upper part is white. The wavy petals are pale yellow-green, veined with brown. The lip is also yellow-green, suffused with brown. (See Fig. 15-9.) The species occurs in Nepal and Assam. It produces flowers in the winter. *P. insigne* has many named varieties, of which the variety 'Harefield Hall' has proved to be outstanding both in itself and as a parent of hybrids. This form is larger than the type, and recent studies have shown it to be a natural triploid (having

three times the usual haploid number of chromosomes). The standard chromosome number of *Paphiopedilum* is twenty-six in the vegetative cell, thirteen in the reproductive cells. 'Harefield Hall' has thirty-nine, or three times thirteen.

P. lawrenceanum. This handsome species has mottled yellow-green foliage and large flowers. The beautiful dorsal sepal is· nearly round, white, with deep purple, flame-shaped veins reaching nearly to the tip. The straight, veined petals are green with purple tips, and both margins carry black warts. The lip is dull purple, tinged with brown and green. It occurs in Borneo and flowers from April to July.

P. lowii. Quite an unusual species, it produces three to six dainty flowers on a long nodding stem. The leaves are light green. The flower parts are slender. The oar-shaped petals are yellow with black spots toward the base, violet at the outer ends. The dorsal sepal is slender at its base, spreading at the top, yellow-green, veined with brownish purple. The lip is brown. This native of Borneo could equally well be included in Section II. It tends to be epiphytic rather than terrestrial, and needs especially good aeration. The blossoms appear in the summer.

P. spicerianum. These medium-sized flowers are distinguished for the large dorsal sepal which is markedly wider than it is tall, yet is folded in a

Fig. 15-8 *Paphiopedilum lawrenceanum.* (*Courtesy J. A. Fowlie*)

turret-like manner. The foliage is dark green. The dorsal sepal is white, with a simple crimson-purple band down the center. Its basal region is green, spotted with red. The petals have wavy margins and are pale green spotted and striped with purple. The lip is rather long, dull purple marked with green. (See Fig. 15-9.) One of the important ancestors of our modern hybrids, it occurs in Assam. The plants are in blossom from October to December.

P. venustum. This species has rather short leaves which are marbled with gray-green on the upper surface, and mottled with dull purple underneath. The flowers, which are produced singly on a tall stem, have a heart-shaped dorsal sepal that is white with dark green veins. The petals have the basal part green with dark warts, and the outer portion dull brownish-purple. The pale yellow lip is tinted with rose, veined and netted with brown. The plants are native to northeast India, and blossom in late winter and spring.

P. villosum. Large, glossy, hairy flowers are produced on rather large plants whose leaves are green above, purple spotted beneath. The dorsal sepal is brownish purple with a green tip. The longish petals are wavy, yellowish brown with a prominent central band of purple. The lip is brownish yellow. (See Fig. 15-9.)

P. villosum var. *boxallii* is sometimes given as a separate species. In this the dorsal sepal is marked in the center with numerous black spots. Var. *boxallii* has been a frequent parent of hybrids. It flowers in January and February. This species, which occurs in Moulmein, has also been found growing as an epiphyte.

Growing Paphiopedilum From Seed

When a group of species as distinct and as beautiful as the paphiopedilums displays itself before you, you cannot down the urge to make hybrids with them. Growers have long worked to blend the best features of several into new combinations, and there are today some stunning hybrids. But the casual observer cannot know the patient work and the many disappointments that lie behind the flower he sees.

The first *Paphiopedilum* hybrid was made in 1869, a cross between *barbatum* and *villosum*. Since then, many successful hybrids have appeared, of which one of the most famous is *P.* Maudiae, the so-called green orchid. Its parentage is *callosum* 'Sanderae' × *lawrenceanum* 'Hyeanum.'

A number of difficulties exist in the breeding of *Paphiopedilum* hybrids. A great deal of effort has gone into the making of crosses in this genus, with less relative success than with other genera. Many of the beautiful hybrids shown today are almost sole survivors of the matings that made them. In the first place, the hybrids are frequently partially or entirely sterile, according to their genetic makeup. This means that often only a small amount of viable seed is produced. In the second place, the seed is hard to germinate, so that much good seed never results in seedlings.

This does not mean that an amateur cannot breed *Paphiopedilum,* for he may hit on a combination that gives a fair amount of good seed. But even if he achieves only a few plants for his effort, he will be rewarded by a justifiable thrill at success under such challenging circumstances.

The pollen does not keep well. Hence it should be used shortly after it has been removed from the two anthers. A toothpick can be used to transfer the granular pollen directly to the stigma.

A seed pod matures in approximately nine to eleven months, occasionally in a shorter or longer time. The technique used for sowing the flasks is essentially the same as that described for *Cattleya.* Calcium hypochlorite solution is usually used as the disinfecting agent. The seed coat is unusually hard and moreover is protected by hairs which make it more difficult to wet with a disinfecting agent. Some workers add a drop or two of a wetting agent, such as Santomerse, to the 140 c.c. of hypochlorite solution to aid its penetration. The exposure to the disinfecting solution is ten or twenty minutes.

A good growing medium is Knudson's "C" solution, with the addition of .05 gram of peptone to one liter of the agar-nutrient mixture. The *p*H should be adjusted to 6 to give the more nearly neutral conditions suited to *Paphiopedilum.*

Often out of a large number of seed sown, only a scant few ever germinate. Experts have germinated several hundred from a single pod, and an occasional amateur has been so fortunate. Contrast this, however, with the many thousands obtainable from almost any cattleya cross. Sometimes seeds germinate after months or even years, but it is almost impossible to maintain the proper growing conditions over long periods. It is, therefore, suggested that a generous amount of seed be sown in each flask.

The reluctant germination suggests the possibility of the presence of an inhibitor in the seed. Burgeff used a soaking technique which improved the percentage of germination. He allowed the seed to stand in sterile water for two weeks to two months before sowing it in the flasks. His growing medium differed slightly from Knudson's "C," and he kept the flasks in the dark until the embryos began to lengthen. The green pod method (see chapter 9) often gives improved germination.

Inheritance in Paphiopedilum

Crosses between certain species have produced hybrids that have proved fairly fertile, and these have been fruitful in the production of other hybrids. Crosses between certain other species have often given hybrids that are almost or entirely sterile. With great patience, breeders have obtained some offspring from the nearly sterile hybrids, as few as a dozen seedlings at times. Thus out of the tremendous numbers of hybrids given in Sanders' "Complete List of Orchid Hybrids" a great many represent crosses from which but few plants were raised. A quick perusal of Sanders' listings gives a very striking introduction to the problems that have been involved in breeding. Under the names of some hybrids there appear long lists of other hybrids made with these parents. Under the names of others but one or two further crosses appear, indicating that these were not fruitful parents. Some of the hybrid names never again appear in the lists, indicating either that these were sterile or were not desirable enough to have been used. A few of the sterile hybrids have come down to us through vegetative propagation, or even by repetition of the crosses that produced them, because they were such lovely things. An example is *P.* Maudiae, an unsatisfactory parent but a very popular plant.

The problems in breeding stem partly from the range of chromosome numbers among the species, and partly from incompatibility even among some species with the same chromosome number. Among the chromosome numbers there are represented 26, 28, 30, 32, 34, 36, 40, 42, and the gametes from these species would contain 13, 14, 15, 16, 17, 18, 20, and 21. The natural triploid, *P. insigne* 'Harefield Hall' has 39 chromosomes, and can produce gametes of 13 and 26 chromosomes.

Species which have 26 chromosomes are: *bellatulum, charlesworthii, delenatii, druryi, exul, fairieanum, hirsutissimum, insigne, niveum, stonei, villosum,* and *villosum* var. *boxalli.* Increasing in chromosome numbers we have *rothschildianum* with either 26 or 28; *praestans* with 28; *spicerianum* with 30, occasionally 28; *callosum* with 32 (and a number of other species, not described in this chapter, with 32); *dayanum* with 34; *lawrenceanum* with 36 and occasionally 40; and *venustum* with 42.

The greatest numbers of modern hybrids have come from the species *insigne, villosum, villosum* var. *boxallii, and spicerianum,* with *bellatulum* also entering into the line. Although *spicerianum* has 30 chromosomes, 4 more than the others, which have 26, these species are quite compatible. Aneuploidy naturally has resulted among the hybrids. Many polyploids also have appeared, having arisen from nonreduced gametes or by a doubling of the chromosome number in some other way during the process of seed formation (see Chapter 8). R. E. Duncan reported the following ranges of chromosome numbers among hybrids: diploid and near-diploid, 26, 27, 28, 29, and 30; triploid and near-triploid, 39, 40, 41, and 42; tetraploid and near-tetraploid, 52, 53, 54, 55, and 56; and one near-pentaploid with 70. The usual reduction of fertility that accompanies polyploidy, and which is further reduced by aneuploidy, is, in the case of the paphiopedilums, additionally reduced by low pollen fertility. Often pollen grains that appear to be normal fail to make tubes and thus cannot function. When we say, therefore, that hybrids from this group of species are fairly fertile, we mean that they are fertile by comparison with the far less fertile hybrids from other groups of species.

Analysis of the chromosome types (shape, size, etc.,) of the various species has enabled cytogeneticists to follow the behavior of these chromosomes in relation to each other when sets from different species are present in the hybrids, and to see what happens to them during reduction division. Failure to pair, is of course, the chief reason for the production of many non-functional reproductive cells. However, it was found that in the primary hybrids among *insigne, villosum,* and *spicerianum* the assortment of chromosomes frequently resulted in distribution of a basic set to the reproductive cells, which then could be functional. Chromosome counts on the progeny from these primary hybrids revealed that reproductive cells with thirteen and fourteen chromosomes had indeed functioned. Such analyses were made upon *P.* Leeanum (*insigne* × *spicerianum*) and *P.* Lathamianum (*villosum* × *spicerianum*), primary hybrids that were the start of the modern hybrids, and which appear many times in the breeding lines. The contribution of the extra chromosome by gametes bearing fourteen allows succeeding generations to build up their chromosome number by adding an extra chromosome here and there, accounting for the aneuploid numbers found among the hybrids. When non-reduced gametes function, these may also carry an extra chromosome or two to the polyploid offspring.

As is true in all species, there is a great amount of variation in color and form to be found among the members of the *Paphiopedilum* species. For instance, in a species which has characteristic spotting, there are forms which are heavily spotted and forms which are spotted only lightly and some not at all. In species that have characteristic red or purple coloring there are rare forms without the red or purple coloring; these are green or pure white. Unfortunately, both the green and white forms are called "albino," and in reading about these forms one must know whether reference is had to "green albinos" or "white albinos." A new term is badly needed here.

Inheritance of color in *Paphiopedilum* is not clearly worked out, but it is a very difficult field. C. C. Hurst, who worked out the white inheritance in *Cattleya* (see Chapter 8) found that the green and white types in *Paphiopedilum* both seem to follow a pattern similar to that of the white cattleyas. Apparently the red and purple pigment depend on the presence of the dominant C and R genes, and pure green or white can show up only when either or both pairs of these genes is recessive. Included in this group of so-called albinos is the yellow *P. insigne* 'Sanderae,' which seems to behave similarly.

Certain features of the species, the color patterns in dorsal sepal and petals, the shape of the parts, etc., are perhaps incompletely dominant. Traces of a feature from this species or that are found in hybrid individuals, often combined with, or superimposed upon, other features. Such fine blendings occur in some of the modern hybrids that it would be difficult to say which feature came from which species. However, these features show up more strongly in some individuals in any cross, and in almost any group of *Paphiopedilum* hybrids one can at a glance pick out flowers that strongly exhibit the characteristics of one ancestor or another.

Mrs. L. Sherman Adams carried out a detailed study of *P. insigne, villosum, spicerianum,* and *bellatulum*—the four species most influential in the formation of the modern hybrids. By modern hybrids we mean the round, compact type currently chosen as the ideal, and sought in the breeding work being done at present. Mrs. Adams included in her study the influence of these species in their earlier hybrids and in modern hybrids descended from this group. Her findings were presented in a series of nine articles in the American Orchid Society Bulletin from January to September, 1954. The modern hybrid chosen was Clementine Churchill (Festivity × Lewis Crampton). This cross involved the repeated use of the species, both directly and by means of their earlier hybrids, to a total of something like 76 crosses before the final Clementine Churchill was reached. In this array, *insigne* is represented 34 times, *villosum* 5 times, *villosum* var. *boxallii* 23 times, *spicerianum* 25 times, and *bellatulum* once. This is of purely historical interest, of course; the number of times a species is used is not important. What is interesting is to see how genes or groups of genes reveal themselves where they have been segregated from parents and brought together in progeny.

We felt it would be of value to see how the characters of the various species showed up in individual flowers of Clementine Churchill, and prevailed upon Mrs. Adams to select examples for us from her huge collection of kodachromes. Costs prevent giving these in color, but much can be seen in black and whites.

In the accompanying display, Figure 15-9, each of the four species is given along with two members of the hybrid which show its influence. The flower to the immediate right of the species in each case is one which more nearly approaches the type of the earlier hybrids, which might be considered intermediate in form between the species, and the "modern" type shown at the far right. This cross is in itself almost a survey of the history of hybridization in *Paphiopedilum*.

A, B, and C, of Fig. 15-9, trace the influence of *villosum*. A is *villosum* 'Cornell #11,' characterized by a tall slender dorsal sepal, curved back at its lower sides. The marking on the dorsal sepal consists of a network of reddish lines, laid on a green ground which extends somewhat beyond the network of lines. The sepal is edged by a fine border of white, not apparent in this picture. The petals widen out from a narrow base, curving forward in a pronounced fashion, and are broadly waved at the edge. They are bi-color, having the upper half red and the lower half green, the two

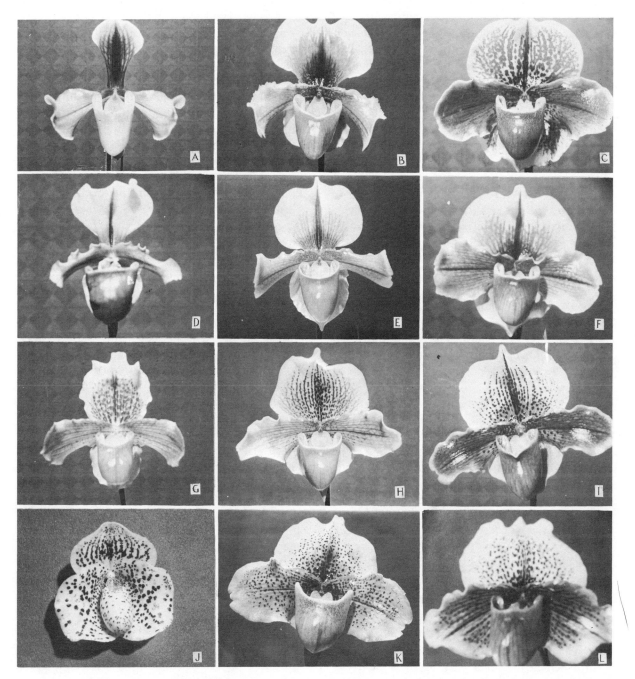

Fig. 15-9 Series showing the influence of the four species that make up the hybrid Clementine Churchill. A, *P. villosum*. B and C, members of the hybrid in which its influence is shown. D, *P. spicerianum*, E and F, individuals of the hybrid in which its influence is strong. G, *P. insigne*, H and I, flowers which show its influence. J, *P. bellatulum*, K and L, individuals which show its influence. In each case the flower to the immediate right of the species is a type that approaches the earlier hybrid style, more full than the species, but not so round and compact as the type preferred at present. The flowers at the far right more nearly approach the "ideal" modern type. (*From kodachromes courtesy Mrs. L. Sherman Adams*)

halves divided by a prominent dark line, and they have a distinct notch at the tip. The pouch is long and narrow, flaring at the top and with long lobes. B, Clementine Churchill #7, shows the *villosum* influence in the markings of the dorsal sepal. The green ground has been lost though the influence of *spicerianum,* so that the markings show up as clear red. The petals have the *villosum* stance, flared outer ends, and dark mid-vein, but show the finer marginal waving of *spicerianum* and *insigne.* With the suppression of green in the flower, the petals have become almost solid red. The pouch shows the flaring of the upper portion and the long lobes of *villosum.* C is Clementine Churchill #61. The dorsal sepal shows a combination of influences. The coloring is exhibited as broken lines or coalesced spots, the influence of the *insigne* pattern upon the *villosum* pattern, while the dark center line comes from *spicerianum.* The petals are broad and flat as in *insigne,* with the *insigne* markings and marginal waving, but they have the notch at the tip that comes from *villosum.* This notch is apparent in almost all of the flowers shown on this page. The pouch, while broadened by the influence of the other species, still has something of the flared shape of *villosum.*

D, E, and F trace the influence of *spicerianum.* D is *spicerianum* 'Babson' with its tall, white dorsal sepal, much broader than it looks because it folds sharply on each side. It has a strong center line of red, and a faint area of green at its base. The petals are rather short and narrow, finely ruffled on the upper edge, and curved slightly forward. The pouch is somewhat blunt. E shows Clementine Churchill #62, which is strongly *spicerianum* both in shape and in the dark center line. The basal markings of the dorsal sepal have been increased somewhat by *villosum,* and spread from green at the base to red at the tips. The petals are a combination of *insigne* and *spicerianum,* with a bit of *villosum* in the dark center line and notch. The pouch is more like that of *villosum* than of *spicerianum.* F is Clementine Churchill #27, in which the dorsal sepal is still strongly *spicerianum* but with more of the *villosum* markings. The petals approach *insigne* quite strongly, but still have something of *spicerianum* and *villosum.* In coloring the petals have reverted to the bi-color type of *villosum.* The pouch is quite close to *spicerianum.*

G, H, and I show *insigne* and flowers in which its influence is strong. G is *insigne,* characterized by a flat rounded dorsal sepal which has two folds

at the tip. It has a green central portion and a broad white border. Within the green ground it is marked by raised spots of reddish brown, arranged over obscure lines. The petals are flat and almost straight, with a slight ruffling at the edges, and a few spots arranged on reticulated lines. The pouch is round, slightly pinched in toward the top and with short lobes. H is Clementine Churchill #108, in which the general pattern and coloring of *insigne* are quite pronounced. The spotting of the dorsal sepal is more refined, and spreads a little closer to the border. The petals are very close to *insigne,* and, while the pouch is a bit more flared, it comes closer to *insigne* than to any of the others. I is Clementine Churchill #70, in which the overall aspect is again very much like that of *insigne.* The concentration of spots in the center of the dorsal sepal suggests the center line of *spicerianum,* and the pouch is quite like *villosum.*

J, K, and L show *bellatulum* and its influence. J is *bellatulum,* with its extremely rounded parts, covered with spots that show a hint of a pattern only in the dorsal sepal. It is entirely white except for the spots, which are purple. The little pouch is long and almost closed. Although this species appeared but once in the long and involved history of this cross, it is interesting to see that there are a number of Clementine Churchills that carry its characteristics. K is Clementine Churchill #115, which has the overall spotting of *bellatulum* in addition to the squat dorsal sepal and the short, broad petals. The pouch shape is not carried over here. L is Clementine Churchill #39, showing even more of the *bellatulum* influence, even to the long, rounded pouch. The petals, however, although much rounded, are spotted on a pattern of lines reminiscent of *insigne.* Neither K or L has the all-white ground of *bellatulum,* both having red and green in the petals and pouch.

PHRAGMIPEDIUM AND SELENIPEDIUM

Phragmipedium, one of the South American genera of the Cypripedium tribe, has about eleven species. It differs from *Paphiopedilum* in that the dorsal sepal is more or less like the petals, and the edges of the lip are infolded giving it a more slipper-like appearance. It has smooth, rather leathery leaves, and can thus be distinguished from *Selenipedium,* which has plicate (pleated) leaves. They may be grown with plenty of heat and moisture from March to November, shaded from the direct rays of the sun. Osmunda fiber is a good medium, allowed to rise above the rim of the pot. After potting, keep on the dry side until growth starts.

P. caudatum. This species has rather stiff, upright leaves, and flower stems one to two feet tall. It is remarkable for its long, ribbon-like petals which grow to a length of three feet. The petals are yellow shaded with brown and tinted with crimson toward the tips. The dorsal sepal is slender and wavy, about six inches long, pale yellow veined with green. The species occurs from Mexico to Peru.

P. sargentianum. The leaves are tufted, six to eight inches long, with golden margins. The flower stem bears two or three blooms. The oval dorsal sepal is pale yellow with red veins. The petals are slightly longer, twisted at the ends, yellow with red margins and veins. The lip is rather long, also yellow marked with red. The plant occurs in Brazil.

P. schlimii. The narrow, foot-long leaves are bright grass-green above, purple underneath. The tall flower stem holds five to eight blooms which are about two inches in diameter, and are covered with a velvety down. The flower parts are oval, rather short, and widespreading. The dorsal sepal

Fig. 15-11 *Phragmipedium schlimii.* (*Courtesy J. A. Fowlie*)

is greenish white tinged with pink, the fused laterals white, veined with green. The petals are white, spotted and stained with rose near the base. The lip is globe-shaped, rose, with the infolded lobes striped rose and white. It is native to Colombia.

Selenipedium. This is the other South American relative of *Cypripedium,* a very rare genus of tall, almost bamboo-like plants, and not amenable to greenhouse culture. The reed-like stems bear large plicate leaves, prominently veined, and at the tips clusters of rather small flowers. *S. chica* reaches more than twice the height of a man.

CYPRIPEDIUM

These are the moccasin-flowers or ladyslippers of our woods and moist meadows. They may be transplanted to our gardens if the new locality is made to imitate their native spot. There are about thirty species. Like the other members of the tribe, these are becoming less numerous with the passing years. Man probably has something to do with this, by using for himself the sunny areas where the plants would do best, so that they are forced to exist in the woods. They are sun-loving plants and do not grow so well in heavy shade. Lovers of these plants ask that instead of removing the wild clumps to your garden, plants be purchased from nurseries. The latter may even do better for you, for they will have been adapted to garden conditions.

Fig. 15-10 *Phragmipedium caudatum* var. *wallisii.* (*Courtesy J. A. Fowlie*)

These native cypripediums require plenty of moisture. A dam around their bed will help to retain water. They do best with some shade at noon.

C. acaule. Pink moccasin-flower. The single flower grows on a rather tall stem. The color is usually pale pink with deeper veining, but deep pink with light veins and pure white are also found. The lip is closed except for a slit in front. This species requires an acid soil and is the most difficult to grow. Often it lasts for a year or two and then dies out. It should be aided by the addition to the soil of such acid material as pine needles. It grows naturally from Newfoundland to North Carolina, and west to the Great Lakes region. The blossoms appear in May and June.

C. calceolus. The beautiful yellow ladyslipper is one of the most handsome of the species and the easiest to grow. The whole flower is bright yellow, with narrow, somewhat wavy petals and a wider dorsal sepal. In culture it requires a porous neutral soil, with plenty of moisture and some shade. It can be found throughout the United States, Canada, Europe, and Asia. The variety *pubescens* is common to our western states, and the variety *parviflorum* to the eastern ones.

C. californicum. Tall plants produce leaves alternately on the stem. From six to twelve flowers occur on the upper part of the stem. They are small, with green sepals and petals and a white lip. The species is native to California and Oregon.

C. candidum. The green flowers have a pretty lip that is white, striped inside with purple. The plant is found in the eastern and mid-western states.

C. montanum. This handsome, fragrant species grows rather tall. One to three flowers are produced on a stem. The petals are wavy-twisted, dull brown, and the lip is whitish veined with purple. It is found in western North America.

C. reginae, or *spectabile,* is truly named the "Queen" ladyslipper. It is tall and robust and produces a wealth of large flowers. The white sepals and petals are set off by the rosy shades of the lip. It requires a sunny spot in the garden and moist, neutral soil. The species occurs from eastern Canada through our northern and mid-western states, and also occurs in western China. It flowers in early summer.

16

THE DENDROBIUM TRIBE

The Dendrobium tribe includes the marvelous genus *Dendrobium* and a few genera of definitely lesser importance. The name is derived from *dendro,* tree, and *bios,* life.

DENDROBIUM

Dendrobiums, which have been loved by amateurs for a hundred years, are enjoying perhaps their greatest degree of popularity right now. From their native lands, where they have always been appreciated, they have been brought first to Europe, and more recently to Hawaii and to the mainland states. We are now benefiting from the loving care and interest bestowed upon them by the growers who have made them a specialty, and who have not only nurtured the species but have created a fascinating succession of hybrids. The Hawaiian growers, especially in recent years, have done intriguing things with the dendrobiums, as they have with the vandas and their relatives.

The very size of the genus *Dendrobium,* with its 1,000 species, promises variety, both in size and character of the plants and of the flowers and the manner in which they are produced. There are kinds which give erect or arching sprays of five to twenty flowers, kinds which give drooping sprays of a dozen to a hundred blooms, and still others in which almost the entire length of the pseudobulb bears clusters of flowers at each node. Many have quite unique and appealing characteristics. The individual flowers are often small, but all are perky or dainty, often of a glistening crystalline texture or velvety softness. The colors are rich, ranging from rose and violet tones, occasionally almost to red, to the most brilliant of yellow and gold. Some species are white.

The plants range in size from miniatures with little wiry or squat pseudobulbs, to a large group of robust species with pseudobulbs from a foot to three feet in height, and on up to kinds that have stems six to eight feet long. Among these are some whose stems bear three to five leaves at the top nodes only, and others whose stems are leafy for almost their entire length. There are deciduous species which lose their leaves the first or second year, and evergreen species which keep their leaves for three or four years. Except for a few in which the stems are truly pseudobulbous, most of them have rather slender, jointed stems that resemble canes. All are epiphytic and all make new growths each year from a rhizome. The growths come close together so that a plant with many stems springs from a rather small basal area.

The flowers are characterized by a "chin" or mentum formed by the joining of the lateral sepals to the foot of the column. In some the base of the fused sepals forms a short spur covering the mentum. The dorsal sepal and the petals are free. The lip narrows at its base to a stalk that is attached to the base of the column foot. The side lobes of the lip usually enfold the short column, while the outer lobe is spreading, pointed or rounded, sometimes fringed. The flowers last for two to three weeks.

The genus ranges over eastern Asia and the

Fig. 16-1 UPPER, *Dendrobium* Millie Sander (*dearei* × *formosum*) is an example of the dearei type of hybrid. Note the long spur. (*Courtesy Wm. Kirch*) LOWER, *Dendrobium phalaenopsis*, a cross between selected strains.

Pacific islands, from the Himalayas through Burma to the Malayan regions, Australia, New Zealand, New Guinea, China, Japan, the Philippines and Fiji. The variety of climatic conditions gives a variety of plant habits, and their cultural needs vary accordingly. Some grow where there is a warm season accompanied by heavy rains, followed by a season of cooler temperatures and little rain. Some come from regions that stay the same temperatures the year round, but where the rainfall is less heavy for part of the year. In some areas the rainfall stays about the same but the temperature cools off for part of the year. In other areas there is little change from

"winter" to "summer." Because of such diversity of native habitat, the species have to be given somewhat individual treatment in a greenhouse. The reputation the dendrobiums have earned, of being somewhat tricky to flower, is perhaps justified, because they need to have everything just right for them. However, the reason one may not flower may be simply that it wants less water after its growths are mature, while another would flower if it were put in a cooler place in the fall.

We shall try to group the species according to sets of conditions that seem most generally suitable. All dendrobiums like good light, some requiring about the same amount as cattleyas, others even more. All thrive with good air circulation. If, from among the groups as we shall list them, some species do not flower for you, try changing the conditions a bit. Move them to a brighter spot, or to one that runs a bit warmer or cooler than the rest of the greenhouse. You can judge the right amount of light by watching the development of the stems and leaves. If they are weak and thin, put the plant in a brighter spot and watch it plump up and spread its leaves during the next few weeks. After the growth is mature, some species need what is loosely spoken of as a "rest," a time during which its active growth is checked to harden the new growth and prepare the plant for flower production. This involves for some a combination of cooler temperatures and less water, for others merely cooler temperatures without a reduction of water, and for still others merely reduction of water while the temperature remains the same.

Group 1. Grow plants in this group with cattleya temperatures, move to cool temperature and restrict watering after growths mature: *D. nobile, chrysanthum,* and *wardianum.* These are deciduous species. *D. nobile* does not lose its leaves until the second year, and it is these growths which produce flowers the second winter. *D. chrysanthum* and *wardianum* lose their leaves the first winter, before or during flowering. All three should be watered and fertilized generously while growing, have good light (*nobile* may not need quite as much as the other two), and temperatures 55° to 60° at night. In the fall, move them to a cool bright greenhouse with a night temperature of 50° (as for cymbidiums). Cut down the frequency of watering, giving just enough to keep plants from shrivelling and cease fertilizing through the winter. After flower buds are well formed, resume normal watering until flowering is finished, and then keep on the dry side until new growths are well started. At this time move back to cattleya temperatures and resume regular watering and fertilizing. If these species are not given "cool-dry" treatment in the fall, vegetative growths will form where flower buds should appear. These vegetative growths may be removed and potted separately when they start their own roots. Hybrids between *nobile* and species of Groups 1 and 2 require the "cool-dry" treatment also.

Group 2. Grow with cattleyas all year round, but keep on the dry side after growths are made up in the fall: *D. anosmum, findlayanum, heterocarpum, parishii,* and *pierardii.* These also are deciduous species. They require a night temperature of 55° to 60° all year round. While the growth is developing and until it is mature, water generously and give ample fertilizer, plenty of light, and good air movement. In the fall, as the last leaf appears, restrict the watering (no fertilizer) to just enough to keep the plants from shrivelling, until flower buds have formed. Then water moderately through flowering and until the new growth (which sometimes starts at flowering time) is well along. After the new growth sends out its own roots, resume more generous watering and start fertilizing again. If *findlayanum* does not flower for you after the first attempt, try keeping it closer to 55° the next winter. If *D. anosmum* does not flower, try it in a spot where the temperature does not go below 60° during the winter. *D. aggregatum* is treated like this group, although it is not deciduous.

Group 3. Grow at cattleya temperatures, move to cool greenhouse for the winter, but do not restrict watering: *D. chrysotoxum, densiflorum, farmeri, fimbriatum, moschatum,* and *thyrsiflorum.* These are evergreen and should not be allowed to dry out at any time of the year. From the time growth starts and until it is mature in the fall, keep them with cattleyas, with the usual good light, water frequently enough to keep the medium moist, and fertilize as for other species. *D. moschatum* may like just a little shade in a bright cattleya house, while the others may be able to take even more light than cattleyas. Syringe the foliage frequently to control red spiders (and spray with a miticide as well) for they find these plants very attractive. In the fall, move to a place where they can be given nights of 50° but continue to water often enough to prevent drying. After flowering and until new growth starts, the plants should be kept cool. After new growth starts, move them back to the cattleya temperature range.

Group 4. Grow moderately cool, with winter nights close to 55°, not over 60°, summer nights close to 60° and summer days not extremely hot. Handle like cattleyas as to water and light except give a short dry period after growth is made up: *D. dearei, formosum, lyonii, infundibulum, macrophyllum, sanderae, schuetzei.* These are evergreen species. They grow well with cattleyas where cattleyas are grown under moderately cool circumstances, but may not do well in the warmest parts of the United States, unless the grower has means for keeping down the temperatures.

Group 5. While this group does not like excessive heat and humidity, it prefers a little more heat than Group 4. Thus this group can be grown with cattleyas almost anywhere, in a spot where the night temperature runs closer to 60°. If possible give them a bit more light than cattleyas, with free air movement: *D. gouldii, stratiotes, taurinum, undulatum, veratrifolium.* These are evergreen species. Some growers grow all of them without a rest period. Others give a short period of lessened water to *D. taurinum, undulatum,* and *veratrifolium* as growth matures. If any of these species seems not to be growing as vigorously as it should, or if the buds drop after they are well formed, put the plant in a spot where the night temperature does not go below 60°. The cultural conditions given here are suitable for hybrids between this group and *D. phalaenopsis, biggibum,* and *superbiens,* described below.

Group 6. Grow with night temperatures that run between 60° and 65°: *D. bigibbum, phalaenopsis,* and *superbiens.* These are evergreen species. Some growers feel that *D. phalaenopsis* and *superbiens* require restricted watering after growth is made up and until the flower spikes start. They do require normal watering during flowering, and restricted watering from then until new growth is well along. New growth sometimes does not start until late summer. During the time of restricted watering, syringe the foliage frequently to keep the plant plump. *D. bigibbum* does not require a drying off period, or at best it needs only a very brief one. These three species are frequently used in hybridization with those of Group 5. The hybrids in which *D. phalaenopsis* figures prominently are often referred to as "Dendrobium Phalaenopsis hybrids." A curious thing about these hybrids is that some of them are much more tolerant of shade than the species and will do well under conditions suitable for phalaenopsis, that is, with about half the amount of light required by cattleyas. Plants have performed nicely for me in an orchid case in the living room, although they have not reached the large size they can achieve in a greenhouse. Note: A few delightful small to miniature species, not included in these groups, are described below.)

General Culture

Potting and dividing. Dendrobiums may be grown in osmunda, a good medium because it gives their fine, wiry roots a firm foothold and tends to hold the sometimes top-heavy plants in place very well. They may also be grown in bark if they are carefully staked. Some growers like to plant them on tree fern logs or slabs, from which they do not have to be removed for a number of years. Some of the deciduous species develop very long stems which cannot hold themselves upright and which therefore grow in a pendant manner. These are best grown in baskets of osmunda or tree fern fiber, or on tree fern logs, or on slabs to which a chunk of osmunda fiber is first wired. Such containers are hung from the top of the greenhouse to give the stems room and

Fig. 16-2 A young plant growing on the pseudobulb that produced the season's flowers. The plantlet may be removed and potted.

light. A few, such as *D. chrysanthum* which would drag the tips of its stems on the floor of the average small greenhouse, may be tied along one side of the greenhouse with a loop of string about every two feet of their length.

Dendrobiums may be divided like other sympodial plants. It is best to wait until the new growths have started. Re-potting and dividing should be done just as new roots show or just before they make their appearance. The evergreen species should be divided to retain three or four older stems along with the new lead. In some kinds the old stems flower for several successive years. In the deciduous species, after a stem has flowered it begins to shrivel and is then no longer of use to the plant. These shrivelled stems should be cut off. Be sure that you do not remove them until they have flowered, or their chance to flower is past (*nobile*, for instance, flowers on growths made the previous year, that is, the flowers come the second winter rather than the winter after the growth is made). Divisions consist of the new growth and the stem from which it arises. The old stem may be removed after it has flowered and the new growth is well along. It is even possible to plant several divisions in the same container to give a spectacular showing.

Small plantlets that develop along the older stems of both evergreen and deciduous species may be separated from the stem as soon as their roots start. When put in their own pots, these grow rapidly, sometimes flowering the first year. Old stems, after flowering, may be cut into sections between the nodes and placed on damp sphagnum moss (or a fine bark and sand mix) in order to encourage plantlets to develop.

In general, dendrobiums do not need as large pots for their size as do many kinds. Their roots are fine and wiry, and they do not grow to any great length. A four- or five-inch pot should accommodate a plant with four or five leads.

Water abundantly while growing. However, new growth on cane types is touchy and may rot if kept wet. Withhold water from the time it starts until new roots develop. In the meantime spray the foliage and the surface of the potting medium, using a fine mist.

Dendrobiums from seed. Dendrobium seed germinates readily and the seedlings grow rapidly. The largest numbers of hybrids come from *nobile* and its relatives (Groups 1 and 2), and *phalaenopsis* and its relatives with the ceratobium section,

Groups 5 and 6. Another group of hybrids stems from intercrossing *dearei, formosum, infundibulum, sanderae,* and *schuetzii.* We should like to point out that the "cultural" groups as we set them up are not meant to follow the lines of botanical relationships, although for the most part they coincidentally do. The genus is divided botanically into sections and sub-sections too numerous to give here. Hybrids in general have been made within the botanical groups. In other words, it has been found that species that are structurally related breed together more readily than species from groups less closely alike. However, there are instances where crosses have been successfully made between species in different botanical sections and sub-sections. For example, *macrophyllum* has been crossed with several members of the group to which *phalaenopsis* belongs; *dearei* has been crossed with *farmeri,* from a different section; and *sanderae* with *nobile,* again from a different section. Perhaps more such crosses will be tried in the future.

The Species

D. aggregatum (syn. *lindleyi*). This charming dwarf species has little chunky four-jointed pseudobulbs bearing a single leaf. The flowers are very round, opening full and flat, with a squarish lip that is downy in the center. They are a delicate orange-yellow to pinkish-yellow, from ten to thirty on a drooping rounded spray. The plants occur in northern India, Burma, and southern China. They flower in the spring. The variety *jenkinsii* is an even smaller plant, a real miniature, with one-inch flowers that have a kidney-shaped lip.

D. anosmum. This plant is also known as *Dend. superbum,* which is actually the name of one of its varieties. Richly colored, they are three-inch flowers of deep magenta with the heart-shaped lip shading into purple at its base. They are produced in pairs from the upper nodes of the three-foot stems. The variety *superbum* has larger flowers and stems that reach five feet; its flowers are fragrant. The species is native to the warm regions in the Philippines. The flowers appear in the spring.

D. bigibbum. Rather slender stems, eighteen inches in height, bear four to eight leaves at their upper nodes. The two-inch flowers are rich magenta, trimmed with a white crest in the center of the notched lip. The flower spray carries a dozen or more blooms, and rises from one of the upper leaf axils. The plants occur in the warm areas of Australia and New Guinea. They flower in winter or spring.

D. chrysanthum. Golden-yellow flowers are produced in clusters of six or so from the nodes toward the end of the extremely long (six to eight feet) stem. The flowers are waxy and have two maroon spots on the lip. As the stems elongate, the lower leaves begin to fall, until finally all the leaves are shed at the time of flowering. This native of Nepal and Burma flowers from late fall to winter.

D. chrysotoxum. The ribbed, cylindrical or spindle-shaped stems are about fifteen inches tall and bear six or eight leaves. The golden yellow flowers are borne in many-flowered erect or drooping sprays from the upper nodes of the stem. They are two inches in diameter, and have a round fringed lip that has a deep orange-yellow spot and red lines in the throat. The species occurs in Burma. It flowers in early spring.

D. cucumerinum. Nicknamed the "cucumber" or "gherkin" orchid because the fat one-inch leaves are covered with little tubercles, it grows from a branching, creeping stem. The tiny greenish white flowers have a very ruffly lip marked with wine-red. They are produced in short sprays, and are said to have a foetid odor. Flowering time is spring. The species is native to Australia.

D. dearei. Pure white flowers with a greenish throat, about two inches in diameter, are borne on sprays that come from the upper nodes of the stems. Each spray has seven to fifteen blooms. The flowers are characterized by a rather long spur and very round flaring petals. The leafy stems grow from a foot to three feet tall. This species forms the starting point for a long line of white "dearei type" hybrids. It is native to the Philippines. The blossoms appear in the summer.

D. densiflorum. This species makes a stunning display with its drooping balloon- or lantern-shaped sprays of sunny yellow flowers, fifty to a hundred completely encircling the stem. The flowers are about an inch and a half across (sometimes a bit larger), golden yellow with an orange lip, of a sparkling crystalline texture, and with a finely toothed edge to the petals and lip. The lip, moreover, is covered with a deep-piled golden down. The plants are sturdy, with stems about fifteen inches tall, somewhat four-angled and a bit knobby at the nodes. The leaves are satiny, rather thick, becoming leathery with age. The plant is native to Nepal and Assam and it flowers in the spring.

D. falcorostrum. In its native New South Wales

this is called the "beech orchid" because it prefers the giant beech trees of the rain forests. It is a cane type with a cluster of twenty or more two-inch flowers rising from its top. They are fragrant, waxy, and have a beautifully open, symmetrical shape. It grows best on a log or tree fern slab with intermediate temperatures.

D. farmeri. Similar to *chrysotoxum* but paler in color, this plant has stems that are four-angled and bear two to four leaves. The rounded flowers are about two inches across and have a downy lip. They are borne on loose sprays that droop from an upper node. The species occurs in Sikkim, Nepal, and Burma. It flowers in the spring and summer.

D. fimbriatum. Best known for its variety *oculatum,* this species is one of the most striking of the "drooping spray, yellow-flowered" types. The sprays are a little smaller than they are in *densiflorum,* carrying about a dozen to twenty flowers. The golden flowers are round, with a round fringed lip that has a deep maroon spot or "eye" in its central portion. The crystalline texture makes them actually sparkle. The stems are about two feet tall, with closely spaced fairly thin leaves clothing almost their entire length. *D. fimbriatum* itself (not var. *oculatum*) is a taller plant whose flowers have an orange eye instead of the maroon spot. It occurs in Nepal and Burma. The flowers come from two- and three-year-old stems, in late spring.

D. findlayanum. Daintily colored flowers are produced in pairs in the late summer from the several nodes near the end of the stems. The petals and sepals are white, tinted with lilac, and the heart-shaped lip is white tipped with pink, yellow in the center. The slender, curved stems have swollen nodes and grow two to three feet long. The species is a native of Burma.

D. formosum. One of the finest of the white dendrobiums, this species has flowers three to four inches across and a variety *giganteum* that has five-inch flowers. The long-lasting flowers, which appear in the fall, are deceptively delicate looking, pure white except for a yellow spot on the lip. They are produced in clusters of three to five from the upper nodes of rather stout, hairy pseudobulbs. The species occurs in Burma.

D. gouldii. A member of a group whose petals are slender and twisted, flaring upward like a pair of horns, this group is called "ceratobium" or, affectionately, the "antelope" orchids. A wealth of yellow blooms are borne on erect sprays from the

Fig. 16-3 *Dendrobium loddigesii,* a lovely miniature whose flowers are delicately fragrant and beautifully fringed.

upper nodes of three-foot leafy stems. The species occurs in New Guinea, and flowers in the fall.

D. heterocarpum. This is the correct name for the species also known as *aureum.* Fragrant, creamy yellow flowers, whose brighter lip narrows to a pointed tongue and is streaked with purple, are borne in two's and three's from the nodes of the previous year's growths (sometimes also from three year old growths). The flowers, which are about two inches across, appear in late winter. Stems are erect, yellow, and grow about eighteen inches tall. The species grows natively from the Himalayas to the Philippines.

D. infundibulum. The three-inch white flowers of this species have lip markings varying from red to yellow, quite similar to *D. formosum.* The plant occurs in Burma and flowers variably.

D. kingianum. This is one of Australia's best loved natives. It has slender, straight stems, slightly enlarged at the base, six to nine inches tall, which bear several leathery leaves on the upper part. The sweetly scented flowers are waxy, about one inch wide borne on somewhat nodding stems four to eight inches long. The color range is marvelous, going from white to pink, rose, and rich purple, and the lip is often spotted. It flowers in the spring, and prefers cool temperatures.

D. linguiforme. This is called the "tongue orchid" because of its tongue-shaped leaves, which are quite like those of *cucumerinum* without the tubercles, having instead a smooth skin and a few parallel depressed lines along the surface. The feathery flower spray is about six inches long and holds thirty or more little creamy or white flowers. It is a native of Australia, where it inhabits many

Home Orchid Growing

different climatic areas, including those with a definite dry season, and benefits from restricted water after new leaves are formed. It is cool growing and flowers in the spring.

D. loddigesii. The slender, branching, creeping stems of this miniature species have something of the habit of a *Dichaea* plant. Tiny leaves clothe the stems and are deciduous eventually. Aerial roots appear where the stem branches. The beautiful, delicately fragrant one-inch flowers come singly along the stem. They have slender rosy-lavender sepals and petals and a round, marvelously fringed lip which has an orange center surrounded by white and a lavender border. Native to Hainan Island, it grows with cattleyas, and flowers in mid-winter.

D. macrophyllum. As the name suggests, this species has unusually large leaves, borne at the top nodes of two-foot ridged stems. The sprays are erect and carry a dozen or fifteen attractive flowers. The oval pointed sepals are hairy on the outside, pale yellow-green, and larger than the white petals. The large lip, its outer lobe long and recurved, is striped with purple. The species occurs in New Guinea, and neighboring islands.

D. moorei. This is a dwarf plant with canes bearing a few slender leaves on the upper parts. The fragrant, half-inch flowers are white, marked with purple, and have slender sepals and petals and a round lip. Native to Lord Howe Island, it flowers in summer with cattleya conditions.

D. moschatum. These plants vary in size from those that reach three feet to some that grow to six feet tall. The lovely and unusual flowers are three inches across, with sepals and petals of pale yellow tipped with rose. The lip is slipper-shaped, downy, with five lines of fringe in the center, and is yellow except for two bright spots of maroon surrounded by orange. The flowers are produced in the winter, sometimes later, on sprays from the uppermost nodes of the previous year's growths. The plants are native to India and Burma.

D. nobile. This delightful species has over eighty named varieties. It was the most widely known of all dendrobiums, together with its hybrids, until the *phalaenopsis* hybrids came along to challenge but not replace them. The charming, brightly colored blossoms are produced in nodding groups of three or so from the nodes along the two-year-old stems. The flowers are three inches in diameter, with sepals and petals white tipped with rosy purple; the rounded lip is velvety, purple in the throat and bordered with white. The winter or spring flowers are long lasting and lend themselves, as do so many others, to dainty corsages. This species occurs at high elevations in India.

D. parishii. Reminiscent of *nobile,* with its flow-

Fig. 16-4 LEFT, *Dendrobium nobile,* flowering in midwinter close to the frosted glass of a cool house. Its velvety flowers come from the leafless canes of the previous years. RIGHT, *Dendrobium fimbriatum* var. *oculatum,* has bright yellow flowers set off by a deep maroon center. (*Courtesy Jack Sweet*)

Fig. 16-5 *Dendrobium gouldei.* Vigor and generosity in flowering characterize this member of the ceratobium or "antelope horn" group of species. *(Courtesy Wm. Kirch)*

ers borne at the nodes along the fifteen-inch stems, these are amethyst purple, with two maroon spots in the throat of the downy lip. The plants occur in Moulmein and flower in spring and summer.

D. pierardii (syn. *aphyllum*). Drooping stems that grow from three to five feet long produce an incredible wealth of flowers in pairs at the nodes. The blossoms are two inches in diameter, pale pink with the yellow lip striped with purple. New growths appear in the early summer at about the same time as the flowers. The plant is native to India.

D. phalaenopsis. A beautifully colored species with many handsome varieties, its flowers appear in the late spring and are borne in dainty arching sprays from the upper nodes of both old and new growths. The stems are from eighteen inches to over two feet tall. The sepals are white flushed with rose, the more rounded petals are mauve veined with a deeper shade. The side lobes of the lip are deep maroon-purple, while the slender pointed middle lobe is pale purple with deeper veins. Among the outstanding varieties of *phalaenopsis* which have entered much into hybridization are: variety *alba* and variety *hololeucum,* both white; 'Schroderianum,' which is very richly colored; and

a long line of selected "strains" chosen for their particular markings, richness of color, or outstanding form. Many of the strains and varieties have been intercrossed to produce lovely things, but these are, of course, not true hybrids. Fascinating hybrids have been made with the "antelope" species, of the botanical section ceratobium. The species occurs in Australia.

D. sanderae. A very lovely species, similar in some ways to *dearei,* it has white, showy flowers, about three and a half inches in diameter. The petals are broad and flaring, and the lip has a wide, spreading outer lobe. The throat is purple, with a few purple stripes extending from the center. There is a variety *parviflorum,* more generally seen in cultivation, which has the flowers a bit smaller but in which the throat is much darker. The flowers appear in the spring in clusters of six to twelve from the upper nodes of the two-foot stems. The species occurs in the mountains of northern Luzon.

D. schuetzii. Another of the *dearei* type, this is a smaller plant. The foot-tall stems are very slender at the base. The large white flowers appear in the fall and are borne in clusters of four or so. They last for many weeks. The plant is native to the Philippines.

D. sophronitis. A most delightful miniature, the plants have brilliant flowers larger than the plants themselves. The pseudobulbs are half an inch tall and the rough, dark green leaves are less than an inch long. The flowers are all shades of red and even range to orange, yellow and white. A native of cool, damp high elevations of New Guinea, it flowers almost continuously. Its flowers last several months.

D. stratiotes. This is one of the attractive "antelope" dendrobiums. Both sepals and petals are twisted or wavy, the long petals standing up like a pair of horns. The sepals are creamy white, the petals pale yellow-green. The lip is white, streaked with purple. It occurs in Indonesia and New Guinea and flowers in the fall.

D. superbiens. This is a striking species, whose crimson-purple flowers have the sepals and petals bordered with white. The broad lip is reflexed and wavy. The two-inch flowers are borne fifteen or more on arching-erect sprays from the top nodes of the three-foot stems. It occurs in Australia and flowers in late summer or fall.

D. taurinum. A strikingly colored member of the "antelope" group, the recurved sepals are pink, while the longer petals, which resemble the horns

Home Orchid Growing

Fig. 16-6 *Dendrobium phalaenopsis* flowers from both old and new growths, giving an array of flowers in rich, soft hues. Shown here is the selected strain 'Delicata'. (*Courtesy Jones and Scully, Inc.*)

of a bull, are reddish brown tinged with purple. The massive lip is rosy marked with raised reddish brown lines, ruffled at its edge. The plant occurs in the Philippines and flowers in the fall. It needs more copious watering than other members of the group.

D. thyrsiflorum. Very close to *densiflorum,* and probably a variety of it, its flowers are identical in shape and size. They are borne in the same lantern-shaped spray and also have the sparkling, crystalline texture. The sepals and petals are white and the lip is deep orange. The plant occurs in Moulmein and Burma and flowers in the winter or spring.

D. undulatum. The flowers of this species are dull yellow, more or less spotted with purple, with extremely twisted sepals and petals. The lip is bright yellow dotted with purple and decorated with five white keels. This species and *taurinum* are about the same size, with three- to four-foot stems, and flower sprays two feet long. *D. undulatum* is native to Australia and New Guinea.

D. veratrifolium. A much larger plant than the other "antelope" species, this one has stems to five feet and flower sprays two and a half feet long bearing many more flowers. Its size and vigor are the characteristics it contributes to hybrids made with various of the other "antelope" species. Its flowers do not have the extreme twisting shown by some; in fact, the oar-shaped petals are not twisted at all but they do stand up tall between the sepals. The lip is broad and open. The flowers are variable in color, mostly white with the lip marked with branching veins of purple. The species occurs in New Guinea.

D. wardianum. The flowers of this species are slightly larger than in *nobile.* They are waxy and white, with the sepals, petals, and lip all tipped with amethyst. The yellow throat is marked with two bright, clear-cut spots of purple. The three-foot stems are pendant and, in the spring, bear pairs of the three-inch flowers for almost their whole length. The plant occurs in Assam and Burma.

Other Members of the Dendrobium Tribe

Authorities differ on the matter of what other genera are closely related to *Dendrobium.* Bailey gives *Inobulbon* and *Sarcopodium.* Others include *Pseuderia, Cadetia, Eria, Porpax,* and *Cryptochilus. Eria* is widespread in the Philippines, where it is enjoyed for its small plants and tiny sprays of flowers.

17

ODONTOGLOSSUM TRIBE

An artist with words might contrive a new adjective to describe the wonders of this tribe of epiphytes. The adjective would have to suggest feathers and pixies, butterflies and pansies, filigree work and the classical ballet. Woven through it would be a feeling of golden sunlight and cool, frosty nights. And when its syllables were cleverly fitted together, it would mean *Odontoglossum, Oncidium,* and *Miltonia,* the three most outstanding members of this tribe.

Odontoglossums and miltonias were widely grown in nineteenth-century England, in the house, the garden, and the greenhouse. A writer of the times described a plant that grew wonderfully in the sitting-room of his home, where it was covered with frost on winter nights and had no heat until the fire was lighted for tea. Sprays of odontoglossums were made into bouquets for "lady musicians" and were used in arrangements for decorations. Single blossoms were considered quite the best boutonnieres for gentlemen. While other kinds of orchids were admired and even grown in quantity, the odontoglossums and miltonias were really the popular orchids of the day.

Oncidium offers variety scarcely to be matched elsewhere in the orchid family. An amateur could easily become an oncidium fancier, for possession of a few of the species provokes a curiosity to know the other elfin forms of the genus. Legend has it that it was *Oncidium papilio* that started the craze of amateur orchid growing.

The genera belonging to the Odontoglossum tribe are so closely related that some botanists consider it merely one large and varied genus. The genera may be freely crossed with one another. So many natural hybrids have been found that the job of marking these from distinct species is far from finished. Whether the tribe is considered one genus or several, certain characters separate the types from each other, and the generic division is helpful in classifying the hundreds of species.

The tribe inhabits tropical America, from Mexico to Bolivia, and climbs from the hot, coastal regions to the cool, misty heights of the Andes. The species from lower elevations can be grown anywhere. Those from the intermediate elevations are a little more restricted, but many of them can be accommodated in greenhouses where cattleyas do well. The cool kinds, from the highest altitudes, especially the "crispum" type of *Odontoglossum,* require conditions not found in many places in this country. The Pacific Northwest offers conditions closest to their needs, and with special handling they can be grown in other areas where cool days as well as cool nights exist during the summer. The introduction of the evaporative cooler to offset our summer heat has widened the possibilities for growing members of this tribe, particularly the borderline species in the groups from intermediate elevations, and it may also make it possible for many growers to experiment with the "crispum" type.

Fig. 17-1 *Miltonia* Charlesworthii, a lovely hybrid that stems from the species *Miltonia vexillaria* and *Miltonia roezlii*. The butterfly marking in the center is typical of many *Miltonia* species and hybrids. (*Courtesy Frederick T. Bonham*)

MILTONIA

Miltonia is affectionately called the "pansy orchid," so named from the most familiar type whose charms are indeed similar to those of the much beloved pansy. Their flowers open flat, with the same frank expression, and their rounded parts are as softly colored. The blossoms are held gracefully on slender stems that appear from the base of mature pseudobulbs and reach a length of from six to eighteen inches. A plant with a number of flower sprays resembles a hand-arranged bouquet, with its pretty, light green foliage forming a background for a compact array of flowers. The pseudobulbs are small, oval-compressed, and smooth; each bears two or more narrow leaves at the apex and a few small ones sheathing the base.

It has taken a good bit of experimentation to learn how to grow miltonias in this country. It is now known that they will thrive with a night temperature of 60° but that they do not like the nights to be much warmer than this even in the summer. As to day temperature, they do best when it does not exceed 80°. Higher day temperatures deplete the plants, unless they prevail just for short periods. They therefore do well with cattleyas in regions of mild summer temperatures, or where summer heat can be carefully controlled.

Potting. Osmunda fiber or tree fern fiber are preferred by many growers, although a seedling grade of fir bark (one-eighth to one-quarter inch) is being used successfully. Drainage must be extremely good, and small pots are used. Rather than risk overpotting, most growers repot every year. Potting should be done during a cool season, either just as the new growths start in the spring, or in the fall.

Light. The species from Colombia and Panama require about the same amount of light as paphiopedilums, 1,000 to 1,500 foot candles in the summer, a bit more perhaps in the winter when the air is cooler. The Brazilian species like about the same amount of light as cattleyas. It is possible to grow both kinds, and their hybrids, in the same greenhouse with the light adjusted by shading according to their individual needs.

Temperature. The day temperature should preferably not exceed 80° and the night temperature should be close to 60°.

Water. Miltonias should not be allowed to become dry. They use more water during warm weather, and care in watering during the summer is essential in order to bring them through the season in good shape.

Humidity. Miltonias must have ample humidity, best furnished by sprayers and fans, or other means of providing moving damp air. A relative humidity of about 60 percent is best, fluctuating between 50 and 70 percent.

Fertilizer. In osmunda fiber, an application of a 10-10-10 fertilizer not more often than once a month seems best. Some growers fertilize only every two months. None is given during the winter where skies are dull, but an occasional application may be given where there is good winter sun. Fertilizing in fir bark and bark mixes should be more frequent, every other watering with a 30-10-10 formula, reduced a bit in winter.

Propagation. Miltonias will do better if not divided too often. Let them grow into plants with many leads and then divide them into clumps of a number of pseudobulbs. Division should be just before new growth starts. They are grown from seed in the same manner as other orchids. There are numerous lovely hybrids in both the Colombian and Brazilian groups, and many crosses between *Miltonia, Odontoglossum, Oncidium, Cochlioda,* and *Brassia.*

The Species

M. anceps. A rather rare species from Brazil, it is of modest size both as to plant and flowers. The latter are about two-and-a-half inches across, with the tips of the yellow-green sepals and petals curved backward. The lip is somewhat fiddle-shaped, white a few longitudinal lines and at their base a few spots of purple. It flowers in May and June, with one bloom to a stem.

M. candida. At first glance this species would not be recognized as a Miltonia, for it has more or less a cattleya shape, with the sides of the lip rolled up around the column. The oval-pointed sepals and petals are equal in size, and can be nearly all brown with yellow edges or yellow with varying degrees of brown markings. The lip is cream color. The flowers are borne three to five to a stem and are about three inches across. Blooming season is autumn; native habitat is Brazil.

M. clowesii. This is a large, handsome species with pseudobulbs up to four inches tall and leaves to eighteen inches long. The flower is of the type with a fiddle-shaped lip. The sepals and petals are slender, pointed, yellow with brown bars. The lip is violet at the basal half, while the pointed outer part is white. The tall flower stem holds seven to ten of the three-inch flowers. Flowering season is fall. The species is native to Brazil.

M. cuneata. Another stunning Brazilian species, this one has slender, pointed sepals and petals that are brown tipped with yellow, and a large square white lip attached by a narrow claw (stalk). The flowers are three inches in diameter, borne five to eight on a tall stem, and appear in early spring.

M. endresii. With white flowers that have a pale pink "bee" in the center, this is a very lovely and dainty species. The flowers are about two inches across, sometimes larger, and are of the type with broad sepals and petals and a much larger rounded lip. They occur three to five to a stem and are delicately fragrant. The plant is small, with flattened pseudobulbs two inches tall, and thin leaves eight to twelve inches long. It occurs in Costa Rica and Panama and flowers in late winter.

M. flavescens. An interesting but less decorative species, this one has star-shaped flowers with narrow, dull yellow sepals and petals and a smaller, pointed, fiddle-shaped lip which is white with some purple streaks. It is native to Brazil and Paraguay and blooms in the summer.

M. phalaenopsis. The pale green, grassy foliage of this species forms a background for the flowers which are held on short stems. The flowers have very much rounded sepals and petals and a broad, four-lobed lip. They are white except for the rich markings of purple on the lip, and are two to two and a half inches in diameter, four or five to a stem. Native to Colombia, it flowers in late summer and early fall.

M. regnellii. Three to five flat subtly tinted flowers are borne on a short stem. The sepals and petals are white, suffused with rose toward the base. The heart-shaped lip is light rose, streaked with a deeper shade and having a white margin. The variety *purpurea* has darker coloring. The plant is native to Brazil.

M. roezlii. This lovely species is often found in the lineage of hybrids. The foliage is pale green and the pseudobulbs are tightly clustered. Two to four large flat flowers are borne on each spike. The sepals and petals are white, the latter having a purple band at the base. The large lip is two-lobed, white with a tinge of purple. It becomes yellow at the base, where two little horns project backward on each side of the column. The species requires especially free ventilation, and plenty of moderated light. It occurs in Colombia and Panama and often flowers twice a year, winter and spring. The popular hybrid *Miltonia* Bleuana is a cross between *Miltonia roezlii* and *Miltonia vexillaria.*

M. schroederiana. See *Odontoglossum confusum.*

M. spectabilis. This was the first miltonia introduced into culture, and comes from Brazil. It is indeed a spectacle when in flower, for large, sturdy plants may bear as many as fifty flowers, each on a separate stem, and all opening at once. The flowers, which occur in the fall, are large, white or cream colored, with a large, wavy lip that is rose-purple

veined with a darker shade. The pseudobulbs are an inch apart, and the foliage is yellow-green.

M. vexillaria. This species has the largest flowers of the genus and is the most popular. It is also the most frequently used in hybridization. The plants are sturdy, easily grown, and generous in the numbers of blooms produced. The richly colored flowers are four inches or more in diameter, and occur two to seven on a spike. A single pseudobulb may give rise to several spikes. The small sepals and petals are bright rose in color, sometimes with a white margin. The huge, bi-lobed lip is the striking feature of the flower and the character desired in its hybrids. It, too, is a rich shade of rose, shading to white at the base, and streaked with yellow and red. Two small horns project from the base of the lip on either side of the column. The plant has pale green foliage, occurs in Colombia, and flowers in spring and summer.

M. warscewiczii. This is a completely charming species, very distinctive in shape and coloring and quite fragrant. The narrow sepals and petals are ruffled along their edges, brown, with a white border and white tips, curled back at their ends. The large lip is square with rounded corners, entirely rose-purple except for a white edge at its outer end. The plant has flattened pseudobulbs four to five inches tall and short, broad leaves. It is native to Panama, Colombia, Ecuador, and Peru, and flowers in the spring.

ODONTOGLOSSUM

Some of the loveliest orchids known to man belong to the genus *Odontoglossum.* They range through Central America and parts of South America, mostly in mountainous regions, having their culmination in the high Andes Mountains. A few species which are little known reach elevations up to 12,000 feet, the "crispum" group lives around 8,000 to 9,000 feet, and still others range on down to 3,000 feet. Even though some of them dwell at elevations comparable to those occupied by cattleyas, they are not as tolerant of our warm summer nights and days, and are better grown as cool orchids, or grown where summer temperatures are quite moderate.

Those that live at the higher altitudes are too touchy as to temperature for most of us to try. These are the "cold" species, or the "crispum" group as they are also called, after the most important species, *O. crispum.* They require an ideal night temperature of 45° in the winter, 50° in the

Fig. 17-2 *Miltonia roezlii,* whose velvety texture and soft markings give it special appeal.

Home Orchid Growing

Fig. 17-3 A "crispum type" bigeneric hybrid, *Odontonia* Epha, which, through several generations, combines the species *Odontoglossum crispum* and *O. harryanum,* and *Miltonia vexillaria* and *M. roezlii.* The flower is white with bright red markings. *(Courtesy Gordon M. Hoyt)*

summer, with the day temperature not exceeding 60°. Hybrids in this group are a little more tolerant of warmer temperatures, but their culture is still restricted to areas where summer days and nights are cool and damp, such as parts of Europe and our Pacific Northwest, or other areas having a similarly fortunate climate. Air conditioning (refrigeration) may make it possible to grow this group where the temperature would normally be too warm, but the expense might be such that few amateurs would wish to indulge in it. The species included in this group are *crispum, luteo-purpureum,* and *odoratum.* Along with the cool temperatures, this group needs a soft damp atmosphere, and, while they cannot take strong light, the light must not be cut below an amount necessary to make good growth and to mature the pseudobulbs.

A better group for the amateur is the cool group, or what we might call the "medium cool" group. Even these do not all lend themselves to summer conditions in the South and some parts of the Midwest, but evaporative coolers make it possible to grow them where it used to be considered impossible. Some of them can easily be grown with cymbidiums, with about half of the amount of light demanded by cymbidiums. Some will make themselves at home with cattleyas, provided the nights stay close to or under 60° in the summer. Those that we suggest you try along with cymbidiums are *bictoniense, cirrhosum, harryanum, insleayi, nobile, rossii,* and *uro-skinneri.* Kinds to grow along with cattleyas are *cariniferum, grande, pendulum, pulchellum,* and *schlieperianum.* A

species which is more tolerant of warmth and does well with cattleyas in warm regions is *pendulum.*

The smooth, bright green pseudobulbs of *Odontoglossum* are oval to round, usually compressed to a sharp edge at the sides. They bear one to two fleshy leaves at the apex, and often have small sheathing leaves at the base. The remarkably varied flowers have sepals and petals that are free and spreading, but an occasional exception has the sepals somewhat united. The base of the lip is parallel to the column, with its outer lobe spreading downward. This habit of the lip is one of the ways by which *Odontoglossum* is distinguished from *Oncidium,* where the lip is never parallel to the column. The graceful stems arise from the base of the newly starting growth in some species, from the mature growth in others.

Potting. Osmunda, tree fern, bark, or mixes can be used. Pot to allow two or three years' growth, as it is not necessary to repot until the material has become broken down. Fertilizer may be given occasionally in osmunda, regularly in the other media.

Light. *O. grande* and *schlieperianum* require the same amount of light as cattleyas; *cariniferum, pulchellum,* and *pendulum* need just a bit less. Those which we have suggested to be grown with cymbidiums will need more shade than the latter, but enough light to keep their foliage a light green.

Water. All require abundant water during the growing season, with good drainage so as not to allow the medium to stay sopping wet. The cold and cool kinds should not be allowed to become dry during the winter, although, of course, they will use less water than they do when growing. The kinds which tolerate warmer temperatures can be allowed to approach dryness between waterings, as can cattleyas. Growers who are successful with *O. grande* in climates warmer than ideal find that it does better for them if allowed to become dry between waterings during the winter.

Humidity. Kinds grown with cattleyas need not be given a higher relative humidity than ordinarily maintained in the greenhouse. The cool growing kinds benefit from a mist spray on bright days. The cold types need a higher relative humidity, around 70 percent if possible, with care to keep the air in circulation to prevent disease. Good air circulation is, with all kinds, contributory to good health.

Temperature. For the cold group, nights should be 45° to 50° and days preferably close to 60° winter and summer. Days can go to 70° when unavoidable, but everything should be done to keep the temperature from going above that level. For the cool kinds, nights should be close to 50°, days preferably not over 80°, ideally around 70°. For the rest, nights should be 55° to 60°, not much over 60° even in summer, days not over 85° except for unusual spells.

Propagation. Most odontoglossums can be easily propagated by division. A few, however, do not respond well. They are readily grown from seed. The flasks of young seedlings must be carefully protected against heat. They mature more quickly than many other genera, in about half the time required for cattleyas.

The Species

O. bictoniense. This was the first odontoglossum to survive the voyage to England and has been popular through the years. It bears three-foot sprays of small yellow-green flowers with a white or rose colored lip. It occurs in El Salvador, Guatemala, and Mexico, and flowers in the fall.

O. cariniferum. Greenish red flowers, bordered with light green, have a white lip which makes the two-inch perky flowers quite distinctive. The spring blossoms are borne on stems three or four feet tall, each of which has short branches with four or five flowers. The sepals and petals are narrow, pointed, not wavy, the edges infolded somewhat and having a keel on the back. The lip is spreading at the outer edge, narrowing to a claw directly under the column. This species occurs in Costa Rica, Panama, and Venezuela.

O. cervantesii. The delightful flowers of this species are almost saucer-shaped with the basal half of the sepals and petals marked with concentric circles of brown lines. The flowers are white or pale pink, two to three inches in diameter, several to a more or less pendant stem. The rounded petals and oval sepals come to a sharp point at their tips. The lip has a round, heart-shaped, ruffled outer lobe, and very tiny side lobes. The plant has small pseudobulbs and leaves six inches long. It is a native of Mexico and Guatemala and blooms variably. It likes a damp, shady spot.

O. chiriquense (syn. *coronarium*). One of the most magnificent of orchids, it has a long, cylindrical head of glorious flowers atop a tall stem.

They are round, very much ruffled in all parts, waxy, and long lasting. The sepals and petals are golden brown, their edges decorated with a yellow frill, and their bases with yellow spots. The lip is a little flaring yellow triangle. Two sharp projections on either side of the basal crest are formed by the fleshy side-lobes of the lip. The plant is straggly, unfortunately, with six to eight inches between pseudobulbs, and has to be grown on a tree fern slab or log. The leaves are short and broad. It is a native of Costa Rica, Panama, Colombia, and Peru and flowers in late summer. A close relative is *O. brevifolium.*

O. cirrhosum. A spray of these dainty flowers, white lightly spotted with rose, is sheer lace. Each part is slender and undulating, prolonged at its tip into a short tail. Even the outer lobe of the lip is but a pointed necktie hanging down. One of the most decorative parts is the basal section of the lip. Here the side lobes form a funnel under the column, bright yellow striped with red, flaring outward to form a portal to aid pollination by birds. Two prominent upward curving projections are situated in the center. The plant is slender, with pseudobulbs to three inches tall and leaves a foot long. It is native to Ecuador and Colombia, flowers in late winter, and is cool growing.

O. confusum. This species has gone under the names of both *Miltonia* and *Odontoglossum schroederianum,* and is one of several closely resembling *O. laeve.* It is quite striking, with stiff flowers borne on a stiff spike. The flowers have slender, pointed sepals and petals, with the latter strongly upright like raised arms, and the lateral sepals often curved backward at their tips. They are green, barred and spotted with brown. The fiddle-shaped lip is rose color on the basal part, white on the outer section. It occurs in Costa Rica, and flowers in early fall.

O. convallarioides. This is a slender little plant with half-inch, waxy, white, globular flowers. The round sepals and petals curve inward, closely surrounding the column, and the lip is flat, shaped somewhat like a bibbed apron, having a basal crest spotted with yellow and red. Although it is quite insignificant compared to its more glamorous relatives, it is nevertheless charming. It is native to Mexico and most of Central America, and flowers in the spring.

O. cordatum. A bold flower, its evenly spreading sepals and petals are broad toward the base and taper to a sharp point. The sepals are almost solid brown with a few yellow stripes at their base; the

A

B

Fig. 17-4 *Odontoglossum cirrhosum.* A, the lacy flower spray. B, a single flower, showing how the sepals, petals and lip are drawn out into points.

petals are yellow with brown spots that become smaller toward their bases. The lip is heart-shaped with a long point at the end, white, with brown spots along the center and a brown tip. It occurs in Mexico, Guatemala, Honduras, and Costa Rica, and blooms from summer to fall.

O. crispum. Connoisseurs often name this species the most beautiful of all orchids. Its lacy two and one-half foot sprays are crowded with flowers, each two and one-half to three inches across. The sepals and petals are pointed, daintily ruffled, with their borders toothed or notched. They are white, some-

times tinged with rose, and may be spotted with crimson or brown. The flower is centered by a speckled lip that is fringed with teeth, and whose borders are even more finely notched than the petals. This species is extremely variable, and more than a hundred varieties have been named. It occurs in Colombia, at an elevation of 9,000 feet and flowers at any time of the year.

O. grande. Large, brilliantly marked flowers make this one of the most widely grown species. The flowers are from five to nine inches across; from four to seven occur on a spike from September to December. The sepals are long and rather slender, yellow, barred with chestnut brown. The wider, wavy petals are brown at the base and yellow at the outer end. The generously rounded lip is white or cream colored, spotted with brown. The waxy flowers last for two weeks or so, and are very decorative. The species occurs in Mexico and Guatemala, and has been nicknamed the "tiger orchid."

O. harryanum. The variegated coloring of this species together with its striking shape make it the valued parent of many hybrids. Four or five three-inch flowers occur to a stem. The wavy sepals and petals are brown with irregular bands of yellow-green. The large shield-shaped lip is flat and wavy, its lower half white, changing to yellow, and its basal part brown, veined with purple. Seven serrated crests decorate its base. This native of Colombia flowers in the fall.

O. insleayi. This species has flowers that resemble those of *grande,* but they are smaller, reaching four inches in diameter. The sepals and petals are yellow, spotted with brown, and the lip is orange-yellow spotted with red-brown. It occurs in Mexico and flowers from October to December.

Fig. 17-5 *Odontoglossum cordatum.* (*Courtesy J. A. Fowlie*)

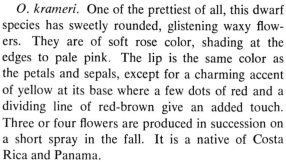

Fig. 17-6 A, *Odontoglossum grande,* the yellow and brown "tiger" orchid. *(Courtesy Rod McLellan Co.)*

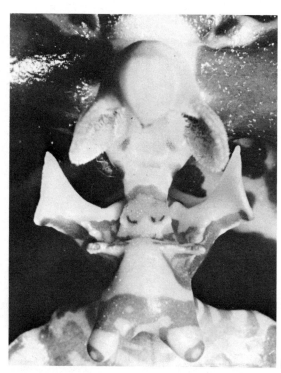

B, the crest of the lip resembles a rubber doll.

O. krameri. One of the prettiest of all, this dwarf species has sweetly rounded, glistening waxy flowers. They are of soft rose color, shading at the edges to pale pink. The lip is the same color as the petals and sepals, except for a charming accent of yellow at its base where a few dots of red and a dividing line of red-brown give an added touch. Three or four flowers are produced in succession on a short spray in the fall. It is a native of Costa Rica and Panama.

O. laeve. Considered the type of a closely related group that includes *confusum* described above, and separated by inconspicuous botanical differences. *O. laeve* has petals a bit wider spread than *confusum;* otherwise it looks very much like it. It has a variety, *auratum,* that is more slender and smaller in all ways, and far less attractive, which has until recently been known as *O. stenoglossum.* While the species *laeve* comes from Mexico and Guatemala, the var. *auratum* is common from Mexico to Costa Rica. The former is spring-flowering, the latter blooms in the summer.

O. luteo-purpureum. This striking and varied species from Colombia produces flowers in horizontal sprays. The wavy, oblong sepals are brownish purple with a yellow margin. The petals are toothed, spotted with purple-brown. The deeply

scalloped yellow lip is fringed and is spotted with purple or rose. The flowers appear in winter and spring.

O. maculatum. This species is distinguished by slender, pointed brown sepals and much broader yellow petals marked with brown spots on their basal half. The lip is a broad triangle, also yellow, marked with two rows of brown spots, much ruffled on its outer edge. On the crest of the lip two tall, stiff keels stand upright, tightly pressed together. A native of Mexico and Guatemala, it flowers in the summer.

O. nebulosum. This resembles *O. cervantesii* in many ways. Instead of the concentric circles of lines it is set off by a filled circle of irregular spots. The flowers are two-and-a-half inches in diameter, produced five to seven to a stem. It occurs in Mexico and blooms in the spring.

O. nobile. This is a good substitute for those who cannot grow *crispum,* but who can furnish quite cool conditions. The long flower spikes carry up to a hundred blooms, each three inches in diameter. The sepals and petals are usually white, sometimes faintly tinged with rose. The kidney-shaped lip is white with a few crimson spots. A native of Colombia, the plants usually flower in the spring.

O. odoratum (syn. *pescatorei*). The flowers of

Min. *Cym.* Evening Star 'Twilight' Min. *Cym.* King Arthur 'San Diego' Min. *Cym.* Sir Galahad 'Grail'

Photographs above courtesy Paul F. Miller

Min. *Cym.* Red Orange (*Courtesy Rod McLellan Co.*)

Min. *Cym.* Lady Bug (*Courtesy Rod McLellan Co.*)

A group of Paphiopedilums: bottom row, Mooreheart, Leyburnense, Wallur; center, three Cinderellas, *sukhakulii,* Mildred Hunter 'Ileana', John Hanes; top row, Claire de Lune, Tendresse. (*Courtesy Rod McClellan Co.*)

Dendrobium aggregatum

Dendrobium densiflorum

Dendrobium thyrsiflorum

Catasetum macroglossum *Catasetum pileatum*

Dendrobium phalaenopsis

(*Rebecca T. Northen*)

Mormodes variabilis *Gongora cornuta*

Stanhopea wardii

Mormodes buccinator

Cycnoches ventricosum var.
   warscewiczii

Coryanthes speciosa

this species are small, but produced in great numbers on branching sprays in winter and spring. They are golden yellow, marked with red-brown, and the wavy narrow lip is covered with down. It occurs in Colombia and Venezuela.

O. pendulum. This is the preferred name for the species familiarly known as *citrosmum*. The drooping sprays carry thick clusters of rounded flowers in pastel hues. The sepals and petals are white to rose, and the extended lip is violet and spreads into two lobes at its apex. The species occurs in Mexico and flowers in late spring.

O. pulchellum. This species is easy to grow and flowers readily. Slender sprays carry six or seven small, waxy, rounded white flowers, each one and one-half to two inches in diameter. Their fragrance suggests lily-of-the-valley. This native of Mexico, Guatemala, El Salvador, and Costa Rica flowers in the spring.

O. retusum. Of solid orange wax, the one-inch flowers of this species are quite eye catching. They are borne on a slender stem, on which they open a few at a time over more than a year. The sepals and petals are similar, fairly broad, with pointed ends that curve forward. The lip is held out almost horizontally, rather concave, with a sharp point at the tip and two fleshy protuberances at its base. It is one of the bird-pollinated species of the high elevations of Ecuador.

O. rossii. One of the loveliest of the genus, this species has short flower stems that bear only two to five blooms, each three inches in diameter. The lack of numbers is compensated for by the beauty of the individual flowers and by their good keeping quality. The sepals are pointed, cream colored to greenish yellow, and barred with dark brown. The blunt, somewhat curled petals are white with a few brown spots at their base. The large, round, wavy lip is pure white. It occurs in Mexico, Guatemala, Honduras, and flowers in the winter.

O. schlieperianum. Another species that resembles a small *grande*. This one has three-inch flowers whose yellow-green ground color is carried into the lip. The markings vary from brown in the type to gold in the variety *flavidum*. Its summer flowering season and the generous number of flowers (eight to fifteen to a spike), make it a worthwhile addition to a collection. This is a native of Costa Rica and Panama.

O. uro-skinnerii. Ten to thirty flowers of striking coloring are produced on long spikes in the spring. The sepals and petals are green, marked with chest-nut-brown, and the large, heart-shaped lip is rose, mottled with white. This species occurs in Guatemala.

ONCIDIUM

Whatever nature's mood may have been when she created the other orchids, surely it was fanciful when she designed the oncidiums. She seems to have caught dancing rays of light, flickering patterns of sun and shadow, little fairy forms not seen by man, and made them into friendly, whimsical, thoroughly delightful flowers. They are meant to be enjoyed with smiles and chuckles and many a held breath. Still generous after endowing so much beauty elsewhere, she seems to have poured out her warmth in this genus.

At least three hundred species of *Oncidium* have been discovered. The description of a mere handful is only a tantalizing glimpse of the whole genus. Favorites among the species are easy to find, and no two fanciers will list the same ones as deserving of attention.

The genus can be found throughout tropical America, from Florida and the West Indies, through Central America to the southern part of Brazil. As with odontoglossums, some are found in low, hot regions, others in the cool upper altitudes. They are more amenable to changes in temperature, however, and most of them will adjust themselves to a moderate greenhouse condition. This makes it easy for the average amateur to include a few oncidiums with almost anything else he grows. As cut flowers, the possibilities they offer are limited only by the imagination of the person working with them. Their filigree-like sprays are charmingly decorative when used alone or as a foil for other flowers. Dainty arrangements for the hair or stunning corsages can be made with groups or with single blossoms.

This genus of epiphytes includes great variety. The pseudobulbs are rounded and flattened at the edges, similar to those of *Odontoglossum,* but some species are without pseudobulbs. The foliage is usually clear green, but is sometimes mottled. The leaves may be fleshy, oval and pointed, with a single prominent mid-vein, or thinner, and many-veined, or terete (cylindrical). The flower sprays are short or long, sometimes drooping, often erect. The blossoms may be large and showy, or small and dainty. All but a few have a lip crest decorated with many protuberances, which adds much to their charm. The unvarying feature that distinguishes

Oncidium from *Odontoglossum* is that in *Oncidium* the base of the lip is never parallel to the column, but forms a right angle to it. The column is short and winged.

Potting. Oncidiums do well in straight osmunda, fir bark or mixes, or can be grown on hanging logs or slabs. Large, robust plants need larger pots for their size than do small plants. Those that produce drooping sprays may be grown in hanging containers. Those that have tall erect sprays need plenty of head room. They need to be repotted only when the medium has broken down.

Temperature. Most of the genus will grow nicely with cattleyas, requiring about the same temperature range and light conditions. Those from the high Andes do best with the 'cool conditions afforded cymbidiums.

Light. Oncidiums all need good light.

Humidity. The humidity conditions necessary for this species are the same as for cattleyas.

Watering. The plants require abundant water during the growing and flowering season, somewhat less at other times.

Fertilizer. The strength of fertilizers and frequency of application are as for cattleyas.

Propagation. Oncidiums respond easily to vegetative propagation, dividing the plants into clumps of three or more pseudobulbs, just before new growth starts. They are also readily grown from seed.

The Species

O. ampliatum. Magnificent panicles, attractively branched and arched, reach a length of three feet. The attractive little dancing doll flowers are clear yellow, spotted with red toward the base of the small sepals and petals. The round flat lip is cream colored on the underside. The round, flattened, ridged pseudobulbs look like turtles. The species occurs from Guatemala to Peru and flowers from March to June.

O. ansiferum. Plants with tall, broad, flat, cardboard-thin pseudobulbs bear sprays of delicate-looking but long-lasting flowers in the summer.

Fig. 17-7 *Oncidium ampliatum*

The flowers are in tones of yellow-green. The side lobes of the spreading lip are large and hold themselves horizontally, looking like an extra pair of petals. This species occurs in Guatemala, Nicaragua, Costa Rica, and Panama.

O. asparagoides. A startling difference marks this species and a few others, among them *abortivum* and *heteranthum,* undoubtedly caused by a mutation in the dim past. Instead of producing flowers along each branchlet of the inflorescence as is normal, flowers occur only at their tips. Where other flowers would be expected, there are only whorls of little green bracts, five in a group, that look like little green stars. These are aborted flowers. In *asparagoides* the effect of many long, sinuous, branched stems with the groups of tiny bracts is reminiscent of asparagus fern. The plant itself is small. The little flowers have greenish yellow sepals and petals barred with green-brown, and a yellow lip. The species is native to Costa Rica and blooms

Fig. 17-8 *Oncidium asparagoides.* All but the end flowers on each branch are aborted and have become mere bracts.

in the fall. *O. abortivum* and *heteranthum* are native to Venezuela.

O. aureum. A lovely species from Ecuador, it produces a tall flower stem, slightly branched, holding twenty to thirty one-inch flowers. They are solid yellow, without crests or markings, and distinguished by the fact that the lip is attached by a slender claw. The sepals are slender, pointed-oval, the petals similar but broader, and the lip is rounded with an indentation at its tip. A plant that looks very much like this occurs in Peru, and is tentatively called *O. dichromum* or *O. aureum* var. *bicolor.* It may be a distinct species. This has red sepals and petals and two teeth in front of the lip claw. Instead of opening its flowers more or less at the same time, as does *aureum,* the unbranched inflorescence gives rise to two or three flowers at a time over a period of a year or more.

O. aurisasinorum. Called *oreja de burro* in its native Honduras, Standley and Williams used this nickname as the basis for its specific name in 1952. It is one of the many "burro ear" species, actually one of the smaller ones. The stiff leaves are attached to very short pseudobulbs, and are light green. The milky white, waxy flowers are produced in a dense cluster at the end of an eighteen-inch stem. They are one and a half inches long, with slender, spreading sepals and petals, the dorsal sepal cupped at the top. The lip is three lobed, the sides of the lateral lobes fold back to make them appear triangular, while the mid-lobe is anchor shaped. It has a toothed callus. Flowering time is fall.

O. batemanianum. Dense heads of small flowers are borne at the top of a four- to six-foot tall stem. They are unusually long lasting, an inch in diameter, and have green sepals, ruffled yellow-green petals barred with brown and a flaring yellow lip decorated at its base with two crests, each consisting of two rows of teeth. It has spherical pseudobulbs that bear a pair of tall, slender leaves. The species is native to Brazil and Peru, where it is often found along rocky road cuts. It flowers in the fall.

O. baueri. Long familiarly known as *altissimum* the robust plants produce flower sprays that sometimes reach twelve feet in length, but usually grow close to six feet. They are gracefully arched or drooping and bear many small blooms. The small sepals and petals are pale yellow spotted with olive-brown, and the larger lip is a brighter yellow with a brown band. This native of the West Indies, Brazil, and Peru flowers in August.

O. cabagre. Almost a miniature, this species has leaves which barely exceed six inches. The dainty

Fig. 17-9 TOP, *Oncidium aurem*, tip of the flower spray. Note the slender claw by which the lip is attached. BOTTOM, a single flower.

little yellow and brown flowers are produced on stems about two feet long. It occurs in Panama and Costa Rica and flowers in the summer.

O. carthagenense. This huge member of the "burro ear" group produces a flowering stem five feet long. The one-inch, round, waxy flowers are much ruffled, with sepals and petals narrowed at the base, broadening suddenly, white with heavy markings of purple or brown-purple. The lip is kidney shaped, colored like the rest of the flower, and has a fleshly, complex crest. The pink column adds a decorative touch. It is very widespread, from Mexico through the West Indies to Venezuela, Brazil, and Colombia, and is summer flowering.

O. cavendishianum. Also a "burro ear" type, this one is not so large as the preceding species. Its flowers occur on a three-foot stem, and tend more to yellow in color, with the sepals and petals often clear yellow but usually marked with red. The bright yellow lip has much ruffled side lobes, and a ruffled, divided mid-lobe. The crest has protuberances in the form of a cross. Native to Mexico and Guatemala, it flowers in early spring.

O. cebolleta. Its name means in Spanish "small onion," referring to the terete leaves that grow

twelve to fifteen inches tall and taper toward the tip. The six-foot flower stem bears a loosely branched panicle at its tip holding many one- to one-and-a-half-inch flowers. The cupped sepals and petals are yellow-brown with dark markings, while the three-lobed lip is yellow with a few brown-red markings on the upper surface, pale yellow underneath. It is common to warm areas throughout the American tropics where it is equipped to endure long dry seasons.

O. cheirophorum. This delightful miniature has little rounded pseudobulbs which are one inch tall and bear two short leaves. They are bright green the first year and become speckled with purple as they age. The flowers, which grow in dense sprays about six inches long, are a bright, clear yellow and very waxy. The plant spreads rapidly to fill its pot and makes a charming show. It is a native of Colombia and southern Central America.

O. crispum. This lovely species and its relatives *forbesii, gardneri,* and *marshallianum* add another variation to the oncidium theme, this time a type with huge petals and dorsal sepal, a large round lip, and lateral sepals partially united and hidden behind the lip. In contrast to the ballerina type

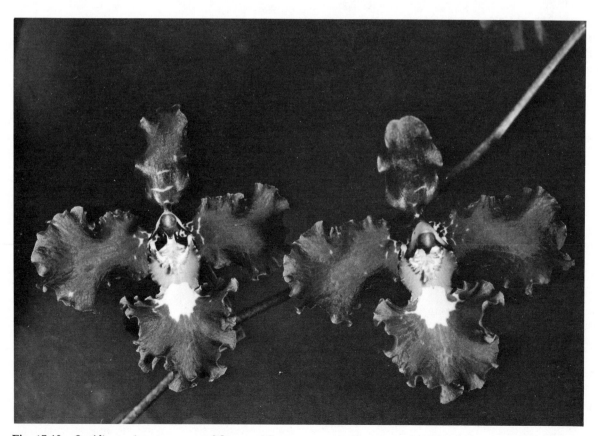

Fig. 17-10 *Oncidium crispum var. grandiflorum.* (*Courtesy J. A. Fowlie*)

such as *varicosum,* these might be feminine members of a folk dancing group, for which the vivacious and audacious *falcipetalum* and its relatives suggest themselves as male dancers. The broad petals of *O. crispum* remind one of the full sleeves of a peasant costume, and the spreading lip the skirt. It is a plant of modest size, with dark green pseudobulbs, compressed and somewhat channelled, each bearing two or three short, rather broadly oval, leathery leaves. The branched inflorescence reaches a height of about eighteen inches and bears ten to twenty two and one-half inch flowers. The blooms are greenish brown with a faint yellow border and a few yellow bars at the base of the parts. The broad petals are ruffled, as are the sepals and lip. The lip has a rectangular basal portion decorated with a finely toothed crest, in front of which is a scalloped patch of clear yellow spreading down onto the ruffled, almost round mid-lobe. The large column has large drooping purple wings. A native of Brazil, it likes a cool spot in the intermediate house, and flowers in the autumn.

O. crista-galli. A lovely dwarf species that produces its bright flowers one to a short stem, but several from a growth. The pseudobulbs are less than an inch tall, and at their tip is an aborted leaf. Leaves come from the base of the pseudobulb, and are three inches tall. The flowers are huge for the plant though but one-and-a-half inches long. They are bright canary yellow, marked with a few red-brown spots at the base of the sepals and petals. The lip is three lobed, with the mid-lobe divided into four parts. The plants grow on the smallest branches in nature, exposed to the morning sun, and in constantly damp forests. They are cool growing, and flower in the fall. The species is native from Mexico through Peru.

O. desertorum. This is one of the many equitant species which have a fan of flat, curved leaves. Actually, each leaf has grown folded together, with only its edges separated to give the appearance of a channel down one side. *O. desertorum* is about two and a half inches tall, and produces a flowering stem a foot high bearing many unique, bright yellow inch-wide flowers, which appear to have three lips. The petals are broadened in an almost exact imitation of the lip, but do not have the crest, and are attached by a brown claw. Native to the Dominican Republic and Haiti, it flowers in the fall.

O. excavatum. A handsome species with large ovoid pseudobulbs and usually a single leaf, it grows both as a complete epiphyte and as a near

terrestrial on grassy slopes of Peru and Ecuador. The tall flowering stem holds a branched panicle of long-lasting flowers. The inch-and-a-half flowers have very large petals and dorsal sepal, and a small lip and winged column. They are yellow except for the brown lip crest and a few brown bars on the other flower parts. The species flowers in the fall and is cool growing.

O. falcipetalum. Whereas with some oncidiums one is reminded of the dainty grace of ballerinas, with the group to which *falcipetalum* belongs one thinks of sheer masculine vigor and exuberance, of flying banners and scarves, of energetic folk dancers. This group of big brown and gold oncidiums is the ultimate for size and showiness. Their three-inch flowers are held on branched stems eight to ten feet long. It includes *macranthum, monachicum, lamelligerum, loxense, superbiens, gyriferum, chrysodipterum,* and perhaps some others. All have in common a short, tongue-shaped lip, and together they are referred to as the group "microchilum" or "cyrtochilum." They have huge sepals and petals, much ruffled and highly decorative, attached by stalks. In *falcipetalum* the dorsal sepal is more rounded and wavy than the laterals, brown with a gold edge or gold marked with brown blotches. The lateral sepals widen out from their long stalks like pantaloons and are solid brown. The petals are smaller, bright yellow with a few brown spots, and are highly ruffled, often curving forward to touch at their tips. The lip and crest are yellow. It is native to high elevations of Peru, Ecuador, and Venezuela, and flowers in the fall.

O. flexuosum. This species is a small member of the popular group of "dancing doll" orchids. Because of the much reduced sepals and petals and the voluminous lip, this group resembles a miniature ballet. The tiny, one-inch flowers of this species occur in dainty showers on a loose, airy panicle atop a tall stem. The sepals and petals are yellow, barred with brown, and the broad, full lip is yellow with a few red spots. It grows and flowers with great freedom and, because of its small size, is welcome in little greenhouses. This native of Brazil flowers at various seasons.

O. forbesii. This could be another feminine member of the folk dancing group. The full, round flowers are two and one-half inches across, shiny brown, with the edges of all parts wavy and marked with a splashed border of yellow. The yellow crest of the lip is dotted with brown and comes to a bodice-like point where the mid-lobe flares out. As a most delightful touch, the column wings, which surround the stigma as well as the anther, are white dotted with red. The inflorescence reaches three feet in length and bears many blooms. Native to Brazil, it flowers in early fall and likes intermediate temperatures.

O. gardneri. Quite similar in shape to *O. crispum,* but daintier, perkier, and more brightly colored, it is delightfully fragrant. The petals are brown, embroidered with a buttonhole stitch in yellow, and the parasol shaped dorsal sepal is yellow barred with brown. The lip is fan shaped, notched in the middle of the outer edge, clear yellow rimmed with a band of brown spots that leave a yellow border. The basal part is briefly narrowed and gives rise to two ear-like side lobes. The crest is decorated with red-brown protuberances. Also native to Brazil, it grows with intermediate temperatures and flowers in late summer or fall.

O. globuliferum. This miniature has the peculiar habit of making long runners that twine around each other and any support they find, forming a spiderweb among their native trees. At each node of the runner there occurs a small plant, which has a flattened round pseudobulb and one leaf. Each plant produces a single flower on a short stem, and then the following year can give rise to another runner. The flowers are large in comparison to the plant. They have abbreviated sepals and petals, yellow, barred with red-brown, and a large, round, undulate lip of bright yellow. It is very difficult to bloom in cultivation. It is native from Costa Rica to Peru and Venezuela, and flowers in the summer.

O. gyriferum. This rare and lovely species from Ecuador belongs to the *falcipetalum* group. Its waxy, dark brown flowers are borne on an eight- to ten-foot stem which has rather widely separated side branches holding several flowers each. The flowering stem has a vining habit that is quite fascinating. The tip of the stem makes circular motions as if groping for a support. When it contacts the stem of a neighboring plant (or a stake) it curls round and round it in an upward direction as it grows. The circular motion is called "circumnutation." Several other species of the *falcipetalum* group are also vining. The flowers of *O. gyriferum* are two inches long, with stalked, oval sepals that come to a graceful point. The petals are also stalked, broad in the middle, and slender-pointed, with ruffled edges of bright yellow. The little strap of a lip curves under and is hidden from view, leaving the voluptuously carved crest as the

Fig. 17-11 *Oncidium gyriferum,* a rare species. One of a group of large brown species from Ecuador that have an extremely small, tongue-shaped lip.

center of attention. The species comes from high elevations in Ecuador, and flowers in the fall, the flowers keeping for two months.

O. henekenii. The lip of this species looks so much like a spider that the people of its native Hispaniola call it the "spider" or "tarantula." The lip even has a crest with six "legs" (the wrong number for a spider, better suiting a bee). The "spider" is velvety, purple-black with a pink "thorax." It grows in warm dry areas where the air is humid, in the Dominican Republic and Haiti. The small dark green leaves are arranged in tiny fans. This is one of the numerous species pollinated by pseudocopulation.

O. incurvum. This small species, which does best when grown a little cooler than the average, produces many dainty, gracefully branched panicles of lovely, one-inch flowers that are pale pink spotted with rosy purple. It comes from Mexico and flowers in late summer and fall.

O. jonesianum. From a plant very similar to *cebolleta,* come the most striking and decorative three-inch flowers, ten to fifteen per stem. The dorsal sepal and the petals arch upward, while the lateral sepals are held behind the flower; all are cream-white, very much ruffled and marked with scattered red spots. The outer lobe of the white lip is broad and flaring, divided in the middle, attached by a claw from which two bright yellow ears spread sideways, and which is decorated with a complicated crest. It likes bright light and not too much water. Native to Paraguay, Brazil, and Uruguay, it flowers in the fall.

O. kramerianum. The "butterfly orchid," which description it shares with its more famous relative, *papilio,* does not grow with the abandon usual to the genus, but it rewards careful attention with a succession of single spectacular butterfly flowers. The petals and the dorsal sepal are drawn out to look like antennae. The lateral sepals are broad, golden yellow spotted with brown; and the large, round, ruffled lip is yellow with the finely toothed border decorated by a band of brown spots. The flowers appear one after another at the tip of a tall jointed stem. The foliage of the plant is green, mottled with brown. This Central American species has a variable flowering season.

O. lamelligerum. This is the most highly ruffled and most decorative member of the cyrtochilum group. It could be the chief dancer in the folk dancing group to which belong *falcipetalum* and the others. The edges of the brown petals and sepals are decorated with a finely toothed yellow border that adds ruffles to the ruffles. The petals are tipped with yellow. The side lobes of the lip are violet, and the white crest is accented with a spot of purple. It is native to Ecuador at moderately high elevations, and was rediscovered a few years ago by the late José Strobel. It blooms in summer and fall.

O. lanceanum. An odd combination of colors makes this a very striking species. The showy flowers are two to three inches across. The sepals and petals are blunt and fleshy, yellow, spotted with chocolate brown or crimson. The spreading lip stands in contrast to the rest of the flower with its rose outer portion and violet base. The robust plants have no pseudobulbs; and the wide, fleshy burro-ear leaves are mottled with brown. The rather short, stout, erect flower stems bear a generous number of blooms in the summer. The species is native to British Guiana.

O. leucochilum. The beautifully colored flowers of this species are about an inch and a half in diameter and are borne on a branched scape that reaches more than ten feet in length. The spatula-shaped sepals and petals are greenish brown barred with red-brown, and the lip has white side lobes and a spreading, wavy mid-lobe. Bright accents are given by the pink tooth of the crest and the pink anther cap and wings of the column. The flowering stem starts in January and takes eight or nine months to bloom, from which time the flowers open in succession over a long period, giving blooms into the winter. It is native to Central America.

O. luridum. Big mule-ear plants give a tall branched flower stem. The flowers, though only an inch in diameter, are truly showy. They are waxy, with sepals and petals white, heavily barred with rose, and a rose lip edged in white. The sepals and petals are short and curving, very wavy on the edges. The side lobes of the lip are rounded but their edges fold back to give the appearance of being square, and they are tinged with orange. The sides of the short mid-lobe also fold back in the center, pinching it in the middle, while the outer lobe flares abruptly. The yellow crest is marked with an orange linear design. This spring-flowering species spreads from Florida through the West Indies and Mexico to British Guiana and Peru.

O. macranthum. This superb flower is the most famous of the cyrtochilum group (described under *O. falcipetalum*). It is a lush and round flower, three to four inches across. The brown sepals and golden yellow petals are about the same size and shape, oval, flat-spreading, gently undulating, attached by slender stalks. The petals are quite ruffled. The side lobes of the waxy lip are purple, the sharply pointed mid-lobe yellow, and the crest is decorated with a burst of white spikes tipped with purple. It blooms in summer and fall on a long, vining, branched stem. It is native to high elevations in Ecuador, and should be grown cool.

O. marshallianum. This is perhaps the most decorative of the feminine folk dancers. The plants are larger and of a lighter green, the inflorescence longer, and the flowers larger and brighter. The less conspicuous dorsal sepal bends forward over the column and is yellow with purple bands. The almost rectangular ruffled petals are slightly fiddle shaped and bi-lobed at their tips, golden yellow with large brown spots down the center. The large, wavy lip is deeply bi-lobed at its outer edge, and

Fig. 17-12, UPPER LEFT, *Oncidium kramerianum*, a spectacular butterfly in yellow and reddish brown, akin to *Oncidium papilio*. (*Courtesy H. A. Dunn and H. Griffin*)

UPPER RIGHT, *Oncidium lanceanum*, a stunning species with large heavy flowers of chocolate and yellow with a pink lip. (*Courtesy Jones and Scully, Inc.*) LOWER, *Oncidium varicosum*.

Fig. 17-13   *Oncidium leucochilum.*

spreads in a broad fan, all clear yellow except for the crest and small side lobes which are spotted with orange-red. Native to Brazil, this one likes a bit cooler temperatures than its relatives, and flowers in the spring.

O. microchilum. The name of this very pretty species must not be confused with the term sometimes used for the group to which *falcipetalum, macranthum,* etc., belong. It is justly named, however, because the mid-lobe of the lip is reduced to a tiny protuberance. The sepals and petals are light or dark brown with yellow markings. The side lobes of the lip are rounded, convex, white marked with purple at the base. It grows natively through Mexico and Guatemala and flowers in the summer.

O. monachicum. This species is quite similar to *falcipetalum.* It, too, is brown except for a delicate border of yellow on its much ruffled parts. The lateral sepals flare out sideways from their narrow stalks, and their broadened outer parts are not quite as large as the dorsal sepal and petals. The tip of the lip curves under. It is native to the cool high elevations of Ecuador, and blooms in late summer.

O. nubigenum. In addition to having attractive flowers, this small species is one of the most fragrant of orchids. The plants have oval compressed pseudobulbs that bear one or two leaves eight to ten inches long. The flowering stem is about a foot tall and bears five to ten flowers, opening more or less at the same time. The green-brown sepals and petals are oval with a sharp little point at their tips, and are somewhat cupped forward. The lip varies from pale to dark rose and is attractively spotted with a darker shade. It has rounded side lobes that are continuous with the mid-lobe. The mid-lobe is rounded but is bi-lobed at its outer end, often quite severely. The crest is composed of two fleshy vertical lobes, each of which is sub-divided into two lesser protuberances. The species occurs in northern Ecuador and Colombia, and flowers in spring and summer.

O. obryzatum. An "almost miniature" Oncidium, these plants are especially vigorous and may outgrow the miniature dimensions. This Central American species is a delightful addition to a collection. Its half-inch brownish flowers appear on dainty sprays in the fall.

O. olivaceum (syn. *cucullatum*) is somewhat larger than *nubigenum* but very similar to it. It differs in that the flowers are larger; the lip is less divided at its end and has a sharp little point in the center; the side lobes of the lip are longer and

Fig. 17-14   *Oncidium macranthum,* another species with the tiny lip, but having a fuller shape. (*Courtesy Margaret Ilgenfritz*)

Fig. 17-15 LEFT, *Oncidium olivaceum,* RIGHT, *Oncidium nubigenum.*

are more sharply set off from the mid-lobe; the crest is a long, single, vertical swelling, undivided and undecorated. The blooms open over an extended period and are less fragrant. It occurs in central Ecuador and flowers in late spring and summer.

O. onustum. This entirely lemon yellow species has nearly round flowers. The sepals are hidden from the front view by the large and rounded petals and lip. The lip is three lobed, with the lateral lobes simulating a pair of petals, and the mid-lobe broad, divided slightly at its tip. The plants have small mottled pseudobulbs each bearing one or two fleshy leaves two to four inches tall. The flowers barely exceed an inch in diameter, but the erect or arching raceme holds a large number. The species occurs in Ecuador, Colombia, Peru, and Panama.

O. ornithorrhyncum. The long specific name means "bird beak," and the drooping, tightly clustered sprays resemble a flock of birds. The rather small plants are easily grown and flower freely. The tiny, fragrant flowers are colored in shades of soft rosy purple. The species, which likes to be grown a little on the cool side, occurs in Mexico and flowers in fall and winter.

O. papilio. This butterfly orchid is said to be

responsible for the orchid craze that has swept the world. It is much like *kramerianum,* described above, but flowers more freely. It was shown at an exhibition of the Royal Horticultural Society soon after its introduction to England in 1823. Here its striking appearance so intrigued the Duke of Devonshire that he was inspired to start an orchid collection of his own. Thus was the fashion for private collections started among wealthy Englishmen. *O. papilio* has longer antennae than *kramerianum,* and the lateral sepals and lip are banded, rather than spotted, with brown. The upper sections of the jointed flower stem are flattened like the parts of a crab's leg. Flowers appear one at a time in succession from both old and new stems, throughout most of the year. The species is a native of the West Indies. See drawing chapter 1.

O. phalaenopsis. A serenely beautiful species, it is quite similar to *nubigenum* except that the flower has a white ground color. The sepals and petals are barred with red-violet, and the lip and its large, scalloped side lobes are dotted with crimson, the dots merging into large areas near the center of the flower. The little flower spike holds five to seven flowers, and the plant itself is small. This native of warmer parts of Ecuador likes in-

Home Orchid Growing

termediate temperatures and blooms in the winter and spring.

O. pumilum. Tiniest of burro-ear species, the rigid little leaves are two to four inches long, and the flowers but a quarter of an inch. The little waxy, yellow blooms are held in clusters along a branched six-inch inflorescence. The sepals and petals are very small, the spreading lip the showy part of the bloom. Oddly, the lateral lobes are larger than the mid-lobe. This spring-flowering species is native to Brazil and Paraguay.

O. pusillum. Flowers the year around are produced by this delightful miniature, one of the equitant species (holding its flat, grown-together leaves in a fan) which is widespread natively through Mexico, Central America, much of South America, and the West Indies. The flowers are typical for the equitant group, with the split mid-lobe of the lip. They are borne on a stem that grows up between the folded edges of the leaf to emerge about half-way along. Each stem produces five or six flowers in succession. The plants require excellent drainage, drying between waterings, but a humid atmosphere. They are perhaps best grown on a tree fern slab which is soaked every other day or so. This one will do well in an orchid case.

O. sarcodes. Even though this species is not technically related to the *O. crispum* group, having the lateral sepals free for one thing, it could well join them in general character and beauty. The large dorsal sepal is yellow with brown bars, as are the smaller lateral ones. The large, wavy petals are broader at their outer ends and are squared off, brown except for a yellow tip. The

Fig. 17-17 *Oncidium pusillum,* one of the equitant species, an exquisite miniature.

large lip is broad and wavy at its outer end, which is separated from two rather large side lobes, yellow with a few red spots. The crest has two large lobes with a small spike between them, and is yellow dotted with brown. It comes from Brazil and flowers in the spring.

O. sphacelatum. This is a large, vigorous species that gives huge panicles of brown and gold flowers. The panicles are particularly attractive because they are upright (and if not, should be tied up) on which the side branches are longest at the bottom, decreasing in length upward, giving a beautiful triangular shape to the spray, an espaliered appearance. The sepals and petals are brown and yellow, the lip pure yellow, brown at the base, the flowers about an inch in diameter. The species is spread through Mexico and Central America and flowers through winter and spring.

O. splendidum. This superb species has three-inch flowers that have a huge, pure yellow, serenely simple lip. The brown- and yellow-barred petals and sepals curve back gracefully at their tips, all except the dorsal sepal which stands straight. The great long lip flares out wide from its narrower mid-section, and has a simple linear crest at its base. The inflorescence is over two feet long, holding the flowers on short side branches of two to three each, widely spaced so that each shows off its charms separately. This is a large one of the burro-ear group. It is found in Mexico and Guatemala and flowers in late winter and spring.

O. stipitatum. This is a terete-leaved plant, native to Honduras, Nicaragua, and Panama, which has a panicle of one-inch flowers. They have yellow, brown-barred sepals and petals and a spreading yellow lip. The side lobes of the lip are often raised to an angle paralleling the petals. The species can be grown warmer than some, in a pendant position,

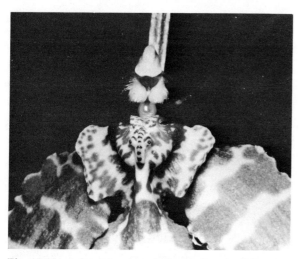

Fig. 17-16 A hand lens reveals fascinating detail in many flowers. Here is the column and lip crest of *Oncidium papilio.*

with care not to over-water. It blooms in the summer.

O. stramineum. This is called "Mexico's rarest orchid" by Stirling Dickinson who found a restricted area where this orchid, seldom seen since its long-ago discovery, still grows. It is a small burro-eared plant, with a panicle of half-inch flowers held in fairly dense clusters. The extremely waxy, cream flowers are delicately spotted with rose. They have rounded, somewhat cupped sepals and petals, and a small, complicated lip of which the side lobes are more conspicuous than the mid-lobe, resembling a pair of up-curving horns. The column is a very pretty part of the flower, with its purple-striped auricles. Although native to a warm, low elevation, it can be grown with cattleyas. Flowering time is spring.

O. superbiens. A little plainer than its fellow members of the cyrtochilum group, it is nevertheless a stunning flower. Its long-stalked sepals are moderately wavy on the edges, and the smaller petals, which are yellow, barred with brown from the middle to the base, are slightly more undulate. The small lip is blackish purple. This species grows natively in Colombia and Venezuela and flowers from winter to spring.

Fig. 17-18 *Oncidium stramineum,* a rare species.

O. teres. Another terete-leaved species, this one has the distinctive characteristic of having its lip plain yellow on the surface but spotted with red-brown on the under side. The half-inch flowers are held on a dense panicle eighteen inches long. A native of Panama, it blooms in late winter and spring.

O. tigrinum. The startling flowers of this species are among the most showy of the genus. They have the appearance of being made of two flowers wired together. The rather large sepals and petals are rich brown, barred with slender lines of yellow. The large, bright yellow lip is in complete contrast to this dark backing. The flowers are about two and one-half inches across, with rather few to a stem. The species occurs in Mexico and flowers in the winter.

O. triquetrum. A veritable jewel among the equitant oncidiums, its one-inch flowers are most unique. (See Fig. 21-6.) The nearly round lip is red or maroon in the center, with lines spreading out into the white border. The broad white petals are marked down the center with red dots. The slender sepals are greenish brown with a lighter border. The leaves are held in a fan of about five. Their edges spread apart a bit, giving a three-edged effect. Native to Jamaica, it flowers in the fall.

O. varicosum. One of the most beloved of the genus, the flower of this species is a "dancing doll" in a beautifully swirling skirt. Literally clouds of these sunny little flowers are borne in lacy, branching sprays. One to two hundred may occur on a single panicle. The sepals and petals are yellow-bronze barred with brown. The lip is pure yellow, sometimes with a brown spot or band at its base, and a curiously toothed crest. The variety *rogersii* is considered by some to be the best of all. It is one that should be included in all collections. This native of Brazil flowers in winter and spring.

O. variegatum. A beautiful and varied species of the equitant group. Withner includes several other species as varieties of this. The flowers are dainty, very prettily marked. The sepals are greenish, the slightly upturned petals white with brown bars toward the base. The side lobes of the lip are almost as large as the petals and parallel them, giving the effect of a second pair of petals. The mid-lobe of the lip is broadly anchor shaped, and has at its base a "t" formed of yellow protuberances on the crest. The various forms come from several of the Caribbean Islands.

Other Genera of the Odontoglossum Tribe

Brassia, a fourth member of this tribe, has spidery flowers which are most unusual and make an attractive showing in spite of their lack of richness of coloring. The sepals and petals are attenuated, giving the appearance of spider legs, and the lip is indeed shaped like the body of a spider. There are about thirty species, all easy to grow with a mixed collection of orchids. They require abundant water during the growing season, and must never be allowed to dry out.

B. antherotes. The extreme length of the sepals of this species make it a curiosity. The dorsal sepals are four to five inches, and the laterals normally ten to twelve, a total of about fourteen to seventeen. It is interesting to watch the spiral buds open, and the sepals unwind as they grow in length to their final mature size. The broad, flat pseudobulbs are about four inches tall and bear a single leaf. The species is widespread through Costa Rica, Panama, Colombia, Ecuador, and Peru, and is spring flowering. The variety *longissima* has flowers with even longer sepals and is a heavier plant. It is less common, however, and appears to occur only in Costa Rica, Panama and Ecuador. It flowers in the fall.

B. caudata. This species has flowers five to eight inches long. All parts are greenish yellow with spots of dark brown toward the base. The slender, pointed lip has fuzzy calli which become tooth-like in the front. It occurs from South Florida to Cuba, and from Mexico, to northern South America. It can flower more than once a year.

B. gireoudiana. These ten- to twelve-inch flowers hold themselves stiffly, with the very slender parts quite straight. The lip is creamy yellow, is not quite as sharply pointed as some, and has two

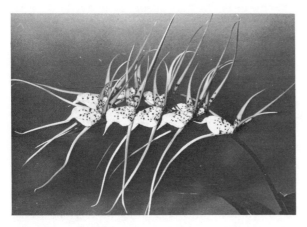

Fig. 17-19 *Brassia verrucosa* 'Horich'.

sausage-shaped crests at its base. Native to Costa Rica and Panama, it blooms in late spring and summer.

B. verrucosa. The whole flower is seven or eight inches long with the dorsal sepal and the shorter petals accounting for three inches of the length, and the longer lateral sepals for the other four. They are pale yellow-green, spotted at the base. The lip is pinched in at the middle and is white with dark green warts. The phalanx of eight to ten flowers is borne in a neat row on a horizontal stem. It occurs from Mexico through Central America and flowers in spring and summer.

Gomesa and **Palumbina** are the remaining genera of the tribe as given by Bailey. Both are pale by comparison to those already described and are therefore seldom grown.

Inter-generic Hybrids

Bi- and tri-generic hybrids are common within this tribe. Crosses between *Miltonia, Oncidium, Odontoglossum* and *Brassia* are not the only possibilities. The genus *Cochlioda*, which Bailey gives as belonging to the Aspasia tribe, hybridizes very easily with all three of these genera, and *Aspasia* has recently been introduced into hybridization. Because its chief importance is in relation to members of the Odontoglossum tribe, we shall include this tribe here.

Cochlioda is similar to *Odontoglossum* in appearance, habitat, and cultural requirements. Its long sprays of small flowers come in shades of rose, red, and red-orange. It is for the sake of the colors that its species are bred with those of other genera.

C. noezliana. This species has arching spikes of small, bright red-orange flowers with a yellow disc on the lip. It occurs in the Andes of Peru.

C. rosea. Flowers of rosy carmine have a pronounced white column. The blossoms are a little less than an inch in diameter but are numerous on the spikes. The plant occurs in Peru and Ecuador.

C. vulcanica. Larger, dark rose flowers grow on erect spikes. The species is native to Ecuador and Peru.

Symphyglossum. This genus has but one species, *S. sanguineum,* which has long been known as *Cochlioda sanguinea,* and has been used in hybridization under that name with several members of the

DIAGRAMMATIC REPRESENTATION
of the known artificial intergeneric crosses

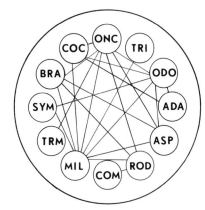

ADA = ADA	ODO = ODONTOGLOSSUM
ASP = ASPASIA	ONC = ONCIDIUM
BRA = BRASSIA	ROD = RODRIGUESIA
COC = COCHLIODA	SYM = SYMPHYGLOSSUM
COM = COMPARETTIA	TRI = TRICHOPILIA
MIL = MILTONIA	TRM = TRICHOCENTRUM

Fig. 17-20 Diagrammatic representation of the known artificial intergeneric crosses in the Odontoglossum tribe. (*Reproduced with the permission of L. A. Garay and the American Orchid Society Bulletin*)

Odontoglossum tribe. *S. sanguineum* is a delightful plant, with slender, somewhat conical compressed pseudobulbs and thin leaves. It bears pendant sprays of small bright pink or rose colored flowers, all on the upper side of the stem. They are waxy, somewhat globular in shape, and long lasting. The flower parts all hold themselves forward to conceal the lip and column except from a front view. This is a winter-blooming species.

Aspasia is a genus of Central American species not as well known as *Cochlioda*. The flowers are fewer and are produced on short stems close within the leaf axils. *Aspasia principissa* has greenish sepals and petals marked with brown, and a near-white lip. *A. epidendroides* is whitish yellow streaked with brown and has a white lip dotted with purple. The species *lunata* and *variegata* carry out similar coloring. *A. pusilla* is a charming dwarf species with green sepals and petals and a bluish lavender lip.

Some of the inter-generic hybrids are beautiful things; others are curiosities with their own appeal. More and more of this work is being done, and it is a field in which the imagination of the amateur may have free play. The warm reddish tones of

Cochlioda, the soft hues and ample proportions of *Miltonia,* the airy grace and generosity of flowers of *Oncidium* and *Odontoglossum,* and the intriguing traits of other genera—all may be combined and re-combined to create new and fascinating things. W. W. G. Moir has led the field in the creation of inter-generic hybrids in this and other tribes, making literally hundreds of successful crosses.

Inter-generic breeding sometimes shows up surprising relationships between genera not previously known to be related. In fact, closeness between species and genera may best be shown by hybridization. One of Moir's crosses, *Miltonia spectabilis* × *Trichopilia suavis* made *Miltonpilia* Magic, not only a new hybrid genus, but one that showed an unexpected relationship between *Miltonia* and *Trichopilia. Trichopilia* is described later, in Chapter 20. Back in the 1920's Ada was crossed with both *Odontoglossum* and *Cochlioda,* but apparently nothing further has been done along this line. Recently *Comparettia* and *Rodriguezia* have both been crossed with various genera of the tribe. These last are described in Chapter 19.

A sampling of bi-generic hybrid names follows:

Adaglossum = Ada × Odontoglossum.   Adioda = Ada × Cochlioda. Brassidium = Brassia × Oncidium. Miltonpasia = Miltonia × Aspasia. Miltonioda = Miltonia × Cochlioda.   Miltonidium = Miltonia × Oncidium.   Odontioda = Cochlioda × Odontoglossum.   Odontocidium = Odontoglossum × Oncidium. Odontonia = Miltonia × Odontoglossum.   Oncidioda = Cochlioda × Oncidium.   Symphyglossonia = Symphyglossum × Miltonia.   Symphodontoglossum = Symphyglossum × Odontoglossum.

Some of the tri- and quadri-generic hybrid names are:

Burrageara = Cochlioda × Miltonia × Odontoglossum × Oncidium.   Charlesworthheara = Cochlioda × Miltonia × Oncidium.   Colmanara = Miltonia × Odontoglossum × Oncidium. Sanderara = Brassia × Cochlioda × Odontoglossum. Vuylstekeara = Cochlioda × Miltonia × Odontoglossum.   Wilsonara = Cochlioda × Odontoglossum × Oncidium.

For other names, consult Garay and Sweet, 1966, and *Handbook on Orchid Nomenclature and Registration,* 1969.

18

CATASETUM AND GONGORA TRIBES

CATASETUM TRIBE

Not content with the devious methods used by other orchids to insure pollination, the members of the Catasetum tribe use a more direct approach—they shoot the pollinia directly at the visiting insect. Each kind has a trigger placed in such a way that the insect is bound to step on it or disturb it in some way. The instant this happens the pollinarium is shot out, the viscid disc flips up, hits the insect, and adheres tightly to its anatomy. The creamy material on the disc is so copious that it actually splatters on contact, precluding any possibility of failure to stick to the hairy surface, and it sets instantly. To attract the proper insect, the flowers exude a potent fragrance, not always detectable to the human nose although often it is quite enjoyable to us as well. The fragrance is not associated with nectar, but is bound in tissues upon which the bee scratches. The tissue is so placed in the flower, at some part of the lip, that the bee in its activity must touch the trigger. The anther is attached to a thin membrane that is stretched like a piece of rubber over a small dome. At the other end of the membrane is fastened the viscid disc. The trigger is inserted just under the edge of the taut membrane, and when it is pressed, it acts as a lever to lift its edge and allow it to snap together, which causes it to fly off, taking the viscid disc and anther with it. When the pollinarium is examined,

it is seen that this membrane substitutes for the stalk or stipe between the pollinia and disc. It can be unrolled and placed back on the dome, but you cannot recreate the same tension that held it in place originally.

Dr. Calaway H. Dodson has made a study of pollination in this group of orchids and in others, and has observed just how the bee is positioned to receive the pollinia, and how the position of the pollinia is associated with placing them on the stigma of the female flower, or, where both sexes are contained in the flower, of placing it on the next one visited. In some, the pollinia are placed "between the shoulders," in others on the end of the abdomen. Furthermore, he analyzes the fragrances with which the flowers lure their pollinators.

So sensitive is the trigger apparatus that it makes it difficult to handle some of these flowers without causing the pollinarium to pop. You can cause it to do so by touching the trigger with your finger or a pencil, and can feel the recoil of the flower as this happens.

In addition to being fascinating performers, the flowers are in most cases very beautiful, and those that cannot be called exactly pretty have a certain lurid appeal. Most of them bloom during fall and winter, but a few wait until spring. They are all deciduous, and with a few exceptions flower while the leaves are falling, or some time after this has taken place.

Catasetum

Best known of the pollen shooters, there are several types of flowers in the genus. Most of them have separately male and female flowers, and though the male flowers are quite distinct in each species, the females all look pretty much alike, with a fleshy hooded lip and a short blunt column. The same plant can produce both, but oddly enough female flowers rarely occur in cultivation, and even in nature are always fewer than the males. Among the types of male flowers, there are some with a large, hood-like lip held uppermost, some with a saucer-shaped lip held ventrally, some that have a definite cup or sac at the base of the lip, and others whose lip is a bearded tongue. A few have perfect flowers, having both sexes in the same flower. The cylindrical pseudobulbs are left with sharp spines after the leaves fall.

It is best to keep the plants quite dry from leaf-fall until new growth begins in the spring, giving occasional water to keep the bulbs plump, once in a while in the pot but mostly by misting. They should be repotted when roots start from the new growth in the spring, and then be watered regularly. They can be grown in any of the media, with generous applications of fertilizer.

C. macrocarpum. This is one of the most widespread, and is typical of the type with a hood lip. (See Fig. 2-6.) The column and its long pointed anther project out from underneath. The pair of triggers extends back under the hood. One is nonfunctional and is curled back, the other, the sensitive one, stands upright. The lip is shiny green, spotted with dull red, heavily on the inside, lightly on the outside. The thin sepals and heavier petals overlap, together surrounding and backing the column. This species is native to Venezuela, Brazil, the Guianas, Trinidad, and Surinam. Some other species of this type are *viridiflavum,* whose lip is gold on top and whose petals and sepals are tinged with gold, native to Panama; *macroglossum,* pure lime green except for a few spots of brown on the petals and sepals and inside the lip, from Ecuador; *oerstedii,* very similar to *macrocarpum* and native to Nicaragua, Costa Rica, Panama, and Colombia; and *collare,* which has a light yellow-green lip whose outer edge is rolled, and dark green sepals and petals, native to Venezuela.

C. pileatum. This is one of the most beautiful of orchids. It is sheer wax, butter yellow, with a pure white column. The lip is a broad, shallow saucer, held downward, and it has a slight coating

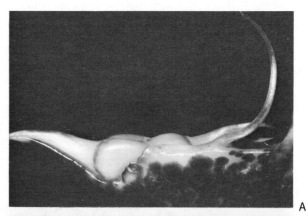

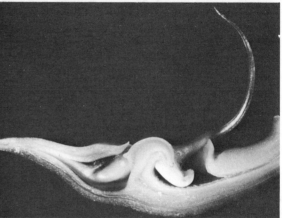

Fig. 18-1 The pollen-shooting mechanism of *Catasetum macrocarpum.*
A. The intact column with pointed anther showing swellings under which are the pollinia. The sensitive trigger curves upward.
B. The column cut in half. Within the cavity near the trigger is the viscid disc, attached to a membrane stretched over a dome of tissue, the other end of which is fastened to the pollinia. Pressing the trigger releases the membrane and the viscid disc flies upward bearing the pollinarium with it.
C. The trigger was pressed and the pollinarium flew up and attached itself to a piece of paper held above the column.

A

B

C

Fig. 18-2 *Catasetum platyglossum* visited by a bee.
A. The bee depresses the trigger.

B. The viscid disc flips downward, fastening itself to the back of the bee. After the bee flies away the anther cap will fall off, leaving the pollinia ready to be deposited on a female flower.

C. A bee with pollinia attached visits a female flower of *C. platyglossum,* and as it crawls into the lip the pollinia will be dragged into contact with the stigma. (*Courtesy Calaway H. Dodson*)

of granular looking papillae at its base, where there is also a small depression. The lateral sepals curve around the rim of the lip, while the dorsal sepal and petals stand up straight, overlapping behind the column. The column sits above the lip with one trigger hanging down, the other curled under. It occurs in Venezuela, Trinidad, and the Amazon region. A similar and also very beautiful species is *platyglossum,* which means "flat lip." This one has a crest on the red-gold lip, and the other parts are yellow tinged with green. It is native to Ecuador.

C. saccatum. Here is a species whose down-hanging lip has a distinct cup or sac at the base, hence its name. Moreover, the lip is three lobed, the side lobes spreading flat beside the sac, and the mid-lobe hanging down in front, all greenish, spotted with brown, and fringed on their edges. The sepals spread at right angles, while the petals stand up beside the dorsal sepal, and they are green spotted with brown. The species occurs in Brazil, Peru, and Ecuador. A variety *christyanum* has at times been considered a separate species. There are several other species with sac-like lips, among them *discolor,* which has a wide, gaping "mouth" with fringed jowls, a pale cream and cream-green flower with pink spots that become wine-red inside the lip, native to Venezuela, Brazil, British Guiana, the Amazons, Colombia, and Surinam; *fimbriatum,* another pink and pale green flower, whose turned-out lip edges are also fringed, from Venezuela, British Guiana, Brazil, Paraguay, Argentina, and Bolivia; and *sanguineum,* a dark brownish green flower with a complicated lip that has a raised border around the sac, overhung by a comb of fleshy, pink projections on each side arising from the outer border of the lip. This last is from Costa Rica, Venezuela, Colombia, and Ecuador.

C. barbatum. This species has many variations that have been given separate specific names at one time or another, such as *appendiculatum* and *cristatum.* All have a narrow, tongue-shaped lip with many white finger-like projections standing up along its borders. These can be thick or thin, sparse or numerous, and it is on the basis of such differences that the separate names have been endowed. In some forms they are so profuse that they hide the whole lip surface. The flower parts are slender, the dorsal sepal and petals standing up together, the lateral sepals spreading down or sideways. The group is widespread through Brazil, Bolivia, Colombia, Ecuador, Peru, the Guianas, Venezuela, and Surinam.

A

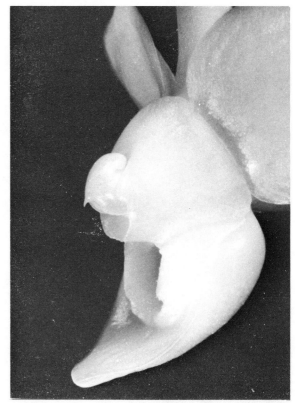

B

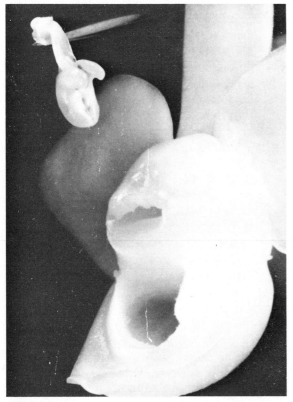

C

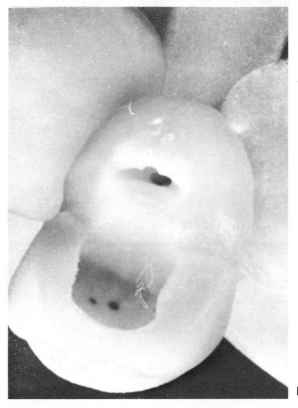

D

Fig. 18-3 *Catasetum suave,* a type with both sexes in one flower.

A. The lowermost flower on the stem has had the pollinia removed.

B. Detail showing column and lip before the pollinia are removed; the stigma is completely covered by the viscid disc.

C. Touching the underside causes the viscid disc to fly out, bringing away the anther with the pollinarium and uncovering the stigma.

D. The stipe of the pollinarium straightens as the bee carries it around for a while so that it can be fitted into the very small cavity of the stigma.

C. suave. This species will introduce those with perfect flowers, although there is quite a variation among them. *C. suave* has very waxy flowers of pure ivory color and delightful fragrance. The fleshy sepals and petals open flat at first but soon fold back sharply to lie along the ovary, leaving the fat, blunt column and scoop-shaped, saccate, lip projecting forward. On first examining the column, it is impossible to see the stigma, but when the pollinarium is shot out by touching the sensitive protuberance on the anther cap, the stigma is revealed, having been covered by the apparatus. This, of course, insures that the flower is not pollinated with its own pollen, since the stigma is not uncovered until the pollinia are removed. The stipe (stalk) of the pollinarium is at first upright so that the pollinia cannot come in contact with the stigma. During the next few moments, it bends forward, by which time the bee would be visiting another flower. Remarkably, according to Dodson, the pollinarium is fastened to the bee either just in front of the first pair of legs or on the basal section of one of these. *C. suave* comes from Costa Rica and Panama. It keeps its leaves for two or three years and does not require as drastic drying as others. It flowers in the summer. *C. eburneum* is very similar to it, and is native to Panama and Colombia.

C. warscewitzii (the spelling of the name continues an error on the part of Lindley, who named it) is also known as *C. scurra*. It is a delicate miniature, another type with perfect flowers. It is rather globe-shaped, with rounded sepals and petals held forward, and a three-lobed lip whose side lobes extend up within the petals, a fringed mid-lobe, and a cup-shaped rear part that hangs down between the lateral sepals. The half-inch flower is almost transparent, striped green and white, and delightfully fragrant. It is found in Mexico, Guatemala, Honduras, Panama, and Venezuela. *C. russellianum,* rather similar, is larger, with bolder flowers also striped green and white but not transparent. The sepals and petals are wide spreading and the lip hangs free with its sides and long mid-lobe rolled out from the saccate base. It occurs in the same countries as the preceding species. *C. roseum,* another perfect flower, is completely charming with its round shape, beautiful rose color, fringed petals, and richly fringed lip. It occurs from Mexico south into South America.

Fig. 18-4 *Catasetum warscewitzii (scurra)*, a miniature species with fragrant green flowers containing both sexes in each flower.

Cycnoches

These are very lovely orchids, worth cultivating for their beauty as well as for their interesting habit. The name means swan's neck, referring to the arching column. The lip in some species is shaped like the body of a swan, adding to the illusion that gives them their name "swan orchid." Plants can produce either male or female flowers, or both at the same time, and occasionally may produce a spray of bi-sexual or hermaphroditic flowers. The pseudobulbs are columnar, bearing five to eight broad graceful leaves. The leaves are notoriously attractive to red spider, and should be sprayed regularly for this pest. They prefer a hanging position in an airy spot, and a daily misting with water. The flower spikes make their appearance from the axils of the leaves. During the development of the flowers the leaves will start to fall. After the leaves have fallen, the plants should be kept quite dry through the winter, with just an occasional syringing. Some growers divide them before carrying them through their rest period, separating the bulbs without cutting back the roots and standing them on the bench, sprinkling them with water occasionally. When new growth has begun its own roots, those left in pots through the winter should be put in fresh medium and the shrivelled pseudobulbs removed, and those separated in the fall should be potted. Regular watering is now resumed. Osmunda fiber may be used, with rather frequent applications of fertilizer. Recently some growers have had exceptional success by adding manure to other media, such as any of the mixes, or bark mixed with tree fern and loamy soil. Cycnoches seem to thrive on a very rich medium. A cymbidium mix might also be used.

Pollination in cycnoches is not as spectacular as in *Catasetum,* but is fascinating nevertheless, as described by Dodson and the late Paul Allen. In those with a rigid lip, such as *chlorochilon* and its relatives, there is a callus on the lip placed in such a way that the bee can hang on only by its front legs to get at the source of the attracting fragrance. This lets its rear end hang down and "tickle" the sensitive viscid disc on the arching column. The pollinarium is thereby sprung, and the pollinia stick to the end of its abdomen. When it visits a female flower, this dangling pair of pollinia are caught by a hook-like notch in the end of the column and sink into the stigma. In types with a fragile, stalked lip, such as *aureum* and *egertonianum,* the weight of the bee clinging to the under side of the lip causes the lip to swing down and bring the tail end of the bee in contact with the trigger. From then on the same sequence of events takes place.

Fig. 18-6 A bee clinging to the lip of *Cycnoches egertonianum.* Its weight causes the lip to bend downward, allowing the tip of its abdomen to touch the sensitive viscid disc and so obtain the pollinia. The one in this picture has already received pollinia from a previous flower. (*Courtesy Calaway H. Dodson*)

Fig. 18-5 A bee with pollinia attached to its rear end scratching at the lip of a female flower of *Cycnoches ventricosum* var. *warscewiczii.* As it leaves the flower the pollinia will be caught by the hook at the tip of the column. (*Courtesy Calaway H. Dodson*)

C. chlorochilon. The plant known by this name and widely grown as the "swan" orchid is actually *C. ventricosum* var. *warscewiczii,* described below. It is difficult to give up the association of the prettier name with the familiar plant. Paul Allen considered *chlorochilon* and *warscewiczii* both to be varieties of *ventricosum.* More recently Garay has returned *chlorochilon* to specific status. The flower is light yellow-green, lightly veined. The lip is pale ivory-green, shading to yellow at the base, and is not clawed. The callus at its base is raised, but there is not a depression around it. As in all of this group, the flowers are upside down. The male and female flowers are much alike, the female having a shorter, stockier column. Occasionally, hermaphroditic flowers are produced; they look like the female but bear pollinia in addition to a stigma. The species occurs in Panama, Colombia, Venezuela, and the Guianas.

Home Orchid Growing

C. egertonianum and its varieties *aureum* and *dianae*. The similarities between these three are evident and it is clear that they are closely related. Formerly considered separate species, the latter two are now generally held to be varieties of *egertonianum*, although not all taxonomists agree. However, var. *aureum* is distinct enough never to be mistaken for *egertonianum* and is by far the most beautiful of the three, while var. *dianae* is about halfway between it and *egertonianum*. All are delicate flowers borne in a long pendant chain, sometimes with as many as thirty flowers open all at once. The male flowers have slender sepals and petals which are of rather thin substance, although the flowers are quite long lasting, a fleshy lip that stands on a stalk and has finger-like processes around the edge, and a long, slender, arching column. The female flowers are fleshy and are much alike in the three types. They have greenish sepals and petals, a very thick waxy lip which is white and without processes, and a short, blunt column. They are borne two or three on a short stem, and to make up for their lack of numbers they keep for two months. Sometimes hermaphroditic flowers occur, but the pollinia are so quickly aborted that unless you spot them soon after the flowers open you may think the flowers were purely female. *C. egertonianum* occurs from Mexico through Central America to Colombia, Ecuador, Peru, Brazil. There are slight differences among those from various areas, for instance, the flowers from Costa Rica are widely spaced on their stem and the lip processes are short, broad, arranged on a flat disc, and few in number, while plants from Ecuador have a more compact inflorescence and the lip processes are numerous, long, and almost filamentous. In general, the sepals and petals are green or greenish brown with veins of darker green or spots of purple. Sometimes the spots are quite dense, giving a very dark flower. The flowers are quite "curly," the sepals tend to curl on the edges and the petals to curl entirely back on themselves, leaving the upward projecting lip on its stalk and the arching column as the conspicuous parts of the flower. When the flower is unfolded it is about two and a half inches long. Flowering takes place in the autumn.

C. egertonianum var. *aureum*. This variety has larger flowers of a pale yellow-green, striped with green and toned with tan. They become more and more yellow with age. The sepals and petals are much broader than in *egertonianum;* the sepals spread wide without curling, the dorsal extending

A

B

Fig. 18-7 *Cycnoches aureum.*
A. The delicate but long-lasting male flowers.
B. Hermaphroditic flowers on the same plant. These are identical in shape to female flowers, but have both a receptive stigma and pollinia. In the flowers shown here the pollinia soon aborted.

back and the laterals forward, while the petals curve backward a bit. The lip is somewhat boat-shaped with the slender processes standing upright. This variety occurs in both Costa Rica and Panama, and flowers in the fall.

C. egertonianum var. *dianae.* This variety is native to Panama. It is pinkish tan with a green tinge, and has less conspicuous markings than either of the others. The lip is more like that of var. *aureum* than like the various forms of *egertonianum* itself, but its edge processes are thicker and are held more rigidly upright and closer together. It, too, is fall flowering.

C. ventricosum. The distinguishing features of this member of the "swan" group are its long lip claw and the fact that the basal callus is only rounded, not particularly raised. Its flowers are waxy, fragrant, and long lasting. They are green at first, fading to yellow. The sepals and petals tend to bend downward. It occurs in Mexico, Guatemala, and Panama.

C. ventricosm var. *warscewiczii.* This is the one long known as *chlorochilon.* Its heavy, waxy, chartreuse flowers are delightfully fragrant. The lip is white, and its basal callus is a projecting, fleshy triangle that arises from a severe depression; both callus and depression are dark green. The flower spike holds four to ten flowers that are four or five inches across. Flowers appear after the growth matures, sometimes before the leaves fall, sometimes afterward. It is native to Panama and Costa Rica.

Mormodes

The name means "weird creature," from the fact that the column is twisted to lie with the back of the anther on the lip. They are also called "goblin" orchids. The position of the column is associated with pollination, and as Dodson recounts it, it is quite unusual. The tip of the anther has a sensitive trigger, and the column is positioned so that an insect crawling across the lip will step on it. The pollinarium flies out and fastens itself to the back of the thorax of the bee. Because the stalk is curled, the bee cannot leave the pollina on that flower. Later on, the stalk straightens out to hold the pollinia upright and the bee leaves them on the stigma of a subsequent flower as it wanders around on the lip. In some flowers the column is not pressed to the lip, but held up somewhat, so that these function only to receive pollen. In other cases Dodson has observed the column to raise up and untwist after the pollinia have been removed, making it more likely that it will receive pollen. Apparently, a flower whose column remains in contact with the lip does not always become pollinated. A fascinating habit, which I have not seen mentioned elsewhere, is that the flowers on the left side of the raceme twist the column to the left; those on the right side have their column turned to the right (see color illustration).

The lip usually has its sides turned down, making it look something like a saddle. The pseudobulbs are fleshy, somewhat lumpy, and have no spines after leaf-fall. They usually flower sometime after the leaves fall, occasionally not until the following spring. Keep them on the dry side through this period of inactivity, resuming watering after the flower spikes start. If new growth has not started by the time flowering is finished, give them another short period of dryness until it does. They need not be repotted each year, though some growers prefer to do so, and can be grown like catasetums.

M. buccinator. The colors of this species range from pure white through shades of yellow, green, and pink, to a dark red, according to the area from which the plants come. The sides of the lip are rectangular giving a squared-off effect viewed from the side. The petals bend forward making an awning over the lip. The species is found throughout tropical America but is most common in Venezuela and Ecuador.

M. colossus. This can be a very large plant, but does not necessarily grow larger than other species. The flowers are nicely shaped, with the sepals and petals held back in a spreading star from the lip, and the sides of the rather longish lip rolled under to meet at their edges. The sepals and petals are golden brown, or yellow, yellow-green, or cream,

Fig. 18-8 In *Mormodes* the column is twisted and bent so that the back side of the anther rests on the lip, exposing the sensitive trigger at its tip. A bee crawling on the lip will touch the trigger and the pollinia will be applied to its back. This is *Mormodes buccinator.*

and the lip a darker shade. It is native to Costa Rica and Panama.

M. hookeri. The most unusual but rather small flowers of this species are dark red with an almost black and very hairy lip. The dorsal sepal bends over the lip, the others and the petals curve backward. It occurs in Costa Rica, Panama, and Colombia.

M. igneum. This species ranges through the same colors as *colossus,* but its parts are more or less spotted with red. The sepals and petals are thin; the dorsal sepal stands up straight, the other parts are bent back. The more fleshy lip is round in outline when spread out, and in natural position has its sides sharply bent down. This one occurs in Costa Rica, Panama, and Colombia.

M. skinneri. This species has its yellow sepals and petals striped with dotted lines of purplish red and the lip marked with large blotches of the same color. The edges of the lip and its center portion are decorated with white hairs. This one is native to Guatemala and Costa Rica.

M. variabilis. A beautifully colored species, with dark rose sepals and petals and a downy, lighter rose lip. The dorsal sepal and petals arch over the column, the laterals are held back a bit. The rounded sides of the lip are turned down and tucked under both front and back, while the tip bears a projection that curves downward. The anther is unusually large, with an exceptionally long point that rests on the lip. This species is found in Ecuador.

GONGORA TRIBE

Within this tribe are some of the most fantastic of orchids as well as some of the most serenely beautiful. All subject their pollinators to the most ignominious treatment, making them fall through the flower, or throwing them backwards against the pollinia, or dumping them in a bucket of water. The lip in every genus is constructed of three parts, marvelously carved with sacs, loops, knobs, and horns. The basal section is the hypochile, the midsection the mesochile, and the tip the epichile. The flowers lure their victims with potent and delightful fragrances, but offer them nothing in the way of nectar. If they give them anything in return for their services, it is merely a momentary pleasure in the fragrances for which they eagerly scratch, and which sometimes causes them to behave in a very silly manner and so distracts them that they do not anticipate what is about to happen to them.

Nor do the "accidents" they endure prevent their coming back for more.

The plants are for the most part epiphytic, with conical to globular pseudobulbs bearing broad, pleated leaves. Many have pendulous flower stems, and these should be grown in a hanging position or be placed on stands. Some have flower stems that bore down through the medium and these are best grown in baskets or bottomless pots. They vary as to seasonal needs, but can be accommodated in an intermediate house.

Coryanthes

This orchid has the notorious reputation of making its pollinators drunk, but like so many good myths, this may have to be toned down a bit. The series of experiences it forces on its pollinators is none the less excruciating, however. The flowers are very complex with the parts marvelously engineered. The very waxy lip is divided into three sections. The end part or epichile is formed into a bucket with a spout, shaped something like an old-fashioned coal bucket; this is attached to the basal part by a stalk, the mesochile; and the basal part is a fat globe from some part of which exudes a tantalizing fragrance. The column, instead of curving toward the lip as in most flowers, hangs down into the bucket and then bends up so that it forms the roof of the spout, with the anther and its viscid disc held just over the end of the spout. The petals and sepals are bent and twisted in various ways to camouflage the opening of the spout and leave open the entrance to the bucket. Two protuberances at the base of the column exude a fluid that drips steadily into the bucket, keeping it full to the spout. With the plants in cultivation and no pollinators around to watch, this in itself is a fascinating procedure to observe. It seems to begin even before the bud opens, for as soon as you can look into the bucket you find it already half full. The strong and delightful fragrance is discernable as soon as the sepals begin to separate.

The late Paul Allen described the events that take place, and Dodson has not only observed the behavior of the bees but has analyzed the fragrances and experimented with their affects on bees in the field. Only male euglossine bees are attracted by the perfumes. Dodson discovered that while the fragrances of the flowers are made up of the same chemical components, they are in different proportions in the various species; thus they attract different species of bees.

A

B

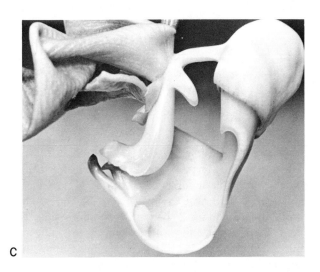

C

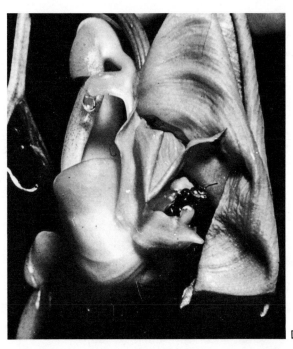

D

Fig. 18-9 *Coryanthes speciosa,* one of the "bucket" orchids. A. The lip is the complicated structure at the right; attached by a narrow stalk, it is carved first into a globe that exudes a potent fragrance (the hypochile), then into a mid-section (the mesochile), and from this it flares out into a bucket (the epichile). The column hangs down into the bucket with its tip bent upward over the spout of the bucket. Lobes at the base of the column secrete fluid that fills the bucket to spout level. The ribbon-like petals drape the spout. The huge sepals curve backward and screen the tip of the column and spout. A bee, scratching at the fragrant tissue and fascinated by it, comes in contact with a drop of the fluid that wets it and plunges it into the bucket. Unable to fly, the bee must crawl out through the spout, and removes the pollinia in the process.

B. Looking into the bucket you can see the opening into the spout with the column curving to form its roof. There is a mound of tissue that acts as a step-stool to assist the bee in finding the spout.

C. The flower is cut in half to reveal its structure and the petals have been removed to show the spout and the tip of the column. Note the tiny beak of the anther.

D. Caught in the act of emerging from the spout, a bee has just tipped up the anther and will fly away with the pollinia on its back. (*D, photo by Paul Allen*)

Home Orchid Growing

The bees arrive warily at a flower, locate the source of the fragrance, and then, losing all caution, begin avidly to scratch or brush at the tissues with bristles on their forelegs. If nothing untoward happens, they fly off, transferring the substance they have acquired to organs on their hind legs. However, something untoward often does happen—frequently a bee will lose its footing (because the waxy surface is slippery, not because the bee is drunk!), or come in contact with a drop of fluid dripping from the column glands, and be felled into the bucket. There it flounders, unable to spread its wings. At last it finds the exit through the spout, helped by a "foot stool" or a "ladder" at its base. The necessity for a bee of the right size becomes apparent, because too small a one would slip through without removing the pollinia, and one that was too large would become stuck in the tunnel. One of the right size, and therefore of the right species, finds the tunnel sufficiently tight-fitting to necessitate a struggle to squeeze through, causing it to press against the anther and remove the pollinia. It then flies away to dry off. When the morning's activities are over, the flowers' fragrance ceases. The events begin again the next day—the flowers are again fragrant, bringing back the bees with pollinia from the day before, and this time the ignominious treatment results in pollination.

The strange behavior of the bees gave rise to the legend that they were drugged or drunk. However, according to Dodson, a bee that falls to the ground instead of into the bucket recovers instantly and flies off, showing that it was probably neither. He believes that since only male bees are attracted, the fragrances must have some special appeal for them—whether sexual or as something they need in their physiological makeup is not known. What they do with the fragrant chemicals also remains a mystery—perhaps they mark their territory with it, or attract females with some product they manufacture from it. At any rate, for flowers to have evolved such a complicated way to lure their pollinators and such a strange way to elicit their services is a remarkable feat of nature.

The roots of the plants in nature are inhabited by ants, who may defend them from natural enemies, and whose excretory material may be nutritive. The plants are difficult to keep in cultivation, but are most rewarding if they live and flower.

C. biflora. A remarkably colored flower in shades of tan and brown, it is marked with lines, dots, and circles of pink and maroon, and with the hypochile covered with silky orange hairs. The mesochile is short, giving a squatty look to the flower, and the bucket is unusually broad and flaring, heavily spotted inside. It is native to Venezuela, Brazil, and Peru.

C. macrantha. Another brownish or yellowish flower, heavily spotted inside and out, its mesochile is decorated with toothed ridges. The bucket is small and less flaring than the preceding. It occurs in Venezuela, British Guiana, Colombia, Peru, and Trinidad.

C. speciosa. This species verges on pure yellow, with a green tinge to the sepals and petals, but some forms are spotted with maroon, lightly everywhere except in the bucket where there may be large blotches. The flowers are three inches across, a bit more modest than the preceding two in size. It is native to most of Central America and northern South America.

Gongora

The small flowers of this genus are borne in pendulous chains. They are pygmies compared to their large flowered relatives, but are fascinating nevertheless. They hang with the column underneath. In most species the dorsal sepal swings down under the column, while the very much abbreviated petals are inserted on the column itself, extending from it like a pair of fins. The waxy, very complicated lip extends horizontally above the column. Dodson relates how the bee must hang to the under surface of the lip to get at the attracting substance. In order to leave the flower it has to drop from the lip, and in so doing it slides down the column bumping into the viscid disc at its tip and so removes the pollinia. The process is repeated on the next flower visited, this time with the pollinia left on the stigma. The petals attached to the column prevent the bee's falling off sideways.

The plants are very pretty, with sharply fluted conical pseudobulbs and prominently veined leaves. They grow readily in an intermediate house, in most potting media, and flower willingly. They do not like to become dry at the roots, but must have good aeration.

G. armeniaca. A cluster of these small golden flowers looks like a conference of bees, held as they are on the stem all facing inward, and evenly spaced. The waxy lip is carved into a hollow at the base from which it swells out, only to be suddenly contracted into a sharp beak at the tip. It is native to Nicaragua, Costa Rica, and Panama.

G. grossa. This species has some apparently distinct differences from *G. quinquenervis.* Most noticeable are the smaller general size of the lip and the fact that the basal horns are long and thick and curve straight downward. Also, the lip is open on its under side. The petals are narrowed abruptly in the middle to form a spike-like outer section. This species occurs in Costa Rica and Ecuador.

G. horichiana. This was once named *G. armeniaca* var. *bicornuta* because of two projections that extend forward on the lip on either side of its beak. It has bright red petals, and the tip of the beak is also red. The beak is long and sharply hooked on the end. This is native to Costa Rica and Panama.

G. quinquenervis. There are so many variations of this species, some of which have formerly been considered separately, that it is difficult to give a description of one type to suit the lot. The flowers can be white, brown, red, or greenish, with or with-

out spots or stripes. The lip is slender, with a tapering projection at the end and two downward pointing horns or whiskers about the mid-point. At its base there may or may not be two more fleshy, down-pointing horns. Apparently the differences among the so-called separate species deal with variations in the lip. At any rate, this is a charming group, with long chains of flowers, thirty or forty at a time. The native range spreads from Mexico south to Brazil and Peru, and to Trinidad.

Stanhopea

Stanhopeas are among the most dramatic looking of orchids. As they hang on their pendulous stems with the long horned lip and arching column, they have the aspect of a bird of prey about to swoop upon a victim. The waxy lip is carved into three sections: a sac-like hypochile, a pinched-in meso-

A

B

Fig. 18-10 A bee visits *Gongora grossa.*
A. The bee clings to the underside of the lip, held in the proper position by its pairs of downward projecting processes.

B. As the bee lets go in order to fly away, it bumps into the column, slides off its tip, and removes the pollinia. It is prevented from falling off sideways by the petals that are attached to the column. (*Courtesy Calaway H. Dodson*)

Home Orchid Growing

Fig. 18-11 *Gongora quinquenervis* is a species with many varieties. Shown here is a distinctive one, also known as *G. truncata* var. *alba.*

chile with a pair of horns, and a triangular flattened epichile. The long column swings down in an arc almost to touch the tip of the lip. The broad sepals flare up like wings, while the smaller and somewhat wavy petals curl up between them. The secret of the weird shape is in the pollination system. A visiting bee, seeking the source of the alluring fragrance, enters the sac of the hypochile. Whether it loses its footing or bumps into the column as it attempts to fly out, it plunges downward between the column and the lip, exiting from the small space between them with the pollinia on its back. On falling through another flower it leaves the pollinia on the stigma. Dodson has found that stanhopeas lure specific bees in the same manner as coryanthes.

The plants have globular or slender, somewhat corrugated pseudobulbs and broad pleated leaves. They grow in moist locations and suffer in too dry an atmosphere, and thrive in moderate shade. They must be grown in an open container so that their flowering stems can grow downward through the medium. We once grew them in square "baskets" made of slats, but on removing some one year found that many flower stems had come up against the slats and failed to develop. Then we tried pots with the bottom knocked out, and these worked except that it was a chore to remove the bottom

without breaking the pot. Now we have discovered wire baskets with an inch and a half or more between the wires, and think these are the answer.

The species vary in the shape of the lip parts and in other ways, but it is very difficult to tell some of them apart without much study and careful charts to go by; even then the assistance of an expert is often necessary. All have a penetrating fragrance, usually quite pleasant. Sadly, the flowers last only three days, but true stanhopea lovers never turn them down because of that.

S. costaricensis. This species is one of the larger forms. It has tan or dull green sepals and petals marked with large purple spots. The broad column does not arch markedly but instead quite parallels the lip. The base of the lip is marked with two large purple eyes. Native to Costa Rica, it flowers in September.

S. ecornuta. This is an odd form, without horns on the lip. It holds its petals closely appressed to the blunt lip and column. It does not depend on a fall-through by a bee, but instead on having the bee enter at the side under the petals, and then, crawl out past the viscid disc of the anther. It is white with a few orange spots on the petals. The base of the lip is orange with red spots. Occurring in Guatemala, Honduras, Nicaragua, and Costa Rica, it flowers in summer or fall.

S. florida. Almost a miniature plant, this species has dainty flowers about three inches long. They are faintly greenish white, with a light stippling of rose. It is native to central Ecuador and flowers in the spring.

S. martiana. A rather lurid species, this one represents a group with a very pronounced sac at the base of the lip or hypochile, with the mesochile almost tucked under it. It is white or light yellow with the tips of the parts clear and a crescendo of spots converging toward the center where they become huge reddish blotches. This occurs in Mexico and flowers in the fall.

S. oculata. The very long and shallow hypochile marks this species, as well as the fact that the column and lip arch widely away from each other before they come close at their tips. The flowers are yellow with circular markings of reddish purple, and also have two eyes on the mesochile. From Mexico, it blooms in the summer.

S. wardii. A widespread and well known species, this is also one of the most beautiful. Its sepals and petals are brilliant yellow marked with dainty spots of reddish brown. The column is

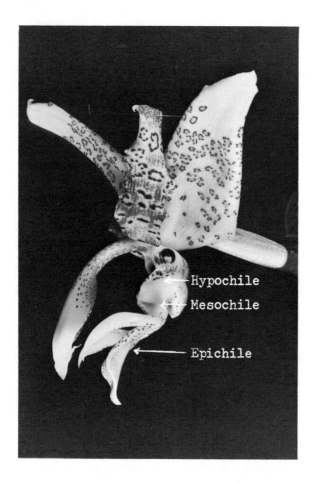

Fig. 18-13 *Stanhopea florida,* a small species native to Ecuador.

Fig. 18-12 UPPER, *Stanhopea wardii,* one of the best known species. Note the pointed tip of the viscid disc near the end of the column, and the pair of horns on the lip guarding it.

LOWER, a bee falling through the space between column and lip. (*Courtesy Calaway H. Dodson*)

ivory or greenish white. The outer half of the lip is white, and the basal half bright orange with two large purple eyes. The species spreads from Mexico to Panama, and into South America. It blooms in the fall.

Other Genera of the Gongora Tribe

Acineta has pendant sprays of lovely, large round flowers, delightfully fragrant, waxy, and richly colored. The broad oval sepals are held forward somewhat, the small petals lie close beside the column, and the very waxy, chunky lip, carved into the three parts typical of this tribe, is almost concealed. The large plants have egg-shaped pseudobulbs and tall plicate leaves. They must be grown in baskets to allow the burrowing inflorescence to emerge from the bottom.

A. barkeri has yellow flowers striped with red-brown, twelve or more in a cluster, and is native to Mexico.

A. chrysantha is globe-shaped, bright yellow spotted with red. The lip is tipped by a projecting horn. This one is native to Costa Rica and Panama.

Home Orchid Growing

A. superba has flowers more open though still cupped. They have a cream ground color and are beautifully speckled with red or rose. The lip is very complicated and has many projecting processes within. It ranges from Panama south to Peru and Venezuela.

Aganisia is a genus of but two species, both requiring a warm greenhouse. The plants are climbers and need to be put on tree fern slabs. The slender pseudobulbs bear a single plicate leaf.

A. cyanea has delightful blue flowers, very prettily shaped, with wavy, oval-pointed sepals and petals and a lip that spreads broadly from its carved and somewhat horny basal part. The flowers are about two inches in diameter and are borne five to seven on an upward-arching stem. The species is native to Venezuela, Colombia, Brazil, and the Amazon regions.

A. pulchella. A less desirable species, the plants more rambling, the flowers smaller and fewer to the stem, it is nevertheless interesting to the collector. The blooms are white with transparent veins and a touch of pink in the lip. It is native to the same general area as above.

Cirrhaea has charms that must surely soon make it better known. It gives long chains of gongora-like flowers that are fragrant, waxy, and variously colored in shades of green, brown, and red, with a very strangely shaped lip consisting of three little lobes on the end of a stalk.

C. dependens and *C. longiracemosa* are both from Brazil, and probably can be accommodated in an intermediate house.

Coeliopsis has but one species, *C. hyacinthosma*, native to Panama and Costa Rica. Its downward boring inflorescence bears a dense head of one-inch, very waxy, globular flowers. Delightfully fragrant, they are white with an orange blotch on the lip. According to its native habitat, it should require intermediate conditions, but it is not easy to grow.

Eriopsis has six species, all distinctive, showy, brightly colored, and waxy. More amenable to cultivation than some of this tribe, they are becoming well known among amateurs.

E. biloba. An erect spike of two feet or more holds many one- to two-inch flowers which are sweetly fragrant. The flower has rather broad some-what cupped sepals, yellow-gold with edges shading to maroon, petals a bit more slender, similarly colored, and a squarish lip whose sides bend up parallel to the column. The outer end of the lip extends in a short, bi-lobed tongue that is white, spotted with dark brown or reddish brown. The plant is variable, and may have rather tall slender pseudobulbs or short, much wrinkled, blackish ones. Three leaves are produced from their tip. From the rhizome grow great masses of roots, sometimes with upward growing, very sharp spikes. The species is native to Costa Rica and Panama and northern South America. It flowers in late winter.

E. sceptrum. Light brownish gold flowers, whose edges shade to a darker tone, are borne many to a two- to three-foot spike. The sepals are broadly oval, the petals a bit narrower and curved down at their tips. The basal part of the lip is yellow densely spotted with maroon. The projecting outer part of the lip is white with widely spaced maroon spots which gives a sharp accent to the flower. The column is creamy green. The plants have conical, wrinkled pseudobulbs, three leaves, and a mass of spiky roots. This species is native to Venezuela, Brazil, and Peru, at somewhat lower elevations than *biloba*.

Houlletia has large, bold, wide-open flowers. Some of the species send the inflorescence down through the medium while others have upright spikes. The sepals and petals of the flowers are slender-oval, and the lip a very complex structure with various horns, crests, or other protuberances. The plants are similar to other members of the tribe.

H. brocklehurstiana. Three-inch, fragrant, waxy flowers are borne on an erect stem up to one and a half feet tall. The sepals and petals are red-brown streaked with yellow and spotted near the base with dark red. The lip is short, the basal part (hypochile) white with black warts and a pair of horns, the trowel-shaped epichile veined with yellow and covered with black warts. This native of Brazil is winter flowering.

H. odoratissima. A terrestrial species with fragrant, somewhat nodding flowers on an upright stem, this one is colored brown on the outside of the sepals and petals, dark maroon on the inner surface. The lip is white with several pairs of horns and a few red dots. It is native to Venezuela, Colombia, Peru, Brazil, and Bolivia.

H. tigrina is also called *H. lansbergii*. It is a smaller plant with a burrowing stem that holds two-

Fig. 18-14 *Houlletia tigrina.* (*Courtesy J. A. Fowlie*)

and-a-half-inch flowers in tones of red-orange with dark red-brown spots. The lip is purple at its base, barred with red, and white at the tip, and has a warty midsection. It occurs in Guatemala, Costa Rica, Panama, Venezuela, and Brazil.

Kegeliella has dwarf plants with drooping (not burrowing) stems of tiny flowers. *K. houtteana,* one of the two species, has half-inch flowers whose pale green sepals and petals are covered with pinkish hairs. The sepals are fairly broad and pointed, the petals thin and ribbon-like. The column is broadly winged, making it the conspicuous part of the flower, while the tiny three-lobed lip is quite inconspicuous. This is native to Panama, Venezuela, Surinam, Jamaica, and Trinidad.

Lacaena has two rare species, one of which, *L. bicolor,* is very handsome. The arching or pendant inflorescence bears twenty to thirty two-inch flowers that have broad wavy sepals and petals, white striped with purple. The three-lobed lip has a triangular mid-lobe that is white with a densely velvety purple patch in its center. It occurs from Mexico to Costa Rica.

Lycomormium. This is a rare genus of two species, having erect or arching spikes of large, globose flowers. The lateral sepals are joined to form a mentum (sac or chin) with the foot of the column. The species *elatum* and *squalidum* are native to Peru.

Neomoorea has but one species, *N. irrorata* which is a magnificent thing. The plant is similar to others of the tribe, but the roots form a dense mat about its base with many upstanding spinous rootlets. Up to twelve large bold flowers are held on an erect spike. The sepals and petals are broad, tapering to a sharp

point and are brownish gold, white at the base. The beautiful yellow lip is small but very decorative, having a pattern of dark lines and spots on the broad side lobes and tiny pointed mid-lobe. Two thin little horns stand up from its mid-section. The species is native to Colombia and occasionally occurs in Panama, and flowers in the spring.

Paphinia is best known for the very famous species, *P. cristata,* although there are a few other attractive ones. The plants are small, with pseudobulbs about two inches tall and plicate leaves six inches tall, but the flowers are large in proportion.

P. cristata. The three-inch, bold, red, star-shaped, flowers hang upside down, each on its own stem from the base of the pseudobulb. The long, slender dorsal sepal and petals are about the same size, while the lateral sepals are a bit shorter and curve outward. The very short lip, which has horns and protuberances on its inner sections, ends in a burst of white hairs that stand like a pompom

Fig. 18-15 *Neomoorea irrorata.*

Home Orchid Growing

Fig. 18-16 *Paphinia cristata*. (*Courtesy J. A. Fowlie*)

over the tip of the column. This species comes from quite hot and humid areas of the Guianas, Venezuela, Trinidad, and Colombia, and is difficult to keep in cultivation. If its secret could be learned, it would be welcome in all collections.

P. grandiflora. This species has flowers up to five inches in diameter. The basal half of the sepals and petals is yellowish banded with chocolate-purple, the outer half entirely the latter color. The lip also ends with white hairs. This one is native to Brazil.

P. rugosa. This species has smaller flowers that are yellow dotted with red and is native to Colombia.

Peristeria has several attractive species, one of which, *P. elata*, is the national flower of Panama. This is nicknamed the "Holy Ghost" or the "Dove" orchid. The plants have heavy, fleshy pseudobulbs topped by two or three very tall pleated leaves. They require warm conditions, and while many people have difficulty flowering them, they have been grown successfully in this country. The leaves fall after the growth matures, and the plants should be kept dry from then until new growth starts. The inflorescence makes its appearance along with new growth. The plants like an open, but quite rich medium.

P. elata. This stately plant is terrestrial. Its huge pseudobulbs require plenty of room and a rich, humusy soil. The erect flower spike bears many round, serenely lovely flowers, waxy white with a sprinkling of fine reddish dots on the outer surfaces. The round sepals and petals overlap to form a perfect cup. Within the cup sits the column between the wings of the hypochile, the "dove" that gives it one of its nicknames. The fleshy, up-turned lip is jointed at the hypochile and is counterbalanced. When a bee enters the flower, its weight tips the lip inward, throwing it against the column so that the pollinia are applied to it. It is native to Panama, Costa Rica, Venezuela, and Colombia, and flowers over a long period in the summer.

P. guttata. This species has a pendant spike of even more cup-like flowers, for the sepals are joined for part of their length. They are yellowish brown with heavy spotting of dark maroon. The wings of the hypochile are green, the outer portion of the lip white with a dark maroon stippling. This is native to Brazil, the Guianas, and Venezuela and blooms in the summer.

P. pendula. This is a smaller plant with very dense heads of small flowers on pendant stems. They are cream colored with very heavy mottling of dark rosy red. This species flowers earlier than

Fig. 18-17 *Peristeria elata*, the "Holy Ghost" or "dove" orchid, exemplifying purity and serenity. It is the national flower of Panama. (*Courtesy H. Dunn and H. Griffin*)

the others. It is a native of Panama and the Guianas.

Polycycnis has long chains of somewhat insect-like flowers, some species quite weird. The plants are similar to the rest of this group, and they can be grown like *Stanhopea*.

P. barbata. This is the most familiar species. The flowers are not too long lasting but are worthwhile nevertheless. Their parts are slender, the petals almost antenna-like. The lip has erect side lobes and a somewhat trowel-shaped end lobe, all covered inside with hairs. The flowers are rather translucent, yellow spotted with red. The species is native to Costa Rica, Panama, Colombia, Venezuela, and Brazil.

P. lepida. A very pretty species, it has long chains of twenty or more pale yellow flowers. The sepals and petals are dotted with dull purple, the lip with chocolate-brown. Two rows of tall, spiky hairs decorate the lip. It is a native of Colombia.

P. muscifera. This one looks like a large mosquito. Its flowers are about an inch across, with their parts all dangling. The sepals are fairly broad, brown with spots of dull red, hairy on the back. The petals are long, thin antennae. The lip is a thick thread covered with bristles. The long, arching column is very thin except for the beaked tip. This is native to Venezuela, Colombia, and Ecuador.

P. vittata. Rather like *barbata* in general aspect, its sepals are dark red with deeper veins, the petals yellow with red veins, and the smooth, three-

Fig. 18-19 *Sievekingia suavis.* (*Courtesy J. A. Fowlie*)

lobed lip pale green with reddish markings. The inflorescence is erect, with many flowers. The roots are a spiny mass inhabited by ants. This species ranges through Brazil, the Guianas, Venezuela, Colombia, and Peru.

Schlimia would not compete with other members of this tribe for beauty, although its strange little flowers are interesting. The species *S. trifida* has tubular flowers with a deep vase-shaped mentum formed by the lateral sepals, and within this is held the tiny lip. The petals barely protrude beyond the opening, and the dorsal sepal lies close over it. Four or five flowers are held on a pendant raceme. The species occurs in Venezuela, Colombia, and Ecuador.

Sievekingia has one species that seems to be well known, and a few others that are very rare. The lovely little *S. suavis* has a pendant spray of four or five waxy flowers. The rather broad, pointed sepals are lemon yellow, and the smaller petals orange. The outer lobe of the lip is cupped and is orange spotted with reddish purple. The plant looks like a seedling *Stanhopea*. This one is native to Costa Rica and Panama. There is another, *S. peruviana* which is not as attractive, its flowers being rather thinner and held more closed. It occurs in Peru.

Fig. 18-18 *Polycycnis lepida.* (*Courtesy J. A. Fowlie*)

Home Orchid Growing

Odontoglossum krameri

Miltonia J. M. Black 'Peter'

Oncidium desertorum

Odontoglossum chiriquense

Oncidium splendidum

Odontoglossum cirrhosum

Oncidium variegatum

(*Rebecca T. Northen*)

Oncidium gardneri

Oncidium aureum

Oncidium macranthum

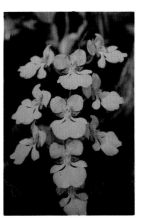

Oncidium onustum

Oncidium carthagenense

Bifrenaria harrisoniana

Comparettia macroplectron

Coelogyne ochracea

Ornithocephalus
cochleariformis

Sobralia xantholeuca

Haraëlla odorata

Chysis tricostata

Maxillaria sanderiana

(Rebecca T. Northen)

Maxillaria juergensis

Bulbophyllum gravidum

Anguloa uniflora

Masdevallia coccinea

19

COLLECTORS' ITEMS

Some of the orchids given in the preceding chapters could just as well have been included here, and some of those in this category are perhaps as well known, if not better known, than some of those described earlier. However, because it is interesting to relate one kind to another, and to know that famous kinds have less well-known relatives, we shall try as far as possible to continue with the tribal arrangement. Do not be disturbed, however, if you find in the future that one or another of the kinds has been moved to another genus, or that separate genera have been combined into one genus. Sometimes it is difficult even for the experts to decide exactly how the orchids are related. To help in locating the genera included in Chapters 19 and 20, we give below an outline of the contents.

Ada Tribe
Ada
Quekettia

Coelogyne Tribe
Coelogyne
Dendrochilum
Neogyne
Pholidota
Pleione

Ionopsis Tribe
Comparettia
Ionopsis
Rodriguezia
Trichocentrum

Lycaste Tribe
Anguloa
Batemania

Lycaste Tribe—continued
Bifrenaria
Lycaste
Xylobium

Maxillaria Tribe
Maxillaria
Scuticaria

Phaius Tribe
Acanthophippium
Aplectrum
Arundina
Bletia
Bletilla
Calanthe
Chysis
Phaius
Spathoglottis

Physurus Tribe
Anoectochilus
Dossinia
Erythrodes (Physurus)
Goodyera
Ludisia (Haemaria)
Macodes

Pleurothallis Tribe
Barbosella
Cryptophoranthus
Lepanthes
Lepanthopsis
Masdevallia
Platystele
Pleurothallis
Restrepia
Scaphosepalum
Stelis

Polystachya Tribe
Ansellia
Galeandra
Neobenthamia
Polystachya

Sobralia Tribe
Calopogon
Sobralia

Zygopetalum Tribe
Bollea
Chondrorhyncha
Cochleanthes
Colax
Huntleya
Kefersteinia
Menadenium
Pescatoria
Promenaea
Zygopetalum

Miscellaneous Genera, Chapter 20
Bulbophyllum
Campylocentrum and *Polyrrhiza*
Coelia
Cyrtopodium
Dichaea
Disa
Eulophiella
Haraëlla
Helcia
Hexisea
Isochilus
Leochilus and *Mesospinidium*
Lockhartia
Meiracyllium
Microcoelia
Mormolyca
Notylia
Oberonia
Ornithocephalus, Dipteranthus, and *Zygostates*
Pinelia and *Pygmaeorchis*
Scaphyglottis
Sigmatostalix
Stenia
Telipogon
Trichoceros
Trichopilia
Tridactyle
Trigonidium
Vanilla

ADA TRIBE

This small tribe has but few species, and since a few hybrids have been made between it and *Odontoglossum* and *Cochlioda,* it should probably be included with that group.

Ada

Two species are known in this genus, both from high elevations in the Colombian Andes, and both brightly colored. It is for their color that hybrids have been made between this genus and members of the Odontoglossum tribe.

Ada aurantiaca. Bright little cinnabar red, bell-shaped flowers are held seven to ten on an arching spray. The sepals and petals hold themselves in a tube for their basal half, with their slender, pointed outer ends spreading in star-like fashion, allowing the little point of the lip to protrude. The flowers appear in the spring.

Ada lehmanni. The flowers of this species are red-orange, more open than the preceding, and have a white lip. It is summer flowering.

Quekettia

This genus of but a few species has all miniature plants.

Q. microscopica. This species has terete channeled leaves that are spotted with purple and may reach four inches in height. The little flower spray is less than two inches long and holds five or six quarter-inch flowers. They are tubular, with the sepals and petals held closely together, the lateral sepals actually joined, and the tips of the parts separating only enough to let the lip and column peek out. The flower is yellow-green with a yellow lip. It occurs in Brazil, Argentina, and Venezuela.

Q. pygmaea. This little plant is much smaller than the foregoing, being about an inch and a half tall. Its little branched flower spray holds about thirty globe-shaped blooms, each one-sixteenth inch in diameter. The sepals and petals are broad, giving the flower a tulip shape. These are white with a pale yellow lip. The plant has terete leaves spotted with purple. It is native to Venezuela and Trinidad.

COELOGYNE TRIBE

The Coelogyne tribe contains several genera, the best known of which is *Coelogyne.* The tribe ranges from China and the Himalayas through Southeast Asia to the Philippines and other Pacific islands. All are characterized by somewhat rounded pseudobulbs, topped by bright green, thin, or rigid leaves. Their flowers are sometimes produced singly, but more often in attractive sprays.

Coelogyne

There are over a hundred species of *Coelogyne.* Some are from high elevations and do best with cool treatment, although both these and those from warmer elevations can be grown in intermediate conditions with care as to their placement. They do well in almost any potting medium that offers good drainage and aeration and can be grown in pots, shallow pans, or hanging baskets. Some have rather a rambling habit and should be given plenty of room in the pot. Repotting and dividing must be done while new roots are starting, else a plant may be badly set back. They are resentful of disturbance at the roots. With such care, however, they reward the amateur with a profusion of blooms. They require copious water during their growing period, but are kept on the dry side during their period of lessened activity, and like moderate shade. In some regions they may be placed out-of-doors in a protected place during the hottest months.

C. cristata. Considered by some to be the most beautiful of East Indian orchids. The combination of sprays of snow-white flowers, apple-green pseudobulbs, and dark green leaves is most attractive. The blooms measure three to five inches, and occur many to the spray which arises from the base of the pseudobulb. The petals and sepals are wavy, and project forward. The lip is three-lobed, the middle lobe decorated inside by five yellow, fringed keels. They keep beautifully and are highly decorative as sprays or for corsages. *Coelogyne cristata* likes fairly cool treatment and does not thrive in great heat. It occurs in the Himalayas and flowers in the winter.

C. dayana. A large plant, with pseudobulbs five to ten inches long and leaves measuring two and one-half feet. The long chain-like sprays bear many flowers which are pale yellow except that the lip is decorated with brown fringed ridges and has brown lateral lobes. This spring- and summer-blooming plant comes from Borneo.

C. lawrenceana. If you looked only at the lip of this and the similar *speciosa,* you would be entranced. Otherwise, they are not very appealing flowers. *C. lawrenceana* is the handsomer of the two, however, with its huge lip decorated on the inside with rows of tall, brown protuberances that look like the tube feet of a starfish. The sepals are fairly broad, the petals very narrow and held back between the sepals. *C. speciosa* has quite droopy sepals and very thread-like petals. Its lip is lined with rows of brown velvety protuberances. *C. lawrenceana* comes from Viet Nam and flowers in the spring; *C. speciosa* occurs in Sumatra and Java and is fall blooming.

C. massangeana. This is one of the loveliest and most popular of the genus, with long sprays of two-inch flowers that are yellow with a very striking and decorative lip. The side lobes of the lip are dark brown inside, and this same color follows around the rows of yellow protuberances that decorate the central portion of the mid-lobe. The sepals and petals are pale yellow, and the flowers very fragrant. They are borne in long drooping chains. Native to Peninsular Thailand, the Malay Peninsula, Sumatra, Java, and Borneo, it blooms from spring through fall.

C. mooreana. A dainty species, it is prettier in some ways than *cristata,* and much easier to grow. The white flowers are held on an erect, arching spray, five to ten at a time. The fairly broad sepals and less wide petals spread in a star shape, and are wavy on the edges. The generous lip has long side lobes and a spreading mid-lobe decorated with yellow inside and two raised keels. It flowers in the winter and comes from Viet Nam.

Fig. 19-1 *Coelogyne mooreana,* white with lines of golden fringe in the lip.

C. ochracea. A perfectly delightful species, it is white with "painted" patches on the lip. The two circular yellow areas are outlined with a neat line of orange, and punctuated in the center with an orange dot or two. The inside of the side lobes of the lip are also "painted" yellow, outlined in orange and striped with brown. This is another easy-to-grow species, and rewarding with many-flowered sprays. It comes from the Himalayas, but does well in an intermediate house. Flowering time is fall.

C. pandurata. Sometimes called the "black orchid," although there are others that fit the name as well, the sepals and petals are emerald-green, and the fiddle-shaped lip is heavily veined and stained with black on a greenish ground. The middle lobe of the lip is ruffled and fringed and carries black warts and ridges. This species does well in the semitropical states. It is a native of Borneo. The blossoms appear in the summer.

C. tomentosa. Pendulous sprays of fifteen to twenty pale orange-red flowers are quite striking in appearance. It occurs in Borneo and Sumatra and flowers in the summer.

Other Genera of the Coelogyne Tribe

Dendrochilum. Although the plants are fairly large, the flowers are minute and are produced in long chains, which gives this genus its nickname "necklace" orchid. *D. cobbianum* has very fragrant flowers, about three-fourths inch in diameter, produced on a twisted chain. They are white with a yellow or orange-yellow lip. *D. filiforme* has one-fourth inch flowers, also white with a yellow lip and fragrant; there are over a hundred on each two-ranked chain. *D. glumaceum* has flowers only faintly fragrant, about one-half inch in diameter, pale yellow with a greenish yellow lip. All three of these are native to the Philippines and flower in spring, summer, or fall. This is the genus that for a long time was known as *Platyclinis.*

Neogyne is a genus of one species, *gardneriana,* which produces small white flowers that quickly wither. It occurs in the Himalayas.

Pholidota has acquired the name "rattle-snake orchid" because the scales of the unopened flower raceme are reminiscent of the rattles of that snake. The flower stem grows from the top of the pseudo-bulb along with the developing leaf. Although the flowers are not colorful, being a yellowish white, a

Fig. 19-2 *Dendrochilum filiforme,* the "necklace" orchid.

only sparsely from November to April, and then regularly during the growing period. *P. humilis* has flowers one to two inches in diameter, which range from white to pale purple. The sepals and petals are spreading, rather narrow. The large lip

A

B

Fig. 19-3 *Pholidota imbricata.* It's nickname of "rattle-snake" orchid does not do justice to the dainty chains of flowers. A, the plant produces a chain from each new growth. B, detail of the flowers.

plant with many slender, trailing stems, each with over a hundred tiny flowers, is most attractive. Each flower peeks out from under a brownish bract. The best known species is *imbricata,* which is easy to grow along with cattleyas. See drawing in Chapter 1. *P. chinensis* is seen in old Chinese paintings, and is native to India and China.

Pleione, "mother of the Pleiades," has large, attractive flowers and peculiar plant habits. The pseudobulbs, which last only a year, are persimmon-shaped, wrinkled and sometimes warty. They bear one or more broad, plicate leaves which fall as the bulbs mature. At the end of the growing season, a new shoot develops from the base of the current pseudobulb, which withers as this takes place. The new shoot produces a flowering stem and roots and then, after flowering, stands still until the following spring. In the spring the resting shoot resumes its growth, forms leaves and pseudobulbs, and repeats the cycle. The plants should be watered

Home Orchid Growing

encloses the column at its base, and then spreads broadly. Its edges are marvelously fringed and the center is keeled and spotted. It comes from Nepal and Sikkim. *P. praecox* has three-inch flowers, fragrant, and of a rich rose-purple. The darker lip is fringed and decorated with fringed crests. This is native to Southern China and Burma.

IONOPSIS TRIBE

The four genera that make up this tribe range natively from Mexico to Brazil. All are small to miniature epiphytes and produce sprays of dainty flowers; some are very striking, for their flowers are large in proportion to the size of the plants.

Comparettia

These are graceful little plants whose flowers are brightly colored and most eye-catching on their arching sprays. The flowers are curiously constructed. The lateral sepals are united and form a spur at their base. The lip has a double spur which fits into that of the sepals. The front lobe of the lip is somewhat heart-shaped, broad and spreading. The petals and upper sepal form sort of a hood behind the column. The plants have tiny pseudobulbs from which arises a single rather broad leaf. They may be grown in small pots or on driftwood or tree fern slabs. They grow natively on small branches in humid forests and must be kept damp in cultivation. A few crosses have been made between *Comparettia* and *Oncidium* and *Rodriguezia*.

C. coccinea has one-inch flowers in tones of yellow shaded with scarlet, and a bright scarlet lip. It is native to Brazil.

C. falcata is similar to *coccinea* but its flowers are of bright cerise, and it has a wider range, spreading from Mexico through Central America and northern South America. In Costa Rica it is found on the merest twigs on the lower parts of trees.

C. macroplectron has beautiful two-inch flowers with an extremely large lip and a very long spur. It is light pink daintily spotted with rose. This is a native of Colombia.

C. speciosa is bright orange with the dorsal sepal and petals veined with a darker shade. It, too, has a very long spur. This one is native to Ecuador.

Ionopsis

These are small plants, which have a many-branched flower stem with innumerable delightful small flowers.

I. satyrioides. This is a lovely small species, apparently without a pseudobulb. The one-third-inch flowers are white. The lip is slender and slightly divided, while the sepals and petals are larger. It's native to the West Indies.

I. utricularioides is a perfectly delightful little plant which gives lacy sprays of half-inch flowers ranging from pink to purple and even white. The prominent lip is broad and flat. The leaf which should arise from the top of the pseudobulb is aborted, and instead there is the merest little point of green in that place. The leaves therefore all come from the base of the pseudobulb. The species ranges from Florida and the West Indies, and from Mexico south to Peru. The species *I. paniculata* has now been combined with this one.

Rodriguezia

The plants are small with delicate sprays of dainty flowers. The lateral sepals are united, and the lip is more or less spurred. Their culture is similar to that of *Laelia* and *Cattleya*.

R. secunda. The whole plant is dwarf in habit, and the six-inch long spray carries twenty to thirty rose-colored flowers, all on one side of the stem. The plants, which occur in Trinidad and Guiana, flower in August.

R. venusta (syn. *bracteata*). The flowers are a little larger than they are in *secunda,* and the sprays more open. They are white, tinged with pink, and the lip is marked with yellow. It occurs in Brazil. Flowering time is variable.

Trichocentrum

This genus is characterized by its odd trowel-shaped lip which is prolonged at its base into a prominent spur. The sepals and petals are free, sometimes longer than the lip and spreading, sometimes smaller and overlapping. The flowers are brightly colored, produced sometimes singly, sometimes several to a stem, and they are large in proportion to the size of the plant. The column is winged and usually covered with short fleshy tubercles.

T. albo-coccineum (*syn. albo-purpureum*). This species has stunning little flowers greenish on the outside, maroon-brown within, with a white lip decorated with two purple spots. It occurs in Ecuador, Peru, and Brazil.

T. panduratum. The sepals and petals of this species are extremely short and overlapping, and the lip is long and narrow with a long tail-like spur. The general appearance of the flower is that of an old-fashioned salt shovel. It occurs in Peru.

T. pulchrum. This is an open flower, with broad sepals and petals that are green, spotted with reddish purple. The rectangular lip is ivory with purple spots. It is native to Venezuela, Colombia, Ecuador, and Peru.

LYCASTE TRIBE

Most orchid collections contain a few members of the Lycaste tribe, particularly of the genus *Lycaste* itself. They are grown not only for their ease of culture, but for their distinct individuality and charm. All members of the tribe are natives of Central or South America or the West Indies. They are mostly high-altitude plants and therefore grow best under fairly cool conditions. The coolest spot in the cattleya house may suit them, with night temperatures in the winter of 50° to 55°. They like to be cool in the summer, too, and shaded from direct sunlight both winter and summer.

Finely chopped osmunda fiber or a mix such as used for cymbidiums will make good potting media. Watering must be handled judiciously so as not to let the medium become soggy. Propagation is by division, cutting through the rhizomes to separate the bulbs in groups of two. Repotting and division should be done just as new growth starts.

Bigeneric hybrids have been made between *Lycaste* and *Anguloa* (*Angulocaste*) and *Lycaste* and *Bifrenaria* (*Lycastenaria*).

Anguloa

The genus *Anguloa* is native to the Andes. They are noted for their fragrance, and for their peculiar globular shape which has given them a number of nicknames, such as "tulip orchid" or "boat orchid." Their hinged lip oscillates gently with the least movement and serves to tip a visiting bee against the column. In its struggle to free itself it removes the pollinia. The large very waxy flowers are serenely beautiful.

The plants themselves are rather striking, with their long, broad, pleated leaves, and the tall, sheathed flower stem rising from the base of the conical pseudobulbs, bearing a single flower. Although they are more or less terrestrial in habit, they will grow in osmunda fiber, to which may be added a third part soil, or possibly some well-dried cow manure, or in a fibrous mix or cymbidium mix. A night temperature of 50° is desirable in the winter, and a cool, shaded environment in the summer. They require ample moisture and water except for

Fig. 19-4 *Anguloa clowesii,* one of the "tulip" orchids. (*Courtesy J. A. Fowlie*)

a brief rest after growth is completed to encourage flowering.

A. clowesii. These lemon yellow flowers are green inside with a white downy lip.

A. uniflora. Creamy white or pale pink blossoms are flushed or dotted inside with deep pink.

A. rueckeri. These flowers are greenish yellow, flushed with brown on the outside, spotted inside with red.

Batemania

Of the two species in this genus, the best known is *B. colleyi.* It is strangely shaped. The broad petals are angled upward like a pair of wings. The base of the lip with its broad side lobes is appressed to the column foot, forming almost a vase, while the mid-lobe curves outward. The lateral sepals do not seem to belong to this flower, for they are slender and trail down, their somewhat frail appearance out of character with the heavy flower. The sepals and petals are dark wine-red, tipped with green, and the lip is white with a reddish flush. The species is native to the Guianas and Brazil.

Bifrenaria

The handsome and showy flowers of this genus are round, waxy, and fragrant. They are all native to Brazil and will do well in either an intermediate or warm greenhouse. The plants are similar to *Lycaste,* and as in that genus the flowers are usually borne on single stems shorter than the leaves. The column has a basal extension called a foot, and the lateral sepals are attached to this in back, their sides folding around it to form a partially open spur.

B. atropurpurea. The two-inch flowers are fleshy, with their rounded sepals and petals wine-red toning to yellow at the base. The lovely full lip with its erect side lobes is white or rose.

B. harrisoniae. This and the species below have all the qualities one could wish for in an orchid—rounded parts, an open aspect, and a full and decorative lip. The flowers are three inches in diameter, very fragrant, with sepals and petals varying from white to greenish yellow with red tones. The lip, covered with short hairs, varies from yellow to wine-purple with dark red veins, and has a hairy yellow crest.

B. tetragona. A smaller flower, this also has a lovely shape. Its sepals and petals are greenish, faintly streaked with brown and the lip is flushed with violet.

Lycaste

The oval, somewhat corrugated pseudobulbs bear broad, pleated leaves which last but a year or two. When the bulbs are newly growing, they are sheathed with smaller leaves which soon fall. The quaint flowers are borne singly on stems that arise from the base of the pseudobulbs starting as the new leaves form. The broad sepals stand out gracefully, while the petals and lip give the impression of a sunbonnet in the center. The petals stand forward, each with its tip gracefully turned out, and surround the small lip which just protrudes from within. The lateral sepals are often united at the base to form a short spur or chin. The blooms last a long time, and a plant may flower for months. The plants are kept fairly dry through the winter, and are watered generously during growth and flowering. The species from Mexico and Central America usually do well in a cool spot in the cattleya house; those from the Andes of northern South America in the cymbidium house, that is, with nights of 50–55°.

L. aromatica. This is an attractive species with flowers about three inches across, yellow, tinged with green. The lip is spotted with orange. It has a

strong, pleasant fragrance. During its resting period it should have considerably less water but should not be allowed to remain dry for long periods. The plants occur in Mexico and flower in winter and spring.

L. ciliata. This large flower has downward-pointing lateral sepals which are quite broad and long, and petals that do not hold as close to the lip as

A

B

Fig. 19-5 A. *Lycaste dowiana,* softly colored appealing little flowers each produced on a single stem. (*Courtesy H. A. Dunn*)
B. *Lycaste xytrophora,* a stunning near twin to *L. dowiana.*

some. The flower is green, with a white, fringed lip. It is native to Colombia and is cool growing.

L. deppei. This interesting species has curiously colored flowers. The sepals are dull green spotted with red, the petals white, and the lip yellow spotted with red. The lateral sepals stand out horizontally. Occurring in Mexico, it is easy to grow, requiring intermediate conditions.

L. dowiana. Prim, quietly colored flowers are produced in profusion. The sepals are olive green on the back, brown in front, and the petals and little fringed lip are pale yellow, or cream. It is native to Costa Rica, Nicaragua, and Panama.

L. leucantha. A very lovely, smallish flower, this has light green sepals, and white petals and lip. The sepals stand at right angles to each other. The lip is sometimes fuzzy in the center. It occurs in Costa Rica.

L. lucusta. One of the most distinctive of all, this has big, heavy, dark green flowers, with a broad fringed lip on which there is a ridged callus. The flower is quite open, the petals flaring sideways rather than over the column. It occurs in Peru.

L. macrophylla. A bright, rather bold flower, this has the typical shape. The sepals are green-brown, sometimes wavy; the petals are white with red markings on the inner surface, which may be dots or a solid patch leaving a white border; and the lip is white, also marked with red. This species is widespread, from Nicaragua to Bolivia.

L. virginalis. This is the preferred name for *L. skinneri,* one of the best of the genus. It can reach six inches in diameter. The flowers are waxy, white, tinged with rose. The middle lobe of the lip is tongue-shaped, marked with purple on the callus or variously dotted with purple. This is one of the easiest to grow. Its flowers last well and can

Fig. 19-6 *Lycaste leucantha,* waxy green with white petals and lip.

be enjoyed for a long time. There are many named varieties, which range from pure white to dark purple. This species requires a much less intense rest period than the more deciduous ones. It is the national flower of Guatemala and occurs in Guatemala, Mexico, and Honduras.

L. xytriophora. This species is similar to *dowiana,* though its sepals are reflexed and its leaves much larger and more luxuriant. A sure way to tell them apart is that *xytriophora* has no spines on the top of the pseudobulbs after the leaves have fallen, while *dowiana* does. *L. xytriophora* is native to Ecuador and flowers in the fall.

Xylobium

This genus cannot compare in beauty to its more showy cousins. Its little pale yellow or straw-colored flowers do not open fully. They are borne on short drooping or erect stems, a dozen to thirty in dense or loose clusters. Fanciers of this tribe and its near relatives may wish to have a few *Xylobiums* as a matter of interest. Species are *elongatum, foveatum, palmifolium, powellii,* etc., and they range from Mexico to Brazil and Peru.

MAXILLARIA TRIBE

Two genera make up this tribe; one, *Maxillaria,* has some three hundred species, and the other, *Scuticaria,* but few.

Maxillaria

There are some very charming species in this genus, and some that are (if you will pardon a species lover for saying so) not particularly attractive. The species range from Florida through the West Indies, and from Mexico to Brazil. They vary tremendously in size, from miniature to those with stems several feet long. There are kinds with tiny pseudobulbs widely spaced on climbing stems that branch and re-branch; kinds with tiny pseudobulbs that do not have a climbing habit; kinds that look like a vanda and grow to quite some heights; plants that have large pseudobulbs and leaves and look like a *Trichopilia* plant, and so on, and on. Most of them can be grown in an intermediate house, a few with cooler temperatures. If you go collecting orchids in the wilds, you are bound to bring back a number of species, some that you will not suspect of being maxillarias.

M. confusa. This little plant, barely three inches tall, rapidly spreads into a mass of tiny pseudo-

Home Orchid Growing

bulbs and leaves and gives great numbers of small, nodding, pointed, white flowers. It is native to Costa Rica.

M. juergensis. This beautiful miniature has pale green pseudobulbs three-fourths inch tall and paired, grass-thin leaves barely an inch long. The cup-shaped, half-inch flowers are green and wine-red. It is a native of Brazil.

M. lepidota. The flowers are strange rather than pretty, with sepals and petals elongated somewhat after the manner of a brassia, yellow and brown, or all yellow. This one is native to Colombia and Ecuador.

M. neglecta. A pretty little plant that would climb if it had something to climb upon, it branches so fast that it will fill a pot like a bouquet. It has tight clusters of waxy, very tiny, white or white and yellow, round flowers at the base of each new growth. It occurs in Honduras, Nicaragua, Costa Rica, and Panama.

M. picta. A very pretty and perky flower, tawny-yellow marked with spots of red, about two and a half inches in diameter, it is native to Brazil.

M. sanderiana. This is the most magnificent of the genus. The flowers are quite like a lycaste in shape and size, borne on rather short stems. They are white, spotted with red, and the base of the sepals and lip are an incredibly rich, almost black-red, very velvety. It occurs at high elevations in Ecuador and must be grown cool.

M. tenuifolia. This is somewhat climbing, with little pseudobulbs each produced higher on the stem than the preceding ones. The leaves are grass-like. The pretty one-and-a-half to two-inch flowers are dark red mottled with yellow. It ranges from Mexico throughout Central America.

M. tigrina. To find when I got home from my first collecting experience in Costa Rica that this plant was a new species was a delightful surprise. I found it on a trip with Clarence Horich. It almost covered a ten-foot stump of an old tree in a cleared area in upper Sarapiqui Canyon. Dr. Charles Schweinfurth described and named it. The plant has small oval pseudobulbs bearing a single leathery leaf, spaced along a rambling rhizome that branches and re-branches, forming festoons that grow in all directions. The tawny, red-striped, inch-and-a-half flowers come in succession from the mature pseudobulbs, on short stems, and are rather long lasting. The oval, sharply pointed sepals stand quite flat, the lateral ones curve downward. The petals curve forward over the column. The hinged lip has a

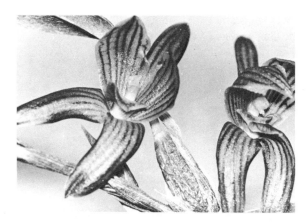

Fig. 19-7 *Maxillaria tigrina,* a new species discovered in Costa Rica, highlight of a collecting trip.

narrow, bluntly pointed mid-lobe, and short, pointed side lobes that are continuous with the folded crest. It stays in bloom from winter into the fall, and grows extremely vigorously, which leads one to wonder why it should be so rare.

M. variabilis. As its name implies, it varies a good bit in coloring, from yellow to red with spots of one or the other color. The flowers are heavy, about three-fourths inch in diameter, and the little pseudobulbs can be quite round or elongated. It grows natively from Mexico to Venezuela.

M. valenzuelana. This is one to grow for the plant alone. The leaves form a beautiful fan, always growing downward. Actually, the leaves are "equitant," that is they grow folded together, with their edges separated only at the base where each overlaps the one next to it. They are bluish green, and pointed, over a foot long. The flowers are very tiny, white or yellow and barely protrude from the folded base of the leaves. It occurs from Honduras to Colombia, Venezuela, and Brazil, and also in Cuba.

M. vitelliniflora. This is similar to *M. juergensis* but the leaves are narrower and twice as long. The tiny flowers are yellow with a dark patch on the lip. It too, occurs in Brazil.

Scuticaria

Of the few species in this genus, *S. steelei* is the best known. It is a remarkable plant, with pendant, terete, whip-like leaves that reach a length of six feet. They arise from pseudobulbs that are mere swellings, but which remain when the old leaves fall. The flowers are three inches in diameter, with rather broad parts and an open aspect. They are fleshy, yellow-green or tan with leopard spots of brown. The three-lobed lip has erect side lobes striped with brown, and a spreading mid-lobe with fewer spots and a downy crest. It is native to Brazil, the Guianas, and Venezuela.

PHAIUS TRIBE

This tribe of mostly terrestrial orchids covers a large part of the world with its various genera. Many are deciduous and flower after the leaves have fallen. Two of the genera, *Phaius* and *Calanthe,* are rather widely grown.

Phaius

A genus of large, handsome plants, *Phaius* is composed of some twenty species that produce tall spikes of showy flowers. There are among the species some that are epiphytic as well as the better known terrestrial ones. The former are seldom grown.

The terrestrial species are native to tropical Asia, Africa, Australia, Madagascar, China, and Japan. They have been cultivated since 1778, when *P. tankervilliae* (*grandifolius*) was imported from China. This is commonly known as the "nun's orchid" or the "veiled nun."

This genus likes an intermediate greenhouse with adequate shade, and night temperatures that do not fall below 55°. The potting compost is a mixture of sandy loam, well-rotted cow manure, and shredded peat moss or osmunda, in equal parts. The pots must have plenty of drainage crock in the bottom. To insure adequate nutrition, the top surface of the soil is covered with a mulch of cow manure. A fertilizer solution may be added after the flower spikes have started. The plants grow vigorously, and require plenty of water all year round.

Plants of *Phaius* may be divided every two or three years, when the blooming season is over. Young plants may be grown from dormant buds on the flower scapes, in the manner described for dendrobium canes. After the flowers have withered, cut the stem, lay it on moist sand in a flat. Cover with glass or muslin to keep in the moisture and provide shade. The little plants that grow from the dormant buds will be large enough in a few months to be potted up.

Dwellers in the southern states may grow members of this genus out-of-doors under the trees. In some regions they may be kept (in their pots) in the garden at least for the summer, being brought into the greenhouse before the nights turn cool.

P. flavus (syn. *maculatus*). Attractive yellow flowers, two to three inches in diameter, are borne in clusters of ten to fifteen on spikes two feet tall. The lip is erect with the front lobe recurved and streaked with orange. The base of the lip forms a prominent spur. The foliage of this plant is attractively variegated with yellow. It occurs in North India and Japan and flowers in the spring.

P. tankervilliae or *tancarvilliae* (syn. *grandifolius*). These are majestic plants, familiarly known as the "nun's orchid." The tall flower spikes carry ten to fifteen flowers whose petals and sepals are white on the back, reddish brown inside. The lip is tubular, with a short spur, a yellow throat, and crimson sides. The species occurs in China and Australia. The flowers appear in winter and spring.

A number of bigeneric hybrids have been made between *Phaius* and *Calanthe,* which are named after both genera, *Phaiocalanthe.*

Calanthe

The name *calanthe* means "beautiful flower," and each of the species known in cultivation lives up to this name. The genus contains some forty or fifty species, some of which are deciduous and some evergreen, but all are terrestrial. The deciduous species have tall, conical pseudobulbs that reach eight or nine inches in height, from which rise the handsome, heavily ribbed leaves. The leaves fall before or at the time of flowering. In the evergreen species the pseudobulbs are lacking and the leaves grow directly from the creeping rhizome.

Mr. Dominy, the original orchid hybridist, made his first cross with *Calanthe.* In 1856 *Calanthe* Dominyi (*C. masuca* × *C. furcata*), the first hybrid orchid, flowered.

Calanthe is potted in the same manner as *Phaius.* The bulbs may be separated once a year, when growth is just starting in the spring, or the plant may be repotted without being divided. New growths come from the base of the old bulbs. A method often used is to separate the bulbs and put several in one large pot, to be assured of a good display of flowers. Water sparingly until growth starts and give the new leaves extra shade for a while. After the leaves are well along, the plants need more light, but, as for cattleyas, the light must be properly moderated. *Calanthe* thrives in warm places in the greenhouse, with a temperature of 55° to 60° at night and with generous daytime humidity.

During their growing season, water the deciduous species generously. The frequency of watering is reduced when the foliage begins to turn yellow in the fall. When the flower spikes show, increase the watering and continue until the blooms are finished. After their winter flowering, the plants must have a decided rest. The pots may be laid on their sides in a cool place and given no water until the following spring. Some growers separate the bulbs, dust them with a fungicide such as Tersan or Arasan (or dip them in a solution), and store them in a dry place at 60°. As soon as root growth begins, the plants must be repotted. The evergreen species are watered all year round.

C. vestita. Once one of the most widely grown of all orchids, this species is still very popular. The lovely sprays of white flowers appear in winter, keep well, and lend themselves to decorations for holiday social affairs or to dainty corsages. The sepals and petals are more or less overlapping, and hold themselves up and back from the long, beautiful lip. The front lobe of the lip is scalloped, and flaring, with a touch of yellow or crimson in the throat. The pseudobulbs are silvery green and the deciduous leaves are nearly two feet long. The flower spike rises to a height of two or three feet. The plants occur in Malaya.

The hybrid *Calanthe* Veitchii (*rosea* × *vestita*) is one of the most popular and is as widely grown as *Calanthe vestita* itself. The flowers are rose colored, and the lip is decorated with a white spot near the base.

The parents of the first hybrid orchid were evergreen calanthes. *C. furcata* bears creamy white flowers generously distributed on a long spike. The plant has large fan-like leaves. *C. masuca* has deep violet flowers on spikes somewhat shorter than those of *C. furcata.* Both require warm, humid growing conditions.

Other Genera of the Phaius Tribe

Acanthophippium comes from the hottest moist jungles of Java, where it grows in heavy shade. The odd flowers are borne on stems that grow from the base of the pseudobulbs. The broad, fleshy sepals enclose the petals and lip, giving the flower the shape of an urn. The species *A. javanicum* has yellow flowers flushed and striped with red.

Aplectrum is a genus that grows wild in our own northern woods. The single species, *A. hyemale,* produces a single evergreen leaf and in the spring a spike of brownish flowers. It is commonly called "Adam and Eve."

Arundina is a genus whose plants resemble sobralias and whose flowers are similar to *Cattleya.* A very tall plant, up to four feet, it needs plenty of room and can be grown out-of-doors in warm climates. The flower scape has few flowers, but the rosy-lilac blossoms are attractive. The popularly known "bamboo orchid," *A. bambusaefolia,* should correctly be called *A. graminifolia.* It occurs in Indo-Malaysia and the Pacific islands.

Bletia is a genus of twenty species native to tropical America. The plants have spherical pseudobulbs, from the apex of which the tall flower spikes are produced. They are terrestrial for the most part but occasionally grow on rocks or fallen logs.

B. purpurea has flowers with pink or rosy sepals and petals and a deep rose-purple lip; *verecunda* produces rose-colored flowers; the blooms of *shepherdii* are deep purple; and those of *sherrattiana* are bright rose. These plants all have leaves from three to four feet long.

Bletilla, a genus from China, includes the species *B. striata,* popularly known as *B. hyacinthina,* often sold in grocery stores and by garden supply companies. It is terrestrial, with small corms underground, and can be grown out-of-doors in most parts of this country. The stem is a foot tall, with several pleated leaves, and bears a spike of small cattleya-like flowers that are amethyst-purple.

Chysis is a genus of handsome plants with lovely flowers, native to tropical America. They have long, heavy, rather club-shaped pseudobulbs which grow in a pendant or horizontal manner. They bear lush, broad, pointed, plicate leaves, often twenty or more, which are deciduous. They require rather warm conditions and plenty of water while growing, and should be kept rather dry after leaf fall and until new growth starts in the spring. Flowering stems arise from the new growth. The inflorescence is usually shorter than the pseudobulbs and bears four to ten blooms. The flowers are lovely, waxy, wide open, with their sepals and petals broad in the middle, pointed at the tips. The lip is very fleshy, three-lobed, with the side lobes erect and the mid-lobe somewhat cup-shaped, partitioned from its base by a crest of teeth.

C. aurea has flowers of brownish yellow, shading to white in the center. The lip has five keels that look like teeth from the front. It occurs from Mexico to Peru and Venezuela and flowers in the summer.

Fig. 19-8 *Chysis bractescens,* waxy flowers of ivory white, the lip toned with yellow and striped with red. (*Courtesy Jones and Scully, Inc.*)

C. bractescens has flowers of ivory white. Its lip is yellow, streaked with red. A native of Mexico, British Honduras, and Guatemala, it blooms in the summer.

C. lemminghei is white, with its parts tipped and marked with purple. Also summer flowering, it occurs in Mexico.

C. tricostata, also known as *C. laevis,* has yellow sepals and petals tinted with lines of red-violet, and a yellow lip marked with red and decorated with three vertical, fleshy keels. It occurs from Mexico to Costa Rica and is summer flowering.

Spathoglottis is a genus of terrestrial orchids native to India and China. They have small corm-like pseudobulbs and grassy foliage. The small, bright flowers are usually produced in small numbers on rather tall spikes. Where they may be grown out-of-doors, for instance in our warm states where the climate is humid, they might be worth a try, for they are very attractive.

PHYSURUS TRIBE

This is the tribe of "jewel" orchids, loved for their beautifully variegated foliage. Their flowers are small, borne on little upright spikes; in past decades people hardly looked at them. Now that the interest in tiny kinds has increased, people have discovered their fascination and are able to see that the flowers are just as interesting as those of many other "botanicals." However, this group has the added advantage of being showy for their foliage alone. They are reputedly difficult to grow, requiring a rich, humusy medium, shade, and high humidity. They are all terrestrial, with fleshy stems and succulent leaves.

The type genus has now had its name changed from *Physurus* to *Erythrodes,* but the tribe is still called Physurus. Some of the species in the various genera have been moved from one to another, and one genus, *Haemaria,* now goes under the name of *Ludisia.*

Anoectochilus

Anoectochilus regalis has velvety leaves with a bright sheen, veined with gold. The flowers are white with the lip marvelously fringed. It comes from southern India and Ceylon.

A. roxburghii comes from the Himalayas and has green leaves with a gold zone in the center and red suffusion toward the margin.

A. sikkimensis, from Sikkim, has dark red leaves with gold veins on the upper surface. The flowers are olive-green and white.

Dossinia

The single species, *D. marmorata,* has almost round leaves of deep green with a network of gold. The flowers are pale brown with white or pink tips. It is native to Sarawak.

Erythrodes (Physurus)

Erythrodes querceticola has yellowish or brownish green leaves with prominent veins. The flowers are yellow-green or white, and have a spurred lip.

E. nobilis is called the "silver" orchid for its beautiful grey-green leaves with a dense network of silver on the surface, and satiny silver undersurface. The small white flowers have a fringed lip.

Goodyera

This genus has American representatives called "rattlesnake plantain" because of their mottled foliage. Some of the Asian species, however, deserve to be included in the group of "jewel" orchids.

Goodyera colorata has almost black leaves veined with red. It occurs in Java, Sumatra, and the Malay Peninsula.

G. hispida has leaves of green flushed with pink and with pink or white veins. It comes from a wide range from the Himalayas to the Malay Peninsula.

Ludisia (Haemaria)

Ludisia discolor has two forms, one that has leaves plain green on the upper surface, red-purple underneath, with a glistening sheen, and a variety *dawsoniana* whose leaves are dull red with veins of pale red or yellow on the surface, reddish on the underneath side. The white flowers have as a striking note the large yellow anther, which is twisted to one side, while the anchor-shaped lip is twisted in the opposite direction. This species is native to Burma.

Macodes

Macodes petola has heavy lengthwise veins and dense, very fine cross veins of gold. The undersurface of the leaves is purple. It occurs from Sumatra to the Philippines. The variety *javanica* has a network of silver veins and is native to Java. Both have red-brown flowers in which the lip is twisted.

M. sanderiana has lengthwise veins of light green, and from these come cross veins of gold. The flowers are brownish with a white lip. This is native to New Guinea.

Fig. 19-9 *Ludisia (Haemaria) discolor,* a jewel orchid whose leaves have a beautiful sheen and are veined with red-gold.

PLEUROTHALLIS TRIBE

There are kinds in this tribe whose flowers are large and spectacular. Others are so small that you have to use a hand lens, even a microscope, to see their parts; when some of these are studied, you find that they are even more fantastic than the large ones. A very large percentage of them, however, appeal only to true lovers of miniatures, for the chief attraction is their very minuteness. If you go collecting orchids in the wilds, you are bound to come home with many members of this tribe, unless you shun them completely. And among those you bring home there may be some quite rare and unusual. They look very much alike when not in flower, and you may pass up something fascinating because you may assume that you already have this one or that one.

Some genera have so many species, and so many of them are superficially alike, that it is difficult for an amateur to identify them (even, I think, for the expert). *Pleurothallis,* alone, is estimated to have a thousand species, *Stelis* five hundred, *Masdevallia* three hundred, some others close to a hundred, and the rest range on down to two. The plants have no pseudobulbs. The somewhat paddle-shaped leaves are carried on slender stems that are covered with bracts. In some, the stem is very short, so that it appears almost as if the flower stem comes from the root area, but actually it does come from the juncture of leaf with stem.

They range all over Mexico, Central America, and South America, living at elevations above 3,000 feet, for the most part, many of them above 8,000 feet. They are epiphytic, inhabiting the damp forests, and like to be kept damp in cultivation. Except for those from extremely high elevations, they can be grown in an intermediate house.

Masdevallia

Masdevallia is the truly showy member of the tribe, and some are among the most spectacular of orchids. The sepals form the conspicuous part of the flower. They are broadened at the base and are joined for part of their length to form a tube, with their tips often extended into tails. Within the tube are the very much reduced petals, lip, and column. A great many of them are from high elevations in the cloud forests and like a cool, gently humid atmosphere. Some come from lower down. If you do not have a cool house, try any that you may obtain in a cool spot in an intermediate house. They are quite susceptible to fungus rot at the point where the leaf joins the stem, so should be watered with care and treated with a fungicide occasionally. Everyone will have their favorites, so the list here will contain only a few distinctive kinds.

M. bella. This species has fragrant flowers whose extended tails give it a length of nine inches. The dorsal sepal is smaller than the laterals whose joined bases are three inches across. The flowers are pale yellow, spotted with purplish brown. It is native to Colombia.

M. chimaera. The name means an imaginary creature or creature of the fancy. This is one of the largest and most spectacular. The fleshy looking sepals are spreading, joined just enough to form a saucer, with tails extended to give it a length of eight or nine inches. They are light brown spotted with dull red and covered with shaggy, disorderly hairs. The reddish, fleshy, grooved lip looks like a piece of meat or fruit rind. This is a native of Colombia.

M. coccinea. This is a neat, velvety, dressy looking flower, two inches across, in shades of red, red-orange and cerise, with some paler forms. The dorsal sepal is narrow and has a stiff tail. The laterals are broadly oval, joined for half their length, and pointed at their tips. The tube is very small and narrow, scarcely revealing the other flower parts. The plant grows easily at cool temperatures, and gives a bouquet of flowers. The variety *harryana* is almost cerise in color. It occurs in Colombia.

M. erinacea (temporarily known as *M. horrida*). One of the miniatures, this is rare and very odd. The little rounded, bell-shaped flowers are greenish, covered with hairs. The short dangling tails have swollen, waxy, yellow tips that an insect could mistake for pollen or for nutritive particles. It is only an inch and a half tall, with grass-like leaves, and occurs in Costa Rica.

M. infracta. A true gem, this one has a tall slender, green, dorsal sepal and broader laterals whose flat, joined area is reddish, verging on purple-black, with a wonderful sheen. The shorter tails of the laterals are green. The tube is fairly open, allowing you to see the little white petals and orange lip. It occurs in Peru and Brazil.

M. minuta. This is another miniature, not as decorative as some, but interesting for its small stature of an inch and a half. The tiny flowers are white, bell-shaped, with the tips of the sepals mere points and yellow in color. It is native to Venezuela, British Guiana, Peru, and Surinam.

M. rolfeana and *M. reichenbachiana.* These are quite similar, both very fine, the former with a more open tube. They are fleshy, waxy, red shading to white inside, with short tails. Both are native to Costa Rica.

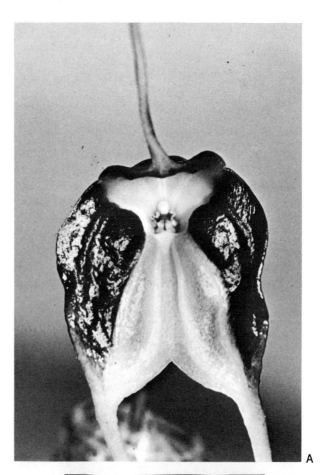

A

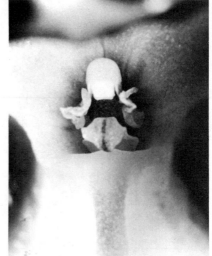

B

Fig. 19-10 *Masdevallia rolfeana,* has a more open tube, A, revealing the petals, lip and column, shown in detail in B.

Home Orchid Growing

M. tovarensis. With pure white flowers, several to a stem, this is one of the best known. The dorsal sepal is narrow and stands up straight, while the laterals are broad and are joined almost to the tip, leaving short slender tails that cross over each other. It occurs in Venezuela.

M. triaristella. Another miniature an inch and a half tall, with dark red, inch-long flowers. The joined area of the lateral sepals is rectangular in shape, with little hair-like tails that point out sideways. The base of the dorsal sepal forms a hood and its tail points upward. This is a native of Nicaragua, Costa Rica, and Colombia.

Pleurothallis

The ten species mentioned here represent but one percent of the total number in the genus, and can give only an inkling of the variety to be found. There are some that reach a height of two feet or more, but their flowers are no larger than those of smaller plants. Those chosen here are all moderate or miniature in size, kinds welcome to any collection.

P. alpina. The peculiar plant form of this and the similar species *sicaria* give them a special appeal. The leaf-bearing stems are fleshy and three-sided, becoming thicker toward the upper end where they merge almost imperceptibly into the leaf. (There is a faint line indicating the joining place.) The long, narrow leaf is fleshy and keeled. From the joining point arises a cluster of tiny, waxy, green flowers that become orange with age. *P. alpina* is native to Costa Rica and Panama; *sicaria* to Venezuela, Trinidad, Colombia, and Ecuador.

P. calyptrostele. One of the smallest of orchids, a miniature miniature, this species spreads like moss on the lower parts of trees in damp forests. The leaves on their tiny stems are barely half an inch tall, and the thread-like flower stems not much more than an inch; in fact, the flowers on their stems are about the size of the fruiting bodies of mosses. The flowers are greenish white, quite transparent, bell-shaped, three or four to a stem. The species occurs in Costa Rica and Panama.

P. cardiochila. This is an example of the many with beautiful heart-shaped leaves, among them plants large and small, with leaves slender or rounded. They make attractive pot plants, capable of competing with many house plants grown for foliage alone. Some have their flowers nestled at the base of the leaf, appearing one or two at a time, while others produce several long stems with many

Fig. 19-11 *Pleurothallis calyptrostele,* a mosslike plant with tiny greenish white flowers.

blooms. *P. cardiochila* has moderately broad leaves which, including their stems, reach a height of ten inches. Two or three plump little clamshell-shaped flowers appear at a time, which are yellow with a tiny red lip. This one comes from Panama. Almost a twin is *P. palliolata* from Costa Rica.

P. gelida. Typical of scores of species that bear fairly tall stems of many small, bell-shaped flowers, this one has flowers of yellowish white, the sepals hairy on the inner surface. It occurs in Florida, Mexico, Central and South America, and the West Indies.

P. immersa. A strange habit characterizes this species. Its flowering stem appears to emerge from the middle of the leaf. On examination it is found to grow up through a tightly closed channel along the mid-vein, which can be split open to reveal the stem—hence the name *immersa.* The flowers droop from the underside of the stem, a row of purple bells. This is found from Mexico to Colombia and Venezuela.

Fig. 19-12 *Pleurothallis gelida.* A hand lens is necessary to see the hairy surfaces of the quarter-inch flowers.

Fig. 19-13 *Pleurothallis immersa* has the curious habit of carrying the flower stem in a closed channel in the leaf.

P. listerophora. The one-eighth-inch flowers of this miniature look like the open jaws of some ferocious animal. They are reddish purple and covered with hairs. The plant is two to three inches tall, and occurs in Costa Rica.

Fig. 19-14 *Pleurothallis listerophora.* The tiny flowers present a ferocious aspect when enlarged from their one-eighth-inch size.

P. raymondi. The little flowers of this species have petals ending in tiny brown boxing gloves, which protrude from the flower in a threatening manner. The flower itself is yellow with brown spots. It is native to Venezuela and Colombia.

P. testaefolia. This beautiful little plant forms festoons of overlapping leaves hanging from a few basal roots. The leaves are spotted with purple-brown, and the spots become raised with age. The flower nestles close to the base of the leaf. It is purple-brown, also, and covered with hairs. This is native to Costa Rica, Venezuela, Colombia, and the West Indies.

Restrepia

This genus is included by some botanists in *Pleurothallis;* by others it is maintained separately. The flowers are quite insect-like, characterized by having the lateral sepals joined almost to their tips. The petals in some are thread-like, ending in little knobs. The plants have their stems enclosed in quite large, papery bracts. The flowers appear singly, usually on stems that are shorter than the leaves, but each growth produces a succession of flowers. Most species grow vigorously, soon filling a good-sized pot. (One tiny plant brought home from Costa Rica five years ago is now overflowing one five-inch pot and two three-inch pots.) There are a number of species, all delightful.

R. filamentosa. The little flowers of this species are slender, with red stripes on a cream base. They stand on wiry stems and jiggle in the breeze. The species is native to Costa Rica and Panama.

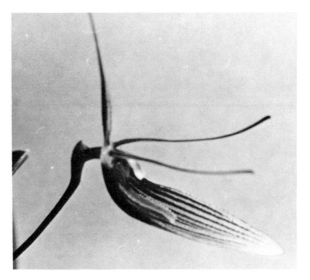

Fig. 19-15 *Restrepia filamentosa* has an insect like appearance.

R. xanthophthalma. These little flowers grow on very short stems, and are therefore held close to the leaf. They are cream or white, densely spotted with red. This one spreads from Mexico through Central America to Panama.

Stelis

In this genus more than in any other, admiration is gratefully extended to the taxonomists with the patience to identify and distinguish between the species! They have the tiniest of flowers in which it is usually impossible to distinguish the inner parts without a strong magnifying glass, even a microscope. The conspicuous part of the flower is the sepals, which are rounded and give an even three-pointed star shape. The extremely tiny and very fleshy petals and lip are scarcely more than little swellings within the center. The plants are indistinguishable from *Pleurothallis* when not in bloom. Even though their identification is frustrating, they make a delightful contribution to any orchid collection. Some of them have the habit of opening their flowers only during part of the day, or even at night, but the same flowers open and close over a long period.

S. argentata. This is a variable species which runs from reddish tones to silvery green, with the sepals plain on the edges or fringed with hairs. It is widespread, from Mexico to Panama and all of northern South America.

S. bidentata. The little red flowers of this species are usually open only at night. It is native to Mexico, Guatemala, and Honduras.

Fig. 19-17 *Barbosella caespitifica,* a rare miniature.

S. leucopogon. The largest of the genus, this has flowers of creamy white almost half an inch across, held on stems that can reach a foot in height. The flowers open and close each day. It occurs in Guatemala, Costa Rica, Nicaragua, and Panama.

Other Genera of the Pleurothallis Tribe

Barbosella is a rare genus of but few species. The plants have paddle-shaped leaves that arise almost without stems from the rhizome. The flowers have their long slender lateral sepals joined completely, while the slender dorsal one stands up straight. The petals are tiny, held horizontally, and the lip barely equals the column in length.

B. caespitifica. The plant is barely two inches tall, with a rose-colored flower a half-inch long. It is native to Ecuador.

B. cucullata. This one has flowers even more slender, with more pointed parts, held on stems twice the height of the leaves. They are pale

Fig. 19-16 *Stelis leucopogon,* the largest of the genus, has flowers almost half an inch wide.

yellow-green. The species is native to Venezuela, Colombia, Ecuador, and Peru.

Cryptophoranthus is a genus called "window orchids." The sepals are joined both at their base and tip, allowing only a small opening, a little slit, into the flower. The lateral sepals form a small chin with the column foot. The flowers look not unlike a bird head. *C. lepidotus* has dark purple flowers, about three-fourths inch long, produced in twos or threes at the base of the leaf. It is native to Panama. Other species range to Cuba and Jamaica.

Lepanthes is a genus of true miniatures. Some are barely a half inch tall while a few reach two or three inches. The flowers are extremely small and can best be appreciated with a hand lens. The stems are covered with funnel shaped bracts that are hairy on the edge. The tiny flower stem comes from the base of the leaf and lies on the back or front surface or stands out sideways. Over many months it produces a series of flowers, and when flowering is finished the little "herring-bone" stem can be seen to have given twenty or thirty flowers,

sometimes in the length of only an inch. The flowers are a sixteenth to three-sixteenths of an inch long, and are very complicated. The sepals are united for part of their length. The petals are bi-lobed and lie like wings on either side of the column. The column is bent downward and is surrounded by the fleshy side lobes of the lip that stand up around it like a collar. Underneath the tip of the column lies the mid-lobe of the lip, a tiny bearded tongue. The flowers are mostly yellow and red, bright little spots of color. The species range from Mexico through Central and South America, and are particularly numerous in the West Indies. Some of the 65 species are *chiriquensis* from Panama and Costa Rica, *obtusa* from Jamaica, *papyrophylla* from Venezuela, Colombia, and Ecuador, *minutipetala* from Peru, and *selenipetala* from the Dominican Republic. New species are constantly turning up. Most are from cool rainforests and like a cool, damp greenhouse. They flower all year around.

Lepanthopsis is related to *Lepanthes*. The plants are similar and equally small, and the flowers are even smaller. The flowers are produced in two

Fig. 19-18 LEFT, the tiny flower of *Lepanthes seleni-petala* lies on the back of its three-quarter inch leaf, a minute symphony of gold sepals, yellow petals, with a touch of red in the center. RIGHT, the even smaller flower of *Lepanthes obtusa* (enlarged here to a greater extent) has wine-red sepals and bright red petals and lip. It has a sparkling, crystalline texture.

ranks on tiny wiry stems that exceed the leaves. The petals are very tiny, simple, and rounded. The lip is also simple, round or somewhat oval, and flat. There are fewer species than of *Lepanthes,* scattered through countries in Central and South America and the Caribbean. One of the most widespread is *L. floripecten.*

Platystele contains several miniatures, among them one of the smallest of flowers. Let G. C. K. Dunsterville * describe one of them, *P. ornata,* a newly discovered species named by Leslie Garay. "Of all miniature orchid treasures, none probably combines smallness of size with greatness of beauty in higher degree than *P. ornata.* A twenty-fifth of an inch in size, each flower is perfect in form and holds itself proudly open—each one-eighth-inch flower spray is a fit corsage for the tiniest of fairies." The plants are an inch and a-quarter tall and live in the tallest of forest trees. The flowers have round sepals, slender, fringed petals, and a broad pointed lip, and are of deep purple with a tinge of green. This is a native of Venezuela. A few other species range from Mexico throughout Central America to Venezuela and Colombia, but none is common.

Scaphosepalum. The name means "bowl-sepals" from the fact that the lateral sepals are united into a bowl. This, plus the fact that the dorsal sepal is free, distinguishes this genus from *Masdevallia* botanically, but actually it looks very different from *Masdevallia.* The flowers are held horizontally, with the dorsal sepal underneath and the bowl curving over to form the top of the flower. The tiny lip and petals are held in the bottom of the bowl. The edge of the bowl (its tip) has a thickening that is different in each species. *S. verrucosum* from Venezuela has the added interest of a pair of tails spreading sideways from the tip. The flowers open one at a time on a wire-thin stem that lengthens through many months. They are an amazing combination of pink, brown, yellow, purple, and white, all in the same flower.

POLYSTACHYA TRIBE

There is great disparity in size and beauty among the genera of the Polystachya tribe, most of which would not casually be suspected of even being related.

* *Introduction to the World of Orchids,* G. C. K. Dunsterville, 1964. Doubleday and Co., Inc., New York.

Ansellia is a genus of continental Africa, of which there are two established species. One species has a great many varieties some of which Dr. Frank Piers feels should be elevated to species rank. Their nickname "leopard orchids" is descriptive of their tawny flowers marked with red or purple-brown spots. They are handsome plants in every way. Some are fragrant, others apparently not, except that some become fragrant when raised in greenhouses. The plants are from eighteen inches to two feet tall, with spindle-shaped, jointed pseudobulbs that bear several pairs of tough, slender leaves at the top. The roots grow in a mass that conceals the rhizome. The branched inflorescenses come from the upper leaf axils, and bear many fleshy, long-lasting two-inch flowers. All are winter flowering.

Ansellia africana. This species, from the dense rain forests and bush of tropical West Africa, has erect racemes of yellow-green flowers boldly marked with dark red-brown bars and spots. Its petals are somewhat broader than the sepals. The mid-lobe of the bright yellow lip is rounded, broader than long, curved back at the tip, and has two keels on its crest. Its range is from Ghana to Uganda.

A. gigantea. Ranging farther south, out of the tropical area, this species has paler, more delicately marked flowers. The mid-lobe of the lip is longer than that of *africana,* and the petals the same width as the sepals. It is native from Natal and Rhodesia to Mozambique.

A. nilotica. Considered by some a variety of *gigantea,* Dr. Piers prefers to consider it a separate species. In its turn it has a great number of varieties ranging through East Africa. In general it has larger, brighter flowers than the other species, with lighter colored markings that in some are quite dense, borne on a downward-arching raceme. The golden lip is oblong and bluntly pointed, with three small, well-developed keels. The somewhat smaller plants and more numerous flowers make it more horticulturally desirable. It grows from Tanzania to Mozambique. A variety *azanica* is more heavily marked and is limited to the East African Coast.

Galeandra is a genus of several species with sturdy pseudobulbs from six to twelve inches tall, bearing several narrow leaves. The flowers are showy, two to three inches across, with the sepals and petals spreading in a fan above the broad lip. The sides of the lip enfold the column, and it is spurred at its base. *G. baueri* has pseudobulbs ten inches tall, and a flower spike of twelve inches which produces flowers for more than one season. They are three inches across, fragrant and long lasting, yellow-brown with a purple and white lip. It spreads from Mexico through Central America and into northern South America. *G. devoniana* is a more compact species. Its three-inch flowers have sepals and petals of brownish purple margined with green, and a white lip striped with purple. The spur is green. This is native to Colombia, the Guianas, and Brazil. Both like a warm spot in a cattleya house.

Neobenthamia. The single, warm-growing species of this genus, *N. gracilis* is grown in many amateur collections although it has six-foot stems. A dense head of little white, tubular flowers is produced directly at the top of the stem. It is native to tropical and East Africa.

Polystachya has many charming little species, and some in which the plants are quite large although the flowers still small. Most of them are native to Africa, but some species occur in Southeast Asia and Indonesia and a few in this hemisphere. *P. affinis* has flat, round two-inch pseudobulbs and rather long leaves. The little hooded, upside down flowers are borne on a one-foot stem. They are a half-inch in diameter, bright yellow-orange, covered with hairs on the outside and striped with brown. This is native to Sierra Leone and the Belgian Congo. *P. pubescens* is a small plant with a stem of twenty or so three-fourths inch flowers that are bright yellow streaked with red. It occurs in Southeast Africa. *P. virginea,* the "snowdrop" orchid of Uganda, is a most delightful miniature with white flowers and a yellow lip.

SOBRALIA TRIBE

The Sobralia tribe is a group of terrestrial orchids which includes two genera, *Sobralia,* native to Mexico and tropical America, and *Calopogon,* native to North America.

Sobralia is a genus of reed-like plants, whose stems grow close together in thick, bushy clumps. They take up quite a bit of room in a greenhouse, but if space can be afforded they are worth growing for their handsome foliage and large, cattleya-like flowers. They vary in height from one to ten feet, and the flowers are from one and one-half to nine inches in diameter. The individual flowers do not last long,

but the plants produce a succession of blooms that give a continuous show.

Sobralia lacks pseudobulbs. The plants require a rich, porous compost, a mixture of loam, leaf mold, osmunda shreds, and cow manure. The pots should be large, with ample drainage to allow for the copious water supply they need during their growing period. During the winter they require somewhat less water, but should never be allowed to become dry at the roots. They may be grown out-of-doors in our subtropical states, but require cool greenhouse treatment farther north with abundant light.

S. fragrans. One of the smallest of the genus, this species has flowers of sulfur yellow, one and one-half to two inches in diameter, borne two to a stem. One of their charms is the fringed lip, which is decorated with many fringed crests. It occurs in Costa Rica, Panama, and neighboring countries.

S. leucoxantha. Plants three feet tall have a profusion of flowers. The sepals and petals are pure white. The gracefully waved lip is white, with its golden throat striped with brown. The species is native to Costa Rica and Panama; it flowers in August.

S. macrantha. Tall, handsome plants reach a height of from four to seven feet, with rose-purple flowers often nine inches in diameter. The sepals are slender and twisted, the petals broader and wavy. The front lobe of the lip is almost round, deep purple, and beautifully ruffled. The throat is whitish with several yellow ridges. This native of Mexico and Guatemala flowers from May to July.

S. xantholeuca. A huge species, this may not be adaptable to greenhouse culture, but can be grown in frost-free areas in full sun. Its tremendous pure yellow flowers are extremely beautiful, with a waxy sheen, and reach nine inches in diameter. They are rather longer lasting than other members of the genus. This species is native to Mexico.

Calopogon

Of the several species in this genus, the well-known *Calopogon pulchellus* grows from Newfoundland to Florida in bogs and moist meadows. It will do well in a shaded place in your garden in a porous soil, with ample water. The plants should not be disturbed very often, but offsets may be separated from the large clumps occasionally. The small offsets take several years to reach blooming size, whereas large clumps bought from collectors will flower immediately. *C. pulchellus* grows in clusters of corms, each producing a single, grassy leaf. The flower stem carries two to twelve attractive flowers that vary in color from magenta-crimson to white. The lip is uppermost in the flower and is bearded with white, yellow, or purple hairs.

ZYGOPETALUM TRIBE

As the amateur wends his way through the name changes in this tribe, he may become frustrated and confused. However, the completely charming and distinctive species are well worth growing whether he knows their right names or not! As he compares the various characteristics of the species, he can understand why the taxonomists are concerned with putting them in their proper places, and will be prepared for any future changes that may come.

Bollea

Beautiful plants have a fan of thin, somewhat keeled leaves and no pseudobulbs. The large, fragrant, waxy flowers are borne singly atop stems that are much shorter than the leaves. The fleshy, ribbed lip crest is prominently raised and covers a good portion of the lip.

B. coelestis. Supposedly blue, its color really tends toward blue violet, or even violet. The broad sepals and petals have white tips, then a broad band of intense violet, and this fades to pale violet at the base. They are somewhat wavy, with the tips of the dorsal sepal and petals sharply pointed. The column is broad, the same color as the dark band on the other parts. From under it comes the neat, rather small lip which is violet in the center, white on the sides, sharply contrasted with the large yellow crest. This species is from the high, cool, damp forests of Colombia, and requires cool treatment. It flowers in the summer.

B. hemixantha. The name means half-yellow. The dorsal sepal is white, tipped with yellow, the laterals are yellow at the tip and longitudinally half yellow and half white. The lip and callus are pure yellow. The huge column is almost as wide as the lip and has broad side wings, white tipped with purple. This is a warm-growing species from Venezuela, which flowers in the summer.

B. lalindei. These fleshy, very fragrant flowers have sepals and petals of pale rose shading into rose-red and tipped with cream yellow, and a large, bright yellow lip. The very broad column is rose colored. This is another cool-growing species from Colombia, and is summer blooming.

Chondrorhynca

This genus has been undergoing revision, with many species removed to *Cochleanthes*. The plants of this genus and of those once included in *Warscewiczella* are quite similar. They have no pseudobulbs; the leaves grow in a fan.

C. aromatica. This species came to me marked *Zygopetalum wendlandii.* It was once named *Z. aromaticum,* and the specific name is most apt. Alex Hawkes now includes this in *Chondrorhynca* as *C. aromatica.* The delightfully fragrant flowers have slender, waxy green sepals and petals, quite long and a bit twisted at the tips. The essentially oval lip is much ruffled and undulated, rose with a white border, spreading from a basal semi-circular crest that has vertical thickenings of purple. Native to Costa Rica and Panama, it blooms in the fall.

C. chestertoni has flowers three inches across, of a pale yellow-green. The sepals and petals are similar, but the lip is broad, yellow spotted with red, and decorated with fringe. The plant should be kept damp throughout the year, and likes a slightly shaded spot in the cattleya house. From Colombia, it is summer blooming.

C. rosea. The flowering stems are about half the length of the leaves, bearing one flower each. The three-inch flowers have green sepals with their edges rolled inward, and broader white petals that hold themselves forward over the lip. The quite tubular lip is green on its under surface, shading on the inside from pale yellow at the base with pink spots to yellow, then to dark pink, to white at the tip. A long, three-ridged crest is situated within the lip, and from it extend three lines. The species is native to Venezuela and requires intermediate greenhouse temperatures.

Cochleanthes

This genus has plants quite similar to those of *Chondrorhynca,* and the flowers are, to the amateur eye at least, also quite similar.

C. discolor. Long known as *Warscewiczella discolor,* this is one of the few orchids to approach blue in some of its color phases. The sepals are pale creamy green; the dorsal one stands more or less upright, the laterals extend back along the ovary. The rich velvety lip is tubular, with the sides enfolding the column and the outer lobe spreading, sometimes a definite blue-violet, sometimes rich red-violet, but always more deeply colored within. The petals hold themselves forward parallel to the lip, and are colored like it on their inner surfaces,

Fig. 19-19 *Cochleanthes discolor* has single flowers on short stems crowded at the base of the leaves. They are creamy green with the lip shading to deep blue.

paler on the outer. The crest is a bright, yellow-toothed callus whose free edge spreads out over the base of the lip. The species flowers from spring to fall and is native to Cuba, Costa Rica, and Panama.

C. marginata. This beautiful pink flower has something of a cattleya shape since its petals spread wide and its sepals are not bent back. The sepals and petals are light pink, the ruffled outer margin of the lip a darker pink, and the inner portion white with a dark pink center. The basal callus is white, as is the column. Native to Colombia, Venezuela, and Ecuador, it grows both in trees and in the fluffy humus on the ground.

Colax

One lovely member of this genus, which has but two or three species, is *C. jugosus.* It has very round, fleshy, long-lasting flowers that are between two and three inches in diameter. The rounded sepals are pure white or ivory, broader than the petals. The petals are white, transversely striped with red or red-violet. The rounded lip and its small side lobes are also white, striped with a bluish violet, as is the column. This native of southern Brazil flowers in the spring.

Huntleya

Among the most striking of orchids, the large, handsome flowers are vivid in color and have a varnished appearance. The plants have a fan of broadly keeled leaves, up to a dozen to a growth, and are without pseudobulbs. One species is very well known, and several others are quite rare.

H. meleagris. It is now accepted that the species *burtii* is synonymous with *meleagris.* This flower is a wide open star with the tapered points of the sepals and petals bent backward. The surface is finely "quilted" and very shiny. The outer two thirds of the sepals and petals is golden brown, and the inner third is white, with a narrow band of yellow in between. At the base of the petals is a splash of dark red with fine lines extending out, almost like a comb. The lip is small, of velvety texture, with a narrow white base and a rounded outer portion of dull red. The crest is a semi-circle of short, white tail-like projections. The large, hooded column is white with a touch of red on its side wings. Native to Costa Rica, Panama, northern South America, and Trinidad, it flowers in the spring.

Among the rare species is *H. lucida,* a beautiful chestnut-brown and white flower. The dark inner portion of the sepals and petals is divided from the less intensely colored outer portion by a yellow-green line. It was discovered long ago but recently found in a restricted area of Venezuela by G. C. K. Dunsterville. *H. fasciata,* a new species from Panama, was named by J. A. Fowlie. It has the outer portion of its yellow-green sepals and petals barred with red-brown, the inner part reddish tan.

Kefersteinia

This genus of small plants has delicate looking flowers, some quite translucent in texture, but they are long lasting nevertheless.

K. graminea. The two-inch flowers are an almost transparent greenish ivory, with slender oval sepals

Fig. 19-20 *Huntleya meleagris,* a bold and striking flower.

Home Orchid Growing

and petals, widespreading, and of about equal size. They are decorated with dotted lines of red over their entire surface. The outer lobe of the lip spreads forward from the basal part that holds itself in an upturned crescent. Within the basal part lies a callus with its two sides sharply upturned. The lip is covered with dotted lines of dark maroon which coalesce in the center. This species is native to Venezuela, Colombia and Ecuador.

K. sanguinolenta. This species has pale green flowers dotted with purple. Its lip is quite stiff at the base and cupped, giving the typical crescent view from the front. The outer portion bends down abruptly and its margin is very wavy and toothed. The markings on the lip are of heavy purple blotches mixed with fine dots, and it has a fine down on its surface. The crest consists of two forward projecting teeth. The species occurs in Ecuador and Venezuela.

K. tolimensis. Most dainty and transparent of all, the flowers are shaped like the preceding, but the lip edge is very much fringed or lacerated. The green sepals and petals are spotted with fine dots of purple which become blotches toward the base. The lip is very heavily dotted with purple, almost solid purple in the center. The callus is a square thickening divided into two parts in the front. The species occurs in Venezuela, Colombia, and Ecuador.

Menadenium

There may be more than one species in this genus, but the one that is best known is indeed lovely. *M. labiosum* has sepals and petals softly shaded brown over green, or maroon over green, and their tapering points curve backward. The petals are held upright, sometimes with their tips crossed. The full, spreading lip is white with pink lines radiating from a semi-circular erect pink crest at its base. The column is a most striking feature, with its long pointed beak and side wings that hang down like the sides of a bonnet. It is native to Venezuela, northern Brazil, and the Guianas, and is summer flowering. The plant is of modest size, with oval pseudobulbs and two rather thin leaves.

Pescatoria

Vegetatively, this genus is indistinguishable from many others of this tribe. The flowers are quite distinctive, very waxy and fragrant, with an unusually large, ridged callus forming a large portion of

Fig. 19-21 *Pescatoria cerina,* white, with a tucked bib of yellow.

the lip. The sepals and petals are oval, rounded and somewhat wavy at the tip.

P. cerina. This pure white flower has such a large lip callus that it appears to have a tucked bib. The ridges of the yellow callus are carried on in lines down the front of the lip, which is also yellow. The corners of the basal part of the lip turn up around the column. This fall- and spring-flowering species occurs in Costa Rica and Panama.

P. dayana. This species has its sepals and petals tipped with green. The lip turns up and out at the end, rather than down as in *cerina.* It is flushed with violet and has rays of violet extending from the base of the very large, red-violet callus. It is native to Colombia and blooms in the winter and spring.

P. klabochorum. The flower is shaped very much like the preceding species. The white sepals and petals are tipped with chocolate-purple. The lip is also white, but is completely covered with rows of purple papillae. The callus is yellow, ridged with nineteen purple lines. From Colombia and Ecuador, it flowers in the summer.

Promenaea

The plants of this genus are miniatures, with pseudobulbs about an inch tall and leaves from two to four inches. They are all from Brazil and are tender and rather warm growing. They are rare in this country at present. The flowers are two inches in diameter, with broad, spreading sepals and petals, and a longish oval lip that has two tall side lobes.

P. stapelioides. The flowers are greenish yellow, densely barred and spotted with purple, the lip almost solid purple.

P. xanthina. This one has flowers of yellow-gold which are fragrant and heavy in substance. The mid-lobe of the lip is yellow, with the side lobes dotted with red.

P. Crawshayana. This is a hybrid between the above species. The flowers are yellow-green, the sepals with but few spots, the petals lightly spotted with red. The spots on the lip become more dense toward the center and cover the side lobes and the tall, semi-circular crest. It blooms in the spring, and is completely delightful.

Zygopetalum

The large pseudobulbous plants, with their broad, heavy, many-veined leaves and bold, strikingly marked flowers well equip this species to be the "granddaddy" of the tribe.

Z. crinitum (by some considered synonymous with *mackayi*). This species has pseudobulbs to four inches tall and leaves eighteen inches long. The flower spike holds five to ten three-inch flowers that are waxy, fragrant, and richly colored. The sepals and petals form a fan, the lateral sepals

Fig. 19-23 *Zygopetalum intermedium,* a stunning and very fragrant species. (*Courtesy Jack Sweet*)

being held horizontally, and are of a green ground color heavily barred with greenish brown. Against this fan stands the lurid violet-striped lip, and the almost reptilian column. Flowering in the fall, it comes from Brazil.

Z. grandiflorum. A most unusual flower, this species has slender, tapering sepals and petals whose points curve backward, the lateral sepals actually flaring sideways. The lip is broad at the base, pointed at the outer end, with tall fin-like side lobes, all fringed at the edge. The whole flower is brightly striped with red, the sepals and petals on a green ground, the lip on white. This species is from Guatemala.

Z. intermedium. Best known of the genus, although usually known by the wrong name, *Z. makayi,* for these two are very much alike. Both have the sepals and petals green, blotched with brown, and a broad white lip veined with branching lines of purple. The chief differences are that in *intermedium* the purple lip lines are actually rows of downy hairs, while the lip of *makayi* is smooth, and the petals of *intermedium* about equal the sepals in length, while those of *mackayi* are shorter. Both are from Brazil, and both are sweetly fragrant and winter flowering.

Fig. 19-22 *Promenaea* Crawshayana, a small plant with quite bold flowers.

Home Orchid Growing

20

COLLECTORS' ITEMS CONTINUED

BULBOPHYLLUM

This huge genus spreads over all the tropical world, but is most heavily concentrated in Africa and Asia and outlying areas. There are among the species some of the most fantastic of orchids, some large, many small, and many with startling details best appreciated with a magnifying glass. Some are fragrant, some not so, and some produce the most foetid odors imaginable. (One to stay away from is *B. beccarii,* which is not only too large for a greenhouse since it climbs a tree like a huge serpent, but its extremely tiny flowers give off an overpowering stench.) Most of them are delightful for their curious flowers. From among the over two thousand species it is possible to describe but a few. However, almost any that come to your hand will prove oddities worth owning.

B. barbigerum. The tiny bearded flowers of this species give it its name. The plant is four inches tall, with a fat pseudobulb having a single leaf. The one-inch flowers would be most inconspicuous, with their slender, dull purple sepals and greatly reduced petals, were if not for the mass of reddish hair thrust out into the breeze by the finger-like lip. These hairs are moved by the merest breath of air, and some are thickened at the end as if to give added motion. The flowers are held on an upright spike, about fifteen or more opening in succession. They are said to have an unpleasant

odor, but apparently this is mild. The species is native to West Africa and flowers in summer.

B. gravidum. A delightful species that produces more than a hundred tiny flowers, a few at a time, from a gradually lengthening spike. The flowers are one-third inch across, very waxy, their sepals and petals triangular, green in color. The tongue-shaped lip is red and is covered with hairs. It jiggles in the slightest breeze and is counterbalanced. The species is found in Malawi and in the West Camaroons and Fernando Poo—the whole continent in between the two locations!

B. lobbii. One of the largest of the genus, this one has spectacular flowers of yellow-gold with tones of purple or red, a sweet fragrance, and a unique shape. The two-inch, egg-shaped pseudobulbs bear a single leaf ten inches tall. Each flower is held on its own stem which is either upright or arching. The tall, narrowly triangular dorsal sepals stand up straight, the lateral ones bend upward like knees. The petals curve out sideways, and the small, tongue-like tip curves forward. The lip is mobile, and like most of this type is counterbalanced so that a little weight, as of an insect, on it at a certain point causes it to tip inward. It comes from the warm tropics of Thailand, Sumatra, Java, Borneo, and the Malay Peninsula, and flowers from late spring to summer.

B. medusae. Perhaps one of the most charming is this species, whose dense heads of straw-colored flowers have their lateral sepals elongated into five-inch threads, giving the effect of very delicate pompoms. They are often spotted with pink. The rest of the flower is less than half an inch long. *B. longissimum* has flowers with even longer sepals, but fewer in a head. *B. medusae* comes from the Malay Peninsula, Sumatra, and Borneo; *longissimum* from Thailand.

B. pachyrrhachis and *brachteolatum*. These might appeal to those who care for the unusual without demanding that they be pretty. Both have tiny flowers inserted on a very fat, cylindrical rachis, almost hidden under their bracts. *B. pachyrrhachis* is from Mexico, Central America, and the West Indies; *brachteolatum*, from Venezuela and the Guianas.

B. picturatum. One of a group long known as *Cirrhopetalum*, this and others of that genus are now included in *Bulbophyllum*. This species has its lateral sepals elongated and broadened, and folded together to look something like a cloak. The tiny dorsal sepal resembles a Chinese hat and has a little waving knobbed hair at its tip. The petals are very much reduced, and are red, as is the tiny, mobile lip. The other flower parts are light brown, somewhat spotted with red. Similar to this species are *cumingii*, which has a fan of rose and white flowers with flatter elongated lateral sepals and fringed dorsal sepal and petals, and *ornatissimum*, whose elongated sepals are much twisted and whose dorsal sepal and petals end in a burst of bristles. *B. picturatum* and *ornatissimum* are from the Himalayas, and *cumingii* from the Philippines.

B. purpureorhachis. A most peculiar habit characterizes this and a number of other species. The flowers are borne in a line down the center of a flat, fleshy rachis, inserted directly on its surface on both sides. The rachis is green spotted with purple, and the half-inch flowers are brown, hairy on the outside, with a tiny, yellow-brown, mobile lip. Other species with this type of rachis are *leucorhachis*, *lindleyi*, *maximum*, and *makakense*, a new species. All are African.

B. reticulatum. One of the larger species, it is a beautiful plant with broad leaves having a network of light green veins on dark green. The flowers are three inches in diameter, and are fleshy and fragrant, produced two to a stem. They are quite similar in shape to *lobbii*, and are white striped with purple. The species occurs in Borneo.

CAMPYLOCENTRUM AND POLYRRHIZA

Leafless plants have a peculiar fascination, for the roots have taken over the process of photosynthesis. Plants in both *Campylocentrum* and *Polyrrhiza* have masses of roots that cling to a branch, and an inconspicuous very small woody stem from which the flowers arise. The former also has species with leaves. The leafless ones, e.g. *Campylocentrum pachyrrhizum* and *porrectum*, give many stems of tiny, yellow-green, spurred flowers. They range natively from Florida through some of the Caribbean islands into Central and South America. *Polyrrhiza funalis* and *lindeni* have large flowers, one or two to a stem. *P. lindeni* is the better known for its five-inch, fragrant, ghost-like greenish white flower that hangs apparently in mid-air. The tails on its lip look like a pair of legs bent at the knee. It comes from Florida and Cuba. Members of both genera are grown successfully by some amateurs who say it is not difficult. The roots are tied gently to a small bare log by many wrappings of soft string, and new roots soon take hold. They must be kept damp by frequent soakings and a humid atmosphere, well shaded in an intermediate or warm greenhouse. *Dendrophylax*, *Microcoelia*, and *Taeniophyllum* are other leafless genera.

COELIA

The best known of this genus is *Coelia triptera*, which produces a brush-like cluster of small white, very fragrant flowers. The plants have a rounded pseudobulb which bears two or three tall, veined leaves. They like a cool spot in the cattleya house. It is native to Mexico, Guatemala, and the West Indies.

Fig. 20-1 *Bulbophyllum picturatum* gives a wheel of little cloaked figures.

Fig. 20-2 *Bulbophyllum gravidum* from Malawi.
A. Up to ten flowers are open at a time on a stem that produces over a hundred through several months.
B. The flower is waxy, green except for the red lip which is edged with golden hairs. The little counterbalanced lips jiggle in the slightest breeze. It was 4½ months from the time this was collected until it reached Wyoming by surface freight.

A

B

CYRTOPODIUM

This genus includes the famous "cigar orchid" of Florida, *Cyrtopodium punctatum,* which also has the nicknames "bee swarm orchid" and "cowhorn orchid." The curved, pointed pseudobulbs grow up to three feet tall, with leaves up to two feet long. In nature they develop into heavy masses of pseudobulbs. The flower spike is up to five feet tall, and bears a showy display of bright yellow flowers spotted with crimson. This species occurs from Florida to South America. The species *C. andersonii* has been known to produce over a hundred flowers to the spike. These epiphytes can be grown in pots with generous applications of fertilizer.

DICHAEA

For sheer beauty of plant form, *Dichaea* is unexcelled. Festoons of gently undulant stems hang from a piece of driftwood or spread in a circular mass over a flat or pot, with closely alternate little leaves. The flowers are tiny, globe-shaped, crystalline in texture. *Dichaea muricata* has very neat, fleshy stems and leaves, and little one-half inch greenish, purple-spotted flowers. *D. panamensis* is more delicate, with the stems more winding. *D. glauca* is a much larger plant, one that grows upright if potted. The leaves are covered with a silvery bloom, and the fragrant, heavy-textured, three-fourths inch flowers are greyish white with light lavender or yellow spots. All range natively through most of Central America and Mexico.

DISA

The "Pride of Table Mountain," *Disa uniflora,* is a magnificent orchid native to Table Mountain and surrounding areas of the Cape Peninsula, South Africa. There are other species there and elsewhere in Africa, but *D. uniflora* is the best known and most handsome. Its four-inch flowers are oddly constructed. The sepals are the conspicuous parts; the vivid red or red-orange dorsal sepal, veined with a darker shade, stands upright, while the broad laterals spread sideways, solid red in color. The lip is a mere strap between the laterals, and the tiny petals stand together in the center of the dorsal. Cultivation is difficult, and raising the plants from seed requires much care. We will not go into this, for if you wish to try these plants it would be best

A

B

Fig. 20-3 *Dichaea muricata.*
A. The plant is beautiful in itself, as it branches and clambers on a hanging mount.
B. Each flower is a jewel with crystalline texture, green with purple spots.

to get directions from experts. They are grown at Longwood Gardens, among the few places in this country. The plants are protected in Africa and exportation prohibited. Seed can occasionally be obtained.

EULOPHIELLA

The warmth-loving species of this genus come from the island of Madagascar. Two species of the four are pretty and worth growing. *Eulophiella elizabethae* has pseudobulbs six inches tall and several narrow plicate leaves, with the flower stem from the base of the plant. The one-and-a-half inch blooms are waxy, fragrant, sweetly rounded, white with a touch of rose. *E. roempleriana* has large flowers on a much heavier plant. They are four inches across, pink with a violet-rose lip. A hybrid between the two is *E.* Rolfei. They like warm conditions, shade, and plenty of water in a well-drained medium.

HARAËLLA

This is a genus of almost-miniature vanda-like plants which have charming flowers. There are few species, perhaps only two. *Haraëlla odorata* bears four or five pair of leaves less than three inches long. The short flower stem holds several flowers in succession, with usually two open at once. The flowers are greenish yellow with small sepals and petals and a large lip. The latter is fiddle-shaped, fringed, and with a large purple patch in the center that sometimes has a bug-like shape. It occurs in Formosa and flowers several times a year under intermediate conditions.

HELCIA

Helcia sanguinolenta is a delightful small plant with large flowers of reptilian coloring and markings. The two-inch, dull green pseudobulbs are somewhat curved and compressed, and bear broad,

Fig. 20-4 *Helcia sanguinolenta,* a flower with reptilian markings.

thin leathery leaves about four inches long. The single flowers come on short stems. The slender, oval sepals and petals are greenish with bars and blotches of light brown neatly outlined in red. The large, ruffled lip is white with a few red lines. A native of Ecuador, it comes from high elevations and likes a cool greenhouse.

HEXISEA

An odd habit is peculiar to this genus and one or two others, that of developing its pseudobulbs one on top of another, in a continuous chain. From the top of each new growth comes a burst of small flowers. In *Hexisea bidentata* the little tulip-shaped blooms are of the brightest scarlet. The sepals and petals are free, the lip adnate to the column for part of its length. This genus is thought to be related in some way to the Cattleya tribe. It ranges natively from Mexico to northern South America.

ISOCHILUS

Isochilus is lovely for itself alone, with its densely tufted, wiry stems loosely clothed with slender, flat leaves. It is very pretty in flower, too, for then the tip of each stem bears a short raceme of tiny rosy flowers. They are tubular, with the points of the sepals, petals, and lip spreading in star-like fashion. There are two species very much alike, *I. linearis* and *major.* They grow easily and spread rapidly so that one soon has a showy plant. Native to Mexico and Central America, the former spreads to Cuba and Argentina, the latter to Jamaica.

LEOCHILUS AND MESOSPINIDIUM

Leochilus is a genus of miniatures, and *Mesospinidium* of almost equally small plants. Both are felt to be related to the Oncidium tribe although no hybrids have as yet been made. They have small, somewhat compressed pseudobulbs and short, thin leathery leaves. The little flowering stems arch gracefully to about the height of the leaves, sometimes a bit more, and bear several half-inch flowers. In both, the flowers are greenish with a white or cream lip, the sepals and petals spotted rather densely with brown, the lip only sparsely marked. In *Leochilus labiatus,* the lateral sepals are free spreading except right at the base, and the lip is a rather long rectangle with a point at the tip, a fat basal callus, and hairs at the base of the column. It is a native of Guatemala, Honduras, Costa Rica, Venezuela, Trinidad, and the West Indies. In

Fig. 20-5 LEFT, *Leochilus labiatus*, a curious little flower from a miniature plant. RIGHT, *Mesospinidium warscewiczii*, another miniature.

Mesospinidium warscewiczii the lateral sepals are united almost to their tips, and are more conspicuous than the small, fleshy, bumpy lip that is held out horizontally. This one is native to Costa Rica and Panama.

LOCKHARTIA

Lockhartia is a genus of beautiful plants which need not bloom to be enjoyed, but which do flower most generously and easily. The foot-tall stems are clothed by little clasping leaves (equitant), which give a braided effect. From the upper leaf axils come clusters of very small and dainty yellow flowers, mottled with red or brown after the manner of *Oncidium,* to which genus they are somewhat related. The little rounded sepals are held back to back above the rest of the flower; the petals, usually folded in half lengthwise, curve upward; and the complicated lip hangs down. The lip in most species has two long side lobes which curve together like arms, a very warty crest vividly marked with brown or red, and a flaring mid-lobe. They vary in size from a half-inch to an inch according to the species. *L. amoena* is one of the larger ones, both as to breadth of leafy stem and

size of flowers, the blooms reaching almost an inch in length. The rounded heart-shaped bracts on the flower stems are especially large in this species, and very decorative. It is native to Costa Rica and Panama. *L. micrantha* is one of the smaller species, with flowers barely half an inch long. It occurs from Nicaragua to Surinam. *L. acuta* has flowers not nearly so ruffly as the others, in fact, quite like some of the equitant oncidiums. It comes from Panama, Colombia, Venezuela, and Trinidad.

MEIRACYLLIUM

Two miniature species belong to the rare genus *Meiracyllium*. Both are rambling little plants without pseudobulbs and with fleshy, rounded leaves not more than two inches tall. Close to the leaf comes a short spray of one-inch dark purplish red flowers. They have spreading sepals and petals and a cup-shaped lip. *M. trinasutum* comes from Mexico and Guatemala; *M. wendlandii* from Mexico, Guatemala, and El Salvador.

MICROCOELIA

Another of the leafless kinds, this little African native produces many stems of tiny, one-eighth inch

Home Orchid Growing

Fig. 20-6 *Lockhartia amoena.*
A. Clusters of complicated little oncidium-like flowers come from the tips of stems clothed with "braided" leaves.
B. Closeup of a single flower.

long flowers that are pure white. The species *M. guyoniana* comes from Zambia, the Belgian Congo, and Angola; *M. physophora* from Zanzibar and Madagascar.

MORMOLYCA

Of the few species in this genus, *Mormolyca ringens* is very common from Mexico to Costa Rica, but *M. peruviana* is rare even in its home country of Peru. The former is the more robust, free-growing plant, and produces flowers over a long period; the latter is smaller, grows slowly, but has much handsomer flowers. The lip in both is reminiscent of the dorsal surface of a bee. This is not so easy to see in *ringens,* but in *peruviana* the velvety surface has just the right markings and shape to resemble a large bee. They are indeed attractive to certain bees for this very reason, the

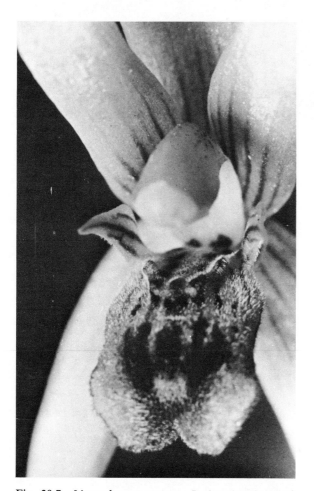

Fig. 20-7 *Mormolyca peruviana.* It doesn't take much imagination to see the lip as a bee with its head buried deep in the flower. This one actually deceives the male bee into thinking the flower is a female bee, and is pollinated by the act of pseudocopulation.

male being sufficiently deceived to attempt copulation with what he thinks is a female of his species. In so doing he removes the pollinia from one flower and places them on another.

M. ringens is about a foot tall with one-inch, round, sharply edged pseudobulbs and slender leaves. Its one-inch flowers are produced singly on six-inch stems, many over a long period. *M. peruviana* is not much over two inches tall, with four-edged pseudobulbs and stiff, keeled leaves. Its flowers are also about an inch long, but have broader parts and are more substantial, with a larger, more furry lip. They come on single stems, once a year in the fall.

NOTYLIA

The tiniest of feathery flowers grace this genus of miniatures. The largest flowers are three-fourths inch in diameter, and some are less than a quarter of an inch. Mrs. G. C. K. Dunsterville found a minute species, later named after her, *Notylia norae,* the mature plant of which was only a quarter of an inch high, with a flower stem an inch long, bearing a pair of quarter-inch flowers. Most species have a cluster or a long chain of the delicate blooms. They have slender or oval sepals and petals, the lateral sepals being joined for part of their length, and a sharply triangular, trowel-shaped lip attached by a stalk. The pollinia lie back on the top of the column, and have an unusually long stipe. *N. peruviana* has a pendant chain of forty or more flowers from a six-inch plant, and comes from Peru, Bolivia, and Venezuela. *N. incurva* has somewhat larger flowers in a shorter and denser spray and is native to Trinidad and Venezuela. *N. nana,* also from Venezuela and Trinidad, is an inch and a half tall, with a chain of blooms longer than the plant. *N. barkeri* is a bit larger plant, with a foot-long stem of flowers that reach a half inch in size. It comes from Mexico and Central America. *N. bicolor,* another Mexican and Central American species, is a three-inch plant with a four-inch flower spray and three-fourths-inch flowers. The flowers in the various species range from white to pale pink and lavender, sometimes delicately spotted.

OBERONIA

Speaking of fairies, it seems that there once was a genus named *Titania,* which now appears to have been combined with *Oberonia.* It must have been done according to botanical priority, but it seems

Home Orchid Growing

more than coincidental that two genera should have been named after the King and Queen of the fairies, and that in the subsequent marriage it was the name of the King that prevailed. *Oberonia* is a genus of small plants with equitant leaves and a tall spike of extremely small flowers, densely packed like the spike of a plantain. The species has a variety of shapes; some are like the little equitant oncidiums and others more like lockhartias. They range natively from the Himalayas through the Malay Peninsula to the Fiji islands. *O. anceps* is one of those with a tallish stem and "braided" leaves. Its flowers are yellow to orange, and it occurs from Sumatra to the Philippines. *O. lunata* is one with a low fan and pink to brownish flowers and is native to Java and India. A form with leaves similar to those of iris and with greenish flowers is *iridifolia,* from the Himalayas and Malaysia.

ORNITHOCEPHALUS AND ITS RELATIVES

Ornithocephalus is the very popular "bird head" orchid, named so because the long beaked column looks like the head of a bird. In fact, depending on the species, you can almost say what kind of a bird it is, a hummingbird or a duck, for instance—that is, if you look with a magnifying glass. The dwarf plants have equitant leaves, arranged in a fan, and have dense little sprays of white or greenish quarter-inch flowers. The sepals and petals are rounded; the lip sometimes round, sometimes tongue or strap shaped, with a fleshy crest. There are subtle differences among the species as to shape of leaves, appearance of the fan, and details of the flowers. *O. bicornis,* whose flowers are fuzzy on the outside, has a long narrow lip with two horns from the crest at its base. It occurs from Guatemala to Panama. *O. gladiatus* has quite flat, open flowers with smooth parts, and a hummingbird beak. It ranges from Mexico through Central and most of South America and many of the Caribbean Islands. *O. cochleariformis,* a native of Panama, has shell-shaped sepals and petals that are fuzzy on the back and are keeled and fringed. The lip is round, curved in on the sides and the end. Its beaked column looks like the head of a duck. *O. inflexus* and *iridifolius* are other species, native to Mexico and parts of Central America.

Dipteranthus, one of the relatives of *Ornithocephalus,* consists of dwarf Brazilian plants with little round pseudobulbs and sprays of tiny, very complicated flowers. *Zygostates* has a fan of leaves rounded at the tip and sprays of delicately formed flowers.

PINELIA AND PYGMAEORCHIS

Pinelia has among the smallest orchids known. In *P. alticola,* a newly discovered species from Venezuela, leaf and pseudobulb are together one-fourth inch tall, and the thread-like stem and minute flower attain a height of three-fourths inch. The flowers are white suffused with maroon.

Pygmaeorchis is, as its name implies, another miniature. *P. brasiliensis* is about half an inch tall, with a fat, round pseudobulb. The flower nestles between the paired leaves, its monstrously fuzzy ovary half the size of the flower itself. This one is from Brazil.

SCAPHYGLOTTIS

Scaphyglottis has the habit of growing one pseudobulb on top of another, and of branching frequently when two are produced instead of one. The tiny flowers are translucent, with something of a cattleya shape. There are many species throughout Central and South America. Most of them have pseudobulbs about two inches long, which, when built on top of each other, can make plants eight or ten inches tall. Others are quite tiny. The flowers are very small, produced in fascicles on short stems from the base of a pseudobulb, and are translucent, ranging in color from greenish to pinkish. *S. cuneata* is a common species spreading through all of Central America, south to Brazil and Bolivia, and to the West Indies. *S. livida* comes from Mexico and Central America.

SIGMATOSTALIX

Sigmatostalix has dwarf plants of great charm. They have tiny pseudobulbs each bearing two or more leaves. The whole plant is about four inches tall. The delicate flower spikes come from the base of the pseudobulbs, and hold a score or so jaunty flowers less than one-quarter inch long. The most outstanding feature of the flower is the long column which is conspicuous in a flower so small, and gives it somewhat the appearance of a miniature cycnoches. In some species the lip is attached by a long claw, giving it the shape of a broad trowel with a handle. In others the lip is "sessile" that is, it has no claw. Many of the species produce a second and third crop of flowers on the same stem. *S. guatemalensis* has green sepals and petals, a lip

A

B

C

Fig. 20-8 *Sigmatosalix*, a genus of miniatures, reveals charming details under a hand lens.
A, *Sigmatostalix racemifera* still perched on the twig on which it lived in the tropics.
B, Closeup of a single flower. The lip is sessile.
C, *Sigmatostalix guatemalensis*, has bright little flowers. The lip is attached by a long claw.

that is long-clawed, brown on the basal half, yellow on the outer part, and a white column striped with red and topped by a bright yellow anther. It occurs in Mexico, Guatemala, Costa Rica, and Panama. In *S. racemifera* the lip is without a claw, and the flowers are very tiny. They are pale translucent pink with a crystalline texture. The spreading portion of the lip is slightly fringed and is spotted with orange. The fleshy, waxy crest is modeled into parallel lobes upturned at the tip, and is bright orange on top. It is native to Panama.

STENIA

Stenia is a rather rare genus of two, possibly three, species, but it makes a choice addition to a collection because of its large flowers produced by a small plant. The leafy plants have very tiny pseudobulbs, or none at all, and produce two-and-

a-half inch, round, almost translucent flowers on single stems. The petals and sepals are broadly oval, pointed at the tips, and spread evenly. The lip is saccate, pinched in the middle. *S. pallida* has greenish white sepals and petals, and a lip that grades from white to yellow, with yellow-green side lobes and a many-toothed callus. It occurs in British Guiana, Venezuela, and Trinidad. *S. guttata* is very much speckled with purple on a straw-colored ground and is native to Peru.

TELIPOGON

Telipogon is a genus of utterly charming little epiphytes that one should know about even if, as it is said, they are difficult to grow, even to bring into the country in a living condition. The flowers are perfect triangles, with the lip almost identical in shape and coloring to the triangular petals. At

Home Orchid Growing

first glance, it is difficult to tell which is the lip, but it is marked by a band of deeper color at its base and is slightly larger. The column has a nose-like beak and is decorated with bristly hairs which remind human beings of insects, although it is not known whether insects see the resemblance. The inconspicuous sepals lie behind the other parts. Colors shade from yellow and green to brownish tones, and the petals and lip are netted and veined with brown or purple. The shape and the netting make the flowers most eye-catching. The species occur in Costa Rica and Panama and spread through northern South America, always at high elevations in the cool, misty cloud forests. There are fifty some species, many with three-inch flowers, but most of them smaller, borne several to a stem arising from a tiny pseudobulbless plant. *T. vargasii, hercules, klotzschianus, gnomus,* and *radiatus* are among the large ones, but are by no means all that are attractive.

TRICHOCEROS

The incredible "fly" orchids, *Trichoceros,* have flowers that look so much like the female of certain species of fly that the male flies attempt to mate with them, an activity called pseudocopulation. Even human beings are deceived, and many visitors to greenhouses where they are in flower will comment "these flowers have bugs on them." They make marvelous conversation pieces; and since they produce flowers through many months, they can be shown to all comers. The plants are small, with tiny pseudobulbs on top of which is an aborted leaf, a mere point. The shiny, rigid leaves come from the base of the pseudobulbs, as does the tall, willowy flower stem. In *T. parviflorus* the flowers are green, spotted with brown. To our eyes, the lip is the "fly"—the pointed mid-lobe the abdomen, the very hairy crest the thorax, and the bristle-shaped side lobes the antennae. The column, which is covered with bristly hairs, is the head. It appears, however, that a fly sees it differently; to him, the shiny stigma resembles the genital opening of the female. The anther holds its viscid disc upright, and the merest touch causes it to stick to whatever surfaces comes in contact with it, in nature the tips of the abdomen of the fly attempting copulation. These plants grow natively on grassy slopes at high elevations, with the plants hidden by the ground cover, and the "flies" hovering in the air. They need a cool greenhouse and are best grown in flats or on a mount over which they can ramble. *Trichoceros parviflorus* is native to Ecuador, Peru, Colombia, and Bolivia, and is greenish brown with dark brown spots. Another species, *Trichoceros muralis,* occurs throughout the same countries. It

Fig. 20-9 A. The "fly" orchid, *Trichoceros parviflorus,* which imitates a female fly so cleverly that male flies

attempt to mate with it, and in so doing perform pollination.
B. *Trichoceros muralis* imitates still another species of fly.

has the same habits, but is a smaller plant and has smaller, somewhat darker flowers. They are reddish-purple, and the side lobes of the lip are not so antenna-like, being rounded and not striped. This evidently imitates another species of fly. Both stay in bloom for many months.

TRICHOPILIA

Trichopilia are strong dark green plants with a flattened pseudobulb bearing a single leathery leaf. The flowers are fragrant, large, with slender sepals and petals and a large wavy lip curled around the column and spreading at its outer edge. The flower stem arises from the base of the pseudobulb and arches upward or curves downward to hang over the edge of the pot. Three, four, or more flowers are borne on each stem. *T. suavis* has lovely white flowers daintily speckled with pink, and a very large, ruffled lip. It is native to Costa Rica, Panama, and Colombia. *T. tortillis* is famous for its ribbon-like sepals and petals, twisted into tight spirals, which are green, in contrast to the white lip. This occurs in Mexico, Guatemala, and El Salvador.

Fig. 20-11 *Trichopilia fragrans* has plain flowers compared to some of its sisters, but has perhaps the sweetest fragrance of all.

T. fragrans, even more fragrant than the others, has greenish white sepals and petals and a white lip with a yellow center. It comes from Cuba, Jamaica, Colombia, and Peru. All can be grown at intermediate temperatures.

Fig. 20-10 *Trichopilia suavis* produces its showy, dainty, fragrant flowers in clusters at the base of the plant.

(*Courtesy H. A. Dunn and H. Griffin*)

Home Orchid Growing

TRIDACTYLE

The increased interest in African species results in more frequent importations. Among them may very likely be *Tridactyle,* especially the species *tridactylites,* which grows natively from the Congo to South Africa. The plant resembles a delicate vanda, with slender stems, narrow leaves bi-lobed at the tip, and thick roots. The tiny and very complicated flowers are borne on short spikes where the leaf joins the stem. The half-inch flowers are somewhat star-shaped, brownish green. The lip is the complex part; it is spurred, with the entrance to the spur showing on its face as a pit. The mid-lobe is divided into a broad center point and two side branches, which are again divided at their tips into little finger-like processes. The plant grows readily, climbing over a piece of driftwood or a tree fern slab, and flowers in the spring.

TRIGONIDIUM

Trigonidium is a lily-like flower, with a tube formed by the sepals, their tips turned out to give a three-part appearance. Two shiny, fleshy protuberances, which can just be seen between the sepals in most species, prove to be thickenings on the tips of the petals, and look rather like eyes. The column and lip are held within the tube. The plants have wrinkled, curved, conical pseudobulbs, and bear one or two slender leaves. The flowers are held singly on stems shorter than the leaves. *T. egertonianum* is pinkish green striped with brown and suffused with rose. The thickenings on the petals are electric blue. It is native to Mexico, Central America, Venezuela, Colombia, and Ecuador. *T. lankesteri* is greenish tan to cinnamon, veined with brown or purple, the petals spotted with purple. It occurs in Costa Rica and Panama.

VANILLA

Vanilla has tremendously long vine-like plants, some with long attractive leaves spaced evenly along the stem, others without true leaves. The species grow natively throughout tropical America, a few in Africa. Several species are grown for the seed pods, which are picked while still green and are cured to produce the flavoring vanilla. The most widely grown commercially is *V. planifolia,* but *pompona* ranks a possible second, and other species may also be in use. Vanilla culture began in Mexico among the Aztecs, and was spread from there to Spain and thence to other countries,

Fig. 20-12 *Tridactyle tridactylites* has short, feathery sprays of dainty little spurred flowers.

with the French developing the largest industry in their tropical possessions. Madagascar is the largest producer today, and Mexico, Tahiti, and other countries also have flourishing vanilla plantations.

The plants grow natively in warm, very humid climates, at relatively low elevations, where there is heavy rainfall. While they thrive with bright sun most of the day, they require some noon shade. The vines are grown from cuttings that include a piece of stem with its aerial roots. These are planted in humusy soil containing a lot of leaf mold, into which the lowermost roots will grow. The vine is trained to a support, preferably one to which the aerial roots can cling. One ingenious grower wrapped a length of hose with osmunda fiber, and tied the vine along it. He could then hook this hose overhead in the greenhouse, and move it at will.

Flowers are produced at the leaf axils, in clusters from which one or two open at a time over about a two week-period. They are fleshy, fragrant, greenish yellow to yellow, somewhat cattleya-like in shape with a trumpet lip, but are very short lived.

Since they open and fade in a day, pollination must be done immediately on the plantations, with the workers going over each vine every day, pollinating from one to two thousand flowers per person. Mostly women and children do the work. Only those flowers that develop in such a position as to allow the beans to grow straight down are used, so that they can be packaged neatly for shipping.

The process of pollination is simple, but was frustrating until, according to the story, a creole worker learned how to do it. The stigma is on the upper surface of a small "shelf" and is covered by a shield formed by the rostellum, which must be lifted in order to expose the stigmatic surface. Plantation workers do not go in for the niceties of sterile technique. Their method is as follows, described by Donovan S. Correll who has made an intensive study of the vanilla industry. The only implements used are the fingers and a splinter of bamboo, or a bit of wood whittled to a point. The worker pushes the lip down out of the way, then holds the column with the fingers of the left hand. With the splinter in the right hand, she lifts the rostellar flap that covers the stigma and folds it upward. With the left thumb, in one downward motion, she "mashes" the pollinia (actually the whole anther) down onto the stigma. It is not known what natural pollinator performs this function or how it is done, but so few flowers are ever pollinated in nature that commercial producers could not rely on insects to do the job. Moreover, the natural pollinators are of course absent in areas to which the species of *Vanilla* are imported.

21

JUNGLE ORCHIDS

Next to seeing orchid plants growing in their native haunts, the most thrilling experience is to receive them fresh from the jungle. You can buy them from people who make a business or a hobby of collecting plants in the wilds, and have them shipped directly to you just as they come from the trees. When you open the box and take out the plants you will be intrigued by their myriad shapes, and as you turn them over in your hands you will find yourself transported in imagination to the places from which they came. Clinging to the stubs of their roots may be pieces of the bark and debris in which they were growing. A small plant may still be perched on a piece of the branch from which it was collected. Their rhizomes assume odd shapes where they wound around a branch, or traveled over a hump or up and down in a crotch. A large plant may have a seedling or some smaller variety nestled among its roots. It will tax your ingenuity to fit them into pots. Some which were growing upward on a tree trunk will naturally lend themselves to being placed upon a slab of tree fern or a slab of wood to which is attached a piece of osmunda fiber. Potting them, caring for them, watching them take hold and grow for you as if they had never left their jungle home, is a rewarding experience.

The range of choice among the wild species is almost limitless. Each collector will furnish a list of things within his area, or you can learn through correspondence what he can get for you. One may have certain species of a genus, another may have different species of that genus. There are many more genera than could be described in the preceding chapters.

You can sometimes persuade a collector in a foreign country to gather little plants for you which do not appear on his list—things that are not found in quantity, odd species that are not widely known. In such a group there are bound to be some whose identity is a mystery even to the collector. It is a special treat to have unknowns and to be surprised when they bloom, and a challenge sometimes to figure out what they are. Some may grow on for years, becoming larger all the time, and you may become discouraged, thinking they will never bloom. Then one day flowering growths appear, and you realize that what you had assumed were mature plants had actually been seedlings! Occasionally in cultivation, plants grow to twice the size they attained in their natural environment—a compliment to your care, or appreciation of more fertilizer, or lack of competition with the plants they lived with in nature.

Since orchids dwell in such varied habitats not all will do equally well in cultivation, however. Some may be greatly set back by fumigation, others may not take kindly to shipping. Bringing plants from many different climates into one greenhouse is a challenge. Their native environment should be taken into consideration when planning what to get and how to care for them. Some may remain static for a long time before showing any sign of new growth—we have had them wait three or four

Fig. 21-1 Nothing can really describe the fun of opening a box of newly arrived jungle orchids. This box contains over a dozen species, many of them miniatures.

years. Do not give them up as long as they have a spark of life!

Many dealers in this country specialize in imported species, and furnish lists of what they offer. Through them you may obtain species you particularly desire, without having to go through the procedure of importing them.

A special aura surrounds plants you collect yourself in foreign countries—they are reminders of the forests, the cliffs, the road cuts from which you gathered them; and they bring back memories of the sights, the people, even the sounds that are so much a part of the total feeling for a land.

It is a revelation to see how many and varied are the habitats where orchids dwell. Most impressive are the great rain and cloud forests. Viewing them from above, from an airplane or, better, from across an extensive valley, you will appreciate the name "cloud" forest. As warm air from below is moved upward, the moisture condenses into a steady succession of clouds that flow through the trees. The rounded heads of the tallest trees stand above a sea of shorter ones. This gives them another name, "storied" forests. At lower elevations there may be three or four distinct stories, or levels of tree height; at higher altitudes, only two. You can see the stories at close range when driving through a forest, or approaching it from an area that has been thinned out. Step into it to see what it is like within. The ground is covered with a dense mass of ferns and other shade-tolerant plants. Aroids cling to the trunks and lower branches, vines disappear up into the foliage above, and rope-like roots hang down from epiphytes overhead. The huge buttressed bases of the largest trees are almost hidden in the vegetation; but if you were to try to walk among them,

you would stumble and slip on their moss-covered surfaces. Everything glistens with moisture in the dim light. You will find but few, if any, orchids within these dense forests; most of them are up in the high tree tops, out of reach and out of sight. But in remnants that border clearings, where the light gets through to the ground, you will find orchids growing lower down.

Then there are the scrub forests composed of small trees, often rich with orchids. They may be a second growth that has come in after deforestation, or they may occur because of climatic conditions. Sunny banks and steep slopes bordering roads offer footholds for orchids. Oddly enough, these are mostly epiphytes whose roots travel through the litter on the ground without penetrating the soil, and you may find the same species in nearby trees. On abandoned coffee fincas or fruit orchards, orchids will have moved in from surrounding forests to inhabit the small trees.

Occasionally you come upon a treasure trove where some of the giants have been felled for timbering or other purposes. As a great tree falls, many of the epiphytes are smashed from its branches, but some may still cling to them and you can thus gather plants that until now were two hundred feet in the air. In Latin America the mountains are the home of families who depend on little gardens they clear from the forests. Where a plot has just been cleared, you can often find still undamaged plants among the slash, and can even rescue some partly damaged ones. The torrential rains soon leach exposed soil, so the families have to move every few years, with the result that these little cleared patches are quite common.

Fig. 21-2 A whole flowering plant smaller than one cattleya flower. Here is a species of *Ornithocephalus*, whose little "bird beak" flowers are individually the size of a single pollinium of the cattleya.

Home Orchid Growing

The vegetation sometimes changes very quickly from place to place. A classic example can be seen as you travel from the mountains to the lowlands, where every few miles you can feel a perceptible change from the raw cold of the high country through a gradual warming until you reach the hot coastal region. The trees change on the way from short and weather-beaten to ever taller and increasingly magnificent specimens. Orchid plants are few at the highest elevations, become more frequent and varied at about 9,000 feet, reach their most prolific state between 6,000 and 3,000 feet, and then taper off again in numbers toward sea level.

In the United States we are accustomed to seeing mountains more heavily vegetated on the north rather than the south-facing slope. Through much of Latin America the Atlantic side is more lush than the Pacific because of the moist Atlantic winds. Along a ridge you may find a damp, moss-festooned forest on the Atlantic side, and just a few feet away on the other side of the ridge, a dry forest. Quite different plants inhabit the two areas.

Land formations govern the air currents and drainage patterns, creating many kinds of microclimates. Swales and swamps, waterfalls and streams, rocky cliffs through which water seeps or which are dry and exposed to the sun—each has its own community of plants. Fog patterns are controlled by the direction of air currents. In one place fog may fill a whole valley at precisely the same hour every day—at one thirty it may still be sunny and clear; at two o'clock you will not be able to see the road ahead of you. In another spot the fog may come streaming through a gap on the Atlantic side to pour across the road and down the Pacific slope as if directed by a hose, wetting everything in its path and leaving areas on either side untouched.

Some regions have rather strict wet and dry seasons, some only seasons of more or less rain. In an area where little rain has fallen for months, you wonder how the epiphytes manage to survive until you realize that they are sustained by the very humid atmosphere. It is well to inquire about the seasons before planning a trip. A daily shower or two does not prevent collecting, but drenching, day-long rains make it difficult and discouraging.

In the damp forests trees are covered with mosses and colorful lichens, pink, yellow, and silver, which are interlaced with the roots of epiphytes. In this soft padding the orchids extend their roots. After seeing this lovely medium and feeling the soft air, it seems miraculous that the plants can adapt to pots of strange media and the ups and downs of artificial conditions. In the dry forests the roots often cling to almost bare bark, offering another example of the adaptability to pots and a greenhouse environment. An occasional little plant is found hanging by one root to the stem of a vine or a root of some other epiphyte. While it is clear that it must obtain nutrients washed from the branches above, you wonder how the seed that gave rise to it ever stayed in that spot long enough to germinate and grow! Tree trunks may be covered with young plants growing from seed drifted from those above. Oddly, one tree may have scores of plants of the same species, while neighboring trees have none of that kind but instead an assortment of others.

It will surprise and confound you to find that you can recognize very few. Perhaps at home you have a wide variety of species and feel quite competent. The chance of finding things you already have is rare, and even if they are present you may not know them. Plants have a way of changing their shape almost from tree to tree, and there will be genera you may never have seen. Plants that look alike may turn out to be different from each other; others that look different may prove to be the same species. You do not often find things in bloom, another fact that makes identification hard; but this adds to the suspense of their flowering after you get them home.

When you see the wealth of epiphytes in which orchids are but a minority—ferns, gesneriads, bromeliads, anthuriums, peperomias, and others—you see how easy it would be to miss a kind here and there. In fact, the fear of missing something made me afraid to move away from the first tree I encountered on my first collecting trip. Even professional collectors can go into the same area time and again and find things they did not see before. Of course, if a few years elapse, plants may be there that were not there the previous time, from seed brought in by winds or birds. Thus it is that even an amateur may come home with some rare kinds, even a new species. And this is a very great thrill.

The deforestation going on in the developing countries causes concern for the conservation of species. It is sad to see the forests decimated. True, there are great areas still left, but no area harbors all the orchids. Some kinds live in quite restricted regions, and when these are cut over the species go with them. What to do about it is a question worrying orchid lovers. Committees have been set up by many orchid societies in hopes of arriving at some plan. At one time it seemed that prevention

A

B

290   Home Orchid Growing

Fig. 21-3 A. Clouds rise steadily from the valleys to bathe the forested mountains of Ecuador.
B. The Sarapiqui Canyon in Costa Rica, typical aspect of the cloud forests. Note the levels of trees in the foreground, with the tallest rising above all the others.

C. A fallen giant in an area cut over for farming. Orchid plants still cling to the branches, and many could be found on the ground. Note the ropelike roots that extended to the ground from epiphytes above.

of collecting offered a solution, but this would not help much where the forests themselves are being destroyed. Some countries forbid the export of orchids, but usually they do not forbid collecting by their own citizens, who can be just as destructive as strangers and who often do not truly value the species. Enlightened groups in some countries are working now toward conservation, however, in full appreciation of their native orchids. Those of us who go collecting should make a real effort to care for the plants we obtain, to share extra ones with others, and to obtain seed from unusual kinds and distribute it to botanical gardens and interested persons. One drawback is that it is not always easy to set seed and obtain pods. No collector should remove all the plants from an area. He should always try to leave enough to propagate themselves naturally, in hopes that they will escape destruction. The exception, of course, is that where the forest is in the process of being cut over, one should rescue everything he can find.

When going into a strange country it is well to contact someone who knows the roads and who might even go with you. There are professional collectors who take people out, and amateurs who will either go with you or tell you where to go. At least in the Central and South American countries where we have been, many roads are not marked. Paved highways are infrequent, sometimes limited to a north-south and an east-west artery. If you get off on unpaved, branching, and winding roads you can easily become lost. As soon as you get away from the cities into the small towns and countryside, you will find no one speaking your language. Your high school or college courses may not have prepared you for the subtle differences in local usage, and you cannot anticipate what odd situations may arise. It is best to have with you someone who knows not only the language but the people and their customs. When we did not have an orchid fancier to go with us, we hired a taxi and its driver for the day. A full day's work is appealing when a

A

B

C

292   Home Orchid Growing

D

E

Fig. 21-4 A. Where roads have been built and the forest thinned orchid seed filtering down from above can germinate on lower trees.
B. Orchids are often found on the rocky walls bordering streams.
C. Crossing a river in Peru, an upper tributary of the Amazon, by a hand-cranked cable car.
D. *Lycaste macrophylla* growing on a rocky cliff in Peru.
E. Mosses and lichens cover the trees. Here a small *Masdevallia* is blooming on a tree trunk in Costa Rica.

driver would otherwise spend hours waiting for fares. We found them most courteous and cooperative, highly amused at the new occupation of orchid hunting (and all the more enthusiastic for that), and anxious to take care of their *locos norteamericanos.* The taxi driver will talk to the people, ask permission to hunt on their land, and fend off trouble if it brews.

Arm yourself with plastic bags large and small, wear heavy waterproof boots, have a waterproof jacket or a raincoat handy, and take suntan lotion. A machete is a handy tool, though you can get along without one. Some collectors carry an extendible pole with a loop or blade at the end. Also, take labels. In the midst of collecting it is difficult to take time to label every plant. But do mark the bag used at each location with the place, date, elevation, type of terrain, climate, and pertinent details about the habitat. Later you can label each plant as you clean it, perhaps with a code number referring to the basic set of data. Virus disease does occur among plants in nature. To help prevent its spread, put plants a few each in small bags as you collect them, and carry them in a larger one. When shipping them also wrap them in small groups before putting them in the carton.

For most of us, the benefit of orchid collecting is not to come home with great masses of plants, but just to be in the places where they grow wild, to breathe the same air, to feel the soft atmosphere, watch the rains and fogs come and go, see how they grow and with what other plants, and gather a few to bring home as treasures.

PROCEDURE FOR IMPORTING ORCHIDS

All plants entering this country must be inspected and treated, and this is done without charge by the United States Department of Agriculture, Plant Quarantine Division at various ports of entry. This is done for your protection as well as that of the whole country. Every day the inspectors of imported plants find pests which, if allowed to reproduce in this country, could become dangerous plant enemies. It is far better to exclude possible enemies than to try to fight them once they have gained a foothold. Orchid growers used to battle pests that we hardly see nowadays, thanks to the service of the United States Department of Agriculture.

Importing orchids includes buying them from collectors who ship them to you, as well as finding them yourself on trips to foreign countries. If you should take such a trip, for your own good have the plants you acquire shipped back to you by way of one of the ports of entry. Perhaps you can plan to return by way of a port of entry and take the plants yourself to the quarantine center. The people there can usually have the plants ready the next day. They will then arrive in your greenhouse free from pests. It is not always easy to detect these yourself. Some bore holes in the rhizomes or pseudobulbs and lay eggs therein, so that even if you can see no insects they may later emerge. Small insects can conceal themselves under the covering scales of rhizomes and leaves. If you should succeed in bringing in plants without inspection, you may regret it later on. If plants are found in your luggage, they will be confiscated. The procedure for importing plants properly is so simple and so worthwhile that everyone should take advantage of it.

First, you must obtain a permit. Even though you do not expect to import any right away, you can obtain the permit so that this matter will be all taken care of if you should later desire to do so. A letter to U. S. Dept. of Agriculture, Permit Section, 209 River St., Hoboken, N. J. 07030, is all that is necessary. State that you wish a permit to import orchid plants. You will be issued a permit number that is good for three years, and which must be renewed every three years in order to be kept active. The permit number goes in their files and in the files at each port of entry. You may import one or a hundred plants, as seldom or as often you wish.

Second, you must obtain shipping labels from the same office, which must accompany each package of plants. The labels bear your permit number and are your tag of identification for the plants as well as your ticket for the services of the laboratory that will inspect and fumigate the plants. Labels are issued for specific ports of entry, so you must know before you order them to which one your shipment will come. From Central and much of South America they will go through Miami or New Orleans; from western South America and the Pacific area, they will arrive at San Francisco; from Mexico, at Brownsville, Texas; and from Europe, at Hoboken, New Jersey.. The collector from whom you buy the plants will tell you, if you ask him, to which port he will ship, and you can then ask for labels for that port. You send the labels to him, and he will put one on the outside of the package.

He must put your name and address inside the package, together with an invoice stating value, and a phytosanitary certificate obtained from the ministry of agriculture in his country.

Third, the matter of how the plants will be shipped should be decided upon between you and the shipper. Those who make a regular business of shipping plants will know how best to send them. It has been our experience that Air Parcel Post is most satisfactory. Not only is it speedy, but the Postal Service will collect the duty on the plants at your door, obviating the necessity of employing the services of a broker to handle this for you at the port of entry. The broker's fee often comes to more than the transportation costs, but a broker is necessary for both air express and air freight. If the plants come by air, they can travel in a closed box, but if they are to be shipped by a slower method, the box should have some holes cut in it for ventilation. Send very small boxes straight Air Mail.

If you wish to send home plants that you acquire in your travels, take the shipping labels with you on your trip. When you are ready to leave for home, pack the plants yourself in a cardboard carton. Wrap them in newspaper, two or three plants to a package, and lay these in the box. Put your name and address inside the box and affix a shipping label to the outside. Pay the postage all the way to your home. The box will go to the port of entry, be opened and inspected and the plants treated, and the original wrapping will be put back on for mailing to your home.

An invoice showing the value of the plants should accompany the package. This can be merely a paper made out by you stating a reasonable figure, and is for the purpose of customs duty. Before shipping plants out of any country, check with the minister of agriculture to get a phytosanitary certificate. If it is necessary to obtain a release for the plants, he will tell you how to go about it.

All kinds of plants arrive at the fumigation center, and the workers do not always know that orchids may be injured by too extensive treatment. Put a note in the box, or ask the shipper to do so, requesting that they be treated gently to prevent injury. Sometimes they will dip them instead of treating them with gas, so you might mention this.

CARE OF JUNGLE PLANTS

As soon as the box arrives, open it and remove the plants. Examine them for any soft areas that show breakdown of plant tissues. It is always wise

Home Orchid Growing

Fig. 21-5 New growth is fairly well along on some jungle plants when they arrive. The growth on this *Cychnoches* appears to be in good condition, but minute bruises on the tender leaves can become infected with fungi or bacteria if care is not taken. It is well to dip new growths in a fungicide solution on arrival.

not a thing that can be done in a moment; rainy seasons interfere and distances are great. Some may have to wait some time before shipment. Those that have growth started should be potted right away. The others can wait for a while. Syringe those lying on the bench once or twice a day to keep them from shrivelling, or to help plump them up.

We have found the polyethylene bags of great help in handling jungle plants. They furnish a wonderfully damp atmosphere that encourages new roots to form and eyes to start growing. The jungle plants can be handled just like backbulbs. Put a little wet medium in the bag, set the plant upon it, close the bag with a rubber band, and stand it upright on the bench so that the new growth will start in the proper direction. When the new roots can be seen starting, remove the plant and pot it just as you would any other plant. Stake it carefully so that it will not wobble in the pot. Keep newly potted plants a bit shaded, and mist the foliage once or twice a day and just the surface of the potting medium, until new roots are growing vigorously. Those which are potted right away are also kept shaded and are given mist sprays until growth is advancing nicely.

It is fun to have some hanging plants, and some lend themselves very well to growing on a slab. A flat piece of osmunda fiber is wired to the slab, and the plant is then fastened on with a wire that encircles both plant and slab. The roots will go through the fiber and cling to the bark, just as they do in nature. After a year or two it is impossible to remove it without cutting the roots, so tightly do they cling. However, plants grown in this way do not have to be changed often, and when it becomes necessary it is not difficult to reestablish divisions on slabs again. A piece of tree fern trunk will serve just as well as the slab with osmunda fiber. Because of the free aeration of a slab or a piece of tree fern, the organic material does not break down as rapidly as it does in a pot, and plants can stay on them for many years. They should be watered quite frequently, and should have a thorough soaking in a bucket every now and then. They appreciate fertilizer every other watering. We have been especially successful with kinds that have a rambling or pendant habit, such as some of the maxillarias, epidendrums, oncidiums, dichaeas, and so forth.

Baskets are decorative, especially those made of redwood slats. Better for such things as *Stanhopea,* and others whose flower stems bore down through the medium, are wire baskets, which allow more

to dip the plants in a fungicide to prevent infection of any part that may have been damaged in handling or shipping. It is not likely that thick, hard leaves will show any injury, but the thin leaves of some kinds may be broken or bruised. Cut off any badly damaged parts and keep a watch over any that have slight damage. (If these later show evidence of infection, treat them again with fungicide.) Lay the plants on a shaded bench where they can have free air circulation.

Some plants will arrive with new growth started; others may be quite dormant. Some may be plump, others shrivelled. For the most part, plants come through the shipping very well. But collecting is

Fig. 21-6 *Oncidium ampliatum* lends itself well to growing on a slab. Wire a piece of osmunda fiber to a slab, as shown in A and B, and then wire the plant in place, C.

Plastic-coated wire is a good type to use. Note the turtle-like pseudobulbs of this species.

space between the barriers than do the slat type. Dime store egg baskets that have the wire covered with plastic are good, as are the plain round wire baskets obtainable from garden centers. Osmunda fiber is the best medium. Lay a tough piece, cut to the right size, on the bottom, and then fill in around the plant with other pieces, packing it tightly enough to hold the plant firmly. If necessary, the plant can be held down by a hoop of wire until it forms a good root system.

For plants which are to be grown in pots, the materials you use for your other orchids will be satisfactory. For terrestrials, a mix such as recommended for cymbidiums is good. If little plants, or those badly shrivelled, have a hard time getting started, put them pot and all into a polyethylene

bag until they become well rooted. Some of the smaller ones seem to do better in osmunda fiber than in plain bark or tree fern.

Miniature gardens can be made in flats, with small plants of contrasting shapes and perhaps one or two a bit taller than the rest for accent. Members of the Pleurothallis tribe lend themselves particularly well to this, as do small epidendrums, maxillarias, oncidiums, and many other little botanicals. The greater ease of keeping a flat damp helps in growing miniature plants. Plastic trays are fine for the purpose. They can be purchased from many dealers, in different sizes. If they come without drainage holes, holes can be burned in with a soldering iron. Burn them from the outside. The plastic melts up around the iron, forming a dike

Home Orchid Growing

Fig. 21-7 UPPER, left and right, "trees" made of drift-   LOWER, Many small plants can be grown together in a flat.
wood support a large number of small orchids.

Jungle Orchids   297

A

Fig. 21-8 A. Imaginative hand-made ceramic containers offer decorative ways to display orchids. Here *Oncidium triquetrum* grows and blooms in a tier of pots with ample drainage holes.

B. Plants can be naturalized on slabs or logs, as has been done with this dwarf species of *Aerangis*. The log is oak. c. *Pleurothallis grobyi* and a young resurrection fern grow on a moss-capped block of redwood. The plants are held by nylon string until they take root. (*Photos by Ted Dully; Courtesy H. Phillips Jesup*) that would impede the flow of water if it were on the inside. Lay a piece of hardware cloth over the holes, and on top of that a layer of gravel. Then fill the tray with your favorite potting mix.

Such flats can be used to keep very tiny pots damp, if you prefer not to put the miniature plants in the flats directly. The little pots plunged in bark or gravel in the tray will not need to be watered so often. And this gives a suggestion for keeping very small pots damp while you are away for a vacation.

Miniature trees are decorative, made from pieces of driftwood or branches cut from trees in your yard. In damp climates you may not need to put pads of osmunda fiber on them, but in drier areas this is a necessity. Stuff the osmunda fiber in crotches and holes or tie it along the limbs. Then wire the plants to the fiber. Sections of small logs with the bark intact are also attractive mounts.

Various imaginative types of pottery can be used. such as strawberry pots or handcrafted containers. Shallow pottery "pans" sold for use with succulents or bonsais are pretty filled with miniature orchid plants.

B

C

22

MINERAL NUTRITION

Man cannot live by love alone. Nor can a plant live by air and water. Every living thing, both animal and plant, depends on certain minerals for the development of its body structure and the maintenance of the living substance within it, protoplasm. Even plants that hang on such a sterile perch as a telephone wire (*Tillandsia*) have a source of minerals to nourish them, dust settling on the wire and minerals dissolved in rain water—small amounts, to be sure, but enough for these particular plants.

It used to be thought that orchids lived entirely on materials taken from the air. Observers overlooked the accumulation of humus material present in breaks in the bark of trees or crevices in weathered rock and in the mosses and lichens thereon, the fertilizing minerals dissolved out of bird droppings and washed down to the plants by rain, and the yearly collection of dead leaves among the bulbs of the plants themselves. Even rain water is not pure, since rain droplets form on dust particles and take up more dust on their way earthward.

A ten-ounce plants consists of nine ounces of water and one ounce of sugars, starches, proteins, fats, waxes, and numerous other substances. This single ounce represents the other chemical substances accumulated by the plant during its lifetime plus the amount of food it has on hand at the moment of weighing. To find out what part of the dry weight of the plant is mineral, the dried plant is ignited and burned to remove carbon, hydrogen, nitrogen, and oxygen. The ash remaining is the total mineral content of the plant, and amounts to approximately 0.076 of an ounce for a ten-ounce plant. A fraction of a cent would buy the chemicals that make up the plant. The value of the living plant is based on the marvelous things its protoplasm, governed by its genes, can do with that minute quantity of nonliving substances.

The minerals, in the form of mineral salts, are absorbed by the roots from the medium in which they grow. The salts are released from the organic matter by slow decay and are put in solution by moisture in the soil. The salts in solution are then taken up by the roots, and transported to every part of the plant, where they enter into various vital activities.

In addition to the minerals, the plant needs water and two things absorbed from the air, oxygen and carbon dioxide. Oxygen, necessary for respiration, is absorbed by the leaves and stems from the atmosphere and by the roots from air in the soil. Carbon dioxide is absorbed by the leaves (and other green parts of the plant) and combined with water taken up by the roots to form sugar, the food of the plant. This process is called photosynthesis because it is carried on only in the presence of light. The simple sugars are turned into complex sugars, starches, and cellulose; and various products formed from carbohydrates are combined with nitrogen, sulfur, and phosphorus to form proteins.

The major mineral elements, necessary in relatively large amounts, and their activities, follow:

Calcium is necessary for cell wall formation and for regulation of cell activities. If calcium is deficient the new growths are stunted and distorted.

Nitrogen, an essential ingredient of proteins and of chlorophyll, is necessary for good vegetative growth. When nitrogen is deficient the plants are stunted and mature too early. Older leaves turn yellow and drop off. Too much nitrogen produces excessive vegetative growth and delayed flowering.

Sulfur is also an ingredient of proteins. Sulfur deficiency may stunt root growth.

Phosphorus, the third important mineral in protein formation, is a catalyst and regulator of vital activity. Sometimes called the "dynamite of living cells." Phosphorus deficiency leads to stunting, but the leaves, instead of turning yellow, become dark green.

Potassium, another important catalyst, regulates many activities. Deficiency results in dwarfness with the edges of the leaves frequently scorched and dead.

Magnesium is part of the chlorophyll molecule, and therefore necessary to the manufacture of food. With lack of magnesium the older leaves become yellow between the veins and the plant does not thrive.

Iron is a catalyst in many reactions, including the formation of chlorophyll. Iron is seldom deficient but is insoluble unless the soil is sufficiently acid. Deficiency of iron causes the younger leaves to become yellow.

Certain other minerals are also necessary, but in extremely minute amounts. Very little is known about their specific activities, and it is thought that they act as catalysts in vital chemical reactions. These minor elements are *boron, molybdenum, manganese, copper,* and *zinc.* They are seldom deficient, for the faint traces found in most soils and as impurities in most chemicals, are enough to supply the needs of the plants. Manganese is the only one of the minor elements that at times needs to be added to nutrient solutions. In fact, in order to do research on the role of the trace elements, workers must first remove the minute amounts of boron, copper, manganese, molybdenum, and zinc contained in the chemicals they will use. They must also redistill water many times before it can be considered pure. They can then study the effects of the minor elements by using them one at a time in measured amounts. It is known that their complete absence causes poor growth, and it is also known

that amounts over the smallest trace are toxic to plants.

We have been talking about the various elements necessary to plant nutrition, but plants can use these elements only in the form of inorganic salts. In nature some inorganic materials are dissolved out of the rock particles in the soil. Additional inorganic salts are released from the humus material in the soil by bacteria and fungi that feed upon it. The same events take place in the potting materials used for orchids. The "breakdown" of organic materials such as osmunda, tree fern fiber, bark, leaf mold, etc., requires the activities of soil bacteria and fungi. We augment the store of chemical salts available to the plant when we apply additional amounts in the form of fertilizers and nutrient solutions. Inorganic salts occur as a variety of compounds, and choices may be made among them. We cannot list all the possibilities, but will give some of the more generally used compounds. Nitrogen may be furnished as nitrate salts or as ammonium salts, for example as ammonium nitrate, ammonium sulfate, potassium nitrate or calcium nitrate. It is generally agreed that plants need nitrogen in both the ammonium form (NH_4) and nitrate form (NO_3), but there is no agreement as to which form should be in greater quantity. Potassium may be furnished as potassium sulfate, potassium nitrate, or potassium chloride; calcium as monocalcium phosphate, calcium nitrate, calcium chloride; phosphorus is furnished in phosphate salts such as calcium phosphate or monopotassium phosphate; iron as ferrous sulfate; magnesium as magnesium sulfate; manganese as manganese sulfate; and sulfur as the sulfate salts just mentioned.

In order for a plant to thrive, it must have a balanced "diet" of the essential minerals. It needs larger quantities of some than of others. And in order to make use of the nutrients, it must have the proper conditions of light, water, and temperature. Curiously, a plant can starve in the midst of plenty if for some reason it is unable to take up the minerals it needs. Overwatering with the resultant inhibition of root function can produce a mineral lack for the plants. Under-watering, not as dangerous as over-watering, can deprive the plant of sufficient materials for growth. Excessive accumulation of salts in the potting medium can prevent the roots from absorbing both water and minerals. Insufficient light can prevent the plant's using the available minerals, through failure to make the necessary amount of sugars, the building blocks for more complicated carbohydrates which, in turn, are combined with minerals from the soil to form proteins, enzymes, etc. The pH of the growing medium is important to root health, for roots function best somewhere between pH 5.2 and pH 6.5. Under proper growing conditions and where an organic medium such as osmunda, tree fern, bark etc., is used, pH seldom becomes a problem. Such media as well as mixes containing a large proportion of organic matter, are more or less self-conditioning, that is, they maintain a pH suitable for plant growth through bacterial action as well as chemical action. The problem of pH in relation to water that is excessively alkaline or acid was discussed earlier, page 32. The control of pH in nutrient solutions used for orchids on an inert medium is a matter for constant attention.

An important contribution to plant nutrition has been made by the introduction of chelates. In a culture solution, or (less likely) in a potting medium, the iron may combine with other ions such as the phosphate ion (PO_4) to form an insoluble compound. This removes the iron from solution and makes it unavailable to the plant. Chlorosis (yellowing) of the leaves will follow, with resultant poor growth. Other metals such as copper, zinc, etc., may be similarly precipitated from solution, although probably iron is the most important to be considered. A chelate is an organic substance which has a chemical attraction for certain elements and which holds them loosely in solution, making them continually available for plant use. The chelate thus prevents precipitation of the particular element. Called the versene compounds, they have quite a complicated structure exemplified by one, called for short EDTA, which is ethylenediamine-tetraacetic acid. It is possible to add this to a culture solution or to a fertilizer solution, but it is probably easier and better to obtain one that has already been combined with iron, such as the product called "Sequestrene." Some manufacturers of orchid fertilizers are including chelates in their prepared products. When used thus, the chelated iron may be substituted for iron sulfate or whatever other iron compound would have been included, or it may be used in addition to it.

Basic nutrient solutions have been worked out for orchids on inert media—seedlings on agar and plants in gravel. As we saw in the chapter on germinating seed, various workers have proposed slightly different formulas for germination, and the same is true for solutions to be used with gravel.

Sometimes substitution of one salt for another gives better results for a certain species. The formulation of fertilizers has been an equally experimental endeavor, and here the matter is complicated by the fact that the materials on which the fertilizers will be used vary so much from each other. The barks of different species of trees contain different amounts of nitrogen, phosphorus, potassium etc.; osmunda fiber collected in different regions varies quite strikingly in content. Any one of these materials may vary in the rapidity with which it releases its minerals under different conditions of watering, temperature, and atmospheric moisture. It is to be expected that fertilizers made up according to the experiences of one grower or another will also vary. There are also organic fertilizers, such as fish emulsion, favored by some. After trying several on your own plants, you yourself may come to have a preference for a certain one. This is good. It shows that all is *en rapport* between you and your plants. Such experiences among growers everywhere show that orchids can get along on quite varied diets, provided they are given the basic essentials.

GRAVEL CULTURE

Gravel culture quite took orchid growers by storm some ten or more years ago. The freedom from toil that it offered gave it the same appeal that bark culture has today. We may now even have the answers to some of the problems that developed with gravel culture and caused many growers to give it up. Certain it is that this method still has some loyal adherents, and it is still a useful method for those who are interested in research on nutrition.

Essentially, gravel culture differs from bark culture only in that gravel is used instead of bark, and that the entire array of necessary minerals must be supplied rather than just a supplemental fertilizer. The chief disadvantage of gravel is that it is heavy.

Plants can be grown in gravel all the way from community pot size to flowering size. For the smallest plants a very fine size is used, between one-sixteenth and one-eighth inch diameter. The size of the gravel is gradually increased as the plants become larger, until for mature plants a size of one-half to three-quarters of an inch is used. The gravel should be from a type of rock that does not readily give materials into solution. For example, limestone is to be avoided. Weathered gravel is preferable to crushed gravel. The manufactured light-weight aggregates such as Idealite, Solite, Holite etc., are excellent. They can be obtained from manufacturers directly or from construction companies.

From the time plants are in three-inch pots, unless they have a good root system to hold them in place, they should be supported with one of the rigid stakes used in bark culture; or should have the rhizomes fastened down by means of a wire extending from one side of the pot to the other.

Plants in small pots have to be watered more often than those in large pots, but all have to be watered more frequently than they do with other media. Each grower must devise his own schedule from observation of his own plants. During the winter, three- and four-inch pots may have to be watered every other day, and in the summer every day. Larger pots may need water every four to six days in the winter, and every three days or so in the summer.

Fertilizer should be a water-soluble, complete formula. Hyponex, Instant Vigoro, or a complete orchid fertilizer can be used. Or you can mix your own according to the formula given below. This formula is the one used in experimental work with orchids in gravel at Ohio State University. The frequency of fertilizing recommended by those who did the work at Ohio State was once a week, with plain water being given in between times when needed. Now that we can give the plants better light because we can keep down the greenhouse temperature by means of cooling apparatuses, I believe that the fertilizing schedule could be stepped up to twice a week or even to every watering during the growing season. They should be flushed with plain water after every few feedings. Once-a-week fertilizing is still probably best during the winter. A concentration of one-half teaspoon of fertilizer to a

gallon of water would be best to start with, but you may wish to vary this experimentally.

The fertilizer can be applied by means of a Hozon attachment, or could be mixed in a tank and applied by a hose. It is best to mix it fresh each time, or at least not to let it stand in the tank for longer than two weeks. Chemical changes can take place in a mixture that is allowed to stand for a long time, and the pH can also change. The plants in gravel do not have a store of minerals from which to draw as they do in organic media, nor do they have the protection from changes in pH furnished by an organic medium.

One of the problems which arises in gravel culture is the accumulation of salts, particularly in the pots. This problem can probably be ameliorated by the use of plastic pots. Plastic pots would also alleviate the rapid drying, making it easier to keep the plants well watered, especially in the smaller sizes. With both clay and plastic pots, however, care must be taken to flush with plain water very thoroughly every week or two.

A second problem with gravel culture is that the iron may become precipitated from the solution, causing chlorosis and abnormal growth. The use of chelated iron should prevent this. It would be well to use a fertilizer containing an iron chelate, or to add a small amount to each batch of fertilizer as it is mixed—approximately 5 grams for each ten gallons of solution.

In preparing this solution dissolve each salt completely in the gallon of water before adding the next salt. Manganese is added by first dissolving one gram of manganese sulfate in 99 cc of water, then 2.5 cc of this solution is used per gallon of nutrient solution. The pH ranges between 5.5 and 6.5, and should be checked before use.

THE OHIO W. P. SOLUTION (to be use half strength)

Name	Symbol	Amount
Potassium nitrate	KNO_3	2.63 grams
Ammonium sulfate	$(NH_4)_2SO_4$	0.44 grams
Magnesium sulfate	$MgSO_4 \cdot 7H_2O$	2.04 grams
Monocalcium phosphate	$CaH_4(PO_4)_2 \cdot H_2O$	1.09 grams
Calcium sulfate	$CaSO_4 \cdot 2H_2O$	4.86 grams
Iron sulfate (Ferrous sulfate)	$FeSO_4 \cdot 7H_2O$	0.5 grams
Manganese sulfate	$MnSO_4$	Make a 1% solution and add 2.5 c.c of this
Water	H_2O	1.0 gallon

A method for watering whole benches of plants at one time, called **subirrigation,** was described in previous editions of this book. The benches were made water-tight, and the water and nutrient solutions were pumped into them and then allowed to drain back into a tank. We no longer recommend this system because of the danger of spreading disease among the plants. The danger would be greatest when the plants were planted directly in gravel with their roots free, somewhat less so if the plants were in pots plunged into the gravel. In either situation, roots would come in contact with each other. Removal of a plant would of necessity allow some roots to be broken, and if these were from a diseased plant, the sap containing disease organisms would infect other plants.

23

PROBLEMS, DISEASES, AND PESTS

Orchid health depends on three fundamentals—good inheritance, proper environment, and freedom from disease and injury. Enough has been said previously about inheritance to emphasize the importance of selecting strong, free-growing, promising plants, whether you acquire them as small seedlings or as mature plants. Environmental conditions that contribute to the health of the plant are the right amount of light, temperature within the proper day-night range, humidity coupled with good air circulation, water to suit the needs of the plants, and proper nutrition combined with root aeration. Deviations from the optimal in any of these conditions may cause variations from the normal thrifty condition of the plant. Diseases are caused by invading viruses, bacteria, or fungi. Prevention of insect injury is an absolute necessity.

AILMENTS ARISING FROM ENVIRONMENTAL CONDITIONS

Light. When the light is too strong, chlorophyll (the green pigment) is destroyed faster than it is made, and leaves become yellow, or even white in young seedlings. Yellowed leaves cannot make as much food as leaves that have the normal amount of chlorophyll. If the condition is not corrected, the older leaves may fall before they should. The general result is a retarded plant.

Sudden exposure to too strong light may burn localized areas. Naturally, the efficiency of a leaf is decreased by the presence of a burned area. The sudden exposure may result from removing too much shading in the fall, from not applying it soon enough in the spring, or by allowing strong light to focus on a plant through a clear area on the glass or through an open ventilator. Flowers are sensitive to the excessive heat produced by too much light, and become dry and thin before their time from its effects.

Insufficient light causes the plants to become a darker green than normal. Even though the dark green plants are handsome to the eye, they are not as healthy as when the foliage is a lighter shade. The plants are usually soft and succulent, susceptible to disease, and their growths do not mature and harden as they should. Flower production is cut down or inhibited entirely.

Temperature. Each kind of orchid has its own temperature requirements. At night temperatures too high for their kind, they will not flower. Growth is poor because food is used faster than it can be made. Often the leaves fall prematurely and death may result.

At temperatures below the specific requirement water and minerals are absorbed but slowly, and formation of chlorophyll is hindered. Yellow foliage and poor development result, and poor flowering is the logical sequel.

There is also an optimal difference between day and night temperatures. Too wide a gap, or not enough drop at night, retards growth.

Orchids can survive short spells of extremely hot weather if everything is done to aid them. The leaves absorb light with its associated heat, and their temperature is therefore usually warmer than the surrounding air. They have some protection from heat in their evaporation of water (transpiration), which acts as a cooling system. For cattleyas, it has been demonstrated that burning occurs if the temperature of the leaves remains at 110° F. for a few hours, or at 120°-125° F. for shorter periods. This means that during hot spells when the greenhouse temperature soars above 100° F., the temperature of the leaves may reach the danger point and sudden burning may occur. I know of a case where every plant in a small greenhouse was burned black when it was accidentally left unattended on a hot day. During hot weather everything must be done to lower the temperatures of leaves. The plants should have cooling mists over the foliage, and proper attention to ventilation, shade, and air circulation.

Burning due to strong light would actually seem to be a heat effect. Concentration of light on one area of a leaf raises the temperature of that area to the burning point.

Flowers are even more sensitive to heat than plants. Flowering plants should therefore be kept as cool as possible under conditions of hot weather to prevent premature fading.

For regions where hot summers are a rule, varieties should be chosen with care as to their particular temperature requirements.

Freezing kills plant tissues just as burning does. However the frozen areas become soft and watery, dirty yellow-green in color and then black. Frozen areas should be cut off and the surfaces be treated with Tersan or other fungicide to prevent infection of the wounds. Do not syringe until the cuts have dried and healed. If severe freezing leaves only a small portion of the plant intact, it should be treated as a potted division until it is actively growing again.

Humidity. Insufficient humidity in the air makes it difficult to maintain an even water supply to the plants. The potting medium dries out quickly, and the plants lose water rapidly through their foliage. This is especially critical for newly potted plants, whose root systems are temporarily non-functioning, and for young seedlings.

Excessive humidity is dangerous for it brings about susceptibility to certain diseases. Flowers may become spotted, either by simple engorgement of water or by fungus growths. *Botrytis* fungus causes pink or brown spots, and flowers may become spotted with a sooty black mold. Plant parts may be attacked by various bacteria and fungi.

The danger of infection during the high relative humidity maintained for the purpose of cooling the plants in the daytime is lessened by good air movement. However, excessively high relative humidity (above 70 percent) contributes to succulent growth which is more susceptible to infection than hard growth.

Watering. Enough has been said about the effects of overwatering on plants and flowers, but we might repeat here that overwatering is one thing to suspect when a plant is not making vigorous growth or when its older leaves are turning soft and yellow. Examine the potting medium and the roots. If the medium is broken down and is wet and mushy it will contain few if any active roots. Repotting is then in order.

Underwatering will cause shrivelling of the leaves and pseudobulbs and new growths will be small. The roots may be thin and starved. If the medium is in good condition (and it probably is since it has been kept dry) simply step up the frequency of watering.

It may take more than a year to bring back the vigor of a plant that has been stunted by one of these conditions, but it is rewarding to see them improve.

Nutrition. Chapter 22 gives the symptoms of various nutritional deficiencies. It is not likely that plants potted in good osmunda will suffer any nutritional lack, provided they are potted firmly. Plants loosely potted will suffer from lack of minerals and perhaps water also. Some of the leaves will turn yellow and die. In bark, yellow leaves are a sign of lack of nitrogen (if it can be ascertained that they are not from root loss). The fertilizers prepared for use with bark contain a higher nitrogen concentration because of the inherent lack of sufficient nitrogen in bark.

Air relations. Industrial regions offer hazards to orchid growing, both by the production of smoke and haze which reduce the light available to the plants, and by the production of noxious fumes. The former is being reduced by modern methods of

Home Orchid Growing

smoke control. The latter is not such a simple problem (see Sepal Wilt, below).

If you live where soot and grime collect on the plants, wash them off with a forceful spray of water at frequent intervals. Dirt collecting on the leaves may plug up the stomata and cut down the working power of the leaf.

Artificial illuminating gas is disastrous to plant life. Even a small amount of the raw gas leaking into the greenhouse will quickly kill the plants. One grower lost a great many when the gas main in the street broke and the gas seeped through the earth into his orchid house. Artificial gas is not safe to use in the greenhouse, nor is gas that has the slightest amount of artificial gas mixed with it. On the other hand, absolutely pure natural gas is perfectly safe, as is bottled gas (butane), provided the heaters are vented to carry off all fumes from combustion.

SEPAL WILT AND PREMATURE AGING

When a flower fades normally, after having lasted its usual length of time, the sepals are the first parts to show signs of deterioration. Starting at the tips, they lose their waxy sheen, become thin and transparent, and finally become tissue-like. The rest of the flower follows suit soon afterward, sometimes remaining in good condition a few days longer than the sepals. Sometimes the aging process sets in prematurely, occasionally almost as soon as the flower opens. There are two types of premature aging, one caused by some failure in cultural, environmental, or inherited factors which prevent the flowers from attaining their normal vigor and substance, and another caused by actual poisoning by substances in the atmosphere. We shall take up the first under the heading "Short Flower Life" and the second under "Sepal Wilt."

Short flower life. Anything which interferes with the health of a plant can result in flowers that are thin in substance and which do not last the normal length of time. Poor potting, improper watering, poor nutrition, excessive temperatures, lack of humidity, insufficient light, root loss—any or all can debilitate a plant. Flowers produced on such plants may be thin from the time they open, never attaining the firm substance expected of them, or they may appear normal for a while but soon fade. Any kind of orchid may respond with poor flowers when the plants are not vigorous. Cattleyas seem

to be the most sensitive to insufficient light, and this is most often the cause of their premature aging. They are also most sensitive to the causal agents of sepal wilt.

A plant brought into the house before the buds are open must be kept in a bright window until the flowers are fully mature, else they will be thin. Long spells of dull weather· may cause cattleya flowers to be less firm than they are normally, with the sepals becoming limp and transparent soon after the bud opens and the rest of the flower lasting only a short time. This condition may be confused with "sepal wilt," but it differs in the fact that the whole flower is thin or becomes thin soon after the sepals shrivel, while in true sepal wilt, the petals and lip are usually quite normal. Premature aging or short flower life, due to insufficient light, occurs in regions with prolonged spells of dull weather. It is also a common complaint where too heavy shading is used at any season.

The sudden fading of a normal flower may result from pollination by a visiting insect. The petals usually fold together and turn papery. Notice whether there are pollinia on the stigma.

Removal or dislodgement of the anther causes premature fading of *Cymbidium, Catasetum, Cycnoches* and possibly some other kinds. A jostling of the buds or open flowers, even by a strong stream of water, may be enough to jar loose the anther in its socket. The fading of one or two flowers on a stem is often a clue to this.

Excessive heat may cause premature fading of flowers throughout the greenhouse, either extreme day temperatures or inordinately high night temperatures. This is particularly likely to happen when the air is too dry in the presence of high temperatures. Too low night temperatures, which do not allow the full development of the flowers, may also be a cause.

When all possible factors are checked, and a plant in apparent good health consistently gives poor flowers year after year, the cause is probably its genetic make-up. Within any species, or in any group of hybrids, there are a few individuals that just do not have the ability to give good flowers. It is not worthwhile to keep such plants. Also, some plants are not good growers, in spite of all the care that you can give them, and because of lack of vigor they flower poorly. These, too, should be disposed of.

Sepal wilt. Sepal wilt, also called dry sepals, is a peculiar condition whose mysteries have required much experimentation and detective work to unravel. Cattleyas are affected most severely. However, the factors that cause sepal wilt in cattleyas may also affect some other kinds in other ways, and may be doing damage not yet realized.

For cattleyas, a typical sequence of events is this: In the midst of a period when flowers are opening in good condition, there comes an interval when some or all opening flowers have thin, dry sepals, brown at the tip. Then, just as suddenly, the interval is over, and flowers are again normal. In affected flowers the sepals wilt as soon as the bud opens. The rest of the flower usually gains its normal substance and lasts well, but the flower is, of course, ruined by the affected sepals. Often the sepals turn soft and leathery before the bud opens, and in many cases the bud is entirely prevented from opening. Observations during short periods of sepal wilt suggest that the causative factors act on the bud just as it is getting ready to open, because (1) flowers already open are not affected, and (2) buds that are still quite green subsequently open normally. The fact that not all flowers are affected, and that the degree of severity varies among affected plants, suggests that some cattleyas are more resistant than others.

Experimental work has shown that ethylene gas will cause sepal wilt. Ethylene gas is used to ripen fruit that has been picked green for shipping. This is essentially an aging process. The gas is present in smog, and in fumes from incomplete combustion of hydrocarbons (coal, oil, gas, gasoline, etc.). Sepal wilt is especially prevalent during periods of smog, frequently occurs in greenhouses heated by open-flame non-vented gas heaters, and is more common in, or close to, industrial areas than in open country. It occurs when the wind brings fumes from factory areas, and is absent when the wind blows the fumes in another direction. It occurs under certain atmospheric conditions when the air hugs the ground and smoke and fumes are layered within it. It is not necessarily connected to light conditions. Growers who have moved their collections away from cities and industrial areas have found that they are more free from sepal wilt. The new techniques for controlling air pollution have improved the situation in some areas.

The reason for the prevalence of sepal wilt among cattleyas is that they are far more sensitive to ethylene gas than other orchids and, indeed, than most other plants. According to O. Wesley Davidson, cattleyas just beginning to split their sepals are affected by one part of ethylene in 300,000,000 to 500,000,000 parts of air. Tomato plants, on the other hand, require as much as one part ethylene gas in 10,000,000 to 20,000,000 parts of air in order to cause their leaves to fold. Carnation flowers become "sleepy" in response to one part ethylene in 20,000,000 to 25,000,000 parts of air. Tomatoes and carnations are therefore not affected by the extremely minute amounts that cause sepal wilt in cattleyas. It would be desirable to have some indicator plant that is more sensitive than cattleyas, but so far we do not know of any.

Other orchids, which are not affected by the small concentration that injures cattleya flowers, may be injured by stronger concentrations. Plants themselves may also be injured. We have had two experiences that have alerted us to these possibilities. Both instances were caused by the rusting through or disconnection of the vent pipe from natural gas heaters in our own greenhouse. Cymbidium plants near the break showed premature aging of the flowers. The flowers turned pink and faded (just as they do when the anthers are removed). Flowers that opened after the break was repaired showed no symptoms. In the other case, the cattleya plants themselves were affected. On the plants near the break (where the fumes were strongest), the older leaves turned a bright orange and fell. For as long as a year afterward, leaves on these same plants continued to age prematurely, although the plants finally recovered. A report from Australia suggests that smog is the cause of a leaf-tip necrosis in cymbidiums. We have heard that cymbidium, paphiopedilum, and odontoglossum flowers were injured at the New York International Flower Show a few years ago when trucks were used to clean the building and the fumes were retained in the building.

Gases other than ethylene may produce the same type of injuries. However, knowing that ethylene is at least one of the culprits removes some of the frustration we suffered in years past when we groped entirely in the dark. We know of nothing, yet, to prevent injury, except to vent all natural gas heaters and keep the plants in top condition. Plants that are not in the best of health may be more vulnerable to attack by the gas.

MECHANICAL AND CHEMICAL INJURIES TO PLANTS

Sharp bending of leaves, particularly the thick, brittle leaves of cattleyas and others, will cause injury to the tissues. The leaves may show a split down the mid-rib, or the end of the leaf beyond the point where it was bent may die. Young leaves are particularly tender and are sometimes unintentionaly broken when a plant is handled. They are also susceptible to bacterial and fungus infections, so if a leaf turns black investigate to see whether its death has been caused primarily by a break or by infection.

Insecticides not specifically recommended for orchids should not be used on them. Those recommended should be used exactly as directed on the label. Injury can be caused by insecticides not compatible with orchids, or by too strong concentrations even of those that are compatible. The injuries appear as burned or blistered spots on leaves. Flower buds may be killed, or blossoms be spotted.

FREAKS

Freak flowers or freak growths, called anomalies, occasionally occur; but for the most part they do not repeat themselves. Sometimes a flower has too few or too many parts, or the parts may be fused to each other. There have been reports of flowers having only two sepals, apparently a dorsal and a ventral sepal, of flowers having no lip or two lips, of flowers in which the lip has reverted to a petal in shape, of flowers in which petals have lip structure, of flowers in which the length of the lip is fused to the column or in which the sepals are fused for part of their length so that the bloom cannot open. Abnormal growths on plants have also been reported. For instance, a cattleya can have a growth with no leaf or a flower stem apparently arising from the base of a pseudobulb instead of from the apex. Sometimes a leaf may be tubular, not opening flat; and sometimes a sheath seems to be part true leaf and part sheath.

Such anomalies are ordinarily accidents in development. They can occur on a plant that has till then given all normal flowers and which thereafter continues to give normal flowers. These are not caused by changes in the genetic make-up of the plant.

However, genetic changes can occur. They are very rare. If a plant gives deformed flowers from the start, the cause is in its genetic make-up. If one flowers normally at first and then starts giving, and continues to give, abnormal flowers, this indicates that some change has taken place in its genes.

Chromosomal aberrations, such as the loss of a chromosome or two, or acquisition of an extra one or two, may cause abnormal growth in a plant. Possession by the plant cells of an odd number of chromosomes (a number over or under an even multiple of the haploid number) is called aneuploidy. This condition may be the basis for some abnormalities.

PARASITIC DISEASES, BACTERIAL, FUNGAL, AND VIRUS

During recent years work on orchid diseases has been intensified. Much has been learned about the diseases, their diagnosis, and the organisms which cause them; and many agents for their control have been developed. Orchid growers are indebted to research workers in many countries, and in the United States particularly to Peter A. Ark, D. D. Jensen, C. I. Kado, Harry C. Burnett, H. H. Murakishi, and Irene Gleason.

In even the best managed greenhouse there is occasionally a diseased plant. Some diseases are mild, doing little damage and easy to control; some are more serious and resist control quite stubbornly but, with persistence, most can be cured. A few come on suddenly and run rampant through a plant, at the same time exposing other plants dangerously. A grower must always be on the alert, ready with

Fig. 23-1 A freak flower that has three equal petals and three anthers. This is a particularly interesting anomaly because it shows an apparent reversion to some possible ancestral type, one in which the third petal had not been modified into a lip, nor the anthers reduced to a single one.

an effective fungicide to treat any suspicious spots, and observant of any spread of disease either in the plant in question or to its neighbors. If your experience with disease has been limited to an occasional incidence it is a compliment to your management. Maintainance of healthy growing conditions is in itself a method of disease control and prevention. The presence of a few diseased plants in a greenhouse where bad conditions exist can set off an epidemic, particularly when the elements conspire to spread infection, with long spells of cold, or warm, cloudy weather.

Bacteria, fungi, and viruses are ever present. Many that attack common garden crops will also attack orchids. Some species of these organisms are parasites on plant tissue and digest the cells for their own food. They enter the plant through wounds, even through such a small injury as an insect puncture, or through the stomata of the leaves. Bacteria reproduce in the plant tissue and come to the surface in minute, oozing droplets. They are spread from plant to plant by contact, contaminated hands or instruments, insects, and splashing water. A fungus usually grows with its cobweb-like body (mycelium) inside of a leaf, pseudobulb, etc., destroying the tissues as it spreads, the only part that appears on the surface being that which bears the spores, the reproductive cells. The spores are carried from plant to plant by the same means as bacteria. Viruses (which have characteristics of both living and non-living entities) reproduce only in living tissue, and travel very rapidly throughout the entire plant. Once infected, a plant contains the virus in all its parts. The infection can be spread to other plants by contaminated cutting tools and by aphids.

Bacterial and fungal diseases in their initial stages can be cured by the use of fungicides and, where necessary, by the removal of diseased parts plus treatment with fungicides. There are some bacterial and fungal diseases that typically advance so rapidly that they are rarely caught in time. As yet no cure has been found for virus diseases. Removal of a part that shows symptoms does not free the plant from the virus because it has traveled into every part (except possibly the minute tip of the growing stem. See p. 112). No chemical has been found which will kill the virus within the plant.

As the orchids themselves require certain conditions for favorable growth, so also do the bacteria and fungi. Many of the latter flourish when temperatures are low and humidity high, conditions that often plague European growers. So readily do diseases occur at such times that the earlier growers thought improper environment itself was the cause of disease. This idea prevailed until the last half of the nineteenth century, when it was demonstrated that plant infections were caused by bacteria and fungi, thriving and multiplying under these very conditions. Other pathogenic organisms thrive under conditions of warmer temperatures coupled with high humidity. Soft, succulent growth is particularly liable to infections.

Moisture is of the greatest significance in the spread of disease. In order for a fungus spore to germinate, or for bacteria to enter a plant, water must be present on rhizome, pseudobulb, leaf, or sheath. Hence good orchid culture calls for watering and syringing early enough in the day to allow the plants to dry off before night. Then, when temperatures are lower and humidity runs up to the saturation point, the plants offers dry surfaces to the potential enemy. Avoid crowding the plants on the bench, as this cuts down air circulation and allows moisture to remain for long periods.

Fans to keep the air circulating are a necessity. A fan in connection with the heater, such as described on page 24, is helpful. Some growers use turbulator fans placed toward the ridge. Another type is a small fan placed here and there to move the air over groups of plants. These can be put underneath the bench and pointed vertically, or they can be placed just over the tops of the plants, always situated to pick up the main stream of air and continue its movement toward one end or the other of the greenhouse.

Sanitation is important. Pathogenic organisms may be perpetuated on plant debris accumulated on or under the benches and may be spread from these sources by splashing water or by insects. Weeds, plant trimmings, old flowers, and all other debris must be cleared away. When treating a diseased plant any parts that are cut off should be burned or should be wrapped and disposed of with trash that is to be burned. Insect control is related to sanitation, since insects play a dual role in plant infection. They inflict wounds through which pathogenic organisms can enter, and they sometimes place in the wound organisms which they have picked up by contact with infected material. Aphids are particularly dangerous since certain species are known to be vectors of virus diseases.

When buying plants, choose those that appear to be disease-free. If you buy by mail, examine the plants carefully when they arrive before putting them with your other plants. If any have soft watery spots, or streaks or patterns of dead tissue in the leaves, reject them.

It is often difficult for an amateur to know what disease he is dealing with from the appearance of spots on his plants, particularly at the onset of the disease. In fact, for a long time it was difficult even for pathologists to do so. In the past few years pathologists have developed methods for culturing bacteria and fungi from tissues of diseased plants, inoculating the pure strains into healthy plants and observing the symptoms, and then recovering the organisms from the inoculated plants. Thus they have been able to study the symptoms produced by specific organisms and follow the course of the disease each causes.

Similarly, viruses have had to be isolated, purified, and inoculated into healthy plants. The virologists are now employing a new method for diagnosis, a *serological test* adopted from the field of immunology. Rabbits are injected with a pure strain of virus, to which they respond by forming antibodies. Juice from an infected plant is then added to a sample of serum taken from the rabbit blood. If the juice contains the specific virus with which the rabbit was inoculated, the antibodies will react with it. A virus test which amateurs can perform is given farther on in this chapter. The descriptions of the various diseases, from their onset through the courses they generally follow, which the pathologists have now made available to us, are a great help to orchid growers.

Laymen are for the most part still not able to pin down each disease to its causative agent, but we can come a lot closer than we could a few years ago. Where a disease is quite specific to a certain kind of orchid, for example miltonia scorch or paphiopedilum crown rot, or when you have seen a certain type a number of times and have learned its course and how it responds to treatment, you become fairly confident in your diagnosing. The viruses are more elusive, although some are so characteristic that an amateur can recognize their patterns. Sometimes diseases may fool you, some little clue may escape you, or you may not notice the disease until it has gone beyond the beginning stages. As far as bacterial and fungal diseases are concerned, those which you cannot treat you will recognize quickly, and for those that can be cured any of a number of fungicides can be used.

The first steps in control are to isolate the diseased plants, cut down the humidity, dispense with syringing, and increase ventilation. This will not only reduce the spread of disease to healthy plants but will help to check its spread in infected ones. Then treat the infected plants. If additional plants in the greenhouse become infected and it appears that the disease is spreading, the whole greenhouse may be sprayed with a fungicide.

CAUTION WITH CHEMICALS

Some of the products on the market today are deadly poisonous. We prefer not to recommend any of these. We see no use in risking injury to human life and health when products of lesser toxicity are available and perform satisfactorily. This does not mean that even those termed "moderately safe" are actually safe, for if used without caution or by persons sensitive to them they can cause serious illness. One should not be soothed by a moderate toxicity rating—*all should be handled with great care.* Any material that will kill a bug can affect a human being.

While many workers believe that they are unaffected by chemicals used as insecticides or fungicides (the "it can't happen to me" attitude), deaths have occurred from their use.* It is possible that a bad headache, a digestive upset, an unaccountable spell of fatigue or dizziness, or a feeling of sleepiness may be caused by them. These are all symptoms of poisoning.

Directions on the label should be followed exactly. Do not depend on memory for quantities as the danger includes injury to plants as well. Keep all chemicals locked up securely at all times. When a container is empty, dispose of it in such a way that it will not come into the hands of a child or a curious person for whom the few remaining drops could be deadly. Wear protective clothing. Take a bath immediately after spraying, and have the clothes worn during the job washed before using them again. Be careful not to inhale fumes, spray, or dust or get them on your skin. Face masks with felt or chemical cartridges are available from supply houses and are a good precaution, as are goggles.

A comprehensive list of chemicals and their toxicity is given in the appendix so that you may check a compound before deciding to use it, and can check those you may have on hand. There is a confusing array manufactured today, and new ones come out frequently. If you do not find the name, perhaps you can find the active ingredient listed.

* Some commercial growers have put all their spraying in the hands of professional contractors.

Before using any new product, find out whether it is safe for orchids as well as for yourself.

Poisons are rated on what is called an LD-50 base; LD stands for Lethal Dose, and 50 means a 50 percent kill of test animals. The number of milligrams per kilogram of body weight necessary to produce the 50 percent kill becomes the LD-50 number. For practical purposes *the lower the LD-50 number, the more poisonous is the material,* which means that it takes less to do damage.

Substances with numbers 1-5 are deadly poisonous; those with numbers 5-50 are violently poisonous. All these should be avoided. From 50-500 substances are poisonous; those with lower numbers should be avoided, those approaching 500 indicate great caution.

Over 500, substances become relatively less poisonous as the number increases, but even those with numbers up to 5,000 can cause illness in a child or a sensitive person.

Over 5,000 substances become relatively safe.

In the list below are a few examples of the deadly poisons on the market today. And following this, a list of substances recommended in this book, so that you can check their toxicity. Even some of these are very poisonous and must be handled with extreme care.

Substances Deadly Poisonous

For a comprehensive list, see Appendix.

Substance	LD-50	Notes
All arsenic compounds	10-50	Injurious to orchids as well as very toxic to man.
All cyanide compounds	5	
All organic mercury compounds	30	
Acti-dione (antibiotic)	5-50	See next list.
Aldrin	55	
BHC (benzene hexa-chloride)	125	
Botran (Dimefox, BFPO)	50	
Ceresan	5	Used in commercial seed treatment. Not advised for home use.
Demeton (Systox)	6	
Dieldrin	40	Banned in some states.
Dithio, Plantfume, Bladafume, Bladex, and other smoke fumigants.	2,5	Never use in home greenhouse. Drift of smoke to home, neighbors, etc., extremely dangerous.
Endrin	5	
Ethion	46	
Guthion	15	

Substance	LD-50	Notes
Lindane	125	
Pano-drench, Panogen	5	
Parathion	3	Banned by law in most states.
Sulfatepp	5	
TEPP	2	
Thimet (phorate)	3	
Vapona (DDVP)	60	
Vapotone (TEPP)	2	
Zectran	16	

Substances in This Book

Substance	LD-50	Notes
Actidione (an antibiotic)	5-50	Extremely toxic. Use only in dire emergency and then with utmost caution.
Anti-Damp	1200	
Aramite	2000	
Arasan	500	Bad reaction with liquor.
Bordeaux	500	
Bioquin 1	5000	
Captan	9000	Can cause injury to flowers.
Chlorobenzilate	3200	
Consan-20	circa 500	
Cygon	215	Not advised. See page 327.
Dimite	500	
Ferbam	5000	
Kelthane	500	
Malathion	880	
Metaldehyde	350	Mask advised if applied as dust.
Natriphene	1200	
Parzate	5000	
Shield	50-500	
Simazine	bet. 500 & 5000	
Tedion	14,000	
Tersan	500	Bad reaction with liquor.
Zineb	5000	

Symptoms of poisoning by the various chemicals include the following, singly or several together: unconsciousness, collapse, convulsions, tremor, nervousness, staggering, loss of coordination, dizziness, sedation (sleepiness), nausea, vomiting, diarrhea, cramps, excessive salivation, difficulty in breathing. If any of these occur, get emergency help at once. Take the container with the patient so that the doctor can know at once what the ingredients are and can contact the nearest poison control center if necessary.

BACTERIAL AND FUNGAL DISEASES

Both bacterial and fungal diseases begin with water-soaked, semi-transparent spots. As the disease spreads a single spot may enlarge until it involves a whole leaf, sometimes spreading from there through the pseudobulb and into the rhizome, or a number of small spots may individually enlarge until they run together. Spots on leaves are easy to detect, but a diseased area on a pseudobulb may escape notice. If the side of a pseudobulb appears to cave in, or if the pseudobulb falls over, investigate to see whether there is an area softened by disease. Some diseases caused by soil-borne organisms may penetrate the plant by way of the roots, progressing to the rhizome and sometimes into the pseudobulbs These are less obvious at their onset because their presence is not suspected until the leaves become soft and wrinkled, or the new lead turns black. In such cases it may be necessary to cut through the rhizome, starting at the older end of the plant, to determine whether the root loss and leaf wilt are caused by disease. If the tissue of the rhizome is clean and white, or cream-colored, it is healthy. If it has black or purple discoloration it is diseased. Before cutting into the rhizome, be sure that the root loss has not been caused by snails.

The list of effective fungicides is long, and new ones are being added to it rapidly. Among them are some with fairly long residual action: Bordeaux Mixture (copper sulfate and lime, an old remedy but still useful), Tersan, Arasan, Ferbam, Zineb, Parzate, Captan, and Bioquin 1 (copper 8-quinolinolate). These are all valuable both as curative sprays and as preventive sprays where large numbers of plants require treating, but they may also be used to spray or sponge individual plants. Some are insoluble in water and are used in a suspension, some are combined with a sticker to make their application more permanent. Bordeaux Mixture may not be as effective as some of the newer fungicides, but if you are faced with the emergency treatment of a plant and cannot readily obtain one of the others, you can usually find Bordeaux Mixture at a local drug or garden store. It can be made into a thick slurry, even a paste, and be applied to wounds or diseased spots. Tersan may be used one teaspoon per gallon of water as a preventive spray, but for infected plants the solution should be one tablespoon per gallon. It may be made into a slurry or a paste and applied to infected areas and to wounds.

With any spray a better spread and quicker drying is obtained by the addition of a wetting agent such as Triton B-1956 or Ortho spreader-sticker, used according to directions. A few drops of a mild household detergent may be used in an emergency, but repeated use of such is not advised as injury may result.

Fungicides which have a shorter residual action but which are very effective are: Natriphene, the sodium salt of o-hydroxydiphenyl, in a concentration of 1:2000, used as a spray or drench; 8-quinolinol sulfate or 8-quinolinol benzoate, the active ingredient in Wilson's Anti-Damp and other preparations, used in a concentration of 1:2000 as a spray or drench. Those that can be used as drenches, in addition to being very effective, are nontoxic to plants; plants from community pot size to adults can be soaked in the solution for several hours at a time.

Not much work has been done as yet with antibiotics on orchids, and we cannot recommend any without reservation at this time. Growers should follow developments in this field for it may be that some will prove safe and useful.

Since diseases can be spread from plant to plant by cutting tools, these should be disinfected after use on each plant. The best method is to boil them or pass them through a flame. An electric cautery tool, if one is available to you, is excellent.

Pythium black rot and damp-off. A water mold, *Pythium ultimum,* causes this disease which results in damp-off of community pot seedlings and which also attacks older plants. It requires free water in order to spread, and since community pots are kept damp and the plants are tender and close together, they are most vulnerable to this fungus. Prevention calls for watering the pots every month or so with Anti-Damp or Natriphene. If a seedling in a pot shows evidence of infection by turning brown and translucent, act quickly. Remove the infected seedling and soak the whole pot in Anti-Damp or Natriphene for several hours. In older seedlings black spots on the basal portion or on the leaves quickly spread to involve the whole plant. Cut out diseased areas and soak as for community pots. Older plants are usually infected through the roots and the disease spreads into the rhizome and thence into the pseudobulbs, but occasionally the route is reversed, starting with a leaf and spreading to the pseudobulbs and thence from one pseudobulb to another. High humidity and cool temperatures favor it. The streaked and blackened tissues sometimes become soft and limp,

Fig. 23-2 Pythium black rot on cattleya pseudobulbs. LEFT, the disease starting at the top. RIGHT, spreading upward from the rhizome. (*Courtesy Peter A. Ark*)

kinds of orchids, among them *Cymbidium* and *Paphiopedilum*. The base of the stem turns light yellow, later dark brown, and the infection spreads to the roots and up into the leaves. The white fungus growth can sometimes be seen on the stems. Later tiny, hard yellow bodies (sclerotia) are formed by the mycelium, which can live for a long time and serve to perpetuate the fungus. The disease thrives with temperatures of about 85° and high humidity. Cut out the diseased portion and immerse the plant in Natriphene for an hour or more.

Heart rot. The fungus, *Phytophthora omnivora*, causes a serious rot that starts in the heart of the plant where the leaves join the stem, and spreads upward through the leaves. This fungus is related to the one that infects the potato, and which ruined the potato crop in Ireland in 1845, causing the famine that killed some 250,000 people. The *Phytophthora omnivora* infection of orchids begins with the appearance of dark, sharply delimited lesions in the very heart of the plant. The infected area spreads rapidly, until within a few days the entire leaf is discolored and falls off. In severe cases the infection spreads from the heart to new leaves formed after the older ones have fallen. In milder instances, the infection may be confined to one of the older leaves, especially if the plant is kept dry. The disease spreads rapidly from plant

and exude water on pressure. As the leaves fall and the contents of the pseudobulbs become completely decayed, all that remain are dried and husk-like remnants of the pseudobulbs. If the disease appears above the level of the rhizome of an adult plant, cut away the streaked and blackened tissue well down into healthy tissue, soak the whole plant, pot and all, for several hours in Anti-Damp or Natriphene, and then let it dry out completely. Spray it with Tersan or Ferbam or one of the other long-lasting fungicides, and give water in the pot only (no syringing) for long enough to ascertain whether the disease is arrested. If the disease spreads upward through the rhizome (see Fig. 23-2), cut between the pseudobulbs until you find a healthy section of the plant. Save only this section and treat as above. If the disease continues to spread the plant may have to be discarded.

Collar rot or orchid wilt. This disease is caused by the fungus *Sclerotium rolfsii,* and affects many

Fig. 23-3 *Sclerotium rolfsii* on the base of cymbidium leaves. Note the white fungus growth and the small round sclerotia. (*Courtesy Peter A. Ark*)

Home Orchid Growing

to plant, injuring especially the highly susceptible *Vanda* and *Phalaenopsis,* but also infecting *Cattleya* and other genera. Young seedlings are very liable to infection. Moist, warm conditions favor its spread. Another species of fungus, *Phytophthora palmivora,* has been isolated from *Dendrobium* in Ceylon and *Vanda* and *Cattleya* in Java. Remove infected leaves or portions of leaves, in hopes of saving the growing point of the plant. Treat with Zineb, or drench with Natriphene, or dip the plant (section above the roots) in Tersan and sprinkle Tersan powder into the heart section. If the growing tip of a vanda is killed, cut the stem well below the tip area and hope for a healthy side shoot. In *Dendrobium* or others, where the top or flowering section of the stem is killed, remove the stem to its healthy base. Repeat treatment with fungicide.

Root Rot. Caused by the fungus *Pellicularia filamentosa,* this is a brown rot that can rapidly kill small seedlings, and bring about the death of older seedlings and mature plants. The brown mycelium infects the roots and progresses through the rhizome and the lower parts of pseudobulbs. Young seedlings are quickly girdled; older plants go into a slow decline as water and nutrient absorption is cut off. Their leaves and pseudobulbs become yellow, twisted, and shrivelled. Soak the plants in Natriphene 1:2000, or treat with Zineb, Tersan, etc. Then repot in fresh medium.

Fusarium wilt. The organisms *Fusarium oxysporum* and *moniliforme* infect the plants through the roots or cut ends of the rhizome. A circle or band of purple discoloration appears in the outer layers of the rhizome, and a pink-purple color travels through the conducting tissue. The entire rhizome may turn purple, and this may extend into the pseudobulbs. Toxic substances produced by the fungus affect the plant, and plugging of the vessels causes failure of transportation of water. The edges of the leaves may turn grayish green and this may progress until the leaves die. To save a plant, all diseased tissue should be removed. This means cutting through the rhizome, sterilizing the knife each time, until perfectly clean tissue is reached. You may not have much plant left, but if it is a valuable one it will be worth the effort to save it. Spray the plant and those that surrounded it on the bench with Actidione, one tablespoon to one gallon of water. (This is also known as Germain's Mildew and Rust Control.) Use great caution as this is extremely toxic. Repeat

Fig. 23-4 Cymbidium tip burn caused by *Botrytis* fungus. (*Courtesy Peter A. Ark*)

every three days, three times. It is possible that this disease is the one described for cymbidiums and illustrated in that chapter.

Cymbidium tip burn. *Botrytis* sp. causes the tip of the leaves to become spotted; as the spots coalesce the whole tip dries. Powdery masses of spores may be seen on dead leaf parts. Diseased tips should be cut off and the plant treated with Tersan or other fungicide.

Anthracnose or leaf spot. Many species of *Gleosporium* and *Colletotrichum* cause this disease in *Cattleya, Paphiopedilum, Epidendrum, Cymbidium, Vanda, Coelogyne, Laelia, Odonto-*

glossum, Oncidium, Phalaenopsis, and others. The fungi are prevalent in most greenhouses and infection is favored by warm temperatures, excessive moisture, and insufficient light. Leaves develop circular or oval sunken spots, that are reddish brown at first, becoming dark brown or gray with age. As the spots dry, black fruiting bodies of the fungus form in the area and these can carry the disease to other plants. Infections are often quite mild, and may be limited by reducing the humidity. However, the whole greenhouse cannot be kept dry in order to control anthracnose, so the plants are

Fig. 23-5 Leaf spot caused by *Gleosporium,* on leaf of *Odontoglossum grande.* (*Courtesy Peter A. Ark*)

best treated. Copper compounds are especially effective, swabbed on the spots, as are Bordeaux Mixture, Tersan, Zineb and other fungicides. If the infection becomes more serious, and the spots enlarge and spread, entire leaves and occasionally a whole plant may be killed. Cut off the badly affected leaves, and repeat treatments with a fungicide until the spread is ended.

One species, *Gleosporium affine,* spreads rather rapidly through leaves of *Oncidium, Odontoglossum* and *Dendrobium.* As the infection progresses toward the base of the leaf the outer portion dies, becoming thin, dry, and light brown. Fruiting bodies of the fungus develop in concentric rings which may be circular or diamond shaped. One's first thought on seeing these is that they may represent a virus infection, but close examination will reveal that the rings are formed by tiny black bodies. If anthracnose is general throughout the greenhouse, spray with one of the long-acting fungicides described earlier.

Leaf Spot. Several species of *Cercospora* cause leaf spot in a variety of orchids. These usually appear as yellow spots which become sunken and turn dark, as small brown spots that become darker and sunken, or as brown streaks. In all cases, the spots enlarge and the affected tissue dies, sometimes with the death of the whole leaf. Small seedlings may be killed. Treatment involves dipping or soaking the plant in one of the recommended fungicides, such as Captan, Ferbam, Zineb, etc., and if the spotting is particularly serious removal of the affected leaves. Surrounding plants should be sprayed with a fungicide as preventative.

Leaf blight. A water mold, *Pythium splendens,* causes leaf blight. The disease starts on a leaf, especially of *Cattleya,* as a round spot of chestnut brown color, often on the edge of the leaf, which enlarges rapidly and turns black. The area becomes thin. Cut out diseased portion well below infected area, and apply Tersan to the whole plant. Keep the plant parts dry and cut down on watering.

Leaf die-back. A fungus, *Glomerella cincta,* causes an infection which starts at the tip of the leaf and spreads toward the base, involving the whole width of the leaf. There is a marked line of distinction between the diseased and the healthy area. The infected area turns soft and brown; later it dries. Cut off the diseased area below the line of infection, and treat the cut edge and remaining part of the leaf with a fungicide such as Tersan. Many kinds of orchids are affected.

Flower speck and blight. *Botrytis cinerea, Sclerotinia fuckeliana* and other fungi cause flower speck and blight. The disease appears at first as tiny water-soaked spots which become larger and turn pink, tan, or brown. It is especially prevalent under damp cool conditions, but can occur at other times. Infected flowers should be removed and destroyed at once as their presence allows for rapid spread of the disease. Old flowers can be a reservoir of infection. Reduce the humidity in the greenhouse and give good ventilation and air movement. If the nights are running too cool, raise the temperature a bit. Spray with a fungicide such as Zineb, Ferbam, etc. Note: Captan can injure flowers and is not suggested for use on them. Keep trash cleaned up as dead plant material can harbor disease-causing fungi.

Black sheaths. Green sheaths are sometimes attacked by one or another of the fungi described, especially under humid conditions and when water is left standing in the pocket between leaf and sheath. If the sheaths are treated in time and are allowed to remain dry, the infection need not spread to the flower buds within. Cut off the sheath

Fig. 23-6 Flower speck caused by *Botrytis cinerea*. (*Courtesy Peter A. Ark*)

above the buds and spray the sheath and buds with Tersan, Zineb, or Natriphene.

Rusts. Many kinds of orchids are subject to attacks by the rust fungus *Hemileia americana*, and possibly by some other species. The fungus produces powdery masses of yellow to yellow-orange spores, which are easily spread from plant to plant. Although plants are seldom killed they can be weakened so that they flower poorly or not at all. Treat with one of the copper-containing fungicides, or with Tersan.

Saprophytic fungi. These are not parasitic, that is, they do not attack living tissue. They live only on dead plant material, such as the dead sheathing leaves of stem, dead sheaths, or parts of leaves that have been killed by other organisms or have died naturally. They thrive under humid conditions where there is not sufficient air movement. Oddly enough, a single plant may show saprophytic fungi on the tissues clothing the stems or rhizomes when others around it are free. Perhaps it is too crowded by surrounding plants to allow the air to move as freely as it should, or the plant may have been kept too wet for a period, allowing the fungus to become established. Drying off the plant will stop the growth of the fungus, although the spots it caused will remain. While the saprophytic fungi are not a threat to the plant they indicate a condition that should be corrected. Perhaps spacing the plants farther apart is all that is necessary.

Snow Mold. A species of *Ptychogaster* produces a white powdery growth on the potting medium which soon covers the roots and rhizome causing suffocation and dehydration. It is quite impermeable to water, and therefore prevents the roots from obtaining it. Treat the pot with Shield 10 percent, one ounce to four gallons of water. If much mold is present, remove all potting medium and treat the plant, then repot it and water it with the Shield solution to prevent regrowth of the fungus. Other molds in the potting medium may be handled in the same way.

Sooty mold. A sooty mold appears occasionally on plants, even on flowers. The organism does not attack the plant parts; it merely grows on the "honey" exuded by them, or on the excrement of aphids or scale insects. It can be washed off with water and a cotton swab. It is fostered by high humidity.

Bacterial brown spot. This disease is caused by *Phytomonas cattleyae,* which enters the plant through wounds or through the stomata. While it attacks *Cattleya* and other genera, it is particularly serious on *Phalaenopsis* and on community pot seedlings. It begins with a small water-soaked spot which is dirty green at first turning brown and sometimes black. The spot enlarges rapidly. On *Phalaenopsis* the spot is blister-like and quickly spreads to the heart of the plant so that if it is not arrested it will kill the plant. Seedlings are also killed quickly. The infected tissues are soft and watery, often breaking open and exuding masses of bacteria which can then quickly spread the infection. On cattleyas, older seedlings and mature plants, the disease does not travel so rapidly, except that a young lead can be quickly killed. Cut out all diseased areas as soon as the disease is detected. Soak community pots, young seedlings, and mature plants for several hours in Natriphene or Anti-Damp. As soon as the plant parts are dry, spray with Tersan, Ferbam, or another long-lasting fungicide.

Miltonia scorch. Also called bacterial tip burn and streak. This is found thus far only on *Miltonia,* and the organism has not yet been identified. It is a cool temperature disease and extremely infectious. It starts as water-soaked spots on the tip or margin of a leaf, often on newly developing leaves, and spreads to the pseudobulb. The pseudobulb becomes yellow to orange in color, and has areas that look eaten or burned away. They become tough and leathery. The diseased parts should be

Fig. 23-8 Miltonia scorch. Also called bacterial tip burn and streak. LEFT, infection originating in the pseudobulbs. RIGHT, originating on the leaves. (*Courtesy Peter A. Ark*)

cut away, and the plant should be immersed in Natriphene or Anti-Damp for several hours.

Brown rot of Paphiopedilum. This disease is caused by the bacillus, *Erwinia cypripedii,* which apparently enters through wounds. It starts as a small chestnut-brown spot on a leaf, usually spreading in both directions so that it soon reaches the crown of the plant. It spreads through successive leaves until a whole growth is affected. Sometimes the growth is killed before the outer ends of the leaves have turned brown. It spreads so rapidly that it can travel through a plant of many leads killing the whole plant. If it is caught soon enough, however, the plant may be saved by cutting off leaves below the infection, cutting out whole growths by severing the rhizome if they have been infected to the base. The plant is then soaked for several hours in Natriphene or Anti-Damp. The soaking should be repeated two or three times at intervals of a few days, else the disease may start up again. After treatment try to keep the foliage dry, watering the pot carefully so as not to splash water on the leaves. In a group of plants where this disease has once occurred, it will help prevent further attacks if they are sprayed with Tersan or other fungicide every three months or so.

Bacterial soft rot. Incurable. This disease is caused by the bacillus, *Erwinia carotovora.* Cattleyas are most seriously affected, although a large number of other kinds are also attacked. The disease is rare, but it is so destructive and infectious that it is suggested that plants be destroyed immediately rather than be treated. The disease

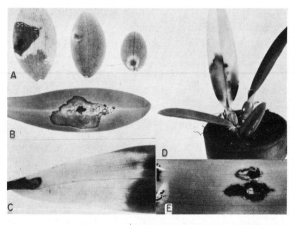

Fig. 23-7 Bacterial brown spot caused by *Phytomonas cattleyae. A, B, C* on Phalaenopsis seedlings and full grown plants; *D* and *E* on *Cattleya trianaei.* (*Courtesy Peter A. Ark*)

starts with a water-soaked dark green spot on the upper end of a leaf. It feels watery and breaks open at a slight touch. The inner tissues of the leaf are rapidly destroyed and the leaf becomes flaccid and wrinkled. The epidermis is so soft that it often breaks open, exuding its watery content and thus contaminating the bench and in fact the whole area surrounding the plant. A foul smell often accompanies the disease. After destroying the plant, thoroughly disinfect the area by drenching bench, posts, and floor with mercuric chloride solution 1:1000 using caution and wearing rubber gloves. Treat neighboring plants with a fungicide.

Bacterial leaf rot. The bacillus *Erwinia chrysanthemi* has recently been found to be the cause of leaf rot in a number of kinds of orchids in Hawaii. In *Grammatophyllum* diseased areas are water-soaked and brownish. In *Dendrobium,* the leaves are water-soaked and yellow. In *Vanda* the disease begins with translucent areas on the leaves, which become dark in color and finally black and sunken. Prevention includes spraying with Natriphene before and during wet weather, and control necessitates removal of the diseased areas and treatment with a fungicide.

VIRUS DISEASES

The study of virus diseases in orchids is a tremendous field; a great deal has been accomplished in the short time of work devoted to it. The study

Fig. 23-9 Bacterial soft rot. Incurable. Caused by *Erwinia carotovora*. The affected leaf shows wrinkling due to collapse of internal tissues. (*Courtesy D. P. Limber and B. A. Friedman*)

is complicated by many things. A certain virus may infect a number of different kinds of orchids, producing different symptoms in each, while different viruses may produce the same symptoms in a single host. In one host a virus may cause only mild symptoms, while in another the same virus may produce a serious disease. Viruses have been isolated from many kinds of orchids. A goodly number of these have been inoculated into species other than those in which they were originally found in an effort to determine whether they are capable of infecting different kinds of plants. It has been found, for instance, that the virus causing severe color breaking in cattleya flowers produces a bar mottle pattern in cymbidium leaves. The virus that produces cymbidium necrotic ringspot infects *Cattleya* and *Spathoglottis* causing death of the new shoots. Cymbidium mosaic virus produces dead areas in the leaves of *Cattleya*. In order to separate just a few of the viruses and determine their action on just a few species, thousands upon thousands of separations of viruses, inoculations into healthy plants, and reverse inoculations from these back to members of the original host species have had to be performed.

Viruses are spread from plant to plant by means of infected cutting tools (sometimes infected in such an apparently harmless way as cutting flowers), and by insect vectors. Divisions of infected plants carry the virus with them. Plants known to be infected should be destroyed. This is a simple matter when the grower can recognize the symptoms, as in cattleyas with color break of the flowers, and when, as Dr. Jensen says, the plant does so poorly that the grower gets rid of it, probably without even knowing that it has had a virus infection. But when the symptoms are obscure or mild enough to pass unnoticed or to be thought not significant, it is not such an easy matter. One cannot always throw away plants on a mere suspicion. If you suspect a plant of having a virus infection, and cannot be sure from descriptions or photographs, keep it somewhat separate from other plants and enlist the aid of some of the experienced growers you know or send specimens away for diagnosis.

To disinfect tools, either flame or boil them.

Virus Diseases in Cattleya

Severe color break of flowers. The color of the flowers is irregularly mottled with light and dark areas and the flowers are often malformed. The

Fig. 23-10 Cattleya severe flower break virus symptoms in *Cattleya* and *Cymbidium*. From LEFT TO RIGHT: flower showing severe color break and some malformation; young cattleya shoot showing rosy mottling; mature cattleya leaf with mosaic of dark-green raised areas; two cymbidium leaves with bar mottle caused by the cattleya severe flower break virus. (*Courtesy D. D. Jensen*)

mottling is evident as dark and light areas in the bud. Leaves formed after infection have a mottling of dark green raised areas, called mosaic mottle. Young growths often have a streaking of rosy color. The virus is transmitted by the green peach aphid, and also by tools. The same virus infects *Cymbidium,* producing **bar mottle** in the leaves, and it can also infect *Oncidium.*

Mild flower breaking. Less severe mottling of the flowers without malformation and milder symptoms in the leaves are caused by the **odontoglossum ringspot virus.** According to Dr. C. I. Kado, this virus is the same as tobacco mosaic virus type "O." Because the symptoms are mild, the disease is sometimes overlooked until valuable plants are attacked. Intergeneric hybrids of *Cattleya* are equally susceptible.

Symmetrical flower breaking. Dark pigment outlines the sepals and covers all but the median area of the petals in flowers that have previously been normal. The disease seems thus far limited to *Cattleya.*

Blossom brown necrotic streak. This serious disease of cattleya flowers is caused by the presence of two viruses in the plant. At present it is not known whether flowers of other genera are affected. The disease shows up from a few days to a week or more after the flowers open, when brown

Fig. 23-11 Cattleya blossom brown necrotic streak. The lesions in general follow the veins of the flower parts, although when the disease has progressed to the point where spots have enlarged and coalesced this is sometimes difficult to ascertain. (*Courtesy Harry C. Burnett*)

Home Orchid Growing

streaks appear along the veins, sometimes showing up first along the mid-vein although this is not always the case. The disease will not usually be mistaken for spotting by *Botrytis,* but if there is any question, watch the plant through its next flowering —if it shows up again you can know that it is the virus-caused disease. Research continues on the nature of the viruses. One has a shape similar to that of cymbidium mosaic virus, the other to that of tobacco mosaic virus type "O." In neither case has it been established that they are identical to the known forms of these. Symptoms may or may not show in the plant. In some cases yellow streaks along the leaf veins have accompanied the disease, but many plants are without symptoms. The brown necrotic streaks are especially noticeable on white flowers, less easy to see on colored ones. The latter should be watched carefully. Plants having this disease should be destroyed.

Leaf necrosis. Caused by the **cymbidium mosaic virus.** The initial infection may kill some of the leaves, and it produces various patterns of dead tissue in others. After the first shock to the plant, leaves formed subsequently may show only mild symptoms and be overlooked. Unless the disease is caught during the early stages, the plant may thus remain in the greenhouse as a reservoir of infection. Necrotic areas may appear as brown sunken pits on the underside of the leaves, as alter-

nate black and chlorotic streaks, or occasionally as rings of dead tissue on the underside. Sometimes the leaves have lengthwise stripes of white or grey and are rough both in appearance and to the touch, and this symptom is easy to distinguish from fungus infections.

Severe leaf necrosis. Caused by the **cymbidium necrotic ringspot virus,** it is deadly, although rather rare. New shoots as well as older leaves are killed, and death of the plant soon follows.

Tobacco mosaic virus "orchid" or "O" type. This virus may be present in *Cattleya* and *Phalaenopsis* without symptoms, or at best showing as light yellow streaks on the leaves. Apparently it does not produce symptoms in the flowers. The danger is that the combination with the virus similar to cymbidium mosaic virus produces the blossom brown necrotic streak. This is a particularly good example of the necessity of caution in handling plants and of sterilizing tools, for one cannot know whether the virus is present or not, at least not without testing every plant.

Virus Diseases in Cymbidium

Cymbidium mosaic. The most common virus disease in orchids. It is this virus with which *Cym.* Alexanderi 'Westonbirt' is infected, and all of the

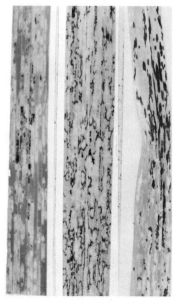

Fig. 23-12 Cymbidium mosaic virus affecting *Cattleya* and *Cymbidium.* The three cattleya leaves at the LEFT show respectively light brown pits on the under surface; streaks of black and yellow tissue; and necrotic rings on the under surface. The three cymbidium leaves at the RIGHT show various mosaic patterns of light and dark green tissue, with some black areas of dead tissue. (*Courtesy D. D. Jensen*)

divisions of that original plant carry the virus. The symptoms first appear as small elongated yellow (chlorotic) streaks on the younger leaves. As growth advances, the chlorotic streaks widen and elongate, and become more sharply defined, sometimes including in their width streaks of green tissue. Necrosis (death of tissues) does not usually occur on the young leaves, but older infected leaves frequently show black streaks and spots, often so severe as to cause the premature death of these leaves. This symptom gave rise to the original name of the disease "black streak." Sometimes the mottling that is present when the leaves are young becomes less conspicuous as the leaves grow old. Plants with mild infection are not greatly affected as to growth and production of flowers, but badly infected plants grow and flower poorly. Viruses extracted from *Laelia anceps, Angraecum eburneum, Epidendrum, Zygopetalum,* and *Oncidium* caused identical symptoms in *Cymbidium* and may be the cymbidium mosaic virus. This virus causes **leaf necrosis in Cattleya.**

Fig. 23-13 Necrotic ringspot virus of *Cymbidium,* the most severe disease of *Cymbidium,* which also causes severe leaf necrosis in *Cattleya.* The first two cymbidium leaves show necrotic rings and spots resulting from the original infection. The next two leaves, produced respectively several months and one year after infection, show necrotic and chlorotic mottling. At the right is a young cattleya leaf with severe necrosis caused by the cymbidium necrotic ringspot virus. (*Courtesy D. D. Jensen*)

Necrotic ringspot. The most severe virus disease in cymbidiums. Instead of causing merely yellowed areas, it produces dead areas—in a pattern of rings, spots, and streaks—on old as well as young leaves. It frequently kills new growths and sometimes the whole plant. This is the virus that causes **severe necrosis in Cattleya** and **Spathoglottis.**

Diamond mottle. The **odontoglossum ringspot virus** (which also causes **mild flower break in cattleyas**) produces elongate chlorotic areas which are often diamond shaped. In older leaves, however, the areas may become necrotic and coalesce to form patterns called "hieroglyphic."

Bar mottle. Caused by the **severe flower-break virus of Cattleya.** Produces very pronounced intermittent lines of rectangular chlorotic areas. Some of the areas may later become necrotic.

Virus Diseases in Odontoglossum

Ringspot. Affecting especially *Odontoglossum grande,* in which it produces concentric rings of necrotic tissue that may enclose some normal green tissue. The rings may coalesce to form varied patterns. Symptoms are worse during the first few months of the disease, and many leaves may fall. After the initial shock wears off, the plant may show few symptoms, although it still carries the virus. The **odontoglossum ringspot virus** causes **mild flower break in Cattleya** and **diamond mottle in Cymbidium.**

Streak. Irregular streaks and small rings, which are light green to yellow at first, later become reddish to black.

Mosaic. Leaves are stunted and have mosaic patterns of light and dark green areas.

Virus Diseases in Spathoglottis

Diamond spot. Chlorotic spots and streaks are followed by reddish brown to black spots, necrotic rings, and diamond-shaped areas, with severely damaged leaves falling prematurely. H. H. Murakishi, searching for a plant that could be used as an indicator of virus in other orchids, especially those with mild or doubtful symptoms, found that *Spathoglottis* is extremely susceptible to infection by a variety of viruses in other genera. Viruses from eight genera—including *Cattleya, Cymbid-*

324   Home Orchid Growing

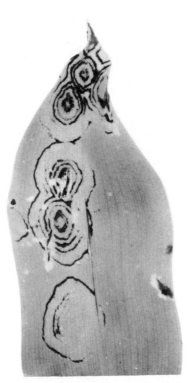

Fig. 23-14 Odontoglossum ringspot virus. LEFT, *Odontoglossum grande* with concentric rings of necrotic tissue enclosing normal or light green tissue. RIGHT, a cymbidium leaf showing diamond mottle as a result of infection with the odontoglossum ringspot virus. (*Courtesy D. D. Jensen*)

ium, Dendrobidium, Miltonia, Vanda, and others —were experimentally inoculated into healthy *Spathoglottis* seedlings. In almost every case, they produced necrotic ringspots and mosaic, the symptoms in *Spathoglottis* being almost identical regardless of the symptoms caused in the plants from which the viruses were taken. A test for virus, using *Spathoglottis,* is described below.

Virus Diseases in Other Orchids

A mosaic disease occurs in *Dendrobidium nobile,* consisting of chlorotic areas varying from small spots to large mottled areas, with occasional rings enclosing green tissue. A **mosaic with flower break** has been reported from Hawaii on *Dendrobium anosmum,* and a **ringspot** on *Dendrobium phalaenopsis,* also from Hawaii.

Severe mosaic streaking occurs in *Oncidium varicosum* and *Oncidium concolor,* characterized by irregular chlorotic spots and streaks in the leaves.

Apparently this is the same virus that causes **cymbidium mosaic** and **cattleya mild flower break.** An infection consisting of **stippled streaks** has been found in *Oncidium flexuosum* and a **light green mosaic mottle** in *Oncidium altissimum.*

Black streak is common in *Epidendrum O'Brianianum* hybrids. It starts with black sunken spots on the underside of the leaves, which show rosy rings on the upper surface. Later the dark areas extend into streaks or lines of spots. When inoculated into cymbidium seedlings, the virus produces mosaic symptoms and may be the **cymbidium mosaic virus.**

A disease called "etch" has been found in a group of plants of *Laelia anceps* in California. Leaves show lines and partial rings of brown to necrotic tissue on the outer portions. Although half of the cymbidum seedlings inoculated with the juice from these plants developed mosaic, the relationship between this and the true cymbidium mosaic virus has not yet been established.

A striking infection was discovered in a group of *Stanhopea* plants imported into California. **Yellow spots and rings** form a sharp contrast to the green leaf tissue. Young leaves acquire the symptoms while small, and the symptoms increase with the age of the leaf.

Work is in progress on viruses in other genera. Viruses that produce known diseases in certain genera may be the cause of infections not yet realized, and others will undoubtedly be discovered.

Testing for Virus

A great help to orchid growers has been the discovery of several non-orchidaceous plants that are specific indicators for cymbidium mosaic virus and tobacco mosaic virus type "O." Each is sensitive to one type of virus only and gives a quick and visible reaction to it. Thus each can be used to show the presence or absence of the particular virus in a suspected orchid.

Cassia occidentalis, Chenopodium amaranticolor * and *Datura stramonium* are used to test for cymbidium mosaic virus. When their leaves are inoculated with the juice from a suspected orchid, they react by developing a sprinkling of brown spots on the leaf surface if this virus is present,

---

* Seeds of these plants may be bought from Harry E. Saier, Dimondale, Michigan. A minimum order of $.50 is requested.

the *Cassia* plants sometimes within four days, the others within ten days.

Chenopodium amaranticolor is also used to test for Odontoglossum ringspot virus.

Gomphrena globosa * and *Chenopodium quinoa* are used to test for tobacco mosaic virus type "O." They react within ten days by showing light sunken areas on the leaf if it is present.

Seedlings are raised from these species in pots in the ordinary manner. They can be used as soon as they have several pairs of well-developed leaves, and function better while young.

The general method of making the test is to brush a leaf with a fine abrasive, and then to apply juice from a suspected plant. A localized reaction results. It takes a bit of practice to perform the test, and it is a good idea to have control leaves treated only with the abrasive for comparison between possible scars from the abrasive and spots due to the virus. You may invent your own procedure, but one will be suggested here.

Select the plants you are going to test and make small paper labels with the plant names or numbers, e.g. Plant #1, Control #1. Tie the little labels with thread to pairs of leaves on the test plant. With a sterile brush (a camel hair water-color brush, boiled and dried) brush the upper surface of both test and control leaves with carborundum 3/F grit. Use a stroke gentle enough not to injure the leaves so much as to produce scars if possible, but firm enough to cause the abrasive to nick the leaf surface or the hairs on the leaf.

In performing the test be careful not to let your fingers become contaminated with juice or you will spread virus from one plant to the next or one test leaf to another. Use a fold of clean paper to hold the tip of a leaf while you cut off a portion with a sterile razor blade. Still holding it with the paper, hold the leaf on a saucer and cut thin slices. Then with a spoon, pressing your finger into its bowl, crush these slices until a little pool of juice collects. Catch a drop of juice on the bottom of the spoon and spread it on the test leaf. Drop spoon, razor blade, and saucer into a pan, to be boiled later.

Repeat the process for each plant to be tested, putting the instruments used with it into the pan directly afterward so that none will be used again before boiling. Boil them for half an hour.

Watch for the reaction through the next several

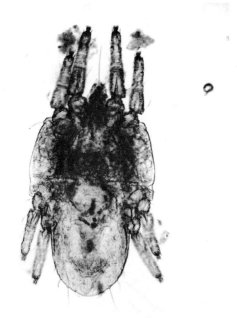

Fig. 23-15 Phalaenopsis mite, *Tenuipalpus pacificus*, one of the false spider mites. (*Courtesy Dr. Irene Gleason*)

days. If in doubt as to the certainty of the test, better repeat it.

Since the reaction in these plants is purely local, the same plants may be used for further tests.

Spathoglottis is apparently sensitive to any virus. If you can obtain seedlings, and are not interested in distinguishing a particular virus, they can be used to denote the presence of a virus infection. Inoculation is done in the same manner as the above. Reaction becomes apparent in four to six weeks, as diamond-shaped spots or rings of necrotic (dead) tissue. A *Spathoglottis* seedling can be used for only one test and must be discarded after showing infection.

Disinfectant for virus. For scrubbing benches and other areas contaminated with virus, and for washing hands after handling infected plants, H. H. Thornberry suggests the use of Trisodium-orthophosphate (also called sodium phosphate, tribasic). To make a concentrated solution, put enough in a quart of water so that some remains undissolved in the bottom of the bottle (do not use an aluminum container). This results in a 1.0 molar solution, and requires 174 grams. There is a heavier form of the salt called the hydrated form, and if you should get this it will take twice as much, for the molecule contains water. Use this 1.0 molar

* Seeds of these plants may be bought from Harry E. Saier, Dimonale, Michigan. A minimum order of $.50 is requested.

solution for scrubbing benches etc., but do not get it on the plants or roots. Use rubber gloves for the process. For washing hands, dilute the concentrated solution by mixing one part with nine of water (a 1:10 solution), and use it along with soap, rinsing thoroughly afterward.

PESTS

Many of the pests that attack orchids in their native habitats, and which used to come into this country with their hosts, are seldom seen in our greenhouses today. The United States Bureau of Entomology and Plant Quarantine bars them at our shores, and modern insecticides have pretty well eliminated those that had gained a foothold here. The pests which concern us now are for the most part kinds that live on garden plants and which invade our greenhouses.

A regular program for control of the various pests is easy to carry out and is better than waiting for populations to build up to high levels. It is difficult to get rid of a heavy infestation of any kind of pest, and a great deal of damage can be done by the pests in the meantime. A very small arsenal of weapons against pests will suffice. Malathion will take care of most insects, and should be kept on hand. A metaldehyde preparation is a necessity for control of snails and slugs. A miticide, preferably one that kills both types of mites prevalent in orchids, such as Dimite or Chlorobenzilate, should also be on hand. To control ants, cockroachs, etc., one might also have chlordane. Where a regular program has not been practiced, and insects have built up to large populations, it is necessary to treat the greenhouse several times at short intervals, perhaps three times ten days apart, with the specific chemical for the particular pests involved. Once the greenhouse has been cleaned up, a spraying every month or six weeks during warm weather, and every two months during cold weather, should keep things under control. In the meantime, be alert for local infestations, and treat these as needed.

It is not yet possible to recommend a systemic insecticide without reservations. Cygon has been used apparently without injury to cattleyas, but it has caused injury to cymbidiums and is not recommended for phalaenopsis or paphiopedilums. It should probably not be used on a mixed collection, particularly not a "species" collection where there may be one each of a hundred or more kinds. It is

very poisonous to human beings, with an LD-50 rating of 215, and should be used with great caution. Plants retain the poison and should themselves be handled with caution. Isotox is reported to injure cattleyas, causing deformity and stunting.

Spider mites. Called red spider or two-spotted mites, these are particularly troublesome on thin-leaved orchids, and seem to have a special affinity for *Cymbidium* and *Cycnoches*. They suck the plant juice and leave tiny white scars on the undersurface of the leaves, where they prefer to live. The result is a fine stippling or silvering of the leaf surface. They are also injurious to the flowers. Their favorite point of attack on flowers is along the seams where the sepals come together in the bud, where they leave small transparent spots surrounding the punctured areas. One such spot is a blemish, but many spots actually ruin the flower. Sometimes as the sepals split apart, the red spiders enter the bud and cause enough damage to distort the flower. Red spiders are very small, one-fiftieth of an inch long, and protect themselves and their eggs with a fine web. They thrive under warm, dry conditions, and their populations can be reduced somewhat by frequent syringing. They belong to the genus *Tetranychus*. The most common is *Tetranychus telarius,* of which one form is bright red and another yellowish or greenish. We have found the best control to be Dimite, although Malathion is also effective against them. Aramite, Chlorobenzilate, Tedion, and Kelthane are also recommended. A second spray in three days is necessary.

False spider mites. These viciously destructive mites are extremely small, impossible to detect without a twenty-power lens. They are different from the spider mites in that they do not spin webs and they feed on both upper and lower surfaces of the leaves. They produce pits of dead tissue and often cause the death of leaves. The most common species are *Brevipalpus californicus,* the omnivorous mite; *Brevipalpus oncidii;* and *Tenuipalpus pacificus,* the phalaenopsis mite. All will do damage to a number of orchids. Dimite, Kelthane and Chlorobenzilate give best control, for they are not killed by Malathion, and Aramite is only partially effective against them. Repeat spray in three days. See under *Phalaenopsis* for more details.

Fungus mites. There are many kinds, but two we have seen are a small, colorless mite, about the size of red spiders but covered with long hairs, and

Fig. 23-16 False spider mite injury on Oncidium leaf. The brown, irregular pits are typical. They first show as yellow flecks that can be mistaken for a virus disease, then enlarge, turn brown and become necrotic. (*Photo by Tom Northen*)

a round dark brown mite which is hard and shiny with a little shield on each side over its legs. These may not do damage to plants, since they apparently feed on decaying organic matter, or on fungi and algae. They are seen only occasionally, but appear in tremendous numbers when they occur. Like Collembola (below), they are an eyesore, and if one is not forewarned about them they can be the cause of great concern. They may appear on an injured part of a plant, or on the new lead to which they are attracted by the honey it exudes, or on algae covering roots or pots. They look like a sprinkling of fine sand. Malathion will get rid of them.

Thrips. These are small chewing insects with narrow tapered bodies, which crawl about rapidly and hide at the slightest disturbance. They are about one-twenty-fifth of an inch long and can be yellow, gray, or black. Some species feed on leaves, on which they produce a fine silvery stippling. They can be particularly injurious to seedlings. Other species feed on flowers, and the little irregularly shaped scars are scattered over the flower surface. Evidence of their presence, if the insects themselves are not seen, are the tiny black dots of their excrement. Species of *Anaphothrips, Taeniothrips,* and others are common on orchids. Malathion is effective against them.

Scale insects. There are two types of scales, the soft scaled and the armored ones. The young stages of both are free moving, but as they mature they select sites, stick their proboscises into the plant tissue, and remain there. The soft scales have a waxy or rubbery covering, while the armored scales secrete a hard shell. The soft scales excrete a sweet substance on which a sooty black mold grows. Eggs or living young are produced in large numbers by the females, and as they emerge from under the bodies of the females, they crawl for a few days. Colonies of scales may cluster under the sheathing leaf of a pseudobulb or rhizome, or at the juncture of leaf and stem, or on the undersides of leaves.

The most common species of soft scale are the soft brown scale, *Coccus hesperidum;* the orchid soft scale, *Coccus pseudohesperidum,* which is less often seen than the former; the hemispherical scale, *Saissetia hemisphaerica;* and the black scale, *Saissetia oleae.* They vary from one-quarter to one-third of an inch long, being in general larger than the armored scales. Repeated spraying with Malathion will give eventual control. It will not kill all of the adults at first, but repetition will kill the crawling stages and eventually the adults.

Among the armored scales the most notorious is the Boisduval scale, *Diaspis boisduvalii.* The shells of the females are a grayish white, oval, somewhat like an oyster shell in appearance. They may occur so thickly as to form an encrustation on the plant. The males occur in cottony masses. They are about one-eighth of an inch long. Many other armored scales occur on orchids, and some of them inject a toxin into the plant in addition to injuring them by sucking the juice. Malathion will kill the young stages, but it will take several repetitions at weekly intervals to kill the adults and control successive hatches of young. Scrubbing badly infested plants with a Malathion solution (using rubber gloves) is an effective way to handle scale on a few plants.

Unlike thrips, aphids, red spiders, etc.—which can enter the greenhouse from the garden—scale does not usually recur in greenhouses regularly treated with Malathion. It can however be brought in on newly acquired plants, especially if these are from collections not properly cared for.

Aphids. Soft-bodied, sucking insects of a number of species, some with wings and some without, can enter the greenhouse, and are particularly attracted to flower buds and open flowers. The females produce living young which take about a week to reach adult size. They may enter the greenhouse by way of the ventilators, or they can be brought in by ants. Their punctures spoil the looks of the flowers. They are particularly troublesome on sprays of small flowers, such as those of *Oncidium* and *Epidendrum,* where their presence may not be noticed at first because of the denseness of the flowers and the minuteness of their parts. They are more easily seen on large flower buds and flower parts, such as those of *Cattleya* and *Cymbidium.* The work of ants can be suspected when isolated infestations are found. The pale green peach aphid (*Myzus persicae*) is commonly found in the greenhouse, and because of its color is not as readily detected as the black bean aphid (*Aphis fabae*), which is another kind commonly found. The latania aphid *Cerataphis latania* has been reported on orchids, but not as often. Malathion gives good general control.

Mealy bugs. A number of species of mealy bugs generally infest greenhouse plants and are reported to be a particular pest on *Phalaenopsis.* They are flat, segmented, whiskery bugs that are coated with wax. Some produce live young and others lay eggs in cottony sacs. The wax they secrete makes their control somewhat difficult, but Malathion used several times at three-week intervals will control them.

Slugs and snails. Slugs are shell-less snails that slide along by means of a foot and lubricate their path with a trail of slime. Often the slime is the clue to their presence. They usually feed at night, and hide in the daytime under the plant parts or the rim of the pot. Young slugs may be only a quarter of an inch long, while adults may reach two inches. The snails that are particularly bothersome are a small, flat-coiled, brown-shelled kind, which reaches about a quarter of an inch in diameter. Both snails and slugs are equipped with a radula, a series of rasps on a moving band, with

which they rasp away plant tissue. They prefer succulent parts such as root tips, young leaves and flower buds. One slug can literally mow down a pot of small seedlings in a night. Both slugs and snails lay eggs within the pot, usually near the bottom. Metaldehyde is the best control. It may be used in dust form, actually dusted on the plants and pots, and then watered into the pot, or it may be applied in liquid form. Either is better than pellets or meal containing arsenic, which cannot be put on the pots, but which must be used on the benches or floor. These are not satisfactory because they do not get the slugs or snails that live in the pots. Repeated treatments are necessary to rid the greenhouse of slugs and snails. They are very stubborn pests and the grower must be equally stubborn.

Ants. While they do not seem to damage plants, ants bring in aphids, mealy bugs, and soft scale. The ants are attracted by the honey secreted by new leads and sheaths. They are killed by Malathion. Chlordane sprinkled on the ground under the benches will help in keeping them out of the greenhouse.

Cockroaches, sowbugs, millipedes. Sowbugs and millipedes are common in the soil and will invade the greenhouse. Cockroaches are prevalent in warm climates. All will feed on orchids. Chlordane sprinkled on the ground or watered into the ground will control the under-bench population.

Collembola. These wingless insects are called springtails because they are equipped with a jumping apparatus on their tails. They are one-eighth of an inch long; may be gray or black, or banded; and live in soil all over the world. They do little damage to the plants, except possibly to root tips when they are present in great numbers, but pots swarming with Collembola are an eyesore. A regular spray program that includes Malathion will keep them under control.

Black fly. Common in greenhouses, this little black fly thrives in over-wet soil or potting medium. Its tiny little white grubs (larvae) dwell in the soil, and the adults flutter up from the soil surface when disturbed. Apparently they do no damage to orchids but, like Collembola, they are a nuisance. Malathion will control them.

Cattleya fly, Dendrobium weevil, Dendrobium beetle. These are specific pests which used to plague orchid growers, and which still do where orchids are grown in the open in tropical areas. They are controlled by Malathion and are now almost never seen in this country.

Other insects. Various beetles, leaf hoppers, etc., occasionally enter the greenhouse, to say nothing of bees. Regular spraying will kill some of them, and hand capturing or swatting will get rid of the rest.

Nematodes. There are many kinds of nematodes, called "eel worms," both soil- and water-dwelling, that are harmless to plants. But some are parasitic on plants, usually definitely associated with certain hosts or groups of hosts. The parasitic kinds are almost microscopic, ranging in length from one-sixty-fourth to one-quarter inch. Among the species that infest plants are some that cause root knots, some that cause root lesions, some that invade leaf and stem tissue, and some that attack flower buds. As far as we know, only three kinds have been found on orchids. These are a species that feeds on and kills the flower buds of terete Vandas in Hawaii; a root-lesion type recently found in cymbidiums of some California areas; and one that infests leaves of cymbidiums and other orchids in New Zealand. The Vanda bud nematodes are being controlled by picking off and burning all infested spikes. There is as yet no safe control for root or leaf nematodes in orchids. The former live in the root tissue and feed upon it. Areas which they destroy are then subject to invasion by fungi and bacteria. Infested plants show rotted and discolored roots, with the root system in general becoming much reduced. The leaf nematodes cause long black streaks. Soil intended for use in potting mixes can be sterilized to free it of nematodes, but chemicals which would kill the nematodes already present are so toxic that they will also kill the plant. It is to be hoped that in the near future some safe control will be developed. It is also hoped that instances of nematode infestation remain as rare as they apparently are at present.

24

HOUSING YOUR ORCHIDS

The first advice to prospective greenhouse owners is to build a greenhouse large enough to hold an expanding hobby. A small greenhouse will look tremendous for a while, compared to the space ordinarily given to house plants. But it is legendary that orchid growers are never satisfied; they are always adding to their collections. Perhaps you will be interested in only one or two kinds at first, and feel you would be satisfied with but a few plants of each. Inevitably you will fall in love with another kind, and then another. You will buy a few seedlings of this and then a few of that. The seedlings will grow to maturity and the mature plants will need dividing. Soon your benches will be overflowing, and you will join in the plaint common to most amateurs, "Oh, for some more space!" We suggest that you drive the old car for a few years longer or take a less expensive vacation in order to build a fairly generous greenhouse.

There are other reasons for not building too small a greenhouse. A very small house is difficult to manage; its small volume of air heats up quickly and cools off quickly, creating a rapid fluctuation of temperature. It is difficult to work in. Large sprays of flowers become entangled with each other. Plants become crowded, causing unhealthy conditions and difficulties in handling.

A very minimum (and this will not hold a large number of plants) would be something in the neighborhood of eight by ten feet. This width would allow two side benches and a center walk. A twelve-foot width would give you two side benches and a center bench. A greenhouse twelve feet wide and fifteen or eighteen feet long is large enough to give space for growing a truly satisfying number of plants, and at the same time is not too large for a busy person to care for in his spare time. The cost of a greenhouse and its equipment does not double when its size is doubled; instead, the cost is about one and one-half or one and one-third. In other words, you can get twice the space for about a half or a third more in cost.

To obtain an idea of types and costs of greenhouses, send for catalogues from various greenhouse manufacturers. Visit some of the home greenhouses in your town. Talk to the owners and find out what faults lie in certain plans, and what good features, so that you can avoid the former and adopt the latter. Inquire about heater efficiency and notice whether certain installations would be satisfactory for orchids. Examine thoughtfully the relation between greenhouse shapes and the amount of bench space allowed.

Perhaps the most economical, from the point of view of space and efficient operation, are the types that have been in use for many years. There are some novelty styles that may appeal to some from the point of view of decorativeness, but before considering one of these be sure that it will give you what you need and want.

Fig. 24-1 Two types of attached greenhouse. UPPER, attached by one end. In another situation this greenhouse could extend to a greater length. (*Courtesy Aluminum Greenhouses, Inc.*) LOWER, a lean-to. Note louvered section at end for ventilation in addition to roof ventilator. (*Courtesy Lord and Burnham*)

A greenhouse may be a free-standing unit, or it may be attached to an existing building. In the latter case, it may be attached by one end, with its length running out from the building, or it may be a lean-to, attached along one side, with the wall of the building substituting for one side wall of the greenhouse. Less desirable for orchids, but still usable, is a breezeway, a glassed-in passageway between two buildings, the house and garage, for instance. A breezeway does not offer as good light, but if the kinds of orchids are chosen for the location, they should do well and give much pleasure.

In locating a greenhouse, the aim is to give it a spot where it will receive as much light as possible throughout the day. If you are planning a greenhouse along with a new home you can assure it a good spot, but it is a challenge sometimes to find an ideal spot in an already established yard. A free-standing type can be placed in any open spot, out of the shadow of the house or nearby buildings, and away from trees. If trees are present, pick a place that receives their shade for the fewest number of hours a day, and then plan to utilize the shade in place of artificial shade on the glass. A clear exposure from the south is important in the winter, because the sun swings to the south at that season. If the greenhouse is to be in a yard facing north, be sure that it stands where the house will not cast a shadow on it in the winter time, or where it will get morning sun if possible. It is generally thought that a greenhouse should run from north to south to allow the sun to travel across it from east to west. Home owners are not always able to achieve this, and should be comforted to know that a greenhouse that runs east and west or north-east and south-west will function very well.

A lean-to should preferably be located so that one side or one end receives light from the east and one side light from the south. A lean-to on the west side is difficult to manage in the summer, although an evaporative or refrigerative cooler may take care of the excessive heat that results from this location.

A place to do the potting and to store materials is a great convenience. The ideal situation (not achieved by all of us, by any means) is to have a potting shed attached to the north end of the greenhouse. If you have hot water heat for the greenhouse, the shed can also house the boiler. If the greenhouse is attached to the garage, or handy to it, perhaps part of the garage may be used for potting. Otherwise, a potting bench may be incorporated in the greenhouse, at the north end so as not to take the best growing space.

MATERIALS AND EQUIPMENT

Aluminum is at present the preferred material for the framework of the greenhouse. It does not rust (as does its antecedent, steel) and need not be painted. The sash bars are narrow and admit more light. Wood is, however, still widely used for home greenhouses and is somewhat less expensive than aluminum. The upkeep of wood is more troublesome, both in labor and cost of paint. Cypress and redwood are chosen for greenhouse construction because they resist decay. Ordinary house paint tends to peel off the wood in a short

Home Orchid Growing

Fig. 24-2 A free-standing greenhouse with attached workroom. Note roller blinds for shading. (*Courtesy* *Lord and Burnham*)

time, actually seeming to be pushed off by moisture moving through the wood from within. Paint stays on the inside far longer than on the outside. We hope that a paint will be developed to fill this need. In the meantime it has been reported that two coats of aluminum paint on the inside provides a moisture barrier against exterior peeling.

Fiberglass is becoming popular to replace glass. Many growers like its diffuse light transmission. It is hail-proof and gives protection against falling tree limbs. Use only white or clear, or a yellow color, not blue or green. Some growers have installed fiberglass panels above glass for hail protection. Up to now, it has had to be scraped and refinished frequently because of weathering. A new type is on the market, called Denverlight C³, whose manufacturers hope will resist weathering longer and cut down drip inside the greenhouse.

The plastic sheeting materials offer tempting savings in construction, but many products that have been put on the market have proved to have much shorter life than was originally expected of them, lasting only months instead of years in some cases. They can be used for seasonal covering, or for temporary covering until glass or fiberglass can be installed.

In many home greenhouse styles, the manufacturers use large panes of double thick glass instead of the older system of many small panes in each section. Construction is made easier by this means. The glass is held in place by patented clips or bar caps, and the owner can easily replace a broken pane.

A masonry foundation is preferable to a wooden one, which will eventually rot out. The foundation walls should be set on a footing that goes below frost level, and may be of brick, stone, cinder block, or any similar material.

Assembling a prefabricated greenhouse is simple. The home owner and his family can put one up by following directions. They come complete with all parts and hardware. Before building the foundation, however, obtain specific details from the greenhouse company for its dimensions and any fittings necessary to hold the sill of the greenhouse. There are definite advantages in buying a complete product designed by greenhouse experts. If you do not want a package unit as offered, often you can buy what parts you wish from the manufacturer to fit a plan of your own. Many growers have built their own greenhouses, from new or used materials, with great success, and have possibly saved a good bit on the cost. A word of caution to the do-it-yourselfers—study standard greenhouse plans and construction first, so that you can come as close to a professional model as possible.

Walks should be at least two feet wide, for plants have a way of hanging out into the aisle.

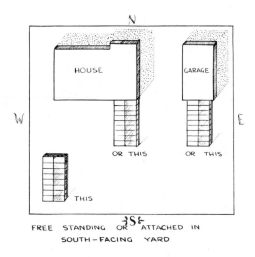

FREE STANDING OR ATTACHED IN
SOUTH-FACING YARD

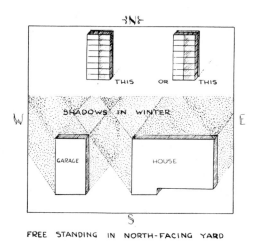

FREE STANDING IN NORTH-FACING YARD

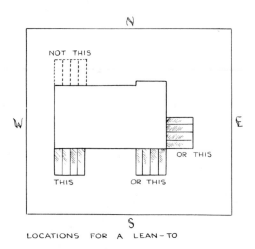

LOCATIONS FOR A LEAN-TO

Fig. 24-3 Suggestions for locating a greenhouse as to exposure and relationship to home.

We feel that it is preferable to leave the ground under the benches bare. The damp earth helps keep the humidity up, and serves as a method of draining off excess water. If you prefer a solid concrete floor, there should be a floor drain and adequate slope to it. Otherwise, you will be wading in water much of the time. Brick paving makes a decorative and useful floor or walk. Brick or concrete can be kept clean with Consan-20.

Prefabricated benches are available. If you wish to build your own, you may make the frames either of wood (painted or treated with a preservative such as Cuprinol or Kopex, *never creosote*) or of pipe or concrete forms. Wooden bench legs should be set on bricks or concrete blocks to keep them from the wet floor. The bottom of the bench should allow free drainage, and free air movement up and through the pots. Such materials as hardware cloth (galvanized wire mesh), steel mesh, or perforated transite are preferred, but wooden slats may also be used. Do not make the benches so high or so wide that you knock over plants in the front row in order to reach those in the back. Stepped benches can be used to give a little more room, provided that they do not cut off the light from plants on either side. A stepped bench is particularly useful on the wall side of a lean-to.

It is well to have both hot and cold water in the greenhouse and a mixing faucet, so that you can warm the water for use in the winter. An extra electrical outlet may come in handy for plugging in an emergency heater or some other piece of equipment.

The heating system is probably the item of largest concern. In a very mild climate or where electricity is cheap, electrical heat may be feasible. An electric heater may be used to boost the temperature when a freak spell of cold weather hits your area. Otherwise, either warm air or hot water heat would be the choice. Hot water is perhaps ideal, but it is also the more expensive of the two. Before installing either, obtain information from a heating engineer as to the capacity of the heater or boiler, amount of pipe, etc., necessary for the size of your greenhouse and the temperature you wish to maintain. If you obtain this information from an expert not in your locality, be sure to give him data on the weather in your region, especially the extremes of cold that can be reached.

The smaller the greenhouse, the larger is the proportionate cost of a heating system for it. This is because certain items in the heating system cost

Fig. 24-4 A greenhouse partitioned to give two sets of temperature conditions, in this case a cool section and an intermediate section. (*Courtesy Aluminum Greenhouses, Inc.*)

the same whether they are for a large or small unit. Also, a heater or a boiler increases in price relatively little for each increase in capacity. However, the basic cost is still higher than we could wish, and it would be desirable to have some ingenious thought applied to the problem.

A hot water system keeps a relatively even temperature. The pipes continue to radiate some heat after the controls shut off the flow. Finned tubing is more efficient than plain pipe, and although it costs more per foot only about a fourth as much is required.

Warm air heaters are used by many orchid growers, fired either by gas or by oil. Both must be vented and be equipped with a thermostat and, for best performance, a blower. Gas heaters must have a safety shut-off valve. If gas is used, it must be 100 percent natural gas or bottled gas. Artificial

gas must never be burned in a greenhouse, nor must gas that has any artificial gas mixed with it. There has been a definite improvement in the types of warm air heaters offered for small greenhouses. Some models are made especially for greenhouses, and some are intended to be used in the home as room heaters or space heaters but are equally satisfactory for greenhouses. Some require a flue or chimney to carry out the fumes from combustion. Others are self-venting, designed to be set in the wall and having a sealed-off firing chamber that operates outside the greenhouse. It is possible to use hot air from the home if a duct system can be conveniently installed.

An aid in heat conservation found useful by many growers is the installation of plastic sheeting under the glass. This also keeps leaves from coming against the freezing glass.

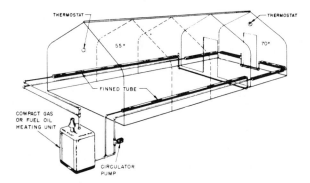

Fig. 24-5 Zone-controlled, automatic, forced-hot-water heat, using finned tubing for circulation of water. The boiler can be fired either by gas or oil. The flow to each of the two sections is controlled separately. (*Courtesy Aluminum Greenhouses, Inc.*)

Emergency heating is a precaution where temperatures are likely to drop below seasonal. Electric heaters may be kept on hand in case of gas failure, and portable butane salamander-type burners in case of power failure.

Cooling systems may be either evaporative or refrigerative, the former being in widest use. Both types come as self-contained units, in a number of sizes. It would be best to obtain the advice of a local expert in air conditioning as to the size required for your greenhouse. It takes a larger unit to cool a greenhouse than it takes for a room of the same size. For most efficient cooling, an evaporative unit should take in air from outdoors. It is therefore best set in an opening in the wall, with the cabinet projecting outside and the opening from the blower flush with the wall. A ventilator at the opposite end should be opened a few inches to allow the air to move through the greenhouse. A cooling thermostat should be installed to operate the unit. This type, which blows cooled air into the greenhouse, is called a "positive pressure" system.

A pad and fan arrangement works on the same principle as an evaporative cooling unit, with the fan thermostatically controlled. An aspen pad is set in one wall. Above it is a perforated trough and below it a trough or pan. Water is conducted to the lower container by a small tube and its level is controlled by a float valve. A pump installed in the lower container moves the water through a tube to the upper trough, from which it trickles down through the pad, to be collected in the lower trough. A fan, placed either directly in front of the pad or in an opening at the opposite end of the greenhouse, pulls outside air through the moist pad. When the fan is directly in front of the pad, a ventilator should

be open at the opposite end. This is another example of the "positive pressure" type. When the fan is in an opening at the opposite end, it pulls the air through the greenhouse and exhausts it, so that no ventilator need be open. This is called a "negative pressure" type.

Shading the greenhouse can be achieved by several possible means. There are certain advantages and disadvantages in all kinds, but this is to be expected when you are trying to adjust the light through various seasons. White shading compound, sprayed or painted (with a paint roller on a long handle) is most widely used. Shading compounds may be obtained from greenhouse suppliers, and are used according to directions. In order to keep the white shading on our greenhouses through spring snows and summer hail we mix it with a small amount of linseed oil. This makes a more permanent paint than many growers would wish, and should probably be used only where it is desirable to have some remain on the glass through the winter, as in areas with very bright winter sun. Without linseed oil, the paint flakes off more readily, and may have to be renewed more often. The advantages of a white shading compound are its low cost and the fact that it can be applied thin or thick according to the season.

Slat shading is made in sections that can be screwed to the sash bars or fastened by brackets. The distance between the slats determines the percentage of outdoor light transmitted. During early spring and late fall perhaps a thin coat of white shading might be used, and the slat shading put up for the warmer months. It can be of wood or aluminum strips on frames of convenient size.

Fig. 24-6 Use of fiberglass in the roof, both for shade and for resistance to hail. (Additional shading may be necessary in many areas.) (*Courtesy Redfern's Prefab Greenhouse Mfg. Co.*)

Diamond Mesh or Hi-Rib Lath can also be used. A louvered aluminum shading has very small louvers that break up the light, but this may give more shade than is needed except in particularly bright exposures. Roller blinds of wood or aluminum strips are often preferred, and can be rolled up on dull days.

Some growers like plastic screening, fiber mesh coated with plastic, which can be fastened either outside or inside the greenhouse. It comes in various grades designed to transmit different amounts of sunlight. The grower chooses the type suitable for his needs. Some growers make use of fiberglass panels as shading. For a bit of extra shade for individual groups of plants, cheesecloth is very satisfactory. It may be tacked up to wooden sash bars, or fastened to a framework of wood or wire, and can be used as thick or as thin as needed.

Ventilation. Automatic vent control is a great help to growers who must be away from home all day. Small motors, in series, are attached to the vent handles and are controlled by a thermostat. An ingenious self-powered vent control is made by Heat Motors, Inc. based on a patent developed by Lockheed Missiles and Space Company. It is a

A

B

C

Fig. 24-7   Perforated plastic tubing for ventilation.
A. Installation of tubing with motorized fan to pull in fresh air and force it through the tubing.
B. Installation without fan. In this case an exhaust fan operating anywhere in the greenhouse causes a vacuum that pulls air in through louvers and through the tubing.
C. Tubing in use in a greenhouse. (*A and B courtesy Acme Engineering and Manufacturing Corp.*)

small, heat-sensitive motor housed in a cylinder. As the motor responds to changes in temperature, it pushes a shaft attached to the vent, opening and closing it with temperature changes from 50° to 90°. No electrical connection or thermostat is needed.

A new method of ventilation for cool weather uses perforated polyethylene tubing, in association with an exhaust fan. The tubing is installed under the ridge, the length of the greenhouse. One end is fastened to a circular frame attached to a set of louvers. The other end is closed. The exhaust fan (this may be one used in connection with pad and fan cooling, or may be installed for the purpose at any convenient spot) is set to turn on at a certain temperature. The louvers may be operated off the same thermostat or may be the free-swinging type that open and close with a slight change of air pressure. When the exhaust fan goes on, it creates a partial vacuum that pulls air in through the louvers and thence through the tubing. This air flows out through the perforations in gentle streams, mixing with the heated air in the upper level of the greenhouse, thus providing fresh, tempered air for the plants. If you prefer, a fan can be installed just inside the louvers to blow air through the tubing, in which case an exhaust fan is not necessary. Other uses for the tubing can be found. It could be used to conduct air from the heater, for instance, running under the center bench in this case.

Humidifiers range from the simple spray nozzle placed in front of a fan (perhaps in front of the heater so that its blower distributes the moist air), to various kinds of mist-making apparatus. The latter are self-contained units which create a fine mist and blow it into the air. If the blower is strong enough, it will also help to circulate the air in the greenhouse.

Temperature alarm. One of the most important pieces of equipment for any greenhouse is a standard high-low temperature alarm, wired to ring a bell in the house when the greenhouse temperature reaches a dangerous level. It has a temperature dial and a hand that moves with the temperature. On each side is a set-hand which you set for the minimum and maximum desired temperatures. When the moving hand comes in contact with a set-hand it makes an electrical contact which rings the warning bell. The mechanism should be wired to batteries so as not to be affected by a power failure. The bell can be placed anywhere in the house where you can hear it easily.

ORCHIDS IN YOUR WINDOWS

For all of the pleasure and ease in the possession of a greenhouse, there is nothing quite like having orchids in your home. Those who would experience the thrill of growing orchids, but for whom a greenhouse is out of the question, should certainly try a few, on a window sill, or in a case made especially for them. Growing orchids in the home is a somewhat different art from growing them in a greenhouse.* However, if you have a bright window, preferably east or south, that will allow them good light all day and direct light for part of each day, you can find kinds that will do well for you. In choosing a window for orchids, avoid one that becomes too hot for any plants, such as some west-facing bay windows or picture windows unfortunately do.

In a place where the night temperature cools off to 55° to 60° you can grow many of the intermediate kinds. Where the night temperature does not fall below 65° you had better try some of the warm kinds. The cool orchids are more difficult to grow in the home because, ordinarily, home temperatures do not go as low as the needed 50°, but if you have a glassed in porch you might try some of these. We do not recommend the kinds that are most demanding of light, in any temperature group, for example, vandas, some dendrobiums, and cymbidiums. Cattleyas and some others which are quite light-demanding, have a fairly wide light range, and in the home during the brightest hours of the day they may receive enough light (perhaps in the neighborhood of 2,000 to 3,000 foot candles when the sun is shining in the window) to enable them to grow and flower fairly well. They will probably not become the heavy, floriferous plants that they would be in a greenhouse, but will do well enough to give you great pleasure.

Some kinds will do better without the protection of a case—among them cattleyas, epidendrums, lycastes, some of the small oncidiums, and some botanicals—because they receive better light when directly in the window. If the leaves become too hot when the sun shines on them, pull a glass curtain or a piece of cheesecloth across the window and give them a mist spray over the foliage. The object is to give them all the light they can take because they do not have as many hours of it in the home as they would in a greenhouse. Water them when they need it, and give fertilizer a bit less frequently

* See Orchids As House Plants, Northen.

than you would for greenhouse plants. Do not let heat from a register blow on the plants. During warm summer nights the window can be left open to bring them the cooler, damper air. Watch for insects and control them as described earlier. Pests from other house plants can attack orchids, and it is well to keep these free from insects also.

The kinds that need the extra humidity of a case are phalaenopsis, paphiopedilums, miltonias and some botanicals. In addition, these require less light than the cattleya group and hence do not suffer from having the light cut down by the extra pane of glass between them and the window. The case should be tall enough to have a good volume of air, and should be equipped with a top and bottom ventilator and a door that opens wide for ease in working with the plants. In the bottom there should be a pan to hold water and to catch the drip from watering. Above the pan is set a grille on which to stand the pots. Depending on the temperature of the spot where the case is to be put, choose the kinds to be grown in it: Phalaenopsis and the mottle-leaved paphiopedilums if the temperature ranges between 60° and 65° or stays close to 65°; miltonias and the plain-leaved paphiopedilums if it ranges between 55° and 60°. An easy way to add humidity to the case is to insert a little electric "one-cup water heater" in the pan below the rack

and plug it in when needed. Don't let it stay on too long as it can eventually overheat the case.

Management of an orchid case follows pretty much the rules for managing a greenhouse. The sun shining in the window can heat up the case just as it does a greenhouse, and it may be necessary to draw a thickness of cheesecloth across the window during the hottest hours. At this time open the top and bottom ventilators and give the plants a mist spray. The case should be ventilated each day, even when the sun is not shining, and the plants may be given a mist spray once a day, allowing them to dry off by night. The air in the case should be kept fresh and buoyant, not stuffy or over-damp. Some of the troubles people have experienced with orchids in cases come from keeping the humidity too high; this causes black sheaths, spotted flowers, and rapid fading of flowers. Plants will dry out faster in the winter, with furnace heat, than in the summer, and this is true both of those in cases and out in rooms. Watering therefore has to be more frequent in the winter, though care against over-watering must always be exercised.

Flasks of seedlings or community pots will thrive in orchid cases. They may be grown in their own case, with shade across the window to subdue the light, or they may share one with larger plants, being placed behind them so as to be shaded. When the seedlings grow larger and need more light, adjustments will have to be made for them.

GROWING WITH ARTIFICIAL LIGHT

The number of amateurs growing orchids indoors under artificial light is increasing every year. With their usual ingenuity they make use of almost any area in the home that can be adapted. A preferred place is the basement which, with its concrete walls and floor, is not subject to damage by water. Since every home is different, and every amateur faces different problems, no two setups are identical. Chief considerations are temperature, air circulation, humidity and watering, the kind of light to use, and the kinds of plants to grow. Some people keep their plants indoors all year around, while others move them outdoors in the summer to benefit from a few months of sunlight.

Benches may be constructed of wood or other materials. Metal trays or benches lined with plastic and filled with gravel catch water and help keep up the humidity. Racks covered with steel mesh or

Fig. 24-8   An orchid case in the living room.

wood slats should be placed over the gravel so that the pots do not stand in water. It is best if the benches stand against walls painted white to reflect light, or covered with special aluminum or spectral Mylar.

The lights must be close to the plants because intensity drops off rapidly as the distance from the plants increases. Fluorescent tubes will not ordinarily burn the leaves. The closer they are placed the better will be growth and flowering—within six inches is ideal. They should be in white reflectors, hung by chains so that their height can be adjusted for differing needs, for instance, to be raised when bloom spikes develop, or lowered if large plants are replaced by smaller ones. Incandescent bulbs will burn the foliage and plants must be arranged to avoid contact with them. Also, the ballasts for the fluorescent tubes become hot and the same caution is advised. If the ballasts can be put out of the growing area it would be wise to do so.

To date, no one type of electric light has been developed capable of duplicating the visible spectrum of sunlight. Visible light ranges from violet through blue, blue-green, yellow, orange, and red. In photosynthesis plants make more use of the blue and red rays than of green or yellow, although the latter do play their roles, and the red end of the spectrum is especially important for mature plants and for flowering. Fluorescent tubes furnish the blue, green, and yellow rays but are deficient in the red. Incandescent bulbs give the red, but fall short in the others. Therefore a combination of the two types is necessary.

The old type Gro-Lux lights proved insufficient for mature plants (although they may be used for flasks and young seedlings). The newer Wide Spectrum Gro-Lux tubes are an improvement in this respect. Of the regular fluorescent tubes, Cool White is better than either the Warm White or Daylight types, but, again, is deficient in the red range. A recently developed tube, called the Optima fluorescent, is said to be superior to any of these, but remains to be fully tested.

At present, best results are to be had by combining the Wide Spectrum Gro-Lux with Cool White, or Cool White alone, with incandescent bulbs. At least four tubes side by side should be used to a bench twenty-four to thirty inches wide. These can be two each of the Wide Spectrum and Cool White. If a wider bench is desired, additional tubes should be used. The tubes should be continuous for the length of the benches; plants placed beyond the ends of the tubes will not get enough light. Four four-foot (40 watt) tubes are sufficient for a bench four feet long. Four eight-foot (75 watt) tubes, or two

Fig. 24-9 A basement setup for orchids under lights. The plants stand on racks over galvanized trays that hold water. Each eight-by-two-foot light fixture holds six 40- watt cool white fluorescent tubes with sufficient incandescent bulbs spaced between them. (*Courtesy Norman Moore*)

sets of four-foot ones, should be used for a bench eight feet long.

Incandescent bulbs should be in an approximate ratio of 1:4. For four 40 watt fluorescent tubes, 40 watts of incandescent light should be used. For four 75 watt tubes, a total of 75 watts of incandescent light is needed. The total wattage of incandescent light can be obtained by spacing the appropriate number of 25 watt bulbs along the length of the fluorescent tubes.

Why plants do well with the lower light intensity of artificial lights can perhaps be explained. In the first place, the light is constant—it is the same intensity from the moment it is turned on until it is turned off, no dawn, no dusk, no cloudy hours or days. In the second place, except when plants that are sensitive to daylength are concerned (see Chapter 7), the lights can be kept on for sixteen hours a day all through the year.

An additional bracket of lights can be installed vertically behind the bench to shine on the sides of the plants. This would allow plant parts normally shaded to receive additional light and thus to make more food. Kinds that are more demanding of light can be placed at the back to receive this extra light.

Temperatures should be managed to suit the needs of the plants, as described in previous chapters. If it is necessary to have a heater, be sure that it is equipped with a fan to distribute the heat evenly and that it does not blow directly on the plants. It is best if the heat is directed against a wall or under the benches so that it is diffused.

Fans for air circulation are a must in any setup. These, also, may be directed against a wall to create a circular current over and around the plants. In hot weather, they may be placed so as to bring air from a nearby window.

Fresh air may be a problem in a room without a window, but perhaps can be solved by circulating air from an adjoining room. Basement growers often find that a window can be opened a crack somewhere near the plants without harm. A baffle may be used to direct the flow of air to the floor, from whence it will be heated before it reaches the plants. Windows may be left open all during the summer, particularly at night to bring about a drop of 10° or more from day temperatures.

A nicely balanced atmosphere includes a relative humidity somewhere between 50 percent and 70 percent. Small humidifiers can be purchased. For a very small group of plants a kind intended for use in a sick room may be adequate. Misting the floors and walls may be sufficient. To combat the growth of algae on these areas and in the trays under the plants, Consan-20 may be used as directed for greenhouses.

As to what kinds to grow, one's own ingenuity is the only limiting factor, together with the size of plants and their natural demands. In one small basement collection miltonias, epidendrums, oncidiums, cattleyas, catasetums, maxillarias, lycastes, odontoglossums, and even vandas all flower together. In this same collection, however, there are others that are not doing well, but this is true of any collection even under the most ideal conditions. Plants may receive a shock when first put under lights and it may take them a while to become acclimated. Newly imported botanicals often need time to recover and may be two or three years reaching blooming condition. As with all plants, patience and experimentation are required. General methods are the same as for greenhouse care—potting, potting materials, watering, and so forth. A word of caution must be given about the use of insecticides in the home. Only those most safe for human beings should be used. If it becomes necessary to use the more toxic ones, take the plants outdoors to treat them.

ORCHIDS IN YOUR GARDEN

Growers in such a fortunate climate as that of Hawaii, Florida, and parts of California can grow orchids in their gardens all year round, using them as an integral part of the landscaping. Those of us not so blessed in the matter of climate can at least have a few plants out-of-doors in the summer. In fact, in areas with quite hot summers, many kinds benefit from being moved outside; these include cymbidiums especially, but also cattleyas, dendrobiums, oncidiums and others.

In regions where orchids can be put outdoors for only part of the year, it is best to hang the pots or baskets on the lower limbs of tall trees, or to place them on a bench and build a lath or screen roof over them. Pots can sometimes be set in places where they will add to the decoration of a patio if the light conditions are right. Plants will dry out faster outside than in a greenhouse, so careful attention to watering is in order. Rain may do the job at times, but it cannot be depended upon. (Sometimes the rain overdoes it!) Guard the plants from the usual array of garden insects by spraying

Fig. 24-10 Orchids in a Florida garden. The plants are naturalized on the tree or hung from the branches. In this group are cattleyas, phalaenopsis, dendrobiums, oncidiums, *Renanthera coccinea,* and Vanda coerulea. (*Courtesy H. F. Loomis*)

grow just as they do in the wilds. Plants that are potted in osmunda can be removed from the pot and the ball of fiber and roots can be firmly wired to a branch or to the trunk. For plants taken from bark, a chunk of fiber should be wired to the branch and the plant then wired in place upon it. The new growth should be next to the bark. As the roots grow, they extend out of the fiber and attach themselves to the tree. Another method is to fasten a half-pot or half a coconut husk to the branch and then settle the plant in the container with enough fiber to keep it firm. Plants naturalized in these ways must be watered regularly when there is not sufficient rain, and should be given frequent applications of fertilizer since they will not have so rich a source of nutrients as they would in jungle trees.

Some kinds can be grown in beds especially prepared for them. Terrestrials such as *Phaius, Bletia, Calanthe* and others need a well-drained bed in which the soil has been replaced with the loose, fluffy type of compost you would use for them in pots. A mixture of sand, gravel or bark, leaf mold, and fibrous loam should be satisfactory. The bed must be located in a spot where the light will be right for the kinds you wish to grow in it.

Epiphytic or semi-epiphytic kinds can also be grown in beds, except that the bed should be raised eighteen to twenty-four inches to allow especially free drainage, somewhat after the manner of a rock garden. The lower foot of its depth is filled with very coarse gravel, and the upper eight to twelve inches with a mixture suitable for epiphytes, perhaps bark mixed with shredded tree fern or leaf mold. Vandas, reed-type epidendrums, some dendrobiums, *Cyrtopodium,* and some of the warmth-tolerant miniature cymbidiums can then be planted in the bed. Tall plants should have some support, perhaps that furnished by a wall to which they can be trained or tied. Plants grouped in the same bed should, of course, have the same light requirements, and the bed should be located to receive the proper amount of sun and shade.

when needed. When moving greenhouse-tender plants outside, do not let them have too much sun at first. Some kinds can be hardened to take clear early morning and late evening sun, with some shade during the hot noon and afternoon hours.

Where orchids can be kept outside all year round, almost all of the greenhouse epiphytes can be naturalized on trees, where they will take root and

25

THE CARE AND USE OF CUT FLOWERS

Even if at first you cannot bear to cut an orchid while it is still fresh, there will come a time when you will want some to wear, to use in a bouquet, to give to a friend, or even to sell. Because of their good keeping qualities, orchids make wonderful corsages that can be worn to one event after another. And because they are in demand commercially, most small growers can find a florist who will be glad to buy an occasional few. Thus an amateur can enjoy his flowers for a few days and then turn them into dollars for the support or expansion of his hobby.

The beauty of growing your own orchids lies in the possibility of having the plants to cherish and the flowers to enjoy in any number of ways.

MAKING CORSAGES

The larger orchids make attractive corsages when only one is used at a time. The smaller ones may be used in groups of two or three, or as a dainty spray if they are very tiny. A single large cattleya is about as much as most women can wear without seeming to be overdressed, but for special occasions, two medium-sized or two of the "cocktail" ones make an elegant corsage. A single cymbidium or paphiopedilum makes a neat, tailored corsage that can be worn with a suit or other daytime attire and is no less lovely when worn with an evening gown.

For more elaborate corsages, cymbidiums and paphiopedilum may be made up two or three together. Among the dozens of orchids described in this book, there are many that would make outstanding corsages, all the more desirable for being unusual. Imagine the comment of your friends if you appeared wearing a corsage of *Peristeria elata, Oncidium splendidum, Diacrium bicornutum,* or their wonder at lacy odontoglossums, or sweetly rounded phalaenopsis.

When you grow your own orchids, you can design the corsages according to your own whims and fancies.

The flowers should be cut only after they have been open forty-eight to seventy-two hours. Colored blooms should reach their richest hue, white ones should have lost all traces of their early green or creamy tinge. At the peak of perfection the fragrant ones will smell their sweetest. With a sterile razor blade, cut the flower from the plant, leaving as long a stem as possible. Hold the stem under water and cut off a thin slice from the end. This prevents air bubbles from entering the cells, and enables the stem to take up water more efficiently. Then put the flower in water in a narrow necked vase so that the water does not touch the flower itself. Set it in a cool, shaded place or refrigerate it at 45°-50° until you are ready for it.

A tiny glass tube of water may be placed on the stem to keep the flower fresh while it is being worn. Special corsage tubes are made for this purpose.

The Care and Use of Cut Flowers   **343**

The stem is placed in it as far as it will go, being certain that the hole in the rubber cap is not so tight that it will pinch the stem, yet tight enough to prevent leakage of the water. In lieu of a tube, the stem may be wrapped in wet cotton and covered with polyethylene film. Stem and tube, or stem and cotton, will be covered with flora-tape or parafilm. Florists often eliminate the tube, but it insures a longer life to the corsage.

Corsage-making kits are available. They contain wires of various thicknesses, ribbons, pins, and the all-important flora-tape or parafilm for wrapping the stems. Since orchids come in so many colors and shades, no kit will always have the right ribbon for every flower. For an occasional corsage you may be able to find suitable ribbon at a notion counter, but if you intend to make many you should lay in a stock of assorted colors from a florist supply house.

The accompanying photographs give the step by step method for making a corsage. The brittle stem must be supported by wire. It is not necessary to puncture the stem of a large flower; the wire is simply laid along the stem and together they are wrapped with parafilm. If the flower is to go into a tube, the wire may be wound around the stem in a spiral manner first, and then the stem and tube can be wrapped together. To apply the parafilm, press the end to the stem just under the flower and wind it several times to give extra support. Then, turning the flower with one hand, draw the tape spirally along the stem pressing it tightly with your fingers. Continue until the wires are also wrapped to the end, as they can be formed into a decorative curl.

An orchid really needs no decoration, but most people feel that the addition of a bit of ribbon completes the dressing of the flower. A very simple bow of only two, possibly three or four, double loops of ribbon is enough. It is a shame to see an orchid so highly dressed that the ribbon is more conspicuous than the flower. The ribbon may blend with the tones of the flower, or perhaps a happy contrast in color may be found. The bow is made by forming the loops with your fingers and then gathering the ribbon in tightly with a fine wire. The ends of the wire serve to fasten the bow to the stem. Stretchy paper ribbon may be used in place of wire.

When a corsage is to be made of several small flowers, it is usually best to separate them and wrap each stem individually. Delicate stems are likely to break at the back of the flower and should have a wire looped over the column and dorsal sepal,

then wound down the stem. The ends of the wire are allowed to extend longer than the stem, and then stem and wire are wrapped with flora-tape, The flowers are then arranged in whatever way you wish, each facing front, and the stems are wired together. After they have been joined, the individual flowers may be turned to give the most effective design. Perhaps a group of small flowers may be made to follow the neckline of a dress, or one flower may stand on the shoulder while the others descend in a graceful curve. There is no limit to what can be done with a spray corsage, and your own ingenuity will produce many lovely arrangements. A spray to be worn in the hair should be light as a feather and may be wired to a comb or a barrette to make it secure. Any group of small orchids is more effective when each flower stands alone in airy grace. A jammed up bunch looks awkward and hides the beauty of the flowers.

A single flower is most attractive worn right side up, as it grows. When several blooms are used in a corsage, the central one should be right side up, and the others may be turned to make a tasteful design. When you put on the corsage, let the pin go through the ribbon, not through the stem.

KEEPING THE CORSAGE

After you have worn your corsage, you will want to keep it fresh for another time. The flowers should be kept in a refrigerator, at a temperature not lower than 45°. Most kinds keep beautifully in an airtight container, without being placed in water. The whole corsage may be laid on a bed of wax paper in a large-mouthed jar with a tight lid. A good procedure is to put the jar in the refrigerator when you put on your orchid, so that it will be cool when you are ready for it. As you take off the lid to put the corsage in it, blow into the jar, so that a film of water vapor covers its sides. Then quickly lay the corsage on the shredded wax paper (to prevent contact with the cold glass), replace the lid, and return the jar to the refrigerator. The moisture retained in the jar is enough to keep the flower fresh for ten days to two weeks.

A bag of polyethylene film may keep the flower even longer. Put some shredded wax paper in the bag and lay the corsage on it. Then fold the end of the bag tightly and fasten it with a couple of paper clips. To avoid having the corsage crushed

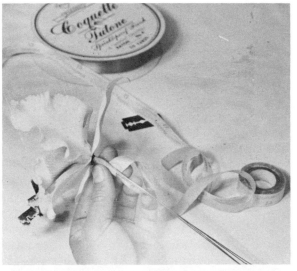
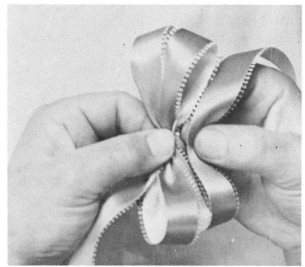

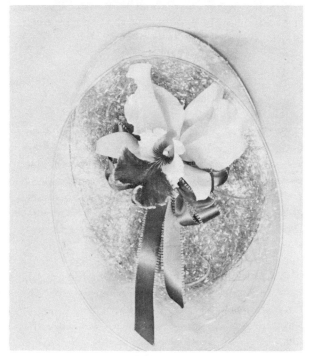

Fig. 25-1 Steps in making a corsage. UPPER LEFT, lay several strands of fine wire along the stem, allowing them to extend some distance beyond. Wrap the stem at its base and the upper ends of the wire snugly with several thicknesses of parafilm. Then spirally wrap the length of the wires. UPPER RIGHT, florists have many ways of making a bow. One is to gather loops one by one, pinching in the center, and holding them firmly. A fine wire or light paper ribbon is then tied tightly around the pinched-in center portion. LOWER LEFT, the bow is snugged up under the lip and lower sepals and tied to the wrapped stem. LOWER RIGHT, the finished corsage. The length of wrapped wire can be curled into a decorative coil. The ribbon chosen here matched the deep tones of the lip.

when things are moved around in the refrigerator, lay it in a small box. The life of many kinds of orchids can be extended after they are cut by keeping them in the refrigerator in polyethylene film. Flowers which you wish to use later for corsages or for other purposes can be cut and stored in this manner.

ORCHIDS AS DECORATIONS

A flowering plant commands attention, even in its red clay pot, and a plant set temporarily in a pretty jardiniere is an addition to any room. There is no danger to the flowers in moving them from the damp greenhouse into the living room. A flowering

The Care and Use of Cut Flowers

plant may even be transported to a hospital room for the pleasure of a sick friend.

But many orchid plants are stiff and ungraceful, and their flowers may be used in a more decorative manner if they are cut. A fine hand with flowers can turn out beautiful things. One orchid in a simple little vase is a spot of beauty for table or mantel. Grand, impressive arrangements using whole sprays of cymbidiums with other flowers, low settings for a few cattleyas, stunning combinations of paphiopedilums with unusual foliage, arrangements of oncidiums with delphinium that are all blue and gold lace, and so on ad infinitum. The flowers used with orchids will have to be renewed from time to time, for the orchids will far outlast them in freshness. Never cut foliage from an orchid plant.

To keep the cut orchids for as long as possible, remove them to a cool place at night. And trim the stems from time to time, holding the tip under water as described above.

SELLING AND SHIPPING BLOOMS

Orchid flowers must be carefully packed in order to arrive at their destination in perfection. Whether you send a corsage to a far away friend or blooms to a wholesaler in the next town, the same packing method is used. Shredded wax paper is obtainable at any wholesale florist house, or possibly from your local florist. This springy, non-absorbent stuff protects the flowers from jostling and keeps the flower parts from rubbing and bruising each other.

A few swatches of shredded wax paper are laid between sepals and petals and around the lip. The flower in its tube of water is then laid on a bed of shredded wax paper in a strong box. The tube must be fastened firmly to the bottom of the box so that the flower will not move from its position. Holes punched in the box on either side of the tube allow wire or a twistem to be tied around the tube, or it may be fastened down with Scotch tape. More shredded wax paper is tucked under the large parts of the flower, and a little put on top to keep them firm.

In moderate weather, the box need be wrapped in only one thickness of paper. But in cold weather, the box is wrapped in layer after layer of newspaper to insulate it. The insulation retains the inside warmth for an hour or two, possibly longer depending on the number of layers. Railway and Air Express are recommended as the best shipping methods, the extra expense being worth the care in handling. A label on the box stating that it contains cut flowers to be protected from heat and cold will insure its being properly cared for.

If you have only two or three cut flowers to market at a time you will do better to sell them to a local florist rather than to a wholesaler. The wholesaler buys flowers either on a commission basis, or outright at a price within the range of their market value. He must make a profit on them, above his cost of handling and bookkeeping. The trouble of opening your occasional small shipment, grading your flowers, and keeping track of their sale is really not a profitable venture for him, compared to what he can make on a shipment of a hundred blooms. Nor is it profitable for you to pay shipping expenses and the sales commission. If you have a steady supply of good quality flowers, and the wholesale florist can count on you for a certain number a week, then it becomes profitable for both of you.

The ups and downs of the market are sometimes disconcerting. Perhaps you ship a box of nice blooms, only to receive fifty cents apiece for them because your contribution arrived at the wholesale house at an inauspicious time. At another time, if orchids are scarce, you may receive three or four times that amount. In general good cattleya flowers wholesale for between one and a half and two and a half dollars, depending on their size and quality. Poor samples sell for very little or are dumped.

In a town where there is not a wholesale florist, the retail florist must send away for his flowers and pay the packing and shipping charges. He may be very glad to buy orchids at home if he can thereby save some expense. Also, the convenience of having a grower nearby from whom he can get a flower at an hour's notice is a factor in your favor. However, if you wish to sell flowers consistently, you must always be certain of their quality and be willing to replace one that does not hold up. If the florist knows that what he gets from you is fresh and of good quality, and that the flowers will last well both for his customers and in his refrigerator, he will continue to buy from you. You must be somewhat dispassionate about pricing and selling flowers. There may be times when to oblige the florist you will have to cut something you had wanted to keep, or sell a fine one for less than its actual value. There will be other times when you have many you would like to sell but for which there is no demand.

The average customer of the average florist is

Home Orchid Growing

not a connoisseur of orchids. He may know one or two kinds, but he will ordinarily not want to pay a premium for a flower that, for instance, has particularly broad petals. To him an orchid corsage should be had for a standard price, and the florist, in order to make the sale, may have to let a fine flower go for less than it would be worth in a more discriminating market. However, if a discerning customer who knows his orchids wants something especially fine, you may be able to make a better sale. Thus unusually fine blooms, or ones of unusual coloring, may command a higher price if there is a demand for them at the moment.

You can encourage the use of less well-known kinds by showing them to the florists, or by inviting them to come to your greenhouse. When we first began growing orchids, even the florists knew only those most commonly used. But now they often request something different for special occasions and encourage their more discriminating customers to let them send corsages of unusual flowers. Prices on the smaller orchids, where several must be used

in a corsage, have to be governed by the number needed to make a fair showing. The florist can help you out here. People are learning that a gift of orchids brings more oh's and ah's from a patient and his friends to say nothing of the doctors and nurses, than a large bouquet of the usual cut flowers. A cattleya in a small vase, a stem of cymbidiums or phalaenopsis, two or three paphiopedilums, a graceful little spray of dendrobiums, epidendrums, or oncidiums, may be the center of attention in a roomful of flowers. Once the customer and the florist have received the plaudits from such a gift, they are sure to want to repeat it.

Over the months you can get great pleasure from your flowers, yet still sell some to make them help support themselves. Even the commercial growers are amateurs at heart and often have collections separate from the plants from which they make their living. For many of us, selling flowers helps us pay for new plants to add to our collections and enables us to have many more kinds than we could otherwise afford.

APPENDIX A
KEY TO THE TRIBES AND GENERA OF THE ORCHID FAMILY

This key is reproduced from the *Standard Cyclopedia of Horticulture* with the kind permission of The Macmillan Company (copyright 1900 and 1914) and its author, Liberty Hyde Bailey, copyright 1928. A few notes have been added (given in parentheses) as explanation to those tribes not described in the text of this book. (Note: A few genera have been added in the text from sources other than Bailey. Nomenclature changes have been made where necessary.)

I. SUMMARY OF TRIBES

A. Fertile stamens 2, with a broad shield-shaped sterile one (staminodium) . . . . 1. CYPRIPEDIUM TRIBE
AA. Fertile stamen 1, with no staminodium.
  B. Anther persistent; pollinia with basal appendages.
    C. The anther erect.
      D. Stigma flat, unappendaged . . . . 2. SERAPIAS TRIBE
      DD. Stigma with appendages . . . . 3. HABENARIA TRIBE
    CC. The anthers placed obliquely . . . . 4. SATYRIUM TRIBE
  BB. Anther usually readily deciduous; pollinia not appendaged or with terminal ones.
    C. Infl. terminal.
      D. Lf.-buds convolute.
        E. Lf.-blade not jointed to stalk.
          F. The anther commonly much exceeding the beak of the column which is not distinctly cut.
            G. Lip without hypochil, usually spurless.
              H. St. short, with only 1 or 2 lvs. . . 5. POGONIA TRIBE
              HH. St. long, with many lvs. . . . 6. VANILLA TRIBE
            GG. Lip with distinct hypochil, which is often spurred . . . . 7. CEPHALANTHERA TRIBE
          FF. The anther commonly about as long as the beak of the column which usually bears a sharp cut or groove.
            G. Pollinia waxy or powdery, not divided.
              H. Lip turned down . . . . 8. SPIRANTHES TRIBE
              HH. Lip turned up . . . . 9. CRANICHIS TRIBE
             GG. Pollinia divided into distinct masses . . 10. PHYSURUS TRIBE
        EE. Lf.-blade distinctly jointed to the petiole.
          F. Pollinia 8: st. slender: fls. usually with spurs or chins . . . . 11. THUNIA TRIBE

FF. Pollinia 4: st. a short pseudobulb: fls. without spurs or chins . . . . . 12. COELOGYNE TRIBE
DD. Lf.-buds conduplicate.
    E. Sepals and petals about equally developed, the lip usually very conspicuous.
        F. Lvs. usually not jointed: column footless . . 13. LIPARIS TRIBE
        FF. Lvs. usually jointed.
            G. Nerves of lvs. 1.
                H. Pollinia 2-4, with very short stalks . 14. POLYSTACHYA TRIBE
                HH. Pollinia 4-8, with distinct caudicles.
                    I. Column-foot forming a chin with the lateral sepals or a short sac with the lip . . . . . 15. PONERA TRIBE
                    II. Column footless . . . . 16. CATTLEYA TRIBE
            GG. Nerves of lvs. several . . . . . 17. SOBRALIA TRIBE
    EE. Sepals much more developed than the petals and lip . . . . 18. PLEUROTHALLIS TRIBE
CC. Infl. lateral, or on separate shoot.
    D. Lf.-buds convolute.
        E. St. slender or gradually swollen.
            F. Pollinia with caudicles but without stalks . 19. PHAIUS TRIBE
            FF. Pollinia without caudicles but with stalks.
                G. Lip jointed to column-foot or forming a spur with it . . . . . . 20. CYRTOPODIUM TRIBE
                GG. Lip not jointed, often with a distinct hypochil . . . . . . 21. CATASETUM TRIBE
        EE. St. a short distinct pseudobulb.
            F. Lip jointed to the column-foot.
                G. Callus-ridges lengthwise . . . . 22. LYCASTE TRIBE
                GG. Callus-ridges transverse . . . . 23. ZYGOPETALUM TRIBE
            FF. Lip continuous with column-foot . . . 24. GONGORA TRIBE
DD. Lf.-buds conduplicate.
    E. St. terminating its growth in 1 year.
        F. Lip movably jointed to foot of column.
            G. Lvs. not strap-shaped: pollinia unappendaged or with either caudicles or stipes, but not with both.
                H. Flowering st. arising from near the apex of the slender st. or from the pseudobulb . . . . 25. DENDROBIUM TRIBE
                HH. Flowering st. arising under the pseudobulb or at the base of the st.
                    I. Pollinia without appendages . 26. BULBOPHYLLUM TRIBE
                    II. Pollinia with distinct stalks.
                        J. Pseudobulbs usually present: flowering st. arising lower than new growth 27. MAXILLARIA TRIBE
                        JJ. Pseudobulbs usually wanting: flowering st. arising higher than new growth . 28. HUNTLEYA TRIBE (included in Zygopetalum Tribe)
            GG. Lvs. strap-shaped: pollinia with broad caudicles and stipes . . . . . 29. CYMBIDIUM TRIBE
        FF. Lip immovably united to foot of column.
            G. Fls. with spurs . . . . . . 30. IONOPSIS TRIBE
            GG. Fls. without spurs.
                H. The fls. narrow, not open . . . 31. ADA TRIBE
                HH. The fls. wide open.
                    I. Lip enrolled around the column . . . . 32. TRICHOPILIA TRIBE
                    II. Lip not enrolled.
                        J. The lip united to column to the middle . . . . 33. ASPASIA TRIBE

Home Orchid Growing

II. KEY TO THE TRIBES

1. Cypripedium Tribe

A. Fl. persistent, withering on the ovary: Lf.-buds convolute . . . . . .   1. *Cypripedium*
AA. Fl. soon deciduous: Lf.-buds conduplicate.
    B. Ovary 3-celled, the placentae central; mouth of lip with broad inturned
      margin . . . .   2. *Phragmipedium*
    BB. Ovary 1-celled, the placentae parietal; mouth of lip usually with no
      broad inturned margins . . . .   3. *Paphiopedilum*

2. Serapias Tribe

(Terrestrial, North Temperate Zone. *Orchis* is the type genus of the orchid
family.)
A. Lip spurred.
    B. Sepals free . . . .   4. *Orchis*
    BB. Sepals united into an arching hood . . . .   5. *Galeorchis*
AA. Lip spurless.
    B. Pollinia glands in a single sac . . . .   6. *Serapias*
    BB. Pollinia glands separate, in 2 distinct sacs . . . . . .   7. *Ophrys*

3. Habenaria Tribe

(Terrestrial, temperate and tropical regions, includes some of our finest native
orchids.)
A. Lip adnate to column at base; stigma broad . . . .   8. *Cynorchis*
AA. Lip free; stigma slender . . . .   9. *Habenaria*

4. Satyrium Tribe

(Terrestrial, South Africa, pretty, but hard to grow.)
Dorsal sepal helmet-shaped . . . .   10. *Disa*

5. Pogonia Tribe

(Terrestrial, mostly North and South America. A few can be grown in gardens.)
A. Fls. on a scape with a terminal whorl of lf.-like bracts . . . . .   11. *Isotria*
AA. Fls. on a leafy st.
    B. Lip crested . . . .   12. *Pogonia*
    BB. Lip not crested . . . .   13. *Triphora*

6. Vanilla Tribe

Sts. rooting at nodes . . . .   14. *Vanilla*

7. Cephalanthera Tribe

(Terrestrial, North Temperate Zone)
A. Fls. with a chin; lip long . . . .   15. *Cephalanthera*
AA. Fls. chinless; lip round . . . .   16. *Epipactis*

8. Spiranthes Tribe

(Terrestrial, mostly tropical, but with a few native species adaptable to
gardens.)
A. Dorsal sepal forming a hood with the petals.
    B. Infl. 1-sided; fls. without a chin . . . .   17. *Spiranthes*
    BB. Infl. not 1-sided; fls. with a chin . . . .   18. *Stenorrhynchus*
AA. Sepals and petals spreading . . . .   19. *Listera*

9. Cranichis Tribe

(Terrestrial, native to tropical America)
Lip and petals inserted upon the elongated column . . . .   20. *Ponthieva*

10. Physurus (Erythrodes) Tribe

A. Lip with a distinct spur.
    B. Lvs. green: lip concave above the spur . . . .   21. *Physurus (Erythrodes)*

    BB. Lvs. usually variegated: lip with a long fimbriate claw . . . .   22. *Anoectochilus*

AA. Lip spurless or nearly so.
    B. Column straight; fls. symmetric.
        C. The lip not clawed . . . .   23. *Goodyera*
        CC. The lip clawed . . . .   24. *Dossinia*
    BB. Column twisted; fls. not symmetric.
        C. The column with 2 upright appendages in front . . . .   25. *Macodes*
        CC. The column without appendages . . . .   26. *Haemaria* (*Ludisia*)

11. Thunia Tribe

Terrestrial, Asia. *Thunia* and *Bletilla* are seen in collections, the latter adaptable to gardens in some regions.)
  A. Fls. without chin.
    B. Sts. without basal pseudobulbs . . . .   27. *Thunia*
    BB. Sts. with basal pseudobulbs . . . .   28. *Bletilla*
AA. Fls. with a distinct chin, formed of lateral sepals and column-foot . . . .   29. *Trichosma*

12. Coelogyne Tribe

  A. Base of lip with sac-like hollow.
    B. Column short, winged above, sepals flat . . . .   30. *Pholidota*
    BB. Column slender; sepals sac-like, concave . . . .   31. *Neogyne*
AA. Base of lip flat.
    B. Column slender, without horns.
        C. Lvs. and pseudobulbs perennial . . . .   32. *Coelogyne*
        CC. Lvs. and pseudobulbs annual . . . .   33. *Pleione*
    BB. Column short, with 2 horns . . . .   34. *Platyclinis*

13. Liparis Tribe

(Terrestrial, North Temperate Zone, many in North America. Best known is *Calypso,* one of our native orchids.)
  A. Lvs. green: fls. without chin.
    B. Lip shoe-shaped . . . .   35. *Calypso*
    BB. Lip not shoe-shaped . . . .
        C. Column short; lip turned upward . . . .   36. *Microstylis*
        CC. Column slender; lip turned downward . . . . . .   37. *Liparis*
AA. Lvs. wanting: fls. with chin . . . .   38. *Corallorrhiza*

14. Polystachya Tribe

  A. Lip spurred.
    B. Plant tuberous: spur slender . . . .   39. *Tipularia*
    BB. Plant not tuberous: spur funnel-shaped . . . .   40. *Galeandra*
AA. Lip not spurred.
    B. The lip 3-lobed.
        C. Column short; chin distinct . . . .   41. *Polystachya*
        CC. Column slender, curved; chin indistinct . . . . . .   42. *Ansellia*
    BB. The lip entire . . . .   43. *Neobenthamia*

15. Ponera Tribe

  A. Lip normal.
    B. St. slender, leafy; no pseudobulbs; pollinia 4 . . . . . .   44. *Isochilus*
    BB. St. a pseudobulb: pollinia 8 . . . .   45. *Coelia*
AA. Lip forming a beaker-like cavity, with the column, or the former hollow at base.
    B. Young shoots at the apex of the old . . . .   46. *Hexisea*
    BB. Young shoots from base of old.
        C. Fls. in dense spikes; pollinia 8 . . . .   47. *Arpophyllum*
        CC. Fls. in short clusters; pollinia 4 . . . .   48. *Hartwegia*

16. Cattleya Tribe

  A. Anther not toothed, nor in an excavation.
    B. Pollinia 4.
        C. Lip adnate to the column, at least at its base.
            D. Ovary produced into a hollow neck . . . . . .   49. *Broughtonia*
            DD. Ovary not so produced . . . .   50. *Epidendrum*
        CC. Lip free.
            D. The lip flat, with 2 elevations on upper side . . . .   51. *Diacrium*
            DD. The lip enrolled about column, with no elevations . . .   52. *Cattleya*
    BB. Pollinia 5-7, some of them often abortive . . . .   53. *Laelio-cattleya*

BBB. Pollinia 8.
    C. Stigma pitted upon the front of the column; anther inclined.
        D. Base of lip gradually merging into blade.
            E. Lip distinctly surrounding the column; sepals and petals
                not wavy . . . . 54. *Laelia*
            EE. Lip not as above; sepals and petals distinctly wavy . 55. *Schomburgkia*
        DD. Base of lip tightly encompassing column, suddenly broadened
            into the broad blade . . . . 56. *Brassavola*
    CC. Stigma running up on 2 extensions of the column-apex; anther
        erect . . . . 57. *Sophronitis*
AA. Anther 2-toothed below, in an excavation in the column . . . . 58. *Leptotes*

17. Sobralia Tribe

A. St. many-lvd., not bulbous at base: lip not bearded . . . . . . 59. *Sobralia*
AA. St. 1- or 2-lvd., bulbous at base; lip bearded . . . . . . 60. *Calopogon*

18. Pleurothallis Tribe

A. Lip turned upward; lateral sepals united into a boat-shaped hood . . . 61. *Scaphosepalum*
AA. Lip turned down.
    B. Sepals united . . . . 62. *Masdevallia*
    BB. Sepals free, or the lateral only united.
        C. Dorsal sepal and petals attenuated into a club-shaped apex . 63. *Restrepia*
        CC. Dorsal sepal and petals not as above . . . . . 64. *Pleurothallis*

19. Phaius Tribe

A. Lvs. not articulated to petiole.
    B. Lip free, encompassing the column . . . . 65. *Phaius*
    BB. Lip adnate to column, the blade spreading . . . . . 66. *Calanthe*
AA. Lvs. articulated to petiole.
    B. Sepals and petals spreading.
        C. Lip with its base tightly enclosing the column, the blade spreading . 67. *Limatodes* (syn.
                        Calanthe)
        CC. Lip not enclosing column.
            D. Fls. with distinct chin . . . . 68. *Chysis*
            DD. Fls. without chin.
                E. Pollinia 8.
                    F. Middle lobe of lip not clawed . . . . 69. *Bletia*
                    FF. Middle lobe of lip clawed . . . . . 70. *Spathoglottis*
                EE. Pollinia 4 . . . . 71. *Aplectrum*
    BB. Sepals and petals erect . . . . 72. *Acanthophippium*

20. Cyrtopodium Tribe

(Both epiphytic and terrestrial, tropical.)
A. Fls. spurred or with sac-like base.
    B. Sepals narrower and less colored than petals . . . . . 73. *Lissochilus*
    BB. Sepals and petals alike or nearly so . . . . . . 74. *Eulophia*
AA. Fls. not spurred nor saccate.
    B. Lip only inserted on column-foot . . . . 75. *Cyrtopodium*
    BB. Lip and lateral sepals inserted on column-foot.
        C. Chin distinct, rectangular . . . . 76. *Warrea*
        CC. Chin indistinct, round . . . . 77. *Eulophiella*

21. Catasetum Tribe

A. Fls. perfect; column twisted . . . . 78. *Mormodes*
AA. Fls. of 2 or 3 forms; column not twisted.
    B. Column stout, straight; fls. with antennae . . . . . 79. *Catasetum*
    BB. Column slender, curved; fls. without antennae . . . . 80. *Cycnoches*

22. Lycaste Tribe

A. Pollinia upon a single stalk.
    B. Fls. globose . . . . 81. *Anguloa*
    BB. Fls. with spreading sepals and petals.
        C. Stalk of pollinia long and narrow; fls. 1 to few.
            D. Infl. of a single erect fl.; lip turned down . . . 82. *Lycaste*
            DD. Infl. of 2 to few drooping fls.; lip turned upward . . 83. *Paphinia*
        CC. Stalk of pollinia short; fls. many . . . . . . 84. *Batemannia*
AA. Pollinia upon 2 Separate stalks . . . . 85. *Bifrenaria*

31. Ada Tribe

A. Lvs. flat.
    B. Sepals free . . . . 118. *Ada*
    BB. Laterals sepals united . . . . 119. *Mesospinidium*
AA. Lvs. cylindric . . . . 120. *Quekettia*

32. Trichopilia Tribe

Lip rolled around the column . . . . 121. *Trichopilia*

33. Aspasia Tribe (See text, with Odontoglossum Tribe)

A. Middle lobe of lip broad . . . . 122. *Aspasia*
AA. Middle lobe of lip narrow . . . . 123. *Cochlioda*

34. Odontoglossum Tribe

A. Lip surrounding column with 2 longitudinal calluses: blade reflexed . . . 124. *Gomeza*
AA. Lip not as above.
    B. Base of lip parallel to column and sometimes adnate to it . . . . 125. *Odontoglossum*
    BB. Lip spreading from base of column.
        C. Lateral sepals united entirely; lip like dorsal sepal . . . . . 126. *Palumbina*
        CC. Lateral sepals free or only partly united; lip unlike dorsal sepal.
            D. Sepals and petals long and much attenuated; lip entire or
                fiddle-shaped . . . . 127. *Brassia*
            DD. Sepals and petals not much attenuated.
                E. The lip entire, flat, broad . . . . 128. *Miltonia*
                EE. The lip mostly 3-lobed, with warts or a cushion at base 129. *Oncidium*

35. Aerides Tribe

A. Lip movably jointed to column.
    B. Middle lobe of spurless lip flat . . . . 130. *Renanthera*
    BB. Middle lobe of spurred lip compressed . . . . 131. *Arachnanthe*
AA. Lip immovably united with column.
    B. Spurless.
        C. Column without a foot.
            D. Summit of lip laterally compressed . . . . . . 132. *Vandopsis*
            DD. Summit of lip not compressed . . . . 133. *Luisia*
        CC. Column with a foot, the lateral sepals attached to it . . . 134. *Phalaenopsis*
    BB. Spurred.
        C. Column without a foot.
            D. Pollinia upon a single stalk.
                E. Spur appendaged.
                      F. With a longitudinal septum . . . . . . 135. *Sarcanthus*
                      FF. With the mouth covered with a plate . . . 136. *Cleisostoma*
                EE. Spur not appendaged.
                      F. Stalk of the pollinia filiform.
                          G. Fls. firm; lip turned downward . . . 137. *Saccolabium*
                          GG. Fls. fragile; lip turned upward . . . 138. *Acampe*
                      FF. Stalk of the pollinia broadened upward or
                        throughout.
                          G. Spur short and broad . . . . . 139. *Vanda*
                          GG. Spur long and slender . . . . . 140. *Angraecum*
            DD. Pollinia on 2 separate stalks, or these united by the gland.
                E. Stalks membranous, the pollinia attached to the face.
                      F. Plants leafy: lip entire . . . . . . 141. *Macroplectrum*
                      FF. Plants without lvs.: lip 3-lobed . . . . 142. *Polyrrhiza*
                EE. Stalks slender.
                      F. Column bent toward the dorsal sepal . . . 143. *Listrostachys*
                      FF. Column straight . . . . 144. *Mystacidium*
        CC. Column with a foot, the lateral sepals attached to it.
            D. Spur curved upward against the lip-blade . . . . 145. *Aërides*
            DD. Spur straight or reflexed.
                E. Lip 3-lobed . . . . 146. *Camarotis*
                EE. Lip entire . . . . 147. *Rhynchostylis*

APPENDIX B
SOURCES OF PLANTS, SUPPLIES, AND SERVICES

Compiled from advertisements. This list is for your convenience in sending for lists and catalogues. No endorsement of the companies is implied, and we take no responsibility for transactions between them and our readers.

ORCHID PLANTS (In addition to these there may be local growers who can furnish plants.)

Alberts and Merkel Bros., Inc., P.O. Box 537 AO, Boynton Beach, Fla. 33435

Keith Andrew Plush, Dorchester, Dorset, England

Armacost and Royston, Inc., 2005 Armacost Ave., West Los Angeles, Calif. 90025

Armstrong and Brown, J. L. Humphreys, Tunbridge Wells, Kent, England

Ashcroft Orchids, 19062 Ballinger Way, Seattle, Wash. 98155

The Bangkrabue Nursery, 15 Klahom's Lane, Bangkrabue, Bangkok, Thailand

M. J. Bates—Orchids, 7911 U. S. 301, Ellenton, Fla. 33532

The Beall Company, Vashon Island, Wash. 98070

Black and Flory, Ltd., Slough, Bucks, England

Black River Orchids, P.O. Box 110, South Haven, Mich. 49090

James Bloom, 1329 N.E. 7th Ave., Fort Lauderdale, Fla. 33304

Blue Grass Orchids, Winchester Rd., R.F.D. 4, Lexington, Kentucky

Paul Brecht Orchids, Costa Mesa, Calif.

Casa Luna Orchids, Star Rte. 1, Box 219A, Beaufort, S. C. 29902

Charlesworth and Co., Ltd., Haywards Heath, Sussex, England

Chow Cheng Orchids, 194 Litoh St., Taichung, Taiwan

Cobb's Orchids, Inc., 780 La Buena Tierra, Santa Barbara, Calif. 93105

Creve Coeur Orchids, 12 Graeser Acres, Creve Coeur, Mo. 63141

Clark Day, Jr., 19311 Bloomfield Ave., Artesia, Calif.

Walter R. Diggleman, 2356 Tiffin Rd., Oakland, Calif.

Dos Pueblos Orchid Co., P.O. Box 158, Goleta, Calif. 93017.

Everglades Orchids, P.O. Box 401, Belle Glade, Fla. 33430

Fennell Orchid Co., Homestead, Fla. 33030

Field's Orchids, 196 N.W. 91st St., Miami, Fla. 33150

Fink Floral Co., 9849 Kimker Lane, St. Louis, Mo. 63127

Fred-Ken Orchids, P.O. Box 660, Homestead, Fla. 33030

Fort Caroline Orchids, 13142 Fort Caroline Rd., Jacksonville, Fla. 32225

Arthur Freed Orchids, Inc., 5731 So. Bonsall Dr., Malibu, Calif. 90265

Fricker Orchids and Greenhouse Mfrs., 5248 Sereno Dr., Temple City, Calif.

Franklin W. Gamble, 62 Shell Rd., Mill Valley, Calif.

G. Ghose and Co., Orchids, Town-End, Darjeeling, West Bengal, India

R. H. Gore Orchids, Box 211, Fort Lauderdale, Fla. 33315

Etta Gray Orchids, 1653 Barnard Rd., Claremont, Calif. 91711

Greenhouse Hawaii, John K. Noa, P.O. Box 180, Waimanalo, Hawaii 96795

Gubler Orchids, 9441 E. Broadway, Temple City, Calif.

Herb Hager Orchids, P.O. Box 544, Santa Cruz, Calif. 95060

Hauserman's Orchids, Inc., P.O. Box 363, Elmhurst, Ill. 60126

Hilo Vanda Nursery, Dr. H. Nishimura, 466 Laukapu St., Hilo, Hawaii 96720

S. M. Howard Orchid Imports, 11802 Houston St., N. Hollywood, Calif. 91607

Gordon M. Hoyt, Orchids, Seattle Heights, Wash. 98063

Margaret Ilgenfritz, Orchids, P.O. Box 665, Monroe, Mich. 48161

H. Iwanaga, 5398 Papae St., Honolulu, Hawaii 96816

J. and L. Orchids, Chestnut Hill Rd., R.D. 2, Pottstown, Pa. 19464

Jones and Scully, Inc., 2200 N.W. 33rd Ave., Miami, Fla. 33142

Patrick O. Kawamoto, 3142 E. Manoa Rd., Honolulu, Hawaii 96822

T. Kazumura Orchid Nursery, 145 N. Judd St., Honolulu, Hawaii 96817

A. J. Keeling and Sons, Westgate Hill, Nr. Bradford, Yorks, England

Kensington Orchids, Inc., 3301 Plyers Mill Rd., Kensington, Md. 20795

Wm. Kirch Orchids, Ltd., 2630 Waiomao Rd., Honolulu, Hawaii 96816

Oscar M. Kirsch, 2869 Oahu Ave., Honolulu, Hawaii 96822

Kodama Orchid Nursery, Ltd., 1039 Kamehameha Rd., Honolulu, Hawaii 96819

Lager and Hurrell, 426 Morris Ave., Summit, N. J. 07901

Landamar Orchids, P.O. Box 698, Tarzana, Calif. 91356

Marcel Lecoufle, 5 Rue de Paris, 94 Boissy-St. Leger, France

Lines Orchids, Taft Highway, Signal Mountain, Tenn. 37377

Stuart Low Co., Jarvisbrook (Crowborough), Sussex, England

Manor Orchids, 970 East Social Row Rd., Dayton, Ohio 45459

Mansell and Hatcher, Ltd., Rawdon, Leeds, Yorks, England

Marcy Orchids, Inc., 6901 S.W. 97th Ave., Miami, Fla. 33143

McBean's Orchids, Cooksbridge, Lewes, Sussex, England

Mrs. Lester McCoy Orchids, 3735 Diamond Head Rd., Honolulu, Hawaii 96803

McKee Jungle Garden, Vero Beach, Fla.

McKeral's Orchid Range, 1801 Hypoluxo Rd., Lantana, Fla. 33460

Rod McLellan Co., 1450 El Camino Real, S. San Francisco, Calif. 94080

Mid-Florida Orchid Center, Inc., S. 9th St., P.O. Box 1031, Winter Garden, Fla. 32787

M. Miyamoto Orchids, 617 Libby St., Honolulu, Hawaii 96792

Moore's Orchids, P.O. Box 2366, Hialeah, Fla. 33012

Muse's Orchids, 3187 S.W. 26th St., Miami, Fla. 33133

Dr. and Mrs. Yoshio Nagano, 261 Eifukucho, Suginami, Tokyo, Japan

Nelson Nurseries, 1975 Opa Locka Blvd., Miami, Fla.

T. Ogawa Orchids, 1454 Kilauea Ave., Hilo, Hawaii

The Orchid House, 699 Sage Ave., Los Osos, San Luis Obispo, Calif. 93401

Orchid Oaks Nursery, 9440 S.W. 107th Ave., Miami, Fla. 33143

Orchids Bountiful, 826 West 3800 South, Bountiful, Utah 84010

Orchids by Turner, Inc., 226 Park St., North Attleboro, Mass. 02760

Orchids of Africa, Helen Cockburn and Frank Piers, F.L.S., Box 2041, Nairobi, Kenya, East Africa

Orchids International, P.O. Box 66560, Burien, Wash. 98166

Orquideario Catarinense, P.O. Box 1, Corupa, Santa Catarina, Brazil

Orquideas Mexicanas, P.O. Box 10-738, Mexico 10 D.F., Mexico

Osment Orchids, 2435 Cleveland St., Hollywood, Fla.

H. Otake Orchid Nursery, 45-270-A Puaae Rd., Kaneohe, Oahu, Hawaii

Pacific Coast Orchid Estate, P.O. Box 281, Moss Beach, Calif. 94038

H. Patterson and Sons, Bergenfield, N. J. 07621

Penn Valley Orchids, 239 Gulph Rd., Wynnewood, Pa. 19096

Joseph R. Redlinger, Orchids, 9236 S.W. 57th Ave., Miami, Fla. 33156

Research Breeders, William West, 753 Kansas Ave., Lovell, Wyo. 82431

Ruben in Orchids, Golden Hours, Inc., 12500 S.W. 46th St., Miami, Fla. 33165

Rapee Sagarick, G.P.O. Box 953, Bangkok, Thailand

David Sanders Orchids, Ltd., Selsfield, East Grinstead, Sussex, England

T. M. Sanders, 12502 Prospect Ave., Santa Ana, Calif. 92705

Santa Barbara Orchid Estate, 1250 Orchid Dr., Goleta, Calif. 93105

Walter Scheeren Orchids, Poestenkill, N. Y. 12140

Shaffer's Tropical Gardens, Inc., 1220 41st Ave., Santa Cruz, Calif. 95060

Sherman Orchid Gardens, Glendora, Calif. 91740

Shimamoto Orchid Nursery, 271 Momi Lane, Wailuku, Maui, Hawaii 96793

Sign of the Coon, Powderville, Mont.

Earl J. Small Orchids, Inc., 6901 49th St., Pinellas Park, Fla. 33565

Ralph Smathers Orchids, P.O. Box 477, Coral Gables, Fla. 33134

Sterling Orchids, Inc., 5502 Sterling Rd., Knoxville, Tenn. 37918

Fred A. Stewart, Inc., 1212 E. Las Tunas Dr., San Gabriel, Calif. 91778

Thornton's Orchids, 3200 N. Military Trail, W. Palm Beach, Fla. 33401

Tradewinds Orchids, Inc., 12800 S.W. 77th Ave., Miami, Fla. 33156

Maurice Vacherot, 31 Rue de Valenton, Boissy-St. Leger (V. de M.) France

Vacherot and Lecoufle, "La Tuilerie," 94 Boissy-St. Leger (V. de M.), France

Voo Doo Orchids, 1340 Jewel Box Lane, Naples, Fla.

J. Milton Warne, 260 Jack Lane, Honolulu, Hawaii 96817

Weeki Wachee Orchids, Rte. 4, Box 65, Brooksville, Fla. 33512

Westenberger Orchid Co., 10150 Foothill Blvd., San Fernando, Calif. 91342

E. C. Wilcox, 1336 N. Michillinda Ave., Arcadia, Calif. 91006

Wilcox's Orchids, 490 Beverly Ave., San Leandro, Calif.

Wilkins Orchid Nursery, 21905 S.W. 157 Ave., Goulds, Fla.

SUPPLIES

Reinfrank and Associates, 5414 Sierra Vista Ave., Los Angeles, Calif. 90038

South Shore Floral Co., Woodmere, Long Island, New York 11598

AGAR AND AGAR-NUTRIENT MIXTURES

Difco Laboratories, Detroit, Mich. 48201

Daniel M. Hill, P.O. Box 1184, Ontario, Calif. 91762

Julius O. Leuschner, 1050 W. 6th St., Los Angeles, Calif. 90017

FLASKING, MERISTEM SERVICE

Armacost and Royston, Inc., 2005 Armacost Ave., West Los Angeles, Calif. 90025

Gallup and Stribling Laboratories, 645 Stoddard Lane, Santa Barbara, Calif. 93103

Hauserman's Orchids, Inc., P.O. Box 363, Elmhurst, Ill. 60126

Iwanaga & Taba Laboratories, 2614 Waiomao Rd., Honolulu, Hawaii 96816

Jones and Scully, 2154 N.W. 33rd Ave., Miami, Fla. 33142

Marion Ryerson, 18320 S.W. 294th St., Homestead, Fla. 33030

VIRUS TESTING SERVICE

Florida West Coast Scientific Labs, P.O. Box 11914, Tampa, Fla. 33610

GREENHOUSES

Aluminum Greenhouses, Inc., 14615 Lorrain Ave., Cleveland, Ohio 44111

Janco Greenhouses, 10788 Tucker St., Beltsville, Md. 20705

Lord and Burnham, Irvington, N. Y. 10533

Mid-America Greenhouse Co., 10907 Manchester, St. Louis, Mo. 63122

National Greenhouse Co., P.O. Box 100, Pana, Ill. 62557

Pacific Coast Greenhouse Mfg. Co., 525 East Bayshore Rd., Redwood City, Calif. 94063

Redfern's Prefab Greenhouses, 55 Mt. Hermon Rd., Scotts Valley, Calif. 95060

Southern Calif. Greenhouse Mfrs., 3266 N. Rosemead Blvd., Rosemead, Calif. 91770

Stearns Greenhouses, 98 Taylor St., Neponset, Boston, Mass. 02122

Sturdi-Built Manufacturing Co., 11304 S.W. Boones Ferry Rd., Portland, Ore.

Texas Greenhouse Co., Inc., 2711 St. Louis Ave., Fort Worth, Tex. 76110

Turner Greenhouses, Box 1260, Goldsboro, N. C. 27530

APPENDIX C
ORCHID LITERATURE

Many kinds of books on orchids are listed below. Some are descriptive of the orchids of particular areas, and are of special interest to those who have a wide variety of kinds in their collections. Others are on culture. Some are old, some are new. Those written before our time, and especially those on culture in other countries, employ terms and describe methods that are strange to us. Nevertheless we can learn much from them. Any grower who is seriously interested in orchids will be well rewarded by reading a few of the old books. Not only will he come to know more about his plants through learning something of their history and their handling in other eras, but he will come to feel a kinship with the growers who nurtured the plants and learned their ways, and who handed on this rich heritage to us. Books that are out of print can often be obtained in used condition through dealers in old books, and some, of course, are rare and quite expensive. They may also be obtained for short periods through the Inter-library Loan Service for a fee that covers handling, postage, and insurance. Reprints of some of the old ones are currently being made, and are available from book dealers.

Ames, Blanche. *Drawings of Florida Orchids,* with explanatory notes by Oakes Ames. 1959. 2nd edition. Botanical Museum of Harvard Univ., Cambridge, Mass. 02138

Ames, Oakes. *Orchidaceae.* Seven fascicles, several out of print. Those available may be obtained from the American Orchid Society, Inc. Botanical Mu-

seum of Harvard University, Cambridge, Mass. 02138.

————. *Orchidaceae of Costa Rica.* Included as part of *Flora of Costa Rica,* Paul Standley. 1937. Field Museum of Natural History, Botanical Series, Vol. XVIII, pp. 197-306. Chicago.

————. *Orchids in Retrospect.* 1948. 172 pages. Botanical Museum of Harvard Univ., Cambridge.

————. *An Enumeration of the Orchids of the U. S. and Canada.* 1924. Boston.

————, and Donovan S. Correll. *Orchids of Guatemala.* 1952-1953. Two vols, 726 pages. Fieldiana: Botany, Vol. 26, Nos. 1 and 2. Field Museum of Natural History, Chicago. Supplement, 1966, by Correll.

————, F. T. Hubbard and C. Schweinfurth. *The Genus Epidendrum in the U. S. and Middle America.* 1936. Available from the American Orchid Society. Cambridge, Mass.

Australia National Herbarium. *Australian Native Orchids.* 1965. Available from the American Orchid Society, Cambridge, Mass.

Bedford, Roger. *A Guide to Native Australian Orchids.* 1969. Angue and Robertson. Sydney, Aust.

Blowers, John W. *Pictorial Orchid Growing.* 1966. 128 pages. Published by the author, 96 Marion Crescent, Maidstone, Kent, England.

————. *Orchids.* 1962. 130 pages. Agent for U. S., St. Martin's Press, 175 Fifth Ave., New York.

Bailey, Liberty Hyde. *Standard Cyclopedia of Horticulture.* Popular edition. 1935. 3 vols., 3,639 pages. The Macmillan Co., New York.

Boyle, Frederick. *The Culture of Greenhouse Orchids, Old System and New.* 1902. London.

Boyle, Louis M. *Growing Cymbidium Orchids and Other Flowers.* 1953. 520 pages. El Rancho Rinconada, Ojai, Calif.

——————. *Cymbidium Orchids For You.* 1950. El Rancho Rinconada, Ojai, Calif.

Brooklyn Botanic Garden. *Handbook on Orchids.* 1967. 81 pages. Brooklyn, N. Y. 11225.

Bruhl, Paul. *A Guide to the Orchids of Sikkim.* 1926. Thaker, Spink and Co., Calcutta and Simla, India.

Burberry, H. A. *The Amateur Orchid Cultivator's Guide Book.* 1899. 3d edition. Liverpool, England.

Burgeff, Hans. *Die Samenkeimung die Orchideen.* 1936. Jena.

Burnett, Harry C. *Orchid Diseases.* 1966. Booklet pub. by University of Florida, Winter Haven, Florida 32882.

Cady, Leo and T. Rotherham. *Australian Orchids in Color.* 1970. 50 text pages, 107 color plates. A. H. and A. W. Reed, Sydney, Aust.

Capps, Anne L. *Source Handbook of Orchid Species.* 1965. 106 mimeographed pages. Available from the author, Rte. 4, Box 376, Vienna, Virginia 22180.

Case, Frederick W., Jr. *Orchids of the Western Great Lakes Region.* 1964. 148 pages. Cranbrook Institute of Sciences, Bloomfield Hills, Michigan.

Cheng, Chow. *Taiwan Native Orchids.* 1967. Chow Cheng Orchids, 194 Litoh St., Taichung, Taiwan.

Cherry, Elaine C. *Fluorescent Light Gardening.* 1965. 256 pages. Information for plants in general. Van Nostrand Reinhold Co., 450 W. 33rd St., New York, N. Y. 10001.

Cogniaux, A. *Orchidaceae Florae Brasiliensis.* 1893-1906. Reprinted 1966.

Costantin, Julien. *Atlas en Couleur des Orchidées Cultivées.* 1000 orchids in color. Circa 1915. Paris.

——————. *La Vie des Orchidées.* 1917. 185 pages. Paris.

Correll, Donovan S. *Native Orchids of North America, North of Mexico.* 1950. 400 pages. Chronica Botanica. Now published by The Ronald Press Co., 15 East 26th St., New York.

——————. *Supplement to Orchids of Guatemala and British Honduras.* 1965. Fieldiana: Botany, Vol. 31, no. 7. Field Museum of Natural History, Chicago, Illinois.

Cox, J. M. *Cultural Table of Orchidaceous Plants.* 1946. Sydney, Australia.

Craighead, Frank S. *Orchids and Other Air Plants of the Everglades National Park.* 1963. 125 pages. University of Miami Press, Coral Gables, Florida.

Curtis, Charles H. *Orchids for Everyone.* 1910. London.

——————. *Orchids.* 1950. 274 pages. Putnam and Co., Ltd., 42 Great Russell St., London.

Darwin, Charles. *On the Fertilization of Orchids by Insects.* 1899. New York.

Davis, Reg. S., and Mona Lisa Steiner. *Philippine Orchids.* 1952. 270 pages. The William Frederick Press, 313 W. 38th St., New York.

de Oca, Rafael Montes. *Hummingbirds and Orchids of Mexico.* 1963. 158 pages. Reproductions of water color paintings. Editorial Fournier, S. A., Apartado Postal 31413, Mexico 20, D. F., Mexico.

Dienum, Dick. *Orchideen van Nederland.* 1944. 174 pages. Text in Dutch.

Dockrill, A. W. *Australian Indigenous Orchids.* 1969. 825 pages. Sydney, Australia.

Dodson, Calaway H. and Robert J. Gillespie. *The Biology of the Orchids.* 1967. 158 pages. Mid-America Orchid Congress, Inc., Nashville, Tenn.

——————, and L. van der Pijl. *Orchid Flowers: Their Pollination and Evolution.* 1967. 214 pages. University of Miami Press. Coral Gables, Florida.

Dunsterville, G. C. K. *Introduction to the World of Orchids.* 1964. 104 pages. Doubleday and Co., Inc., Garden City, New York.

——————, and Leslie A. Garay. *Venezuelan Orchids Illustrated.* Vols. I, II, III, IV. 1959-1966. Covering 650 species. Andre Deutch, Ltd., 105 Great Russel St., London WC 1.

Duperres, A. *Orchidées d'Europe.* 1955. 239 pages. Native orchids of Europe. Text in French.

Duval, L. *Les Cattleya: Traité de culture practique.* 1907. Paris.

——————. *Les Odontoglossum.* 1900. Paris.

——————. *Les Orchidées.* 1905. Paris.

Eigeldinger, O. *Orchids for Everyone.* 1957. 144 pages. John Gifford Ltd., 125 Charing Rd., London, WC2.

Erickson, Rica. *Orchids of the West.* 2nd ed. 1966. 107 pages. Terrestrial orchids of Western Australia. Paterson Brokensha Pty. Ltd., 65 Murray St., Perth, Western Australia.

Fawcett W., and A. B. Rendle. *Flora of Jamaica:* Vol. 1, *Orchids.* British Museum, London.

Fennell, T. A., Jr. *Orchids for Home and Garden.* 1956. Revised 1959. 160 pages. Rinehart and Co., Inc., New York.

Firth, M. J. *Native Orchids of Tasmania.* 1965. 90 pages. C. L. Richmond, Tasmania.

Fowlie, Jack A. *A List of Diagnostic Illustrations of the American Orchid Society Bulletin,* Vols. 1-30. Available from the author, 5201 LaForest Dr., La Canada, Calif. 91011.

Garay, Leslie A. and Herman R. Sweet. *Natural and Artificial Hybrid Generic Names of Orchids.* 1966. 212 pages. Botanical Museum Leaflets, Vol. 21, no. 6. Harvard University, Cambridge, Mass. 02138

Garrard, Jeanne. *Growing Orchids for Pleasure.* 1966. 302 pages. A. S. Barnes and Co., Inc., South Brunswick, N. J.

George, A. S. and Herb Foote. *Orchids of Western Australia.* Westviews Pty. Ltd., Perth, Australia.

Ghose, B. N. *Beautiful Indian Orchids.* 1959. 155 pages. G. Ghose and Co., Town-End, Darjeeling, Indian Union. Second edition 1969.

Gilbert, P. A. *The Charm of Growing Orchids.* 1952. 2nd edition. Shepherd Press, Sydney, Australia.

——————. *Orchids: Their Culture and Classification.* 1951. 252 pages. Shepherd Press, Sydney, Australia.

Graf, Alfred Byrd. *Exotica 3. Pictorial Cyclopedia of Exotic Plants.* 1963. 1,828 pages. Includes 901 illustrations and descriptions of orchids. Roehrs Co., Rutherford, N. J.

Gratiot, J. *Les Orchidées, Leur Culture.* 1934. Paris.

Grubb, Roy and Ann Grubb. *Selected Orchidaceous Plants.* Parts 1, 2, and 3. 1961-1963. Drawn and hand printed by the authors, 62 Chaldon Common Rd., Caterham, Surrey, England.

Hamilton, Robert M. *Orchid Flower Index.* A world list of reproductions in color in books and periodicals 1736 to 1966. 1967. 124 pages. Pub. by the author, 921 Beckwith Rd., Richmond, British Columbia, Canada.

Handcock, Ralph, and Margaret Smith. *You, Too, Can Grow Orchids.* Circa 1955. 60 pages. Daymark's Book Arcade, Ltd., Sydney, Australia.

Harrison, C. Alwyn. *Commercial Orchid Growing.* 1914. London.

———. *Orchids for Amateurs.* 1911. London.

Harvard Univ., Botanical Museum Leaflets. By subscription, or separately from Amer. Orchid Soc., Inc.

Hawkes, Alex D. *Orchids: Their Botany and Culture.* 1961. 297 pages. Harper and Bros., New York.

———. *Encyclopaedia of Cultivated Orchids.* 1965. 602 pages. Faber and Faber Ltd., London.

Hoehne, F. C. *Flora Brasilica: Orchidaceae.* 1940-45, 1953. In parts, incomplete. Instituto de Botanica, Sao Paulo, Brazil.

Hogg, Bruce. *Orchids: Their Culture.* 1957. 139 pages. Cassell and Co., Ltd., Melbourne and Sydney, Australia.

———. *Orchids for Everybody.* 1946. Abbotsford, N. S. W., Australia.

Holttum, R. E. *A Revised Flora of Malaya.* Vol. 1, *Orchids of Malaya.* 1953. Government Printing Office, Singapore, Malaya.

Hooker, Sir Joseph Dalton. *Century of Orchidaceous Plants.* 1851.

———. *Himalayan Journals.* 1854.

———. *Flora of India.* 1855.

———. *Century of Indian Plants.* 1895. Reprint 1967.

———, and George Bentham. *Genera Plantarum.* An important contribution to plant classification. 1862-83.

Hopp, W. *Blütenzauber der Orchideen.* 1957. 250 pages. Text in German.

Hurst, Charles C. *Experiments in Genetics.* 1925. Cambridge University Press, Cambridge, England.

———. *Mechanism of Creative Evolution.* 1932. Cambridge University Press, Cambridge, England.

Jackson, B. D. *A Glossary of Botanical Terms.* 1928. 4th edition. Reprinted, 1948. Duckworth and Co., London.

Kamemoto, H., R. Tanaka, and K. Kosaki. *Chromosome Numbers of Orchids in Hawaii.* 1962. 28 pages. Hawaii Ag. Exp. Sta. Bulletin 127. University of Hawaii, Honolulu.

Kano, Kunio. *Studies on the Media for Orchid Seed Germination.* 1965. 80 pages. Memoirs No. 20, Faculty of Agriculture, Kagawa University, Mikityo, Kagawa-ken, Japan.

King, R., and R. Pantling. *The Orchids of the Sikkim-Himalaya.* 1898. Reprinted 1967.

Kramer, Jack. *Growing Orchids at Your Windows.* 1963. 151 pages. D. Van Nostrand Co., Inc., New York.

Kupper, Walter. *Orchidées.* Translated from German to French. Circa 1955. 100 color plates. Service d'Images Silva, Zurich, Switzerland. English translation also available.

Kränzlin, F. *Beiträge zu Orchideenflora Sudamerikas.* 1911. Uppsala and Stockholm.

Lawrence, W. J. C. *Practical Plant Breeding.* 1951. Revised 3d edition. 166 pages. George Allen and Unwin, Ltd., London.

Lecoufle, Marcel, and Henri Rose. *Orchids.* 1957. 112 pages. English edition. Crosby and Lockwood and Son, Ltd., 26 Old Brompton Road, S. W. 7, London.

Lemmon, Kenneth. *The Covered Garden.* 1962. 284 pages. Historical Museum Press Ltd., London.

Leon, Hermano. *Flora de Cuba,* Part 1 (pp. 341-404) *Orchids.* 1946. Havana, Cuba.

Lindley. *Folia Orchidacea.* 1852. Reprinted by A. Asher and Co., Amsterdam. 1964.

Logan, Harry B., and Lloyd C. Cosper. *Orchids Are Easy to Grow.* 1949. 312 pages. Ziff-Davis Publishing Co., Chicago.

Long, John C. *Native Orchids of Colorado.* 1965. 34 pages. Museum Pictorial No. 16. Denver Museum of Natural History, Denver, Colorado.

Marston, Margaret E., and Pisit Voraurai. *Multiplication of Orchid Clones by Shoot Meristem Culture.* A review of the literature. Misc. Publication No. 17. University of Nottingham, Dept. of Horticulture, Sutton Bonington, Loughborough, England.

McLeish, John, and Brian Snoad. *Looking at Chromosomes.* 1957. 87 pages. Macmillan and Co., Ltd., London.

Millican, Albert. *Travels and Adventures of an Orchid Hunter.* 1891. London.

Morris, F., and E. Eames. *Our Wild Orchids.* 1929. New York.

Moulen, Fred. *Orchids in Australia.* 1958. 148 pages, 100 colored figures. Australia Edita Pty. Ltd, Sydney, Australia.

Nicholls, W. H. *Orchids of Australia.* 129 pages of text, 476 pages of color. Thomas Nelson (Aust.) Ltd. Sydney. 1969.

Nicolai, W. *Orchideen.* 1939. Frankfurt (Oder).

Noble, Mary. *You Can Grow Cattleya Orchids.* 1968. 148 pages. Published by author, 3003 Riverside Ave., Jacksonville, Fla. 32205.

———. *You Can Grow Orchids.* 1954. Revised. 152 pages. Published by author. 1964.

———. *Florida Orchids.* 1952. 88 pages. State Dept. of Agriculture, Tallahassee, Fla.

Northen, Rebecca T. *Orchids as House Plants.* 1955. 122 pages. Van Nostrand Reinhold Co., 450 W. 33 St., New York, N. Y. 10001.

O'Brian, James. *Orchids.* 1890. London.

Ospina, Mariano. *Orquideas Colombianas.* 1958. 305 pages. Publicaciones Tecnicas Ltda., Bogotá, Colombia.

Osorio, L. F. *Colombian Orchids.* 1941. Medellin, Colombia.

Piers, Frank. *Orchids of East Africa.* 1968. 2nd fully revised and enlarged edition. 300 pages. Wheldon and Wesley Ltd., Codicote nr. Hitchin, Herts, England.

Poddubnaya-Arnoldi, V. A., and V. A. Selenzneva. *Orchids and Their Culture.* 1957. 175 pages. Text in Russian. Academy of Sciences of the USSR, Moscow.

Rasbach, Kurt. *Orchideen in Deutschland.* 1958. 25 color photographs, unbound, of native orchids. Heinz Werner Haase, Uetersen Holst., Gr. Sand 16, Germany.

Reusch, Glad. *Orchid Corsages and Leis.* 1963. 33 pages. Earl J. Small, Orchids, Inc., P.O. Box 11207, St. Petersburg, Florida.

————, and Mary Noble. *Corsage Craft.* 1951. 148 pages. Van Nostrand Reinhold Co., 450 W. 33rd St., New York, N. Y. 10001.

Richter, Walter. *Die Shönsten aber Sind Orchideen.* 1958. 280 pages. 64 color plates. Neumann Verlag, Dr. Schmincke-Allee 19, Radebeul 1, Germany. English translation and revision under new title *The Orchid World,* 1965. E. P. Dutton and Co., Inc., New York.

Riehl, Matthias. *Grosse Liebe zu Orchideen.* 1958. 112 pages. Falken-Verlag Erich Sicher, Schellendorffstrasse 29, Berlin-Dahlem, Germany.

Rittershausen, R. R. C. *Successful Orchid Culture.* 1953. 136 pages. London. Printed in New York by Transatlantic Arts., Inc.

Rolfe, R. A., and C. C. Hurst. *The Orchid Stud Book.* 1909. List and discussion of hybrids to that date. Kew Herbarium, London.

Rotor, Gavino B. *Daylength and Temperature in Relation to Growth and Flowering of Orchids.* 1952. Cornell Experiment Station Bulletin #885, Cornell University, Ithaca, New York.

Rupp, H. M. R. *Orchids of New South Wales.* 1943. National Herbarium, Sydney, Australia. Reprint 1969.

Sander, David. *Orchids and Their Cultivation.* 1962. Revised edition of earlier book by the Sanders of St. Albans. Blandford Press, London.

Sander, (C. R., F. K., and L. L.). *Sander's Orchid Guide.* 1927. Revised edition. Reprinted.

Sander, Fred. *Reichenbachia.* 1888-1894. 4 vols. Plates are now collectors' items.

Sanders. *Complete List of Orchid Hybrids.* Compilation of hybrids to 1946, in first volume. Addenda: three volumes, 1946-48, 1949-51, 1952-54. *One Table List of Orchid Hybrids,* 1946-1960. Addenda, 1963, 1966. England. Available from American Orchid Society, Inc., Botanical Museum of Harvard Univ., Cambridge, Mass. Addenda published from time to time, will also be available from American Orchid Society.

Schelpe, E. A. C. L. E. *An Introduction to the South African Orchids.* 1966. 109 pages. MacDonald and and Co., Ltd., Gulf House, 2 Portman St., London W 1.

Schlechter, Rudolph. *Die Orchideen.* 1927. 2nd edition. Berlin.

Schultes, Richard Evans. *Native Orchids of Trinidad and Tobago.* 1960. 257 pages. Pergamon Press, New York.

Schweinfurth, Charles. *Orchids of Peru.* 1958-1961. Fieldiana: Botany, Vol. 30, Nos. 1, 2, 3, 4. 1,005 pages. Field Museum of Natural History, Chicago, Illinois.

————, and Alvaro Fernandez Berez. *Flora de la Real Expedicion Botanica del Nuevo Reino de Granada:* *Orchidaceae,* I. 1963. Reproduction of plates made in 1760-1817. Several volumes to follow. Ediciones Cultura Hispanica, Madrid.

Seidenfaden, Gunnar, and Tem Smitinand. *The Orchids of Thailand.* 1959. Two parts of six or seven projected. The Siam Society, Bangkok, Thailand. Order from Munksgaard, 6 Norregade, Copenhagen K., Denmark.

Summerhayes, V. S. *Wild Orchids of Britain.* 1951. 366 pages.

Thomale, Hans. *Die Orchideen.* 1954. 189 pages. Eugen Ulmer, Ludwigsburg, Germany.

U. S. Public Health Service. *Clinical Handbook on Economic Poisons.* Revised 1963. 143 pages. U. S. Government Printing Office, Washington, D. C. 20402. By Wayland J. Hayes, Jr.

University of California. *The U. C. System for Producing Healthy Container-Grown Plants.* 1957. Manual #23. Agricultural Publications, Grinnell Hall, University of California, Berkeley 4, Calif.

Vacherot, Maurice. *Charme et Diversité des Orchidées.* 1957. 68 pages. Paris, France.

————. *Les Orchidées.* 1954. 270 pages. Librairie J. B. Baillière et Fils, 19 rue Hautefeuille, Paris, France.

Veitch and Sons, *Manual of Orchidaceous Plants.* 1887. 2 vols. London. Reprinted 1962.

Veitch, James. *Hortus Veitchii.* 1906. London.

Warner, Robert, and B. S. Williams. *Orchid Album.* 11 vols. 1881-1896. England.

Watkins, John V. *ABC of Orchid Growing.* 1948. 3d edition, 1956. 190 pages. Prentice-Hall, Inc., Englewood Cliffs, New Jersey.

Watson, W., and H. J. Chapman. *Orchids: Their Culture and Management.* 1903. Revised edition. London.

White, E. A. *American Orchid Culture.* 1927. Revised 1942. A. P. DeLaMare Co., Inc., New York.

Williams, B. S. *The Orchid Grower's Manual.* 7th edition revised by Henry Williams. 1894. Reprinted, 1960. Wheldon and Wesley, Ltd., Codicote, Hitchin, England.

Williams, Louis O. *The Orchidaceae of Mexico.* 1952. Four parts, as Vol. 2 of "Cieba." Escuela Agricola Panamericana, Tegucigalpa, Honduras.

————, and Paul H. Allen. *Flora of Panama,* Part III, Fascicles 2, 3, and 4: *Orchidaceae.* 1946-49. Annals of the Missouri Botanical Garden, St. Louis, Mo.

Willoughby, Adelaide. *Orchids and How To Grow Them.* 1950. 135 pages. Oxford University Press, New York.

Wilson, Margaret. *A Bibliography of South African Orchids.* 1957. Available from the American Orchid Society.

Withner, Carl L. *The Orchids: A Scientific Survey.* 1959. 648 pages. The Ronald Press Co., 79 Madison Ave., New York, N. Y. 10016.

Wright, J. C. *Cymbidium Hybrids and Awards.* List from 1860 to 1957. Addenda. Cymbidium Society, Inc.

Wright, N. Pelham. *Orquideas de Mexico.* 1958. 120
pages. Bi-lingual text. La Prensa Médica Mexicana,
Copilco-Universidad, Mexico 20, D. F.

PERIODICALS AND HANDBOOKS
PUBLISHED BY ORCHID SOCIETIES

It is of benefit to an amateur to belong to an orchid
society, a group of growers with whom he can ex-
change information and share mutual interests, either
on a person-to-person basis or through the pages of a
publication. Most of the larger societies publish a
periodical which is included with membership fees.
In addition to news about orchids and growers,
methods and problems, the periodicals offer the advertisements of dealers from whom the amateur can
obtain plants and supplies.

American Orchid Society Bulletin. 12 issues a year.
American Orchid Society, Inc., Botanical Museum
of Harvard University, Cambridge, Mass. 02138.
> *Orchid Culture.* Information Pamphlet No. 1.
> *Beginner's Handbook Series.* Unbound reprints of
> 32 Chapters from 1955-57 Amer. Orch. Soc. Bul-
> letin.
> *Growing Orchids Indoors.* Reprints of several
> articles from the Amer. Orch. Soc. Bulletin.
> *Handbook on Pests and Diseases.* Reprints of four
> articles from Amer. Arch. Soc. Bulletin.
> *Mertistem Tissue Culture.* Reprints of four articles
> from the Amer. Orch. Soc. Bulletin.
> *Handbook on Orchid Nomenclature and Registra-
> tion.* 1969. 118 pages. Prepared by the Hand-
> book Committee at the authorization of the Inter-
> national Orchid Commission on Classification,
> Nomenclature, and Registration. Available from
> the American Orchid Society, Inc.

The Orchid Digest. The Orchid Digest Corporation.
26 La Cresta Road, Orinda, Calif. 94563. 10 issues
a year.
> *The Whys and Wherefores of Orchid Culture.* Sig-
> nificant selections from the *Orchid Digest.*

The Florida Orchidist. 4 issues a year. The South
Florida Orchid Society, 2708 NE 29th Court, Ft.
Lauderdale, Florida 33306.

The Orchid Advertiser (a newspaper) P.O. Box 495,
Cocoa, Florida 32922.

Oregon Orchid Society Bulletin. 11 mimeographed
issues a year. Oregon Orchid Society, 1916 S. W.
Madison, Portland, Oregon 97205.
> *Your First Orchids and How to Grow Them.* Kept
> up to date by frequent revisions by the Oregon
> Orch. Soc.
> *An Orchidist's Lexicon.* Oregon Orchid Soc. Inc.

Orchidata. 6 issues a year. The Greater New York
Orchid Society, 183 Fox Den Road, Bristol, Conn.
06010.

Bulletin of the Pacific Orchid Society of Hawaii. 4
issues a year. Pacific Orchid Society of Hawaii,
P.O. Box 1091, Honolulu, Hawaii 96808.

Handbook for the Growing of Orchids in Hawaii.
Vol. 19, Nos. 3 and 4. Pacific Orch. Soc. of Hawaii.

Na Pua Okika o Hawaii Nei. 4 issues a year. Honolulu Orchid Society, 1710 Pali Highway, Honolulu,
Hawaii 96813.

Bulletin of the National Capitol Orchid Society. 4
mimeographed issues a year. National Capitol Orchid Society, Inc., 3604 Thornapple St., Chevy
Chase, Maryland 20015.

Cymbidium Society News. 9 issues a year. The Cymbidium Society of America, Inc., P.O. Box 4202,
Downey, Calif. 90241.

The Orchid Review. 12 issues a year. The Orchid
Review Ltd., 62 Chaldon Common Rd., Chaldon,
Caterham, Surrey, England.

Orquideologia. 5 issues a year. Sociedad Colombiana
de Orquideologia, Apartado Aéreo 4725, Medellín,
Colombia.

Australian Orchid Review. 4 issues a year. Published
by affiliated societies of Australia. Subscription
address: Shepherd and Newman Pty. Ltd., Yurong
St., Sydney, N. S. W. 2000, Australia.

New Zealand Orchid Review. 4 issues a year. The
New Zealand Orchid Society, 24 McIntyre Rd.,
Mangere, New Zealand.

Philippine Orchid Review. 3 issues a year. The National Museum, Herron and Taft Aves., Manila,
R. P.

PROCEEDINGS OF WORLD ORCHID
CONFERENCES

Containing all of the papers presented.

Proceedings of the Second World Orchid Conference.
1958. Harvard University Printing Office, Cambridge, Mass. Can be procured from American
Orchid Society.

Proceedings of the Third World Orchid Conference.
1960. The Royal Horticultural Society, Vincent
Square, London, S. W. 1.

Proceedings of the Fourth World Orchid Conference.
1963. The Straits Times Press Ltd., Times House,
River Valley Rd., Singapore 9. Also available from
the American Orchid Society.

Proceedings of the Fifth World Orchid Conference.
1966. Available from The American Orchid Society.
Index for this volume prepared by and available
from Robert M. Hamilton, 921 Beckwith Rd.,
Richmond, B.C.

Proceedings of the Sixth World Orchid Conference
(in preparation)

APPENDIX D
POISONS: THEIR USE AND TOXICITY

* Reference number indicates other name. Use indicated is as follows: I = insecticides; F = fungicides; M = miticides; S = slug; H = herbicides; SI = systemic insecticides; FU = fumigation.

The LD-50 means the amount of the chemical necessary to obtain a 50 percent kill with a single dose. The doses are given in milligrams of chemical per kilogram of body weight.

Toxicity	mg. per kg.	Deadly amount for 150-lb. man
Lethal	1 mg. to 5 mg.	5-7 drops
Highly Toxic	5 mg. to 50 mg.	7 drops to 1 teaspoon
Toxic	50 mg. to 500 mg.	1 teaspoon to 1 ounce
Moderately Toxic	500 mg. to 5000 mg.	1 ounce to 1 pint
Moderately Safe	5 gm. to 15 gm.	1 pint to 1 quart
Safe	15 gm. +	1 quart +

The route of poisoning is: O = oral, or taken by mouth; I = for inhalation, spray or gas; S = for application to skin; E = for eye. It is important to remember that vehicles such as oil, kerosene, xylene, etc., may greatly enhance absorption. Great care is advised in handling all poisons, with protective clothing and masks for all with LD-50 under 500

Name	Cross reference to other name	Use	LD-50 in mg.	Route
1. Aldrin		I	55	O-I-S
2. Antidamp	99	F	1200	
3. Aramite		M	2000	
4. Arasan		F	500	O
5. Arbortox # 7 Powder	110-115	S	450	O
6. Arsenate, calcium		I-H	40	S-O
7. Arsenic acid		I-H	20	S-O
8. Arsenite, sodium		I-H	10	S-O
9. Azobenzine		M	500	

* Slightly modified and used with permission of the author, Henry G. Morton, M.D. and the American Orchid Society Bulletin from an article in that publication, Oct., 1966.

Name	Cross reference to other name	Use	LD-50 in mg.	Route
10. Basic Copper Sulfate	20	F	500	O
11. Benzene Hexachloride		I	125	O-S
12. BFPO	66	S-I	7	O-S
13. Bidrin		I	15	O-I-S
14. Bioquin 700	99	F	5000	
15. BHC	11	I	125	O
16. Bladafume	183	I	5	O-S I-E
17. Bladex	179	I	2	O-S I-E
18. Bladan	179	I	2	O-S I-E
19. Borax		H	1000	O
20. Bordeaux		F	500	O
21. Botran	62	F	50	S-O

Name	Cross reference to other name	Use	LD-50 in mg.	Route
22. Bugetta	6-110	S	50	S-O
23. Calcium Arsenate	6	I-H	40	S-I
24. Carbaryl		I	500	O-S-I
25. Carbophenothion		I-M	28	O
26. Captan		F	9000	O
27. Carbon Disulfide		I-FU	500	O-I
28. Carbon Tetrachloride		I-FU	500	O-I
29. CDT	164	H	5000	O
30. Ceresan		F	5	O-I
31. CES	3	M	2000	
32. Chlorobenzilate		M	3200	O
33. Chlorobenzylate	32	M	3200	O
34. Chlorbenside		M	10,000	O
35. Chlordane		I	457	S-O
36. Chlorocide	34	M	10,000	O
37. Chloroparicide	34	M	10,000	
38. Chlorophenothan	52	I	250	O-I
39. Chlorthion		I-M	1500	
40. CMU	101	H	3400	
41. Copper aceto-arsenite	142	F	22	O
42. Copper A Compound		F	500	O
43. Copper 53 Fungicide	20	F	500	O
44. Copper Hydro Bard	20	F	500	O
45. Co-Ral		I	200	O
46. Cube	160	I	132	O
47. Cyano guanidino	139	F	5	I-O
48. Cygon	68	S-I	215	O
49. DBD	91	I	15	O
50. DCPC	70	M	500	O
51. DDD	176	I	2280	O
52. DDT		I	250	O-I
53. DDVP		I	60	S-O
54. Delnav		M	50	O
55. Demeton		S-I	6	O-S I-E
56. Derrin	160	I	500	O
57. Derris	160	I	500	O
58. Dexon		F	50	O-S
59. Diazinon		I	100	O
60. Dibrom	122	I	430	O
61. Dichlone	153	F	500	O
62. Dichloran		F	50	O
63. Dichloricide	138	I	2526	O
64. Dicophane	52	I	250	O-I
65. Dieldrin		I	40	O-S-I
66. Dimefox		S-I	7	I-S
67. Dimetan		S-I	90	O
68. Dimethoate		S-I	215	O
69. Dimeton	55	I	6	O
70. Dimite		M	500	O
71. Dipterex		I	500	O
72. Dithane	196	F	5000	O
73. Dithio	183	I-M	5	O-I S-E
74. Dithione	183	I-M	5	O-I S-E
75. Diuron	101	H	3400	O
76. DMC	70	M	500	O
77. DMDT	115	I	800	O
78. Dylox	71	I	500	O
79. Endosulfan		I	110	O-S
80. Endrin		I	5	O-S-I
81. EPN		I-M	14	O-S
82. Ethylene (causes sepal wilt)			gas	I
83. Ethyl Mercury Chloride	30	F	5	O-I
84. Ferbam		F	500	O
85. Folpet		F	10,000	O
86. Fosvex	179	I-M	2	O-I E-S
87. Fulex A-D-O	99	F	1200	
88. GBH	105	I	125	O-I-S
89. Gamma Benzene	105	I	125	O-I-S
90. Gesarol	52	I	250	O-I
91. Guthion		I	15	O
92. Heptachlor		I	90	O-S-I
93. Hexachloride	105	I	125	O-I S
94. Hexamite	179	I-M	2	O-I E-S
95. Hexone	105	I	125	O-I-S
96. HHDN	1	I	55	O-I-S
97. Hydrocyanic Acid	98	I	1	O-I-S
98. Hydrogen Cyanide		I	1	I
99. Hydroxyquinoline		F	1200	O
100. Isotox	105	I	125	O-I-S
101. Karmex		H	3400	O
102. Kelthane		M	500	O
103. Korlan	159	I	1740	
104. Lead Arsenate		I	50	O
105. Lindane		I	125	O-S-I
106. Malathion		I	880	O
107. Maneb		F	500	O
108. Manzate	107	F	500	O
109. Metacide	116	I	9	O-S I-E
110. Metaldehyde		S	350	O
111. Meta	110	S	350	O
112. Metaceldehyde	110	S	350	O
113. Methyl Bromide		I	50	I
114. Meta-Systox		S-I	70	S-O
115. Methoxychlor		I	800	O
116. Methyl Parathion		I	9	O-S I-E
117. M Fixed Copper	20	F	500	O
118. Mineral Oil			10,000	O
119. Mitox	34	M	10,000	O
120. Monuron		H	3200	O
121. Nabam		F	395	O
122. Naled		I	43	O
123. Natriphene		F	2000	O
124. Navadel	54	M	50	O
125. Neburon		H	5000	O
126. Neocid	52	I	250	O-I
127. Niagaramite	3	M	2000	O
128. Nicotine		I	1	O-S E-I
129. Nifos	179	I-M	2	O-I E-S
130. Nifos-T	179	I-M	2	O-I E-S
131. Octalene	1	I	55	O-I-S
132. OMPA	162	S-I	30	O-S
133. Orthocide	26	F	5000	O
134. Ovotran		M	2000	O
135. Oxine	99	F	1200	O
136. Oxyquinoline	99	F	1200	O
137. Paracide	138	I	2526	O
138. Paradichlorobenzene		I	2526	O
139. Pano-Drench		F	5	I-O
140. Panogen	139	F	5	
141. Parathion		I-M	3	O-S E-I
142. Paris Green		I-F	22	O
143. Parzate	196	F	5000	O
144. PDB	138	I	2526	O
145. Pentac		M	3160	
146. Pennacap		F	500	O
147. Petroleum Oil			10,000	O
148. PCNB	146	F	500	O
149. Pestox 111	162	S-I	30	O-S
150. Phaltan	85	F	10,000	O
151. Phorate	184	S-I	3	O-S-I
152. Phosdrin		I	6	O-S-I
153. Phygon		F	500	O
154. Piperonyl Butoxide		I	11,000	O
155. Pyrenone		I	500	O
156. Pyrethrins		I	15,000	O
157. 8-Quinolinol Benzoate		F	1200	O
158. Rhothane	176	I	2280	O
159. Ronnel		I	1740	
160. Rotenone		I	132	O
161. Ryania		I	750	O
162. Schradan		S-I	30	O-S
163. Sevin	24	I	500	O-S-I
164. Simazine		H	5000	O
165. Slug Kill	110	S	350	O
166. Sodium Arsenite	8	I-H	10	S-I
167. Spectrocide	59	I	100	O
168. Sulfatepp	183	I-M	5	O-I S-E
169. Sulfatep	183	I-M	5	O-I S-E
170. Sulphur		I-M	10,000	
171. Systox	55	S-I	6	O-S I-E
172. Tedion		M	14,000	O
173. Tepp	179	I-M	2	O-I E-S

Name	Cross reference to other name	Use	LD-50 in mg.	Route
174. Tetradifon	172	M	14,000	
175. Telvar	101	H	3400	
176. TDE		I	2280	O
177. Tersan	4	F	500	O
178. Terraclor	146	F	500	O
179. Tetraethyl Pyrophosphate		I-M	2	O-S I-E
180. Tepp	179	I-M	2	O-S I-E
181. Tep	179	I-M	2	O-S I-E
182. Tetron	179	I-M	2	I-S O-E
183. Tetraethyl dithionopyrophosphate		I-M	5	O-I
184. Thimet		S-I	3	O-I-S
185. Thiodan	79	I	110	O-S
186. Thiram	4	F	500	O
187. Toxophene		I-M	60	S-O
188. Trithion	25	I-M	28	O
189. Trolene	159	I	1740	

Name	Cross reference to other name	Use	LD-50 in mg.	Route
190. Vapotone	179	I-M	2	O-I S-E
191. Vapona	53	I	60	O-S
192. Warfarin		Rats	400	O
193. Wilson's Anti-Damp	157	F	1200	O
194. Zectran		I	16	O
195. Zerlate	197	F	100	O
196. Zineb		F	5000	O
197. Ziram		F	100	O

To this list should be added:
Actidione (cyclohexamide), an antibiotic for agricultural use. LD-50 = 5-50. A single oral dose of 10 mg. causes intense nausea in human beings.

Consan-20. LD-50 = 500
Ethion LD-50 = 46 } Both related to
Plantfume LD-50 = 2 } Parathion.
Shield LD-50 = 50-500

Home Orchid Growing

INDEX

The bold numbers indicate pages on which illustrations appear.